4x 12/14 ct 5/14

BY NORA EPHRON

FICTION
Heartburn

ESSAYS
I Remember Nothing
I Feel Bad About My Neck
Nora Ephron Collected
Scribble Scribble
Crazy Salad
Wallflower at the Orgy

DRAMA
Love, Loss, and What I Wore (with Delia Ephron)
Imaginary Friends

SCREENPLAYS
Julie & Julia
Bewitched (with Delia Ephron)
Hanging Up (with Delia Ephron)
You've Got Mail (with Delia Ephron)
Michael (with Jim Quinlan, Pete Dexter, and Delia Ephron)
Mixed Nuts (with Delia Ephron)
Sleepless in Seattle (with David S. Ward and Jeff Arch)
This Is My Life (with Delia Ephron)
My Blue Heaven
When Harry Met Sally . . .
Cookie (with Alice Arlen)
Heartburn
Silkwood (with Alice Arlen)

The MOST of Nora Ephron

The MOST of Nora Ephron

 Alfred A. Knopf · New York · 2013

THIS IS A BORZOI BOOK
PUBLISHED BY ALFRED A. KNOPF

Copyright © 2013 by the Estate of Nora Ephron
Introduction copyright © 2013 by Robert Gottlieb

All rights reserved. Published in the United States by Alfred A. Knopf,
a division of Random House LLC, New York,
and in Canada by Random House of Canada Limited, Toronto,
Penguin Random House Companies.

Acknowledgments can be found on page 559.

www.aaknopf.com

Knopf, Borzoi Books, and the colophon
are registered trademarks of Random House LLC.

Library of Congress Cataloging-in-Publication Data

Ephron, Nora.
[Essays. Selections]
The Most of Nora Ephron / by Nora Ephron. —First edition.
    pages cm
"This is a Borzoi book."
ISBN 978-0-385-35083-9 (hardcover)
I. Title.
PS3555.P5A6 2013
814'.54—dc23
2013016426

Jacket photograph by Elena Seibert
Jacket design by Carol Devine Carson

Manufactured in the United States of America
First Edition

Contents

Personal · 467

Introduction

A couple of years before Nora's death in 2012, she and I sat down to begin putting together the table of contents for this book. Then other things got in the way—her play, *Lucky Guy;* a movie script she was working on—and it was set aside. Perhaps, too, knowing how ill she was, she began to see the book as a memorial and that made her uncomfortable—she never said. But although I was aware of her dire medical situation, the original impulse behind the book was not to memorialize but to celebrate the richness of her work, the amazing arc of her career, and the place she had come to hold in the hearts of so many readers.

The reaction to her death was an outpouring of disbelief and grief. Before the publication of her two final collections—*I Feel Bad About My Neck* and *I Remember Nothing*—she was, of course, admired and enjoyed for both her writing and her movies, but the readership of these last books seemed to me to be on another level. It was personal. Her readers not only felt that they knew her but that she knew them. Obviously, not all the people—more than a million of them!—who bought *Neck* were women who identified with her or sensed her identification with them, but certainly many of them were. She had become a model, an ideal, or at the very least, an example—she was telling them things about herself that were also about them, and giving them permission to think these things and feel these things. And she was also telling them what to look out for, what lay ahead. Her honesty and directness, and her unerring prescience, had made her a *figure*—someone whose influence and authority transcended her individual achievements, extraordinary as they were.

In her later years, her movies brought her tremendous response and reward, both for their quality and because she was the first woman of her time to become a successful commercial film director. How did she do it? By her talent, naturally—her uncanny ability to give us romance as seen through a gimlet eye. Some people complained that her movies were sentimental—those happy endings! But those happy endings were actually realistic: She had lived one herself, through her long third marriage, one of the happiest marriages I've ever witnessed.

The determination and persistence—and clarity—that saw her prevail in Hollywood were the qualities that earlier had propelled her to the heights of journalism, first as a reporter, then as an outspoken commentator. Her abiding principle was the reality principle. And of course she had a not-so-secret weapon: She was funny, even when she was furious; funny through thick and (as we know from *Heartburn*) thin. And she was openly and generously personal without being egotistical. She saw everything wryly, including herself. She also looked great.

This book is structured around the many genres and subjects she explored and conquered. As you'll see, it's autobiographical, sociological, political. It adds up to a portrait of a writer, a log of a writer's career, and an unofficial—and unintended—report on feminism in her time. She's a reporter, a profilist, a polemicist, a novelist, a screenwriter, a playwright, a memoirist, and a (wicked) blogger—blogging came along just in time for her to lash out fiercely at the bad old days of Bush/Cheney. And let's not forget that she was an obsessed foodie. Even her novel has recipes.

What was she like in real life? To begin with, she was a perfect spouse: She and her Nick could have given lessons to that earlier exemplary Nick-and-Nora, the Thin Man and the Thin Man's lady. She adored her two boys, and nobly tried not to micromanage them. (A real sacrifice: Managing things was one of her supreme talents—and pleasures.) She was a fanatical friend, always there for anyone who needed support, encouragement, or kindness. She was also, I can report, a wonderfully responsive colleague. We worked together on all her books after her first collection, *Wallflower at the Orgy*, without a single moment of contention. As a result, I think I know what she would have wanted this book to be, and her family allowed me to shape it. My immediate reward was having a professional excuse to reread everything she ever wrote. No other editorial job I've ever performed has been so much fun.

·   ·   ·

A few notes on the text. Since almost all of this material has previously appeared in print but in a variety of venues, we've justified such technical matters as spelling and punctuation. There are some places (surprisingly few, actually) where, over the years, Nora repeated certain stories (sometimes with minor variations) or remade certain points—as in her memories of her early role model, "Jane." We've left these as they originally appeared so that they can be read in context. The brilliant introduction she wrote for the published version of *When Harry Met Sally*... originally preceded the text of the script, but now it follows it—I felt it gave away too many of the surprises to come. The recipes—she might not have been pleased—remain untested.

—*Robert Gottlieb*

✷ *The Journalist*

Introduction to Wallflower at the Orgy

Some years ago, the man I am married to told me he had always had a mad desire to go to an orgy. Why on earth, I asked. Why not, he said. Because, I replied, it would be just like the dances at the YMCA I went to in the seventh grade—only instead of people walking past me and rejecting me, they would be stepping over my naked body and rejecting me. The image made no impression at all on my husband. But it has stayed with me—albeit in another context. Because working as a journalist is exactly like being the wallflower at the orgy. I always seem to find myself at a perfectly wonderful event where everyone else is having a marvelous time, laughing merrily, eating, drinking, having sex in the back room, and I am standing on the side taking notes on it all.

I am not, I must tell you, entirely happy with this role. There are times when I would much prefer to be the one having the fun; there are times when I am seized with an almost uncontrollable desire to blurt out, in the middle of interviews, *"Me! Me! Me!* Enough about *you.* What about *me?"* But then I remember that, like so many journalists, I am stuck on the sidelines not just because I happen to be making a living at the job but because of the kind of person I am and the reason I was drawn to this business.

Everyone I know who writes has an explanation for it, and for years I went around collecting them, hoping that someone else's reason would turn out to be mine. The first person who gave me what seemed like a good one was a colleague on the *New York Post* (where I worked for five years), who told me during my first week there that the reason she loved her work was that every day, on the way home from work, she could see people on the subway reading her articles. For four years I looked around the subway to find someone reading mine. No one ever was. And finally, one day, it happened: the man next to me opened to a story of mine, folded the paper carefully back to settle in for a long read, and began. It took him exactly twenty seconds to lose interest, carefully unfold the paper, and turn the page.

Then I remember asking a man who had no real reason for working at a daily newspaper why he was there. "I'll tell you," he said. "I can't think of any place I would rather have been the day the president was killed than in a newspaper office." And that seemed like a wonderful reason—and I thought of the day President Kennedy was shot and the perverse sense of pleasure I got from working under deadline that day, the gratitude for being able to write rather than think about what had happened, the odd illusion of somehow being on top of the situation.

But in the end, the reason I write became quite obvious to me—and it turned out to have much more to do with temperament than motivation. People who are drawn to journalism are usually people who, because of their cynicism or emotional detachment or reserve or whatever, are incapable of being anything but witnesses to events. Something prevents them from becoming involved, committed, and allows them to remain separate. What separates me from what I write about is, I suspect, a sense of the absurd that makes it difficult for me to take many things terribly seriously. I'm not talking about objectivity here (I don't believe in it), nor am I saying that this separateness makes it impossible to write personal journalism. I always have an opinion about the orgy; I'm just not down on the floor with the rest of the bodies.

I feel that I should tell you a little about myself before letting the book begin. I feel this largely because I have just read the introductions to nine other collections of magazine articles, and all of them are filled with juicy little morsels about the people who wrote them. I think, however, that there is quite enough of me in most of these articles for me to forgo telling you how I love eating McIntosh apples and Kraft caramels simultaneously. That kind of thing. I should say that almost everything in this book was written in 1968 and 1969, and almost everything in it is about what I like to think of as frivolous things. Fashion, trashy books, show business, food. I could call these subjects Popular Culture, but I like writing about them so much that I hate to think they have to be justified in this way—or at least I'm sorry if they do.

One night not too long ago I was on a radio show talking about an article I had written for *Esquire* on Helen Gurley Brown [see p. 82] and I was interrupted by another guest, a folk singer, who had just finished a twenty-five-minute lecture on the need for peace. "I can't believe we're talking about Helen Gurley Brown," he said, "where there's a war going on in Vietnam." Well, I care that there's a war in Indochina, and I demonstrate against it; and I care that there's a women's liberation movement, and I demonstrate for it. But I also go to the movies incessantly, and have my hair done once a week, and cook dinner every night, and spend hours in front of the mirror trying to make my eyes look symmetrical, and I care about those things, too. Much of my life goes irrelevantly on, in spite of larger events. I suppose that has something to do with my hopelessly midcult nature, and something to do with my Hollywood childhood. But all that, as the man said, is a story for another time.

—May 1970

Journalism: A Love Story

What I remember is that there was a vocational day during my freshman year in high school, and you had to choose which vocation you wanted to learn about. I chose journalism. I have no idea why. Part of the reason must have had to do with Lois Lane, and part with a wonderful book I'd been given one Christmas, called *A Treasury of Great Reporting.* The journalist who spoke at the vocational event was a woman sportswriter for the *Los Angeles Times.* She was very charming, and she mentioned in the course of her talk that there were very few women in the newspaper business. As I listened to her, I suddenly realized that I desperately wanted to be a journalist and that being a journalist was probably a good way to meet men.

So I can't remember which came first—wanting to be a journalist or wanting to date a journalist. The two thoughts were completely smashed up together.

I worked on the school newspaper in high school and college, and a week before graduating from Wellesley in 1962 I found a job in New York City. I'd gone to an employment agency on West Forty-second Street. I told the woman there that I wanted to be a journalist, and she said, "How would you like to work at *Newsweek* magazine?" and I said fine. She picked up the phone, made an appointment for me, and sent me right over to the Newsweek Building, at 444 Madison Avenue.

The man who interviewed me asked why I wanted to work at *Newsweek.* I think I was supposed to say something like, "Because it's such an important magazine," but I had no real feelings about the magazine one way or another. I had barely read *Newsweek*; in those days, it was a sorry second to *Time.* So I responded by saying that I wanted to work there because I hoped to become a writer. I was quickly assured that women didn't become writers at *Newsweek.* It would never have crossed my mind to object, or to say, "You're going to turn out to be wrong about me." It was a given in those days that if you were a woman and you wanted to do certain things, you were going to have to be the exception to the rule. I was hired as a mail girl, for $55 a week.

I'd found an apartment with a college friend at 110 Sullivan Street, a horrible brand-new white-brick building between Spring and Prince. The rent was $160 a month, with the first two months free. The real estate broker assured us that the South Village was a coming neighborhood, on the verge of being red-hot. This turned out not to be true for at least twenty years, by which time the area was called SoHo, and I was long gone. Anyway, I packed up a rental car on graduation day and set off to New York. I got lost only once—I had no idea you weren't supposed to take the George Washington Bridge to get to Manhattan. I remember being absolutely terrified when I realized that I was accidentally on the way to New Jersey and might never find a way to make a U-turn; I would drive south forever and never reach the city I'd dreamed of getting back to ever since I was five, when my parents had thoughtlessly forced me to move to California.

When I finally got to Sullivan Street, I discovered that the Festival of St. Anthony was taking place. There was no parking on the block—they were frying zeppole in front of my apartment. I'd never heard of zeppole. I was thrilled. I thought the street fair would be there for months, and I could eat all the cotton candy I'd ever wanted. Of course it was gone the next week.

There were no mail boys at *Newsweek,* only mail girls. If you were a college graduate (like me) who had worked on your college newspaper (like me) and you were a girl (like me), they hired you as a mail girl. If you were a boy (unlike me) with exactly the same qualifications, they hired you as a reporter and sent you to a bureau somewhere in America. This was unjust but it was 1962, so it was the way things were.

My job couldn't have been more prosaic: mail girls delivered the mail. This was a long time ago, when there was a huge amount of mail, and it arrived in large sacks all day long. I was no mere mail girl, though; I was the Elliott girl. This meant that on Friday nights I worked late, delivering copy back and forth from the writers to the editors, one of whom was named Osborn Elliott, until it was very late. We often worked until three in the morning on Friday nights, and then we had to be back at work early Saturday, when the Nation and Foreign departments closed. It was exciting in its own self-absorbed way, which is very much the essence of journalism: you truly come to believe that you are living in the center of the universe and that the world out there is on tenterhooks waiting for the next copy of whatever publication you work at.

There were telex machines in a glass-enclosed area adjacent to the lobby, and one of my jobs was to rip off the telexes, which usually contained dispatches from the reporters in the bureaus, and deliver them to the writers and editors. One night a telex arrived concerning the owner of *Newsweek,* Philip Graham. I had seen Graham on several occasions. He was a tall, handsome guy's guy whose photographs never conveyed his physical attractiveness or masculinity; he would walk through the office, his voice booming, cracking jokes, and smiling a great white toothy grin. He was in a manic phase of his manic depression, but no one knew this; no one even knew what manic depression was.

Graham had married Katharine Meyer, whose father owned the *Washington Post,* and he now ran the *Post* and the publishing empire that controlled *Newsweek.* But according to the telex, he was in the midst of a crack-up and was having a very public affair with a young woman who worked for *Newsweek.* He had misbehaved at some event or other and had used the word "fuck" in the course of it all. It was a big deal to say the word "fuck" in that era. This is one of the things that drives me absolutely crazy when I see movies that take place in the fifties and early sixties; people are always saying "fuck" in them. Trust me, no one threw that word around then the way they do now. I'll tell you something else: they didn't drink wine then. Nobody knew about wine. I mean, someone did, obviously, but most people drank hard liquor all the way through dinner. Recently I saw a movie in which people were eating take-out pizza in 1948 and it drove me nuts. There was no take-out pizza in 1948. There was barely any pizza, and barely any takeout. These are some of the things I know, and they're entirely useless, and take up way too much space in my brain.

Philip Graham's nervous breakdown—which ended finally in his suicide—was constantly under whispered discussion by the editors, and because I read all the telexes and was within earshot, even of whispers, I was riveted. There was a morgue—a library of clippings that was available for research—at *Newsweek*; morgues are one of the great joys of working in journalism. I went to it and pulled all the clips about Graham and read them between errands. I was fascinated by the story of this wildly attractive man and the rich girl he'd married. Years later, I read their letters in Kay Graham's autobiography, and realized that they'd once been in love, but as I went through the clips, I couldn't imagine it. It seemed clear he was an ambitious young man who'd made a calculated match with a millionaire's daughter. Now the marriage was falling apart, before my very eyes. It was wildly dramatic, and it almost made up for the fact that I was doing entirely menial work.

After a few months, I was promoted to the next stage of girldom at *Newsweek*: I became a clipper. Being a clipper entailed clipping newspapers from around the country. We all sat at something called the Clip Desk, armed with rip sticks and grease pencils, and we ripped up the country's newspapers and routed the clips to the relevant departments. For instance, if someone cured cancer in St. Louis, we sent the clipping to the Medicine section. Being a clipper was a horrible job, and to make matters worse, I was good at it. But I learned something: I became familiar with every major newspaper in America. I can't quite point out what good that did me, but I'm sure it did some. Years later, when I got involved with a columnist from the *Philadelphia Inquirer*, I at least knew what his newspaper looked like.

Three months later, I was promoted again, this time to the highest rung: I became a researcher. "Researcher" was a fancy word—and not all that fancy at that—for "fact-checker," and that's pretty much what the job consisted of. I worked in the Nation department. I was extremely happy to be there. This was not a bad job six months out of college; what's more, I'd been a political science major, so I was working in a field I knew something about. There were six writers and six researchers in the department, and we worked from Tuesday to Saturday night, when the magazine closed. For most of the week, none of us did anything. The writers waited for files from the reporters in the bureaus, which didn't turn up until Thursday or Friday. Then, on Friday afternoon, they all wrote their stories and gave them to us researchers to check. We checked a story by referring to whatever factual material existed; occasionally we made a phone call or did some minor reporting. Newsmagazine writers in those days were famous for using the expression "tk," which stood for "to come"; they were always writing sentences like, "There are tk lightbulbs in the chandelier in the chamber of the House of Representatives," and part of your job as a researcher was to find out just how many lightbulbs there were. These tidbits were not so much facts as factoids, but they were the way newsmagazines separated themselves from daily newspapers; the style reached an apotheosis in the work of Theodore H. White, a former *Time* writer, whose *Making of the President* books were filled with information about things like President Kennedy's favorite soup. (Tomato, with a glop of sour cream.) (I ate it for years, as a result.)

At *Newsweek,* when you had checked the facts and were convinced they were accurate, you underlined the sentence. You were done checking a piece when every word in it had been underlined. One Tuesday morning, we all arrived at work and discovered a gigantic crisis: one of the Nation stories in that week's *Newsweek* had been published with a spelling error—Konrad Adenauer's first name was spelled with a *C* instead of a *K*. The blame fell not to the writer (male) who had first misspelled the name, or to the many senior editors (male) and copy editors (male) who had edited the story, but to the two researchers (female) who'd checked it. They had been confronted, and were busy having an argument over which of them had underlined the word "Conrad." "That is not my underlining," one of them was saying.

With hindsight, of course, I can see how brilliantly institutionalized the sexism was at *Newsweek.* For every man, an inferior woman. For every male writer, a female drone. For every flamboyant inventor of a meaningless-but-unknown detail, a young drudge who could be counted on to fill it in. For every executive who erred, an underling to pin it on. But it was way too early in the decade for me to notice that, and besides, I was starting to realize that I was probably never going to be promoted to writer at *Newsweek.* And by the way, if I ever had been, I have no reason to think I would have been good at it.

The famous 114-day newspaper strike (which wasn't a strike but a lockout) began in December 1962, and one of its side effects was that several journalists who were locked out by their newspapers came to *Newsweek* to be writers, temporarily. One of them was Charles Portis, a reporter from the *New York Herald Tribune* whom I went out with for a while, but that's not the point (although it's not entirely beside the point); the point is that Charlie, who was a wonderful writer with a spectacular and entirely eccentric style (he later became a novelist and the author of *True Grit*), was no good at all at writing the formulaic, voiceless, unbylined stories with strict line counts that *Newsweek* printed.

By then I had become friends with Victor Navasky. He was the editor of a satirical magazine called *Monocle,* and it seemed that he knew everyone. He knew important people, and he knew people he made you think were important simply because he knew them. *Monocle* came out only sporadically, but it hosted a lot of parties, and I met people there who became friends for life, including Victor's wife, Annie, Calvin Trillin, and John Gregory Dunne. Victor also introduced me to Jane Green, who was an editor at Condé Nast. She was an older woman, about twenty-five, very stylish and sophisticated, and she knew everyone too. She introduced me to my first omelette, my first Brie, and my first vitello tonnato. She used the word "painterly" and tried to explain it to me. She asked me what kind of Jew I was. I had never heard of the concept of what kind of Jew you were. Jane was a German Jew, which was not to say she was from Germany but that her grandparents had been. She was extremely pleased about it. I had no idea it mattered. (And by the way, it didn't, really; those days were over.)

I could go on endlessly about the things I learned from Jane. She told me all about de Kooning and took me to the Museum of Modern Art to see pop art and op art. She taught me the difference between Le Corbusier and Mies van der Rohe. She'd gone out with a number of well-known journalists and writers, and long before I met them I knew, because of Jane, a number of intimate details about them. Eventually, I went to bed with one of them and that was the end of my friendship with her, but that's getting ahead of things.

One day after the newspaper strike was about a month old, Victor called to say he'd managed to raise $10,000 to put out parodies of the New York newspapers, and asked if I would write a parody of Leonard Lyons's gossip column in the *New York Post*. I said yes, although I had no idea what to do. I'd met Lyons—he appeared nightly at Sardi's, where my parents often had dinner when they were in New York—but I'd never really focused on his column. I called my friend Marcia, who'd recently babysat Leonard Lyons's son's dogs, and asked her what the deal was with Lyons. She explained to me that the Lyons column was a series of short anecdotes with no point whatsoever. I went upstairs to the morgue at *Newsweek* and read a few weeks' worth of Lyons's columns and wrote the parody. Parodies are very odd things. I've written only about a half dozen of them in my life [see pp. 50–54; 124–125]; they come on you like the wind, and you write them almost possessed. It's as close as a writer gets to acting—it's almost as if you're in character for a short time, and then it passes.

The papers Victor produced—the *New York Pest* and the *Dally News*—made their way to the newsstands, but they didn't sell. Newsstand dealers really didn't understand parodies in those days—this was long before *National Lampoon* and the *Onion*—and most of them sent them back to the distributor. But everyone in the business read them. They were funny. The editors of the *Post* wanted to sue, but the publisher, Dorothy Schiff, said, "Don't be ridiculous. If they can parody the *Post* they can write for it. Hire them." So the editors called Victor and

Victor called me and asked if I'd be interested in trying out for a job at the *Post*. Of course I was.

I went down to the *Post* offices on West Street a few days later. It was a freezing day in February and I got lost trying to find the entrance to the building, which was actually on Washington Street. I took the elevator to the second floor and walked down the long dingy hall and into the city room. I couldn't imagine I was in the right place. It was a large dusty room with dirty windows looking out at the Hudson, not that you could see anything through the windows. Sitting in a clump of desks in the winter dark was a group of three or four editors. They offered me a reporting tryout as soon as the lockout was over.

There were seven newspapers in New York at that time, and the *Post* was the least of them, circulation-wise. It had always been a liberal paper, and it had had glory days under an editor named James Wechsler, but those days were over. Still, the paper had a solid base of devoted readers. Seven weeks into the lockout, Dorothy Schiff bolted the Publishers Association and reopened the paper, and I took a two-week leave of absence from *Newsweek* and began my tryout. I'd prepared by studying the *Post,* but more important, by being coached by Jane, who'd worked there briefly. She explained everything I needed to know about the paper. She told me that the *Post* was an afternoon newspaper and the stories in it were known as "overnights"; they were not to be confused with the news stories in the morning papers. They were feature stories; they had a point of view; they were the reason people bought an afternoon paper in addition to a morning paper. You never used a simple "Who What Where Why When and How" lead in an afternoon paper. She also told me that when I got an assignment, never to say, "I don't understand" or "Where exactly is it?" or "How do I get in touch with them?" Go back to your desk, she said, and figure it out. Pull the clips from the morgue. Look in the telephone book. Look in the crisscross directory. Call your friends. Do anything but ask the editor what to do or how to get there.

I arrived for my tryout expecting the city room to look different from the way it had on that dark winter day I'd first come there, but except for brighter lighting, it didn't. It was a relic, really—a period set for a 1920s newsroom. The desks were old, the chairs were broken. Everyone smoked, but there were no ashtrays; the burning cigarettes rested on the edges of desks and left dark smudge marks. There were not enough desks to go around, so unless you'd been there for twenty years, you didn't have your own desk, or even a drawer; finding a place to sit was sort of like musical chairs. The windows were never cleaned. The doors leading into the city room had insets of frosted glass, and they were so dusty that someone had written the word "Philthy" on them with a finger. I couldn't have cared less. I had spent almost half my life wanting to be a newspaper reporter, and now I had a shot at it.

I had four bylines my first week. I interviewed the actress Tippi Hedren. I went to the Coney Island aquarium to write about two hooded seals that were refusing to mate. I interviewed an Italian film director named Nanni Loy. I covered a murder on West Eighty-second Street. On Friday afternoon, I was offered a permanent job at the paper. One of the reporters took me out for a drink that night, to a bar nearby called the Front Page. That's what it was called, the Front Page. Later that night, we took a taxi up Madison Avenue and we passed the Newsweek Building. I looked up at the eleventh floor, where the lights were ablaze, and I thought, Up there they are closing next week's edition of *Newsweek*, and nobody really gives a damn. It was a stunning revelation.

I loved the *Post*. Of course, it was a zoo. The editor was a sexual predator. The managing editor was a lunatic. Sometimes it seemed that half the staff was drunk. But I loved my job. In my first year there, I learned how to write, which I barely knew when I began. The editors and copy editors brought me along. They actually nurtured me. They assigned me short pieces at first, then longer pieces, then five-part series. I learned by doing, and after a while, I had an instinctive sense of structure. There was a brilliant copy editor, Fred McMorrow, who would walk my story back to me and explain why he was making the changes he was making. Never begin a story with a quote, he said. Never use anything but "said." Never put anything you really care about into the last paragraph because it will undoubtedly be cut for space. There was a great features editor, Joe Rabinovich, who kept my occasional stylistic excesses in line; he saved me from woeful idiocy when Tom Wolfe began writing for the *Herald Tribune* and I made a pathetic attempt to write exactly like him. The executive editor, Stan Opotowsky, came up with a series of offbeat feature assignments for me. I wrote about heat waves and cold snaps; I covered the Beatles and Bobby Kennedy and the Star of India robbery.

The *Post* had a bare-bones staff, but more women worked there than worked at all the other New York papers combined. The greatest of the rewrite men at the *Post* was a woman named Helen Dudar. *Hello, sweetheart, get me rewrite.* In those days, the *Post* published six editions a day, starting at eleven in the morning and ending with the four-thirty stock market final. When news broke, reporters in the street would phone in the details from pay phones and rewrite men would write the stories. The city room was right next to the press room, and the noise— of reporters typing, pressmen linotyping, wire machines clacking, and presses rolling—was a journalistic fantasy.

I worked at the *Post* for five years. Then I became a magazine writer. I believed in journalism. I believed in truth. I believed that when people claimed they'd been misquoted, they were just having trouble dealing with the sight of their words in cold, hard print. I believed that when political activists claimed that news organizations conspired against them, they had no idea that most journalistic enterprises were far too inept to harbor conspiracy. I believed that I was temperamentally suited to journalism because of my cynicism and emotional detachment; I sometimes allowed that these were character flaws, but I didn't really believe it.

I married a journalist, and that didn't work. But then I married another, and it did.

Now I know that there's no such thing as the truth. That people are constantly misquoted. That news organizations are full of conspiracy (and that, in any case, ineptness is a kind of conspiracy). That emotional detachment and cynicism get you only so far.

But for many years I was in love with journalism. I loved the city room. I loved the pack. I loved smoking and drinking scotch and playing dollar poker. I didn't know much about anything, and I was in a profession where you didn't have to. I loved the speed. I loved the deadlines. I loved that you wrapped the fish.

You can't make this stuff up, I used to say.

I'd known since I was a child that I was going to live in New York eventually, and that everything in between would be just an intermission. I'd spent all those years imagining what New York was going to be like. I thought it was going to be the most exciting, magical, fraught-with-possibility place that you could ever live; a place where if you really wanted something you might be able to get it; a place where I'd be surrounded by people I was dying to know; a place where I might be able to become the only thing worth being, a journalist.

And I'd turned out to be right.

—November 2010

How to Write a Newsmagazine Cover Story

You Too Can Be a Writer

Y ou can learn, in your spare time, to write articles for publication, and if you master the art, you can be paid to do it on a full-time basis.

Of course, there are all sorts of writers. There are reporters, for example. Reporters have to learn how to uncover FACTS. This is very difficult to learn in your spare time. There are also serious journalists. But serious journalists have TALENT. There is no way to learn to have talent. There are also fiction writers. But fiction writers need IMAGI-NATION. Either you have imagination or you don't. You can't pick it up in a manual.

But there is one kind of writer you can learn to be and you will not need FACTS, TALENT, or IMAGINATION. You can become a newsmagazine cover story writer. Just master the six rules enumerated below and you will know all you need to about how to write a newsmagazine cover story—or at least the kind of newsmagazine cover story dealing with lifestyle, soft news, and cultural figures.

RULE ONE

Find a subject too much has already been written about.

To do this, read with care the following: *Women's Wear Daily, Vogue,* Joyce Haber's column, Suzy's column, the "Arts and Leisure" section of the Sunday *New York Times, Rolling Stone,* and the movie grosses in *Variety.*

Any name mentioned more than four or five hundred times in the last year is a suitable subject for a newsmagazine cover.

RULE TWO

Exaggerate the significance of the cover subject.

Study the following examples to see how this is done by the experts:

"Today, a few weeks shy of twenty-six, Liza has evolved in her own right into a new Miss Show Biz, a dazzlingly assured and completely rounded performer. The Justice Department should investigate her. She is a mini-conglomerate, an entertainment monopoly" (*Time* on Liza Minnelli, February 28, 1972).

"At thirty-five, Coppola stands alone as a multiple movie talent: a director who can make the blockbuster success and the brilliant, 'personal' film" (*Newsweek* on Francis Ford Coppola, November 25, 1974).

"Finally, the film confirms that Robert Altman, the director of *Nashville*, is doing more original, serious—yet entertaining—work than anyone else in American movies" (*Newsweek* on *Nashville* and Robert Altman, June 30, 1975).

"At twenty-nine, salty Lauren Hutton is America's most celebrated model of the moment—and the highest-paid in history, as well. . . . Her extraordinarily expressive face and throwaway sex appeal, captured in the strong, spirited photographs of Richard Avedon, have made Hutton a permanent fixture in the pages of *Vogue* and at least a passing fancy in five movies. And in contrast to the exotic stone-faced beauties of the 1960s, her natural gap-toothed, all-American good looks epitomize the thoroughly capable, canny, contemporary woman of the Seventies" (*Newsweek* on Lauren Hutton, August 26, 1974).

"Margaux is the American Sex Dream incarnate, a prairie Valkyrie, six feet tall and one hundred thirty-eight pounds. . . . Effortlessly, Margaux stands out in a gallery of fresh young faces, newcomers who are making their names in modeling, movies, ballet, and in the exacting art of simply living well. They add up to an exhilarating crop of new beauties who light up the landscape in the U.S. and abroad" (*Time* on Margaux Hemingway and the New Beauties, June 16, 1975).

RULE THREE

Find people who know the subject personally and whose careers are bound up with the subject's. Get these people to comment on the subject's significance.

"Add to all this her beliefs in the trendy cults of mysticism and metaphysics and she becomes thoroughly modern Marisa, aptly crowned by the *International Herald Tribune*'s society chronicler Hebe Dorsey as 'the girl who has everything plus'" (*Newsweek* on Marisa Berenson, August 27, 1973).

"'This event is the biggest thing of its kind in the history of show business,' modestly declared David Geffen, the thirty-year-old human dynamo, 'Record Executive of the Year,' chairman of the board of Elektra/Asylum Records, who just pulled off one of the great coups in the music business—signing Dylan away from Columbia Records" (*Newsweek* on Bob Dylan's concert tour, January 14, 1974).

"This is Roy Halston Frowick . . . known simply as Halston—the premier fashion designer of all America. . . . Halston's creative strength derives from personally dressing the most famous and fashionable women in the world, and while his name is not yet a household word, his impact on fashion trend setters is considerable. 'Halston is the hottest American designer of the moment,' says James Brady, the former publisher of *Women's Wear Daily* and now publisher of *Harper's Bazaar*. Fashion consultant Eleanor Lambert goes even further. 'Along with Yves St. Laurent,' says Miss Lambert, 'Halston is the most influential designer—not only in America, but in the world' " (*Newsweek* on Halston, August 21, 1972).

RULE FOUR

Try, insofar as it is possible, to imitate the style of press releases.

"On the one hand she is very American, with deep roots in the South and an almost apple-pie adolescence (from cheerleader to campus queen). There is about her a touching innocence, openness, expansiveness, and vulnerability. But at the same time she is no bright-eyed square. She breathes sophistication, elegance, grace, passion, experience. Dunaway has become more than a star—she is a style and a symbol" (*Newsweek* on Faye Dunaway, March 4, 1968).

"She is the rural neophyte waiting in a subway, a free spirit drinking Greek wine in the moonlight, an organic Earth Mother dispensing fresh bread and herb tea, and the reticent feminist who by trial and error has charted the male as well as the female ego" (*Time* on Joni Mitchell, December 16, 1974).

"There are many things gorgeous about Robert Redford. The shell, to begin with, is resplendent. The head is classically shaped, the features chiseled to an all-American handsomeness just rugged enough to avoid prettiness, the complexion weather-burnished to a reddish-gold, the body athletically muscled, the aura best described by one female fan who says: 'He gives you the feeling that even his sweat would smell good' " (*Newsweek* on Robert Redford, February 4, 1974).

RULE FIVE

Use statistics wherever possible. Better yet,
use statistics so mind boggling that no reader will bother to do
simple arithmetic to determine their impossibility.

One example will suffice here:

"[There are] one hundred million dogs and cats in the U.S. . . . Each day across the nation, dogs deposit an estimated four million tons of feces" (*Time* on the American Pet, December 23, 1974).

RULE SIX

Study the examples.

Read more newsmagazine cover stories.

Learn to use adjectives like "brilliant," "gorgeous," "original," "serious," and "dazzling" with devil-may-care abandon.

Learn to use clichés with devil-may-care abandon.

Master this technique and you too will be able to get a job writing back-of-the-book cover stories at a newsmagazine. You too will be able to take a subject, any subject, and hype it to the point where it bears no resemblance to reality. Whoever you write about will never be able to live up to what you write about him, but never mind. The important thing is that people will talk about YOUR STORY. They will talk about it for years. They will say how strange it was that the career of whoever you wrote about seemed somehow to slip after the cover *you wrote* appeared. They will allude ominously to the Newsmagazine Cover Curse. But you will know better.

So begin now, before it's too late. If it doesn't work out, you can always go work at a fan magazine.

—October 1975

The Assassination Reporters

Hugh Aynesworth and Bob Dudney work in a little office just off the city room of the *Dallas Times Herald*, and things were running fairly normally there the day I dropped in to see them. A woman had just telephoned to say that she knew for a fact that Jack Ruby's brain had been controlled by a television station near the Dallas airport. The day before, a little man in high-topped sneakers had come by, whispered about some inside information he claimed to have, and finally confided that the Jews had killed President Kennedy.

Dudney, twenty-five, was in the eighth grade when John F. Kennedy was shot. He is new to the assassination beat, and he is still a little amazed by the people he meets on it. But Aynesworth, forty-four, has been covering the story on and off since November 22, 1963, and nothing fazes him anymore. "In 1963 only the most brazen kooks came out," he says, "but by the time Jim Garrison started in in 1966 and 1967, even the timid ones were getting into it. People want to be involved in this. I've heard five or six people confess that they were part of a conspiracy to kill Kennedy—only it turns out they were in jail, or in a loony bin in Atlanta, at the time. There were about five hundred people in Dealey Plaza that day. In twenty years, there'll be ten thousand."

The day of the assassination, Aynesworth was working as science and aviation editor of the *Dallas Morning News*, and he decided to walk over and have a look at the president's motorcade. He was standing catty-corner to the School Book Depository when he heard three shots. "I thought the first one was a motorcycle backfiring," he says, "but by the time I heard the second, I knew what it was. People started reacting in a very violent way. They threw their children down and started screaming. There was one big black woman who had been thrilled to death because she was wearing a pink dress the same color as Jackie Kennedy's. She threw up within five seconds of the shots."

After a while, Aynesworth saw a group of people running toward the Depository building. "On the fifth floor we saw three black guys pointing up to the sixth-floor window. There were FBI cars and a radio car. And then a funny thing happened. This shows what bad luck can do for you. There was a long-time police reporter for the *Dallas News* there named Jim Ewell. The FBI was working up floor by floor in the Depository building, and here comes a call over the radio: 'This is a citizen, an officer's been shot.' It was on Tenth Street, three or four miles away. I said to Ewell, 'You stay here, I'll go after that one.' He stayed, and of course he saw no one. I ran off with two TV guys and a Channel Eight news car, and we go to the Tippit killing. Then a call came in that there was something going on at the Texas Theater. I got there, and there was Jim Ewell, and I said, 'Jim, you take the upstairs and I'll take the downstairs.' Turned out Oswald was downstairs. I just got there in time. Oswald came up with his fist, which had a gun in it, and slugged McDonald, and the other cop jumped him from the back.

"Within a few minutes of that, I got a tip from someone at the police station about the two addresses in Oswald's wallet. We went tearing over to the Elsbeth address, where he wasn't living—I burst in on some wino and his girl shacked up together. Then we went to 1026 Beckley, where he actually lived. We were twenty minutes behind the FBI. There was that little old room, it couldn't have been more than eight by ten. The only thing they left in it was a banana peel.

"On Sunday morning, Jim Ewell had the assignment at the jail, but he got a flat tire on the way. I went over just to see what was going on and saw Ruby kill Oswald. It was pure luck that I saw it and he missed it all. He feels snakebit, I'm sure."

Today Jim Ewell is still a police reporter in Dallas, and Hugh Aynesworth—well, Aynesworth is still a reporter too, but he is also an odd sort of footnote to the assassination, the journalist who has spent more time on the story than any other. He is a walking compendium of names of FBI agents, New Orleans informers, assistant district attorneys, bus drivers, and cabbies. He was the first reporter to print Oswald's diary and he sat shivah with Jack Ruby's family.

Aynesworth became so emotionally involved in the Clay Shaw trial that one of his dreams influenced the outcome of the case. "Suddenly one night I awakened out of a nightmare," he told James Kirkwood, author of *American Grotesque*. He had dreamed that District Attorney James Garrison produced a surprise witness who came in "and sat down and captivated the jury, winning the case hands down." He was so shaken by the dream that he wrote a letter to Shaw's lawyer, urging him to hire a private detective to investigate one of Garrison's witnesses, a dapper man named Charles Spiesel who claimed he had heard Shaw discuss the possibility of assassinating Kennedy. The detective discovered that Spiesel had filed a sixteen-million-dollar lawsuit charging the New York police and a psychiatrist with hypnotizing him and preventing him from having normal sexual relations; the information was crucial in discrediting Spiesel's testimony.

In some way, of course, Aynesworth is probably as addled about the assassination as some of the genuinely crazy people who come to see him. Unlike them, though—and unlike most of the buffs—he continues to believe that John F. Kennedy was killed by Lee Harvey Oswald, acting alone. "I sort of feel like a damn fool," he says. "There's nobody on earth who'd rather prove a conspiracy than me. I'd love to write it—if there was any damn thing that made me believe it." It's an odd position: investigative reporters try to bring conspiracies to light; Aynesworth has spent much of his time knocking them down.

"Let me tell you how the story about Oswald's being an FBI informer got started," he said. "There was a note in Oswald's papers with the name James Hosty on it. Hosty was an FBI agent, and in the beginning we thought Oswald was some kind of a spy or paid informer. I worked the FBI stuff, and we'd run down everything you could imagine. I even got Hosty's phone records. I called the phone company and I just asked, 'How do you get phone records if you've moved?' I never actually said I was Hosty—she just assumed I was, and she sent them. Anyway, we couldn't put it together except for these interviews where Hosty had come to see Marina. And that's where Lonnie Hudkins came along.

"Lonnie Hudkins was on the *Houston Post*, and he'd been sent to Dallas to work on the story. He called me up all the time, he would bug me and give me all these tips that were nothing. I just didn't want him bugging me anymore. So one day he called up and said, 'You hear anything about this FBI link with Oswald?' I'd just about had it. I said to him, 'You got his payroll number, don't you?' 'Yeah, yeah,' said Lonnie. I reached over on my desk, and there was a telex number on a telegram, S. 172 I think it was, and I told it to Lonnie. 'Yeah, yeah,' he said, 'that's it. That's the same one I've got.' Lonnie could see the moon coming out at high noon." The number eventually became part of the lore of the assassination.

Aynesworth stayed on the *News* until 1966, did some work for *Life*, and was on the staff of *Newsweek* from 1967 to 1974. The story would die down for a while and then crop up again. "Something was always coming up," he said. "*Look* magazine bought the Manchester book, so *Life* felt it had to have something to counteract it. They put an investigative team on it, and in 1966 they were digging around. They moved to New Orleans and worked with Garrison, did a lot of investigation for him. Jack Fincher, the San Francisco bureau chief, comes up with a little fag from New Orleans, a short-order cook who told him a story about Oswald and Ruby being seen in New Orleans as lovers, and then at the YMCA in Dallas. He wove a great tale. Fincher didn't know enough to know whether it was good, so they told him in New York to run it by Dallas and see what Hugh thinks.

"We got a motel room at the Executive Inn out by the airport, and we taped this story, and he really had it down. There was no way I could break him. I was beginning to wonder myself. He was going on and on, he'd seen them swimming, hugging and kissing, and he said they'd even tried to entice him. Finally, I looked at him and said, 'Wasn't that a terrible scar on Ruby's leg, that shark bite? Which leg was it on, anyway?' He said, 'It was the right leg.' He took a pause. 'No,' he said, 'it was the left leg. I remember now.' I said, 'You little son of a bitch, he didn't have a scar on his leg.' He started crying. I felt sorry for him—he'd been promised a good bit of money for his story."

Last year, after working a spell as a private investigator, Aynesworth joined the *Times Herald* and began working with Dudney. They make an interesting pair: Aynesworth is stocky and square, Dudney is lean and long-haired; Aynesworth is disorganized, Dudney is a compulsive file keeper; Aynesworth works the phone, Dudney writes. The *Times Herald*, under the byline of its publisher Tom Johnson, broke the story last fall of the threatening letter Oswald wrote to the FBI prior to the assassination; Aynesworth and Dudney did much of the legwork and wrote the backup stories. Their biggest story, both agree, was a nonstory that took them weeks to put together. An FBI clerk named William Walter, who was working in the New Orleans office in 1963, told them that five days before the assassination he saw a Teletype saying there would be an assassination attempt in Dallas and that no one had done anything about it.

"When we first talked to him on the phone," Dudney said, "we were both extremely excited. The guy was very convincing."

"We interviewed him twenty-some times," said Aynesworth, "and we talked to everybody who ever knew him."

"We got red flags everywhere," said Dudney.

"We gave him a polygraph," said Aynesworth, "and he didn't pass it."

"We never could get the one bit of information that proved it or disproved it," said Dudney.

"When we were three weeks into it," Aynesworth said, "CBS got onto it. Dan Rather called and asked me what I thought. I said, 'I'm ninety percent sure he's lying, but I'm not sure.' They did some film with him, chartered a plane to get it out, and once again Dan and I were back and forth on the phone. I gave him the results of the polygraph—with

Walter's permission. Finally, CBS went with it—but in a very positive manner. So we came back with a detailed, massive study. Knocking these stories down is no good—but you have to do it. There's a lack of willingness in this business to say that nothing is there. Especially after a few bucks have been spent."

There is a reason there are only a handful of reporters working the Kennedy assassination—and that is that a lot of smart reporters have kept as far away from it as is possible. This is a story that begs for hundreds of investigators, subpoena power, forensics experts, grants of immunity; it's also a story that requires slogging through twenty-seven volumes of the Warren Commission report and dozens of books on the assassination. A lot of people are dead. Some of the ones who are alive have changed their stories. The whole thing is a mess. And while it's not likely that Aynesworth and Dudney will get to the bottom of it—that would be a little like shooting a bear with a BB gun—it's nice to know they are still down there in Dallas plugging away.

"The other night I was at a party," Bob Dudney said, "and we were talking about certain great events that shaped the lives of people my age. The emergence of the Beatles and the Vietnam war were obvious influences. And I said that I thought the assassination of Kennedy was a big influence—and as soon as I said it I corrected myself. Oswald's death was more an influence than Kennedy's. Had he lived, so much more would have come out. His death left us a legacy of suspicion and doubt that's turned in on everybody. It's unusual. Such a neurotic little man, who was really such a loser, you know, and he's left a very profound influence. The country would have recovered from the death of John Kennedy, but it hasn't recovered yet from the death of Lee Harvey Oswald and probably never will."

—February 1976

The Palm Beach Social Pictorial

I am sitting here thinking a mundane thought, which is that one picture is worth a thousand words. The reason I am sitting here thinking this is that I am looking at one picture, a picture of someone named Mignon Roscher Gardner on the cover of the *Palm Beach Social Picto-*

rial, and I cannot think how to describe it to you, how to convey the feeling I get from looking at this picture and in fact every other full-color picture that has ever appeared on the cover of this publication.

The *Palm Beach Social Pictorial* appears weekly throughout the winter season in Palm Beach and I get it in the mail because a friend of mine named Liz Smith writes a column in it and has it sent to me. There are several dozen of us on Liz Smith's list, and I think it is safe to say that we all believe that the *Palm Beach Social Pictorial* is the most wonderful publication in America. Beyond that, each of us is very nearly obsessed with the people in it. My particular obsession is Mignon Roscher Gardner, but from time to time I am unfaithful to her, and I get involved instead with the life of Anky Von Boythan Revson Johnson, who seems to live in a turban, or Mrs. Woolworth Donahue, who apparently never goes anywhere without her two Great Danes nuzzling her lap. One friend of mine is so taken with Helene (Mrs. Roy) Tuchbreiter and her goo-goo-googly eyes that he once made an entire collage of pictures of her face.

Mignon Roscher Gardner, who happens to be a painter of indeterminate age and platinum-blond hair, has appeared on the cover of the *Pictorial* twice in the last year, both times decked in ostrich feathers. Anyone who appears on the cover of the *Pictorial* pays a nominal sum to do so; Mrs. Gardner's appearances usually coincide with an opening of her paintings in Palm Beach, although the last one merely coincided with the completion of her portrait of Dr. Josephine E. Raeppel, librarian emeritus of Albright College in Reading, Pennsylvania. Most of the painters whose work appears on the cover of the *Pictorial* are referred to as "famed, international" painters, but Mrs. Gardner is a local, and the furthest the *Pictorial* will go in the famed-international department is to call her prominent. "Prominent artist-aviatrix," for example—that's what they called her last February, when she appeared on the cover in her hair and turquoise ostrich feathers along with a painting from a new series she called "The Cosmobreds." The painting was of a naked young man on a flying black horse, and according to the *Pictorial*, it was a departure from her usual work in animals and sailboats and portraits because "Mignon wanted to combine her love for horses and for flying." In back of the painting of the Cosmobred and Mrs. Gardner herself are some curtains, and if you ask me, they're the highlight of the photograph. They are plain white curtains, but the valances are covered with chintz daisies, and the curtains are trimmed, but heavily trimmed, with yellow and green pompons, the kind drum majorettes trim their skirts and boots with.

Inside the *Palm Beach Social Pictorial* are advertisements ("Dress up your diamond bracelet"), columns, and pictures. The pictures show the people of Palm Beach eating lunch, wearing diamonds in the daytime, eating dinner, attending charity functions, and wearing party clothes. Most of the people are old, except that some of the women have young husbands. It is apparently all right to have a young husband if you are an old woman in Palm Beach, but not vice versa; in fact, the vice versa is one of the few things the columnists in the *Social Pictorial* get really upset about. Here, for instance, is columnist Doris Lilly writing about the guests at a recent party she attended: "Bill Carter (now U.N. ambassador to U.N.I.C.E.F.) proved he really does love children by bringing his latest airline hostess." And here from another columnist, Maria Durell Stone, is another guest list: "Then there were the Enrique Rousseaus, she's Lilly Pulitzer, and even Lilly's ex, Peter, was there with, well, as someone said, 'I don't think it's his daughter but she just might be.'" Every so often, the *Pictorial* prints pictures of people they describe as members of Palm Beach's Younger Set; they all look to be in their mid-forties.

There are two types of columnists who write for the *Pictorial*—locals, and correspondents from elsewhere. There are two advantages to being a correspondent from elsewhere: you don't have to spend the winter in Palm Beach, and you get a lofty title on the masthead. Wally Cedar, who writes from Beverly Hills and Acapulco, is the *Pictorial's* International Editor, and Liz Smith, who writes from New York, is the National Editor. With one exception—and I'll get to her in a minute: she's Maria Durell Stone—the local columnists in the *Pictorial* have tended to be relentlessly cheerful women whose only quibbles about life in Palm Beach have to do with things like the inefficiency of the streetlights on Worth Avenue. Cicely Dawson, who owns the *Pictorial* along with her husband, Ed, whom she always refers to as "our better half," writes a goings-on-about-town column in which she manages to summon unending enthusiasm and exclamation points for boutiques, galleries, parties, and new savings banks in town. "Congratulations to Nan and James Egan of the James Beauty Salon on their recent twenty-fifth anniversary," Dawson once wrote. "No client would guess from the cheerful attitude of this wonderful couple what hardship they have had these past few months. After an illness-free life, James was diagnosed as having chronic kidney failure last December. Oh that Palm

Beach County had an Artificial Kidney Center! . . . because that's what James needs."

In all fairness, Mrs. Dawson is almost a grouch in comparison to Leone "Call Me the Pollyanna of Palm Beach" King, who until her retirement in 1973 could not find enough good things to say about the place. Where else, Mrs. King once asked in a long series of rhetorical questions, "could you find families offering living quarters to people of low incomes, without at least making some sort of charge? . . . Where could you find friends with splendid flower gardens leaving a message with their gardeners to send certain people bouquets during the winter while they are off on a trip around the world? Where could you find big bags of fruit from a Palm Beach orange grove on your doorstep at regular intervals? . . . Don't let fabulously rich people throw you. They are just the same as anyone else except they can do what they jolly well please when they jolly well please. They have likes and dislikes, aches and pains, problems. They are just people."

Maria Durell Stone has left the *Palm Beach Social Pictorial*—she has been stolen away by the West Palm Beach daily paper—but her two years on the weekly coincided, and not coincidentally either, with what I think of as the *Pictorial*'s Golden Era, so I cannot leave her out of this. Mrs. Stone is a Latin-looking lady with a tremendous amount of jet-black hair who is divorced from architect Edward Durell Stone and has taken not one but two of his names along with her. She began writing for the *Pictorial* three years ago, and no one writing in any of the Palm Beach publications comes near her gift for telling it like it is. "I've done nothing but praise the Poinciana Club since it opened," she wrote last year, "but being a critic means that every now and then one must speak the truth and I am sorry to say it, but Bavarian Night there was a disaster."

Mrs. Stone's main problem in life—and the theme of her column too—had to do with being a single woman in a place where there are few eligible men. There are a lot of us with this problem, God knows, but she managed to be more in touch with it than anyone I know. Not a column passed without a pointed remark to remind the reader that this Mrs. Stone was looking for a Roman spring. "I met Vassili Lambrinos this week and he's divine," she wrote one week. "Dorothy Dodson, petite, refreshing and vivacious, gave a luncheon for him and I got to know him better—unfortunately not as much as I would like to, but what's a poor bachelor girl to do?" Another week, Mrs. Stone went to a charity auction: "There were numerous items to bid on and I did covet that stateroom for two on the S.S. *France*, but as luck would have it, someone else got it. I wouldn't have known who to take with me anyway, so it's probably just as well." Age was no barrier: "One of the best things of the evening," she wrote of the Boys' Club Dinner, "was the Boys' Club Chorus, which consisted of adorable little boys of unfortunate circumstances who sang many lively numbers at the top of their divine adolescent voices. It was heartwarming to hear." Apparently, Mrs. Stone's subtlety was not lost on her readers: "Stanton Griffis, that amazing ex-ambassador who sat next to me at the Salvation Army luncheon the other day, told me that if I really wanted to get the right man, I should put an ad in my column saying, 'Wanted: Intelligent, handsome, lean, tall, romantic type with kindness and money.' Well, now that I've said it, let's see if my octogenarian friend is right."

From time to time, something sneaks into the *Pictorial* that has to do with the outside world, and when it does, it is usually in Liz Smith's column. Miss Smith writes for the publication as if she were addressing a group of—well, a group of people who winter in Palm Beach. She interrupts her column of easygoing gossip and quotes to bring her readers little chautauquas; last year's were about Richard Nixon ("Hope all you people who couldn't stomach poor old Hubert are happy these days," one of them concluded) and this year's are about oil and the Middle East. ("So here are the most fascinating and frightening statistics I've read recently, from *The New Republic*. You remember *The New Republic*—it's liberal, left, and riddled with integrity, but even so, don't ignore the statistics.")

The rich are different from you and me; we all know that, even if some of the people in Palm Beach don't. But it is impossible to read the *Social Pictorial* without suspecting that the rich in Palm Beach are even more different. One of my friends tells me that Palm Beach used to be a rather nice place and that now it's become a parody of itself; I don't know if she's right, but if she is, the *Social Pictorial* reflects this perfectly. If there were more communities like it, I don't think I would find the *Palm Beach Social Pictorial* so amusing. But there aren't, so I do.

The *Palm Beach Social Pictorial*, P.O. Box 591, Palm Beach, Florida. By subscription, $10 a year.

—May 1975

The Boston Photographs

I made all kinds of pictures because I thought it would be a good rescue shot over the ladder . . . never dreamed it would be anything
else. . . . I kept having to move around because of the light set. The sky
was bright and they were in deep shadow. I was making pictures with a
motor drive and he, the firefighter, was reaching up and, I don't know,
everything started falling. I followed the girl down taking pictures . . . I
made three or four frames. I realized what was going on and I completely turned around, because I didn't want to see her hit."

You probably saw the photographs. In most newspapers, there were
three of them. The first showed some people on a fire escape—a fireman,
a woman, and a child. The fireman had a nice strong jaw and looked
very brave. The woman was holding the child. Smoke was pouring from
the building behind them. A rescue ladder was approaching, just a few
feet away, and the fireman had one arm around the woman and one
arm reaching out toward the ladder. The second picture showed the fire
escape slipping off the building. The child had fallen on the escape and
seemed about to slide off the edge. The woman was grasping desperately at the legs of the fireman, who had managed to grab the ladder.
The third picture showed the woman and child in midair, falling to the
ground. Their arms and legs were outstretched, horribly distended. A
potted plant was falling too. The caption said that the woman, Diana
Bryant, nineteen, died in the fall. The child landed on the woman's
body and lived.

The pictures were taken by Stanley Forman, thirty, of the *Boston
Herald American.* He used a motor-driven Nikon F set at 1/250, f 5.6–
8. Because of the motor, the camera can click off three frames a second.
More than four hundred newspapers in the United States alone carried
the photographs; the tear sheets from overseas are still coming in. The
New York Times ran them on the first page of its second section; a
paper in south Georgia gave them nineteen columns; the *Chicago Tribune,* the *Washington Post,* and the *Washington Star* filled almost half
their front pages, the *Star* under a somewhat redundant headline that
read: SENSATIONAL PHOTOS OF RESCUE ATTEMPT THAT FAILED.

The photographs are indeed sensational. They are pictures of death
in action, of that split second when luck runs out, and it is impossible to
look at them without feeling their extraordinary impact and remember-

ing, in an almost subconscious way, the morbid fantasy of falling, falling off a building, falling to one's death. Beyond that, the pictures are classics, old-fashioned but perfect examples of photojournalism at its most spectacular. They're throwbacks, really, fire pictures, 1930s tabloid shots; at the same time they're technically superb and thoroughly modern—the sequence could not have been taken at all until the development of the motor-driven camera some sixteen years ago.

Most newspaper editors anticipate some reader reaction to photographs like Forman's; even so, the response around the country was enormous, and almost all of it was negative. I have read hundreds of the letters that were printed in letters-to-the-editor sections, and they repeat the same points. "Invading the privacy of death." "Cheap sensationalism." "I thought I was reading the *National Enquirer.*" "Assigning the agony of a human being in terror of imminent death to the status of a side-show act." "A tawdry way to sell newspapers." The *Seattle Times* received sixty letters and calls; its managing editor even got a couple of them at home. A reader wrote the *Philadelphia Inquirer*: "*Jaws* and *Towering Inferno* are playing downtown; don't take business away from people who pay good money to advertise in your own paper." Another reader wrote the *Chicago Sun-Times*: "I shall try to hide my disappointment that Miss Bryant wasn't wearing a skirt when she fell to her death. You could have had some award-winning photographs of her underpants as her skirt billowed over her head, you voyeurs." Several newspaper editors wrote columns defending the pictures: Thomas Keevil of the *Costa Mesa* (California) *Daily Pilot* printed a ballot for readers to vote on whether they would have printed the pictures; Marshall L. Stone of Maine's *Bangor Daily News*, which refused to print the famous assassination picture of the Vietcong prisoner in Saigon, claimed that the Boston pictures showed the dangers of fire escapes and raised questions about slumlords. (The burning building was a five-story brick apartment house on Marlborough Street in the Back Bay section of Boston.)

For the last five years, the *Washington Post* has employed various journalists as ombudsmen, whose job is to monitor the paper on behalf of the public. The *Post*'s current ombudsman is Charles Seib, former managing editor of the *Washington Star*; the day the Boston photographs appeared, the paper received over seventy calls in protest. As Seib later wrote in a column about the pictures, it was "the largest reaction to a published item that I have experienced in eight months as the *Post*'s ombudsman. . . .

"In the *Post*'s newsroom, on the other hand, I found no doubts, no second thoughts . . . the question was not whether they should be printed but how they should be displayed. When I talked to editors . . . they used words like 'interesting' and 'riveting' and 'gripping' to describe them. The pictures told something about life in the ghetto, they said (although the neighborhood where the tragedy occurred is not a ghetto, I am told). They dramatized the need to check on the safety of fire escapes. They dramatically conveyed something that had happened, and that is the business we're in. They were news. . . .

"Was publication of that [third] picture a bow to the same taste for the morbidly sensational that makes gold mines of disaster movies? Most papers will not print the picture of a dead body except in the most unusual circumstances. Does the fact that the final picture was taken a millisecond before the young woman died make a difference? Most papers will not print a picture of a bare female breast. Is that a more inappropriate subject for display than the picture of a human being's last agonized instant of life?" Seib offered no answers to the questions he raised, but he went on to say that although as an editor he would probably have run the pictures, as a reader he was revolted by them.

In conclusion, Seib wrote: "Any editor who decided to print those pictures without giving at least a moment's thought to what purpose they served and what their effect was likely to be on the reader should ask another question: Have I become so preoccupied with manufacturing a product according to professional traditions and standards that I have forgotten about the consumer, the reader?"

It should be clear that the phone calls and letters and Seib's own reaction were occasioned by one factor alone: the death of the woman. Obviously, had she survived the fall, no one would have protested; the pictures would have had a completely different impact. Equally obviously, had the child died as well—or instead—Seib would undoubtedly have received ten times the phone calls he did. In each case, the pictures would have been exactly the same—only the captions, and thus the responses, would have been different.

But the questions Seib raises are worth discussing—though not exactly for the reasons he mentions. For it may be that the real lesson of the Boston photographs is not the danger that editors will be forgetful of reader reaction, but that they will continue to censor pictures of death precisely because of that reaction. The protests Seib fielded were really a variation on an old theme—and we saw plenty of it during the Nixon-Agnew years—the "Why doesn't the press print the good news?" argument. In this case, of course, the objections were all dressed up and cleverly disguised as righteous indignation about the privacy of death. This is a form of puritanism that is often justifiable; just as often it is merely puritanical.

Seib takes it for granted that the widespread though fairly recent newspaper policy against printing pictures of dead bodies is a sound one; I don't know that it makes any sense at all. I recognize that printing pictures of corpses raises all sorts of problems about taste and titillation and sensationalism; the fact is, however, that people die. Death happens to be one of life's main events. And it is irresponsible—and more than that, inaccurate—for newspapers to fail to show it, or to show it only when an astonishing set of photos comes in over the Associated Press wire. Most papers covering fatal automobile accidents will print pictures of mangled cars. But the significance of fatal automobile accidents is not that a great deal of steel is twisted but that people die. Why not show it? That's what accidents are about. Throughout the Vietnam war, editors were reluctant to print atrocity pictures. Why *not* print them? That's what that war was about. Murder victims are almost never photographed; they are granted their privacy. But their relatives are relentlessly pictured on their way in and out of hospitals and morgues and funerals.

I'm not advocating that newspapers print these things in order to teach their readers a lesson. The *Post* editors justified their printing of the Boston pictures with several arguments in that direction; every one of them is irrelevant. The pictures don't show anything about slum life; the incident could have happened anywhere, and it did. It is extremely unlikely that anyone who saw them rushed out and had his fire escape strengthened. And the pictures were not news—at least they were not national news. It is not news in Washington, or New York, or Los Angeles that a woman was killed in a Boston fire. The only newsworthy thing about the pictures is that they were taken. They deserve to be printed because they are great pictures, breathtaking pictures of something that happened. That they disturb readers is exactly as it should be: that's why photojournalism is often more powerful than written journalism.

—November 1975

Russell Baker

I have come to my devotion to the columns of Russell Baker later than most of the people I know, and I'm not sure whether this is because I am slow to catch on, or because Russell Baker is even better than he used to be. The answer, I suspect, is a little of both. In the last year, Baker has moved from Washington to New York, and the column he writes for the *New York Times* and its news service has shifted away from politics and toward urban life in general. I was about to go on to say something or other about that, but I realize that I have already begun to be unfair to Baker. Which is one of the problems of writing about him: as soon as you start to describe what he does, you do him an injustice. Urban life indeed. Baker did a column the other day that began with Franco dying and going straight to the New York Department of Motor Vehicles; it was brilliant, and there is no way to distill or describe it. You had to be there. And in any case, when I went to interview Baker and told him that column was a perfect description of urban life in New York, he assured me it was about urban life in Russia.

Baker is, of course, usually referred to as a humor columnist and usually lumped together with Art Buchwald, and that, too, is unfair. He is to Buchwald what Saul Steinberg is to Peter Arno: he tends to humor that is abstract, almost flaky, off the wall, cerebral, a bit surrealistic. He almost never writes a column that is a long joke; because of this, and because he builds on mood and nuance, a neat paragraph summary of a typical Baker column doesn't work at all. So I thought I would just go see him and let him talk, and the hell with anyone who wants a decent description of his writing. I should probably tell you that Baker is fifty, a tall, skinny man who looks a little like a hayseed. He is extremely low-key, terribly nice, and often seems on the verge of being embarrassed, particularly by praise of any sort.

Q: How did anyone at the *Times* know you would write a funny column?

BAKER: Nobody knew what the column was going to be. I didn't, the *Times* didn't. I was in the *Times* Washington bureau, and I had a reputation for being a "writer" in quotation marks— the quotation marks implied that there were reporters and then there were writers. I did a lot of feature-type stuff.

There was no expectation that the column was supposed to be funny. I'd outlined what was essentially an idea for a casual essay column, the sort of thing *The New Yorker* had done in the late forties in "The Talk of the Town." The style would be casual, monosyllabic, simple sentences, small ideas. I did know at the outset that I was interested in the ironies of the public condition. I was fascinated by irony. But what you project on a piece of paper and what finally emerges are two wildly different things. When I sat down to write, what came out was what was in me. The first column ever printed was a spoof, a send-up of a Jack Kennedy press conference. Very quickly I began doing basic satires, traditional forms like dialogues, fantasies, hoaxes, parodies, burlesques.

Q: Was it difficult?

BAKER: At the start, yes. I didn't know what it was going to be. Now it has a rigid identity, and there are days when it writes itself. When you start a column, you're in a very creative state; you're building a personality in a piece of writing. It's a strange kind of business. After a while the column becomes a tyrant. You've created a personality that is one aspect of yourself, and it insists on your being true to it every time you sit down to write. As time passes and you change, you may become bored with that old personality. The problem then is how you escape the tyranny of it. In a way, it's always a struggle between you and this tyrant you've created that is a piece of yourself. In the last year I've gone back to the essay form and abandoned the satirical form.

Q: Is that because of moving to New York?

BAKER: I'm not so aware of that. The change is the subject matter. It's so easy to do Washington. You have nothing but subject matter. But what happens in New York? Who, after all, knows who Abe Beame is, or Hugh Carey? I've had to work a lot harder, to take special subject matter and make it mean something to people outside New York.

Q: Someone once said something to the effect that he'd never known a writer who had a happy childhood.

BAKER: I've had an unhappy life, thank God. I suspect all childhoods are unhappy. My father died when I was five—it's my first memory—and I was lugged off from Virginia to New Jersey to live with a brother of my mother. He was the only member of the family who was employed, and he was making thirty-five dollars a week. He was married to a lovely Irishwoman who ran the household. My mother had a job where she sewed smocks for twelve dollars a week, and I was raised in a matriarchy. I was imbued with the business that you've got to get ahead. I always had a job, an awful job, usually selling *Saturday Evening Post*s. I was just terrible at it. They'd open the door and I'd say, "Well, I guess you don't want to buy a *Saturday Evening Post*," and they'd slam the door in my face.

Q: How did you get into journalism?

BAKER: I'd always been a drifter. When I was at Johns Hopkins, I was the only guy on the campus who didn't know what he wanted to be. Everyone wanted to be a doctor or a scientist or an engineer. It was very depressing. In a vague way I wanted to be Ernest Hemingway—that was in the days when he was still read. There was a guy on the faculty who lectured on T. S. Eliot and also wrote for the *Sun*, and he told me about this job. I went to see the managing editor, and he offered me a job, and I thought, It's a good way to kill time until I get around to writing a novel someone can publish. It was 1947 and I did police reporting at night. I never went to the office, never wrote anything. I drifted from police station to police station, hung around hospitals listening to people die, and phoned in police-blotter stuff. I did that for two years. I was in love at the time; I was leading this strange upside-down existence, hanging out with raffish characters all night and sleeping till one or two in the afternoon. I kind of liked it. I was getting an education. But after a year, I decided to go ahead and write a novel. I spent a summer and wrote a ninety-thousand-word novel in three months. You know Capote's famous comment on Kerouac—"That's not writing, it's typing." That's what the novel was. I was a self-taught typist, and I was combining the typing exercises with the writing of a novel. It was very valuable to me later. I'm a very fast typist.

Q: And what happened to the novel?

BAKER: Shipped it around a few places and then I put it in the attic. It was about what it was like to be twenty-three years old. I discovered then that the world I was living in was so much more interesting than the world I was capable of conceiving. I was hooked on journalism. That was the end of it. I never went back to writing fiction.

Q: How did you get to the *Times*?

BAKER: The *Sun* sent me to London as its correspondent. I was twenty-seven, very young to be in London, but very adventurous. Things were very difficult in England then, and most of the American reporters went to the PX for food. I didn't. I lived like an Englishman off the English economy, and I lost a lot of weight. I was hungry all the time. I cut myself off from the American community. Most of the reporters hung around the foreign office to get the diplomatic poop. I felt the AP would provide that. I went to Parliament and wrote about the nature of British political debate. I wrote about what Sunday afternoon was like, and British eccentrics. I was really a kind of travel writer. Everybody was writing about the British economy and taxes except me. So I began to attract some attention. Scotty Reston was head of the *Times* Washington bureau, and he wrote and asked me to come work there. I said no. I was happy—the *Sun* was about to bring me back to be White House correspondent, and that was my idea of paradise. I mean, what more was there? I came back, and after two weeks I realized I had made the worst decision of my life. I'd given up London for this pocket of tedium. I was sitting in this awful lobby waiting for Jim Hagerty to come out with a handout. At one point I was vacationing in Denver—when you covered Eisenhower you were always vacationing in Denver, writing stories on how many fish he had caught that day, or what he'd said at the first tee. Reston came through and offered me the job again. So I came to the *Times* on the condition I get off the White House. I went up to the Hill for a while, and the following year I was back at the White House. I got to Denver in time to cover Eisenhower's first heart attack. I handled the first presidential bowel movement in the history of the *New York Times*.

Q: I read somewhere that you eventually became unhappy in the Washington bureau.

BAKER: I didn't have a period of unhappiness where I was unhappy with the *Times*. I was just at the end of my rope. It wasn't possible to deal with Washington in a very sophisticated way, and the *Times* was not a paper where you could be very creative or innovative. For a long time I was more than willing to trade all that for the education. It was the best graduate school of political science in the world. If you wanted to know what was going on in the Senate, you went up there and Everett Dirksen explained it to you. But I'd spent over seven years doing it. I knew the personalities. I knew what speeches they were going to make on any issue. I became restless. It was really a matter of discontent with myself—I knew the limitations of the *Times*. Then the editor of the *Sun* offered me a column, a blank check, really, any kind of column I wanted. I thought, Yeah, that's what I want to do. It was a great out for me. There was an intimation it would lead to a bigger job at the *Sun*. We shook hands on it. I told Reston I was leaving and he was appalled. I was shocked that anybody cared. I went home and that night Orvil Dryfoos, the publisher, called and said, We're not going to let you leave the *Times*, and then they began making offers to me, and that's how the column began.

Q: And why did you decide to move to New York?

BAKER: Basically it was because a pipe burst in my home in Washington on a Saturday morning. I was very depressed. I suddenly realized I was going to have to put a lot more money into this house, and I said, "Let's sell the son of a bitch and get out of here."

—April 1976

The Detroit News

A few months ago, Seth Kantor went and laid an egg. Kantor works in Washington as an investigative reporter for the *Detroit News*, and in October 1976 he broke a big one, a scoop on the Michigan Senate race, a front-page story that he clearly thinks ought to have earned him praise, if not prize nominations; instead, it got him nothing but criticism. Two columnists on his own paper attacked him. Mike Royko of the *Chicago Daily News* suggested that the *Detroit News* be awarded a large bronze laundry hamper for "the most initiative in poking around in somebody else's dirty underwear." Even Kantor's wife thought he went a little overboard.

Kantor's story said that Democrat Don Riegle, a Michigan congressman then running for the Senate, had had an affair in 1969 with a young woman who tape-recorded several of their conversations with his permission. (In 1969 Riegle was married to his first wife; he is now married to his second.) The *News* printed selected portions of the taped transcripts. Seth Kantor claims that the episode "tells you a lot about a man's judgment as well as his stability." A *News* editorial that endorsed Riegle's opponent Marvin Esch claimed that the story revealed Riegle's "arrogance, immaturity, cold-bloodedness and consuming political ambition."

The voters of Michigan apparently felt otherwise. The day Kantor's story appeared, Riegle had slipped to a bare 1 percent edge in the polls; on election day three weeks later he won the Senate seat by a 6 percent margin, and his staff considered sending the *News* a telegram reading: "Thanks. We couldn't have done it without you."

In the year or so since Fanne Foxe jumped into the Tidal Basin, journalists have begun to debate a number of extremely perplexing questions concerning the private lives of political figures. How much does the public have the right to know? How much does an editor have the right to determine what the public has a right to know? Where do you cross the line into invasion of privacy? Last summer, in the most successful book promotion stunt ever pulled off, Elizabeth Ray brought down Wayne Hays—but she was an editor's dream, the-mistress-on-the-payroll-who-can't-type. What about mistresses who *can* type? Editors justify printing just about anything about a politician on the grounds of character. Are those adequate grounds? These questions are worth thinking about, but they all assume that decisions on what to print will be made by responsible journalists. As it happens, that may not be the correct assumption in the case of the *Detroit News*.

The *News* is the largest afternoon newspaper in America (circulation 613,000), and until last year, when the *Detroit Free Press* overtook it, it was one of the few big-city afternoon papers that sold more copies than the local morning paper. The decline in *News* circulation is generally attributed to a number of factors: editorial lethargy, a rising number of white-collar workers within the city as well as overall population decline, and an increased antagonism toward the paper in Detroit's black community. On the editorial page, the *News* supports civil rights; but following the 1967 riots, publisher Peter Clark bricked up the first-floor windows of the *News* building; the paper also began printing a daily roundup of minor crimes, identifying suspects by race. In 1971, under a photograph, the *News* ran this caption: "Milton B. Allen, fifty-three, of Baltimore, isn't letting the fact that he's the city's first Negro state's attorney deter him from his crusade against narcotics, crime and corruption." Last year, Mike McCormick, news editor of the *News*, sent his staff a memo that leaked to Mayor Coleman Young, who attacked it in a widely reported speech. "We are aiming our product," McCormick wrote, "at the people who make more than $18,000 a year and are in the twenty-eight to forty group. Keep a lookout for and then play—well—the stories city desk develops and aims at this group. They should be obvious: they won't have a damn thing to do with Detroit and its internal problems."

Since 1959, the *News* has been run by Martin S. Hayden, a conservative who was one of the few editors of a major newspaper to oppose the printing of the Pentagon Papers. Hayden is the last of a breed—a power broker as well as an editor; one *News* political reporter recalls a recent Detroit mayoral campaign in which Hayden persuaded *both* candidates to run. In 1969, Hayden and publisher Clark were supporters of the missile program; during the ABM debate in Congress, Hayden sent a memo to the *News* Washington bureau that read: "The Washington staff should watch our editorial page, know our policy and help support it" by looking for "interpretative pieces and sidebars that help drive home the editorial point of view." Hayden insists he never asks reporters to slant the news, but several journalists who have been offered jobs in the Washington bureau got the impression that he expected them to investigate Democrats slightly more carefully than Republicans.

Now sixty-four, Hayden is retiring in June, and in the last year his power has become less than absolute. In 1975, a group of *News* employees met to discuss ways to improve the paper; they discovered that part of the problem was that the paper was perceived as stodgy and conservative. This group, which subsequently became known as the Kiddie Committee, set to work to hire younger reporters and columnists who were "with it" or "hip" or merely bearded. Meanwhile, publisher Clark offered a column to the *News*'s most outspoken critic, a local talk-show host named Lou Gordon. Gordon and the new columnists began to snipe regularly at each other and at the way the *News* handled various stories. Hayden was not amused. "It's too much of a discussion of the newspaper business," he says. "I've always disliked reporters who make themselves part of the story. It wasn't the way I was brought up." Hayden continues to keep a close eye on the Washington bureau, while the other editors deal directly with the local staff; as a result, the paper occasionally seems schizophrenic. During the Riegle-Esch campaign, for instance, two young local political reporters wrote a story saying that Republican Esch had lied about his role in passing a piece of legislation; twelve days later, John Peterson of the Washington bureau wrote a story saying that Esch's lie was only a *little* lie.

Seth Kantor reported directly to Martin Hayden on all three stories he wrote about Don Riegle. The first, which ran in September, said that Riegle had signed his estranged wife's name to a tax rebate check in 1971 and then failed to give her half the refund. This was followed by a story quoting a Jack Anderson study that called Riegle one of the ten most unpopular members of Congress. Both stories were attacked by Riegle: the first was clearly a shabby episode in an acrimonious divorce, the second a harsh way of describing an unsurprising fact—congressmen who switch parties (as Riegle did, in 1973) are bound to be unpopular. Then Kantor got the tapes story.

In 1976, following the Elizabeth Ray revelations, a writer named Robin Moore (*The Green Berets, The Happy Hooker*) came to Washington to write a paperback about congressional sex. He was introduced to one Bette Jane Ackerman, who had had an affair with Riegle in 1969 while she was an unpaid staff worker in his office; during that period, she made some tapes of her conversations with him and supposedly replayed them like love letters while she was home sick. Eventually, the romance ended; Riegle divorced his wife and married another staff member. Last summer, Miss Ackerman accepted five hundred dollars from Robin Moore for her help as a go-between with other Washington women, and she played her tapes for New York *Daily News* reporter Joe Volz, who was then working with Moore. The tapes are predictably adolescent, childishly dirty, and thoroughly egomaniacal. "I'll always love you," Riegle tells Miss Ackerman. "I—I—God, I feel such super love for you. By the way, the newsletter should start arriving."

Kantor got hold of a transcript of the tapes. He also obtained some love letters Riegle wrote to Miss Ackerman. And at some point, with editor Hayden's approval, he drew up and signed an agreement with Miss Ackerman's lawyer, David Taylor, pledging that he would not use her name in the stories. Kantor then flew to Detroit and went to confront Riegle with the story. Kantor's version will give you an idea of the tenor of the meeting:

"He agreed to meet me with a lawyer. They had a tape recorder. I had a tape recorder. I asked him about this relationship with this unpaid staff worker, taped with his knowledge, and I got a strong blast at both the *Detroit News* and at me. He said it was a well-known fact in Washington that I had been assigned by my editor to get him. I asked him who had told him that. He refused to tell me. He said I was absolutely the worst journalist in Washington. I said, Well, if I can't be the best, I'd just as soon be the worst. Well, he said, we all have to make a living."

Both Seth Kantor and Martin Hayden deny that anyone at the *News* was out to get Don Riegle—but somebody must have been; there's no other way to explain the decision to run the story Kantor turned in. Written in pulp-magazine style, it's loaded with phrases like "sex-tainted," "provocative brunet," "kiss-and-playback romance," "tell-tale tapes," "boudoir antics," and so forth. It refers to Miss Ackerman as "Dorothy"—allegedly her code name on the tapes—and fails to mention the fact that she was paid by Robin Moore. It also leaves out something that Kantor and Hayden knew—that Miss Ackerman had been what newspaper reporters call "close" with South Korean lobbyist Tongsun Park, as well as several other congressmen. The lead of the story says that Riegle once described the affair as "more important than 'a lousy subcommittee hearing.'" Later in the article, it becomes clear that Riegle used the expression in a casual, offhand way: "In one of their conversations, Riegle said he had to break away 'to go to a lousy subcommittee hearing now.'" Kantor added sanctimoniously: "It is in the subcommittees that Congress does its basic legislative work."

The article backfired totally, of course. *News* columnists Lou Gordon and Fred Girard wrote columns protesting it. The Associated Press and United Press International refused to run the story the day it broke. Says AP executive editor Louis Boccardi: "We try to make a decision like this based on whether there's some relevance to the individual's public responsibility, and we couldn't satisfy ourselves that was the case here." Within days, Riegle was the recipient of a wave of sympathy; he took the offensive, attacking the *News* and charging the paper with conspiring with his opponent to smear him.

Two weeks later, Saul Friedman of the *Detroit Free Press* wrote the other half of the story—he identified Miss Ackerman by name, linked her to Park, and revealed the financial details of her transaction with Moore. Which proved that in a healthy, competitive, two-newspaper town, the public is occasionally subjected to twice as much trash.

When I interviewed Martin Hayden in Detroit after the election, he did not believe he had made a mistake in running the Riegle story. "Seth said that all this information was coming out in Moore's book," said Hayden. "What if the book came out and people said, 'Did you know about this?'" Did Hayden ever consider not printing the transcript of the tapes? "Not after we had them. Without the tapes I don't know if there would have been any story. The question was of his judgment, not his sexual morality." Did he think the story was heavy-handed? "As a matter of fact, we went easy. Before we were through we became convinced this was not an isolated case." Did Hayden meet with Kantor or any *News* editors to discuss whether the story should be printed? "No. I handled it. Whatever blame there is is mine."

Should Hayden have printed the story? Probably not—the fact that it would eventually be printed in a quickie paperback is hardly justification. But if he decided to go ahead, he ought to have printed the whole story—including Miss Ackerman's name and details about her financial transactions concerning the tapes. In order to nail Riegle, the *News* gave up half the story.

Was the piece justified on the grounds that, finally, Riegle's character was revealed? No. Anyone who reads Riegle's book, *O Congress*, is perfectly able to perceive his "arrogance, immaturity, cold-bloodedness and consuming political ambition." Among other things.

Should Hayden have used the tapes? No. I can't make a rule about what constitutes an invasion of privacy, but I know one when I see one.

For some time after I came back from Detroit, I wondered what all this proved. Certainly it was clear that the voters of Michigan were more sophisticated than Seth Kantor and Martin S. Hayden, but that wasn't much of a point: so is my cat. Then, on November 7, Larry Flynt published a full-page advertisement in the *Washington Post* promising to pay $25,000 to any woman who would tell her story about sex with a congressman to *Hustler* magazine, and I looked for some way to tie that in, but I couldn't. I'm afraid, in fact, that I can't come up with a real point to any of this. Which may be the point. Nobody really cares. Newspaper editors have stumbled into a whole new area they're now allowed to publish stories about, and they're publishing ridiculous, irrelevant, hypocritical, ugly little articles that aren't dirty enough for *Hustler* or relevant enough for the papers that print them. "Maybe I'm on the wrong side of the pendulum swinging," Seth Kantor said to me. Maybe so.

—February 1977

The Ontario Bulletin

Two years ago, my husband bought a cooperative in the Ontario Apartments in Washington, D.C. The Ontario is an old building as Washington apartment buildings go, turn of the century, to be imprecise, and it has high ceilings, considerable woodwork, occasional marble, and views of various capital sights. It also has the *Ontario Bulletin*. The *Ontario Bulletin* is a mimeographed newsletter that arrives every month or so in the mailbox. It is supplemented by numerous urgent memos and elevator notices; many of these concern crime. The Ontario is located in what is charitably called a marginal neighborhood, and all of us who live there look for signs that it is on the verge of becoming less marginal. The fact that the local movie theater is switching from Spanish-language films to English-language films is considered a good sign. The current memo in the elevator is now: "During the past eight weeks, FIVE ONTARIO WOMEN HAVE HAD THEIR PURSES SNATCHED on the grounds or close by. Three of these events occurred this week." This memo, written by Sue Lindgren, chairperson, Security Committee, goes on to state: "Fortunately, none of the victims was seriously injured and no building keys were lost." We were all relieved to read this, though I suspect that Christine Turpin was primarily relieved to read the part about the keys. Mrs. Turpin was president of the Ontario during the crime wave of May 1976, when she wrote a particularly fine example of what I think of as the Turpin School of memo writing:

"There have been *three purse snatchings* at the Ontario's front door in the last *two weeks* causing *lock changes twice* in the same period. All three incidents occurred in daylight hours; the three 'victims'—all women—were returning from grocery stores on Columbia Road. Two of the three had ignored repeated and publicized advice: DO NOT CARRY BUILDING KEYS IN YOUR POCKETBOOKS. They also ignored other personal safety precautions. Much as we sympathize with them over their frightening experience and over the loss of their personal belongings, the fact remains that had these 'victims' heeded the warnings, everyone at the Ontario would have been spared the inconvenience of a second lock/key change in two weeks as well as the expenditure of $250 for replacements."

As far as I can tell, several of the early warnings Mrs. Turpin refers to appeared in the *Ontario Bulletin*, but I can hardly blame the "victims" for not noticing them. Until recently, the *Ontario Bulletin* was written by Mildred A. Pappas, who appears to be as blithe and good-humored as Mrs. Turpin is the opposite. Here and there Mrs. Pappas tucks in a late-breaking crime story: "As we were going to press Security Chairman Sue Lindgren called to say that the cigarette machine in the basement had been vandalized and that both cigarettes and some change were missing. There were no known suspects at the time of the call." But Mrs. Pappas has a firm editorial philosophy, which she expressed in the January 1975 *Bulletin*: "Both the trivial and the important are vital in portraying a clear picture of life in the Ontario—or anywhere else." And she has such a charming way with the trivial that her readers really ought to forgive her apparent tendency to skip over the important. In the February 1975 *Bulletin*, for example, Mrs. Pappas does mention the business of not putting keys into pocketbooks, but that item pales next to the report on the revival of a limp African violet at the Houseplant Clinic, and it fades into insignificance next to the tantalizing mention of the removal of a hornets' nest from Elsie Carpenter's dining room window.

The information on the hornets' nest appeared in a regular feature of the *Bulletin* called "News and Notes," which includes birthdays, operations, recent houseguests, and distinguished achievements of residents, as well as bits of miscellaneous information like the announcement of the founding of the Ad Hoc Friends of the Pool Table Committee. Other regular sections of the publication are "The Travelers Return," a list of recent trips by residents; and "Committee Reports," summaries of the doings of the various building committees, of which there are nine. (This figure does not include the committee for the pool table, which has since disbanded, having successfully restored the table to use in the basement Green Room, which was recently and unaccountably painted yellow during the 1976 Painting Project.) The Ontario is surrounded by trees and gardens, so the *Bulletin* often mentions the planting of a new azalea or juniper tree, and it recently devoted an entire page to the final chapter of the eight-year controversy of the Great Red Oak, cut down on August 27, 1976, after the board of directors overruled what was known as the "wait and see" policy of the High Tree Subcommittee. Articles like these are often illustrated with simple drawings of birds and leaves. Occasionally, a photograph is used, but only on a major story like the flap over the water bill.

Ontario residents first learned of the water-bill flap in a July 1975 *Bulletin* article headlined A SHOCKING BILL FOR A SHOCKING WASTE:

"Chairman Chris Turpin has just announced that a staggering (and unbudgeted) $1,660.94 water bill for the last quarter has just been received, adding that the amount is more than *three* times the amount for the preceding quarter. A wrong billing? No. Uncommon usage for bad water, etc.? No. . . . The water company has advanced the opinion that only one malfunctioning toilet allowed to run continuously can be the cause. . . . The chairman stated that the board will decide on a method of payment of the unprecedented bill at its July meeting, the alternatives being (1) to find the resident or residents responsible and to bill accordingly, or (2) to specially assess *all* residents (owners and tenants alike) approximately $10 each to settle the bill."

For a month, we anxiously awaited word of what was up. Would ten dollars be added to the maintenance? Or would Chairman Turpin lead the Ad Hoc Committee on the Unprecedented Water Bill through each apartment in search of the hypothetical malfunctioning toilet? Finally, the July *Bulletin* appeared, with a terse report suggesting that the investigation was closing in: the prime suspect turned out to be not some irresponsible resident but the building's thirty-five-year-old water meter, which had just been removed for inspection by the water company. Meanwhile, Clarence K. Streit, a resident who was apparently unaware that human error was about to be ruled out, made a guest appearance in the *Bulletin* as the author of the Flask Water Dollar Saver. "It is quite practical," he wrote, "to save three pints of water every time one flushes a toilet. We have been doing it for a couple of years." According to Streit, if everyone in the building placed three pint flasks in his toilet tank, the Ontario could save 150,000 gallons of water a year—or, as he put it, *150,000* gallons of water a year. Mrs. Pappas urged residents who took up Streit's suggestion to submit their names for publication in order to encourage others. No one did; at least I assume no one did from the fact that Mrs. Pappas never again referred to the Flask Water Dollar Saver Plan. In the August *Bulletin*, however, the water meter was definitely fingered; it turned out to be not just out of order but thoroughly obsolete. A photograph of the new water meter appeared as an illustration.

If I have any complaint at all about the *Ontario Bulletin*, it is simply that its even-handed approach occasionally leaves something to be desired. Accurate reporting was simply not enough to convey the passions engendered by the paint selections of the 1976 Painting Project, nor was it adequate to describe the diabolical maneuverings of President Turpin and the Ontario board in the face of these passions. Residents who read the loving tribute in the August *Bulletin* to the Great Red Oak and the account of its mysterious incurable disease could hardly have been prepared for the stunning moment at the annual meeting in September when it was moved that no tree be cut down without a membership vote. Mrs. Pappas's low-key description of the restored iron grille entrance doors—"Unfortunately, the 'Ontario' inscription now faces the interior of the building since it could not be relocated from its solid iron casting to the outside"—does not quite do justice to the situation.

And I cannot imagine that *Bulletin* readers were in any position to judge the item in March 1976, which announced Dr. Allan Angerio's resignation as House Maintenance Committee Chairman. "In protest of the Board's sanction of extensive remodeling in a neighboring apartment, Dr. Allan Angerio has resigned five months after his appointment. In a recently circulated letter to all residents Dr. Angerio states that during the extended period of renovation he was 'unable to use my apartment for either business or pleasure.' He also states that his letter has engendered a considerable response from the membership, many of whom have indicated interest in a proposed revision of the Bylaws and House Rules of the Corporation to preclude further extensive structural 'modernization' efforts in the Ontario." This is certainly a fair summary of what happened—but it is not enough. I know. I am married to the man who hired the contractor who accidentally drilled the hole into Dr. Angerio's bedroom wall.

In any case, mine are small complaints. The main function of a newspaper is to let its readers know what's going on, and I doubt that there are many communities that are served as well by their local newspapers as this tiny community is by the *Ontario Bulletin*. And I would feel even more warmly toward the publication than I do but for the fear I have, each month, that I will pick it up to read: "The residents of 605 had a fight last Thursday night over the fact that one person in the apartment never closes her closet doors." I like neighborhoods, you see, but I worry about neighbors. Fortunately, my husband and I also have an apartment in New York. And I was extremely pleased several weeks ago when we moved to new quarters there in an extremely unfriendly-looking brownstone on an extremely haughty block. In the course of the week's move, we carried some garbage out of the apartment and left it on the street for the garbage collectors. Ten minutes later—*ten minutes later*—a memo arrived from the 74th Street Block Association concerning the block rules on refuse. I'm not going to quote from it. All I want to say is that its author, Emma Preziosi, while not in the same league with Christine Turpin, definitely shows promise.

—March 1977

Gentlemen's Agreement

Esquire *refused to run this column. It was printed in* [MORE], *the journalism review.*

In November 1975, *Esquire* magazine published an article by a young writer named Bo Burlingham. It was called "The Other Tricky Dick," and it was a long reporting piece, ten thousand words or so, on Richard Goodwin, author, speechwriter to presidents, and then-fiancé of Lyndon Johnson's biographer Doris Kearns. I was the editor on the piece. Burlingham portrayed Goodwin as an ambitious, crafty manipulator, a brilliant man who loved to outsmart his friends and associates to further his career. The article was carefully reported, the facts in it checked by the magazine's research department, and *Esquire*'s lawyer and managing editor grilled Burlingham on his sources for the article. All of us on the editorial side of the magazine believe that Burlingham's article was solid. Which does not explain how it came to pass that a few weeks ago, Esquire, Inc., decided to pay Goodwin $12,500 and to print the apologetic column about the article which appears in the November issue.

Magazines settle libel suits out of court all the time, of course. Not all magazines—*The New Yorker* has a strict policy against it; but many other magazines believe that it is cheaper to settle than to pay the high costs of litigation. At *Playboy*, I'm told, they say that they have never lost a libel case; the reason is that the magazine settles before it gets to court. All of this is a fairly well-kept secret in the magazine business; in fact, one of the arguments put to me against my writing this column was that if it becomes known that *Esquire* settles out of court, every joker whose name is mentioned in the magazine might end up suing. I rather doubt that will happen—but in any case, my concern is not with future nuisance suits, merely with this one.

The trouble with Goodwin began in August 1975, before Burlingham's article even appeared in the magazine. Doris Kearns, who is now Goodwin's wife, came to New York to see me and Don Erickson, editor of *Esquire*. She asked us to kill the article. She said that Goodwin had become so nervous about what it might contain that he had taken to his bed on Cape Cod and had been there for two weeks. At that point, the article was on the presses and could not have been killed if Rich-ard Goodwin dropped dead. We told her this. Then, a few days before publication, a telegram arrived—I can't remember whether it was from Goodwin or from a friend of Goodwin—putting the magazine on some sort of legal notice. A rumor came floating through that Goodwin had hired President Nixon's former lawyer James St. Clair and was planning to sue *Esquire* for libel. Then nothing for a while.

In the early months of 1976—I'm sorry to be so fuzzy about dates, but I didn't know what was going on—a man named Arnold Hyatt telephoned the president of Esquire, Inc., A. L. Blinder. Hyatt, a Boston shoe manufacturer and contributor to Democratic campaigns, knew both Blinder and Goodwin, and he apparently suggested the two men get together and work this thing out like gentlemen. A couple of points about Abe Blinder. The first is that a few years ago, he and the rest of the magazine's management were slightly traumatized by the result of a lawsuit William F. Buckley filed against *Esquire* over an article by Gore Vidal. *Esquire*'s lawyers wanted to fight the suit; they were certain it would be dismissed in a summary judgment. But it wasn't, and the ultimate cost to the company, including the eventual out-of-court settle-ment, was in the neighborhood of $350,000. A second point is that Blinder takes pride in the fact that he rarely interferes in the magazine's editorial matters. When I interviewed him about the Goodwin matter, he told me that he probably would not allow this column to be printed in the magazine—but he added that he had vetoed only one other article in his thirty-three-year history at *Esquire*. "It was about Morris Lapi-dus, the architect of the Fontainebleau Hotel," he said, "and it was very negative, very uncomplimentary. The Tisch brothers are good friends of mine, and they called and told me it would be bad for the hotel business if we printed it."

After Hyatt's call, Blinder spoke to Goodwin and arranged a lunch for himself, Goodwin, Kearns, and Arnold Gingrich, the editor in chief and founder of *Esquire*. Goodwin arrived at the lunch with a set of papers containing a legal complaint and an itemization of grievances against the article. Blinder told Goodwin he had three alternatives: he could write a letter to the editor, he could sue, or he could forget it. Goodwin said that a letter to the editor would simply be his word against Burlingham's. But he indicated that he would be willing to work something out short of a lawsuit. At this point, Arnold Gingrich made a suggestion. He wrote a monthly column in which he often commented on articles in the magazine, and he might be able to write something that would reflect Goodwin's version of events. A token payment of one thousand dollars was mentioned, and everyone went home. A few weeks later, Goodwin met with Gingrich to draft the column. The next day, Gingrich was hospitalized with lung cancer; he died in July.

While Gingrich was ill, the column that appears in this issue was written by Don Erickson, now editor in chief of the magazine. In it, Gingrich relates that after reading Burlingham's article, which portrayed Goodwin as a Sammy Glick, he was surprised to meet Goodwin and find no trace at all of the ruthlessness Burlingham alluded to. Burlingham's portrait, said Gingrich, "is sufficiently at odds with the man himself that an appraisal is in order. . . . The piece made him out to be a guy who didn't pay his debts. But what we didn't say was that he had never had his credit withdrawn anywhere and that, with his holdings in Maine, he has assets several times his liabilities. And we made him out to be a man who goes around scaring people, including women, with guns. We didn't report that his gun hobby has never gone further than shooting at small birds and clay pigeons. He never owned a handgun, he told me. The one we reported on turned out to be a toy belonging to his son, he said. We implied that he had a streak of kleptomania and produced an incident that didn't prove it."

As it continues, the column is extremely clever. It is framed as one man's opinion, not as a formal apology, so there was no need for the magazine to show it to the author or editor involved. It is full of "he said" and "he told me," so that nothing is actually denied; still, the impression is that there was somehow faulty, incomplete, or inaccurate reporting. Gingrich claims to be speaking as an editor in disagreement with the other editors of the magazine, but this is not really accurate. Gingrich was not just the founder of the magazine but its guiding spirit, and a reappraisal from him is considerably more loaded than a simple difference of opinion among equals.

But there's more to the story. Erickson's draft was sent to Goodwin for approval. Then, in June, *Esquire* received a letter from James St. Clair, who turned out to be Goodwin's lawyer after all, demanding sixteen thousand dollars for Goodwin to pay the legal fees entailed in reaching the settlement. This came as a surprise to the management. Blinder was under the impression that the token payment of one thousand dollars was agreed upon; he also believed that this was to have been a transaction among gentlemen, not lawyers. *Esquire*'s house counsel, Ron Diana, replied to St. Clair on July 7. He said the magazine was completely unwilling to pay such a high fee, particularly because it continued to believe in the accuracy of Burlingham's article; Diana instead offered five thousand dollars. Arnold Hyatt, the shoe man, then resurfaced. He called Blinder to say that Goodwin was shocked at the belligerent tone of Diana's letter; Goodwin, all injured innocence, could not understand how things had gotten so unpleasant. Blinder was apparently persuaded by the call, and the $12,500 fee was arrived at. Blinder then sent Hyatt a case of champagne.

Out-of-court settlements are extremely complicated, or so I have found from talking to lawyers in the past couple of weeks. They're reached as a result of a combination of practical and ethical consider-ations. Generally speaking, though, if a magazine is willing to settle, the rule is this: if the magazine believes its article was right, it may set-tle for practical considerations and pay a token amount to avoid court costs. If the magazine is wrong, it may settle not only by paying off but also by printing a retraction, correction, or apology. What is extremely rare—so rare that none of the lawyers I interviewed could recall a simi-lar case—is for a magazine that believes it is right to pay off *and* print a retraction of sorts.

I can't quarrel with the financial settlement Goodwin got. I don't like it, but it's a business decision, I suppose. But Goodwin got the money *and* the apology. This is a tribute to him: he is as crafty and manipula-tive and brilliant as Bo Burlingham said he was. But it's a bad moment for this magazine. Abe Blinder told me that he had no problem with the settlement because: "There is no principle involved." I would like to state the principle involved. It's very simple. A magazine has an obliga-tion to its writers and readers to stand by what it prints.

In any case, the Goodwin business is over. Bo Burlingham got $1,250 for his article and Dick Goodwin got $12,500 and an apology. There are all sorts of lessons to be drawn here, but the only one that seems to me at all worth mentioning is that I will henceforth try, when assigning articles on controversial subjects, to find writers who know the Tisch brothers.

In our conversation, Abe Blinder said that another reason he would probably not allow this column to run in *Esquire* was that Arnold Gin-grich is dead and cannot defend himself. I am deeply sorry that Arnold is dead, for many reasons. For one thing, he was a man who could change his mind, and I like to think that by now he might have come around to Burlingham's way of seeing Dick Goodwin. For another, I think he meant it when he said what he did at the end of his monologue on Goodwin: "I've always said that this is a magazine of infinite surprises where people can say what they damn please, even to the extent of the editors disagreeing among themselves." If he were alive, I think that on those grounds he would have allowed me to print this column in the magazine: he would also have admitted that I outfoxed him just a little bit on that one small point.

One last thing. I speak only for myself, but I would like to apologize to Bo Burlingham.

—November 1976

I Just Want to Say: The World Is Not Flat

Last week I went to one of those Internet conferences I get invited to now and then, and of course *New York Times* columnist Thomas Friedman was there. He wasn't actually there in person. It wasn't that important a conference. He sent a tape of himself. He took the entire thesis of his best-selling book *The World Is Flat* and squished it down into twenty minutes. Coincidentally, two nights earlier, I had found myself standing across from Friedman, in person, at a craps table in Las Vegas. As he rolled the dice to make a five, I shouted, "This is it, Tom, this is your chance to make up for being wrong on Iraq." But he rolled a seven and crapped out.

And then there he was at this conference. There was a big banner over the screen that said THE WORLD IS FLAT, and all the bright, young Internet people watched Friedman talk about globalization and say that technology had flattened the walls of the world. They were enthralled by him and actually managed to stay focused and off their mobile devices for the entire time he was speaking. Afterward, instantly, they all turned their mobile devices back on, and the huge conference room was suddenly illuminated by hundreds of small boxes and orchestrated by the sound of thousands of tiny fingers tapping away.

Friedman, of course, is not just a columnist for the world's most powerful newspaper—he's something else. He's a panelist. There's an entire population of panelists today, mostly guys, who make a living in some way or other but whose true career consists of appearing at conferences like this. Some of these panelists are players and some are merely journalists, but for a brief moment, the panel equalizes them all. The panelists perform in front of audiences that include ordinary people, but their real performances are for one another at places like the Four-square Conference in New York and Herbert Allen's summer CEO-fest in Sun Valley; the panelists' job is to put into perspective whatever conventional wisdom happens to apply at the moment, and to validate it.

In fact, these conferences tend to be validating in every way, and it's no surprise that at the last two I attended, there were representatives from Walmart who appeared onstage and were never once asked about their public-relations difficulties over pesky things like the way they treat their employees. (At both conferences, though, the men from Walmart were cheerfully asked about their company's policy of requiring executives to fly tourist and sleep two-in-a-room on business trips. Both times the men from Walmart cheerfully replied. Both times the audience cheerfully chuckled along.)

Anyway, it interests me that every time I go to one of these conferences, there's a piece of absolutely unarguable conventional wisdom about the Internet that seems sooner or later to turn out to be wrong. It's not easy to be wrong about the Internet—the Internet consists of pretty much everything in the universe. So pretty much anything you say about it is going to turn out to be partly true in some way or other. Nonetheless, it turns out not to be.

For example, when I started going to these conferences, it was a given that the Internet was going to set everyone free; this was back in the day, when we understood the Internet to mean e-mail. The world was full of executives and panelists who took the position that it was much simpler to return twenty e-mails than ten telephone calls. But executives now return hundreds of e-mails every day, and life is not remotely simpler. They return e-mails day and night. They never go home from their e-mail. What's more, they absorb almost nothing that happens, because the minute it does, their BlackBerrys are blinking at them.

Then the dot-com boom began, and a new piece of conventional wisdom emerged: the dot-coms would make us rich. This was true. They did. And then, suddenly, the dot-coms crashed. So not quite true.

Time for a new piece of conventional wisdom: there was no money in the Internet. This was confounding: it seemed that an amazing, unheard-of, completely mystifying episode had occurred in the history of capitalism. A huge business had emerged, but there was no profit in it. Warren Buffett, who is the king of the panelists, the überpanelist, the second-richest man in America, the sage of Omaha who plays online bridge with the first-richest man in America, gave a speech during this period, and reminded all his acolytes that between 1904 and 1908 there were 240 automobile companies in business; by 1924, 10 of them accounted for 90 percent of revenues. This sentence was quoted as if it had come straight from the Mount, although no one was entirely sure what it meant. Was everyone going to go out of business, or just almost everyone? The guys who'd started in garages would make money, of course—they'd already made money. The guys who'd invented the technology and the software would be rich. But everyone who'd come afterward would be doomed.

Many panels were held on this point, and many panelists were thoughtful and interesting (and puzzled) about the bleak future ahead. But one thing was clear: there was no money in the Internet. And advertising was not the answer: advertising would never work because the people using the Internet would never ever accept it. The Internet was free. The Internet was democratic. The Internet was pure. Ads would never fly. What's more, in the TiVo world we now live in, the ads would be blocked by Internet users who would never stand for them.

Which brings me to this conference on the Internet I attended last week, where, it will not surprise you to hear, there was a new piece of conventional wisdom: there were billions of dollars to be made in the Internet. It had suddenly become clear that there was a lot of advertising money out there, and all you had to do was provide content so that the ads had something to run alongside of. It crossed my mind that the actual definition of "content" for an Internet company was "something you can run an ad alongside of." I found this a depressing insight, even though my conviction that all conventional wisdom about the Internet turns out to be untrue rescued me somewhat from a slough of despond on the subject.

And by the way, the world is not flat. There are walls everywhere. If there weren't, we wouldn't have gone into Iraq, where everybody crapped out, not just Tom Friedman.

—March 2006

The Making of Theodore H. White

He was alone, as always.
A man who finishes a book is always alone when he finishes it, and Theodore H. White was alone. It was a hot, muggy day in New

York when he finished, or perhaps it was a cold, windy night; there is no way to be certain, although it is certain that Theodore H. White was certain of what the weather was like that day, or that night, because when Theodore H. White writes about things, he notices the weather, and he usually manages to get it into the first paragraph or first few pages of whatever he writes. "Hyannis Port sparkled in the sun that day, as did all New England" (*The Making of the President 1960*). "It was hot; the sun was blinding; there would be a moment of cool shade ahead under the overpass they were approaching" (*The Making of the President 1964*). "Thursday had been a cold day of drizzling rain in Manhattan, where Richard Nixon lived" (*The Making of the President 1968*). "I could see the fan of yellow water below shortly before the plane dipped into the overcast" (*The Making of the President 1972*). And now Theodore H. White looked at the opening line of his new book, *Breach of Faith*: "Wednesday dawned with an overcast in Washington—hot, sticky, threatening to rain—July 24th, 1974." It had worked before and it would work again.

White flicked a cigarette ash from his forty-sixth Marlboro of the day and took the last sheet of one hundred percent rag Strathmore parchment typing paper from his twenty-two-year-old IBM Executive typewriter. It was the 19,246,753rd piece of typing paper he had typed on in his sixty years. He was tired. He was old and tired. He was also short. But mainly he was tired. He was tired of writing the same book over and over again. He was tired of being taken in, taken in by John F. Kennedy, Lyndon Johnson, Robert Kennedy, General Westmoreland, Richard Nixon, tired of being taken in by every major politician in the last sixteen years. He was tired of being hornswoggled by winners. He was tired of being made to look like an ass, tired of having to apologize in each successive book for the mistakes he had made in the one before. He was tired of being imitated by other journalists, and he was tired of rewriting their work, which had surpassed his own. He was tired of things going wrong, tired of being in the wrong place at the wrong time; the night of the Saturday Night Massacre, for example, he found himself not in the Oval Office but on vacation in the South of France, where he was reduced to hearing the news from his hotel maid. He was tired of describing the people he was writing about as tired.

We must understand how Theodore H. White got to be that way, how he got to be so old and so tired. We must understand how this man grew to have a respect and awe for the institutions of American government that was so overweening as to blind him to the weaknesses of the

men who ran them. We must understand how he came to believe that all
men in power—even base men—were essentially noble, and when they
failed to be noble, it had merely to do with flaws, flaws that grew out of
a massive confluence of forces, forces like PR, the burgeoning bureaucracy, television, manipulation, and California. We must understand
his associates, good men, tired men but good men, men he lunched with
every week, men who worked at newsmagazines which had long since
stopped printing run-on sentences with subordinate clauses attached to
the end. And to understand what has happened to Theodore H. White,
which is the story of this column, one would have to go back to earlier
years, to the place where it all started.

Time magazine.

That was where it all started. At *Time* magazine. Not everything
started at *Time* magazine—Theodore H. White developed his infuriat-
ing style of repeating phrases over and over again later in his life, after
he had left *Time* magazine—but that is where most of it started. It was
at *Time* magazine that White picked up the two overriding devices of
newsmagazine writing. The first was a passion for tidbits, for small
details, for color. President Kennedy liked to eat tomato soup with sour
cream in it for lunch. Adlai Stevenson sunned himself in blue sneakers
and blue shorts. Hubert Humphrey ate cheese sandwiches whenever he
was in the midst of a crisis.

The second was omniscience, the omniscience that results when a
writer has had a week, or a month, or a year to let events sift out, the
kind of omniscience, in short, that owes so much to hindsight.

Until 1959, when Theodore H. White began work on the four-
hundred-one-page, blue-bound *Making of the President 1960*, no
reporter had written a book on a political campaign using these two
devices. White did, and his book changed the way political campaigns
were covered. He wrote the 1960 campaign as a national pageant, a
novelistic struggle for power between two men. He wrote about what
they wore and what they ate and what they said behind the scenes. He
went to meetings other reporters did not even ask to attend; the participants at the meetings paid scant attention to him. And then, of course,
the book was published, became a best seller, and everything began to
change.

Change.

Change begins slowly, as it always does, and when it began, White
was slow to notice it. He covered the 1964 campaign as he had covered
the one before; he did not see that all the detail and color and tidbits and

dialogue made no difference in that election; the political process was not working in the neat way it had worked four years before, with hard-fought primaries and nationally televised debates and a cliff-hanger vote; the 1964 election was over before it even began. Then he came to 1968, and the change, mounting like an invisible landslide, intensified, owing to a massive confluence of factors. The first was the national press, which began to out-report him. The second was White himself. He no longer went to meetings where he was ignored; he was, after all, Theodore H. White, historian to American presidential elections. Had he been a student of physics and the Heisenberg uncertainty principle, instead of a student of history and all the Cicero he could cram into his books, he might have understood what was happening. But he did not. The change, the invisible landslide of change, eluded him. He wrote a book about a new Nixon, an easier, more relaxed, more affable Nixon. He missed the point. He missed the point about Vietnam; he missed the point about the demonstrations. Larry O'Brien used to be important; now it was these kids; who the hell were these kids to come along and take politics away from Theodore H. White? He missed the point about the Nixon campaign too. And so, in 1969, came the first great humiliation. A young man named Joe McGinniss, a young man who had gone to low- and mid-level meetings of the Nixon campaign, where the participants had paid him scant attention, produced the campaign book of the year, *The Selling of the President*, and even knocked off Theodore H. White's title in the process. Then, before he knew it, it was 1972, another campaign, another election, and White went through it, like so many other reporters, ignoring Watergate; months later, as he was finishing the 1972 book, he was forced to deal with the escalating scandal; he stuck it in, a paragraph here, a paragraph there, a chapter to wrap it all up, all this sticking out like sore thumbs throughout the manuscript. That year, the best book on the campaign was written not by White but by Timothy Crouse, who had stayed at the fringes, reporting on the press. To make matters worse, Crouse's book, *The Boys on the Bus*, included a long, not entirely flattering section on Theodore H. White, a section in which White complained, almost bitterly, about the turn things had taken. He spoke of the night McGovern won the nomination in Miami:

"It's appalling what we've done to these guys," he told Crouse. "McGovern was like a fish in a goldfish bowl. There were three different network crews at different times. The still photographers kept coming in in groups of five. And there were at least six writers sitting in the corner—I don't even know their names. We're all sitting there watching him work on his acceptance speech, poor bastard. He tries to go into the bedroom with Fred Dutton to go over the list of vice presidents, which would later turn out to be the fuck-up of the century, of course, and all of us are observing him, taking notes like mad, getting all the little details. Which I think I invented as a method of reporting and which I now sincerely regret. If you write about this, say that I sincerely regret it. Who gives a fuck if the guy had milk and Total for breakfast?"

White sat in the Harvard chair given to him by the Harvard Alumni Association and looked with irritation at his new manuscript, *Breach of Faith*. Here it was 1975 and he had a new book coming out. What in Christ was he doing with a book coming out in 1975? He wasn't supposed to have to write the next one until 1977. Theodore H. White shook his close-cropped, black-haired head. It was these damned politicians. He'd spent the best years of his life trying to train these assholes, and they couldn't even stay in office the full four years.

White stared at the title. Breach of faith. The new book's thesis was that Richard Nixon had breached the faith of the American people in the presidency; that was what had caused him to be driven from office. But deep down, Theodore H. White knew that the faith Nixon had breached had been his, Theodore H. White's. White was the only American left who still believed in the institution of the presidency. Theodore H. White was depressed. Any day now, he might have to start work on the next book, on *The Making of the President 1976*, and where would he ever find a candidate who measured up to his own feelings about the United States and its institutions? The questions lay in his brain cells, growing like an invisible landslide, and suddenly Theodore H. White had the answer. He would have to run for president. That was the only way. That was the only way to be sure that the political processes would function the way he believed they ought to. That was the only way he could get all those behind-the-scenes meetings to function properly. That was the only way he could get all those other reporters out of his story. White realized that something very important was happening. And so he did what he always does when he realizes something very important is happening: he called the weather bureau.

It was forty-nine degrees and raining in Central Park.

—August 1975

✳ *The Advocate*

Vaginal Politics

We have lived through the era when happiness was a warm puppy, and the era when happiness was a dry martini, and now we have come to the era when happiness is "knowing what your uterus looks like." For this slogan, and for what is perhaps the apotheosis of the do-it-yourself movement in America, we have the Los Angeles Self-Help Clinic to thank: this group of women has been sending its emissaries around the country with a large supply of plastic specula for sale and detailed instructions on how women can perform their own gynecological examinations and abortions. Some time ago, two of its representatives were in New York, and Ellen Frankfort, who covers health matters for the *Village Voice*, attended a session. What she saw makes the rest of the women's movement look like a bunch of old biddies at an American Legion Auxiliary cake sale:

"Carol, a woman from the . . . Clinic, slipped off her dungarees and underpants, borrowed somebody's coat and stretched it out on a long table, placed herself on top, and, with her legs bent at the knees, inserted a speculum into herself. Once the speculum was in place, her cervix was completely visible and each of the fifty women present took a flashlight and looked inside.

" 'Which part is the cervix? The tiny slit in the middle?'

" 'No, that's the os. The cervix is the round, doughnut-shaped part.' "

Following the eyewitness internal examination, Carol and her colleague spoke at length about medical ritual and how depersonalizing it is, right down to the drape women are given to cover their bodies; they suggested that women should instead take the drape and fling it to the ground. If the doctor replaces it, they suggest throwing it off again. And if he questions this behavior (and one can only wonder at a doctor who would not), they recommend telling him that California doctors have stopped draping. "And if you're in California, tell him that doctors in New York have stopped this strange custom." The evening ended with a description of the most radical self-help device of all: the period extractor, a syringe-and-tube contraption that allows a woman to remove her menstrual flow, all by herself, in five minutes; if she is pregnant, the embryo is sucked out instead. Color slides were shown: a woman at home, in street clothes, gave herself an early abortion using the device. "I hesitate to use the word 'revolutionary,' " Frankfort wrote of the event, "but no other word seems accurate. . . ."

Ellen Frankfort's report on this session is now reprinted as the opening of her new book, *Vaginal Politics* (Quadrangle Books). When I first read it in the *Voice*, I was shocked and incredulous. At the same time, it seemed obvious that at the rate things were going in the women's movement, within a few months the material would not be surprising at all. Well, it has been over a year since the Los Angeles Self-Help Clinic brought the word to the East, and what they advocate is as shocking and incredible as ever. I mean, it's awfully perplexing that anyone would suggest throwing linens all over an examination room when a simple verbal request would probably do the trick. And when Frankfort informs us, as she does at the end of her book, that "there are several groups of women who get together in New York City and on their dining room tables or couches look at the changes in the cervix," it is hard not to long for the days when an evening with the girls meant bridge.

On the other hand . . .

On the other hand, the self-help movement and the concern with health issues among women's groups spring from a very real and not at all laughable dissatisfaction with the American medical establishment, and most particularly with gynecologists. In New York, the women's movement has turned this dissatisfaction to concrete achievement in placing paid women counselors in major abortion clinics and in working to lower rates and change procedures at these clinics; in Boston, the Women's Health Collective has produced a landmark book, *Our Bodies, Our Selves*, a comprehensive compilation of information about how the female body works. But the animosity against doctors has also reached the point where irresponsibility, not to mention hard-core raunchiness, has replaced reason. When Frankfort asked Carol about the possible negative effects of period extraction, her question was taken as a broad-scale attack on feminism. The fact is that if doctors were prescribing equipment as untested as these devices are, equipment which clearly violates natural body functions, the women's health movement would be outraged. It has been justifiably incensed that birth-control pills were mass-marketed after only three years' observation on a mere 132 women. The Los Angeles women are advocating a device that has not been tested at all for at-home use; in hospitals, it has been used safely, but by doctors, and primarily for early abortion. There is a horrifying fanaticism to all this, and it springs not just from the zeal to avoid doctors entirely, but from something far more serious. For some time, various scientists have been attacking women's liberation by insisting that because of menstruation, women are unfit for just about everything several days a month. In a way, the Los Angeles women are supporting this assertion in their use of period extraction for non-abortion purposes; what they are saying, in effect, is, yes, it *is* awful, it is truly a curse, and here is a way to be done with it in five minutes. I am not one of those women who are into "blood and birth and death," to quote Joan Didion's rather extraordinary and puzzling definition of what it means to be female, but I do think that the desire to eliminate the first of these functions springs from a self-hate that is precisely parallel to the male fear of blood that underlies so many primitive taboos toward women.

In any event, the extremist fringe of the self-help movement in no way invalidates the legitimate case women have against gynecologists. These doctors are undoubtedly blamed for a great deal that is not their fault; they are, after all, dealing in reproductive and sexual areas, two of the most sensitive and emotionally charged for women. Still, I have dozens of friends who have been misdiagnosed, mismedicated, mistreated, and misinformed by them, and every week, it seems, I hear a new gynecological atrocity tale. A friend who asks specifically not to be sedated during childbirth is sedated. Another friend who has a simple infection is treated instead for gonorrhea, and develops a serious infection as a side effect of the penicillin. Another woman tells of going to see her doctor one month after he has delivered her first child, a deformed baby, born dead. His first question: "Why haven't you been to see me in two years?" Beyond all this, there are the tales of pure insensitivity to psychological problems, impatience with questions, preachy puritanism particularly toward single women, and, for married women, little speeches on the need to reproduce. My usual reaction to these stories is to take a feminist line, blame it all on complicated sexism or simple misogyny. But what Ellen Frankfort has managed to do in *Vaginal Politics*—and what makes her book quite remarkable—is to broaden women's health issues far beyond such narrow analyses. "The mystique of the doctor, profound as it is, is not the only negative feature of the present health system," she writes. "Unfortunately, the women from the Los Angeles Self-Help Clinic . . . seemed to be focusing mainly on this aspect of the problem while ignoring the need for institutional change. Feminist politics cannot be divorced from other political realities, such as health care and safety."

The problems women face with doctors stem not just from their own abysmal lack of knowledge about their bodies, and not just from female conditioning toward male authority figures. (The classic female dependency on the obstetrician, Frankfort notes, transfers at childbirth to dependency on the pediatrician, all this "in perfect mimicry of the dependency relationship of marital roles.") They stem also from inequities in the health system and from the way doctors are educated. The brutalizing, impersonal training medical students receive prepares them perfectly to turn around and treat their patients in exactly the same way: as infants. Writes Frankfort: "We feel hesitant to question their procedures, their fees or their hours, and often we're simply grateful that we're able to see them at all, particularly if they're well recommended." My sister-in-law, who is pregnant, told me the other day that she was afraid to bother her gynecologist with questions for fear of "getting on his wrong side." As Frankfort points out: "The fear that a patient will be punished unless he or she is totally submissive reveals a profound distrust of the people in control of our bodies." (I have, I should point out, exactly the same fears about my lawyer, my accountant, and my maid. Generally speaking, none of us is terribly good at being an employer.)

Vaginal Politics covers a wide range of health subjects: the New York abortion scene, drugs, psychoanalysis, breast cancer, venereal disease, the law, the growth of the consumer health movement in America. At times, the tone is indignant to the point of heavy-handedness. Also, I caught several factual errors. But Frankfort has written with contagious energy and extraordinary vitality; without exaggeration, her book is among the most basic and important written about women's issues, and I hope it will not be overlooked now that the more faddish women's books have had their day.

The tendency in reviewing this book, of course, is to stress the more outlandish and radical aspects of the health movement, but Frankfort's real strength lies in her painstaking accumulation of political incidents. There is the case of Shirley Wheeler, who had an abortion and was convicted for manslaughter under an 1868 Florida law. The condition of her probation: marry the man she lives with, or return to her parents in North Carolina. If she refused, if she, for example, lived instead with a woman, her parole would be rescinded and she would be sent to jail. There are the guidelines for sterilization proposed by the American College of Obstetricians and Gynecologists: no woman can be sterilized unless her age multiplied by the number of children she has borne is 120 or more. Writes Frankfort: "The logic behind this sliding scale of reproductive output has it that in order to earn her right to not have children, a woman must first produce some." For men, under the same guidelines, voluntary sterilization is available to anyone over twenty-one. Period. Another incident in the book, and one that is particularly compelling, is the case of Dr. Joseph Goldzieher, who is at the Southwest Foundation for Research and Education in San Antonio, Texas. Some years ago, Dr. Goldzieher got to wondering whether one reason birth-control pills prevent conception might simply be psychological, and he decided to run a test to see. There were 398 women, most of them Chicanos, coming to the clinic, and one fifth of them were given placebos instead of contraceptives. Within a year, six of the women, all mothers of at least three other children, had given birth. Writes Frankfort: "The ethics of a researcher who considers an unwanted child an unfortunate 'side effect' of an experimenter's curiosity needs no further commentary. However, what should be pointed out . . . is that not only does Dr. Goldzieher work at a research institute where poor nonwhite women are selected for experimentation, but he is also a consultant to several drug companies. In fact, the experiment was sponsored by Syntex, a leading pill manufacturer. . . ."

And so the doctors work for the drug companies and prescribe accordingly, the hospitals take advantage of the poor, the laws are antiquated, it goes on and on. Knowing what your uterus looks like can't hurt, I suppose, and knowing more about your body can only help, but it seems a shame that so much more energy is being directed into this sort of contemplation and so little into changing the political structure. There is a tendency throughout the movement to overindulge in confession, to elevate The Rap to a religious end in itself, to reach a point where self-knowledge dissolves into high-grade narcissism. I know that the pendulum often has to swing a few degrees in the wrong direction before righting itself, but it does get wearing sometimes waiting for the center to catch hold.

—December 1972

Miami

It's about this mother-of-us-all business.

It is Sunday morning in Miami Beach, the day before the Democratic Convention is to begin, and the National Women's Political Caucus is holding a press conference. The cameras are clicking at Gloria, and Bella has swept in trailed by a vortex of television crews, and there is Betty, off to the side, just slightly out of frame. The cameras will occasionally catch a shoulder of her flowered granny dress or a stray wisp of her chaotic graying hair or one of her hands churning up the air; but it will be accidental, background in a photograph of Gloria, or a photograph of Bella, or a photograph of Gloria and Bella. Betty's eyes are darting back and forth trying to catch someone's attention, anyone's attention. No use. Gloria is speaking, and then Bella, and then Sissy Farenthold from Texas. And finally . . . Betty's lips tighten as she hears the inevitable introduction coming: "Betty Friedan, the mother of us all." That does it. "I'm getting sick and tired of this mother-of-us-all thing," she says. She is absolutely right, of course: in the women's movement, to be called the mother of anything is rarely a compliment. And what it means in this context, make no mistake, is that Betty, having in fact given birth, ought to cut the cord. Bug off. Shut up. At the very least, retire gracefully to the role of senior citizen, professor emeritus. Betty Friedan has no intention of doing anything of the kind. It's her baby, damn it. Her movement. Is she supposed to sit still and let a beautiful thin lady run off with it?

The National Women's Political Caucus (N.W.P.C.) was organized in July 1971 by a shaky coalition of women's movement leaders. Its purpose was to help women in and into political life, particularly above the envelope-licking level. Just how well the caucus will do in its first national election remains to be seen, but in terms of the Democratic Convention it was wildly successful—so much so, in fact, that by the time the convention was to begin, the N.W.P.C. leaders were undergoing a profound sense of anticlimax. There were 1,121 women delegates, up from 13 percent four years ago to nearly 40 percent. There was a comprehensive and stunning women's plank in the platform; four years ago there was none. There were battles still to be fought at the convention—the South Carolina challenge and the abortion plank—but the first was small potatoes (or so it seemed beforehand) and the second was a guaranteed loser. And so, in a sense, the major function for the N.W.P.C. was to be ornamental—that is, it was simply to be *there*. Making its presence felt. Putting forth the best possible face. Pretending to a unity that did not exist. Above all, putting on a good show: the abortion plank would never carry, a woman would not be nominated as vice president this year, but the N.W.P.C. would put on a good show.

Nineteen seventy-six, and all that. Punctuating all this would be what at times seemed an absurd emphasis on semantics: committees were run by "spokespersons" and "chairpersons"; phones were never manned but "womanned" and "personned." All this was public relations, not politics. They are two different approaches: the first is genteel, dignified, orderly, goes by the rules, and that was the one the women planned to play. They got an inadvertent baptism in the second primarily because George McGovern crossed them, but also because politics, after all, is the name of the game.

In 1963, Betty Friedan wrote *The Feminine Mystique* and became a national celebrity. She moved from the suburbs to Manhattan, separated from her husband, and began to devote much of her time to public speaking. She was a founder of the N.W.P.C. and of the National Organization for Women (N.O.W.), from whose national board she resigned voluntarily last year. This year she ran and lost as a Chisholm delegate to the convention. Among the high points of her campaign was a press release announcing she would appear in Harlem with a "Traveling Watermelon Feast" to distribute to the natives. In recent months, her influence within the movement has waned to the point that even when she is right (which she is occasionally, though usually for the wrong reasons), no one pays any attention to her. Two weeks before the convention, the N.W.P.C. council met to elect a spokesperson in Miami and chose Gloria Steinem over Friedan. The election was yet another chapter in Friedan's ongoing feud with Steinem—the two barely speak—and by the time Betty arrived in Miami she was furious. "I'm so disgusted with Gloria," she would mutter on her way to an N.W.P.C. meeting. Gloria was selling out the women. Gloria was ripping off the movement. Gloria was a tool of George McGovern. Gloria and Bella were bossing the delegates around. Gloria was part of a racist clique that would not support Shirley Chisholm for vice president. And so it went. Every day, Friedan would call N.W.P.C. headquarters at the dingy Betsy Ross Hotel downtown and threaten to call a press conference to expose the caucus; every day, at the meetings the N.W.P.C. held for press and female delegates, movement leaders would watch with a kind of horrified fascination to see what Betty Friedan would do next.

And Gloria. *Sic transit*, etc. Gloria Steinem has in the past year undergone a total metamorphosis, one that makes her critics extremely uncomfortable. Like Jane Fonda, she has become dedicated in a way that is a little frightening and almost awe-inspiring; she is demanding to be taken seriously—and it is the one demand her detractors, who prefer to lump her in with all the other radical-chic beautiful people, cannot bear to grant her. Once the glamour girl, all legs and short skirts and long painted nails, David Webb rings, Pucci, Gucci, you-name-it-she-had-it, once a fixture in gossip columns which linked her to one attractive man after another, she has managed to transform herself almost totally. She now wears Levi's and simple T-shirts—and often the same outfit two days running. The nails are as long as ever, but they are unpolished, and her fingers bare. She has managed to keep whatever private life she still has out of the papers. Most important, she projects a calm, peaceful, subdued quality; her humor is gentle, understated. Every so often, someone suggests that Gloria Steinem is only into the women's movement because it is currently the chic place to be; it always makes me smile, because she is about the only remotely chic thing connected with the movement.

It is probably too easy to go on about the two of them this way: Betty as Wicked Witch of the West, Gloria as Ozma, Glinda, Dorothy—take your pick. To talk this way ignores the subtleties, right? Gloria is not, after all, uninterested in power. And yes, she manages to remain above the feud, but that is partly because, unlike Betty, she has friends who will fight dirty for her. Still, it is hard to come out anywhere but squarely on her side. Betty Friedan, in her thoroughly irrational hatred of Steinem, has ceased caring whether or not the effects of that hatred are good or bad for the women's movement. Her attack on Steinem in the August *McCall's*, which followed the convention by barely a week, quoted Steinem out of context (Steinem's remark, "Marriage is prostitution," was made in the course of a speech on the effects of discrimination in marriage laws) and implied that Gloria was defiantly anti-male, a charge that is, of course, preposterous. I am not criticizing Friedan for discussing the divisions in the movement; nor do I object to her concern about man-haters; if she wants to air all that, it's okay with me. What I do not understand is why—for any but personal reasons—she chooses to discredit Steinem (and Bella Abzug) by tying them in with philosophies they have absolutely nothing to do with.

At a certain point in the convention, every N.W.P.C. meeting began to look and sound the same. Airless, windowless rooms decked with taffeta valances and Miami Beach plaster statuary. Gloria in her jeans and aviator glasses, quoting a female delegate on the gains women have made in political life this year: "It's like pushing marbles through a sieve. It means the sieve will never be the same again." Bella Abzug in her straw hat, bifocals cocked down on her nose, explaining that abortion is too a Constitutional right and belongs in a national platform. "I would like an attorney to advise us on this," says a New York delegate who believes it is a local matter. "One just did," Bella replies. Clancy and Sullivan, two women delegates from Illinois whose credentials are being challenged by the Daley machine, stand and are cheered. Germaine Greer, in overalls, takes notes quietly into a tiny tape recorder. Betty looks unhappy. The South Carolina challenge is discussed: the women want to add seven more delegates to the nine women already serving on the thirty-two-member delegation. "Are these new delegates going to be women or wives?" asks one woman. "Because I'm from Missouri and we filed a challenge and now we have twelve new delegates who turned out to be sisters of, wives, daughters of. . . . What is the point of having a woman on a delegation who will simply say, 'Honey, how do we vote?'" The microphone breaks down. "Until women control technology," says Gloria, "we will have to be dependent in a situation like this." The days pass, and "Make Policy Not Coffee" buttons are replaced by "Boycott Lettuce" buttons are replaced by "Sissy for Vice President" buttons. The days pass, and Betty is still somewhat under control.

The task Friedan ultimately busied herself with was a drive to make Shirley Chisholm vice president, something Shirley Chisholm had no interest whatsoever in becoming. Friedan began lobbying for this the Friday before the convention began, when she asked the N.W.P.C. to endorse Chisholm for vice president; the council decided to hold back from endorsing anyone until it was clear who wanted to run. And meanwhile it would be ready with other women's names; among those that came up were Farenthold, Abzug, Steinem, and Representative Martha Griffiths. Jane Galvin Lewis, a black who was representing Dorothy Height of the National Council of Negro Women at the convention, had suggested Steinem at the meeting. The night Shirley Chisholm was to arrive in Miami, Lewis went up to the Deauville Hotel to welcome her and bumped into Betty Friedan in the lobby.

"What are you doing here?" Friedan asked.

"I'm here to meet Shirley," said Lewis.

"You really play both ends, don't you?" said Friedan.

"Explain that," said Lewis.

"What kind of black are you anyway?"

"What are you talking about?"

"You didn't even want to support Shirley Chisholm," Friedan said, her voice rising. "I heard you. I heard you put up somebody else's name."

"That was after we decided to have a list ready," said Lewis. "Stop screaming at me."

"I'm going to do an exposé," shouted Friedan. "I'm going to expose everyone. If it's the last thing I do, I'm going to do it. I'm going to do it." She turned, walked off to a group of women, and left Jane Lewis standing alone.

"It's like pushing marbles through a sieve," Gloria is saying. Monday, opening day, and the N.W.P.C. is holding a caucus for women delegates to hear the presidential candidates. Betty has publicly announced her drive to run Chisholm for vice president. The ballroom of the Carillon Hotel, packed full of boisterous, exuberant delegates, activists, and press, gives her suggestion a standing ovation; minutes later, it is hissing Chisholm with equal gusto for waffling on the California challenge. I am sitting next to Shirley MacLaine, McGovern's chief adviser on women's issues, and she is explaining to fellow delegate Marlo Thomas that McGovern will abandon the South Carolina challenge if there is any danger of its bringing up the procedural question of what constitutes a majority. McGovern, she is saying, plans to soft-pedal the challenge in his speech here—and here he is now, pushing through another standing ovation, beaming while he is graciously introduced by Liz Carpenter. "We know we wouldn't have been here if it hadn't been for you," she says. "George McGovern didn't talk about reform—he did something about it." The audience is McGovern's. "I am grateful for the introduction that all of you are here because of me," says the candidate rumored to be most in touch with women's issues. "But I really think the credit for that has to go to Adam instead. . . ." He pauses for the laugh and looks genuinely astonished when what he gets instead is a resounding hiss. "Can I recover if I say Adam and Eve?" he asks. Then he goes on to discuss the challenges, beginning with South Carolina. "On that challenge," he says, "you have my full and unequivocal support." Twelve hours later, the women find out that full and unequivocal support from George McGovern is considerably less than that.

. . .

"We were screwed," Debbie Leff is saying. Leff is press liaison for the N.W.P.C., and she is putting mildly what the McGovern forces did to the women. Monday night, the caucus, under floor leader Bella Abzug, delivered over 200 non-McGovern delegate votes on South Carolina—100 more than they had been told were necessary—and then watched, incredulous, as the McGovern staff panicked and pulled back its support. Tuesday night, the fight over the abortion plank— which was referred to as the "human-reproduction plank" because it never once mentioned the word "abortion"—produced the most emo- tional floor fight of the convention. The McGovern people had been opposed to the plank because they thought it would hurt his candidacy; at the last minute, they produced a right-to-lifer to give a seconding speech, a move they had promised the women they would not make. "Because of that pledge," said Steinem, "we didn't mention butchering women on kitchen tables in our speeches, and then they have a speaker who's saying, 'Next thing you know, they'll be murdering old people.'" Female members of the press lobbied for the plank. Male delegates left their seats to allow women alternates to vote. The movement split over whether to have a roll call or simply a voice vote. At four in the morn- ing, Bella Abzug was screaming at Shirley MacLaine, and Steinem, in tears, was confronting McGovern campaign manager Gary Hart: "You promised us you would not take the low road, you bastards." The roll call on the plank was held largely at Betty Friedan's insistence. She and Martha McKay of North Carolina were the only N.W.P.C. leaders who were willing to take the risk; the rest thought the roll call would be so badly defeated that it would be best to avoid the humiliation. Friedan was in this case right for the wrong reasons: "We have to find out who our enemies are," she said. Incredibly, the plank went down to a thor- oughly respectable defeat, 1572.80 against, 1101.37 for.

Thursday. A rumor is circulating that Gloria Steinem is at the Doral Hotel to speak with McGovern. I find her in the lobby. "I didn't see him," she says. "I don't want to see him." She is walking over to the Fontainebleau for a meeting; and on the way out of the Doral, Bob Anson, a former *Time* reporter, who interviewed her for a McGovern profile, says hello.

"At some point I'd like to talk to you about the socks," Gloria says.

"What do you mean?" asks Anson.

"You said in that article that I give him advice about socks and shirts. I don't talk to him about things like that. He listens to men about clothes."

Anson apologizes, claims he had nothing to do with the error, and as we leave the hotel, I suggest to Gloria that such incorrect facts stem from a kind of newsmagazine tidbit madness.

"That's not it," says Gloria. "It's just that if you're a woman, all they can think about your relationship with a politician is that you're either sleeping with him or advising him about clothes." We start walking up Collins Avenue, past lettuce-boycott petitioners and welfare-rights pamphleteers. "It's just so difficult," she says, crying now. I begin babbling—all the pressures on you, no private life, no sleep, no wonder you're upset. "It's not that," says Gloria. "It's just that they won't take us seriously." She wipes at her cheeks with her hand, and begins crying again. "And I'm just tired of being screwed, and being screwed by my friends. By George McGovern, whom I raised half the money for in his first campaign, wrote his speeches. I can see him. I can get in to see him. That's easy. But what would be the point? He just doesn't understand. We went to see him at one point about abortion, and the question of welfare came up. 'Why are you concerned about welfare?' he said. He didn't understand it was a women's issue." She paused. "They won't take us seriously. We're just walking wombs. And the television coverage. Teddy White and Eric Sevareid saying that now that the women are here, next thing there'll be a caucus of left-handed Lithuanians." She is still crying, and I try to offer some reassuring words, something, but everything I say is wrong; I have never cried over anything remotely political in my life, and I honestly have no idea of what to say.

And so Friday, at last, and it is over. Sissy Farenthold has made a triumphant, albeit symbolic, run for the vice-presidency and come in second; as a final irony, she was endorsed by Shirley Chisholm. Jean Westwood is the new chairperson of the Democratic National Committee, although she prefers to be called chairman. I am talking to Martha McKay. "I'm fifty-two years old," she is saying. "I've gotten to the point where I choose what I spend time on. Look at the situation in North Carolina. Forty-four percent of the black women who work are domestics. In the eastern part of the state, some are making fifteen dollars a week and totin'. You know what that is? That's taking home roast beef, and that's supposed to make up for the wages. We're talking about bread on the table. We're talking about women who are heads of households who can't get credit. They hook up with a man, he signs the credit agreement, they make the payments, and in the end he owns the house. When things like this are going on in the country, who's got time to get caught in the rock-crushing at the national level? I'm just so amazed that these gals fight like they do. It's so enervating."

—November 1972

Reunion

A boy and a girl are taking a shower together in the bathroom. How to explain the significance of it? It is a Friday night in June, the first night of the tenth reunion of the Class of 1962 of Wellesley College, and a member of my class has just returned from the bathroom with the news. A boy and a girl are taking a shower together. No one can believe it. Ten years and look at the changes. Ten years ago, we were allowed men in the rooms on Sunday afternoons only, on the condition the door be left fourteen inches ajar. One Sunday during my freshman year, a girl in my dormitory went into her room with a date and not only closed the door but put a sock on it. (The sock—I feel silly remembering nonsense like this, but I do—was a Wellesley signal meaning "Do Not Disturb.") Three hours later, she and the boy emerged and she was wearing a different outfit. No one could believe it. We were that young. Today boys on exchange programs from MIT and Dartmouth live alongside the girls, the dormitory doors lock, and some of the women in my class—as you can see from the following excerpt from one letter to our tenth-reunion record book—have been through some changes themselves:

"In the past five years I have (1) had two children and two abortions, (2) moved seriously into politics, working up to more responsible positions on bigger campaigns, (3) surrendered myself to what I finally acknowledged was my lifework—the women's revolution, (4) left my husband and children to seek my fortune and on the way (5) fallen desperately, madly, totally in love with a beautiful man and am sharing a life with him in Cambridge near Harvard Square where we're completely incredibly happy doing the work we love and having amazing life adventures."

I went back to my reunion at Wellesley to write about it. I'm doing a column, that's why I'm going, I said to New York friends who were amazed that I would want anything to do with such an event. I want to see what happened, I said—to my class, to the college. (I didn't say that I wanted my class and the college to see what had happened to me, but that of course was part of it, too.) A few years ago, Wellesley went through a long reappraisal before rejecting coeducation and reaffirming its commitment to educating women; that interested me. Also, I wondered how my class, almost half of which has two or more children, was dealing with what was happening to women today. On Friday evening, when my classmate and I arrived at the dormitory that was our class headquarters, we bumped into two Wellesley juniors. One of them asked straight off if we wanted to see their women's liberation bulletin board. They took us down the corridor to a cork board full of clippings, told us of their battle to have a full-time gynecologist on campus, and suddenly it became important for us to let them know we were not what they thought. We were not those alumnae who came back to Wellesley because it was the best time of their lives; we were not those cardigan-sweatered, Lilly Pulitzered matrons or Junior League members or League of Women Voters volunteers; we were not about to be baited by their bulletin board. We're not Them. I didn't come to reunion because I wanted to. I'm here to write about it. Understand?

Wellesley College has probably the most beautiful campus in the country, more lush and gorgeous than any place I have ever seen. In June, the dogwood and azalea are in bloom around Lake Waban, the ivy spurts new growth onto the collegiate Gothic buildings, the huge maples are obscenely loaded with shade. So idyllic, in the literal sense—an idyll before a rude awakening. There was Wellesley, we were told, and then, later, there would be the real world. The real world was different. "Where, oh where are the staid alumnae?" goes a song Wellesley girls sing, and they answer, "They've gone out from their dreams and theories. Lost, lost in the wide, wide world." At Wellesley we would be allowed to dream and theorize. We would be taken seriously. It would not always be so.

Probably the most insidious influence on the students ten years ago was the one exerted by the class deans. They were a group of elderly spinsters who believed that the only valuable role for Wellesley graduates was to go on to the only life the deans knew anything about—

graduate school, scholarship, teaching. There was no value at all placed on achievement in the so-called real world. Success of that sort was suspect; worse than that, it was unserious. Better to be a housewife, my dear, and to take one's place in the community. *Keep a hand in.* This policy was not just implicit but was actually articulated. During my junior year, in a romantic episode that still embarrasses me, I became engaged to a humorless young man whose primary attraction was that he was fourth in his class at Harvard Law School. I went to see my class dean about transferring to Barnard senior year before being married. "Let me give you some advice," she told me. "You have worked so hard at Wellesley. When you marry, take a year off. Devote yourself to your husband and your marriage." I was incredulous. To begin with, I had not worked hard at Wellesley—anyone with my transcript in front of her ought to have been able to see that. But far more important, I had always intended to work after college; my mother was a career woman who had successfully indoctrinated me and my sisters that to be a housewife was to be nothing. Take a year off being a wife? Doing what? I carried the incident around with me for years, repeating it from time to time as positive proof that Wellesley wanted its graduates to be merely housewives. Then, one day, I met a woman who had graduated ten years before me. She had never wanted anything but to be married and have children; she, too, had gone to see this dean before leaving Wellesley and marrying. "Let me give you some advice," the dean told her. "Don't have children right away. Take a year to work." And so I saw. What Wellesley wanted was for us to avoid the extremes, to be instead that thing in the middle. Neither a rabid careerist nor a frantic mamma. That thing in the middle: a trustee. "Life is not all dirty diapers and runny noses," writes Susan Connard Chenoweth in the class record. "I do make it into the real world every week to present a puppet show on ecology called *Give a Hoot, Don't Pollute.*" The deans would be proud of Susan. She is on her way. A doer of good works. An example to the community. Above all, a Samaritan.

I never went near the Wellesley College chapel in my four years there, but I am still amazed at the amount of Christian charity that school stuck us all with, a kind of glazed politeness in the face of boredom and stupidity. Tolerance, in the worst sense of the word. Wellesley was not alone in encouraging this for its students, but it always seemed so sad that a school that could have done so much for women put so much energy into the one area women should be educated out of. How marvelous it would have been to go to a women's college that encouraged impoliteness, that rewarded aggression, that encouraged argument. Women by the time they are eighteen are so damaged, so beaten down, so tyrannized out of behaving in all the wonderful outspoken ways unfortunately characterized as masculine; a college committed to them has to take on the burden of repair—of remedial education, really. I'm not just talking about vocational guidance and placement bureaus (which are far more important than anyone at these schools believes) but also about the need to force young women to define themselves before they abdicate the task and become defined by their husbands. *What do you think? What is your opinion?* No one ever asked. We all graduated from Wellesley able to describe everything we had studied— Baroque painting, Hindemith, Jacksonian democracy, Yeats—yet we were never asked what we thought of any of it. *Do you like it? Do you think it is good? Do you know that even if it is good you do not have to like it?* During reunion weekend, at the Saturday-night class supper, we were subjected to an hour of dance by a fourth-rate Boston theater ensemble which specializes in eighth-rate Grotowski crossed with the worst of *Marat/Sade*. Grunts. Moans. Jumping about imitating lambs. It was absolutely awful. The next day, a classmate with the improbable name of Muffy Kleinfeld asked me what I thought of it. "What did *you* think of it?" I replied. "Well," she said, "I thought their movements were quite expressive and forceful, but I'm not exactly sure what they were trying to do dramatically." *But what did you think of it?*

I am probably babbling a bit here, but I feel a real anger toward Wellesley for blowing it, for being so damned irrelevant. Like many women involved with the movement, I have come full circle in recent years: I used to think that anything exclusively for women (women's pages, women's colleges, women's novels) was a bad idea. Now I am all in favor of it. But when Wellesley decided to remain a women's college, it seemed so pointless to me. Why remain a school for women unless you are prepared to deal with the problems women have in today's society? Why bother? If you are simply going to run a classy liberal-arts college in New England, an ivory tower for $3,900 a year, why not let the men in?

Wellesley *has* changed. Some of the changes are superficial: sex in the dorms, juicy as it is, probably has more to do with the fact that it is 1972 than with real change. On the other hand, there are changes that are almost fundamental. The spinster deans are mostly gone. There is a new president, and she has actually been married. Twice. Many of the hangovers from an earlier era—when Wellesley was totally a school for the rich as opposed to now, when it is only partially so—have been eliminated: sit-down dinners with maids and students waiting on tables; Tree Day, a spring rite complete with tree maidens and tree plantings; the freshman-class banner hunt. Hoop rolling goes on, but this year a feminist senior won and promptly denounced the rite as trivial and sexist. Bible is no longer required. More seniors are applying to law school. "They are not as polite as you were," says history professor Edward Gulick, which sounds promising. Yet another teacher tells me that the students today are more like us than like the class of 1970. The graduation procession is an endless troupe of look-alikes, cookie-cutter perfect faces with long straight hair parted in the middle. Still, there are at least three times as many black faces among them as there were in my time.

And there is the graduation speaker, Eleanor Holmes Norton, a black who is New York City Commissioner of Human Rights. Ten years ago, our speaker was Santha Rama Rau, who bored us mightily with a low-keyed speech on the need to put friendship above love of country. The contrast is quite extraordinary: Norton, an outspoken feminist and mesmerizing public speaker, raises her fist to the class as she speaks. "The question has been asked," she says, " 'What is a woman?' A woman is a person who makes choices. A woman is a dreamer. A woman is a planner. A woman is a maker, and a molder. A woman is a person who makes choices. A woman builds bridges. A woman makes children and makes cars. A woman writes poetry and songs. A woman is a person who makes choices. You cannot even simply become a mother anymore. You must *choose* motherhood. Will you choose change? Can you become its vanguard?" It is a moving speech, full of comparisons between women today and the young blacks of the 1960s; midway through, a Madras-jacketed father, absolutely furious, storms down the aisle, collars his graduating daughter, and drags her off to tell her what he thinks of it. She returns a few minutes later to join her class in a standing ovation.

As for my class, two things are immediately apparent. The housewives, who are openly elated at being sprung from the responsibility of children for a weekend, are nonetheless very defensive about women's liberation and wary of those of us who have made other choices. In the class record book, the most common expression is "women's lib notwithstanding," as in this from Janet Barton Mostafa: "I'm thrilled to find, women's lib to the contrary notwithstanding, that motherhood is a pretty joyful experience. Shakespeare will have to wait in the wings a year or two." *You cannot even simply become a mother anymore. You must* choose *motherhood.* "I steeled myself against coming," one of the housewives said at reunion. "I was sure I was going to have to defend myself." Neither she nor any other housewife will have to defend herself this trip; we are all far too polite. Still, it is interesting that the housewives—not the working mothers or the single or divorced women—are self-conscious. Which brings me to the second trend: the number of women at reunion who are not just divorced but proudly divorced, wearing their new independence as a kind of badge. I cannot imagine that previous Wellesley reunions attracted any divorced women at all.

On Saturday afternoon, our class meets formally. The meeting is conducted by the outgoing class president, B. J. Diener, the developer of Breck One Dandruff Shampoo. She has brought each of us a bottle of the stuff, a gesture some of the class think is in poor taste. I think it is sweet. B. J. is saying that the college ought to do more for its alumnae—hold symposia around the country, provide reading lists on selected subjects, run correspondence courses for graduate-school credits. I find myself involved in a debate about the wisdom of all this—I hadn't meant to get involved, but here I am, with my hand up, about to say that it sounds suspiciously like suburban clubwomen. As it happens, I am sitting in the back with a small group of fellow troublemakers, and we all end up waving our hands and speaking out. "It seems to me," says one, "that all this is in the same spirit of elitism we've tried to get away from since leaving Wellesley." Says another: "Where is the leadership of Wellesley when it comes to graduate-school quotas for women? If Wellesley is going to stand out and be a special place for women, it should be standing up and making a loud noise about it." One thing leads to another, and the Class of 1962 ends up passing a unanimous resolution urging the college to take a position of leadership in the women's movement. It seems a stunning and miraculous victory, and so, giddy, we push on to yet another controversial topic. That morning, graduation exercises had been leafleted by a campus group urging Wellesley to sell its stocks in companies manufacturing products for war; we think the class should support them. President Diener thinks this is a terrible idea, and she musters all her Harvard Business School expertise to suggest instead that we ask the college to vote its shares against company management. Hands are up all over the room. "The whole purpose of Wellesley's investment is to make money," says one woman, "and I for one don't care if they want to invest it in whorehouses." The motion to urge the college to sell its war stocks is defeated 30–8. The eight of us leave

together, flushed with the partial success of our troublemaking, and
suddenly I feel depressed and silly. We had come back to make a little
trouble but, like the senior who won hoop rolling and denounced it, we
all tend toward tiny little rebellions, harmless nips at the system. We
will never make any real trouble. Wellesley helped see to that.

And the nonsense. My God, the nonsense. At reunion, most of the
students are gone and classes are over for the year. All that remains is
a huge pile of tradition. Singing on the chapel steps. Fruit punch and
tea in the afternoon. Class cheers and class songs. On Sunday morning, the last day of a hopelessly overscheduled weekend, the reunion
classes parade down to the alumnae meeting. Each class carries a felt
banner and each woman wears a white dress decorated with some kind
of costume insignia, also in class colors. My class is holding plastic
umbrellas trimmed with huge bouquets of plastic violets and purple
ribbons. The Class of 1957 is waving green feather dusters. Nineteen
thirty-two is wearing what look like strawberry shortcakes but turn
out to be huge red crowns; 1937 is in chefs' hats and aprons with signs
reading, " '37 is alive and cooking!" I am standing on the side, defiant
in my non-umbrellaness, as the Class of 1952 comes down the path
with red backpacks strapped on; in the midst of them I see a woman I
know, a book editor, who is marching with her class but is not wearing
a backpack. I start to laugh, because it seems clear to me that we both
think we are somehow set apart from all this—she because she is not
wearing anything on her back, I because I am taking notes. We are both
wrong, of course.

I can pretend that I have come back to Wellesley only because I want
to write about it, but I am really here because I still care, I still care
about this Mickey Mouse institution; I am foolish enough to think that
someday it will do something important for women. That I care at all,
that I am here at all, makes me one of Them. I am not exactly like
them—I may be a better class of dumb—but we are all dumb. This college is about as meaningful to the educational process in America as a
perfume factory is to the national economy. And all of us care, which
makes us all idiots for wasting a minute thinking about the place.

—October 1972

Commencement Address to Wellesley Class of 1996

President Walsh, trustees, faculty, friends, noble parents . . . and dear class of 1996, I am so proud of you. Thank you for asking me to speak to you today. I had a wonderful time trying to imagine who had been ahead of me on the list and had said no; I was positive you'd have to have gone to Martha Stewart first. And I meant to call her to see what she would have said, but I forgot. She would probably be up here telling you how to turn your lovely black robes into tents. I will try to be at least as helpful, if not quite as specific as that.

I'm very conscious of how easy it is to let people down on a day like this, because I remember my own graduation from Wellesley very, very well, I am sorry to say. The speaker was Santha Rama Rau, who was a woman writer, and I was going to be a woman writer. And, in fact, I had spent four years at Wellesley going to lectures by women writers, hoping that I would be the beneficiary of some terrific secret—which I never was. And now here I was at graduation, under these very trees, absolutely terrified. Something was over. Something safe and protected. And something else was about to begin. I was heading off to New York, and I was sure that I would live there forever and never meet anyone and end up dying one of those New York deaths where no one even notices you're missing until the smell drifts into the hallway weeks later. And I sat here thinking, "Okay, Santha, this is my last chance for a really terrific secret, lay it on me," and she spoke about the need to place friendship over love of country, which I must tell you had never crossed my mind one way or the other.

I want to tell you a little bit about my class, the class of 1962. When we came to Wellesley in the fall of 1958, there was an article in the *Harvard Crimson* about the women's colleges, one of those stupid, mean little articles full of stereotypes, like "girls at Bryn Mawr wear black." We were girls then, by the way, Wellesley girls. How long ago was it? It was so long ago that while I was here, Wellesley actually threw six young women out for lesbianism. It was so long ago that we had curfews. It was so long ago that if you had a boy in your room, you had to leave the door open fourteen inches, and if you closed the door you had to put a sock on the doorknob. In my class of, I don't know, maybe

375 young women, there were six Asians and five blacks. There was a strict quota on the number of Jews. Tuition was $2,000 a year, and in my junior year it was raised to $2,250 and my parents practically had a heart attack.

How long ago? If you needed an abortion, you drove to a gas station in Union, New Jersey, with five hundred dollars in cash in an envelope and you were taken, blindfolded, to a motel room and operated on without an anesthetic. On the lighter side, and as you no doubt read in the *New York Times Magazine* and were flabbergasted to learn, there were the posture pictures. We not only took off most of our clothes to have our posture pictures taken; we took them off without ever even thinking, "This is weird, why are we doing this?" Not only that; we had also had speech therapy—I was told I had a New Jersey accent I really ought to do something about, which was a shock to me since I was from Beverly Hills, California, and had never set foot in the state of New Jersey . . . not only that; we were required to take a course called Fundamentals, Fundies, where we actually were taught how to get in and out of the backseat of the car. Some of us were named things like "Winkie." We all parted our hair in the middle. How long ago was it? It was so long ago that among the things that I honestly cannot conceive of life without, that had not yet been invented: pantyhose, lattes, Advil, pasta (there was no pasta then, there was only spaghetti and macaroni)—I sit here writing this speech on a computer next to a touchtone phone with an answering machine and a Rolodex, there are several CDs on my desk, a bottle of Snapple, there are felt-tip pens and an electric pencil sharpener . . . well, you get the point: it was a long time ago.

Anyway, as I was saying, the *Crimson* had this snippy article which said that Wellesley was a school for tunicata—tunicata apparently being small fish who spend the first part of their lives frantically swimming around the ocean floor exploring their environment, and the second part of their lives just lying there breeding. It was mean and snippy, but it had the horrible ring of truth; it was one of those do-not-ask-for-whom-the-bell-tolls things, and it burned itself into our brains. Years later, at my twenty-fifth reunion, one of my classmates mentioned it, and everyone remembered what tunicata were, word for word.

My class went to college in the era when you got a master's degree in teaching because it was "something to fall back on" in the worst-case scenario, the worst-case scenario being that no one married you and you actually had to go to work. As this same classmate said at our reunion, "Our education was a dress rehearsal for a life we never led." Isn't that the saddest line? We weren't meant to have futures; we were meant to marry them. We weren't meant to have politics, or careers that mattered, or opinions, or lives; we were meant to marry them. If you wanted to be an architect, you married an architect. *Non ministrare sed ministrari*—you know the old joke, not to be ministers but to be ministers' wives.

I've written about my years at Wellesley, and I don't want to repeat myself any more than is necessary. But I do want to retell one anecdote from the piece I did about my tenth Wellesley reunion. I'll tell it a little differently for those of you who read it. Which was that, during my junior year, when I was engaged for a very short period of time, I thought I might transfer to Barnard my senior year. I went to see my class dean and she said to me, "Let me give you some advice. You've worked so hard at Wellesley, when you marry, take a year off. Devote yourself to your husband and your marriage." Of course it was a stunning piece of advice to give me because I'd always intended to work after college. My mother was a career women, and all of us, her four daughters, grew up understanding that the question "What do you want to be when you grow up?" was as valid for girls as for boys. Take a year off being a wife. I always wondered what I was supposed to do in that year. Iron? I repeated the story for years, as proof that Wellesley wanted its graduates to be merely housewives. But I turned out to be wrong, because years later I met another Wellesley graduate who had been as hell-bent on domesticity as I had been on a career. And she had gone to the same dean with the same problem, and the dean had said to her, "Don't have children right away. Take a year to work." And so I saw that what Wellesley wanted was for us to avoid the extremes. To be instead that thing in the middle. A lady. We were to take the fabulous education we had received here and use it to preside at a dinner table or at a committee meeting, and when two people disagreed we would be intelligent enough to step in and point out the remarkable similarities between their two opposing positions. We were to spend our lives making nice.

Many of my classmates did exactly what they were supposed to when they graduated from Wellesley, and some of them, by the way, lived happily ever after. But many of them didn't. All sorts of things happened that no one expected. They needed money, so they had to work. They got divorced, so they had to work. They were bored witless, so they had to work. The women's movement came along and made harsh value judgments about their lives—judgments that caught them by surprise, because they were doing what they were supposed to be doing, weren't they? The rules had changed; they were caught in some kind of strange time warp. They had never intended to be the heroines of their own lives; they'd intended to be—what?—First Ladies, I guess, First Ladies in the lives of big men. They ended up feeling like victims. They ended up, and this is really sad, thinking that their years in college were the best years of their lives.

Why am I telling you this? It was a long time ago, right? Things have changed, haven't they? Yes, they have. But I mention it because I want to remind you of the undertow, of the specific gravity. American society has a remarkable ability to resist change, or to take whatever change has taken place and attempt to make it go away. Things are different for you than they were for us. Just the fact that you chose to come to a single-sex college makes you smarter than we were—we came because it's what you did in those days—and the college you are graduating from is a very different place. All sorts of things caused Wellesley to change, but it did change, and today it's a place that understands its obligations to women in today's world. The women's movement has made a huge difference, too, particularly for young women like you. There are women doctors and women lawyers. There are anchorwomen, although most of them are blond. But at the same time, the pay differential between men and women has barely changed. In my business, the movie business, there are many more women directors, but it's just as hard to make a movie about women as it ever was, and look at the parts the Oscar-nominated actresses played this year: hooker, hooker, hooker, hooker, and nun. It's 1996, and you are graduating from Wellesley in the Year of the Wonderbra. The Wonderbra is not a step forward for women. Nothing that hurts that much is a step forward for women.

What I'm saying is, don't delude yourself that the powerful cultural values that wrecked the lives of so many of my classmates have vanished from the earth. Don't let the *New York Times* article about the brilliant success of Wellesley graduates in the business world fool you—there's still a glass ceiling. Don't let the number of women in the workforce trick you—there are still lots of magazines devoted almost exclusively to making perfect casseroles and turning various things into tents.

Don't underestimate how much antagonism there is toward women and how many people wish we could turn the clock back. One of the things people always say to you if you get upset is "Don't take it personally," but listen hard to what's going on and, please, I beg you, take it personally. Understand: every attack on Hillary Clinton for not know-ing her place is an attack on you. Underneath almost all those attacks are the words "get back, get back to where you once belonged." When Elizabeth Dole pretends that she isn't serious about her career, that is an attack on you. The acquittal of O. J. Simpson is an attack on you. Any move to limit abortion rights is an attack on you—whether or not you believe in abortion. The fact that Clarence Thomas is sitting on the Supreme Court today is an attack on you.

Above all, be the heroine of your life, not the victim. Because you don't have the alibi my class had—this is one of the great achievements and mixed blessings you inherit: unlike us, you can't say nobody told you there were other options. Your education is a dress rehearsal for a life that is yours to lead. Twenty-five years from now, you won't have as easy a time making excuses as my class did. You won't be able to blame the deans, or the culture, or anyone else: you will have no one to blame but yourselves. Whoa!

So what are you going to do? This is the season when a clutch of suc-cessful women—who have it all—give speeches to women like you and say, to be perfectly honest, you can't have it all. Maybe young women don't wonder whether they can have it all any longer, but in case you are wondering, of course you can have it all. What are you going to do? Everything, is my guess. It will be a little messy, but embrace the mess. It will be complicated, but rejoice in the complications. It will not be anything like what you think it will be like, but surprises are good for you. And don't be frightened: you can always change your mind. I know: I've had four careers and three husbands. And this is something else I want to tell you, one of the hundreds of things I didn't know when I was sitting here so many years ago: you are not going to be you, fixed and immutable you, forever. We have a game we play when we're waiting for tables in restaurants, where you have to write the five things that describe yourself on a piece of paper. When I was your age, I would have put: ambitious, Wellesley graduate, daughter, Democrat, single. Ten years later not one of those five things turned up on my list. I was: journalist, feminist, New Yorker, divorced, funny. Today not one of those five things turns up in my list: writer, director, mother, sister, happy. Whatever those five things are for you today, they won't make the list in ten years—not that you still won't be some of those things, but they won't be the five most important things about you. Which is one of the most delicious things available to women, and more particu-larly to women than to men. I think. It's slightly easier for us to shift, tŏ change our minds, to take another path. Yogi Berra, the former New York Yankee who made a specialty of saying things that were famously maladroit, quoted himself at a recent commencement speech he gave. "When you see a fork in the road," he said, "take it." Yes, it's supposed to be a joke, but as someone said in a movie I made, don't laugh, this is my life, this is the life many women lead: two paths diverge in a wood, and we get to take them both. It's another of the nicest things about being women; we can do that. Did I say it was hard? Yes, but let me say it again so that none of you can ever say the words "Nobody said it was so hard." But it's also incredibly interesting. You are so lucky to have that life as an option.

Whatever you choose, however many roads you travel, I hope that you choose not to be a lady. I hope you will find some way to break the rules and make a little trouble out there. And I also hope that you will choose to make some of that trouble on behalf of women. Thank you. Good luck. The first act of your life is over. Welcome to the best years of your lives.

—May 1996

✳ *The Profiler: Some Women*

Helen Gurley Brown: "If You're a Little Mouseburger, Come with Me. I Was a Mouseburger and I Will Help You."

I don't know anyone who has had professional contact with Helen Gurley Brown who is not fascinated by her. You probably don't believe that, but it's true. In the three years I wrote for Cosmopolitan, *she managed to drive me absolutely crazy with her passion for italics, exclamation points, upbeat endings, and baby simpleness. She once insisted on translating all the common French phrases I had used in an article—and translated almost every one of them wrong. But still, there is something about her. . . .*

They are still screaming at her after all these years. They are still saying that Helen Gurley Brown is some kind of scarlet woman, for God's sake, leading the young women of America into reckless affairs, possibly with married men. And every time they say it she sits there, little puckers beginning in her chin, and waits for the moment when the talk show will be over and she can run offstage and burst into tears. You might think that by now they would stop screaming—after all, this small, thin, dreadfully sincere woman is not to blame for the moral turpitude in America; you might think that by now Helen Gurley Brown would stop crying—after all, her attackers simply do not, cannot understand. But no. Just the other night, it happened again. On *The Merv Griffin Show* or *The Joey Bishop Show.* One or the other. She was just sitting there, talking in her underslung voice about how a single girl must go to lunch with married men, that a single girl with no other men in her life must somehow make the men who are there serve a purpose. She finished her little spiel and the screaming began. A singer on the panel started it. "Is this the kind of thing we want the young women of our country to listen to?" he said. "I wouldn't want any daughter of mine to go and date a married man." Then he turned to the audience and said, "Everyone out there who agrees with me, raise your hand or clap." And it began. Thunderous applause. Hundreds of hands flapping on the monitors. And as soon as the show was over, Helen Gurley Brown began to cry.

As it happens, Helen Gurley Brown cries quite a lot. She cried for three hours at Trader Vic's the night Jerry Lewis attacked her on *The Tonight Show.* She cried one day in the beauty parlor just after returning from a trip to see her mother. She cried the day a Hearst executive refused to let her run a cover of *Cosmopolitan* magazine because there was too much boosom showing. (That's the way she pronounces it. *Boo*som.) She cried the day Richard E. Berlin, president of the Hearst Corporation, put his foot down over a cover line that said, "The Pill That Makes Women More Responsive to Men." She cries all the time because people don't understand her. Jerry Lewis does not understand her, her mother does not understand her, and from time to time, the Hearst Corporation does not understand her. They don't understand what she is trying to do. They don't understand that she knows something they don't know. She knows about the secretaries, the nurses, the telephone-company clerks who live out there somewhere, miles from psychiatrists, plastic surgeons, and birth-control clinics. Only 8 percent of *Cosmopolitan*'s readers are in New York City—the rest are stuck in the wilds, coping with their first pair of false eyelashes and their first fling with vaginal foam and their first sit-down dinners and their first orgasms. These are the girls who read Helen Gurley Brown's *Single Girl's Cookbook* and learn—yes, *learn*—that before guests arrive for dinner it is smart to put out the garbage. These are the girls who buy *Cosmopolitan* and swallow whole such tidbits of advice as: "Rub your thighs together when you walk. The squish-squish sound of nylon . . . has a frenzying effect." These are the girls who have to be told How to Tell If He's a Married Man. You don't believe there are girls who cannot tell if a man is married? Listen, then, to this letter to Helen Gurley Brown from a young lady in Savannah, Georgia:

> My problem is a common one. I am an expectant unwed mother. . . . The father of my child turned his back on me after he found out. Besides, he was married. However, I was not aware of this until after our affair had begun, and too weak to break it off until I realized he had never been serious about me. By this time it was too late.

Helen Gurley Brown knows about these girls. She understands them. And don't you see? *She is only trying to help.*

. . .

We are sitting in her yellow-and-orange office across the street from Hearst headquarters at Fifty-seventh Street and Eighth Avenue in New York. On the floor is a large stuffed tiger. On the bulletin board is a picture of her husband, David. She calls him Lambchop. On the wall is a long magazine rack containing, along with a number of popular periodicals, the last twelve months of *Cosmopolitan* magazine. Read all about it. Why I Wear My False Eyelashes to Bed. I Was a Nude Model. I Was Raped. I Had a Hysterectomy. On her desk—along with some dental floss she uses before all editorial meetings—is a tearsheet of the next in a series of advertisements she writes for *Cosmopolitan*; this one, of a luscious girl, her hand poised deftly over her cleavage, has the following to say:

> What does a girl do if she's wearing a hairpiece and she and her date are getting quite romantic? Well, we all know that a hairpiece can't live through very much in the way of stress and strain so I just take out the pins and take mine off. So far no boy I've known has ever fainted dead away because everything that basically *counts* is me . . . adding extra hair is just an *accessory*. When I think of all the subterfuge and pretending girls once had to go through I'm thankful I live now when you can be truthful . . . and there's a wonderful magazine to help me be the honest female-female I really am. I love that magazine. I guess you could say I'm That COSMOPOLITAN Girl.

Helen Gurley Brown is now in her fifth year as editor in chief of *Cosmopolitan*. She took it over when she was forty-three and it was in trouble, turned it around, breathed new life and new image into it, became the only editor in America to resurrect a dying magazine. She is now forty-eight and tiny, with tiny wrists, tiny face, tiny voice. "I once heard her lose her temper," a former *Cosmo* editor recalls, "and it sounded like a little sparrow—she was chirping as loud as she could but you still couldn't hear her." She wears Rudi Gernreich dresses, David Webb jewelry, a Piaget watch, expensive hairpieces, custom-cut false eyelashes— but it never quite seems to come together properly. An earring keeps falling off. A wig is askew. A perfect matched stocking has a run. All of which not-quite-right effect is intensified because Helen Gurley Brown relentlessly talks about her flat chest, her nose job, her split ends, her adolescent acne, her forty-minute regimen of isometrics and exercises to stay in shape. She does not bring up these faults to convince you she is unattractive but rather to show you what can be done, what any girl can do if she really tries. "Self-help," she says. "I wish there were better words, but that is my whole credo. You cannot sit around like a cupcake asking other people to come and eat you up and discover your great sweetness and charm. You've got to make yourself more cupcakable all the time so that you're a better cupcake to be gobbled up." That's the way she talks when she gets carried away—exhortation, but in the style of girlish advertising copy. She talks about "hot-fudge-sundae-kind-of-pleasure" and "good-old-fashioned-popcorn-eating-being-transported-to-another-world-going-to-the-movies." Ten years as an advertising copywriter pays off for this girl. Yes sir. She can package anything. Titles for articles fall out of her mouth involuntarily. A staff member will suggest an article idea, and if she likes it, she has the title in an instant. The Oh-So-Private World of the Nurse, she will squeal. Or The Bittersweet World of the Hillbilly Girl. Or The Harried, Happy World of a Girl Buyer. One day someone suggested an article about how most girls worry about having orgasms. "Yes!" cried Mrs. Brown. "We'll call it 'It Never Really Happens to Me.'"

I am in Helen Gurley Brown's office because I am interviewing her, a euphemism for what in fact involves sitting on her couch and listening while she volunteers answers to a number of questions I would never ask. What she is like in bed, for example. Very good. Whether she enjoys sex. Very much. Always has. Why she did not marry until she was thirty-seven. Very neurotic. Wasn't ready. It all seems to pour out of her, her past, her secrets, her fears, her innermost hopes and dreams. Says her husband, David, "Whether it was group therapy or what, there's nothing left inside Helen. It all comes out."

It all comes out—in interviews, on television, in editorial conferences, in memoranda, in the pages of her magazine. Helen Gurley Brown spends twelve hours a day worrying, poring over, agonizing about her magazine; if her insomnia is acting up, she may spend most of the night. She writes endless memos, in lower-case letters, to her writers, full of suggestions for articles she is particularly concerned about. "would like to go into a little detail about what goes through a girl's *head* as she is unable to have an orgasm," went one recent memo. "maybe a soliloquy. this subject has been treated so *clinically* . . . as though she couldn't do pushups. . . ." She writes memos to her editors praising them, nudging them, telling them how to fix stories that need fixing. "She has a very clear picture of what will and will not fit her magazine," said Hearst editor-at-large Jeannette Wagner. "If she sends you back an article with a note that says, 'I want a lead that says thus-and-such,' you go back and do exactly what she says."

She works over every piece that goes into the magazine, doing the kind of line-by-line editing most editors leave to their juniors— rewriting, inserting exclamation points and italics and capitalized words and *Cosmopolitan* style into everything. "I want every article to be baby simple," she often says. Not surprisingly, most of the magazine sounds as if it were written by the same person. And, in a way, it is. *Cosmopolitan is* Helen Gurley Brown. Cute. Girlish. Exhortative. Almost but not quite tasteless. And in its own insidious, peculiar way, irresistible. Says *Cosmo* articles editor Roberta Ashley: "Helen manages to walk that line between vulgarity and taste, which isn't easy. The magazine is like a very sexy girl—you don't mind that her dress is cut down to her navel because her hair is clean. If her hair were dirty, you'd be revolted."

And if, at times, Helen Gurley Brown and her magazine are offensive, it is only because almost every popular success is offensive. Mrs. Brown—like Hugh Hefner and Dorothy Schiff, to name two other irritating publishing successes—offends because she is proving, at sizable financial profit, the old Mencken dictum that no one ever went broke underestimating the intelligence of the American public. She is demonstrating, rather forcefully, that there are well over a million American women who are willing to spend sixty cents to read *not* about politics, *not* about the female liberation movement, *not* about the war in Vietnam, but merely about how to get a man.

I have not been single for years, but I read *Cosmopolitan* every month. I see it lying on the newsstands and I'm suckered in. How to Increase the Size of Your Bust, the cover line says. Or Thirteen New Ways to Feminine Satisfaction. I buy it, greedily, hide it deep within my afternoon newspaper, and hop on the bus, looking forward to—at the very least—a bigger bra size and a completely new kind of orgasm. Yes, I should know better. After all, I used to write for *Cosmopolitan* and make this stuff up myself. But she gets me every time. I get home—or sometimes, if I simply can't wait, I open it on the bus, being careful to remove my glove so that onlookers will see my wedding band and will know I'm not reading *Cosmopolitan* because I'm That COSMOPOLITAN Girl. And there it is. Buy a padded bra, the article on bustlines tells me. Fake it, the article on orgasm says. And I should be furious. But I'm not. Not at all. How can you be angry at someone who's got your number?

. . .

In a recent article in the *Antioch Review* linking *Cosmopolitan* and *Playboy*, Peter Michelson wrote, "*Cosmopolitan*, or more likely the Hearst hierarchy, recognized how *Playboy* was making the world safe for pornography, and it very neatly cut itself in on the sex-profit nexus." That explanation, while interesting, gives the Hearst Corporation more credit than it is due. In 1964 about all the Hearst people realized was that *Cosmopolitan* was in bad shape. Circulation had dropped to under eight hundred thousand copies a month, below the advertising guarantee. Advertising was down to twenty-one pages an issue. Early in 1965 Helen Gurley Brown came to see Richard Deems, president of the Hearst Magazine Division, with a dummy for a new magazine. He had vaguely heard of her, had no idea she was at all controversial, and had never read her 1962 best seller, *Sex and the Single Girl*. But he liked her, he liked her idea for a magazine aimed at single women, and most of all, he liked her long list of companies that might be willing to advertise in such a magazine. It is safe to say that if Deems had thought that Helen Gurley Brown was going to turn *Cosmopolitan* into something that would repeatedly be called the female counterpart to *Playboy*, he would not have employed her. "We happen to be a company with a conscience about what it publishes," he said. "Our paperback division is the only book company that doesn't have a married-sex book. We're very studious about this kind of thing."

There are, of course, many similarities between *Cosmopolitan* and *Playboy*. Both magazines contain nudity. Both are concerned with sexual freedom of a sort. Both are headed by people who are the products of repressed, WASP backgrounds. Both publish the worst work of good writers. Both exalt material possessions. Both are somewhat deprecating to the opposite sex: *Playboy* turns its women into sexual objects; *Cosmopolitan* makes its men mindless creatures who can be toppled into matrimony by perfect soufflés, perfect martinis, and other sorts of perfectible manipulative techniques.

Recently Helen Gurley Brown even commissioned a *Playboy*-type foldout picture—of actor James Coburn, nude, his vital parts somewhat obscured by a potted palm. "It was a very pretty picture," said Mrs. Brown. "But . . . I don't like to be in the position of turning James Coburn down . . . but the particular picture I needed didn't come out of this shooting. The pictures were very hippie and mystical, strange and ethereal and a little sad, and Jesus, that isn't what I had in mind at all. I wanted a cute, funny, wonderful foxy picture, with that great mouth and marvelous teeth. I *am* going to do a foldout—I'll take another whack at it—but I haven't got the picture I want yet."

There is one major difference between *Playboy* and *Cosmopolitan*. The *Playboy* man has no problems. The *Cosmopolitan* girl has thousands. She has menstrual cramps, pimples, budget squeeze, hateful roommates. She cannot meet a man. She cannot think of what to say when she meets one. She doesn't know how to take off her clothes to get into bed with him. She doesn't know how to find a psychiatrist. She even gets raped, though only by rapists with somewhat unlikely dialogue. (In "I Was Raped," *Cosmopolitan* introduced the only rapist in history who lay down on his victim and murmured, "Let's make love.")

"It drives my management wild to be compared with *Playboy*," said Mrs. Brown. "We are not like *Playboy*. We are all the things we've been talking about—onward, upward, be it, do it, get out of your morass, meet some new men, don't accept, don't be a slob, be everything you're capable of. If you're a little mouseburger, come with me. I was a mouseburger and I will help you. You're so much more wonderful than you think. *Cosmopolitan* is shot full of this stuff although outsiders don't realize it. It is, in its way, an inspiration magazine."

There is very little that has happened to Helen Gurley Brown that she has not managed to extricate a rule from. Or learn a lesson from. Or make a maxim of. Or see, in hindsight, that it was all part of a plan. If it weren't for her unhappy childhood, she says, she wouldn't be enjoying herself so much now. If it weren't for her years of difficulty, she would never have had such a drive to improve her lot. She has led a hard life, a perfect life out of which to build inspirational books and an inspirational magazine.

She was born in Green Forest, Arkansas, in the Ozarks, the second daughter of Cleo and Ira Gurley. Both her parents were schoolteachers, but her father turned to politics and was elected to the state legislature. In 1925 he moved his family to Little Rock. He was killed in a freak elevator accident in the State Capitol Building seven years later. His daughter Helen was ten and his daughter Mary was fourteen.

"That really changed our lives considerably," Helen Gurley Brown remembered one day recently. "That sort of finished things, finished a phase of my life which I never will get back. The security. . . . They say a great deal of your life is formed by the time you're about seven, so these drives and rages and ambitions and yearnings and needings and cravings of mine must have been formed before that time, some of them. I never have gotten to the bottom of all that. Why am I so driven? It seems logically to have derived from things that happened to me after my father died, but some of it must be residual from very early. I don't know.

"But anyway, here we are in Little Rock, little fatherless children. I don't think my mother and father were particularly happy together, but my father's death was a horrendous thing in her life. She and my father had been very poor. She gets disgusted with me because I keep carrying on about how poor I was. I always ate. I always looked okay. I really never was eating pork and beans out of a can and putting cardboard in the soles of my shoes. But it's what you get in your head, it's how it seemed to you that motivates you. Whereas my parents were really poor, and just about the time things were beginning to go rather well, she and my father resolved whatever differences they had, poosh, he's taken away, snapped off.

"We stayed in Little Rock for about three years after my father's death," she continued. "But he left a limited amount of insurance and our house was mortgaged to the hilt. So because Mother felt we couldn't keep up the nice little standard of living in Little Rock on this particular stipend she had been left, she decided we'd all go move to Los Angeles. It was very brave and gutsy of her. But my sister didn't want to go to California. I didn't either. And my mother didn't level with us, because you didn't in those days. She said, 'Oh, I think it would be nice to go to California, we have relatives there.' So we move to California and Mary gets polio." She paused. "She was nineteen. There was no March of Dimes and there was nobody to help. Shlurp, in one big thing, in one year, it took all the money we had. I really got good and scared out of my wits about that time." Another pause. "I just didn't know what was going to become of us. It was still the end of the Depression, jobs were very hard to get and my sister—she's never walked again. I don't know, we were sort of a pitiful little tribe." Her voice cracked and she began to cry. "My word," she said. "I never talk about this anymore." She daubed at her eyes with a handkerchief. "Well, this is the way I was for years. It was the three of us sort of huddled together. My sister was in a wheelchair and needed constant care. My mother couldn't go back to work or do anything for a number of years." Tears continued to roll down her face. "I was terrified," she said.

The Gurleys moved to the East Side of Los Angeles near the Los Angeles Orthopaedic Hospital, and Helen enrolled at John H. Francis

Polytechnic High School. Her memories of that period—aside from her sister's illness—have mainly to do with having acne. "I was kind of a cute little girl, but who could see past these pus pustules?" Like that. She became a student leader, graduated as valedictorian, and was taken to the prom by the student-body president. "It was the coup of the year," she recalled with some amusement. "He had a real case on me, because he got close enough to find out what I was like. I always have to get men close enough to me to be interested in me. I have to do what I call Sinking In before they pay attention. I'm never anybody that some man sees at a party and says, 'Get me her.' Never. But once they get near me and I turn on what I call Plain Girl Power—well, it worked with the student-body president."

Following high school and a year at Woodbury Business College, Helen went to work answering fan mail at radio station KHJ to pay for her second year at college. Her mother worked in the marking room at Sears Roebuck. Her sister did telephone work for the Hooper rating service. Then Mrs. Gurley and Mary moved back to Arkansas and Helen was left as a single girl in Los Angeles. Friends who knew her in the 1940s, when she held eighteen consecutive secretarial jobs, remember her as a shy, self-effacing, attractive girl who always did the sorts of clever things that seemed astonishing twenty years ago, like putting egg in spinach salad. She was, they recall, completely neurotic about money. She sent one week's salary each month to her family and she was convinced no one would ever marry her because of her financial obligations.

To make ends meet, she took the bus to work, drove her car only on weekends with gas she pumped at the serve-yourself station on Beverly Boulevard, brought her lunch to the office in a paper sack, read other people's newspapers, made her own clothes, traveled by Greyhound bus. She tried every angle. Because she washed her hair in Woolite, she wrote the president of the company to tell him—and he sent her a free box of the stuff. She wrote an unsolicited memo to the proprietor of the beauty salon in her office lobby telling him how to hype up business— and he did her hair for nothing. She entered the *Glamour* magazine Ten Girls with Taste Contest three years in a row, and finally won. "I used to enter all the contests," she said. "I bought so many bars of Lux soap to enter the 'I like Lux soap because . . .' contest. I couldn't enter under my own name because I worked in an advertising agency, so I would send them to Mary and say, 'Please, Mary, have a picture made of yourself in a wheelchair and send these off.' Well, that didn't work. That's one that failed. But I did it. I tried."

She tried everything. Vitamin therapy. Group therapy. Psychoanalysis. Hair therapy. Skin therapy. Her persistent self-improvement dazzled her friends. "She decided the kind of person she wanted to be, the milieu in which she wanted to live, how she wanted to look," said one long-time California associate. "In a very real sense, she invented herself." There were a number of men in Helen Gurley's life—two agents, a married advertising executive, and a Don Juan whom she spent nine years off and on with—but to hear her tell it, her job always came first. She became secretary to Don Belding, a partner in Foote, Cone & Belding, and after five years she was made a copy writer. "It was so heady," she recalled in a near whisper. "I adored it. Instead of making a hundred dollars a week I'm making ten thousand dollars a year, and this is in 1955 and that was considerable money for a girl then, very heady. You know, everything adds up. It's what I keep saying in my books and in *Cosmo*. If you do every little thing you can do in your own modest position, one thing leads to another. So *do* it and *be* it and *write* the letters and *make* the phone calls and get *on* with it. And this is what I was doing every hour of the day, every day of the year.

"But I'm still living in my frugal way. I'm still bringing my lunch to the office. And I was conservative enough to have saved a little money. I had managed to save eight thousand dollars." One day Helen Gurley walked into a Beverly Hills used-car lot and paid five thousand dollars for a Mercedes-Benz. Cash. "The next weekend I went to the Beldings' ranch in total shock because of this money I spent. It just was not like me. I was in pain, physical pain. Everyone told me all the reasons I should have that car—that I was a successful writer and a gifted girl— they pumped me up and held my hand. But every time they looked at me I was sitting over in the corner in a catatonic heap thinking of the money.

"A week or so later a friend of mine set up this famous date with David Brown, whom she'd been saving for me. I thought it was going to be a big thing. I felt it in my bones before I met him. She'd been talking about him for three years, and it felt right. It was an interesting, lovely evening. And he took me to my car after dinner. I could see him looking at this car, this nice car. And I said, 'Yes, I just bought it and I paid all cash for it.' And that was a nice thing, he liked the fact that I'd been able to save all that money, because he had been married to very extravagant women, particularly his last wife."

Helen Gurley and David Brown were married one year later, in September 1959, at the Beverly Hills City Hall. He is now vice president and chief of story operations at 20th Century-Fox, and his wife continually says she could never have become what she has become without him. He gave her the idea of writing *Sex and the Single Girl*. He gave her the idea of aiming a magazine at single women. He was once an editor of *Cosmopolitan*; and in her early days there, he helped her run the magazine, rushing over in taxicabs for street-corner conferences about copy. He still writes all the cover blurbs for the magazine. Both Browns live work-oriented lives—long office hours, dinners out with business friends. They spend at least one night a week at Trader Vic's with Darryl Zanuck; they travel to Palm Springs and the Riviera with Richard Zanuck. Several nights a week they eat at home, in their Park Avenue apartment, and spend the evening working.

At one point last year, Mrs. Brown was also emceeing a television show and overseeing the editing of Hearst's *Eye* magazine. Both operations are now defunct, and she is left with just *Cosmopolitan*. Now selling 1,073,211 copies a month. Now pulling in 784 advertising pages a year—compared with 1964's 259. There are still the little setbacks, of course: old friends who are jealous; reader complaints over increasing nudity in the magazine; the Hearst Corporation's censorship. But though Helen Gurley Brown cries frequently, she cries much less now than she used to.

Why just the other day she managed to get through a major flap without crying once. It all had to do with the breast memorandum. Perhaps you remember it—one of her staff members leaked it to *Women's Wear Daily*, and every newspaper in the country picked it up. The memo began, "We are doing an article on how men should treat women's breasts in lovemaking. It will either help us sell another 100,000 copies or stop publication of *Cosmopolitan* altogether." Its purpose? "To help a lot of men make a lot of girls more happy." It went on to say . . . But stop. Let her tell the story.

"It started with my idea of how boosoms should be handled," she said. "Ninety-nine percent of the articles here are assigned by the other editors, but this particular thing was a secret of mine that I felt only I understood. I called my own writer in California and told her about it. She tried it and turned it in and it was beautiful, but *God*, it didn't have *anything* to do with how men should treat women's boosoms. It had to do with *love* and it had to do with *companionship* and the wonderful relationship between men and women, but it just didn't have *anything* to do technically with the subject. I wanted techniques. What does she like and how does she tell him and what does he do and how does he shape up. So I called my writer and said, 'This is your personal reminiscence of all your love affairs, and fascinating as it is, it doesn't have *anything* to do with boobs.' And she said, 'I know. Can you supply me with any material?'

"That's when I sat down and wrote my memo to the girls in the office. Just give me your thoughts about boosoms, I said. Has anybody ever been a real idiot in making love to you? How could men improve their techniques? What would you like done that's not being done? I just got a wonderful response. All the girls responded except two. I'd like to know who the two were because I don't think they'd be happy at *Cosmopolitan*, but I had no way of knowing because a lot of girls didn't sign their memos. I've sent many memos before—give me your definition of a bitch, have you ever dated a very wealthy man—and this was just another one of those memos. Then I saw it in *Women's Wear Daily* and I really did hit the roof. A lot of people said, Ho, ho, ho, how lucky can you be? You probably mailed it yourself in an unmarked envelope. But that's not true, because I tread a very careful path with Hearst management and I don't want to get them exercised about anything. If I just very quietly develop these articles and show them the finished product, it's much better. But this big brouhaha started because this little bitch, whoever she was, sent the memo to *Women's Wear*, and I would still fire her if I knew who she was. Because then the turmoil started. My management said to me, We want to see a copy of the boosom article the minute it's finished. I didn't want this attention to be called to what I was doing. Furthermore, we have trouble with supermarkets in the South and I didn't want them stirred up ahead of time.

"Well, the girls wrote their wonderful memos, I put two other writers on the story—because the girl in California suddenly got very haughty and said she didn't want to deal with the material. She just went absolutely crackers about the whole thing. So these two writers took it on and between them they turned in wonderful stuff, their own ideas plus all my material. I got this fantastic article. But my management won't let me run it. The actual use of anatomical words bugs them. Well, you cannot talk about love and relationships when you're talking about how to handle a breast. You must be anatomical. You've got to say a few things about what to do. I'm not mad at them—they do it because they're afraid we'll have too much flack. But I plan to lie low for a while and come back with my boosom article later. I read it tenderly, like a little love letter, every so often. I'll try it again after a while."

.   .   .

One day a couple of years ago, a *Cosmopolitan* editor named Harriet LaBarre called me and asked if I wanted to write an article on how to start a conversation. They would pay six hundred dollars for one thousand words. Yes, I would. Fine, she said, she would send me a memo Helen had written on the subject. The memo arrived, a breezy little thing filled with suggestions like "Remember what the great Cleveland Amory says—shyness is really selfishness" and "Be sure to debunk the idea that it is dangerous to approach strangers." I read it and realized with some embarrassment that I had already written the article the memo wanted, in slightly different form—for *Cosmopolitan,* no less. I called Harriet LaBarre and told her.

"Omigod," she said. "And I even edited it."

We talked it over and decided that I might as well take the assignment anyway.

"After all," said Mrs. LaBarre, "if it doesn't bother us to *run* the same article twice, it shouldn't bother you to *write* it twice."

"I have just one question, though," I said. "What is this about the great Cleveland Amory and his theory that shyness is just selfishness?"

"Did she say that?" said Mrs. LaBarre. "She must be kidding—I don't even think she likes Cleveland Amory."

A few weeks later I turned the article in, and Harriet LaBarre called. "We're going to run it," she said, "but there are two things we want to change."

"All right," I said.

"First of all, I was wrong about Cleveland Amory," she said. "I'm afraid we do have to say that shyness is really selfishness."

"But shyness *isn't* really selfishness," I said.

"Well, I know, but that's the way we have to put it."

"What's the second thing?" I said.

"Well, it's just one little change Helen made, but I wanted to read it to you. You have a sentence that reads, 'It is absurd to think that any girl who asks a nice-looking man how to get to Rockefeller Center will be bundled up in a burlap bag and sold into a Middle Eastern harem.'"

"Yes," I said, realizing it wasn't much of a sentence.

"Well, Helen changed it to read, 'The notion that any girl who asks a nice-looking man how to get to Rockefeller Center is immediately bundled up in a burlap bag and sold into a Middle Eastern harem is as antique and outmoded a myth as the notion that you can't take a bath while you're menstruating.'"

"What?"

"Is that all right?" she said.

"Is that all *right*? Of course it's not all right. How did that particular image get into my article?"

"I don't really know," said Harriet LaBarre. "We're thinking of doing a piece on menstruation and maybe it was on her mind."

I hung up, convinced I had seen straight to the soul of Helen Gurley Brown. Straight to the foolishness, the tastelessness her critics so often accused her of. But I was wrong. She really isn't that way at all. She's just worried that somewhere out there is a girl who hasn't taken a bath during her period since puberty. She's just worried that somewhere out there is a girl whose breasts aren't being treated properly. She's just worried that somewhere out there is a mouseburger who doesn't realize she has the capability of becoming anything, anything at all, anything she wants to, of becoming Helen Gurley Brown, for God's sake. And don't you see? *She is only trying to help.*

—February 1970

Dorothy Schiff and the New York Post

I feel bad about what I'm going to do here. What I'm going to do here is write something about Dorothy Schiff, and the reason I feel bad about it is that a few months ago, I managed to patch things up with her and now I'm going to blow it. She had been irritated with me for several years because I told the story about her and Otto Preminger's sauna on the radio, but we managed to get through a pleasant dinner recently, which made me happy—not because I care whether or not Dorothy Schiff is irritated with me but simply because I have a book coming out this summer, and if she were speaking to me, I might have a shot at some publicity in the *New York Post.* Ah, well. It's not easy being a media columnist. The publicity I had in mind, actually, was this little feature the *Post* runs on Saturdays called "At Home With," where semi-famous people tell their favorite recipes. Mine is beef borscht.

Dorothy Schiff is the publisher, editor, and owner of the *New York Post*, America's largest-selling afternoon newspaper. I used to work there. The *Post* is a tabloid that has a smaller news hole than the New York *Daily News*—five front pages, various parts of which are often

rented out to Chock full o' Nuts and Lüchow's. It also has a center magazine section containing mostly *Washington Post* columnists, a first-
rate sports section and drama critic, and Rose Franzblau, Earl Wilson,
and Dear Abby. It takes about eleven minutes to read the *Post*, and there
are more than half a million New Yorkers like me who spend twenty
cents six days a week to kill eleven minutes reading it. It is probably safe
to say that fewer and fewer young people read the *Post*, and that fewer
and fewer young people understand why anyone does. It is a terrible
newspaper.

The reason it is, of course, is Dorothy Schiff. A great deal has been
written about Mrs. Schiff in various places over the past years, and some
of it—I'm thinking here of Gail Sheehy's article in *New York* at the end
of 1973—has captured perfectly her coquettish giddiness, her penchant
for trivia, and her affection for gossip. It is taken for granted in these
articles that Dolly Schiff is a very powerful woman—she is in fact very
powerful for a woman and not particularly powerful for a newspaper
publisher. What is rarely discussed is her product. In Sheehy's article, I
suppose this was partly because Mrs. Schiff had manuscript approval,
and partly because the publisher of *New York*, like so many other men
Mrs. Schiff toys with, thinks that someday he will buy the *New York
Post* from her. But it is a major omission: There is no other big-city
newspaper in America that so perfectly reflects the attitudes and weaknesses of its owner. Dorothy Schiff has a right to run her paper any way
she likes. She owns it. But it seems never to have crossed her mind that
she might have a public obligation to produce a good newspaper. Gail
Sheehy quite cleverly compared her with Scheherazade, but it would be
more apt, I think, to compare her with Marie Antoinette. As in let them
read schlock.

In 1963, when I went to work there as a reporter, the *New York Post*
was located in a building on West Street, near the Battery. The first day
I went there, I thought I had gotten out of the elevator in the fire exit.
The hallway leading to the city room was black. Absolutely black. The
smell of urine came wafting out of the men's room in the middle of the
long hallway between the elevator and the city room. The glass door
to the city room was filmed with dust, and written on it, with a finger,
was the word "Philthy." The door was cleaned four years later, but the
word remained; it had managed to erode itself onto the glass. Then,
through the door, was the city room. Rows of desks jammed up against
one another, headset phones, manual typewriters, stacks of copy paper,
cigarette butts all over the floor—all of it pretty routine for a city room,

albeit a city room of the 1920s. The problem was the equipment. The
staff of the *Post* was small, but it was too large for the city room and
for the number of chairs and desks and telephones in it. If you arrived at
the *Post* five minutes late, there were no chairs left. You would go hunt
one up elsewhere on the floor, drag it to an empty space, and then set off
to find a phone. You cannot be a newspaper reporter without a phone.
The phones at the *Post* were the old-fashioned headset type, with an
earpiece-mouthpiece part that connected to a wire headpiece. Usually
you could find the earpiece-mouthpiece part, but only occasionally was
there a headpiece to go with it, which meant that you spent the day with
your head cocked at a seventy-degree angle trying to balance this tiny
phone against your shoulder as you typed. If you managed to assemble
a complete telephone in the morning, it was necessary to lock it in your
desk during lunch, or else it would end up on someone else's head for
the afternoon. The trouble with that was that half the staff did not have
desks, much less desk drawers to lock anything in.

None of this was supposed to matter. This was the newspaper business. You want air conditioning, go work at a newsmagazine. You want
clean toilets, go work in advertising. Besides, there was still a real ele-
ment of excitement to working at the *New York Post* in 1963. The paper
had been a good paper once, when James Wechsler was the editor, and
for a while it was possible to believe that it would be again. Mrs. Schiff
had kicked Wechsler upstairs, had changed the focus of the paper from
hard-hitting, investigative, and left-wing to frothy, gossipy, and women-
oriented, but we all thought that would change eventually. At some
point in the next few years, several New York papers would shut down.
None of us really thought the *Post* would. "The most depressing thing
about the *Post*," a reporter who once worked there used to say, "is
that it will never shut down." When the other papers folded, the *Post*
would have to get better. It would have to absorb the superior financial-
page reporters from the other afternoon papers, the superior columnists from the *Herald Tribune*. It would have to run two more pages of
news, enlarge its Washington bureau, beef up its foreign coverage, hire
more staff, pay them better, stop skimping on expense accounts. Why I
believed this I don't know, but I believed it for years. The managing editor, Al Davis, who once dumped four gallons of ice water on my head
in an attempt to tell me how he felt about the fact that I was leaving the
Post for a while to go live in Europe, was fired in 1965, and we all had
several months of euphoria thinking his replacement would make a difference. Blair Clark, the former CBS newsman and thread millionaire,

came in as Mrs. Schiff's assistant—he too thought he would be able to buy the *Post* from her—and we all thought he would make a difference. The *Trib* folded, and the *Journal*, and the *World Journal Tribune*, and we all thought that would make a difference. Nothing made a difference.

I first met Mrs. Schiff a few weeks after I started working at the *Post*. I was summoned to lunch in her office, a privilege very few other reporters were granted in those days, and the reason for it had mainly to do with the fact that my parents were friends of her daughter, and I suspect she felt safe with me, thought I was of her class or some such. "You're so lucky to be working," she said to me at that meeting. "When I was your age, I never did anything but go to lunch." Mrs. Schiff's custom during these lunch meetings—perhaps as a consequence of spending so much of her youth in expensive restaurants at midday—was to serve a sandwich from the fly-strewn luncheonette on the ground floor of the *Post* building. A roast beef sandwich. Everyone who had lunch with her got a roast beef sandwich. Lyndon Johnson, Bobby Kennedy, and me, to name a few. She thought it was very amusing of her, and I suppose it was. She would sit on one of her couches, looking wonderful-for-her-age—she is seventy-two now, and she still looks wonderful-for-her-age—and talk to whoever was on the other couch. There was, as far as I could tell, almost no way to have an actual conversation with her. She dominated, tantalized, sprinkled in little tidbits, skipped on to another topic. Once, I remember, she told me apropos of nothing that President Johnson had been up to see her the week before.

"Do you know what he told me?" she said.

"No," I said.

"He told me that Lady Bird fell down on the floor in a dead faint the other day, with her eyes bulging out of her head."

"Yes?" I said, thinking the story must go on to make a point, to relate to whatever we'd just been talking about. But that was it.

In the course of that first meeting, I asked Mrs. Schiff a question, and her answer to it probably sums her up better than anything else she ever said to me. The newspaper strike was still on—she had walked out of the Publishers' Association a few weeks before and had resumed publication—and I was immensely curious about what went on during labor negotiations. I didn't know if the antagonists were rude or polite to one another. I didn't know if they said things like "I'll give you Mesopotamia if you'll give me Abyssinia." I asked her what it had been like. She thought for a moment and then answered. "Twenty-eight men," she said. "All on my side." She paused. "Well," she said, "I just ran out of things to wear."

That was Mrs. Schiff on the 114-day newspaper strike. She took everything personally, and at the most skittishly feminine personal level. There was always debate over what made her change her endorsement from Averell Harriman to Nelson Rockefeller in the 1958 gubernatorial election, but the only explanation I ever heard that made any sense was that a few days before the election, she went to a Harriman dinner and was left off the dais. She was obsessed with personal details, particularly with the medical histories of famous persons and the family lives of Jews who intermarried. I once spent two days on the telephone trying to check out a story she heard about Madame Nhu and a nervous breakdown ten years before, and I was constantly being ordered to call back people I had written profiles on in order to insert information about whether they were raising their children as Jews or Episcopalians or whatever.

Every little whim she had was catered to. Her yellow onionskin memos would come down from the fifteenth floor, and her editors, who operated under the delusion that their balls were in escrow, would dispatch reporters. In 1965, during the New York water shortage, she sent the one about Otto and the sauna. "Otto Preminger has added two floors to his house under my bedroom window," she wrote. "One, I understand, is for a movie projection room and the other, a sauna bath. Frequently, I hear water running for hours on end, from the direction of the Preminger house. It would be interesting to find out if a substantial amount of water is or is not required by such luxuries. Please investigate." The memo was given to me, and I spent the next day writing and then rewriting a memo to Mrs. Schiff explaining that saunas did not use running water. This did not satisfy her. So Joe Kahn, the *Post*'s only investigative reporter, was sent up to Lexington Avenue and Sixty-second Street to find the source of the sound of running water. He found nothing.

Ultimately, I discovered what union negotiations were like. I became a member of the grievance committee and the contract committee, and the head of the plant and safety committee. About the plant and safety committee—I was also the only member of it, and I think it is accurate to say that everyone at the *Post* thought I was crazy even to care. It wasn't precisely a matter of caring, though. I was physically revolted by the conditions at the newspaper, none of which had changed at all since I began there. The entrance to the lobby was still black, "Philthy" and the dust were still on the door, and there was a slowly accumulating layer of soot all over the city room. Then there were the bathrooms. They were cleaned only once a day and had overflowing wastebaskets and toilets. The men's room in the entrance hall still had no door, and there was something wrong with the urinals. In the summertime, it was especially unpleasant to walk past it.

I first began to bring up my complaints about plant conditions to management in the grievance committee. Mrs. Schiff was not present. I asked that the hallway be painted. I asked for a snap lock on the men's room door. I asked for more chairs and phones in the city room. I asked if it were possible to hire a few more maintenance people—there was one poor man whose job consisted of cleaning all the bathrooms and of sweeping out the city room each day. Nothing happened. About a year after I began to complain, I was summoned to lunch again by Mrs. Schiff because of a memorandum I had written about Betty Friedan. I asked her about the possibility of cleaning the city room and repainting the entrance, and she looked at me as if the idea had never occurred to her. (The next week, the hallway was in fact painted and the city room cleaned for the first time in four years.) Then I mentioned the bathrooms, which she referred to for the rest of the conversation as the commodes. She listened to me—as just about everyone did—as if I were addled, and then said that she didn't really see the point of keeping the commodes clean because her employees were the kind of people who were incapable of not dirtying them up. I tried to explain to her that if the plant were clean, her employees would not be careless about dirtying it. I suggested that she had exactly the same sort of people working for her as there were at the *Daily News*, and the bathrooms at the *Daily News* looked fine. I don't think she understood a word I said.

One more thing about that lunch. We were talking about Betty Friedan. I had written a memo about an article she had written for the magazine section of the Sunday *Herald Tribune*; I thought we could develop a series about women in New York from it. The memo had been sent up to Mrs. Schiff, who wanted to talk about it. It turned out that she was upset with Betty Friedan and seemed to think that *The Feminine Mystique* had caused her daughter, a Beverly Hills housewife, to leave her household and spend a lot of money becoming a California politician. Mrs. Schiff thought I wanted to write a put-down of Mrs. Friedan—which was fine with her. I explained that that wasn't what I had in mind at all; I agreed with Betty Friedan, I said. "For example," I said, reaching for something I hoped Mrs. Schiff would understand, "Betty Friedan writes that housewives with nothing else to do often put a great deal of nagging pressure on their husbands to earn more money so they can buy bigger cars and houses."

Mrs. Schiff thought it over. "Yes," she said. "I've often thought that was why the men around here ask for raises as much as they do."

Top pay for reporters at that time was around ten thousand dollars a year. Mrs. Schiff had no idea that it took more than that to raise a family. She had no idea how the people who worked for her lived. She did not know that one hundred dollars was not a generous Christmas bonus. She did not even have a kind of noblesse oblige. She just sat up there serving roast beef sandwiches and being silly.

Jack Newfield, another *New York Post* alumnus, wrote an article about the paper in 1969 for *Harper's*, and in it he quoted Blair Clark, who was then assistant publisher of the *Post* for a brief interlude. "Dolly's problem," said Clark, "is that her formative experience was the brutal competitive situation the *Post* used to be in. She doesn't know how to make it a class newspaper." In the lean years, she survived by cutting overhead, keeping the staff small, cutting down on out-of-town assignments, paying her employees as little as possible. And all this still goes on, not just because she still thinks she is in a competitive situation but also because she survived, and she did it her way. She did it by being stingy, and she did it by being frothy and giddy; she was vindicated and she sees no reason to do things differently.

The last time I saw her, she mentioned that she had heard the things I said about her on the radio. "Nora," she said to me, "you know perfectly well you learned a great deal at the *Post*." But of course I did. I even loved working there. But that's not the point. The point is the product.

Nora Ephron's Beef Borscht

Put 3 pounds of beef chuck cut for stew and a couple of soupbones into a large pot. Add 2 onions, quartered, and 6 cups beef broth and bring to a boil, simmering 15 minutes and skimming off the scum. Add 2 cups tomato juice, the juice from a 1-pound can of julienne beets, salt, pepper, the juice of 1 lemon, 1 tablespoon cider vinegar, 2 tablespoons brown sugar, and bring to a boil. Then simmer slowly for 2½ hours until the beef is tender. Add the beets left over from the beet juice, and another can of beets and juice. Serve with huge amounts of sour cream, chopped dill, boiled potatoes, and pumpernickel bread. Serves six.

—April 1975

Dorothy Parker

Eleven years ago, shortly after I came to New York, I met a young man named Victor Navasky. Victor was trying relentlessly at that point to start a small humor magazine called *Monocle*, and there were a lot of meetings. Some of them were business meetings, I suppose; I don't remember them. The ones I do remember were pure social occasions, and most of them took place at the Algonquin Hotel. Every Tuesday at 6 p.m., we would meet for drinks there and sit around pretending to be the Algonquin Round Table. I had it all worked out: Victor got to be Harold Ross, Bud Trillin and C.D.B. Bryan alternated as Benchley, whoever was fattest and grumpiest got to be Alexander Woollcott. I, of course, got to be Dorothy Parker. It was all very heady, and very silly, and very self-conscious. It was also very boring, which disturbed me. Then Dorothy Parker, who was living in Los Angeles, gave a seventieth-birthday interview to the Associated Press, an interview I have always thought of as the beginning of the Revisionist School of Thinking on the Algonquin Round Table, and she said that it, too, had been boring. Which made me feel a whole lot better.

I had never really known Dorothy Parker at all. My parents, who were screenwriters, knew her when I was a child in Hollywood, and they tell me I met her at several parties where I was trotted out in pajamas to meet the guests. I don't remember that, and neither, I suspect, did Dorothy Parker. I met her again briefly when I was twenty. She was paying a call on Oscar Levant, whose daughter I grew up with. She was frail and tiny and twinkly, and she shook my hand and told me that when I was a child I had had masses of curly black hair. As it happens, it was my sister Hallie who had had masses of curly black hair. So there you are.

None of which is really the point. The point is the legend. I grew up on it and coveted it desperately. All I wanted in this world was to come to New York and be Dorothy Parker. The funny lady. The only lady at the table. The woman who made her living by her wit. Who wrote for *The New Yorker.* Who always got off the perfect line at the perfect moment, who never went home and lay awake wondering what she ought to have said because she had said exactly what she ought to have. I was raised on Dorothy Parker lines. Some were unbearably mean, and some were sad, but I managed to fuzz those over and remember the ones I loved. My mother had a first-rate Parker story I carried around for years. One night, it seems, Dorothy Parker was playing anagrams at our home with a writer named Sam Lauren. Lauren had just made the word "currie," and Dorothy Parker insisted there was no such spelling. A great deal of scrapping ensued. Finally, my mother said she had some curry in the kitchen and went to get it. She returned with a jar of Crosse & Blackwell currie and showed it to Dorothy Parker. "What do they know?" said Parker. "Look at the way they spell Crosse."

I have spent a great deal of my life discovering that my ambitions and fantasies—which I once thought of as totally unique—turn out to be clichés, so it was not a surprise to me to find that there were other young women writers who came to New York with as bad a Dorothy Parker problem as I had. I wonder, though, whether any of that still goes on. Whatever illusions I managed to maintain about the Parker myth were given a good sharp smack several years ago, when John Keats published a biography of her called *You Might As Well Live.* By that time, I had come to grips with the fact that I was not, nor would I ever be, Dorothy Parker; but I had managed to keep myself from what anyone who has read a line about or by her should have known, which was simply that Dorothy Parker had not been terribly good at being Dorothy Parker either. In Keats's book, even the wonderful lines, the salty remarks, the softly murmured throwaways seem like dreadful little episodes in Leonard Lyons's column. There were the stories of the suicide attempts, squalid hotel rooms, long incoherent drunks, unhappy love affairs, marriage to a homosexual. All the early, sharp self-awareness turned to chilling self-hate. "Boy, did I think I was smart," she said once. "I was just a little Jewish girl trying to be cute."

A year or so after the Keats book, I read Lillian Hellman's marvelous memoir, *An Unfinished Woman.* In it is a far more affectionate and moving portrait of Parker, one that manages to convey how special it was to be with her when she was at her best. "The wit," writes Hellman, "was never as attractive as the comment, often startling, always sudden, as if a curtain had opened and you had a brief and brilliant glance into what you would never have found for yourself." Still, the Hellman portrait is of a sad lady who misspent her life and her talent.

In one of several unbelievably stupid remarks that do so much to make the Keats biography as unsatisfying as it is, he calls Parker a "tiny, big-eyed feminine woman with the mind of a man." There are only a few things that remain clear to me about Dorothy Parker, and one of them is that the last thing she had was the mind of a man. *The Portable Dorothy Parker* contains most of her writing; there are first-rate stories in it—"Big Blonde," of course—and first-rate light verse. But the worst work in it is characterized by an almost unbearably girlish sensibility. The masochist. The victim. The sentimental woman whose moods are totally ruled by the whims of men. This last verse, for example, from "To a Much Too Unfortunate Lady":

> He will leave you white with woe
> If you go the way you go.
> If your dreams were thread to weave,
> He will pluck them from his sleeve.
> If your heart had come to rest,
> He will flick it from his breast.
> Tender though the love he bore,
> You had loved a little more. . . .
> Lady, go and curse your star,
> Thus Love is, and thus you are.

What seems all wrong about these lines now is not their emotion—the emotion, sad to say, is dead on—but that they seem so embarrassing. Many of the women poets writing today about love and men write with as much wit as Parker, but with a great deal of healthy anger besides. Like Edna St. Vincent Millay's poetry, which Parker was often accused of imitating, Dorothy Parker's poetry seems dated not so much because it is or isn't but because politics have made the sentiments so unfashionable in literature. The last thing I mean to write here is one of those articles about the woman artist as some sort of victim of a sexist society; it is, however, in Parker's case an easy argument to make.

And so there is the legend, and there is not much of it left. One no longer wants to be the only woman at the table. One does not want to spend nights with a group of people who believe that the smartly chosen rejoinder is what anything is about. One does not even want to be published in *The New Yorker.* But before one looked too hard at it, it was a lovely myth, and I have trouble giving it up. Most of all, I'm sorry it wasn't true. As Dorothy Parker once said, in a line she suggested for her gravestone: "If you can read this, you've come too close."

—October 1973

Lillian Hellman: Pentimento

I met Lillian Hellman just before her memoir *Pentimento* was published in 1973. I was working as an editor at *Esquire* and we were publishing two sections from the book, one of them called "Turtle." It was about Hellman and Dashiell Hammett. I'd never seen any of Lillian Hellman's plays, and I'd struggled with Hammett's mysteries, but I read "Turtle" in galleys before we printed it, and I thought it was the most romantic thing ever written. It's a story about a vicious snapping turtle that Hellman and Hammett kill. They slice its head off and leave it in the kitchen to be made into soup. It somehow resurrects itself, crawls out the door, and dies in the woods, prompting a long, elliptical, cutthroat debate between Hammett and Hellman about whether the turtle is some sort of amphibious reincarnation of Jesus.

I have no excuse for my infatuation with this story. I was not stupid, and I was not particularly young, both of which might be exculpatory. Like many people who read *Pentimento*, it never crossed my mind that the stories in it were fiction, and the dialogue an inadvertent parody of Hammett's tough-guy style. I thought it was divine. I immediately called the *New York Times Book Review* and asked if I could interview Hellman on the occasion of *Pentimento*'s publication. They said yes.

Hellman was already on her way to her remarkable third act. She'd published *An Unfinished Woman*, a memoir, which had been a best seller and National Book Award winner, and now with *Pentimento* she was on the verge of an even bigger best seller. She turned up on talk shows and charmed the hosts as she puffed on her cigarettes and blew smoke. With her two successful books, she'd eradicated the memory of her last few plays, which had been failures. Eventually the most famous story from *Pentimento*, "Julia," was made into a movie, with Jane Fonda as Lillian Hellman, Jason Robards as Hammett, and Vanessa

Redgrave as Julia, the brave anti-Nazi spy whom Hellman claimed she'd smuggled $50,000 to in Germany in 1939, in a fur hat. The end of Hellman's life was a train wreck, but that came later. I wrote a play about it, but that came even later.

Lillian was sixty-eight when I met her, and by any standard, even of the times, she looked at least ten years older. She had never been a beauty, but once she'd been young; now she was wrinkled and close to blind. She had a whiskey voice. She used a cigarette holder and one of those ashtrays that look like beanbags, with a little metal contraption in the middle for snuffing out the ash. Because she could barely see, the question of whether the perilously ever-lengthening ash would ever make it to the ashtray without landing in her lap and setting her on fire provided added suspense to every minute spent with her.

But in some strange way that you will have to take my word for, she was enormously attractive—vibrant, flirtatious, and intimate.

I went to see her at her home on Martha's Vineyard, which sat on a rocky beach near Chilmark. The interview is an embarrassment. I did not ask a tough question, and, by the way, I didn't have one. I was besotted. She was the woman who had said to the House Un-American Activities Committee: "I cannot cut my conscience to fit this year's patterns." She had loved the toughest guy there was, and although he had been drunk for almost their entire time together, he loved her back. Now it turned out she had practically stopped Hitler.

In the afternoon after our first interview, I went for a walk down to Lillian's beach. I'd been there no more than a few minutes when a man turned up. I had no idea where he'd come from. He was older, gray-haired, fleshy. He asked if I was staying with Lillian. I immediately became nervous. I stood up and made some sort of excuse and walked as quickly as I could over the rocks and back to the house. Lillian was sitting out on the patio in a muumuu.

"How was the beach?" she asked.

"Fine," I said.

"Was anyone else there?"

"A man," I said.

"Older?" she said. "Fat?"

"Yes," I said.

"That does it," she said.

She stood up and took off toward the beach.

A few minutes later she came back. The intruder had vanished. She was in a rage. She was apparently in an ongoing war with the man. Goddamn it, she'd told him to stay off her beach. Goddamn it, she'd told him to stop trying to have conversations with her friends. She would tell him again, if he ever dared to come around and she caught him lurking there. She was furious that he'd disappeared before she'd had the chance to order him away. I couldn't believe it. She was dying for a fight. She loved confrontation. She was a dramatist and she needed drama. I was a journalist and I liked to watch. I was in awe.

After my very bad interview with her appeared in the *Times*, Lillian and I became friends. "Friends" is probably not the right word—I became one of the young people in her life. She wrote me letters all the time, funny letters, mostly typed, and signed Miss Hellman. She sent me recipes. She came to my apartment and I went to hers. It was hard to imagine Lillian had ever been a Communist, I have to say that. I'd grown up knowing a lot of left-wing people in Hollywood who lived well, but there was no trace of the Old Left in Lillian's apartment at 630 Park Avenue—no Mexican art, for instance, or Ben Shahns; it was furnished in a style that fell somewhere between old WASP and German Jewish—brocade sofas, small tables made of dark wood, oil paintings of the sea, Persian rugs.

She held small dinners for six or eight, and she always had rollicking stories to tell that I now realize were exaggerated, but which at the time were hilarious. She'd had a run-in with a saleswoman one Sunday in the fur department of Bergdorf Goodman. Jason Epstein had set her kitchen on fire making Chinese food. Lillian was fun. She was so much fun. She had a great deep laugh, and she always had a subject for general conversation. "My great-uncle has died," she said one night at her table, "and the lawyer called to say, 'He has left you a pleasant sum of money.' How much money do you think is a pleasant sum of money?" What a game! What a wonderful game! We eventually agreed, after much debate, that $675,000 was our idea of a pleasant sum of money. She said we had guessed it on the nose. Was it true? Was any of it true? Who knows? I listened, enthralled, as she told me how Hammett had once run off with S. J. Perelman's wife, how Peter Feibleman (to whom she eventually left her home on the Vineyard) had hurt her feelings by trying to make a date with one of her good friends, how she'd once seen a young woman she thought might be Julia's daughter. This last episode took place on a cliff, as I recall. Lillian and Dashiell Hammett had been standing on a cliff when a young woman came up to her, touched her arm, and ran away. "I've always wondered," she said. "Because she looked so much like Julia."

Here is a letter she wrote me about delicatessens, my father, Henry
Ephron, and me:

*I am sitting in P. J. Bernstein's Delicatessen, a place I visit about
once a month. I have long been sentimental about middle-aged
ladies who have to use their legs and several of the waitresses,
being Jewish, have pounced on this unspoken sympathy. One of
them knows that I do something, but she does not know exactly
what I do; that doesn't stop her from kissing me as I order my
knockwurst.*

*A few days ago, when she finished with the kissing, she said,
"You know Henry Aarons?" "No," I said, "I don't." She pushed
me with that Jewish shoulder-breaking shove. "Sure you do," she
said, "his daughter." "Maybe," I said, my shoulder alive. When
she returned with the knockwurst, she said, "His daughter, some
fine writer, eh?" I said I didn't know, my shoulder now healed.
She said, "What kind of talk is that? You don't know a fine writer
when you hear a fine writer?" "Where does Mr. Aarons live?" I
said, hoping to get things going in a better direction. "Do I go
there?" she said. "He comes here." Well, in the next twenty minutes, by the time I had indigestion, it turned out it was your father
she was talking about who, by coincidence, two hours later, called
me to say that he had seen Julia.*

*I don't know why I tell you this, but somewhere, of course, I
must wish to make you feel guilty.*

It's a delightful letter, isn't it? I have a pile of her letters. When I look
through them, it all comes back to me—how much I'd loved the early
letters, how charmed I'd been, how flattered, how much less charming
they began to seem, how burdensome they became, and then, finally,
how boring.

The story of love.

Here was a thing Lillian liked to do: the T.L. Most people nowadays
don't know what a T.L. is, but my mother had taught us the expression,
although I can't imagine why.

T.L. stands for Trade Last, and here's how it works: you call someone up and tell her you have a T.L. for her. This means you've heard a
compliment about her—and you will repeat it—but only if she first tells
you a compliment someone has said about you. In other words, you will
pass along a compliment, but only if you trade it last.

This, needless to say, is a strange, ungenerous, and seriously narcissistic way to tell someone a nice thing that has been said about them.

"Miss Ephron," she would say when she called, "it's Miss Hellman. I have a T.L. for you."

The first few times this happened, I was happy to play—the air was full of nice things about Lillian. She was the girl of the year. But as time passed, the calls became practically nightmarish. Everything was starting to catch up with her. She'd written another book, *Scoundrel Time*, a self-aggrandizing work about her decision not to testify before HUAC, and followed it with her somewhat problematical decision to pose for a Blackglama mink ad. People were talking about her, but not in any way that gave me something to trade. Not that I was hearing much of it—I was living in Washington, and people in Washington don't talk about anyone who doesn't live in Washington, and that's the truth.

But there she was, on the other end of the phone, waiting for me to come up with my end of the T.L. My brain would desperately race trying to think of something I could say, anything. I had to be careful, because I didn't want to get caught in a lie. And if I made up a story, I had to be sure I was quoting a man, because despite her warmth to me, Lillian didn't care about nice things women said about her. And I couldn't say, "I'm in Washington, no one here is talking about you." So I would eventually make something up, usually about how much my husband adored her (which was true). But it never really satisfied her. Because what Lillian really wanted to hear, T.L.-wise, was that I'd just spent the evening with someone like Robert Redford (to pick an imaginary episode out of the air) and that he'd confessed that he desperately wanted to sleep with her.

When my marriage ended and I moved back to New York, Lillian was shocked. She couldn't imagine why I'd left him. She called and asked me to reconsider. She said I ought to forgive him.

Neither my husband nor I had the remotest interest in our getting back together, but Lillian was determined, and she kept pressing me. Can't you forgive him? I took the moment to slip out of her life.

I told myself that I could never have gone on with the friendship because of the way Lillian had reacted to the divorce.

Then, about a year later, a woman named Muriel Gardiner wrote a book about her life as a spy before World War II, and it became clear that Hellman had stolen her story. There was no Julia, and Lillian had never saved Europe with her little fur hat.

I told myself I could never have gone on with the friendship because Lillian had turned out to be a pathological liar.

Then Lillian sued Mary McCarthy for calling her a liar.

And I told myself I could never have gone on with the friendship because I could never respect someone who had turned against the First Amendment.

I actually did. I actually told myself that.

But the truth is that any excuse will do when this sort of romance comes to an end. The details are just details. And the story is always the same: the younger woman idolizes the older woman; she stalks her; the older woman takes her up; the younger woman finds out the older woman is only human; the story ends.

If the younger woman is a writer, she eventually writes something about the older woman.

And then years pass.

And she herself gets older.

And there are moments when she would like to apologize—at least for the way it ended.

And this may be one of them.

—November 2010

Jan Morris: Conundrum

As I suppose everyone knows by now, James Morris was four years old and sitting under the piano listening to his mother play Sibelius when he was seized with the irreversible conviction that he ought to have been born a girl. By the age of nine, he was praying nightly for the miracle. "Let me be a girl. Amen." He went on to the army, became a journalist, climbed Mount Everest with Sir Edmund Hillary, won awards for his books, and had four children with a wife who knew that all he really wanted was a sex change. Almost two years ago, he went off to a clinic in Casablanca that had dirty floors, shaved off his pubic hair, "and went to say goodbye to myself in the mirror. We would never meet again, and I wanted to give that other self a long last look in the eye and a wink of luck." The wink of luck did that other self no good at all: the next morning, it was lopped off, and James Morris woke up to find himself as much a woman as hormones and surgery could make him. He promptly sold his dinner jacket and changed his name.

This entire mess could doubtless have been avoided had James Morris been born an Orthodox Jew (in which case he could have adopted the standard Jewish prayer thanking God for *not* making him a woman) or had he gone to see a good Freudian analyst, who might have realized that any young boy sitting under a piano was probably looking up his mother's skirt. But no such luck. James Morris has become Jan Morris, an Englishwoman who wears sweater sets and pearls, blushes frequently, bursts into tears at the littlest things, and loves having a gossip with someone named Mrs. Weatherby. Mrs. Weatherby, Morris writes, "really is concerned . . . about my migraine yesterday; and when I examine myself I find that I am no less genuinely distressed to hear that Amanda missed the school outing because of her ankle."

Conundrum is Jan Morris's book about her experience, and I read it with a great deal of interest, largely because I always wanted to be a girl, too. I, too, felt that I was born into the wrong body, a body that refused, in spite of every imprecation and exercise I could manage, to become anything but the boyish, lean thing it was. I, too, grew up wishing for protectors, strangers to carry my bags, truck drivers to whistle out windows. I wanted more than anything to be something I will never be—feminine, and feminine in the worst way. Submissive. Dependent. Soft-spoken. Coquettish. I was no good at all at any of it, no good at being a girl; on the other hand, I am not half-bad at being a woman. In contrast, Jan Morris is perfectly awful at being a woman; what she has become instead is exactly what James Morris wanted to become those many years ago. A girl. And worse, a forty-seven-year-old girl. And worst of all, a forty-seven-year-old *Cosmopolitan* girl. To wit:

"So I well understand what Kipling had in mind, about sisters under the skin. Over coffee a lady from Montreal effuses about Bath—'I don't know if you've done any traveling yourself' (not too much, I demurely lie) 'but I do feel it's important, don't you, to see how other people really live.' I bump into Jane W—— in the street, and she tells me about Archie's latest excess—'Honestly, Jan, you don't know how lucky you are.' I buy some typing paper—'How lovely to be able to write, you make me feel a proper dunce'—and walking home again to start work on a new chapter, find that workmen are in the flat, taking down a picture-rail. One of them has knocked my little red horse off the mantelpiece, chipping its enameled rump. I restrain my annoyance, summon a fairly frosty smile, and make them all cups of tea, but I am thinking to myself, as they sheepishly help themselves to sugar, a harsh feminist thought. It *would* be a man, I think. Well it would, wouldn't it?"

It is a truism of the women's movement that the exaggerated concepts of femininity and masculinity have done their fair share to make a great many people unhappy, but nowhere is this more evident than in Jan Morris's mawkish and embarrassing book. I first read of Morris in a Sunday *New York Times Magazine* article that brought dignity and real sensitivity to Morris's obsession. But Morris's own sensibility is so giddy and relentlessly cheerful that her book has almost no dignity at all. What she has done in it is to retrace his/her life (I am going to go crazy from the pronouns and adjectives here) by applying sentimental gender judgments to everything. Oxford is wonderful because it is feminine. Venice is sublime because it is feminine. Statesmen are dreadful because they are masculine. "Even more than now," Morris writes of his years as a foreign correspondent, "the world of affairs was dominated by men. It was like stepping from cheap theater into reality, to pass from the ludicrous goings-on of minister's office or ambassador's study into the private house behind, where women were to be found doing real things, like bringing up children, painting pictures, or writing home."

And as for sex—but let Morris tell you about men and women and sex. "You are doubtless wondering, especially if you are male, what about sex? . . . One of the genuine and recurrent surprises of my life concerns the importance to men of physical sex. . . . For me the actual performance of the sexual act seemed of secondary importance and interest. I suspect this is true for most women. . . . In the ordinary course of events [the sex act] struck me as slightly distasteful, and I could imagine it only as part of some grand act, a declaration of absolute interdependence, or even a sacrifice."

Over the years, Morris saw a number of doctors, several of whom suggested he try homosexuality. (He had tried it several times before, but found it aesthetically unpleasant.) A meeting was arranged with the owner of a London art gallery. "We had a difficult lunch together," Morris writes, "and he made eyes at the wine waiter over the fruit salad." The remark is interesting, not just because of its hostility toward homosexuals but also because Jan Morris now makes exactly those same sorts of eyes at wine waiters—on page 150 of her book, in fact.

As James turns into a hermaphrodite and then into Jan, the prose in the book, which is cloying enough to begin with, turns into a kind of overembellished, simile-laden verbiage that makes the style of Victorian women novelists seem spare. Exclamation points and italicized words appear with increasing frequency. Everything blushes. James Morris blushes. His "small breasts blossomed like blushes." He starts talking to the flowers and wishing them a Happy Easter. He becomes even more devoted to animals. He is able for the first time ("the scales dropped from my eyes") to look out a plane window and see things on the ground below not as cars and homes seen at a distance but "Lo! . . . as dolls' houses and dinky toys." Shortly before the operation, he and his wife, Elizabeth, whose understanding defies understanding, take a trip, both as women, through Oregon. "How merrily we traveled!" Morris writes. "What fun the Oregonians gave us! How cheerfully we swapped badinage with boatmen and lumberjacks, flirtatious garage hands and hospitable trappers! I never felt so liberated, or more myself, nor was I ever more fond of Elizabeth. 'Come on in, girls,' the motel men would say, and childish though I expect it sounds to you, silly in itself, perhaps a little pathetic, possibly grotesque, still if they had touched me with an accolade of nobility, or clad me ceremonially in crimson, I could not have been more flattered." The only thing Morris neglects to write into this passage is a little face with a smile on it.

Morris is infuriatingly vague about the reactions of her children (she blandly insists they adjusted perfectly) and of Elizabeth (she says they are still the closest of friends). "I am not the first," Morris writes, "to discover that one recipe for an idyllic marriage is a blend of affection, physical potency and sexual incongruity." (Idyllic marriage? Where your husband becomes a lady? I suppose we owe this to creeping Harold-and-Vitaism; still, it is one of the more ridiculous trends of recent years to confuse great friendships with great marriages; great marriages are when you have it all.) As for her new sex life, Jan Morris lyrically trills that her sexuality is now unbounded. But how?

Unfortunately, she is a good deal more explicit about the details of what she refers to as "truly the symptoms of womanhood." "The more I was treated as a woman, the more woman I became," she writes. "I adapted willy-nilly. If I was assumed to be incompetent at revers-ing cars, or opening bottles, oddly, incompetent I found myself becom-ing. If a case was thought too heavy for me, inexplicably I found it so myself. . . . I discovered that even now men prefer women to be less informed, less able, less talkative, and certainly less self-centered than they are themselves; so I generally obliged them. . . . I did not particularly want to be good at reversing cars, and did not in the least mind being patronized by illiterate garage-men, if it meant they were going to give me some extra trading stamps. . . . And when the news agent seems to look at me with approval, or the man in the milk-cart smiles, I feel absurdly elated, as though I have been given a good review in the Sunday *Times*. I know it is nonsense, but I cannot help it."

The truth, of course, is that Jan Morris does not know it is nonsense. She thinks that is what it is about. And I wonder about all this, wonder how anyone in this day and age can think that this is what being a woman is about. And as I wonder, I find myself thinking a harsh feminist thought. It *would* be a man, I think. Well, it would, wouldn't it?

—June 1974

Pat Loud: No, But I Read the Book

I suppose it is completely presumptuous for me to write even one word on the saga of Pat and Bill and Lance and Kevin and Grant and Delilah and Michele Loud. Last year, I managed to miss every single episode of *An American Family*. But I did catch the Louds on the talk shows, and it seemed to me at the time that, with the possible exception of Tiny Tim, no group of people had ever passed so quickly from being celebrities to being freaks. I was amazed at the amount of time they lingered on, being analyzed in print, taking up space on the air, stealing valuable time from any number of people I would prefer to have read about or seen, even including Shecky Greene. Finally, though, like a toothache, the Louds went away. And the other day, when Pat Loud's book arrived in the mail, I felt terrible that I had not spent the months of their absence grateful for it; it is always easier to have a toothache return when you have at least had the sense to appreciate how wonderful it was not to have had one.

Pat Loud: A Woman's Story was written by Mrs. Loud with Nora Johnson, and the publicity director at Coward, McCann & Geoghegan assures me that its style—which is slick and show-biz rat-a-tat-tat—reflects Mrs. Loud's way of speaking exactly. "Gloria was a lamb chop." "Rose gardens he doesn't walk through." Like that. The book itself is sad and awful, and at times quite fascinating and moving. All these adjectives ring a bell: it seems to me that they were applied to the television series as well. In fact, the only thing about Pat Loud's book that is different from the television series that propelled her into her book contract is that no one who reads it will ever wonder Why She Did It. She did it because she wanted to tell her side. She did it because she had very little else to do. And she did it because she has come to believe that her brand of letting-it-all-hang-out candor is valuable to others in her position. Will she ever learn?

"Every other writer and cocktail circuit sociologist is contemplating the problem of the 46-year-old mother-housewife who suddenly isn't needed anymore," Mrs. Loud writes. "But most of these 'problem women' never had what has saved me, at least so far, from that devastating moment of truth: instant fame." The television show may not have saved Pat Loud from the truth—her own head seems to have done that job perfectly well. But the experience certainly confused her, and confused the issues involved to boot. Pat Loud's book is not the straight I-found-myself-through-divorce women's lib confessional; her case is too unusual. Rather, it is a rambling, perplexing, contradictory account by a woman who is trying, and failing, to make some sense out of a series of events that probably defy sensible explanation.

The real story of the Loud marriage, as told in this book, is a good deal more complicated and tacky, mainly tacky, than what I gather came out in the television series. The Louds and their five children lived in Santa Barbara, California, Pat working hard at being Supermom, Bill at his strip-mining-equipment business. As the marriage went on and the number of children increased, Mrs. Loud began finding telltale clues around the house. First a love letter to Bill from another woman, then a loose glove in his suitcase, lipstick on his handkerchiefs, a brochure from a Las Vegas hotel. The love letter enraged her so that she packed her four children into the family car—she was pregnant with the fifth—and drove off into the night. As it turned out, she did not get very far; Mrs. Loud, who has no selectivity index whatsoever, explains: "When I'm pregnant, I have the trots all the time, and sometimes it's really essential to get to a john fast . . . and there wasn't any gas station. . . . So finally I turned around and went home." In 1966, she found a set of her husband's cuff links, engraved "To Bill, Eternally Yours, Kitty," and all hell broke loose. Her husband assured her he had bought the cuff links in a pawn shop, but she did not believe him. So she snuck off, had an extra set of his office keys made, and while he was off on a business trip she went to look through his files.

"It was all there," she writes, "as though it had been waiting for me for years—credit card slips telling of restaurants I'd never been to and hotels I'd never stayed at, plane tickets to places I'd never seen, even pictures of Bill and his girls as they grinned and screwed their way around the countryside."

Bill Loud returned from his business trip. Pat Loud slugged him, in front of the children. He slugged her back, in front of the children. They both went to see a psychiatrist. They both stopped seeing the psychiatrist. They spent night after night getting drunk as Bill Loud recited the intimate sexual details of his infidelities. The subject of open marriage was introduced. Pat Loud began going to local bars during lunch and picking up businessmen. "We would have a few drinks and some tortillas," she recalls. "Then we would let nature take its course." She threatened divorce. He started seeing his women again. And in the midst of this idyllic existence, Craig Gilbert, a filmmaker with a contract from public television, came into their home and told them he was looking for "an attractive, articulate California family" to do a one-hour special about.

It is impossible to read this book and not suspect that Craig Gilbert knew exactly what he was doing when he picked the Louds, knew after ten minutes with them and the clinking ice in their drinks that he had found the perfect family to show exactly what he must have intended to show all along—the emptiness of American family life. Occasionally, in the course of this book, Pat Loud starts to suspect this, nibbles around it, yaps like a puppy at the ankles of truth, then tosses the idea aside in favor of loftier philosophical pronouncements. "If he knew it," she concludes, "it was not necessarily because he actively smelled it about us, but because he knew in a way what we didn't—that life is lousy and it's tragic and it's supposed to be and you can pretend otherwise if you want, but if you do, you're wrong."

Gilbert had no trouble persuading the Louds to cooperate. Bill had always been outgoing and exhibitionistic. Pat, for her part, saw the show as a way to appear as she had always wanted to—the perfect mother, cheerfully beating egg whites in her copper bowls. When Gilbert informed them that the show was going to be so good that he would shoot enough for five specials and then twelve, the Louds consented, apparently without a tremor of anxiety.

"Of course," Pat Loud writes, "if you're going to be in print or on the radio or TV, you can't help thinking of all the people who will read or see you, and the first ones I thought of were all Bill's women. There they would sit in frowzy little rented rooms scattered about California, Oregon, Washington, and Arizona, little gifts from Bill here and there, a memento from some trip or something he'd bought them, pathetic scraps of forgotten pleasure in their failed and lonely worlds. Their bleached blond hair would be falling sloppily out of its hairpins and their enormous breasts would be falling equally sloppily out of their torn, spotty negligees as they clutched their glasses of Scotch and rested their fat ankles on footstools to relieve their aching, varicose veins. . . . In pathetic, panting interest they would turn on their televisions to look at the Louds, and they would weep. . . . If they'd had Bill for a few hours or days, if they'd had a few sessions of what they probably thought of as blinding ecstasy, I had had him a thousand times more."

Pat Loud offers a number of other explanations as to why her family agreed to Gilbert's proposal—the one she seems to believe most firmly is that anyone would have. But she is less sure about why the reaction to the show was so enormous. "What nerve have we touched?" she asks at one point. "I would like to know; I would really like to know." I suspect I know. I think the American public has an almost insatiable need to feel superior to people who appear to have everything, and the Louds were the perfect vehicle to fill that need. There they were, a beautiful family with a beautiful house with a beautiful pool, and one son was a homosexual, the rest of the children lolled about, uninterested in anything, and the marriage was breaking up. All of it was on television, in *cinéma vérité*—a medium that at its best (I'm thinking of the Maysleses' *Salesman* and the Canadian Film Board's *Lonely Boy* and *The Most*) has always tended to specialize in a certain amount of implicit condescension.

It is on the subject of the making of the series that Pat Loud is most interesting. *Cinéma vérité* filmmakers have always insisted that after a time, their subjects forget the cameras are there, but as Pat Loud makes clear, it's just not possible. "You can't forget the camera," she writes, "and everybody's instinct is to try and look as good as possible for it, all the time, and to keep kind of snapping along being active, eager, cheery, and productive. Out go those moments when you're just in a kind of nothing period. . . . You don't realize how many of those you have until you're trying not to have them. . . . And what you also don't realize is that you *have* to have them—they're like REM sleep."

Ultimately, Pat Loud seems to have come to believe that she owed more to the filmmakers than she did to herself or her husband; any concept of dignity or privacy she may have had evaporated in the face of pressure from them. Again she nibbles around the edges of this, almost but not quite getting it, but the suggestions of what happened are there: the illiterate Californians trying to impress the erudite Easterners; the boring, slothful family attempting to come up with a dramatic episode to justify all that footage; the woman who had always tried to please men—first her father, then her husband—now transferring it all to Craig Gilbert.

And when, in the course of events, Pat Loud decided she wanted a divorce, Craig Gilbert convinced her that she owed it to him, to all of them, to do it on the air. "If I decided to divorce during the filming," Mrs. Loud says Gilbert told her, "I must be honest enough to do it openly and not confuse the issue further by refusing to allow it to be shot." Again she almost has it, almost sees how she was conned, and then falls into utter nonsense. "Couldn't it be," she asks, "that since circumstance and fate had put me in a position to rip away the curtain of hypocrisy, that maybe, just maybe, we could help other families face their problems more honestly?" And then she switches gears, and makes sense again: "A psychiatrist told a friend of mine recently that in his experience he'd found that there is almost always a third force present when divorce finally happens. The miserable marriage can wobble on for years on end, until something or somebody comes along and pushes one of the people over the brink. . . . It's usually another man . . . or another woman . . . or possibly a supportive psychiatrist; in my case, it was a whole production staff and a camera crew. . . ."

And so the marriage and the television series ended, and along came the notoriety. And now there is the book, and there will be more: more talk shows, more interviews. It all seems sad; there is no way to read this book and not feel that this bumbling woman is way over her head. She has made a fool of herself on television, and now she is making a fool of herself in print. She does not understand that it is just as hard to be honest successfully as it is to lie successfully. And now, God help her, she has moved to New York. She will get a job, she tells us at the end of the book, and perhaps she will be able to fulfill her fantasy. Here is Pat Loud's last fantasy. She's at this swell New York cocktail party, "exchanging terribly New York in-type gossip about who's backing what new play and who got how much for the paperback rights to Philip Roth's latest," and there is this man who takes her to dinner, and then to bed, and they have a wonderful affair. "I'm not saying he would solve everything, or pick up the pieces, or even make me happy. Nor is he as important as a good job. But the nice thing about fantasies is that you don't have to explain them to anybody. They are absolutely free." There she goes again, almost making sense, talking about the importance of work, and the need not to look to anyone for the solution of her problems, and then she blows it all. "They are absolutely free." That's the thing about fantasies. They're not absolutely free. Sometimes you pay dearly for them. Which is something Pat Loud ought to have learned by now. Will she ever?

—March 1974

Julie Nixon Eisenhower: The Littlest Nixon

She comes down the aisle, and the clothes are just right, Kimberly-knitted to the knee, and she walks in step with the government official, who happens to be H.E.W. Secretary Caspar Weinberger, and her face is perfect, not smiling, mind you—this is too serious an event for that—but bright, intent, as if she is absolutely fascinated by what he is saying. Perhaps she actually is. They take their places on the platform of the Right to Read Conference at Washington's Shoreham Hotel, and he speaks and she speaks and the director of Right to Read speaks. Throughout she listens raptly, smiles on cue, laughs a split second after the audience laughs. Perhaps she is actually amused. On the way out, she says she hopes she will be able to obtain a copy of the speech she has just sat through. Perhaps she actually thought it was interesting. There is no way to know. No way to break through. She has it all down perfectly. She was raised for this, raised to cut ribbons, and now that it has all gone sour, it turns out that she has been raised to deal with that, too.

The Washington press corps thinks that Julie Nixon Eisenhower is the only member of the Nixon Administration who has any credibility—and as one journalist put it, this is not to say that anyone believes what she is saying but simply that people believe *she* believes what she is saying. They will tell you that she is approachable, which is true, and that she is open, which is not. Primarily they find her moving. "There is something about a spirited and charming daughter speaking up for her father in his darkest hour that is irresistibly appealing to all but the most cynical." That from the *Daily News*. And this from NBC's Barbara Walters, signing off after Julie's last appearance on the *Today* show: "I think that no matter how people feel about your father, they're always very impressed to see a daughter defend her father that way."

There *is* something very moving about Julie Nixon Eisenhower—but it is not Julie Nixon Eisenhower. It is the *idea* of Julie Nixon Eisenhower, essence of daughter, a better daughter than any of us will ever be; it is almost as if she is the only woman in America over the age of twenty who still thinks her father is exactly what she thought he was when she was six. This idea is apparently so overwhelming in its appeal that some Washington reporters go so far as to say that Julie doesn't seem like a Nixon at all—a remark so patently absurd as to make one conclude either that they haven't heard a word she is saying or that they have been around Nixon so long they don't recognize a chocolate-covered spider when they see one.

I should point out before going any further that I have a special interest in presidents' daughters, having spent a good thirty minutes in my youth wanting to be Margaret Truman. And even back then, I knew it was not a perfect existence—Secret Service men trailing you everywhere, life in a fishbowl, and so forth. Still, whatever the drawbacks, it seemed clear that if you were the president's daughter, you at least got to date a lot. The other attraction to the fantasy, I suppose, had to do with the fact that the role of the president's daughter is the closest thing there is in America to being a princess, the closest thing to having stature and privilege purely as a result of an accident of birth. It is one of life's little jokes that both America and Britain have suffered through remarkably similar princesses in recent years: the Johnson girls, the Nixon girls, and Princess Anne are all drab, dull young women who have managed to acquire enough poise and good grooming to get through the public events their parents do not have time to attend.

Julie and Tricia were born just as their father was beginning public life. They grew up in Washington as congressman's daughters, senator's daughters, and vice president's daughters. Then they moved to California to be gubernatorial candidate's daughters, and later to New York to be presidential contender's daughters. After graduating from the Chapin School, Tricia went on to Finch College, Julie to Smith. There she began dating, and married—not a commoner, but a president's grandson. (David Eisenhower, with his endless tables of batting averages and illogical articles on the American left, is the perfect Nixon son-in-law. Still, he is not stupid. Last summer, after working as a sportswriter for the Philadelphia *Bulletin*, he was asked if he had any observations on the American press. "Yes," he reportedly said. "Journalists aren't nearly as interesting as they think they are.")

Marriage—which might logically have been expected to move Julie into a more removed and private existence—has instead strengthened and intensified her family connections and political role. During college, the Eisenhowers spent their summer vacations in a third-floor suite at the White House and took time off from school to campaign for Nixon's re-election. These days, they see Julie's parents several times a week; the Nixons often sneak off to eat with Julie and David in the $125,000 two-bedroom Bethesda home that Bebe Rebozo bought and rented to the Eisenhowers, presumably at well below its market price.

A few months ago, Julie took a full-time job at $10,000 a year at Curtis Publishing, where she is assistant editorial director of children's magazines and assistant editor of *The Saturday Evening Post*. She announced at the time that the children's magazine field attracted her because it would be impossible for her, as the president's daughter, to write for adult magazines on sensitive political subjects. An upcoming article for *The Saturday Evening Post*, however, while hardly on anything sensitive or political, is nonetheless on a topic that could not be more calculated to draw attention to her position: it is a profile of Alice Roosevelt Longworth, who is now eighty-nine and in the seventy-third year of her career as a president's daughter.

Julie, of course, is nothing like Alice Roosevelt, or any of the other flibbertigibbet presidents' daughters in the history of this country. In the months since the Watergate hearings began, she has become her father's principal defender, his First Lady in practice if not in fact. "It was something I took on myself," she said. "I just thought I had a story to tell, that there were certain points I could make, and I was very eager to do it. The idea that my father has to hide behind anyone's skirts is of course ludicrous." In any case, Julie's skirts were the only ones available: Pat Nixon is uncomfortable in press and television interviews, and Tricia is in New York. (Washington rumor has it that her husband, Edward Cox, and the president do not get on.) "And that leaves me," said Julie.

It has left her to make two appearances on the *Today* show, a television hookup with the BBC, a guest shot on Jack Paar's show. She has survived Kandy Stroud of *Women's Wear Daily* and lunch with Helen Thomas of the U.P.I. and Fran Lewine of the A.P. Odd little personal details about the president have slipped out during these interviews—whether deliberately or not. She has said that her father sometimes doesn't feel like getting up in the morning, that he took the role of devil's advocate in a family discussion on whether he should resign, that he often sits alone at night upstairs in the White House playing the piano. During her last appearance with Barbara Walters, whose interviews with her have been dazzling, she even came up with a sinister-influence theory of her own to explain everything: "Sometimes I think we were born under an unlucky star."

Her performances are always calm and professional and poised, her revelations just titillating enough, and after all, she's only a girl—and the combination of these has tended to draw attention away from the substantive things she is saying and the way she is saying them. Julie Eisenhower has developed—or been coached in—three basic approaches to answering questions. The first is not to answer the question at all. During her BBC appearance, an American woman living in England phoned in to say, "I would like Mrs. Eisenhower to know that her father's actions have made our position abroad untenable . . . it would be better if he came forward and answered questions himself instead of putting you in his place." Julie replied, "I'd like to ask . . . how she thinks my father can answer more on Watergate without pointing the finger at people who have not been indicted." This answer—in addition to skirting the question and making Nixon look like a man whose sole thought is of the Constitution—utterly overlooks the fact that almost everyone connected with Watergate has been called to testify, a good many have been indicted, and some have even been convicted.

The second approach is to point to the bright side. Thus, when she is asked about Watergate, she talks instead of her father's successes with China, Russia, and the Middle East crisis. When she is asked about the number of presidential appointees who have been forced to resign, she mentions Henry Kissinger and Ron Ziegler, whom she once called "a man of great integrity." "And I'd go beyond that," she said once. "I'd say that many of these people we're talking about, these aides, were great Americans, really devoted to their country, and they didn't make any money on Watergate, they didn't do anything for personal gain. They made mistakes, errors in judgment. I don't think they're evil men."

The third, and most classic, of Mrs. Eisenhower's techniques is simply to put the blame elsewhere—on the press. She combines the Middle American why-doesn't-the-press-ever-print-good-news theme with good old-fashioned Nixon paranoia. I spoke with her the other day for five minutes, and she spent most of that time complaining that her mother had met the day before with a group from the Conference on the Role of Women in the Economy, and not one word about it had been printed in the papers. "Instead we get all these negative things," she said. When she was asked recently what she thought of Barry Goldwater's charge that her father's credibility was at an all-time low, she replied: "Barry Goldwater also had a press conference during this whole period . . . and he said that the press were hounds of destruction. I don't think he meant all of the press, but, um, Goldwater *is* a quotable man, isn't he? I didn't hear *that* on the networks. But when he says [my father's] credibility is at an all-time low, that *is* on the networks."

The only questions that stump Julie Eisenhower at all are the ones that concern her father's personality. She has said that she is sick of telling reporters what a warm, human person he is—a fact that fortunately has not stopped reporters from pressing her to give examples. One story she produced recently to show what a card her father can be in his off moments concerned the time her husband, David, took the wheel of Bebe Rebozo's yacht—and the president, in response, appeared on deck wearing not one but two life preservers. "He is quite a practical joker," she said on another occasion. "He likes to tease and he likes to plan surprises when he can. Things like getting birthday candles for a cake that don't blow out. You know, all nice and lit and you sit there huffing and puffing and they don't go out. . . . Things like that."

There is no point in dwelling too heavily on the implications of a daughter who has managed to play a larger role in her father's life than his wife seems to. And there is also no point in wondering what is going to happen to Julie Eisenhower's view of her father if the fall actually comes. It is safe to say that breeding will win out, and all the years of growing up in that family will protect her from any insight at all, will lead her to conclude that he was quite simply done in by malicious, unpatriotic forces. What is clear, though, is that Julie Nixon Eisenhower is fighting for herself and her position as hard as she is fighting for her father and his. She once said that if her father was forced out of office, she would "just fold up and wither and fall away." What is more likely is that she will deal with that, too, vanish for a couple of years, and then crop up in politics again. That, after all, is what Nixons do, and that, in the end, is all she is.

—December 1973

Lisbeth Salander: The Girl Who Fixed the Umlaut

There was a tap at the door at five in the morning. She woke up. *Shit. Now what?* She'd fallen asleep with her Palm Tungsten T3 in her hand. It would take only a moment to smash it against the wall and shove the battery up the nose of whoever was out there annoying her. She went to the door.

"I know you're home," he said.

Kalle fucking Blomkvist.

She tried to remember whether she was speaking to him or not. Probably not. She tried to remember why. No one knew why. It was undoubtedly because she'd been in a bad mood at some point. Lisbeth Salander was entitled to her bad moods on account of her miserable childhood and her tiny breasts, but it was starting to become confusing just how much irritability could be blamed on your slight figure and an abusive father you had once deliberately set on fire and then years later split open the head of with an ax.

Salander opened the door a crack and spent several paragraphs trying to decide whether to let Blomkvist in. Many italic thoughts flew through her mind. *Go away. Perhaps. So what.* Etc.

"Please," he said. "I must see you. The umlaut on my computer isn't working."

He was cradling an iBook in his arms. She looked at him. He looked at her. She looked at him. He looked at her. And then she did what she usually did when she had run out of italic thoughts: she shook her head.

"I can't really go on without an umlaut," he said. "We're in Sweden."

But where in Sweden were they? There was no way to know, especially if you'd never been to Sweden. A few chapters ago, for example, an unscrupulous agent from Swedish Intelligence had tailed Blomkvist by taking Stora Essingen and Gröndal into Södermalm, and then driving down Hornsgatan and across Bellmansgatan via Brännkyrkagatan, with a final left onto Tavastgatan. Who cared, but there it was, in black-and-white, taking up space. And now Blomkvist was standing in her doorway. Someone might still be following him—but who? There was no real way to be sure even when you found out, because people's names were so confusingly similar—Gullberg, Sandberg, and Holmberg; Nieminen and Niedermann; and, worst of all, Jonasson, Mårtensson, Torkelsson, Fredriksson, Svensson, Johansson, Svantesson, Fransson, and Paulsson.

"I need my umlaut," Blomkvist said. "What if I want to go to Svavelsjö? Or Strängnäs? Or Södertälje? What if I want to write to Wadensjö? Or Ekström or Nyström?"

It was a compelling argument.

She opened the door.

He handed her the computer and went to make coffee on her Jura Impressa X7.

She tried to get the umlaut to work. No luck. She pinged Plague and explained the problem. Plague was fat, but he would know what to do, and he would tell her, in Courier typeface.

`<Where are you?>` Plague wrote.

`<Stockholm.>`

`<There's an Apple Store at the intersection of Kungsgatan and Sveavägen. Or you could try a Q-tip.>`

She went to the bathroom and got a Q-tip and gently cleaned the area around the ALT key. It popped into place. Then she pressed "U." An umlaut danced before her eyes.

Finally, she spoke.

"It's fixed," she said.

"Thanks," he said.

She thought about smiling, but she'd smiled three hundred pages earlier, and once was enough.

—July 2010

✳ *The Novelist*

Heartburn

One

The first day I did not think it was funny. I didn't think it was funny the third day either, but I managed to make a little joke about it. "The most unfair thing about this whole business," I said, "is that I can't even date." Well, you had to be there, as they say, because when I put it down on paper it doesn't sound funny. But what made it funny (trust me) is the word "date," which when you say it out loud at the end of a sentence has a wonderful teenage quality, and since I am not a teenager (okay, I'm thirty-eight), and since the reason I was hardly in a position to date on first learning that my second husband had taken a lover was that I was seven months pregnant, I got a laugh on it, though for all I know my group was only laughing because they were trying to cheer me up. I needed cheering up. I was in New York, staying in my father's apartment, I was crying most of the time, and every time I stopped crying I had to look at my father's incredibly depressing walnut furniture and slate-gray lamps, which made me start crying again.

I had gotten on the shuttle to New York a few hours after discovering the affair, which I learned about from a really disgusting inscription to my husband in a book of children's songs she had given him. *Children's* songs. "Now you can sing these songs to Sam" was part of the disgusting inscription, and I can't begin to tell you how it sent me up the wall, the idea of my two-year-old child, my baby, involved in some dopey inscriptive way in this affair between my husband, a fairly short person, and Thelma Rice, a fairly tall person with a neck as long as an arm and a nose as long as a thumb and you should see her legs, never mind her feet, which are sort of splayed.

My father's apartment was empty, my father having been carted off to the loony bin only days before by my sister Eleanor, who is known as the Good Daughter in order to differentiate her from me. My father leads a complicated psychological life along with his third wife, who incidentally happens to be my former best friend Brenda's sister. My father's third wife had been wandering up Third Avenue in a towel the week before, when she was spotted by Renee Fleisher, who went to high school with Brenda and me. Renee Fleisher called my father, who was in no position to help since his crack-up was halfway there, and then she called me in Washington. "I don't believe it," she said. "I just bumped into Brenda's big sister and she says she's married to your father." I myself had found it hard to believe when it happened: to have your father marry your mortal enemy's older sister is a bit too coincidental for my taste, even though I go along with that stuff about small worlds. You have no choice if you're Jewish. "It's fine with me if you marry Brenda's sister," I had said to my father when he called to say he was about to, "but please have her sign a prenuptial agreement so that when you die, none of your fortune ends up with Brenda." So Brenda's big sister signed the agreement, that was three years ago, and now here's Renee Fleisher on the phone to say, hi ho, Brenda's sister married your father and by the way she's wandering up Third Avenue wearing a towel. I turned all this over to my sister Eleanor, who put on her goodness and went over to my father's apartment and got some clothes onto Brenda's sister and sent her to her mother in Miami Beach and took my father to a place called Seven Clouds, which is not an auspicious name for a loony bin, but you'd be amazed how little choice you have about loony bins. Off went my father to dry out and make ashtrays out of leaves, and there sat his apartment in New York, empty.

I had the keys to my father's apartment; I'd stayed there often in the past year because we were broke. When Mark and I got married we were rich and two years later we were broke. Not actually broke—we did have equity. We had a stereo system that had eaten thousands of dollars, and a country house in West Virginia that had eaten tens of thousands of dollars, and a city house in Washington that had eaten hundreds of thousands of dollars, and we had *things*—God, did we have things. We had weather vanes and quilts and carousel horses and stained-glass windows and tin boxes and pocket mirrors and Cadbury chocolate cups and postcards of San Francisco before the earthquake, so we were worth something; we just had no money. It was always a little mystifying to me how we had gone from having so much money to having so little, but now, of course, I understand it all a little better, because the other thing that ate our money was the affair with Thelma Rice. Thelma went to France in the middle of it, and you should see the phone bills.

Not that I knew about the phone bills the day I found the book of children's songs with the disgusting inscription in it. "My darling Mark," it began, "I wanted to give you something to mark what happened today, which makes our future so much clearer. Now you can sing these songs to Sam, and someday we will sing them to him together. I love you. Thelma." That was it. I could hardly believe it. Well, the truth is I didn't believe it. I looked at the signature again and tried to make it come out some other name, a name of someone I didn't know as opposed to someone I did, but there was the *T* and there was the *a* plain as day, even if the letters in the middle were a little squishy, and there's not much you can do with a name that begins with a *T* and ends in an *a* but Thelma. Thelma! She had just been to our house for lunch! She and her husband Jonathan—actually, they hadn't come for lunch, they'd stopped by afterward for dessert, a carrot cake I'd made that had too much crushed pineapple in it but was still awfully good compared to Thelma's desserts. Thelma always makes these gluey puddings. Thelma, her husband Jonathan (who knew all about the affair, it turned out), my husband Mark—all three of them sat there while I waddled around in a drip-dry maternity dress serving carrot cake to the rest of the guests and apologizing about the crushed pineapple.

It may seem odd to you that their coming to lunch bothers me as much as it does, but one of the worst things about finding out about a thing like this is that you feel stupid, and the idea that I actually invited them over and they actually accepted and all three of them actually sat there thinking I was some sort of cheese made it that much worse. The most mortifying part of it all is that the next day Thelma called to say thank you and asked for the carrot cake recipe and I sent it to her. I removed the crushed pineapple, of course. "Here is the carrot cake recipe," I wrote on a postcard, "with the kinks out of it." I'm afraid I put a little face with a smile next to the recipe. I am not the sort of person who puts little faces on things, but there are times when nothing else will do. Right now, for instance, I would like to put a little face at the very end of this sentence, only this one would have a frown on it.

I should point out that although I could hardly believe Mark was having an affair with Thelma, I knew he was having an affair with someone. That was how I came upon the songbook in the first place: I was poking around in his drawers, looking for clues. But Thelma! It made me really angry. It would have been one thing if he'd gotten involved with a little popsy, but he'd gone off and had an affair with a person who was not only a giant but a clever giant. I cannot tell you how many parties we'd come home from while this affair was being secretly conducted and I'd said, while taking off my clothes, "God, Thelma said such an amusing thing tonight." Then I would repeat it, word for word, to Mark. Talk about being a fool! *Talk about being a fool!* I even knew Thelma was having an affair! Everyone did. She had taken to talking indiscriminately and openly about the possibility that her husband Jonathan would be dispatched to some faraway State Department post and she would stay behind in Washington and buy a condominium.

"She's talking about condominiums," my friend Betty Searle called up to say one day. "Obviously she's involved with someone."

"Are you sure?" I said.

"Of course I'm sure," said Betty. "The question is who." She thought for a minute. "Maybe it's Senator Campbell," she said. "He's talking about condominiums, too."

"Senators always talk about condominiums," I said.

"That's true," said Betty, "but who else could it be?"

"I'll ask Mark," I said.

"Do you think Thelma Rice is having an affair with Senator Campbell?" I said to Mark that night.

"No," he said.

"Well, she's having an affair with someone," I said.

"How do you know?" he said.

"She's talking about buying a condominium if Jonathan is sent to Bangladesh," I said.

"Jonathan's not going to be sent to Bangladesh," said Mark.

"Why not?" I said.

"Because we still care about Bangladesh," said Mark.

"Then Upper Volta," I said.

Mark shook his head, as if he couldn't believe he'd been dragged into such a hopelessly girlish conversation, and went back to reading *House & Garden*. Shortly after that, the talk of condominiums stopped.

"Thelma's not talking about condominiums anymore," Betty called up to say one day. "What do you think it means?"

"Maybe it's over," I said.

"No," said Betty. "It's not over."

"How do you know?" I said.

"She had her legs waxed," said Betty, and then, very slowly, added, "for the first time." And then, even more slowly: "And it's not even summer yet."

"I see what you mean," I said.

Betty Searle really was a witch about these things—about many things, in fact. She could go to a dinner party in Washington and the next day she could tell you who was about to be fired—just on the basis of the seating plan! She should have been a Kremlinologist in the days when everything we knew about Russia was based on the May Day photograph. Twitches, winks, and shrugs that seemed like mere nervous mannerisms to ordinary mortals were gale force indicators to Betty. Once, for example, at a cocktail reception, she realized that the Secretary of Health, Education, and Welfare was about to be canned because the vice president's wife kissed him hello and then patted him on the shoulder.

"Anyone pats you on the shoulder when you're in the cabinet, you're in big trouble," Betty said the next day.

"But it was only the vice president's wife," I said.

Betty shook her head, as if I would never ever learn. Later that day, she called the Secretary of Health, Education, and Welfare and told him that his days were numbered, but he was so busy fighting with the tobacco lobby that he paid no attention. Two days later, the tobacco lobby rented the grand ballroom of the Washington Hilton to celebrate his ouster, and the Secretary of Health, Education, and Welfare started preparing to go on the lecture circuit.

"So who do you think Thelma's involved with?" Betty said.

"It could be anyone," I said.

"Of course it could be anyone," said Betty, "but who is it?"

"What about Congressman Toffler?" I said.

"You think so?" said Betty.

"She's always talking about how brilliant he is," I said.

"And she seated him next to herself at her last dinner party," said Betty.

"I'll ask Mark," I said. "He was seated on her other side."

"Do you think Thelma Rice is having an affair with Congressman Toffler?" I asked Mark that night.

"No," said Mark.

"Well, whoever she's having an affair with, she's still having it," I said.

"How do you know?" said Mark.

"She had her legs waxed," I said. "And it's only May."

"The Ladies' Central is busy this week, isn't it?" said Mark. "Who'd you hear that from?"

"Betty," I said.

Mark went back to reading *Architectural Digest*, and shortly thereafter Thelma Rice went to France for a few weeks, and Betty and I moved on to the subject of the president's assistant, who was calling Betty in the middle of the night and saying, "Meet me in the Rotunda and I'll tickle your tits," and other bizarre remarks encompassing Washington and sex.

"What should I do about it?" Betty said one day at lunch.

"Tell him if he does it again you'll call the newspapers," I said.

"I did," said Betty, "and you know what he said? He said, 'You haven't lived till you've squeezed my Washington Post.' Then he cackled madly." She poked at her Chicken Salad Albert Gore. "Anyway, I can't prove it's him," she said, "although Thelma always says he's a notorious letch."

"That's what Mark always says, too," I said.

I should have figured it out, of course. By the time I did, the thing had been going on for months, for seven months—for exactly as long as my pregnancy. I should have known, should have suspected something sooner, especially since Mark spent so much time that summer at the dentist. There sat Sam and I in West Virginia, making air holes in jars full of caterpillars, and there went Mark, in and out of Washington, to have root canals and gum treatments and instructions in flossing and an actual bridge, never once complaining about the inconvenience or the pain or the boredom of having to listen to Irwin Tannenbaum, D.D.S., drone on about his clarinet. Then it was fall, and we were all back in Washington, and every afternoon, Mark would emerge from his office over the garage and say he was going out to buy socks, and every evening he would come home empty-handed and say, you would not believe how hard it is to find a decent pair of socks in this city. Four weeks it took me to catch on! Inexcusable, especially since it was exactly the sort of thing my first husband said when he came home after spending the afternoon in bed with my best friend Brenda, who subsequently and as a result became my mortal enemy. "Where were you the last six hours?" I said to my first husband. "Out buying light bulbs," he said.

Light bulbs. Socks. What am I doing married to men who come up with excuses like this? Once, when I was married to my first husband, I went off to meet a man in a hotel room at six in the morning and told my husband I was going out to be on the *Today* show; it never even crossed his mind to turn on the television set to watch. Now, that's what I call a decent job of lying! Not that it does any good to prove my ingenuity; it doesn't matter how smart you are if both your husbands manage to prove how dumb you are as easily as mine had.

Of course, my fling with the man in the hotel room happened a long time ago—before my divorce, before I met Mark, before I decided to marry him and become an incorrigible believer in fidelity. It is of course hideously ironic that the occasion for my total conversion to fidelity was my marriage to Mark, but timing has never been my strong point; and in any case, the alternative, infidelity, doesn't work. You have only a certain amount of energy, and when you spread it around, everything gets confused, and the first thing you know, you can't remember which one you've told which story to, and the next thing you know, you're moaning, "Oh, Morty, Morty, Morty," when what you mean is "Oh, Sidney, Sidney, Sidney," and the next thing you know, you think you're in love with both of them simply because you've been raised to believe that the only polite response to the words "I love you" is "I love you too," and the next thing you know, you think you're in love with only one of them, because you're too guilty to handle loving them both.

After I found the book with the disgusting inscription in it, I called Mark. I'm embarrassed to tell you where I called him—okay, I'll tell you: I called him at his shrink's. He goes to a Guatemalan shrink over in Alexandria who looks like Carmen Miranda and has a dog named Pepito. "Come home immediately," I said. "I know about you and Thelma Rice." Mark did not come home immediately. He came home two hours later because—are you ready for this?—THELMA RICE WAS ALSO AT THE SHRINK'S. They were having a double session! At the family rate!! I did not know this at the time. Not only did Thelma Rice and Mark see Dr. Valdez and her Chihuahua, Pepito, once a week, but so did Thelma's husband, Jonathan Rice, the undersecretary of state for Middle Eastern affairs. Mark and Thelma saw Chiquita Banana together, and Jonathan Rice saw her alone—and that man has something to do with making peace in the Middle East!

When Mark finally came home, I was completely prepared. I had rehearsed a speech about how I loved him and he loved me and we had to work at our marriage and we had a baby and we were about to have another—really the perfect speech for the situation except that I had misapprehended the situation. "I am in love with Thelma Rice," he said when he arrived home. That was the situation. He then told me that although he was in love with Thelma Rice, they were not having an affair. (Apparently he thought I could handle the fact that he was in love with her but not the fact that he was having sex with her.) "That is a lie," I said to him, "but if it's true"—you see, there was a part of me that wanted to think it was true even though I knew it wasn't: the man is capable of having sex with a venetian blind—"if it's true, you might as well be having an affair with her, because it's free." Some time later, after going on saying all these lovey-dovey things about Thelma, and after saying he wouldn't give her up, and after saying that I was a shrew and a bitch and a nag and a kvetch and a grouse and that I hated Washington (the last charge was undeniably true), he said that he nonetheless expected me to stay with him. At that moment, it crossed my mind that he might be crazy. I sat there on the couch with tears rolling down my face and my fat belly resting on my thighs, I screwed up my courage, and when Mark finished his sixteenth speech about how wonderful Thelma Rice was compared to me, I said to him, "You're crazy." It took every ounce of self-confidence I had.

"You're wrong," he said.

He's right, I thought. I'm wrong.

Well, we went around in circles. And then he asked me if I wanted to be alone for a while. I guess he wanted to drive over to Thelma's to tell her he had held fast to their love. It didn't matter. He drove off and I scooped up Sam and a suitcase full of Pampers, called a taxi, and left for the airport.

Two

One thing I have never understood is how to work it so that when you're married, things keep happening to you. Things happen to you when you're single. You meet new men, you travel alone, you learn new tricks, you read Trollope, you try sushi, you buy nightgowns, you shave your legs. Then you get married, and the hair grows in. I love the everydayness of marriage, I love figuring out what's for dinner and where to hang the pictures and do we owe the Richardsons, but life does tend to slow to a crawl. The whole summer Mark was secretly seeing Thelma Rice while pretending to be at the dentist, I was cooking. That's what I do for a living—I write cookbooks. And while I did discover a fairly revolutionary and absolutely foolproof way to make a four-minute egg, and had gotten to the point where I simply could not make a bad vinaigrette, this was not exactly the stuff of drama. (Even now, I cannot believe Mark would want to risk losing that vinaigrette. You just don't bump into vinaigrettes that good.) Before that, there had been a lot of time spent on swatches and couches and floor plans. It was almost as if Mark had a career as a columnist and I had a career as a food person and our marriage had a career as a fighter with contractors. First we fought with the Washington contractor, who among other atrocities managed to install our carpet on the sixth floor of a Washington department store; then we fought with the West Virginia contractor, who forgot the front door. "No one uses front doors in the country anyway," he said when we pointed it out, which was also what he said about the paper-towel rack and the medicine cabinet. Then we hired Laszlo Pump, a Hungarian troubleshooter, to clean up the mess the other two contractors had made, and that was when the real trouble began. Laszlo ripped out the living room wall and vanished. We called him at home and got his wife. She said his father had died. A week later she said his dog had died. A week later she said his analyst had died. Finally we reached Laszlo. He said he had cancer.

"He has cancer," I said when I hung up the phone.

"Bullshit," said Mark.

"People don't lie about that," I said.

"Yes they do," said Mark. "Contractors do. They lie about everything. Look, we'll go to his house. We'll see how he looks. If he looks okay I'll kill him."

"We can't go to his house," I said.

"Why not?" said Mark.

"Because we don't know where he lives."

"We'll look it up," said Mark.

"We can't look it up," I said. "He has an unlisted address."

"What are you talking about?" said Mark.

"It's the latest thing," I said.

"What kind of person has an unlisted address?" Mark said. "I'll tell you what kind. The kind that doesn't want to be dead. The kind that people are trying to kill all the time."

"Why are you angry at me?" I said.

"I'm not angry at you," said Mark.

"Then why are you shouting at me?" I said.

"Because you're the only one who's here," said Mark.

I burst into tears. "I hate it when you get angry," I said.

"I'm not angry at you," said Mark. "I love you. I'm not angry at you."

"I know," I said, "but it scares me. It reminds me of my father."

"I'm not your father," said Mark. "Repeat after me, 'Mark Feldman is not my father.'"

"Mark Feldman is not my father," I said.

"Am I fat?" said Mark.

"No," I said.

"Am I bald?"

"No."

"Do I smell of Dr. Scholl's foot pads?"

"No," I said.

"I rest my case," said Mark.

It always ended up like that in the end—us against the world, Washington's bravest couple in combat with the entire service industry and their answering machines—but the point I want to make is this: I sat on that plane to New York in a state of total misery, yet part of me was secretly relieved to be done with swatches and couches and fights with contractors, and that part of me was thinking: Okay, Rachel Samstat, finally something is happening to you.

That's my name—Rachel Samstat. It's always been Rachel Samstat. I held on to it through both my marriages—through the first because I never liked my first husband's last name enough to change mine to it, and through the second because I was by then known in a small and modest way as Rachel Samstat. The cookbooks I write do well. They're very personal and chatty—they're cookbooks in an almost incidental way. I write chapters about friends or relatives or trips or experiences, and work in the recipes peripherally. Then, of course, the television show came along, which made the books sell even better.

How I got my own show is probably something you're wondering. I'm not exactly a conventional television personality, although I suppose I'm somewhat conventional when it comes to public television, which is what my show was on, not network. "Too New York" is what the last network that was approached about me responded, which is a cute way of being anti-Semitic, but who cares? I'd rather be too New York than too anything else. Anyway, I don't belong on a network. I have the kind of odd and interesting features that work out all right in life but not at all on the screen, so I'm far better off on public television, where the producers and cameramen are used to Julia Child and are pathetically grateful that I'm not quite as tall. Also, there's my blink. I blink. "Hi, I'm Rachel Samstat"—saying that, looking directly at the camera, I blink fifty or sixty times minimum. It's the looking at the camera that makes me do it; when I'm looking at a person, or a pork roast, my blinks go down to near normal.

After we taped the first show and discovered the blink, Richard, my producer, suggested I go see a professional television coach, who specialized in voices but was willing to undertake a little eyelid work on the side. She kept telling me she'd never had a failure, probably to encourage me, but the effect was to make me absolutely determined to be her first, which I was.

"I don't think I can fix the blink," she told Richard after several sessions, "but I can probably do a little something with the voice."

"We like the voice," said Richard, and thank God, because there wasn't much left of me by then that someone hadn't taken a swipe at, usually using the definite article. The voice. The blink. The hair. The chin. "She has a quality onscreen not unlike Howard Cosell," someone high up at the station is supposed to have said, and even though I choose to think he meant it as a compliment—he meant I'm the sort of person you feel strongly about one way or another—Howard Cosell was not exactly what I had in mind. What I had in mind was Imogene Coca or Elaine May. Anyway, the important thing is that I do happen to have a funny voice, and it makes people laugh. It works on television, although there's no way a voice coach would understand that, since her job is to teach everyone to sound like David Brinkley.

It's really because of Richard that the television show came up at all. I was on a talk show promoting *My Grandmother's Cookies* when Richard saw me. Actually, it was Phil Donahue he saw me on. Richard is hooked on Phil Donahue. He says that if Sigmund Freud had watched Phil Donahue he would never have wondered what women want. There I was, fielding questions about piecrust and doing my Jewish prince routine, when Richard got the idea it might make a series—me and my relatives and my friends and a few famous strangers, talking about food, talking about the role food plays in life, doing a little cooking, a middlebrow Julia Child crossed with a highbrow Dinah Shore. How we got away with it I don't know, except that we threw Proust and his madeleines into the opening credits, and I managed to get Isaac Bashevis Singer to make noodle kugel on the pilot. Also, the show cost next to nothing to produce, and what little it cost was underwritten by an oil company where someone I used to date is now in charge of parceling out money to public television. I dated him when he was Jewish—now that he works at the oil company you can't exactly tell. He was so Jewish when I dated him that he taught Hebrew school, and I, who at that point had had no Jewish education whatsoever, learned about Purim and good Queen Esther and the wicked Haman from him one night in a dormitory at Harvard while he stuck one and then two and then three fingers into me. This was before the discovery of the clitoris, when there was far too much sticking of fingers into things and not nearly enough playing around with the outsides; still, it was a nice enough introduction to the origins of Hamantaschen pastries, and I retain a special and absurd affection for Purim in spite of the fact that I have always hated Hamantaschen. That isn't true. Mark's aunt Florence makes good Hamantaschen. Aunt Florence, who raised Mark, is a great cook; her triumph, which she serves on Thanksgiving along with the turkey, is a brisket cooked with sauerkraut and brown sugar, and it sounds perfectly awful, I know, but it's truly one of the most delicious things I've ever eaten.

I'd been planning to have Mark's aunt on the next thirteen-week cycle of my television show to discuss the brisket, as well as her tzimmes and gefilte fish, but I don't really see how I'm going to be able to now that all this has come about. I don't like blaming family members for what goes wrong with children, because someday when my kids are arrested for grand larceny I don't want anyone looking accusingly at me, but Mark's behavior was so obviously Florence's fault that even Florence knew it. "It must be my fault" were in fact her first words on the subject when I called to tell her I had gone to New York because her nephew had fallen in love with Thelma Rice. "Don't be silly," I said in reply, but what I was thinking was: You bet your sweet ass it is. Jewish princes are made, not born.

RACHEL SAMSTAT'S JEWISH PRINCE ROUTINE

You know what a Jewish prince is, don't you?
   (Cocks her eyebrow)
If you don't, there's an easy way to recognize one. A simple sentence. "Where's the butter?"
   (A long pause here, because the laugh starts slowly and builds)
Okay. We all know where the butter is, don't we?
   (A little smile)

The butter is in the refrigerator.

(Beat)

The butter is in the refrigerator in the little compartment in the door marked "Butter."

(Beat)

But the Jewish prince doesn't mean "Where's the butter?" He means "Get me the butter." He's too clever to say "Get me" so he says "Where's."

(Beat)

And if you say to him—

(Shouting)

"in the refrigerator"—

(Resume normal voice)

and he goes to look, an interesting thing happens, a medical phenomenon that has not been sufficiently remarked upon.

(Beat)

The effect of the refrigerator light on the male cornea.

(Beat)

Blindness.

(A long beat)

"I don't see it anywhere."

(Pause)

"Where's the butter" is only one of the ways the Jewish prince reveals himself. Sometimes he puts it a different way. He says, "Is there any butter?"

(Beat)

We all know whose fault it is if there isn't, don't we.

(Beat)

When he's being really ingenious, he puts it in a way that's meant to sound as if what he needs most of all from you is your incredible wisdom and judgment and creativity. He says, "How do you think butter would taste with this?"

(Beat)

He's usually referring to dry toast.

(Beat)

I've always believed that the concept of the Jewish princess was invented by a Jewish prince who couldn't get his wife to fetch him the butter.

I was not raised as a Jewish princess. Sometimes I'm accused of being one because I'm not exactly the outdoor type, but I grew up a scrappy little athlete with a scrappy little mother who wanted me to have a flashy career like her own. I wonder what she would have made of my work. My mother was a good recreational cook, but what she basically believed about cooking was that if you worked hard and prospered, someone else would do it for you.

My mother was an agent in Hollywood, a lady agent, a classic forties career woman: she had short hair and bangs, she wore suits with shoulder pads, and she talked in a gravelly voice. She handled what were known in the business as specialty acts, which is to say mostly midgets. After they stopped making movies like *The Wizard of Oz*, the midget market dried up and she moved into actors with scars. In the meantime, we had a lot of midgets hanging around the house, and as a result my mother often served food that was a little too bite-sized. My sister Eleanor gets very churlish about my mother's cooking, and she always points out that my mother's fling with rumaki lasted considerably longer than it should have; but Eleanor hates to give credit where credit is due, and the fact is that my mother had enormous flair when she was paying attention, and when she didn't feel like paying attention she threw in a lot of butter. She could also Keep Help, which I was raised to believe was no small thing; indeed, I was raised to believe that almost the worst thing that could be said about you after you grew up was that you couldn't.

Every New Year's Day, my parents had a big party, and their friends came over and bet on the Rose Bowl and argued about which of the players on either team were Jewish, and my mother served her famous lox and onions and eggs, which took her the entire first half to make. It took her so long, in fact, that I really don't have time to give you the recipe, because it takes up a lot of space to explain how slowly and painstakingly she did everything, sautéing the onions over a tiny flame so none of them would burn, throwing more and more butter into the pan, cooking the eggs so slowly that my father was always sure they wouldn't be ready until the game was completely over and everyone had gone home. We should have known my mother was crazy years before we did just because of the maniacal passion she brought to her lox and onions and eggs, but we didn't. Another thing my mother was famous for serving was a big ham along with her casserole of lima beans and pears. A couple of years ago, I was in Los Angeles promoting *Uncle Seymour's Beef Borscht* and a woman said to me at a party, "Wasn't your mother Bebe Samstat?" and when I said yes, she said, "I have her recipe for lima beans and pears." I like to think it would have amused my mother to know that there is someone in Hollywood who remembers her only for her lima beans and pears, but it probably wouldn't have. Anyway, here's how you make it:* Take 6 cups defrosted lima beans, 6 pears peeled and cut into slices, ½ cup molasses, ½ cup chicken stock, ½ onion chopped, put into a heavy casserole, cover, and bake 12 hours at 200°. That's the sort of food she loved to serve, something that looked like plain old baked beans and then turned out to have pears up its sleeve. She also made a bouillabaisse with Swiss chard in it. Later on, she got too serious about food—started making egg rolls from scratch, things like that—and one night she resigned from the kitchen permanently over a lobster Cantonese that didn't work out, and that was the beginning of the end.

Shortly after that, she went into her blue-chip stamp phase. She wasn't alone, of course. It was 1963, and there were a lot of American women who were saving blue-chip stamps and green stamps and plaid stamps and whatever stamps their supermarkets were giving out; still, ladies in suits with shoulder pads were supposed to have more sense. My mother, who had spent years avoiding supermarkets, made at least one trip a day to the local Thriftimart. (The scar-face market had gone pretty dry on her at this point, and she had very little else to do.) She would get into her 1947 Studebaker and set off for a day in the aisles. She developed passionate and brief attachments to new products. One month she fell in love with instant minced onions. Another month it was Pepperidge Farm raspberry turnovers. The next it was frozen chopped chives. She would return home with her bags of groceries, leave them in the kitchen for the housekeeper to empty, and go up to her bedroom, where the card table was equipped with one of those little sponge-and-jar contraptions you use when you have a lot of stamps to stick.

I was living in New York at the time, and I heard about most of this from my sister Eleanor, who was perfecting her sanctimoniousness under the aegis of my mother's progressive insanity, but I saw a little of it firsthand when my mother arrived in Manhattan one day with a ten-speed blender she had purchased for me with twenty-six books of blue-chip stamps. She had carried it onto the plane and held it on her lap all the way to New York. The next day my apartment was burglarized, and they took the blender, complete with warranty. They also took my typewriter, the television set, and my gold bracelet. My mother surveyed the wreckage and then, instead of just going out to buy a new

---

* See page 392 for the missing ingredient.

blender for sixteen dollars, went off to the nearby A & P and spent six hundred dollars on groceries, just for the plaid stamps. Then she returned to my apartment and began pasting them into stamp books. That's what she was doing when the police finally arrived—sitting there at the table, laughing her gravelly laugh and licking every so often as the two policemen told us what they thought were a lot of rollicking stories about New Yorkers who'd been burglarized of all the presents under their Christmas trees. We all had a drink, and then we all had another, and four hours later my mother was singing "When that midnight choochoo leaves for Alabam'" and the policeman whose lap she was sitting on was taking little nips at her shoulder. Then she got up and did a tap dance to "Puttin' On the Ritz" and passed out in the middle of it. It was a fabulous pass-out as those things go. She was in midair when it happened—she had both her legs up to one side, and she'd just managed to click her heels together when her eyes clanged shut and she slid on one side of her leg to the floor. I put her to bed.

"Was I very bad?" she said on the way to the airport the next day.

"Not really," I said.

"Please say I was," she said.

My father was a specialty act himself, though not in any formal sense. He was a character actor—he worked under the name of Harry Stratton, the name he still uses—but he played the kind of characters who have no character: he played kindly lawyers and kindly doctors and kindly teachers, and he said kindly things to whatever leading actor was about to lose heart in his fight to discover penicillin or defeat the outlaws or rout the Nazis. He made a lot of money—so did my mother—and they invested it in Tampax stock, and one day they were rich, and a good thing they were, because my mother's medical bills were enormous. She drank and drank and drank and finally one day her stomach swelled up like a Cranshaw melon and they took her to a very fashionable hospital for rich people with cirrhosis and the doctors clucked and said there was nothing that could be done. My parents had moved to New York by this time, and my mother's hospital room had a view of the East River. She lay there slowly dying, with my father impatiently standing by. "Pull the plug," he would say to the doctors, and the doctors would calmly explain that there was no plug, there was just the wasting away of life. A few of her former clients came to see her—the scar faces frightened the nurses and the midgets made whoopee on the electric wheelchairs—and now and then she came into focus and made deals. "I think we can get you a hundred thou on the next one," she would say; she hadn't handled a client in years, but she went rattling on about points and box office and below the line and above the line. The nurse would bring lunch. "I think I'll take it in the commissary," she'd say. One day my father called and said, "You'd better come. I think this is it." Of course, he telephoned every day and said that, but it always sounded like wishful thinking; now, finally, I knew he must be right. I went straight to the hospital, and when I went into her room she was sleeping. Suddenly she opened her eyes and looked at me. "I just screwed Darryl Zanuck on the remake," she said, and gave a little croak, which I didn't know at the moment was a significant thing, the actual croak—I thought it was just her gravelly laugh—and died.

"Mother's gone," said the nurse. Not "Your mother" but "Mother." I stared at the nurse, stunned not so much by my mother's death, which after all had been promised for months and, as far as my father was concerned, was long overdue, but by the nurse's presumption. "You can call your mother Mother," I snapped, "but you can't call my mother Mother." The nurse gave me one of those withering looks that are meant to make you feel as if your thoroughly understandable rage is mere female hysteria. She pulled the sheet over my mother's face. "We're going to take Mother away now," she said in a tone so condescending that I became even more wild with anger. "She's not your mother," I shouted. "On top of which, she's not gone, she's dead. Do you hear me? *Dead*. And what you're going to take away is her body, so call it a body. Call it a corpse, for Christ's sake." The nurse was now looking at me with an expression of complete horror, which I thought at the time was on account of my behavior, but it wasn't really; it was complete horror at what was happening behind me, which was that my mother had chosen that moment to make a full recovery. The sheet began rising like a slow-motion poltergeist, and then, in a burst, my mother whipped off the cloth and shouted: "Ta da!" Then she fainted. "Fainted dead away" is what the nurse said, which just goes to show you another anomaly of hospital life, which is that they only use the word "dead" when it doesn't apply.

"We thought you were dead," I said a few minutes later, when my mother came to.

"I was," she said, "I was." She shook her head slightly, as if trying to remember a fuzzy dream. "I floated away in a white organdy dress and black patent-leather Mary Janes," she said. "I looked like Baby Snooks. I tried to get something to wear that was more dignified, but the dignified clothes were being used on another set." She nodded; it was all coming back now. "I looked down, and there was your father, clicking a clapboard that read: 'Bebe's Death, Take One.' The camera started rolling. I was floating farther and farther away. I was definitely dead. Your father sold the Tampax stock and bought himself a Borsalino hat. 'Print,' he said. 'It's a wrap.' " She began tapping her breastbone defiantly. "*I* was the one who sat next to Bernard Baruch at a dinner party in 1944 and heard him say, 'Buy something people use once and throw away.' *I* was the one who stuck a Tampax into my twat in 1948 and came out of the bathroom and said, 'See if this is traded over the counter.' *I* was the one who made us rich, and now the bastard is going off and spending my money on bimbos while I'm stuck in goyishe heaven in an inappropriate costume. Fuck this, I said to myself, and at that moment I came back."

The next day, when I went to see her, she was sitting up in bed smoking Kools and doing the Double-Crostic. "I have experienced a miracle," she said. "You know what that means, don't you?"

"No," I said.

"It means there's a God," she said. "If you believe in miracles you have to believe in God. One follows from the other."

"No it doesn't," I said. "It doesn't follow at all. It doesn't have to be the sort of miracle someone's in charge of. It could just have been an accident of some sort. Or a dream. Or a misdiagnosis on the part of the nurse."

My mother shook her head. "I was dead," she said. "You should have seen it up there. Fluffy white clouds, and little angels with pink cheeks playing tiny harps."

"Lyres," I said.

"Miss Smart and her college education," said my mother.

A week later, she checked out of the hospital, filed for divorce, and went to New Mexico to find God. And she did. She found God and she married him. His name was Mel, he honestly believed he was God, and as my first husband Charlie said at the time, "If there's one thing we know about God, it's that he's not named Mel." Mel took my mother for every penny she had, plus Charlie's old Swedish-modern couch and a set of flatware I was very attached to. Then she died again, this time for good.

I would like to ask her what a person who is seven months pregnant is supposed to do when her husband turns out to be in love with someone else, but the truth is she probably wouldn't have been much help. Even in the old days, my mother was a washout at hard-core mothering; what she was good at were clever remarks that made you feel immensely sophisticated and adult and, if you thought about it at all, foolish for having wanted anything so mundane as some actual nurturing. Had I been able to talk to her at this moment of crisis, she would probably have said something fabulously brittle like "Take notes." Then she would have gone into the kitchen and toasted almonds. You melt some butter in a frying pan, add whole blanched almonds, and sauté until they're golden brown with a few little burned parts. Drain lightly and salt and eat with a nice stiff drink. "Men are little boys," she would have said as she lifted her glass. "Don't stir or you'll bruise the ice cubes."

Three

Maybe you think I walked out on Mark awfully fast if I was really so in love with him, but I probably wouldn't have if it wasn't for my therapist. I left that part out, and I hate to bring it up because until now you've been thinking that Mark was the one with the unconventional shrink, and now you're going to see we both were. Oh, well. I have a therapist named Vera Maxwell. She's fifty-eight years old and quite beautiful, she has creamy white skin and curly black hair and she wears bright red lipstick and caftans. She's famous, really, she goes on talk shows and has a lot of celebrity patients, and every so often she has to fly off to co-host Merv Griffin, or she has to take a phone call in the middle of a session from someone having a crisis at the Cannes Film Festival.

Vera is a wonderful therapist. She is loving, caring, giving, and unrelenting. Of course, when I first went to her, I was unhappily married to Charlie, and now nine years had passed and I was unhappily married to Mark, and that might not sound like progress. But trust me. You'll have to trust me, because there's no real way to convey what she does in her office that doesn't sound like some sort of Yiddish mumbo jumbo. She tells the kreplach joke a lot, and the one about the man from Minsk meeting the man from Pinsk. I will tell you the kreplach joke, but the truth is you need an accent to tell it well; I would throw in a recipe for kreplach as well, but it's a pain in the ass to make kreplach.

THE KREPLACH JOKE

Once upon a time there was a little boy who hated kreplach. Every time he saw a piece of kreplach in the soup he screamed, "Aaaaah, kreplach!" So his mother decided to teach him not to be afraid of kreplach. She took him into the kitchen and rolled out some dough. "Just like a pancake," she said. "Just like a pancake," said the little boy. Then she took a piece of meat and rolled it into a ball. "Just like a meatball," she said. "Just like a meatball," said the little boy. Then she rolled up the meat in the dough and held it up. "Just like a dumpling," she said. "Just like a dumpling," said the little boy. Then she dropped it into the soup and put it in front of the little boy, and he screamed, "Aaaaah, kreplach!"

Anyway, the thing about Vera is that she's very direct; she's not one of those shrinks who sit there impassively and say "Mmmmhmmm" every so often. After Mark told me he was in love with Thelma Rice and left me to be alone for a while, I called up Vera in New York and told her what had happened, and do you know what she said? She said, "He's disgusting." That threw me a little, because even though I knew that Vera was no slouch at calling a spade a spade, it seemed awfully strong.

"What should I do?" I said.

"What should you do?" Vera replied.

That may not look like a direct response, but it was. She said "What should you do?" with her voice rising on the word "do," and it was as if there was only one possible thing to do and how could I possibly wonder what it was. But I hung in there; I tried to get her to be a little more specific.

"Yes, what should I do?" I said.

"Is this what you want?" Vera said. "Is this what you want in a husband?"

Well, of course it wasn't what I wanted in a husband. On the other hand, what I wanted in a husband was Mark. At least that's what I'd thought I wanted. Could I help it if Mark didn't measure up to Vera's ideas of a husband? Vera has a husband to match her ideas—his name is Niccolo, and he has a white beard and he wears crisp seersucker suits and straw hats that he tips, and Vera says that the sex she has with Niccolo is as good after twenty years of marriage as it was in the beginning, which is almost the most depressing thing she says since no one else can say that except Vera, but if Vera says it there must be something to it; and what's more, what's worse in a way, is that Vera says she is never bored by Niccolo and he is never bored by her because they never tell the same stories twice. She told me this one day when I was still married to Charlie.

"Never?" I said.

"Never," said Vera, but if she ever did tell a story twice, she said, she would change it around a little so that Niccolo would still find it interesting. Myself, I never change a story. I never even change an *inflection* in a story once it's working. Mark, on the other hand, changes his stories every time he tells them, by making them longer. He has a story he tells about his first day of work in the newspaper business. He went to his office his first day in the newspaper business in a brand-new white suit, and they told him he had to wash the carbon paper, and he believed them, and he went into the men's room and turned on the water and the carbon splattered all over his brand-new white suit. It's a good story. Mark told it to me the night we met. We all have stories like that, stories we rely on to establish our charm in the beginning of relationships. I tell one about wanting to play the ukulele in the school orchestra. They asked me what instrument I wanted to play, and I said the ukulele, and they said, but there's no ukulele in the school orchestra, and I said, then what can I play that's like the ukulele, and they said the viola. That story doesn't sound so charming on the page, but I tell it very well. In any case, by the time Mark fell in love with Thelma Rice, the story about his first day in the newspaper business had turned into a novella.

"Well, is it?" said Vera. "Is this what you want in a husband?"

"I guess not," I said weakly, and left for the plane.

I worry about telling you this kind of story. Psychoanalysis has done strange things to my dialogue, and when I talk about it I sound a little like one of those starlets on *The Tonight Show* who's just stumbled onto Eastern philosophy or feminism or encounter therapy or any other system of thought that explains everything in the universe in eight minutes. Pick a dream, any dream—I'll analyze it and give you a pep talk. This used to cause a lot of friction between me and Mark. When I first met him, he had a recurrent nightmare that Henry Kissinger was chasing him with a knife, and I said it was really his father and he said it was really Henry Kissinger, and I said it was really his father and he said it was really Henry Kissinger, and this went on for months until he started going to the Central American shrinkette, who said Henry Kissinger was really his younger sister. That's almost the only good thing I can say about Our Lady of the Castanets: Mark's going to her at least ended our conflict over psychoanalysis. In fact, he was converted overnight. "What's really bothering you?" he would say. Or: "What does that remind you of?" Or: "That sounds hostile to me." Or: "I'm not your mother." All this happened before we got married, and I found it incredibly seductive.

So we got married and I got pregnant and I gave up my New York apartment and moved to Washington. Talk about mistakes. There I was, a regular at the Thalia, a connoisseur of the latest goat cheeses, an expert on alternate routes to Long Island—there I was, trying to hold up my end in a city where you can't even buy a decent bagel. I don't mean to make it sound as if it's all about being Jewish, but that's another thing about Washington. It makes you feel really Jewish if that's what you are. It's not just that there are so many Gentiles there; it's that the Gentiles are so Gentile. Listen, even the Jews there are sort of Gentile. Not that I complained. I can work anywhere, I said bravely. I had a new husband, and then I had a new baby, and then I had another baby coming, and meanwhile I had my friends and a kitchen stove with six burners. *Uncle Seymour's Beef Borscht* made the best-seller list and two weeks later I was in the Sunday *Times* crossword puzzle, 26 across— Uncle Seymour's niece, it said.

Every so often I would fly to New York for one thing or another, and would go by to see Vera. I had really graduated from therapy by then, but I liked to stop in for an oil check from time to time. I would tell her I was okay, really I was, I was working hard, things were good with me and Mark, the baby was wonderful, and then, after the session, I would walk into Balducci's and there would be the arugola and radicchio and fresh basil and sorrel and sugar snap peas and six kinds of sprouts, and I would think to myself: Even the vegetables in New York are better.

It's not just the vegetables, of course. I look out the window and I see the lights and the skyline and the people on the street rushing around looking for action, love, and the world's greatest chocolate chip cookie, and my heart does a little dance. The little dance my heart was doing as I looked out the window of my father's apartment was not exactly a polka, but at least I was where I wanted to be. If I couldn't have Mark, I could finally be back making sorrel soup. Take 4 cups of washed sorrel and cut off the stems carefully. (If you don't, the soup will be hairy, and no one will know it's the sorrel's hair and not the cook's.) Sauté the sorrel in 4 tablespoons butter until wilted. Add 2½ quarts chicken stock and 4 chopped peeled potatoes. Cook 45 minutes until potatoes are tender. Purée in a blender and add salt, pepper, and hot red pepper flakes. Chill and add more salt and the juice of 1 lemon and 1 cup heavy cream. Serve with lemon slices.

.   .   .

The next morning the doorbell rang. I'd been up all night waiting for Mark to turn up to say it was all a terrible mistake, he really loved me, he must have been crazy, he didn't know what had gotten into him, and he would never see Thelma again if I would just come back to Washington immediately. I flung open the door to tell him I never wanted to see him again but I might consider coming back under certain circumstances, and who should it be but Jonathan Rice, the undersecretary of state and my partner in cuckoldom. I burst into tears and we fell into each other's arms.

"Oh, Jonathan," I said, "isn't it awful?"

"It's awful," he said. "What's happening to this country?" (Jonathan never takes anything personally; he always sees himself as a statistical reflection of a larger trend in society.)

Sam toddled into the living room and began methodically removing the books from the bookshelves, and Jonathan and I sat down and started on vodka mixed with Red Cheek apple juice. It turned out that Jonathan had been up half the night discussing the situation with Thelma and Mark, and when he realized neither of them was going to do a thing about it, he'd hopped on the shuttle and come to my father's, where Mark said I probably was.

"I had to talk to you," Jonathan said. "I love my wife." I'll skip the direct quotes, because it's too sickening—in less than twenty-four hours I'd had to listen to two grown men talking like saps about Thelma. He loved Thelma, Jonathan said, he had never loved anyone but Thelma, he had loved Thelma for nineteen years and would always love her even though Thelma didn't give a rat's ass about him and never had. She was a hysteric, Jonathan said, and a hopeless romantic; he'd been through this half a dozen times with her other men—the worst, he said, had been her affair with the undersecretary of the Nationalist Chinese embassy; she'd nearly had a nervous breakdown when Nixon recognized China and the Nationalists had to leave the country. "She got into bed and stayed there for weeks," said Jonathan. "Imagine my dilemma: there I was, on the Asia desk." He sighed. "Of course, normalization was psychologically hard on many Americans."

Still, Jonathan went on, he'd never seen Thelma quite so smitten with anyone as she was with Mark, and vice versa, and off went Jonathan on a long description of the presents Mark had given Thelma and the restaurants he'd taken her to and the meals they'd ordered and the business trips she'd gone along with him on and the hotels they'd stayed in and the room service (room service! he'd even had room service with her!) and the flowers that had arrived the next day. Just thinking about the flowers made me want to die, just thinking about the flowers he'd sent her while occasionally bringing me home a bunch of wilted zinnias. Mark is such a campaigner; he never just *does* something, he crusades for it. To realize, as I was suddenly beginning to realize, that all his energy had been going into Thelma Rice for all these months made me so sad I could hardly breathe. Jonathan went rattling on, pouring on detail after detail, to the point that I accused him of bugging his own telephone—he knew so much, he knew actual dialogue—but he claimed that Thelma simply told him everything. "We have an honest marriage," Jonathan said, and he glared at me as if I were somehow responsible for this whole mess because my marriage was so hopelessly dishonest. For months I'd been doing nothing but boiling eggs and teaching my child to differentiate between the cat in the hat and the fox in socks, and Jonathan Rice, the undersecretary of state, was actually angry at *me*! It's stuff like this that got us into Cambodia. Anyway, since Jonathan knew so much, I asked him if he happened to know exactly what it was that Mark and Thelma had been doing four days earlier, on the day the inscription in the children's book was dated. *I wanted to give you something to mark what happened today, which makes our future so much clearer. . . .* And of course he knew; the man knew everything. Four days earlier, my husband, Mark Feldman, had taken his paramour, Thelma Rice, to the Bloomingdale's furniture department, where they had looked at couches for his office. Bloomingdale's! The ultimate perfidy!

"But his office has a couch," I said.

"His *new* office," Jonathan said.

"What new office?" I said.

"The new office he wants to rent on Connecticut Avenue," said Jonathan. "And of course it needs a couch." He paused for emphasis. "You can't have a love nest without a couch." He paused again. "A convertible couch."

"I know I'm slow," I said, "but I did manage to figure the convertible part out."

The couch Thelma liked was green, Jonathan said, but Mark liked a brown tweed one, and they almost compromised on a pale yellow one but Thelma thought it would show the dirt, and just when I was becoming really sorry I'd asked, Jonathan came to the point—there was a point to his visit, it turned out—and said that he believed that if I came back to Mark, the two of us could wait the two of them out. He'd talked to the Guatemalan whiz-bang, he said—that's when I found out all three of them were seeing her—and she'd assured him that Mark's affair with Thelma would never last, because Mark had too much Jewish guilt and would never give up his children.

"Also," said Jonathan, "there's a lot Mark doesn't know about Thelma, and when he finds it out I'm sure he won't love her anymore."

"There's a lot Thelma doesn't know about Mark, too," I said.

"Like what?" said Jonathan.

"It doesn't matter," I said. "You know all this awful stuff about Thelma and you still love her, and I know all this awful stuff about Mark and I still love him, so what makes you think they're going to stop loving each other when they find out what we know about them?"

"Tell me some awful stuff about Mark," said Jonathan.

I couldn't think of much. Mark has to be reminded to clean his nails, and sometimes he says he's read a book when he's read only the first fifty pages of it, and he doesn't visit his great-aunt Minnie in the Hebrew Home as much as he should, but the truth is that the only really awful thing I knew about Mark Feldman was that he had betrayed me. That was a terrible thing, I don't mean to downplay it, but it wasn't the sort of thing Jonathan was looking for; Jonathan wanted to be told that Mark was a notorious plagiarist, or a shoplifter, or a scofflaw, and then he wanted to take the information home to Thelma like an old bone. Poor Jonathan. Poor pathetic doggie. The man actually believed he was going to argue her out of it. On top of everything else (not that I was going to tell him, although Thelma undoubtedly already had), Jonathan was up against a real piece of work in the sack, and it's hard to compete with that if you're the spouse who's been around for years; it's hard to compete with *anyone* new in the sack if you're the spouse who's been around for years. I really wanted to say something consoling to Jonathan, but every time the urge came over me to do so, he would drop one more piece of the betrayal into my lap: he was like a six-year-old boy who comes up to you with a shy smile, takes your hand, and gently presses a snake into it. No wonder Thelma had fallen in love with Mark; if I'd spent nineteen years with Jonathan Rice, I would have run off with a delivery boy from the Fleet Messenger Service.

"I'm not going back to Mark," I said. "I'm not going to sit there while the two of them go on seeing each other on their convertible couch. I'm not going to wait this out."

"You're my only hope," Jonathan said.

I started crying again, and Jonathan put his arms around me and began muttering something about how the economy was in bad shape too, and there we were, hugging each other while Jonathan went on about the gross national product, when my father walked into the living room. He'd escaped from the loony bin in a jogging outfit.

"I'd like you to meet Jonathan Rice," I said.

"You're doing this in front of the kid?" said my father.

"It's not what you think," I said. "Mark is in love with Jonathan's wife."

"Who's Mark?" said my father.

"My husband," I said.

"It's the Thorazine talking," said my father. "They shoot you up with so much of it you can't even remember your son-in-law's name. Who was Charlie?"

"My first husband," I said.

"He's a fool," said my father.

"I thought you liked Charlie," I said.

"Not Charlie. Mark. Mark's a fool."

"What am I going to do?" I said. I started to sob. My father gave a little nod to Jonathan Rice, a little move-over-Buster-you're-in-the-way nod, and Jonathan untangled himself and stood up and my father sat down and tangled himself, and I shook and heaved and wheezed and snorted all over his sweatsuit. My father said a lot of terrific daddy things to me that made me cry even harder, partly because the dialogue was completely lifted from an obscure Dan Dailey movie he'd played a pediatrician in, and partly because he nevertheless delivered the lines so very well.

"What am I going to do?" I said.

"There's nothing you can do, baby," said my father.

"Of course there's something she can do," said Jonathan. "She can come back to him. If we both stick with it, we can sit this thing out."

"Jonathan is the undersecretary of state in charge of Middle Eastern affairs," I said.

My father looked at Jonathan. "I suppose they don't give that job to Jews," he said.

"That's right," said Jonathan.

"You want to make a pact with someone," said my father, "go call up the president of Egypt. Leave Rachel out of this." Then he told Jonathan to have a nice flight back and showed him to the door. Then he telephoned Lucy Mae Hopkins, the maid, and asked her to move into the apartment for a while to help take care of Sam. Then he called the Chinese restaurant down the block and ordered shrimp fried rice, which is something I love to eat when I'm feeling blue, shrimp fried rice with Chinese mustard and ketchup. Then, after Lucy Mae and the Chinese food arrived, he announced that he was going back to the loony bin because there wasn't room for all of us to sleep in the apartment.

"Men," he said as he left. "I hate them. I've always hated them. You wonder why I always hang around with women and never with men, it's because men do things like this." He waved his hand vaguely at me and my stomach, and jogged off into the night.

Of course, I knew he wasn't going back to the loony bin at all; he was going to see Frances. Frances is my father's mistress. She works at a paper company, and she has remained true to my father even though he keeps marrying other women and leaving her with nothing but commissions on his stationery orders. He orders an enormous amount of stationery, partly to keep a hand in with Frances, partly to have plenty of pieces of paper on which to write to me and my sister Eleanor about his will. Two or three times a month, my father threatens to cut me out of his will, and then he changes his mind, and each of these developments requires a letter. He also writes a lot of letters to Frances, promising that he'll end up with her eventually; I know this because once he accidentally put a letter to her into an envelope to me and vice versa. Frances got very excited when she opened the letter meant for me, because it had no salutation and she thought he was cutting *her* out of his will, which she hadn't realized she'd been written into in the first place. Why she puts up with him I don't know. Why any of us puts up with him I don't know. The truth is that if my father weren't my father, he would be one of the men he hates; he is incorrigibly faithless and thoroughly narcissistic, to such an extent that I tend to forget he's also capable of being a real peach.

(Another thing I like to eat when I'm feeling blue is bacon hash. Cut some bacon into small pieces and start to cook it over a slow flame so that some of the fat is rendered. Then add diced cooked potatoes and cook slowly until the potatoes and bacon are completely crunchy. Eat with an egg.)

Four

The shock of catapulting from the peanut-butter-and-jellyness of my life into High Drama was so great that the first morning I woke up, I was honestly stunned to discover it wasn't all a bad dream. That's a hopelessly banal metaphor, but that's just what it felt like, one of those bad dreams in which you realize you're having a bad dream and then you wake up in the dream to the same old bad dream—the dream equivalent of the cereal box with the baby on it eating breakfast next to the cereal box with the baby on it eating breakfast, forever and ever.

By the second morning, I'd given up on that. I woke up and lay there, watching the baby inside me make waves on my belly, and wondered what would become of me. Mark would turn up eventually, of course— but what if he didn't? What would I do? Where would I live? How much money would I need? Who would sleep with me? This last question interested me deeply, because I couldn't imagine that I'd ever be my normal shape again. I will be seven months pregnant forever, I thought, as the tears started to drip slowly into my ears, and after that I will be eight months pregnant forever, and after that I will be nine months pregnant forever. The only men I'd have a shot at would have to be used to thoroughly misshapen women, and that pretty much ruled out everyone but doctors. Under other circumstances, doctors would never have crossed my mind. I went out with one when I was in college. I was suffering from a finger that got abscessed when I stuck a ballpoint pen into a hangnail. He took one look at it and said, "Abscesses. Diabetes." This terrified me, because it's always seemed to me that there's a lot of diabetes among Jews, even though it's hard to pin anyone down on the question. Once, in fact, I tried to; I met a diabetes specialist, and I said to him, "May I ask you a question?"

He replied: "You want to ask me if Jews have more diabetes than anyone else."

"Yes," I said.

"Everyone asks me that," he said. "They don't. There's a sect in India that has more diabetes than Jews."

This reminded me of those feminists who are always claiming that male domination is not the natural state because there's one tribe in New Guinea where the men lie around weaving and the women hunt bears. Anyway, I didn't have diabetes, I merely had an abscessed finger.

I have never since been remotely interested in doctors. But who else would bother with me? There I was, seven months gone, swaybacked, awkward, bloated, logy, with a belly button that looked like a pumpkin stem and feet that felt like old cucumbers. If pregnancy were a book, they would cut the last two chapters. The beginning is glorious, especially if you're lucky enough not to have morning sickness and if, like me, you've had small breasts all your life. Suddenly they begin to grow, and you've got them, you've really got them, breasts, darling breasts, and when you walk down the street they bounce, truly they do, they bounce bounce bounce. You find yourself staring in the mirror for long stretches of time, playing with them, cupping them in your hands, pushing them this way and that, making cleavage, making cleavage vanish, standing sideways, leaning over, sticking them out as far as they'll go, breasts, fantastic tender apricot breasts, then charming plucky firm tangerines, and then, just as you were on the verge of peaches, oranges, grapefruit, cantaloupes, God knows what other blue-ribbon county-fair specimens, your stomach starts to grow, and the other fruits are suddenly irrelevant because they're outdistanced by an honest-to-God watermelon. You look more idiotically out of proportion than ever in your life. You feel such nostalgia for the scrawny, imperfect body you left behind; and the commonsense knowledge that you will eventually end up shaped approximately the way you began is all but obliterated by the discomfort of not being able to sleep on your stomach and of peeing ever so slightly every time you cough and of leaking droplets from your breasts onto your good silk blouses and of suddenly finding yourself expert in mysteries you hadn't expected to comprehend until middle age, mysteries like swollen feet, varicose veins, neuritis, neuralgia, acid indigestion, and heartburn.

Heartburn. That, it seemed to me as I lay in bed, was what I was suffering from. That summed up the whole mess: heartburn. Compound heartburn. Double-digit heartburn. Terminal heartburn. The tears poured from my eyes as I lit on the image, and the only thing that might have made it even more satisfyingly melodramatic and masochistic would have been to be lying in the bathtub; nothing like crying in the tub for real self-pity, nothing like the moment when every last bit of you is wet, and wiping the tears from your eyes only means making your face even wetter.

I considered staying in bed all day. I considered getting out of bed and into the bathtub and staying *there* all day. I wondered if even considering these two alternatives constituted a nervous breakdown. (Probably not, I decided.) I contemplated suicide. Every so often I contemplate suicide merely to remind myself of my complete lack of interest in it as a solution to anything at all. There was a time when I worried about this, when I thought galloping neurosis was wildly romantic, when I longed to be the sort of girl who knew the names of wildflowers and fed baby birds with eyedroppers and rescued bugs from swimming pools and wanted from time to time to end it all. Now, in my golden years, I have come to accept the fact that there is not a neurasthenic drop of blood in my body, and I have become very impatient with it in others. Show me a woman who cries when the trees lose their leaves in autumn and I'll show you a real asshole.

I picked up the remote control unit and turned on the television set. There was Phil Donahue. He was interviewing five lesbians, who had chosen the occasion of their appearance on Donahue to come out of the closet. I could just imagine the five of them, waiting through the years for the right offer, turning down Merv, turning down Kup, turning down Cavett, watching contemptuously as their friends chose mundane occasions like Thanksgiving with Mom and Dad for the big revelation, waiting for the big one, Phil himself, to finally come clean. I contemplated lesbianism. Lesbianism has always seemed to me an extremely inventive response to the shortage of men, but otherwise not worth the trouble. It occurred to me that if I stayed in bed much longer, I would be forced to watch a soap opera. That seemed redundant, so I got up and went to group.

Under normal circumstances, I probably wouldn't mention my group. There's a real problem in dragging a group into a book: you have to introduce six new characters, bang bang bang, six new characters who are never going to be mentioned again in any essential way but who nonetheless have to be sketched in, simply because I can't really leave out of this story what happened to my group. Maybe you remember reading about it, I don't know. You'd probably remember if you did—because Vanessa Melhado is in my group. The advantage of having Vanessa Melhado in my group is that at least I don't have to introduce all six patients, since you've seen at least one of them in the movies. The other patients I'm going to have to describe by first name only: one of the many rules of group therapy is that you're not to know anyone's last name. With Vanessa, of course, you can't help knowing, she's too famous; and when my books started being published, everyone in the group learned mine; but until we all ended up on the front page together, we never knew anyone else's.

I hadn't been to my group in two years; when I moved to Washington, I'd graduated. The group held a special session in my honor, and it was really quite lovely. Everyone managed to say nice things to me except Diana, and I managed to say nice things to everyone except Diana, and Eve brought *grieven,* which are pieces of rendered chicken fat cooked with onions, and Ellis brought champagne, and even Dan, who never brings food and when he does it's only a tiny little container of cole slaw that doesn't go around, even Dan brought a cheesecake I'd given him the recipe for.

I got the cheesecake recipe from my father's second wife, Amelia, who was my family's housekeeper for years before she married him. Amelia, in fact, was what people were referring to when they said my mother was so gifted at Keeping Help. She was black—high yellow, to be exact—and ample (I think ample would be a polite way of describing her size) and covered with so many moles that she looked like a poppy seed cookie. And although it was clear that my father married her mostly to get even with my mother for marrying the Mel who thought he was God, it was still pretty inexcusable as these things went. What made it inexcusable, as far as I was concerned, was not that she was black and fat and looked like a poppy seed cookie, but that my father, in marrying her, got her to do for nothing exactly what she had been doing for a rather pleasant salary; this, it seemed to me, was going too far in the Keeping Help department. What made it inexcusable as far as my sister Eleanor was concerned was that she was sure Amelia was after my father's fortune. Since the Mel who thought he was God had already bankrupted my mother, Eleanor was positive the other half of the Tampax money would vanish as well and end up invested heavily in Amelia's only vice: wigs. "She's got at least forty of them now," Eleanor would say. "Imagine how many she'll have after he's gone."

Once I tried to engage Eleanor on the question of whether Amelia and my father had ever slept together, but she was in such a rage about the marriage there was really no dealing with her; she couldn't even enjoy empty speculation about it. Which was a shame, because Amelia was much too good-hearted to have been a gold digger, and she made my father happy, which is more than I can say of Eleanor and me, who were busy leading our own lives. Amelia cooked my father perfect meals and then sat down and giggled merrily at everything he said. In fact, she giggled merrily at everything everyone said. This put the burden of being amusing on whoever was with her, but my father loved it. My father occasionally says things like "A flying nun covers a multitude of sins" and then looks for a laugh, and it was a great comfort to him that Amelia was always good for one even if everyone else in the room was trying to ignore him.

What a cook she was! Everything she made was the lightest, the flakiest, the tenderest, the creamiest, the whateverest. She would stand at the kitchen counter—kneading dough for yeast rolls, making curls from carrots, rolling butter into balls—and tell me her secrets. She knew the mystery of my grandmother's cookies (sour cream), and she insisted there was only one true road to piecrust (Crisco). She had burn scars from her fingertips to her elbows, and she could tick them off: this one from a chicken fry for her mother's ninetieth birthday, this one from the first time she made potato pancakes, this one from a cast-iron pot she'd tended over a fire when she was growing up in the bayou. I owe her a huge debt—and her ending up with a big chunk of my father's money and a roomful of wigs would have been fine with me. But Amelia died after a year of marriage, and the only thing she ever got out of my father was a very nice grave somewhere in Louisiana.

Here's Amelia's cheesecake recipe; she always said she got it from the back of the Philadelphia cream cheese package. Make a nice graham cracker crust and pack it into a 9-inch pie pan. Then mix 12 ounces cream cheese with 4 well-beaten eggs, 1 cup sugar, and a teaspoon vanilla. Pour into the pie shell and bake 45 minutes at 350°. Remove and cool 15 minutes. Then spread gently with 2 cups sour cream mixed with ½ cup sugar and bake 10 minutes more. Cool and refrigerate several hours before serving.

I took the subway to group. I always took the subway to and from Vera's; it cleared my head. I sat down, remembered to twist my diamond ring inward so the muggers wouldn't see it, and tried to concentrate on how I was going to tell the group what had happened to me. I felt mortified. Two years earlier, I had walked off into the sunset—cured! it's a miracle! she can walk!—and now I was back again, a hopeless cripple. I looked around the subway car. A Japanese man was taking pictures of the passengers. He was undoubtedly a tourist, but he was making everyone in the car uncomfortable. I tried not to look at him, but it was impossible. Once I saw an exhibitionist on the subway, and I tried not to look at him, too, but the funny thing about exhibitionists—and the reason I'm never really offended by them—is that you can't help sneaking a peek now and then to see if the damned thing is still sticking out.

I looked at the Japanese man in a way that I hoped implied that I didn't really care if he took my picture, and that if he did take my picture I didn't really care that he was shooting my bad side, but then I decided I did care. So I smiled. I look much better when I smile. In fact, when I don't smile, I look as if I'm frowning even though I'm not.

The Japanese man took my picture and nodded his head to me in a grateful fashion. I nodded back, and a man in a plaid shirt sitting next to me looked at me and winked. I immediately wondered whether he was single, and if so, whether he was a college graduate and straight. Then I thought of how awful it would be to be single again, how awful to be back on the market with the old New York ratio going against me, two hundred single women to every straight single man, packs of Amazons roaming the streets looking in vain for someone genuinely eligible and self-supporting who didn't mind a little cellulite. It was such a depressing thought that I almost began to cry—but then I remembered the Japanese man with the camera. I did not want anyone, even a stranger on the subway, to take a picture of me crying.

The man in the plaid shirt winked again, and I realized that even if he was single and a college graduate and straight, the odds were unlikely that I would ever get involved with an indiscriminate winker at pregnant women on subways. Anyone who winks at pregnant women on subways must have something wrong with him, it seemed to me. Of course, everyone has *something* wrong with him, that's for sure, but this guy probably had something *really* wrong. Perhaps he's a rapist, I thought, or a mugger. I figured that in my present physical condition I was fairly safe from rapists, but in case he was a mugger and knew how to recognize a diamond ring even when it was turned inward, I twisted the ring off in what I hoped was a thoroughly discreet manner, made an ambiguous gesture as if I were pulling at the skin on my throat, and cleverly dropped the ring into my bra.

The subway came to Union Square and I got out. There was Ellis. Ellis is in my group. He was buying popcorn at the nut stand in the subway station, and when he saw me he looked so pleased that he threw the entire contents of the box of popcorn over his head, and just stood there grinning as it settled onto and around him. He was like a living version of a snowman in a glass ball you shake the snow inside of. I was glad to see him, too, but I couldn't tell him that because another rule of group is that members are not allowed to have conversations of any sort outside the group room, so we walked together without saying a word all the way to Vera's office.

Vera was sitting at the low, round table, opening the containers of food the group members had brought for lunch. Vanessa was there, and Eve and Diana and Sidney and Dan—and they clucked over the photographs of Sam and asked when the new baby was due and looked truly horrified when I told them why I was there.

"My husband is in love with someone else" is hard to say flat out. "My husband thinks he's in love with someone else" is as close as I came before bursting into tears. Even Diana looked truly horrified, which surprised me because Diana always gets a little smile on her face when something awful happens to me. Years earlier, I had come into group one day and burst into tears, and Diana had gotten that little smile on her face; she was really disappointed to discover that the reason I was crying was that I'd been assaulted by a cabdriver; no doubt she'd been hoping for a more personal tragedy, with longer-lasting effects. Well, now she had one.

Sidney handed me a box of Kleenex. Sidney never really says much in group—he just passes the Kleenex and looks solicitous. I wiped my eyes and managed to stop sobbing long enough to get most of the story out. Then I burst into tears again, and so did Diana.

"Why does everything happen to Rachel and nothing ever happens to me?" she cried.

"Stick it up your ass, Diana," said Ellis.

"You'd like to, wouldn't you?" said Diana. "That's the only way you like it, I bet."

"I like it all ways, which is more than I can say for your husband," said Ellis.

"Who brought the chopped liver?" asked Dan.

"I did," said Eve.

"Did you make it?" asked Dan.

"I bought it," said Eve. "Is that all right with you?"

"I was about to tell you it was delicious," said Dan. "Now I don't feel like telling you."

"Nothing's ever enough for you, is it?" said Eve.

"Every week you complain about the food," said Vanessa. "When's the last time *you* brought food to group? When's the last time you brought anything to group?"

"What did I do now?" said Dan.

"What did you do *now*?" said Eve.

"You know what this reminds me of?" said Vera.

"The old woman from Vladivostok and the camel," said Ellis.

"Please don't tell that one again," said Vanessa.

"I won't," said Vera. "But that isn't even the point. Why don't you want to talk about Rachel?"

"I'm too threatened to talk about Rachel," said Eve. "I believe in Rachel. I believe in Rachel and Mark. If they can't make it, who can?"

"Vera and Niccolo," said Ellis.

"They don't count," said Vanessa.

Everyone nodded glumly.

"Who's the other woman?" said Diana.

"It doesn't matter," I said.

"It matters to Diana," said Ellis. "All Diana cares about is finding out people's last names."

I told them a little about Thelma. I said she had a nose as long as a thumb and walked like a penguin; that made me feel better. I said Mark was a schmuck; that made me feel even better. I told the part about all three of them going to see the Central American charlatan and her dwarf dog, and I said how unfair it was that I couldn't even date.

"She must be feeling better," said Ellis. "She's making jokes."

"She makes jokes even when she's feeling terrible," said Vera. "Don't let her fool you."

"Why do you have to make everything into a joke?" asked Diana.

"I don't have to make everything into a joke," I said. "I have to make everything into a story. Remember?"

"How do you feel?" asked Eve.

"Hurt. Angry. Stupid. Miserable." I thought for a minute. "And guilty."

"You didn't do this," said Eve. "*He* did."

"But I picked him," I said.

"Anyone would have picked Mark Feldman," said Vanessa.

"No last names in group," said Vera.

"Anyway, it's not over," said Eve. "He'll be back."

"And then what?" I said. "It's like a beautiful thing that suddenly turns out to be broken into hundreds of pieces, and even when you glue it back together it's always going to have been horribly broken."

"That's what a marriage is," said Sidney. "Pieces break off, and you glue them back on."

"Look at it this way," said Vanessa, "it's not a total loss. At least you got Sidney to say something."

Sidney looked quite pleased with himself.

"Are you done, Sidney?" asked Ellis.

"Yes," said Sidney.

"Because if you are," said Ellis, "I just want to say that I don't think that's what a marriage is."

"That *is* what a marriage is," said Dan. "After a certain point it's just patch, patch, patch."

"That's not what Vera and Niccolo's marriage is," said Eve.

Everyone nodded glumly again.

"Sometimes I wish you and Niccolo would get a divorce," I said to Vera. "Your marriage is very hard on the rest of us."

"I saw Niccolo last week," said Vanessa, "and he told me that occasionally at the end of the day he and Vera get irritable with each other."

"I would kill for merely irritable," I said.

"Under what circumstances did you see Niccolo last week?" Diana asked.

"He and Vera came to a screening of my new movie," said Vanessa.

"And when you become a movie star, Diana, I'll come to a screening of your new movie, too," said Vera.

"Thanks a lot," said Diana. Diana is a computer programmer.

"What do you want?" said Vanessa. "Mark is going to turn up, and you have to know what you want when he does."

I thought about it.

"I want him back," I said.

"What do you want him back for?" said Dan. "You just said he was a schmuck."

"I want him back so I can yell at him and tell him he's a schmuck," I said. "Anyway, he's my schmuck." I paused. "And I want him to stop seeing her. I want him to say he never really loved her. I want him to say he must have been crazy. I want her to die. I want him to die, too."

"I thought you said you wanted him back," said Ellis.

"I do," I said, "but I want him back dead."

I smiled. It was the first time I'd smiled about the situation. I looked around the room, expecting everyone to be smiling back, but they were all looking in my direction as if something strange was going on. Ellis was the first to speak. "You haven't by any chance hired an assassin without telling us first, have you?"

I turned to look behind me. A man wearing a nylon stocking over his head was standing at the door, holding a snub-nosed revolver. He grabbed me around the neck, pulled me to my feet, and pressed the gun against my temple. "On the table," he said. "Money, jewelry, anything you've got that I want. Hold anything back and I'll kill the lady just like this—" And for an instant, he aimed the gun at the wall, pulled the trigger and fired. Everyone jumped at the explosive crack and turned to watch a framed photograph of Theodor Reik break into shards and fall to the floor. A second later, a framed Chivas Regal ad with a caption that said "The bottle is either half empty or half full depending on how you look at it" fell off the wall, too.

"I always hated that picture," said Sidney.

"This is not the time to talk," said Vera.

She took off the strands of antique beads from around her neck, and her three lacy wedding bands, and put them into the middle of the table. Everyone started to throw money onto the pile. Vanessa unsnapped the gold necklace she'd been given after something (though not that much) had happened between her and John Wayne in Mexico. Diana made a great show of removing her plastic bracelets and throwing them ceremoniously into the taramasalata.

The man in the nylon stocking pressed the gun into my temple so hard that I almost cried out. I closed my eyes. "Your turn, lady," he said.

I could feel the diamond ring I had slipped into my bra pressing against my breast. Mark had given me the ring when Sam was born. We had gotten to the hospital when the contractions were coming only five minutes apart, and Mark sat in the labor room, next to me, holding my arm, whispering, singing, making little jokes, doing everything right. I'd been absolutely positive that he wouldn't—that he'd turn into the kind of hopeless father who goes through the whole business under the delusion that it's as much his experience as it is yours. All this starts in Lamaze classes, where your husband ends up thinking he's pregnant, and let me tell you he's not. It's not his body, it's not his labor, it's not his pain—it's yours, and does any man give you credit or respect for it? No. They're too busy getting in on the act, holding their stopwatches and telling you when to breathe and when to push and taking pictures of the kid coming out all covered with goo and showing them to your friends at dinner parties and saying what a beautiful and moving experience it was. Not Mark. He just sat there helping me to get through, and he stayed completely calm when the doctor said there was something wrong, perhaps the umbilical cord was around the baby's neck; and he looked so impassive when he glanced over at the fetal monitor and saw that the baby had stopped breathing that I didn't even realize how serious the situation was; he just kept on whispering and singing and making little jokes as they rushed me into the operating room and knocked me out for the emergency Caesarean.

When I came to, he was standing next to me. He was wearing a green surgical smock and a mask, and he was crying and laughing, and in his arms was Sam, our beautiful Sam, our sunray, pink and gold and cooing like a tiny dove. Mark laid him on me, and then he lay down next to me on the narrow slab, and held us both until I fell asleep again.

Two hours later, when I woke up, he gave me the ring. He'd just gone out and bought it. The diamond was in an antique setting surrounded by tiny little diamonds; it looked like a delicate ice flower. The next day Mark took it back to the jeweler and had it engraved: "Rachel and Mark and Sam."

I've always wondered what I would have done about the diamond ring in my bra under other circumstances. If I'd had a choice. I didn't have a choice, because the man in the nylon stocking was the man in the plaid shirt, and he'd seen me put the ring in my bra on the subway. But suppose he hadn't? Would I have handed it over? Would I have risked my life to hold on to the ring? I don't know. All I know is that when the man in the plaid shirt and nylon stocking said, "Your turn, lady," he was gesturing toward my bra. So I reached into the bra and gave it to him. He motioned to Eve to put the other things into a bag, and she did.

"Now everyone lie down on the floor," he said. He kept the gun pressed against my head and began backing out of the room, holding me against him. "No one calls the police," he said. "Otherwise I hurt the lady." He opened the door to the hallway and took off the nylon stocking. We got into the elevator and started down.

"I'm sorry about your ring," he said.

"Don't say things you don't mean," I said.

He stepped out into the vestibule and ran out the door of the building to the street. I rode back up and walked into Vera's office. Everyone stood up, looking a little embarrassed, and Vera went to call the police. There was a lot of hugging while she was out of the room. Hugging is against the rules, too, but so is robbery, so no one cared.

"They'll be here in a few minutes," Vera said when she came back. She looked around the room. "You must all feel that I failed to protect you."

"Don't blame Vera," I said. "It was my fault."

"You always think it's your fault," said Vanessa. "You're much too guilty."

"Can't anything ever be Rachel's fault?" asked Diana.

"He saw me on the subway," I said. "He saw me take my ring off and stick it into my bra. He must have followed me here, only I was walking with Ellis so he couldn't rob me on the way."

"I hope you and Ellis weren't having a conversation outside the group room," said Dan.

"We weren't," said Ellis, "but if we had been, we probably would have been talking about what a creep you are."

There was a long silence.

"This is going to get into the papers," said Vanessa. "That's going to be my fault." Everything Vanessa did ended up in the papers.

"Good," said Diana. "We're going to find out everyone's last names."

"I have something terrible to say," said Ellis. "I was attracted to him." He looked thoroughly ashamed of himself. "He had a nylon stocking over his face and I was attracted to him."

"I saw him without the nylon stocking," I said.

"And?" said Ellis.

"And I was attracted to him, too."

"But you're desperate," said Ellis.

"That's true," I said. "But don't rub it in."

Five

One afternoon, some months before all this happened, I was working in the kitchen in our house in Washington trying to perfect my system for a four-minute egg. Here's how you make a four-minute egg: Put an egg into cold water and bring it to the boil. Turn off the heat immediately and put the lid on the saucepan. Let it sit. In three minutes, you will have a perfect four-minute egg. It just so happens that the world is not waiting breathlessly for a three-minute way to make a four-minute egg, but sometimes, when you are a food person, the possible irrelevance of what you are doing doesn't cross your mind until it's too late. (Once, for example, when I was just starting out in the food business, I was hired by the caper people to develop a lot of recipes using capers, and it was weeks of tossing capers into just about everything but milkshakes before I came to terms with the fact that nobody really likes capers no matter what you do with them. Some people *pretend* to like capers, but the truth is that any dish that tastes good with capers in it tastes even better with capers not in it.)

Anyway, there I was, boiling eggs at three-twenty on a Thursday afternoon. I know the exact time, because I looked at the clock as soon as I heard the shout. A man was shouting—screaming, actually. A fight, I thought. A terrible fight, I thought. A fight so terrible that someone is going to get killed, I thought. I went to the front door and opened it. The shouting stopped. I went back to the eggs. That evening, when Mark came home, I said, "If someone was murdered on this block this afternoon, it happened at three-twenty." Mark paid no attention at all. At the time I thought this was because he thought I was turning into the sort of melodramatic woman who is forced to imagine excitement and romance and intrigue because she's stuck at home all day; but I realize now that his affair with Thelma was just beginning, and his reaction was simply the one you affect when you're becoming involved with someone else and you're determined not to be remotely interested in or amused or touched by the person you're married to.

Now that I think about it, perhaps I *was* turning into a certain kind of melodramatic woman—not the kind who fantasizes because she's housebound but the kind who's simply trying to get her husband's attention because she knows that he's somewhere else, with someone else. Even then, back when the affair was starting, mustn't I have had an inkling? I can't bear that I didn't, but that's not the reason I'm telling the story about the man down the block who was murdered, so I'll get back to it.

Three days later. A Sunday. Mark and I were on our way out to lunch. The police. A half-open door to the house across the street. On the floor of the foyer, a huge brownish stain. "If there's a dead body in there," I said to the policeman outside, "it happened at three-twenty on Thursday afternoon." There was. It was Mr. Abbey, a meek little man who had had his last fling with rough trade. And I was the only witness! I don't mean to get so excited here, but I've always wanted to be a witness. I've always wanted to swear to tell the truth, the whole truth, and nothing but the truth and spar with lawyers and be sketched by courtroom artists. Now my time had come! And I knew nothing. It really was depressing, and not just for me, but for the homicide detective on the case, who kept trying to pry information out of me.

"You know more than you think," Homicide Detective Hartman kept saying, as he urged me to search my memory for the additional details he was certain were buried there.

"No I don't," I said.

A few days after Mr. Abbey's body was discovered, Homicide Detective Hartman came back to take another crack at my subconscious. He was full of interesting information. He told me that Mr. Abbey had spent the last morning of his life at a furniture auction. Afterward, a friend who was there had asked him to lunch. Mr. Abbey refused. He said he had seen a beautiful black man cruising the bus terminal the night before, and was going back to find him. And that was the last anyone saw of Mr. Abbey.

I was fascinated by the story. I couldn't believe that anyone would be so sexually driven that he might actually skip lunch—and after an auction! I think of myself as a healthy person with a strong sex drive, but it's never occurred to me to forgo meals. I said this to Mark later. I said, perhaps this is the difference between homosexuals and heterosexuals, perhaps this relentless priapism is characteristic of the obsessive, casual sex that lasts so much later in the lives of homosexuals than in heterosexuals. And Mark got this look on his face, this incredulous look, that at the time I thought meant he couldn't believe I could have such a short memory. Had I forgotten the first months of our courtship? The hours and hours of sex, the smell of it everywhere, in the air, on the sheets, on my hands, in my hair—had I managed to forget all that? (Of course I hadn't; on the other hand, we never once had less than three meals a day, so there.) Now, of course, I know about Thelma, and I realize that Mark's incredulity arose simply because I knew so little about him and *his* relentless priapism, knew so little about *men*. When will I ever learn? When will I ever understand that what's astonishing about the number of men who remain faithful is not that it's so small but that there are any of them at all?

I see that once again I've gotten off the track, that I've drifted back to Mark, to Mark and Thelma, but I can't help myself. When something like this happens, you suddenly have no sense of reality at all. You have lost a piece of your past. The infidelity itself is small potatoes compared to the low-level brain damage that results when a whole chunk of your life turns out to have been completely different from what you thought it was. It becomes impossible to look back at anything that's happened—from the simplest exchange between the two of you at a dinner party to the horrible death of Mr. Abbey—without wondering what was really going on. See the couple. See the couple with the baby. See the couple with the baby having another baby. *What's wrong with this picture?* Everything, as it happens.

But I was telling you about Mr. Abbey's death for a reason, and it has nothing to do with betrayal. I simply wanted you to understand that when my group was robbed, I was almost grateful: it gave me another shot at being a witness to a crime. And this time I knew stuff, I really knew stuff. I had actually laid eyes on the bugger. I couldn't wait to be deposed, or whatever it is they call what they do to you.

They took us to the station house in a paddy wagon. This was fairly insulting, since we were the victims, but the detective in charge of the case had so many statements to take that he wanted to do it with stenographers and typewriters and tape recorders nearby. We spent the afternoon in a small green room and each waited his turn. First the police talked to Vera, because she was in charge of the premises, as they say, and then they talked to Vanessa, because she was the most famous and beautiful (I've come to terms with the fact that Vanessa is the most famous and beautiful, but it really irritated me that day since after all I was the one who knew the most about what happened), and then they talked to Diana because she insisted she would hold them responsible if she missed her Supersaver flight to Los Angeles. Finally Detective Nolan got to me.

I told him everything. I said the robber was about six feet tall. Sandy hair. Watery blue eyes. A little squint. Pinkish complexion. A long, thin nose on a wide, shiny face. Weighed about 165—I can never be sure what men weigh. A fat neck. A red and green plaid cotton shirt, a khaki jacket, jeans and running shoes. I first noticed him when a Japanese man on the subway took my picture. My guess is that the Japanese man has a picture of the robber.

"What did the Japanese man look like?" asked Detective Nolan.

"Japanese," I said. "You know."

"I know," said Detective Nolan. "Small and Oriental and wearing a dark gray suit, with a camera around his neck."

"Yes," I said.

"What kind of camera?"

I shrugged. "I thought I was doing pretty well till we got to this part," I said.

"You are doing very well," said Detective Nolan.

"You say that to everybody," I said.

"No I don't," he said.

"Yes you do," I said. "I was a witness to something else recently, and the detective kept telling me how well I was doing, but I wasn't really."

"What else were you a witness to?" said Detective Nolan.

"A murder in Washington," I said. "I wasn't actually a witness—I just heard the shouting. Why?"

"I just wondered," said Detective Nolan.

"You just wondered if I was the kind of woman who attracts criminals the way other women attract alcoholics or sadists." (I have a friend who attracts dwarfs. Every time she turns around, a dwarf is following her. It's very disturbing.)

"No," said Detective Nolan. "What made you notice the man on the subway?"

"He winked at me," I said.

"I see," said Detective Nolan.

"It was probably my fault," I said, "because I was smiling at the Japanese man, because I'd rather have my picture taken when I'm smiling because when I'm not smiling I look as if I'm frowning, and that's when the robber winked at me, so I wondered if he was single, and then he winked again and I wondered if he was a mugger, and that's when I put my diamond ring into my bra."

"You mean you just looked at him and automatically wondered if he was single?"

"Well, he winked at me," I said.

"What made you think he might be a mugger?"

"I didn't really *believe* he was a mugger," I said. "I just realized that he might not be a suitable object for fantasy. I didn't even know if he'd gone to college."

"Are you sure there wasn't some detail you can't quite remember that alerted you in some way?"

"Like the bulge of his revolver under his jacket?" I said.

"Yes," said Detective Nolan.

"I don't think so," I said, "but it's possible that he was looking at my ring before I twisted it backwards, and I knew that. Subconsciously, I mean."

"Subconsciously," said Detective Nolan.

"I just remembered something," I said. "The Japanese man was wearing a little identification card. The kind they give you at conventions."

"Excellent," said Detective Nolan, and left the room. A few minutes later he came back and sat down.

"How long do you think it would take me?" he said.

"To find the Japanese man?" I said.

"To have therapy," he said. "How long would it take?"

"What's wrong with you?" I said.

"Nothing much," he said.

"Nine years," I said.

"How long did it take you?" he said.

"Nine years," I said. "Of course, I've had two years off for good behavior, but now I'm back. And there was nothing much wrong with me, either. That's why I graduated in the first place. The ones there's really something wrong with are in forever."

"Why did you start nine years ago?" asked Detective Nolan.

"I wanted a divorce," I said.

"From this guy who's being so terrible to you now?"

"From the first one," I said. I looked at him. "Diana told you, didn't she? I know she did. That bitch."

"I'm sorry to bring it up," said Detective Nolan. "It's not even relevant. Although it might explain why you were wondering whether the guy on the subway was single."

"That's true," I said.

"I was thinking of going into therapy because I can't decide whether to have a hair transplant," said Detective Nolan.

"You already have an awful lot of hair," I said.

"It's not mine," said Detective Nolan.

"It looks pretty good," I said.

"You think so?" he said.

"Yes," I said.

"I'm just telling you that so you know something about me, and since I know something about you, we're even."

"I don't think you need therapy," I said. "You might be the only person in America who doesn't."

I finished being interviewed by Detective Nolan, and gave him my father's telephone number and my number at home in Washington just in case. It wasn't until I was past the newspaper photographers and on the subway that I wondered whether Detective Nolan was single. He wasn't exactly my type, but look where my type had gotten me. Then I wondered if he was uncircumcised. Then I wondered if I could be happily married to a policeman. Then I wondered why I was so hopelessly bourgeois that I couldn't even have a fantasy about a man without moving on to marriage. Then I stopped wondering. For one thing, the subway arrived at my stop and I got off. For another, it seemed clear to me that it would never matter. When I got to my father's apartment, I was sure, Mark would be there.

And he was.

Six

I met Mark Feldman at a party in Washington at my friend Betty's. Betty Searle and I went to college together, and we always used to talk about living together afterward; but one day Betty said that I was a brunette and belonged in New York and she was a blonde and belonged in Washington, and she was right. Betty went off to Washington and became famous for her local television show, her dinner parties, and her affairs with a first-rate cross section of the American left wing. Every Christmas she had a party that everyone in Washington came to, and there, one Christmas, was Mark. I recognized him the minute he walked in because I'd seen him on *Meet the Press*, and once you see that beard you never forget it. He has a black beard, but the part of it that's on the left side of his chin has a little white stripe in it, where the skin underneath has no pigment. Just like a skunk is what you're thinking, and you're right, but it can look very odd and interesting. I've always liked odd and interesting-looking men because I'm odd and interesting-looking myself, and I always figured I had a better shot at them than at the conventionally good-looking ones. (Water seeks its own level, et cetera.) My mother would have loved Mark Feldman's beard. "A scar but not" is what she would have called it.

Mark is a syndicated columnist, that's why I'd seen him on television. He writes about Washington as if it's a city like any other (it's not), filled with rich and interesting characters (it's not). He's known for being chronically perverse about politics. For instance, some people think it's terrible that Washington doesn't work, but Mark thinks it's wonderful, because if it worked, something might actually be accomplished and then we'd really be in bad shape. This is a very clever way of being cynical, but never mind.

"Stay away from him," Betty said, when she saw me looking over at him.

"Why?" I said.

"He's trouble," she said.

"Please don't throw me in the brier patch," I said.

So Mark Feldman and I went out to dinner. He told me the story of his first day in the newspaper business. I told him the story of wanting to play the ukulele in the school orchestra. And then we went to bed. We stayed there for about three weeks. Every so often he got up to write a column, and I got up to call my answering machine in New York to see if there was any reason not to be in Washington for a while longer. There wasn't.

At some point in those three weeks, we had gotten out of bed for some reason or other, and we were taking a walk near the Pension Building. It's a huge, block-square structure with a frieze of Civil War soldiers, thousands of soldiers moving cannons and guns and wagons and horses slowly around the perimeter of the building. We went up the stairs to the entrance, and the guard let us into the inner courtyard. It was barely lit. The guard went down the hall and turned on the lights, and suddenly I could see the huge open space in the center of the building, pillars three stories high, leaded glass at the top. For many years, the inaugural balls were held in the Pension Building. We could hear the guard's radio, with an old Sinatra song coming from it. Mark held out his hands.

"I can't dance," I said. "I've never been able to."

"I believe in you, Rachel," he said.

We started to dance.

"You didn't believe me," I said.

"I'm not going to step on your foot," Mark said.

"I know that," I said.

"No you don't," he said.

He stepped back and put his right hand on the front of his waist and his left hand on the back.

"Right here," he said. "That part of you is mine for the next three minutes. After that I'll give it back. But you have to give it to me for now."

"I have to trust you," I said.

"Right."

"I have to *follow* you," I said.

"Right."

"Oh, God," I said.

"You can do it, Rachel," he said, and he put his arms out again. We started to dance. I closed my eyes. And I relaxed. People are always telling me to relax—the hairdresser tells me to relax, and the dentist, and the exercise teacher, and the dozen or so tennis pros who have attempted to do something about my backhand—but the only time I think I've ever really relaxed in my entire life was for three minutes in the Pension Building dancing with Mark Feldman.

"I'm dancing," I said.

"I love you," he said.

So we were in love. We were madly in love. We flew back and forth on the Eastern shuttle and we called each other on various WATS lines and I became best friends with his best friends and he became best friends with my best friends, and there were presents and concerts and three-pound lobsters at the Palm, and then one day I came down to Washington and walked into his apartment and found a Virginia Slim cigarette butt in an ashtray. *Who's been eating my porridge?* Mark said it was the maid's. I pointed out that the maid smoked Newports. Then he said it was his sister's. I pointed out that his sister had stopped smoking. Then he said he had bummed it from a copy girl at the office. I said that even copy girls at the office weren't naive enough to smoke Virginia Slims. Then he got angry and said if he'd wanted to live with a detective he'd live with a detective and why didn't I trust him? Then I got angry and said if he was going to bum cigarettes he ought to bum Marlboros so I wouldn't think he was cheating on me, and why didn't he at least have the decency to empty the ashtray into the garbage disposal.

Next thing you know, we were at a party—a party for his book about Washington—and I looked across the room and saw him talking to a reporter from the *Sydney Morning Herald*, and she started laughing, and even her laugh had an Australian accent. I walked over and carefully linked my arm through his. "Oh," she said, "Mark was just telling me the most amusing story about his first day in the newspaper business."

Then off he went on his book tour.

"Hi, I'm Irv Kupcinet, and my guests tonight are Mark Feldman, syndicated columnist and author of the new best-seller Return to Power; *Toby Bright, director of the Institute of Sexual Analysis and herself the best-selling author of* Good in Bed; *former British Prime Minister Harold Wilson; and Graham Kerr, the Galloping Gourmet, who is here today to talk about Jesus Christ."*

A couple of days after I saw the show on television, I was having lunch with my friend Marie, at the omelet place on Sixty-first Street.

"I met Mark," Marie said.

"When?" I said.

"I was in Chicago a few days ago when he was on his book tour."

"Where did you meet him?

"*Playboy* had a party for some book."

"And?"

"He seemed nice," Marie said. "I couldn't really tell that much. It was crowded and all." She started playing with her ratatouille filling.

"Marie?"

"I keep thinking about it," Marie said. "You know. If it were reversed, what would I want you to do? What do you think?"

"I think it takes two people to hurt you," I said. "The one who does it and the one who tells you."

"I know," said Marie. "Shit."

"But I'd want you to tell me," I said. "Who was she?"

"The one who wrote the sex book," said Marie.

"They were together at the party," I said.

"And later," said Marie. "At the hotel."

"That bastard," I said.

"Look," said Marie, "he's got a big book, he's having a fling, it'll go away."

"Listen," I said. "I had a book. I did the Kup show. And I didn't fuck the Galloping Gourmet, and he wasn't into Jesus Christ then, either."

"I feel terrible," said Marie.

"Don't you dare steal feeling terrible from me," I said.

"This isn't fair," said Marie. "You're so much better at this than I am. You've been in group."

Of course, we could talk for days about why Marie told me. I'm glad she told me—it saved me from finding out at a later time—but still you have to wonder. Anyway, Mark and I broke up. I flew down to Washington and collected my things and had a big fight with Mark in which he accused me of the thing men think is the most insulting thing they can accuse you of—wanting to be married—and he took me to the airport and my duffel bag burst in the middle of the National Airport parking lot and all the whisks and frying pans and cookbooks fell out on the ground and then we had another big fight over whether it was his Julia Child or mine that I was taking back to New York (it was his) and that was that.

"Well, you knew he was trouble from the very beginning, didn't you?" said Vera after it was over. Which is the kind of thing Vera is always saying, and which I fundamentally agree with but nonetheless get extremely irritable about.

"Of course I knew that," I said. "I told it to you right after I met him. And you know what you said? You said, 'Everybody has a past.'"

"I never said that," said Vera.

"You certainly did say that," I said.

"What I said was that people are capable of change," said Vera. "If you don't think people can change, what are you doing here?"

"Investing my money in caftans," I said.

The telephone rang and Vera answered it. "What's the split on the paperback?" she said to whoever was calling. "What does your agent say?" She nodded. "Well, hold out for sixty-forty over two hundred fifty thousand." She hung up and looked at me.

"You think I picked Mark because I knew what was going to happen," I said.

"Did I say that?" said Vera.

"You don't have to say it, Vera."

"Well?" she said.

"No," I said. "No."

"An old man goes to buy a horse," said Vera. "Have I told you this story?"

"I can't tell yet," I said. "They all sound alike in the beginning."

"Goes to buy a horse," said Vera. "The horse trader says, 'I can sell you a very nice horse for five hundred rubles.' 'What else do you have?' says the old man. The horse trader says, 'Well, for one hundred fifty rubles I can sell you a donkey. He won't live as long, but he'll get you from Kiev to Vilna.' The old man buys the donkey, and two weeks later it drops dead. So he goes back to the horse trader and says, 'How was I to know?'"

"Is that a story about how smart you are, or how dumb I am?" I said.

"Both," said Vera.

"Well, at least this time I get to be a person in the story. The last time you told one of your Russian parables I was a bag of chickens."

There was a long pause.

"Well?" said Vera.

"It's not as simple as that, Vera," I said. "You want everything to be simple. You think I'm just standing there, and this army of men is walking by, shouting, 'Choose *me*, choose *me*,' and I always pick the turkey. Life's not like that. I can't even find a man who lives in the same city I do."

"Of course you can," said Vera.

Well, of course I couldn't. The next man I was involved with lived in Boston. He taught me to cook mushrooms. He taught me that if you heat the butter very hot and put just a very few mushrooms into the frying pan, they come out nice and brown and crispy, whereas if the butter is only moderately hot and you crowd the mushrooms, they get all mushy and wet. Every time I make mushrooms I think of him. There was another man in my life when I was younger who taught me to put sour cream into scrambled eggs, and since I never ever put sour cream into scrambled eggs I never really think of him at all.

Two months passed. I flew to Boston every other weekend. The man in Boston flew to New York every other weekend. I was deeply involved in piecrust. I was perfectly happy. And Mark turned up. Mark turned up full of repentance and bearing gifts. He sent flowers. He sent jewelry. He sent chocolates, and not those overly refined Swiss ones either— nice chewy, nutty American ones. He called up and said psychoanalytic things on the phone. He said he had made the worst mistake of his life and he wanted me back and he would love me forever and he would never hurt me again. He said he wanted to marry me. He said he was going to marry me. He said I might as well get used to the idea. He asked me to marry him on the IRT downtown local, and he asked me to marry him on the Forty-ninth Street crosstown bus. He asked me to marry him so often—and I refused so often—that when he failed to ask me for a day or so, I started to worry. He campaigned for me. He spoke of babies. Forever and ever. "Let's sing all the songs we know about marriage," he said to me one morning. Picture a little love nest, he sang, out where the roses cling. Picture the same sweet love nest, I sang back, think what a year can bring.

There were two reasons I didn't want to marry Mark. First of all, I didn't trust him. And second of all, I'd already been married. Mark had already been married, too, but that didn't really count; it certainly didn't count in the way it usually counts, which is that it makes you never want to get married again. Mark's first wife was named Kimberly. (As he always said, she was the first Jewish Kimberly.) Mark and Kimberly were married for less than a year, but he had enough material from her to last a lifetime. "My wife, the first Jewish Kimberly," Mark would begin, "was so stingy that she made stew out of leftover pancakes." Or: "My wife, the first Jewish Kimberly, was so stingy she once tried to sell a used nylon stocking to a mugger." In truth, the first Jewish Kimberly really was stingy, she recycled everything, and she once blew up their apartment and most of what was in it while making brandy out of old cherry pits.

My first husband was stingy, too, but that was the least of it. My first husband was so neurotic that every time he had an appointment, he erased the record of it from his datebook, so that at the end of the year his calendar was completely blank. My first husband was so neurotic he kept hamsters. They all had cute names, like Arnold and Shirley, and he was very attached to them and was always whipping up little salads for them with his Slice-o-Matic and buying them extremely small sweaters at a pet boutique in Rego Park. My first husband was so neurotic he would never eat fish because he'd once choked on a fishbone, and he would never eat onions because he claimed he was allergic to them, which he wasn't. I know, because I snuck them into everything. You can't really cook without onions. "Is this an onion?" Charlie would say, his eyes narrowing as he held up a small, translucent object he had discovered floating in the sauce that covered his boneless dinner. "No, it's a celery," I would say. It didn't really fool him; at the end of every meal he would leave a neat little pile of small, translucent objects on his plate. God, was he neat. My first husband was so neat he put hospital corners on the newspaper he lined the hamster cage with.

The reason my marriage to Charlie broke up—although by now you're probably astonished that it lasted even a minute—was not because he slept with my oldest friend Brenda or even that he got crabs from her. It was because Arnold died. I felt really sad when Arnold died, because Charlie was devoted to Arnold and had invented a fairly elaborate personality for Arnold that Arnold did his best to live up to. Hamsters don't really do that much, but Charlie had built an entire character for Arnold and made up a lot of hamster jokes he claimed Arnold had come up with, mostly having to do with chopped lettuce. Also, and I'm sorry to tell you this, Charlie often talked in a high, squeaky voice that was meant to be Arnold's, and I'm even sorrier to tell you that I often replied in a high, squeaky voice that was meant to be Shirley's. You enter into a certain amount of madness when you marry a person with pets, but I didn't care. When Charlie and I were married, I was twenty-five years and eleven months old, and I was such a ninny that I thought: Thank God I'm getting married now, before I'm twenty-six and washed up.

Anyway, when Arnold the hamster died, Charlie took him to one of those cryogenic places and had him frozen. It wasn't at all expensive, because the body was so small, on top of which there wasn't any additional charge for storage because Charlie brought Arnold home in a nice Baggie with a rubber band around it and simply stuck him into the freezer. I could just see Cora Bigelow, the maid, taking Arnold out one Thursday thinking he was a newfangled freeze-dried potato treat in a boil bag; boy, would Charlie be in for a shock the next time he went to put an eensy-weensy bouquet of flowers next to Arnold's final resting place, directly to the right of the ice cube tray. I mean, what are you supposed to do with a first husband like that? I'll tell you what: divorce him. I'll tell you something else: when you divorce a first husband like that, you never look back. You never once think: God, I wish Charlie were here, he'd know how to handle this. Charlie never handled anything if he could help it. He just made a note of it in his Mark Cross datebook and erased it when the problem had cleared up.

I left Charlie after six years, although at least two of those years were spent beating a dead horse. There have always been many things you can do short of actually ending a bad marriage—buying a house, having an affair, and having a baby are the most common, I suppose— but in the early 1970s there were at least two more. You could go into consciousness raising and spend an evening a week talking over cheese to seven other women whose marriages were equally unhappy. And you could sit down with your husband and thrash everything out in a wildly irrelevant fashion by drawing up a list of household duties and dividing them up all over again. This happened in thousands of households, with identical results: thousands of husbands agreed to clear the table. They cleared the table. They cleared the table and then looked around as if they deserved a medal. They cleared the table and then hoped they would never again be asked to do another thing. They cleared the table and hoped the whole thing would go away. And it did. The women's movement went away, and so, in many cases, did their wives. Their wives went out into the world, free at last, single again, and discovered the horrible truth: that they were sellers in a buyers' market, and that the major concrete achievement of the women's movement in the 1970s was the Dutch treat.

I left Charlie everything—the cooperative apartment, the house in the country, and Shirley, Mendel, Manny, and Fletcher. I took my clothes and my kitchen equipment and two couches I had brought to the marriage. I asked Charlie for a coffee table, but he wouldn't give it to me. The moving man sat there reading the section on vaginal self-examination in my spare copy of *Our Bodies, Ourselves* while Charlie and I fought about furniture. I said we had three coffee tables; the least he could do was to give me one. He said I had both couches and where was he supposed to sit anyway. I said that I'd brought both couches to the marriage, but that all three coffee tables had been accumulated *during* the marriage and I ought to get *something* that had been accumulated during the marriage. He said I could have Mendel. I said Mendel was a washout, even for a hamster. He said he'd brought furniture to the marriage, too, but that I'd given it to my mother when she'd run off with the Mel who was God and it had never been seen again. I said the furniture we'd given to my mother was Swedish modern and revolting and we owed the Mel who was God a big favor for taking it off our hands. He said he would never give me the coffee table because he'd just realized I'd packed the carrot peeler along with my kitchen equipment and now he had no way to make lunch for Shirley and the boys. On his way out to buy another carrot peeler, he said he would never forgive me for what I'd said about Mendel. At the end of the move, the mover shook my hand solemnly and said, "I had five others this week just like this one. Yours wasn't so bad."

Of course, afterward Vera said I'd set it up so it would happen that way, set it up so that there would be no way Charlie could possibly give me the coffee table and I could therefore walk away from the marriage with the happy knowledge that Charlie was as stingy as I'd always said he was. "You picked him," Vera said, "because his neuroses meshed perfectly with yours." I love Vera, truly I do, but *doesn't anything happen to you that you don't intend?* "You picked him because you knew it wouldn't work out." "You picked him because his neuroses meshed perfectly with yours." "You picked him because you knew he'd deprive you the way your mother or your father did." That's what they're always telling you, one way or another, but the truth is that no matter whom you pick, it doesn't work out; the truth is that no matter whom you pick, your neuroses mesh perfectly and horribly; the truth is that no matter whom you pick, he deprives you the way your mother or your father did. "You picked the one person on earth you could have problems with." "You picked the one person on earth you shouldn't be involved with." There's nothing brilliant about that—that's life. Every time you turn around you get involved with the one person on earth you shouldn't get involved with. Robert Browning's shrink probably said it to *him*. "So, Robert, it's very interesting, no? Of all the women in London, you pick this hopeless invalid who has a crush on her father." Let's face it: *everyone* is the one person on earth you shouldn't get involved with.

And what is all this about *picking*, anyway? Who's picking? When I was in college, I had a list of what I wanted in a husband. A long list. I wanted a registered Democrat, a bridge player, a linguist with particular fluency in French, a subscriber to *The New Republic*, a tennis player. I wanted a man who wasn't bald, who wasn't fat, who wasn't covered with too much body hair. I wanted a man with long legs and a small ass and laugh wrinkles around the eyes. Then I grew up and settled for a low-grade lunatic who kept hamsters. At first I thought he was charming and eccentric. And then I didn't. Then I wanted to kill him. Every time he got on a plane, I would imagine the plane crash, and the funeral, and what I would wear to the funeral and flirting at the funeral, and how soon I could start dating after the funeral.

Is this inevitable, this moment when everything leads to irritation, when you become furious that he smokes, or that he coughs in the morning, or that he sheds crumbs, or that he exaggerates, or that he drives like a maniac, or that he says "Between you and I"? You fall in love with someone, and part of what you love about him are the differences between you; and then you get married and the differences start to drive you crazy. You fall in love with someone and you say to yourself, oh, well, I never really cared about politics, bridge, French, and tennis; and then you get married and it starts to drive you crazy that you're married to someone who doesn't even know who's running for president. This is the moment when any therapist will tell you that your problem is fear of intimacy; that you're connecting to your mother, or holding on to your father. But it seems to me that what's happening is far more basic; it seems to me that it's just about impossible to live with someone else.

And soon there's nothing left of the marriage but the moments of irritation, followed by the apologies, followed by the moments of irritation, followed by the apologies; and all this is interspersed with decisions about which chair goes in the den and whose dinner party are we going to tonight. In the end, what's left is a social arrangement. You are a couple. You go places together. And then you break up, and the moving man tells you yours wasn't so bad. But it was. Even when you end a marriage you want to end, it's awful.

I started out telling you all this because I wanted you to understand why I so resisted getting married again. It seemed to me that the desire to get married—which, I regret to say, I believe is fundamental and primal in women—is followed almost immediately by an equally fundamental and primal urge, which is to be single again. But there was Mark. With his big brown eyes and his sweetheart roses. Forever and ever, he said. Forever and ever and ever, he said. *I'll be loving you always. . . . Not for just an hour, not for just a day, not for just a year, but always.*

For a long time, I didn't believe him. And then I believed him. I believed in change. I believed in metamorphosis. I believed in redemption. I believed in Mark. My marriage to him was as willful an act as I have ever committed; I married him against all the evidence. I married him believing that marriage doesn't work, that love dies, that passion fades, and in so doing I became the kind of romantic only a cynic is truly capable of being. I see all that now. At the time, though, I saw nothing of the sort. I honestly believed that Mark had learned his lesson. Unfortunately, the lesson he learned wasn't the one I had in mind: what he learned is that he could do anything, and in the end there was a chance I'd take him back.

Seven

"Your husband's here," Lucy Mae Hopkins said, as she opened the door to my father's apartment for me. Then she rolled her eyes. Lucy Mae Hopkins had given up men for Jesus forty years earlier, and she couldn't understand why anyone else wouldn't, given the choice. I walked into the living room. Mark was sitting on the couch, reading a book to Sam. He looked up and gave me a nod and went on reading. I sat down in a chair and noticed a blazer Mark had draped over the back of it. A new blazer. The man had broken my heart and then gone out and bought himself a new blazer! To make matters worse, it was a nice blazer. I fingered the material.

"Britches," said Mark. Britches is a store in Washington where Mark buys his clothes. The man had broken my heart and had then gone out and bought himself a new blazer and the first word out of his mouth was Britches!

Mark finished reading to Sam and sent him off to the kitchen for a cookie. He looked at me. "I'd like you to come back," he said.

I shook my head no, not because I was refusing but because I couldn't believe that that was all he had to say. Not a word about Thelma. Not a word about how he must have been crazy. Not a word about how he was sorry. Perhaps this is Mark's way of being understated, I thought. And then again, perhaps not. In fact, probably not. I kept on shaking my head. I couldn't stop shaking my head. "I love you," he said. He said it with the animation of a tree sloth. "I want you to come home," he said. "You belong at home."

"I'm not coming home if you're going to see her anymore," I said.

"I'm not going to see her anymore," he said.

There was a long silence. I kept expecting him to reach out for my hand, or touch my face. He didn't. Rachel, I said to myself, this will not do. You cannot go anywhere, much less home, with a man whose idea of an apology does not include even a hypocritical show of affection. Say no. Tell him to drop dead. Crack one of your father's atrocious lamps over his head. Go into the kitchen and invent the instant waffle. Anything.

"I know this is difficult for you," Mark said, "but it's difficult for me, too."

And then Mark started to cry. *Mark* started to cry. I couldn't believe it. It seemed to me that if anyone was entitled to cry in this scene, it was going to be me; but the man had run off with my part. "I'm in a lot of pain," he said.

There has been a lot written in recent years about the fact that men don't cry enough. Crying is thought to be a desirable thing, a sign of a mature male sensibility, and it is generally believed that when little boys are taught that it is unmanly to cry, they grow up unable to deal with pain and grief and disappointment and feelings in general. I would like to say two things about this. The first is that I have always believed that crying is a highly overrated activity: women do entirely too much of it, and the last thing we ought to want is for it to become a universal excess. The second thing I want to say is this: beware of men who cry. It's true that men who cry are sensitive to and in touch with feelings, but the only feelings they tend to be sensitive to and in touch with are their own.

Not that I knew this at the time. If I had, I could have stayed in New York with my pathetic dreams of Detective Nolan and six kinds of smoked salmon. What I actually did, though, is that I looked at Mark, sitting there, a picture of misery, and I crumbled. I can't stand to see a man cry, that's the truth. I can't stand to see a woman cry either, but the only woman I ever really see crying to any extent is me, and even though you may think I do an awful lot of it for someone who can't stand to see it, the fact is that I cry much less now than I used to. When I was young, a rude salesman at the hardware store could make me cry.

"All right," I said to Mark. "I'll come home."

"Good," said Mark, and he stopped crying. "You can put the ring back on now," he said.

I shook my head no.

"For God's sake, Rachel," he said. "Put the ring back on."

"I gave it away," I said.

"You what?" he said.

"I gave it away."

"To whom?" he said.

"To a celebrity auction," I said.

"Is this a joke?" he said.

"Yes," I said, "and not a bad one, all things considered."

"Put the ring back on," he said.

"Only part of it was a joke," I said.

"Which part?" said Mark. Mark used to like the fact that I make jokes in adverse circumstances, but clearly the charm of that had begun to wear thin.

"The part about the celebrity auction was a joke," I said. "The part about giving it away wasn't."

"You gave the ring away," said Mark.

"Not of my own free will," I said.

"Someone took it away from you," said Mark.

"Yes," I said.

"Do you want me to guess who it was?" he said.

"My group was robbed," I said.

"That's funny," said Mark. He started to laugh. "By an outsider, or by someone in the group?"

"By an outsider," I said, "and it's not funny. He held a gun to my head."

"Just because you don't think it's funny doesn't mean I don't think it's funny," said Mark. "Maybe I can get a column out of it." He began to nod slowly, the way he does whenever he gets an idea for a column and it's just started ticking away. Mark writes three columns a week, and while most of them are about political life, just enough of them are about domestic life that I sometimes felt as if I were living with a cannibal; things barely finished happening before Mark was chewing away at them, trying to string them out, turn them upside down, blow them up into 850 words for tomorrow's newspaper. Sometimes, when he was really worried about what to write about next, he would sit at dinnertime, his eyes darting desperately around the room. Was there a column in the salt and pepper shakers? In the paper napkins? In the Cuisinart food processor? "Have you noticed how hard it is to peel a hard-boiled egg?" he'd say. "Yes," I'd say. "You think there's anything to it?" he'd say. Or: "Have you noticed that English muffins don't taste as good as they used to?" he'd say. "Yes," I'd say. "You think there's anything to it?" he'd say. I don't mean to sound innocent and passive about all this; I loved looking for things for Mark to write columns about. I brought home anecdotes about parking lot attendants and supermarket checkers for him to munch on. In fact, it occurs to me that one of the reasons I sometimes felt that nothing had happened to me since my marriage was that every time something *did* happen, Mark got a column out of it and in essence made it all seem as if it had happened to him. You should see the column he got out of Mr. Abbey's murder. *My* murder, my very own personal murder, and he ran off with it and turned it into an essay on homosexuals and urban crime and practically got us all killed by the Gay Rights League. He even raided Sam's life. Sam was barely two years old, and the column about the time he swallowed the nail polish remover had run in 109 papers and the one about his first dead guppy was about to be anthologized by the Oxford University Press. Someday Sam was going to grow up and sit down to write about his life and there wouldn't be anything left of it to write about.

"You can't get a column out of my group's robbery," I said.

"Why not?" said Mark.

"Because it happened to *me*," I said. "On top of which, it was really awful."

"I'm sorry," said Mark. "Did he hurt you?"

"He twisted my arm," I said.

"Show Daddy where," said Mark.

"Oh, shut up," I said. Then I smiled. I couldn't help it. And so did he.

"I'll buy you another ring," said Mark.

"We don't have the money for another ring," I said.

"That's true," said Mark. "We didn't even have the money to insure this one."

We sat and looked at each other for a moment.

"It's sort of fitting," I said.

"Meaning what?" said Mark.

"Meaning it was a symbol of how good things were, and now that things aren't, it's just as well it's not here to remind me."

"I hate it when you say things like that," said Mark.

"I know," I said. "Do you still love her?"

"I don't want to talk about it," he said.

"But you're not going to see her anymore," I said.

"I already said that," he said.

"And the two of you aren't going to see that Guatemalan frittata together anymore, either."

"Rachel."

"Just say yes or no."

"I told you I wasn't going to see Thelma anymore, so obviously we're not going to see Dr. Valdez together anymore, either."

"Good," I said.

"Thelma doesn't really believe in that stuff anyway," he said.

"I wouldn't either," I said, "if all I had to go on was that refried taco who calls herself a therapist."

"Rachel."

"Yes."

"If we leave now we can make the last plane."

.   .   .

The last Eastern Airlines shuttle between New York and Washington leaves at nine o'clock at night. When Mark and I were single and he lived in Washington and I lived in New York, we could never have a serious fight late at night, because there was no way to slam out the door and go home. There was something I liked about the fact that our lives and temperaments were controlled by an airline schedule, but the truth is that there were many things I liked about the Eastern shuttle. Not the comfort, and not the courtesy of the flight attendants, both of which were negligible. But the things you were supposed to like. The fact that it tended to leave when it said it was going to and to get there on schedule an hour later. The fact that you didn't need a reservation and always got a seat. The fact that there was something so utterly no-nonsense about it, just like its passengers. No one ever seemed to be going from one end of the Eastern shuttle to the other for fun. No one ever seemed to be *traveling*. They were all simply going to meetings that were in offices that happened to be in another city. Everyone carried a briefcase. Everyone was dressed for success. Everyone was serious. Indeed, it seems to me that the Eastern shuttle was almost a perfect reflection of the Puritan tradition in its attempt to make a virtue out of suffering, abstinence, and plainness; and it always seemed fitting that one Eastern shuttle flies New York to Boston, where the Puritan tradition began, and the other flies New York to Washington, where those produced by that tradition are rewarded with the power to force the rest of the country to heel to its values. I loved that it took such an austere conveyance to get me to Mark; there was something wonderfully romantic about it. I looked like everyone else on the shuttle, I dressed like everyone else, I carried the *New York Times* and the *Washington Post* and the *Wall Street Journal* like everyone else. But everyone else was on their way to work, and I was on my way to Mark.

Then, one day, Mark and I were on the Eastern shuttle and he asked me to marry him. This was when he was asking me to marry him a couple of times a week, but he had never asked me on the Eastern shuttle.

"This is your chance to say yes on the Eastern shuttle," he said.

"No," I said.

"This is your chance at a really bad metaphor," he said.

"No," I said.

"This is your last chance," he said. "I'll ask you to marry me again and again, but I'll never again ask you on the Eastern shuttle."

So I said yes.

Our friends the Siegels gave us ten shares of Eastern Airlines stock for a wedding present. Ha ha. The fare on the shuttle went to fifty dollars. And to fifty-four dollars. And to fifty-eight dollars. Arthur Siegel said: "It's a good thing you two met before the fare went up, because no fuck is worth $116 round trip." Ha ha. I moved to Washington and Sam was born and Arthur said that the money I saved not taking the Eastern shuttle almost paid for the baby's diapers. Ha ha. Eastern shuttle jokes. Not particularly funny jokes, but what do you expect?

Anyway, just try flying the Eastern shuttle with a baby. Try flying any plane with a baby if you want a sense of what it must have been like to be a leper in the fourteenth century, but try the shuttle for the ultimate in shunning. All those men in suits, looking at you as if your baby is going to throw up over their speech drafts; all those men in suits who used to look at me with respect when I pulled out my American Express gold card, now barely able to conceal their contempt for me and my portable Wet Ones.

And just try flying the Eastern shuttle with a baby *and* with a husband who is barely speaking to you. Mark deserted me the minute we got to the terminal at La Guardia and went off to buy magazines and newspapers and to call the office to make sure something important hadn't happened while he was off in New York on a trivial personal errand. I got on line for the plane. Sam was cranky and tired, and I was holding him and the duffel bag and the shopping bag full of Pampers and trying to write out my boarding pass with a pencil stub and my glasses fell off my nose and when I leaned over to pick them up, a stack pack of Ritz crackers fell out of my pocket onto the floor. The man next to me in line picked them up and asked me if he could help. I almost cried; I wanted to cry, but I was afraid crying would make my glasses fall off my nose again. He was a dark-skinned man with a rather thrilling foreign accent I couldn't place. Gratefully I handed him the shopping bag, and he carried the duffel bag to the baggage conveyor belt. When he came back, he smiled, and I noticed he had three subcutaneous cysts on his face—those little lumps that save Robert Redford from being too handsome. I wondered if he'd consider having his subcutaneous cysts removed if we got married. I wondered if I could live with someone with a foreign accent. I wondered where he was from, and how his family would feel about his marrying a Jew. I wondered if wherever he was from was the kind of place where they refer to Jewish women as Jewesses.

"Where are you from?" I said.

"From?" he said.

"What country are you from?" I said.

"My cauntry," he said with a smile, "ees bery beautiful."

I nodded. He nodded. I nodded. He nodded. So much for marrying foreigners, I thought. So much for my vow not to have marital fantasies about strangers.

I took an aisle seat on the plane, put Sam in the middle, and saved the window for Mark. He turned up a few minutes later and handed me the early edition of the *Daily News*. There was Vanessa, on page one, coming out of the police precinct; she looked wonderful. Inside was a riveting story about the glamorous group and the robbery. The story identified me as a "cookbook author," which always irritates me a little bit since they aren't merely cookbooks, but at least it didn't say that I was a distraught, rejected, pregnant cookbook author whose husband was in love with a giantess. According to the article, Sidney and Dan not only discovered each other's last names at the police precinct but also discovered that they were distant cousins. I wasn't sure what the readers of the *Daily News* were going to make of that detail, but I was positive my group would waste hours discussing its possible relevance. In fact, it seemed to me it might make sense to disband the group entirely, since we were bound to be spending so much time in the next year talking about the robbery and its effect that we would never again have time to discuss anyone's actual life. I wondered whether Mark had read the story, but I knew that if I asked him what he thought of it he would simply use it as yet another occasion to insult my adventures in psychoanalysis in order to punish me for insulting his. I looked over at him. He was immersed in *Casa Vogue*. It was as if he were pretending he wasn't with me, that I was just some hopeless woman who didn't even bother to space her pregnancies, much less respond properly to sitting in the same row with important Washington journalists who are trying to concentrate on home-decorating tips. And I'll tell you the capper. The stewardess came down the aisle to collect the fares. Now, Mark and I always split things up. I paid my way; I always paid my way. We both earned money, and the money we earned went to pay for what we did. But wouldn't you think that on this night of all nights he ought to have put my shuttle fare on his credit card? Well, he didn't.

I looked at him and was about to say something, when Meg Roberts poked her head over the back of the seat in front of us.

"I thought I was going to see you at Betty's the other night," she said.

"Fare, please," said the stewardess.

I fished in my bag for my credit card and handed it to her.

"At Betty's?" I said.

"At her birthday party," Meg said.

"Omigod," I said. I looked at Mark. He shook his head; he had forgotten, too. I was off in New York crying my eyes out, and he was in Washington fucking his brains out, and we had both forgotten Betty's thirty-ninth birthday party. The only way Betty would ever forgive me would be for me to tell her why, and if I told her why she'd tell everyone in Washington, and then everyone in town would know something about our marriage that I didn't want them to know. I know all about Meg Roberts's marriage, for example, because Meg confides in her friend Ann, who confides in Betty, who confides in me. What I know is that Meg Roberts sleeps with presidential candidates, and her husband sleeps with presidential candidates' press secretaries' secretaries. They seem very happy.

"How was the party?" said Mark.

"Wonderful," said Meg, and popped back down.

Actually, there is no possible way a seated dinner party in Washington can ever be wonderful. After only half an hour of drinks, you are seated, seated forever, trapped between two immensely powerful men who think it's your function as their dinner partner to draw them out. You draw them out. You ask them about the SALT talks. You ask them about the firearms lobby. You ask them about their constituencies. You ask them about the next election. Dinner ends and everyone goes home. It always amazes me that women like Meg Roberts ever manage to get anything sexual going in Washington, although obviously she knows something about drawing men out that I don't.

Sam threw up on Mark's new blazer.

"Shit," said Mark.

"I'm sorry," I said. Sam started to cry. There was a kind of odd murmur in the seats around us, as the smell began to penetrate to the adjoining rows. At any moment the murmur would probably build to a hiss, and then to a chorus of boos, and ultimately Sam and I would be stoned to death with Bic pens.

"What am I apologizing for?" I said. "It's not my fault."

"I know it's not," said Mark. "I'm sorry."

"It's not your fault either," I said.

"This whole thing is my fault," he said.

"If you really believed that, you would have paid my shuttle fare," I said.

I picked up Sam and stood up to go to the bathroom with him. Mark began to wipe off his blazer with his handkerchief.

"You bought that blazer with Thelma Rice, didn't you?" I said, and started for the back. I didn't even have to hear the answer. Mark's impulse to fall in love is always accompanied by his impulse to purchase clothes with the loved one looking on. Sometimes it seemed to me that I had spent half my marriage in the men's department watching small white-haired tailors on their knees making chalk marks on Mark's trouser cuffs.

I went back to the bathroom and laid Sam on the top of the toilet seat to change his clothes. Toilet seats in airplane bathrooms are not even big enough to change baby piglets on. Sam's head kept flopping off the cliff sides of the toilet seat as I changed his overalls and T-shirt and diaper. When I finished, I checked out the mirror to see if I looked older, or sadder, or wiser. I didn't; I just looked tired. Well, I was going home. I was going home with my husband. I loved my husband. The city of New York was a wonderful place, but it seemed terribly unimportant next to my marriage. So much for sorrel soup. I had never thought my marriage could survive an infidelity, but it would. It had been unrealistic of me to expect that the situation would never come up. They say all marriages go through something like this. I became dizzy as the clichés raced through my head. I put Sam on the bathroom floor and threw up. In the main cabin, the pilot was announcing our descent to the Washington area. Yes indeed, I thought. I wiped myself off and went back to my seat.

Eight

I see that I haven't managed to work in any recipes for a while. It's hard to work in recipes when you're moving the plot forward. Not that this book has an enormous amount of plot, but it has more plot than I've ever dealt with before. My other books just meandered from one person to the next, whereas this one has a story with a beginning and an end. That's one of the things that make it different from most of what has happened to me in my life: I know when it began and when it ended. When my first marriage collapsed, I made a lot of notes about the hamsters and the fight over the coffee table, but I could never be sure whether the end of my marriage to Charlie was the beginning of a story or the end of one. But the story I'm telling here began the day I discovered the affair between Mark and Thelma, and it ended exactly six weeks later. It has a happy ending, but that's because I insist on happy endings; I would insist on happy beginnings, too, but that's not necessary because all beginnings are intrinsically happy, in my opinion. What about middles, you may ask. Middles are a problem. Middles are perhaps the major problem of contemporary life.

In any case, all I meant to say was that because this book tells a story, there aren't as many recipes in it as there are in my other books, so if you bought it because you thought there were going to be lots of recipes in every chapter, I'm sorry.

On the other hand, I've gotten to the point in the story where I return to Washington, and that brings me to the Siegels, finally to the Siegels; and therefore it brings me to the linguine alla cecca recipe. The four of us went to Italy a few years ago, and Julie Siegel and I managed to wangle the recipe from the proprietor of a restaurant in Rome. We also spent quite a lot of time after that trip working in pesto, because we went to Italy in 1977, and in 1977 everyone was eating pesto. As Arthur Siegel said one day: "Pesto is the quiche of the seventies." Arthur had a way of saying things like that—of summing up the situation so perfectly that you never wanted another spoonful of pesto again—and whenever he said something like that, Mark always ran off with it and turned it into a column. Arthur used to complain bitterly about having his best remarks stolen, but the truth is he rather liked it; he was a running character in Mark's columns, and he enjoyed a certain notoriety at Georgetown Law School, where he taught criminal law while waiting for the Kennedys to return to power. As for the linguine alla cecca, it's a hot pasta with a cold tomato and basil sauce, and it's so light and delicate that it's almost like eating a salad. It has to be made in the summer, when tomatoes are fresh. Drop 5 large tomatoes into boiling water for one full minute. Peel and seed and chop. Put into a large bowl with ½ cup olive oil, a garlic clove sliced in two, 1 cup chopped fresh basil leaves, salt, and hot red pepper flakes. Let sit for a couple of hours, then remove the garlic. Boil one pound of linguine, drain, and toss with the cold tomato mixture. Serve immediately.

Arthur and Julie and Mark and Rachel. The Siegels and the Feldmans. It's not just that we were best friends—we dated each other. We went steady. That's one of the things that happens when you become a couple: you date other couples. We saw each other every Saturday night and every Sunday night, and we had a standing engagement for New

Year's Eve. Our marriages were tied together. We went to Italy, we went to Ireland, we went to Williamsburg, we went to Montreal, we went to St. Martin, and Mark drove and I navigated and Julie suggested wrong turns and Arthur fell asleep. Then, when we got to wherever we were going, Mark wanted to eat and I wanted to see the market and Julie wanted to go to the museum and Arthur wanted to take a crap. We had flat tires together and we ran out of gas together; in some fundamental sense, we were always on the road, merrily on our way to nowhere in particular. Two of us liked dark meat and two of us liked light meat and together we made a chicken.

I suppose that I honestly believed that if I couldn't save our marriage, the Siegels could. Which is why I called them from New York the night I discovered Mark's affair. They were shocked. They were astonished. There was consternation in every syllable they uttered. All of this was a relief to me—suppose they'd known! Suppose they'd known and hadn't told me! Suppose they'd known and told me!

"With Thelma Rice?" Julie said on the phone. "Omigod."

"Julie, what am I going to do?" I said.

"Pick up the phone, Arthur," said Julie. "It's Rachel."

"Hello," said Arthur.

"I'm sorry to call so late," I said.

"That's okay," said Arthur. "Obviously you've finally figured out who Thelma Rice is having the affair with and you're calling to tell us, and I appreciate it even if it is one in the morning."

"It's Mark," I said.

"Did something happen to Mark?" said Arthur. "Jesus Christ, Rachel. What is it?"

"Arthur," said Julie, "Thelma Rice is having the affair with Mark."

"He says he's in love with her," I said.

"He told you this?" said Arthur.

"Yes," I said.

"Why did he tell you this?" said Arthur.

"I found a book she'd given him with an inscription in it, and when I confronted him, he said he was in love with her."

"He said he was in love with her or he said he was fucking her?" said Arthur.

"He said he was in love with her but he said he wasn't fucking her," I said.

"Where are you?" said Julie.

"In New York," I said. "At my father's."

"Where's Sam?" said Julie.

"With me," I said.

"Does he know what's happening?" said Arthur.

"I don't think so," I said. "I've been crying for eight hours now, and he hasn't even noticed."

"I know," said Julie. "When Alexandra was two I cried for eight *months* and she never noticed."

"Does Mark know you're there?" said Arthur.

"I don't know," I said.

"That fuckhead," said Arthur. "He's gone crazy."

"That's what I said to him," I said. "But he denied it."

"Of course he denied it," said Arthur. "That's the truest sign of insanity—insane people are always sure they're just fine. It's only the sane people who are willing to admit they're crazy."

"Did you know about this, Arthur?" said Julie.

"Of course I didn't know about it," said Arthur. "How could you think I would know about it and not tell you?"

"I told him he had to stop seeing her," I said.

"And what did he say?" said Arthur.

"He said he wouldn't. And he said I should stay with him anyway and have the baby. He said, 'I am in love with Thelma Rice. I still have feelings about you, of course, and we are going to have another baby, so I suggest we just get from day to day.' "

"Oh, shit," said Julie.

"Listen, Rachel, sit tight," said Arthur. "I'm going to talk to him."

Arthur and Julie will go over there and beat some sense into Mark, I thought when I hung up the phone. Arthur and Julie will glare at him until he withers under the moral opprobrium of their gaze. Arthur and Julie will take the power of our friendship and club him into submission. This was not exactly the romantic scenario I had had in mind—I would have preferred Mark to have a more voluntary kind of blinding vision— but it would have to do. After all, Mark might be willing to give me up, and my vinaigrette, but he would never give up the four of us. And Thelma would never fit in. For one thing, she was too tall. Arthur and Julie and Mark and I were all approximately the same size, which is one reason we traveled so well together. It's hard to walk in lockstep with people a lot taller than you are, because they take longer strides, and you always feel like a little puppy scampering to keep up. For another thing, Thelma Rice really didn't care about food—that was clear from her gluey puddings—while the four of us had a friendship that was a shrine to food. We had driven miles to find the world's creamiest cheesecake and the world's largest pistachio nut and the world's sweetest corn on the cob. We had spent hours in blind taste testings of kosher hot dogs and double chocolate chip ice cream. When Julie went home to Fort Worth, she flew back with spareribs from Angelo's Beef Bar-B-Q, and when I went to New York, I flew back with smoked butterfish from Russ and Daughters. Once, in New Orleans, we all went to Mosca's for dinner, and we ate marinated crab, baked oysters, barbecued shrimp, spaghetti bordelaise, chicken with garlic, sausage with potatoes, and on the way back to town, a dozen oysters each at the Acme and beignets and coffee with chicory on the wharf. Then Arthur said, "Let's go to Chez Helene for the bread pudding," and we did, and we each had two. The owner of Chez Helene gave us the bread pudding recipe when we left, and I'm going to throw it in because it's the best bread pudding I've ever eaten. It tastes like caramelized mush. Cream 2 cups sugar with 2 sticks butter. Then add 2½ cups milk, one 13-ounce can evaporated milk, 2 tablespoons nutmeg, 2 tablespoons vanilla, a loaf of wet bread in chunks and pieces (any bread will do, the worse the better), and 1 cup raisins. Stir to mix. Pour into a deep greased casserole and bake at 350° for 2 hours, stirring after the first hour. Serve warm with hard sauce.

For the most part, Arthur Siegel is remarkably content. Once when we played Do You Have Any Regrets, the only thing he could come up with was that we hadn't ordered some fried onion rings at Chez Helene along with the bread pudding. When we played What Do You Wish You Were Named, I wanted to be named Veronica because it's luscious and I'm not, Julie wanted to be named Anthea because it's thin and she's not, Mark wanted to be named Sasha because it's dashing and he's not, and Arthur thought it over and said it seemed to him his name suited him just fine. It does. Arthur is chunky but solid, as an Arthur should be, and he has a red handlebar mustache that almost compensates for the fact that he is almost completely bald. I'll tell you how sensible Arthur is: he doesn't even mind being bald.

Arthur and Mark had grown up together in Brooklyn. They went to Columbia, and then Mark went to journalism school there and Arthur went off to law school at Yale. They both ended up in Washington. Julie was a legislative assistant on Capitol Hill when Arthur met her. She has curly blond hair and goo-goo-googly eyes and big pearly teeth like the girl in the Coca-Cola ad, and every so often Arthur stares across the room at her as if he cannot believe she's his. All of this is mystifying to Julie, who believes she's just a fairly average plump girl from Texas who snagged a nice Jewish husband solely due to what she calls shiksa madness.

The Siegels got married and moved into a two-bedroom apartment on Connecticut Avenue, and Mark would bring his girlfriends to breakfast on Sundays. The first Jewish Kimberly passed through their lives. Then more girlfriends. Then Mark turned up with me, and suddenly there we were, the four of us. Together. We would sit around, doing nothing, nothing at all, lazy Sundays with clouds in the coffee and papers all over the living room and dusty Sunday light coming through the color-coordinated Levolor blinds. Arthur would say that the trouble with Washington was that there wasn't a decent delicatessen. Julie would say that the trouble with Washington was that there weren't any late movies on television. I would say that the trouble with Washington was that it was so goyish. Mark would say that the trouble with Washington was that too many people there spent too much time figuring out what the trouble with it was. We would all say these things as if we had never said them before, and argue over them as if we had never argued over them before. Then we would all decide whether we wanted to be buried or cremated. Then we would move on to the important matters. Should they paint their living room peach? Should they strip down their dining table? Should they buy a videotape recorder? Should they re-cover the couch?

"I don't see what was wrong with it before," said Arthur after they re-covered the couch.

"Nothing was wrong with it before," said Julie.

"What color is this anyway?" said Arthur.

"Taupe," said Julie.

Arthur shook his head. "I've always been terrible at colors," he said. "It comes from having grown up with the single-row box of crayons instead of the big box. If I'd had the big box I would now know taupe and cerise and ecru. Instead, all I know is burnt sienna. And what good does it do me? Never once have I heard anything described as burnt sienna. Never once have I heard anyone say, 'Follow that burnt sienna car.'"

"I think there's a column in this," said Mark.

"Goddammit, Feldman," said Arthur.

"You can have it if you want it," said Mark.

"What do you mean, I can have it if I want it?" said Arthur. "It's *mine*. *I'm* the one who gets to say 'You can have it if you want it.' Not you."

"What are you going to do with it?" said Mark. "Write it up for the *Yale Law Review*?"

"He doesn't have to do *anything* with it," I said. "He can simply add it to his repertoire."

"Thanks, Rachel," said Arthur. He looked at Mark. "Don't break up with her, okay?" he said. "Promise me you won't."

"Jesus Christ," said Mark. "You'd think *you* were going with her."

"We are," said Arthur. "The two of us are going with the two of you."

"You used to like me when I was unattached," said Mark.

"Not as much as I like you as a couple," said Arthur, and he gave Mark a playful punch on the arm.

"You're punching me because you want me to think you're kidding, but you're not," said Mark.

"You'll never know, will you?" said Arthur. "The truth is, I wish you two would get married."

"Arthur, for God's sake," said Julie.

"I can't help it," said Arthur. "I like being married. I want everyone I care about to be married. That's the kind of guy I am. Warm. Generous. Expansive. Charming."

"You just want everyone to be in the same pot you're in," said Mark.

"I like the pot I'm in," said Arthur. "I like how it goes along. What's for dinner and which movie should we see and where are my socks."

"Where are your socks?" said Mark. "Where are my socks? Where are all the missing socks?"

"They're in heaven," said Arthur. "You die, you go to heaven, and they bring you a big box, and it's got all your lost socks in it, and your mufflers and your gloves, and you get to spend eternity sorting them all out."

"I think there's a column in this," said Mark.

"Goddammit, Feldman," said Arthur.

Mark and I got married. You should have seen Arthur at the wedding. He stood with his head cocked at a jaunty angle, winking wildly and uncontrollably at the judge. He had done it. He had talked Mark into it. By the simple example of his own contentment, he had persuaded his best friend to give up bachelorhood. At the end of the ceremony, he whipped a glass from his pocket and placed it on the ground, and when Mark smashed it into the judge's Oriental rug, Arthur whooped around the room and danced the kazatsky. Three months later, I was walking up Connecticut Avenue, through the park at Dupont Circle, and there were Arthur and an unidentified female in a mad clinch on the park bench.

"I saw Arthur this afternoon," I said when I got home. "Kissing a . . ." I gestured absently with my hand and shook my head.

"Woman," said Mark.

"How long have you known about it?" I said.

"I don't know anything about it," said Mark. "I was just finishing the sentence. With Arthur, he's kissing a woman or a bagel. I took a guess." He looked at me. "Who was she?"

"I don't know."

"What did she look like?"

"Thin. Pretty. Big tits. Your basic nightmare."

We looked at each other.

"Should we do anything?" I said.

"He's my friend," said Mark. "We don't meddle in each other's lives."

"Of course we do," I said, "we meddle constantly. That's what true friendship is about."

"What did you have in mind?" said Mark.

"I don't know," I said.

"Maybe it's just a fling," said Mark. "He's almost forty, he probably feels nothing's happening to him—"

"It's just a passage," I said angrily.

"Yeah," said Mark.

"Shit," I said.

"Look, I hated the book as much as you did," said Mark.

"I know," I said. "I just feel betrayed. Never mind Julie—he's cheating on us, you know what I mean?"

"I know what you mean," said Mark.

"One of the things I love about you is that you know what I mean even when I don't," I said.

"Actually, I don't," said Mark. "I just say I do."

"Maybe it's not serious," I said.

"Maybe it's just a fuck," said Mark.

"Yeah," I said.

"And I'm a ballerina," said Mark.

Two nights later, Arthur rang the bell in the middle of the night and announced that he was in love.

"A stewardess?" said Mark.

"A flight attendant," said Arthur.

"You must really be in love," said Mark.

"I am," said Arthur.

"Is this a midlife crisis or something?" said Mark.

"Don't reduce my life to some dime-store philosophy so it's easier for you to handle," said Arthur. "For twenty years I've watched you fuck around and fuck up and cheat on this one and cheat on that one. Did I ever judge you? Did I ever purse my lips? Did I ever say tch tch tch? Did you ever hear those words from me?"

"Tch tch tch?" said Mark. "Those words? I never heard those words because your tongue was so busy hanging out of your mouth you couldn't get them out. Listen to me. You're married. You've been married eight years. You've got a kid. Don't throw it away for a fuck."

"I suppose you're going to tell me things are going to be the same in bed with you and Rachel after eight years," said Arthur.

"No," said Mark, "but it'll still be good."

"It just won't be as often," said Arthur. "Instead of a couple of times a week it'll be a couple of times a year."

"I'll be almost fifty in ten years," said Mark.

"You know how old you have to be before you stop wanting to fuck strangers?" said Arthur. "Dead, that's how old. It doesn't stop. It doesn't go away. You put all this energy into suppressing it and telling yourself it's worth it because of what you get in exchange, and then one day someone brushes up against you and you're fourteen years old again and all you want to do is go to a drive-in movie and fuck her brains out in the backseat. But you don't do it because you're not going to be that kind of person, so you go home, and there's your wife, and she wears socks to bed."

"Socks again," said Mark.

On and on they went. It was late. Two in the morning. Three in the morning. We sat around the kitchen table in the yellow glow of the high-crime lights on the street, and I listened to Mark. Marriage was a trust, he said. Betray that trust and you have nothing, he said. I felt so smug. My husband the convert. My husband the true believer. My husband the husband. See a marriage counselor, he said. Do something.

And they did. The Siegels went to see a very nice marriage counselor named Gwendolyn. Gwendolyn left her husband three months later, but the Siegels survived. The four of us resumed normal activities. We went to Ohio for the shoofly pie and we went to Virginia for the ham. We were able to discuss other friends' marital difficulties without Julie's looking hurt and Arthur's looking guilty. Last summer they came to visit us in West Virginia, and Julie and I spent a week perfecting the peach pie. We made ordinary peach pie, and deep-dish peach pie, and blueberry and peach pie, but here is the best peach pie we made: Put 1¼ cups flour, ½ teaspoon salt, ½ cup butter, and 2 tablespoons sour cream into a Cuisinart and blend until they form a ball. Pat out into a buttered pie tin, and bake 10 minutes at 425°. Beat 3 egg yolks slightly and combine with 1 cup sugar, 2 tablespoons flour, and ⅓ cup sour cream. Pour over 3 peeled, sliced peaches arranged in the crust. Cover with foil. Reduce the oven to 350° and bake 35 minutes. Remove the foil and bake 10 minutes more, or until the filling is set.

I keep thinking about that week in West Virginia. It was a perfect week. We swam in the river and barbecued ribs and made Bellinis with crushed peaches and cheap champagne. We lay out on the lawn, the sunlight dappling through the copper beech, and Alexandra got her kite into the air and Sam applauded madly and scampered behind her, screaming with joy. Is it hot enough for you, we said, and the water isn't cold once you get in. We methodically rubbed sun block onto the arms of our children and poured another pitcherful into our glasses. So we were grownups. So what? Arthur lifted his glass. "I love you," he said. "I love us." The phone rang. Mark ran to get it and then called me into the house. We stood with the phone between us and listened to the lady in the hospital say that she had the results of the amniocentesis. The baby was normal. It was a boy. We ran back to the Siegels and drank to the baby. "You're going to have a brother," we told Sam. He started to cry. "Nathaniel," I said. "Can you say Nathaniel?" "No," said Sam. "Tummy hurts." Mark took him then, and walked him down to the river. They found a frog. Sam held it cupped in his hands, and giggled. I remember thinking: Lucky me, lucky us, lucky Sam, lucky Nathaniel. *What's wrong with this picture?*

Nine

Arthur and Julie lived just a few blocks from our house. The morning after Mark and I got back to Washington, I slid out of bed and went over to see them. Arthur opened the door and gave me the kind of look you give someone who's just had a death in the family and hugged me in a long, speechless, what-can-I-say sort of way.

"How are you?" he said.

"I'm back," I said. "How am I?"

"You're back," he said.

"Mark came to New York yesterday," I said. "He said he would stop seeing Thelma, so I came back."

Arthur nodded.

"What do you think?" I said.

"I don't know," said Arthur.

Julie came out from the bedroom. She put her arms around me and patted me quite a lot, and I cried on the shoulder of her terry-cloth bathrobe.

"Did you see him?" I said.

They nodded.

"I even saw her for a few minutes," said Arthur.

"Look," I said, "I'm putting you in an awkward position here."

"No, no," said Julie.

"What did he say?" I said.

"It doesn't matter," said Arthur.

"Why doesn't it matter?" I said.

"Because he's crazy," said Arthur.

We went into the kitchen and sat down with some of Arthur's fetish-istically brewed coffee. Arthur makes coffee by putting eggshells and cinnamon sticks and an old nylon stocking into the coffeepot. His coffee tastes like a very spicy old foot.

"The week you came to West Virginia two months ago," I said.

"What about it?" said Arthur.

"Did we have a good time that week?"

"Terrific," said Julie.

"Did Mark and I seem happy?"

"Yes," said Julie.

"I was wondering about it," I said, "because Mark told me that our marriage had been terrible for a long time, and now I can't remember whether or not it was."

"He told us that, too," said Arthur.

"What else did he tell you?" I said.

"He said you were mean to him," said Arthur.

"I probably am," I said.

"Don't be ridiculous," said Julie.

"I am," I said. "All summer long I was snapping at him because he was never there."

"Of course you were snapping at him," said Julie. "He was having an affair."

"But I didn't know," I said.

"You must have known," said Arthur. "I knew."

"I thought you said you didn't know," said Julie.

"I didn't know about Thelma," said Arthur, "and I didn't know for sure, but I thought he was up to something. All those trips to the dentist."

"What was the matter with me?" I said. "If you could see it, why couldn't I?"

"Stop beating up on yourself," said Julie. "You trusted him. You have to trust someone you're married to, otherwise you'd spend your entire life going through the phone bills and American Express receipts."

"It's going to be all right," said Arthur.

"You're only saying that because you have to leave to teach a class and it's a good exit line," I said.

"I'm saying it because I have to leave and teach a class," said Arthur, "but it's true. He'll come to his senses. Jesus Christ, Rachel. Sam's still a baby and you're pregnant."

Arthur kissed us both goodbye and went out the door. Julie waited until she was sure he'd taken the elevator.

"I didn't know Mark was having an affair," said Julie. "I want you to know that. I don't know what I would have done if I'd known, but I didn't know."

"I know," I said. "What should I do, Julie?"

"Go home. Go on working. Take care of Sam. Have the baby. Wait the thing out. Eventually he'll get tired of her. Eventually she'll turn into as big a nag as he thinks you are. Eventually he'll get just as bored in bed with her as he is with you. And when that happens, he'll decide that it's less trouble to stay with you."

"But Mark isn't going to see Thelma anymore," I said. "So how is he going to get tired of her?"

"He will," said Julie.

"He will what?" I said.

"He'll see her again, and he'll get tired of her."

"And I'm supposed to sit there like a lox in the meantime?"

"Yes," said Julie. "If you want to stay married."

"That's a terrible thing to say," I said.

"I know," said Julie, "but it works. I did it. Sometimes I don't know why I did it, because it's so horrible and painful and humiliating, waiting the damned thing out. Sometimes I think I'd have been better off if I'd just left."

"Aren't you glad you're still with Arthur?"

"Oh, sure," said Julie.

"Then what is it?"

"I don't know," said Julie. "Sometimes the idea of being single interests me. For example, I woke up this morning and realized I'm never going to have bondage. It's just never going to come up with me and Arthur. I don't want to have it particularly, but it's never going to come up."

"I've never done it either," I said, "though I guess if I wanted to I could always ask."

"Arthur would just laugh at me," said Julie.

"Although I'm not sure what Mark would tie me to," I said, "since we don't have a headboard. You pretty much need a headboard, don't you think?"

"I don't know," said Julie. "That's the whole point."

"I guess you could always check into a hotel," I said. "Hotel beds have headboards."

"You could call room service for the rope," said Julie.

"It's really bad, isn't it?" I said.

"It's always bad when it happens," said Julie. "And then it gets better. You'll see. In a while, you'll be able to spend entire fifteen-minute periods without thinking about what they did together."

"And in the meantime," I said, "I can think about all the things in my future if it doesn't work out."

"What besides bondage?" said Julie.

"Amyl nitrates," I said. "Threesomes. Japanese movies. Roller disco. Thai food."

"I thought you hated Thai food," said Julie.

"I do," I said, "and if my marriage breaks up, I'll never have to have it again. It may be worth it."

Julie looked at me. "I think something happens to them," she said.

"You mean men," I said.

"I'm not saying they're worse," said Julie. "I'm saying they're different."

"You are too saying they're worse," I said.

"I know," said Julie.

"So what do we do?" I said.

"We hang on," she said, "and if it doesn't work, we try again with the next one."

.   .   .

When I got home, Mark was out in his office writing a jolly column about the Eastern shuttle. I walked into the kitchen and found Sam with Juanita, the maid. She was teaching him to say "Lie down with dogs, get up with fleas" in Spanish, which in some ways is the motto for Juanita's life. Juanita had lain down for twelve years with her husband, Hernando, and when he finally crawled out of her life, taking her Sears, Roebuck charge card with him, he left behind a rash of bad debts and old girlfriends and faulty automobile parts that seemed destined to dominate Juanita's life forever. At least once a week she would turn up late for work, and explain through sobs that the Sears credit department was about to seize a stereo component she knew nothing about, or that her husband had stolen the spare tire from her car trunk, or that someone named Theresa had turned up at the front door asking for Hernando's stopwatch. "I tol' her he takes two minutes, drunk or sober," said Juanita. "What she need to time it for?" Juanita was a very brave woman, really—she was singlehandedly supporting her three children—and I always tried very hard to love her, but she made it difficult because she was so disaster-prone. One morning, for example, on her way to work, she was stuck in a traffic jam on the Beltway, and when she got out of her car to see what was holding things up, in that split second, someone crept in through the passenger door of her car and stole her purse. Another time, she was standing in line in the Georgetown Safeway when a woman in front of her collapsed, and after Juanita revived her with mouth-to-mouth resuscitation, the woman tried to have her arrested for making improper advances.

Juanita looked up from Sam when I came in and burst into tears.

"Juanita," I said, "I'm not up for this. Whatever it is, I'm not up for it."

"Oh, Missee Felman, I feel so bad for ju," said Juanita. Even Juanita knew about it! The day after I'd left for New York she'd turned up to discover Mark and Thelma having a heart-to-heart talk on the living room couch.

"I know that lady," said Juanita. "She no good."

"I know," I said.

"*I* know," said Juanita. "I work for her ten years ago."

"What's wrong with her?" I said.

"She very messy," said Juanita.

Juanita gave me a big hug, which was awkward since she was only about four feet six inches tall, and a hug from her felt like the Heimlich maneuver. Then she pulled back and managed a huge smile that was meant to cheer me up—but instead revealed her mouthful of gold teeth, which only served to remind me of the time I had spent two days on the telephone with her dentist, negotiating a long-term payment for Hernando's root canal work.

"Everything be okay," she said. "You see."

I went up to the little room on the third floor that I used for an office. In the typewriter was an article I'd been writing about potatoes. I took it out of the typewriter and put in a fresh sheet of paper. I must write all this down, I thought. Someday I may write something that's not a cookbook, and this will all be grist for it. But I couldn't. To write it down was to give it permanence, to admit that something real had happened. I walked around the room trying to pretend that nothing had happened. I thought about potatoes. The first time I made dinner for Mark I made potatoes. The first time I made dinner for just about anyone I ever cared for I made potatoes. Very very crisp potatoes. I must make some potatoes tonight, I thought; mashed potatoes. Nothing like mashed potatoes when you're feeling blue. I could hear Mark's typewriter from the office over the garage; I kept hoping he would leave, go out for more socks, so I could dash into his sanctuary and go through the phone bills and the American Express receipts, but he was still there, tapping away. Maybe *he's* making notes for a novel, I thought. Worse, maybe he's making notes for a *column*. That would really do it. There would be my entire marital disaster, reduced to an 850-word column in 109 newspapers. I knew just how he'd write it, too. He'd write it in that dumb Hemingway style he always reserved for his slice-of-life columns. *The old man had told him it would happen. The old man had said to him, Sasha, it will happen someday. You will be on the river. You will be going downstream. You will hit a log.*

The phone rang.

I picked it up.

"Rachel, it's Betty."

"Oh, God," I said. "I'm so sorry."

"I know, I know," said Betty.

"You know?" I said.

"It must have been awful," said Betty.

"How do you know?" I said.

"It's in the paper," said Betty.

"In the paper?" I said.

"Why didn't you tell me that Vanessa Melhado was in your group?" said Betty.

"The robbery's in the paper?" I said.

"In the Style section," said Betty.

"We're not allowed to tell anyone who's in the group," I said.

"What's she like?"

"We're not allowed to tell that either," I said. "Listen, I feel terrible about missing your party."

"I understand," said Betty. "I knew something awful must have happened to you if you weren't there, and now I see that it did."

"Yes," I said. "It was awful."

"Anyway, it doesn't matter," said Betty, "because I found out who Thelma Rice is having the affair with."

"Who?" I said.

"You're not going to like it," said Betty.

"Who is it?" I said.

"Arthur," said Betty.

"Arthur Siegel?" I said.

"Yes," said Betty. "They were having drinks in the Washington Hilton yesterday afternoon. Nobody has drinks in the Washington Hilton unless something secret's going on."

"Arthur isn't having an affair with Thelma Rice," I said. "Nobody is having an affair with Thelma Rice."

"How do you know?" said Betty.

"I just know," I said.

"Tell me," said Betty.

"Okay," I said, "but you can't tell this to anyone."

"I promise," said Betty.

"I saw Thelma at the gynecologist's, and that's when I found out."

"What?" said Betty.

"She has this horrible infection," I said. "You don't even want to know about it."

"Oh, God," said Betty.

"She made me promise not to tell anyone," I said, "but she almost didn't have to because it's so disgusting I almost couldn't. I'm only telling you because I want you to know it's not true about her and Arthur."

"Then why was she having a drink with him?" said Betty.

"That's part of it," I said.

"What are you talking about?" said Betty.

"She wanted some legal advice," I said. "She got the infection in a Vietnamese restaurant in Virginia, and she wants to sue them."

"She got it from something she ate, or from the toilet seat?" said Betty.

"The toilet seat, I guess," I said, "although I'm not sure. Maybe from the spring rolls."

"Oh, God," said Betty. "Poor Thelma."

"Poor Thelma?" I said.

"I feel so sorry for her," said Betty.

"Don't feel too sorry for her," I said. "It's curable. Eventually."

"Maybe I should have her and Jonathan to dinner," said Betty.

"Don't," I said.

"Why not?" said Betty. "It's not catching, is it?"

"No," I said, "it's just that she's so depressed, she's no fun to be around."

"I think we should have a dance," said Betty.

"What?" I said.

"The three of us. You, me, and Thelma."

"I hate dances," I said.

"It'll be fun, Rachel," said Betty.

"I can't dance," I said.

"Come on," said Betty. "Where do you think we should do it?"

"The White House," I said.

"That's a great idea," said Betty. "They're always talking about opening it up to the public. I'll call the social secretary."

"Betty—"

"And let's have lunch, the three of us, next week. Tuesday."

"Tuesday I have to be in New York to do a cooking demonstration."

"Rachel, you really are impossible," said Betty. "Thelma and I will have lunch on Tuesday. We will plan the dance. It will make Thelma feel better about her infection, and you'll have something to take your mind off the robbery—"

"My mind isn't *on* the robbery," I said.

"Good," said Betty. "Start making your guest list."

"Thelma's going to want to invite the Kissingers," I said. "Is that the kind of dance you want to have?"

"Goodbye," said Betty, and hung up.

POTATOES AND LOVE: SOME REFLECTIONS

The beginning

I have friends who begin with pasta, and friends who begin with rice, but whenever I fall in love, I begin with potatoes. Sometimes meat and potatoes and sometimes fish and potatoes, but always potatoes. I have made a lot of mistakes falling in love, and regretted most of them, but never the potatoes that went with them.

Not just any potato will do when it comes to love. There are people who go on about the virtues of plain potatoes—plain boiled new potatoes with a little parsley or dill, or plain baked potatoes with crackling skins—but my own feeling is that a taste for plain potatoes coincides with cultural antecedents I do not possess, and that in any case, the time for plain potatoes—if there is ever a time for plain potatoes—is never at the beginning of something. It is also, I should add, never at the end of something. Perhaps you can get away with plain potatoes in the middle, although I have never been able to.

All right, then: I am talking about crisp potatoes. Crisp potatoes require an immense amount of labor. It's not just the peeling, which is one of the few kitchen chores no electric device has been invented to alleviate; it's also that the potatoes, once peeled, must be cut into whatever shape you intend them to be, put into water to be systematically prevented from turning a loathsome shade of bluish-brownish-black, and then meticulously dried to ensure that they crisp properly. All this takes time, and time, as any fool can tell you, is what true romance is about. In fact, one of the main reasons why you must make crisp potatoes in the beginning is that if you don't make them in the beginning, you never will. I'm sorry to be so cynical about this, but that's the truth.

There are two kinds of crisp potatoes that I prefer above all others. The first are called Swiss potatoes, and they're essentially a large potato pancake of perfect hash browns; the flipping of the pancake is so wildly dramatic that the potatoes themselves are almost beside the point. The second are called potatoes Anna; they are thin circles of potato cooked in a shallow pan in the oven and then turned onto a plate in a darling mound of crunchy brownness. Potatoes Anna is a classic French recipe, but there is something so homely and old-fashioned about them that they can usually be passed off as either an ancient family recipe or something you just made up.

For Swiss potatoes: Peel 3 large (or 4 small) russet potatoes (or all-purpose if you can't get russets) and put them in cold water to cover. Start 4 tablespoons butter and 1 tablespoon cooking oil melting in a nice heavy large frying pan. Working quickly, dry the potatoes and grate them on the grating disk of the Cuisinart. Put them into a colander and squeeze out as much water as you can. Then dry them again on paper towels. You will need more paper towels to do this than you ever thought possible. Dump the potatoes into the frying pan, patting them down with a spatula, and cook over medium heat for about 15 minutes, until the bottom of the pancake is brown. Then, while someone is watching, loosen the pancake and, with one incredibly deft motion, flip it over. Salt it generously. Cook 5 minutes more. Serves two.

For potatoes Anna: Peel 3 large (or 4 small) russet potatoes (or Idahos if you can't get russets) and put them in water. Working quickly, dry each potato and slice into 1/16-inch rounds. Dry them with paper towels, round by round. Put 1 tablespoon clarified butter into a cast-iron skillet and line the skillet with overlapping potatoes. Dribble clarified butter and salt and pepper over them. Repeat twice. Put into a 425° oven for 45 minutes, pressing the potatoes down now and then. Then turn up the oven to 500° and cook 10 more minutes. Flip onto a round platter. Serves two.

The middle (I)

One day the inevitable happens. I go to the potato drawer to make potatoes and discover that the little brown buggers I bought in a large sack a few weeks earlier have gotten soft and mushy and are sprouting long and quite uninteresting vines. In addition, one of them seems to have developed an odd brown leak, and the odd brown leak appears to be the cause of a terrible odor that in only a few seconds has permeated the entire kitchen. I throw out the potatoes and look in the cupboard for a box of pasta. This is the moment when the beginning ends and the middle begins.

The middle (II)

Sometimes, when a loved one announces that he has decided to go on a low-carbohydrate, low-fat, low-salt diet (thus ruling out the possibility of potatoes, should you have been so inclined), he is signaling that the middle is ending and the end is beginning.

The end

In the end, I always want potatoes. Mashed potatoes. Nothing like mashed potatoes when you're feeling blue. Nothing like getting into bed with a bowl of hot mashed potatoes already loaded with butter, and methodically adding a thin cold slice of butter to every forkful. The problem with mashed potatoes, though, is that they require almost as much hard work as crisp potatoes, and when you're feeling blue the last thing you feel like is hard work. Of course, you can always get someone to make the mashed potatoes for you, but let's face it: the reason you're blue is that there *isn't* anyone to make them for you. As a result, most people do not have nearly enough mashed potatoes in their lives, and when they do, it's almost always at the wrong time.

(You can, of course, train children to mash potatoes, but you should know that Richard Nixon spent most of his childhood making mashed potatoes for his mother and was extremely methodical about getting the lumps out. A few lumps make mashed potatoes more authentic, if you ask me, but that's not the point. The point is that perhaps children should not be trained to mash potatoes.)

For mashed potatoes: Put 1 large (or 2 small) potatoes in a large pot of salted water and bring to a boil. Lower the heat and simmer for at least 20 minutes, until tender. Drain and place the potatoes back in the pot and shake over low heat to eliminate excess moisture. Peel. Put through a potato ricer and immediately add 1 tablespoon heavy cream and as much melted butter and salt and pepper as you feel like. Eat immediately. Serves one.

Ten

I don't want to string this part out. You don't really need to hear a blow-by-blow account, because it isn't all that interesting. The first night back I made shrimp curry. (The recipe's in *Uncle Seymour's Beef Borscht* if you want it.) The next night chicken stuffed with lemons. (Marcella Hazan.) The next night, takeout from Scott's Bar-B-Q. Mark and I sat at dinner and made conversation. The word desultory applies. We talked about everything except what had happened. I tried not to cry. I tried hard not to ask where he went in the afternoon. I tried hard not to go into his office and turn it upside down looking for more evidence, but finally I decided what the hell, go take a look, how much worse can it get, and it turned out Mark had locked his office door and

I couldn't get in. At one point over the weekend Mark asked me how I made my vinaigrette, but I wouldn't tell him. I figured my vinaigrette was the only thing I had that Thelma didn't (besides a pregnancy), and I could just see him learning it from me and then rushing over to her house with a jar of Grey Poupon mustard (the essential ingredient) and teaching her the wrist movement and dancing off into a sunset of arugola salads. I must seem to be putting too much emphasis on this vinaigrette of mine, but war is war.

Perhaps you are wondering whether we had sex. Normally I don't like to get into this area, because it embarrasses me, but since it's probably crossed your mind I'd better deal with it. We had sex. We always had sex. That's one of the most perplexing parts of the story; that's one of the reasons why Mark's relationship with Thelma had come as such a surprise to me. Now that I look back on it, we hadn't been doing anything particularly inventive in that department of late, but I have never been big on invention in that department. Why kid around? Every so often I browse through books full of tasteful line drawings of supplementary positions—how to do it standing and in the swimming pool and on the floor—and I'm always mystified. On the floor! Why would anyone want to do it on the floor when a bed was available? I'll tell you the truth: even sex on a beach seems to me to be going too far.

On Tuesday morning I took the shuttle to New York for my food demonstration in the Macy's housewares department. I do food demonstrations from time to time, although I do more talking than actual demonstrating. Occasionally, serious food people come to observe, and I can see them sneer as they watch my hopelessly sloppy chopping. Serious food people do not take me seriously, and they're right not to. I more or less backed into the food writing business, and before anyone in the food establishment could decide what to do with me, there I was, writing articles and doing demonstrations and appearing on television and essentially taking money from their pockets.

What they say about me is I have no real training as a cook, I'm basically a performer, I clip recipes from other people's cookbooks and pass them off as my own, I don't have an original point of view, and I am a sellout. (This last accusation always makes me cross, because I would love to be a sellout if only someone would ask.) They used to say that I was wrong about nouvelle cuisine, but I turned out to be right about it, so they don't say that anymore. My position on nouvelle cuisine is that it's silly.

What I say about them is they use too many adjectives. I hate adjectives. I also hate similes and metaphors, just can't do them, never have been able to. Anyone who wants to write about food would do well to stay away from similes and metaphors, because if you're not careful, expressions like "light as a feather" make their way into your sentences, and then where are you? The problem, though, is how to do without adjectives. If you write about food, you can't really do without them; but if you do *with* them, you run the risk of writing sentences like "The fish was juicy but the sauce was lumpy," or "The sauce was creamy but the veal was stringy," or, to sum up, "The noun was (complimentary adjective) but the other noun was (uncomplimentary adjective)." This is a particular danger for food writers who review restaurants, which I have never done and never will. You have to draw the line somewhere.

Obviously I didn't start out in life wanting to be a food writer. These days there are probably people who do—just as there are now people who start out wanting to be film critics, God help us—but I started out wanting to be a journalist. Which I became. I was a reporter for the *New York World-Telegram and Sun* and I lived in a junior two-and-a-half, and whenever I was home alone at night I cooked myself a perfect little dinner. None of your containers of yogurt for me; no, sir. I would pick a recipe from Michael Field or Julia Child and shop on the way home and spend the first part of the evening painstakingly mastering whatever dish I had chosen. Then I would sit down to eat it in front of the television set. At the time I thought this was wildly civilized behavior, but the truth is it was probably somewhat Mamie Eisenhowerish. In any case, I learned to cook. Everyone did—everyone my age, that is. This was the mid-1960s, the height of the first wave of competitive cooking. I'm always interested when people talk about the sixties in the kind of hushed tone that is meant to connote the seriousness of it all, because what I remember about the sixties was that people were constantly looking up from dessert and saying things like: "Whose mousse is this?" Once, I remember, one of my friends called up to say his marriage had ended on account of veal Orloff, and I knew exactly what he meant. It was quite mad, really. I was never completely idiotic—I never once made a quiche, for example—but I held my own, and I'm afraid that I'm still known in certain circles as the originator of a game called If You Had to Have Only One Flavor Soufflé for the Rest of Your Life, Would It Be Chocolate or Grand Marnier?

Anyway, there I was at the *World-Telegram* when the food editor retired. There was a pause before the next food editor arrived, and I was asked to fill in and write the "A Visit With" column. You know the kind of column it was: I would go to interview famous people in their homes, and they'd talk about their dinner parties and their decorators and their indispensable housekeepers, and then, in the end, they'd give me a recipe. The recipes weren't much—you'd be amazed at how many legendary hostesses tried to get away with newlywed garbage like chicken Divan and grapes with sour cream and brown sugar—but the interviews were really quite fascinating. People would say the oddest things about the servant problem and the extra-man-at-the-dinner-party problem and tipping at Christmas and how you could tell the economy was getting worse because of all the chicken you were starting to see at dinner parties. "Dark-meat chicken," one woman said to me contemptuously.

It was just a mild little column in a newspaper no one read, but as a result of it, I began to have a field of expertise. That's probably putting it too strongly—it wasn't as if I had become an expert in law or economics or seventeenth-century England—but that's how it felt: having spent my life knowing nothing much about anything (which is known as being a generalist), I suddenly knew something about something. I certainly knew enough to make jokes in the food-world language. I learned that the words "monosodium glutamate" were almost automatically funny, especially aloud, as were "The R. T. French's Mustard Tastemaker Award," "The Pillsbury Bake-Off," and "The National Chicken Cooking Contest." This gave me an edge as a food writer that almost made up for the fact that I think that certain serious food-world subjects, like coulibiac of salmon (another automatically funny phrase), are not worth bothering with.

(Another argument I have with serious food people is that they're always talking about how *creative* cooking is. "Cooking is very creative" is how they put it. Now, there's no question that there are a handful of people doing genuinely creative things with food—although a lot of it, if you ask me, seems to consist of heating up goat cheese or throwing strawberry vinegar onto calves' liver or relying excessively on the kiwi. But most cooking is based on elementary, long-standing principles, and to say that cooking is creative not only misses the point of creativity—which is that it is painful and difficult and quite unrelated to whether it is possible to come up with yet another way to cook a pork chop—but also misses the whole point of cooking, which is that it is totally mindless. What I love about cooking is that after a hard day, there is something comforting about the fact that if you melt butter and add flour and then hot stock, *it will get thick!* It's a sure thing! It's a sure thing in a world where nothing is sure; it has a mathematical certainty in a world where those of us who long for some kind of certainty are forced to settle for crossword puzzles.)

Normally I enjoy doing food demonstrations—I like giving my speech, I like the way it laces in and out of the subject of food. But when I was about halfway through the demonstration at Macy's—I was right in the middle of cooking Lillian Hellman's pot roast—I realized I was in trouble. Lillian Hellman's pot roast is the sort of recipe that makes my reputation in the food world what it is, since it contains all sorts of low-rent ingredients like a package of onion soup mix and a can of cream of mushroom soup. It even has something called Kitchen Bouquet in it, although I always leave it out. You take a nice 4-pound piece of beef, the more expensive the better, and put it into a good pot with 1 can of cream of mushroom soup, an envelope of dried onion soup, 1 large chopped onion, 3 cloves chopped garlic, 2 cups red wine, and 2 cups water. Add a crushed bay leaf and 1 teaspoon each thyme and basil. Cover and bake in a 350° oven until tender, 3½ hours or so.

The reason the pot roast recipe gets to me is that it's an occasion for a point I like to make about couples in America. What I say is that I think Lillian Hellman had a remarkable effect as a literary heroine, although not the effect she was always accused of having. I have no problem with her political persona, or with her insistence on making herself the centerpiece of most of the historical conflicts of the twentieth century; but it seems to me that she invented a romantic fantasy about her involvement with Dashiell Hammett that is every bit as unrealistic as the Doris Day movies feminists prefer to blame for society's unrealistic notions about romance. The Doris Day fantasy, you may recall, is that the big man and the little woman march into the sunset together and live happily ever after. The Lillian Hellman fantasy is that the big man and the *big* woman march into the sunset together, fighting and cursing and drinking and killing turtles, but they, too, live happily ever after (until, of course, one of them dies, leaving the other free to reinvent the romance). I'm not saying that Lillian Hellman was the first writer to animate this fantasy couple—and even Hammett had a hand in it, with his Nick and Nora Charles. But Hellman's version was presented as fact, not fiction, so it makes you think it's possible. And is it?

It's a small point, just an aside that gets me through measuring the liquid ingredients, but it occurred to me as I delivered it yet another time that I had always zipped through that part of the speech as if I had somehow managed to be invulnerable to the fantasy, as if I had somehow managed to escape from or rise above it simply as a result of having figured it out. I think you often have that sense when you write—that if you can spot something in yourself and set it down on paper, you're free of it. And you're not, of course; you've just managed to set it down on paper, that's all. The truth is that I'm at least as big a sap about romance as old Lillian was, probably even bigger.

I'll give you another example. I've written about cooking and marriage dozens of times, and I'm very smart on the subject, I'm very smart about how complicated things get when food and love become hopelessly tangled. But I realized as I stood there doing my demonstration in the middle of the Macy's housewares department that I had been as dopey about food and love as any old-fashioned Jewish mother. I loved to cook, so I cooked. And then the cooking became a way of saying I love you. And then the cooking became the easy way of saying I love you. And then the cooking became the only way of saying I love you. I was so busy perfecting the peach pie that I wasn't paying attention. I had never even been able to imagine an alternative. Every so often I would look at my women friends who were happily married and didn't cook, and I would always find myself wondering how they did it. Would anyone love me if I couldn't cook? I always thought cooking was part of the package: Step right up, it's Rachel Samstat, she's bright, she's funny, *and she can cook!*

I got so depressed and angry thinking about all this that I gave the onion an enormous whack and sent it flying into the front row of spectators, right into some lady's Literary Guild tote bag. Everyone laughed, and I tossed my head blithely as if it were the sort of thing I do all the time—which it's not—and that's when I saw Richard. Richard is my producer. (I love being able to say things like that. My producer. My doctor. My accountant. My floor man. My agent. My maid.) Richard Finkel, who produced my television show, is tall and red-haired and cannot see even with his glasses on, and he was squinting through the crowd at Macy's while I retrieved the onion. As if he weren't obvious enough already, he began to wave wildly at me, and I immediately felt better. I love Richard. That I should have spotted him at that exact moment was really quite odd: the first night Richard and I slept together, he did an imitation of his father eating an onion, and I can almost never think of raw onions without remembering him, lying naked in bed, taking mad, passionate bites of an imaginary onion and producing spectacular belches. It's a miracle I didn't fall in love with Richard on the spot, because I'm silly enough to think that any man who would imitate his father eating an onion is a suitable love object; but I didn't. I'll tell you who would have fallen in love with Richard had she been there: Brenda, my former friend and current step-relative-once-removed. Brenda was always falling in love with men whose attraction utterly mystified me, and whenever I would ask her what she saw in them, she would say things like: "He does a wonderful Sophie Tucker." Brenda fell in love with her husband Harry because he did a brilliant bit about a two-thousand-year-old man, and she always said she knew the marriage was over a week after it had begun, when she discovered that Harry had lifted the entire routine from Mel Brooks.

Richard and I slept together only a few times. We had one of those affairs that you begin by saying, "We're making a big mistake," and what you mean by that is not that you're getting in over your head but that you're just killing time. Richard and I killed a little time and then went back to being friends. Then I started seeing Mark, and Richard started seeing Helen, and things got complicated. Richard never really liked Mark, and I didn't really like Helen—that was the complication. Helen is one of those people who never say anything, not because she's shy but because she's learned—in a way I always mean to—that if you don't say anything, you make people far more nervous and self-conscious and careful around you than if you do. People like me, we just rush into the vacuum of silence people like Helen float around in; we blather and dither and yakyakyak, and people like Helen just sit there and smile into the wind.

"Does she hate me?" I said to Richard after I first met Helen.

"Of course not," said Richard.

"Then why doesn't she ever say anything?" I asked.

"She's shy, that's all," said Richard.

"I don't think so," I said.

"You always underestimate how intimidating you are," said Richard.

"Bullshit," I said.

"He's wrong about Iran," Richard said after he first met Mark.

"Tell him," I said. "Don't talk to me about Iran. I couldn't care less."

"I tried to tell him," said Richard, "but it's very hard to interrupt a monologist."

"He's not a monologist," I said. "He just likes to talk. Some people like to talk."

"Leave Helen out of this," Richard said.

"I wasn't even thinking of Helen," I said.

"Bullshit," said Richard.

Then we all got married. It's hard when you don't like someone a friend marries. First of all, it means you pretty much have to confine your friendship to lunch, and I hate lunch. Second of all, it means that even a simple flat inquiry like "How's Helen?" is taken amiss, since your friend always thinks that what you hope he's going to say is "Dead." You feel irritated because your darling friend has married beneath himself, and he feels irritated because you don't see the virtues of his beloved. Then, if your friend's marriage fails, he becomes even more irritated at you, because if you had been a real friend, you would have prevented him physically from making the mistake, you would have locked him up in a closet until the urge to get married had passed. Of course, I tried that with Brenda, and it didn't work either. Long before we learned that Harry had pilfered the two-thousand-year-old-man routine from Mel Brooks, it was clear that he wasn't good enough for Brenda, and I made the mistake of telling her so. And when I turned out to be right, when they finally broke up after eight miserable years, was she grateful to me for tipping her off in the first place? No indeed. She slept with my husband Charlie, and as an extra bonus we all ended up with Harry's crabs.

I was dreading having to tell Richard about Mark and me; I could just imagine the look of smug satisfaction that would cross his face. But that wasn't what happened. What happened was that I finished my food demonstration and Richard swept me off to a dark bar and said, "I have to talk to you," and before I could even hold up my hand to indicate that I had to talk to him, too, he began.

"I had a vision that something horrible was wrong," said Richard. "And it is."

"A vision?" I said. It's not like Richard to talk of visions. Richard doesn't even like to hear about dreams.

"I went to have my hair cut yesterday," said Richard. "I was sitting there, trying to read the paper, and Melanie, who cuts my hair, was working away, and it suddenly crossed my mind to ask her how things were with her and Ray. She's been engaged to Ray for a couple of years. So I ask her. And she rolls her eyes. And she tells me he's fallen in love with someone else. He's come to her, he's told her he's in love with someone else, but he still wants to be friends. So she says to him, I don't want to be friends with you. And he says, why not? And she says, because you're a real shithead, that's why. Melanie looks at me and says,

'Can you believe it? Can you believe his nerve? You know what he says to me after that? He says, "You mean you're not even going to cut my hair anymore?" Can you dig this? The guy falls in love with someone else while he's engaged to me and he actually thinks I'm going to go on cutting his hair. Fuck him. What do I want with him if he wants to be such an asshole?' She rolls her eyes again, and she's snipping away, and suddenly I'm looking dead ahead into the mirror, and something weird starts to happen to me. Maybe a vision is putting it too strongly, but that's what it felt like. I thought to myself: Do not ask for whom the bell tolls, Richard Finkel, it tolls for you."

"Richard," I said, "what are you talking about?"

"I *knew*," said Richard. "At that moment I *knew*."

"You knew what?" I said.

"I knew Helen was in love with someone else."

"Helen," I said.

"My wife," said Richard. "Helen. Remember? The one you hate."

"I don't hate Helen," I said. "Helen hates me."

"It was suddenly clear," Richard said. "Helen was in love with someone else, and she was going to tell me about it, and there wasn't the remotest chance that when she did I was going to be as healthy and strong about it as this girl who cuts my hair."

"And *is* Helen in love with someone else?" I said.

"Yes," said Richard. "I came home and I told her about my vision, and when I got through, do you know what she said to me? She said, 'I think we'd better have a talk.'" Richard shook his head. "'I think we'd better have a talk' are the seven worst words in the English language."

"Helen is in love with someone else," I said.

"Yes," said Richard.

"That is really weird," I said.

"You don't know the half of it," said Richard.

"Yes I do," I said. "Ask me how Mark is."

"How's Mark?" said Richard.

"He's in love with someone else," I said.

"You're just saying that to make me feel better," said Richard.

"No I'm not," I said. "Mark has fallen in love with someone else, and he's treating me like an old beanbag."

"Oh, sweetie," said Richard, and he gave me a big hug. Then he ordered two more drinks. Doubles. Then he gave me another hug. One thing I have to say about marital crises is that people certainly do hug you a lot when you're going through them.

"Is it a boy or a girl?" said Richard.

"Is what a boy or a girl?" I said.

"The person Mark's fallen in love with," said Richard.

"I know you don't like Mark," I said, "but that is truly an absurd question."

"It's a girl, right?" said Richard.

"Right," I said.

"That's what Helen's fallen in love with, too," said Richard.

"Oh, sweetie," I said.

We looked at each other. It was a tricky moment. It's always a tricky moment when a friend tells you his marriage is in trouble: you have to be very careful what you say, in case he rides it out. This moment, however, was trickier than most. It would have been a terrible mistake, for example, for me to have said "Good riddance to bad rubbish" to Richard, although that's what I thought. It would have been an even bigger mistake for me to have introduced the word "dyke" into the conversation, but I didn't have to worry about that.

"Did you know she was a dyke?" said Richard.

"There's no way to tell if someone's a dyke," I said. "All sorts of attractive, feminine women are dykes. In fact, if anything, I would say that Helen isn't quite attractive enough to become one."

"That's not funny," said Richard.

"Yes it is," I said. "Anyway, she's not necessarily a dyke; she's just having a thing with a woman."

"I suppose you're going to tell me that it's normal and natural, and that all women have tendencies of that sort."

"No," I said, "but it's not as much of a stretch for women as it is for men. It's not that big a deal."

"It's a big deal if it's your wife," said Richard. "And I'll tell you the worst part of it. The worst part of it is that she's fallen in love with someone that I introduced her to. She's fallen in love with her secretary, and I got her the job."

"I'm not following you," I said.

"Joyce Raskin," said Richard. "The secretary. She used to work at Channel Thirteen, and she got laid off. I'd always liked her, and Helen was looking for a secretary, so I gave Joyce Helen's number and now she's sleeping with my wife."

"Well, don't blame Joyce," I said.

When my friend Brenda slept with my first husband, Charlie, I made that mistake—I blamed Brenda. It seemed quite unsurprising that

Charlie would betray me—he, after all, was a man, and men had been betraying me since the first grade. *But she was my friend!* She had been my friend since the day we'd met, when we were both five years old and standing on line for books in kindergarten; and I have never forgotten that moment because she turned around and I looked at her and decided she was the most beautiful thing I'd ever seen. Her flaxen hair came to her waist, her eyes were deep green, her skin was white as snow, just like a stupid fairy tale. I always hoped that Brenda would eventually lose her looks—my theory being that I would grow up and gain mine, she would lose hers, and we'd end up more or less even—but she never did. What made this worse when we were young was that every summer we went to camp together and performed as an act in the camp talent show, and she always got to be the girl and I always had to be the boy. I had been deeply and smolderingly resentful of Brenda for years simply because I so wanted to be the girl and never got to be, and the truth is that I was secretly pleased when she slept with Charlie because I was exonerated from the guilt of all those years of feeling jealous of her and was plunged suddenly into a warm bath of innocent victimization.

That's the catch about betrayal, of course: that it feels good, that there's something immensely pleasurable about moving from a complicated relationship which involves minor atrocities on both sides to a nice, neat, simple one where one person has done something so horrible and unforgivable that the other person is immediately absolved of all the low-grade sins of sloth, envy, gluttony, avarice, and I forget the other three.

It wasn't until years later, when the extent of the betrayal was finally revealed to me, that I realized how wrong I'd been to blame Brenda. Years later, Brenda, the creep, turned up at my father's wedding to her big sister and came up to me, dripping with earnest, weepy sincerity.

"I really hope we can be friends again," she said.

"I seriously doubt we're ever going to be," I said.

"But I miss you so much," said Brenda. She started to cry.

"Don't pull that on me," I said. "I didn't do anything to you, you did it to me. Remember?"

"Yes," said Brenda. "And I'll never forgive myself. Please forgive me."

Be reasonable, Rachel, I said to myself. This woman is now a relative. Are you never going to speak to her again because of one afternoon's indiscretion? Because of one afternoon your husband went out to buy lightbulbs and didn't?

"Please forgive me," Brenda went on. "If I could take back any week of my life, it would be that week in Florida."

That week in Florida! I couldn't believe it! Months before the afternoon of the lightbulbs, Brenda had been so forlorn about her marriage to Harry that Charlie and I had taken her along with us to the Pillsbury Bake-Off. To perk her up! Can you imagine? I had spent the week wandering through the Grand Ballroom of the Fontainebleau Hotel, judging the Sweet 'n Creamy crescent crisps, and now it turned out that Brenda and Charlie had spent the week watching X-rated movies on the pay TV upstairs and fucking like rabbits. There I was at my father's wedding reception, there was my father telling yet another worn-out anecdote about how he told Howard Hawks to stuff it, there was my new stepmother passing the guacamole, and I was in such a rage about that week in Florida I could hardly see straight. I wasn't angry at Brenda, you understand. I'd spent so many years being angry at Brenda that I didn't have the energy to be any angrier. It was Charlie I wanted to kill. I'll admit it was a delayed reaction, but I honestly wanted to call him up and tell him to go to hell and threaten never to see him again. Since I really hadn't seen him since our marriage ended five years earlier, this would have been a fairly empty gesture, but I still felt like making it. I was in a real mess with Mark, no question of that, but at least I knew whom to blame.

"Why shouldn't I blame Joyce?" Richard said to me. "She was my friend."

"But Helen is your wife," I said.

"But I never trusted Helen," said Richard. "She just used to sit there and drink her Tab, and I could never figure out what was going through her head."

"Well, now you know," I said.

"What's that supposed to mean?" said Richard.

"I don't know," I said, "but it was meant to make you feel better, not to make you mad."

"I'm sorry," said Richard. "Tell me about you and Mark."

We went out to the street. It was a clear October day, and we started walking uptown, arm in arm. When you're pregnant, it's especially nice to walk arm in arm with someone who's tall, because your stomach fits in so neatly. I told him about me and Mark and Thelma. By the time I got through, we had walked all the way from Macy's to Central Park, and when we got to the park, Richard kissed me. Richard kisses very nicely. So does Mark, but one of the things that happens in marriage is that the kissing stops. We walked over to the zoo, watched the Delacorte clock strike five, and sat down on a bench facing the seal pond. Richard kissed me again.

"I think I cooked too much for him," I said.

"You're crazy," said Richard.

"I think I was so entranced with being a couple that I didn't even notice that the person I thought I was a couple with thought he was a couple with someone else."

Richard put his hand on my stomach. It was hard and round as a basketball. "I think you should come home with me," he said.

I shook my head no.

"I mean it, Rachel," said Richard. "It'll be terrific. I've never slept with anyone who was seven months pregnant."

"I'm sure Helen will like it, too," I said.

"Helen moved out this morning," said Richard. "So you can move in if you want to. There's even room for the kids. I'm serious, Rachel. I once did a documentary on Lamaze, so I'm prepared to go into labor with you. We can go take a refresher course."

"I'm not big on Lamaze," I said.

"Then we can go take a class in anti-Lamaze," said Richard.

"But we're not in love," I said.

"How do you know?" said Richard.

"Because I'm still in love with Mark. And you're still in love with Helen. And we would just huddle together, two little cuckolds in a storm, with nothing to hold us together but the urge to punish the two of them for breaking our hearts."

"Marry me," said Richard. He stood up and said it again, loudly. "Marry me, Rachel."

There were a dozen people sitting on benches and wandering around the seal pond, and I could see them turning to watch.

"I mean it, Rachel," said Richard, very loudly now. "I want to marry you. I should have married you in the first place."

"Marry him, Rachel," shouted a young man sitting two benches away. "Give the kid a father."

There was a cheer from a couple on another bench, and scattered laughs.

"Richard, sit down," I said. "Please."

"Do you want to bring a child into the world under these circumstances?" he shouted. He was moving toward the seal pond now, and he jumped onto the parapet surrounding it. "I want to marry you and you want to marry me—you just aren't in touch with it. Marry me, Rachel. I'm constant. I'm immutable. I'm probably drunk, but I mean every word of this. When I say forever, I mean forever. And if you want me to sit down and stop shouting at you and making a public spectacle of myself, you'll have to say yes." There was a huge cheer from the spectators. "You hear this?" said Richard. "There's a groundswell of support here." He looked at me and raised both hands in the air in a victory salute. "Marry me," he shouted, "and you will never have to set foot in the city of Washington again. Marry me and you will never have to pretend you know the difference between Iran and Iraq. Marry me and you will never again have to listen to someone tell you who he thinks the next assistant foreign editor of the *Washington Post* is going to be." He tossed his head and smiled in what I'm sure he thought was an extremely handsome gesture. Then he turned around and leapt backward into the seal pond. There was a huge flapping of flippers as the seals who were lying on the rocks dove into the water. Everyone ran to the fence and watched as Richard swam several circles around the pond in a perfect Australian crawl and then pulled himself up to dry on the rocks. "Think it over," he shouted to me, and then fell backward in a mock collapse. About a minute later, he was arrested by the park police for disturbing the peace. He was extremely good-humored about it. They wrapped him up in a horse blanket and took him to the precinct in the park and wrote out a ticket and sent him home. I made him some eggs and put him to bed.

"Stay here," he said.

"No," I said.

"Where are you going?"

"To my father's for the night. I've missed the last plane."

"Rachel," said Richard, "it had nothing to do with how much you cooked for him. It had nothing to do with how much you wanted to be a couple. It had nothing to do with you."

"It must have had something to do with me," I said.

"Why?" said Richard.

"Because if it didn't, there's nothing I can do about it."

"That's my point," said Richard.

"I know that's your point," I said, "but I can't accept it."

"Well, if you ever do," said Richard, "you ought to do what I did. I feel much, much better."

"Are you suggesting I ask someone I'm not in love with to marry me and then jump into the seal pond?" I said.

"I'm suggesting that you make a wild and permanent gesture of size," said Richard, "and mine was to ask you to marry me and jump into the seal pond. Yours can be anything you want."

"The only wild and permanent gesture of size that has ever crossed my mind," I said, "is to have my hair cut."

"You'll think of something," said Richard. "And when you do, I'll be here." Then he smiled and fell asleep.

Eleven

The next morning, I flew back to Washington. I felt better; at least someone wanted to be married to me. It wasn't the person I was married to, but it was better than nothing. I took a cab home. Maybe he's missed me, I thought as we came around the corner. Maybe he's come to his senses. Maybe he's remembered he loves me. Maybe he's full of remorse. There was a police car parked in front of the house. Maybe he's dead, I thought. That wouldn't solve everything, but it would solve a few things. He wasn't, of course. They never are. When you want them to die, they never do.

Mark was sitting in the living room with two Washington policemen. The police were telling Mark how much they liked his column and drinking beer. It's always a shock to me that the police are willing to drink your beer. I spent so many years as a child watching Jack Webb turn down beer on *Dragnet* that I've come to believe it's practically insulting to offer a policeman even a cup of coffee. When I walked in, both policemen stood up, and one of them shook my hand and announced solemnly that he had come to return my diamond ring. There was a receipt, which I signed, and then he handed me a small brown envelope tied with string. I opened it. The ring was inside, wrapped in tissue, along with a letter from Detective Nolan. "Dear Ms. Samstat," it said, "I am sending this to Washington, as I understand from your therapist that you are living there again. We caught the perpetrator and he confessed, so it will not be necessary for you to appear in court. If you turn up in New York at any point, give me a call. I am bald now." There was a phone number and his name, Andrew Nolan. Andrew. Not a bad name. Andy. AndyAndyAndy. No, Andy. Please, Andy. Yes, Andy. Don't stop, Andy. I love you, Andy. I started to put the ring back on my finger, but the diamond was loose in the setting. A sign. I was sick and tired of signs. I showed it to Mark. He glared at me. Another sign.

The police left, and Sam came rushing downstairs, shouting, "Mommy, Mommy," and jumped into my lap.

"Thelma called yesterday," Mark said, "and she's very angry at you, and I am, too."

"Where were you, Mommy?" said Sam.

"New York City," I said, "but I'm back now."

"She had lunch with Betty yesterday," said Mark, "and Betty told her you said she had herpes."

"I never said herpes," I said.

"You must have said something," said Mark.

"I said she had an infection," I said.

"Well, she's furious at you," said Mark.

"*She's* furious at *me*," I said. "That's rich." All my life I had wanted to say "That's rich." Now I finally had gotten my chance. "That's really rich," I said. "Listen, you bastard. You tell Thelma that if she keeps calling here, I'll tell Betty she has the clap."

"Clap hands," said Sam, and clapped his together.

"I'll get it into 'The Ear,' too," I said. " 'What hopelessly tall and ungainly Washington hostess has a social disease, and we don't mean her usual climbing?' "

Mark stood up and strode out of the room and slammed the door behind him. I heard the car start, and he drove off.

I read Sam a story, but I could barely concentrate. When is this going to stop hurting? I wondered. How was I ever going to get through? There was one bright spot in my life, my child, and I couldn't even focus on him. I've been shot in the heart, I thought. I've been shot in the brain, I thought, and all I can come up with are clichés about being shot in the heart. I knew there were women who understood these things, who could walk around as if they were under water until the smoke cleared, who could keep their big mouths shut, who could even manage the delicate moment when they confronted their rivals at a dinner or the supermarket or the Saks Jandel winter clearance sale, but I clearly wasn't one of them. My mother once caught my father kissing someone at a party, and she never forgot it; every time she got tanked she brought it up. A mere kiss. What would she have done with a full-fledged love affair during a pregnancy?

I knew it wasn't Thelma's fault that any of this had happened. She was never my friend. We had never even had lunch! And I had long since ceased to believe in the existence of that mystical sisterly loyalty women are alleged to feel toward one another. But knowing all this, I nonetheless hated her with every swollen inch of my being. I hated her for turning Mark from the man I had fallen in love with into a cold, cruel stranger; it was almost as if he had become her mirror image, and was treating me the same way Thelma treated her husband Jonathan.

I could just imagine the next Washington evening all four of us were invited to. I could just imagine Thelma doing her gracious lady number, holding out her hand like the Queen of England ready to mend a fence with an unruly colonial nation, paying me a totally hypocritical compliment about the black *schmatta* I had been stuck wearing since my fifth month of pregnancy. "Oh, Rachel," she would say, "I always find that dress so very becoming." I wanted more than anything to be a good girl under those circumstances. To button my lip. To let one go by. I wanted more than anything to be the kind of cool and confident person who could treat her as if she were no more trouble to me than an old piece of chewing gum I had accidentally stepped in. But clearly I wasn't cut out to be that kind of person.

And what would happen if everyone found out? What would happen if this tacky little mess became common knowledge; what would happen when the four of us became that year's giggle, or gossip, or simply what Walter Winchell used to call a Dontinvitem? It was hard enough putting a marriage back together without becoming known publicly as a marriage-in-trouble; a marriage-in-trouble is welcomed with about as much warmth as cancer.

I took Sam into the kitchen and handed him over to Juanita. Then I went out the back door and over to Mark's office. The door to it was open, as I'd expected; he'd left the house in such a hurry he hadn't locked it. I sat down in his desk chair and opened the drawer and pulled out the file with the phone bills in it. It was all there, as I knew it would be: local phone calls that Mark had charged to our home number; long-distance calls to France in May; calls in August to Martha's Vineyard. I pulled out the American Express bills. (What did masochistic women do before the invention of the credit card?) I went through the receipts: the Marriott Hotel in Alexandria, the Plaza Hotel in New York, the Ritz-Carlton in Boston. And the flowers—so many flowers.

I felt like a character in a trashy novel; I even knew which trashy novel I felt like a character in, which made it worse: *The Best of Everything*. At least I wasn't going through the garbage, but that was only because it hadn't turned out to be necessary. The first flowers were sent in mid-March. Mid-March. I suddenly remembered: in mid-March, when the nuclear power plant at Three Mile Island overheated, I had become so worried about its blowing contaminated air in our direction that I had taken Sam with me to a food demonstration in Atlanta. For years, Mark had been haranguing me about my total lack of interest in politics, and finally I had got interested—so interested I had actually left town—and where had it got me? It had got me and Sam to Atlanta, and my husband and Thelma to bed. That would teach me to be political.

I put the papers back into the files and shut the drawer. Then I sat there, looking out the window. There was a newspaper open on the desk. I glanced down at it and realized that I hadn't seen that day's *Post*. I stared—it *wasn't* that day's *Post*. It was the Sunday real estate section. I felt a knot in my stomach, and lost my breath for a moment. I opened it to Houses—D.C. Mark had been through the section carefully. He had marked all the houses with four bedrooms or more in decent northwest Washington locations. I closed my eyes to stop the dizziness. So they were looking at houses. Well, why was I surprised? They were looking at blazers and couches; could houses be far behind? There were little scribbled notes next to a few of the listings. Addresses. Information about maids' rooms. One of the houses appeared to have a pool.

I went back to the kitchen and sat with Sam while he had lunch. I sang "The Itsy Bitsy Spider" fourteen times. Sam went up for his nap, and I borrowed Juanita's car. I drove to Cleveland Park, where the Rices lived. I drove past their house. The shades were drawn in front; it looked as if no one was home. I was about half a block past the house, thinking about tootling over to the Marriott Hotel in Alexandria and bursting in on them with a can of Raid, when I saw our car. I stopped short and backed up. Our car, definitely. I parked and got out and stood on the curb, staring into it. There was Sam's baby seat, strapped into the back. Sam's baby seat was always strapped into the back of the car, but somehow, at this moment, it seemed the ultimate obscenity—Mark's involving even the baby seat in his affair.

I walked up to the house and looked for signs of life. The Rices lived in a large wood house bordered by rhododendron and azalea bushes. I stepped onto the lawn and tried to see through a crack below a drawn window shade, but the bushes were in the way. I was trying to move quietly, but there were crunching leaves and twigs everywhere I stepped. Suddenly I tripped and fell. I realized I'd twisted my ankle, and for a moment I thought I'd strained my stomach muscles, but the pain went away. I looked to see what I'd tripped on and saw that it was a wire that surrounded the house. I began to follow it to see where it led, turned the corner, and gasped. There was a body lying face down on

the ground under a rhododendron bush. Jonathan Rice. Maybe he's
dead, I thought. It crossed my mind as his leg twitched that I had had
that thought twice in less than two hours about two completely different men, and I couldn't decide which of them I was more disappointed
to find out I was wrong about.

Jonathan was lying there wearing a set of earphones. He turned and
looked at me. He barely blinked. He took off the earphones and sat up.

"You really shouldn't have said that thing about the herpes, you
know," he said. "Thelma was very fond of you."

"But now she's not," I said.

"Now she's not," said Jonathan. "Now she's very angry. And they're
looking at houses. And they found something they like on Twenty-first
Street, but Thelma thinks they need five bedrooms and Mark thinks
they can make do with four."

I wondered who was handling the Middle East while Jonathan was
out spying in the bushes, but he had put on the earphones again, and
now he was shaking his head. "They're talking about buying it right
away and getting it all ready, and a few months after you have the baby
Mark and Thelma will move in. He thinks he can get joint custody."

I was having trouble breathing again, and I put my hand on my
stomach.

"What's the matter?" said Jonathan.

"I tripped on your wire," I said, "and I think I strained my stomach
muscles."

A few minutes later, as Jonathan was giving me the next bulletin—
something about how Mark and Thelma were going to finance the purchase with a bank loan, which Jonathan took as an occasion to lecture
me on rising interest rates—I had another pain.

"Jonathan," I said.

Jonathan put his fingers to his lips, as if something really cosmic were
going on in the house.

I pulled the earphones from his head.

"Jonathan," I said. "I'm in labor."

I don't remember very much. I remember that Jonathan sprang to his
feet and bounded into the house. I remember that Mark came out a few
minutes later. I remember the drive to the hospital: I accused Mark of
looking at houses; he accused me of snooping in places I didn't belong.
I remember the labor room, and my obstetrician suddenly appearing,

Marvin, my obstetrician, taking charge, being a professor, explaining my labor to a group of interns: the baby is in the transverse position and we can't risk waiting for it to turn itself, given the prematurity; another Caesarean is indicated. Are there any questions? One of the interns raised his hand. "I really enjoy your column," he said to Mark. The interns left. "Your husband can watch," Marvin said to me. "It really isn't allowed with Caesareans, but we'll sneak him into the delivery room." He was so pleased with himself, Marvin was, so pleased that he would be able to give this lovely couple he was on a first-name basis with the opportunity to share in the birth of their second child. Wrong couple, I wanted to say; that was last year's couple. This year things are different. This year my husband is a stranger. Do not let this stranger see me eviscerated.

The anesthetist put the needle into my back and I waited for the epidural to grab hold. Mark was standing next to me. One contraction. Two contractions. Three. Then the dullness, the easing off, the mermaid sensation. I watched the fetal monitor bleeping steadily as they wheeled me into the delivery room.

"Tell me about when Sam was born," I said to Mark.

He looked at me.

"Start where the doctor says there's something wrong," I said.

Mark nodded. "The doctor took me outside the labor room and said there was something wrong, they were losing the heartbeat. And we went back in and he told you the baby was in distress. And you said, 'Is our baby going to die?' "

I had heard this dozens of times.

Mark went on: "And he said, 'We're going to do an emergency Caesarean.' And they took you away. You were really brave. I was terrified. And I sat out in the waiting room, and the man sitting across from me was eating a sausage pizza. And fifteen minutes later the doctor came out, and took me into the delivery room, and there was Sam, making these funny little noises. They put him into my arms, and you woke up and you said, 'Is that our baby?' And I laid him down on you. And I lay down next to you."

I was crying.

"That was a great day," I said.

"Can you feel this?" said the doctor. The knife.

"Yes," I said. "A little."

I turned my head away from Mark. A nurse wiped my face and said, hold on, it's going to be all right. The pediatrician, our pediatrician, came into the delivery room. "If I am going to be your pediatrician," he had said when Sam was born, "we are going to have to understand something. You are never to call me and say, 'I'm sorry to bother you.' You are never to call me and say, 'This is probably nothing.' If you think it's worth a phone call, I want to hear about it. Got it?" Mark and I had sat there with our floppy little bundle. We were so proud—so proud of ourselves, of our baby, even of our pediatrician's patter. We marched into parenthood so full of hubris. We were on our second marriages; we had got the kinks out of the machinery; we would bring up our children in a poppy field of love and financial solvency and adequate household help. There would be guns for our daughters and dolls for our sons.

After Sam was born, I remember thinking that no one had ever told me how much I would love my child; now, of course, I realized something else no one tells you: that a child is a grenade. When you have a baby, you set off an explosion in your marriage, and when the dust settles, your marriage is different from what it was. Not better, necessarily; not worse, necessarily; but different. All those idiotically lyrical articles about sharing child-rearing duties never mention that, nor do they allude to something else that happens when a baby is born, which is that all the power struggles of the marriage have a new playing field. The baby wakes up in the middle of the night, and instead of jumping out of bed, you lie there thinking: Whose turn is it? If it's your turn, you have to get up; if it's his turn, then why is he still lying there asleep while you're awake wondering whose turn it is? Now it takes *two* parents to feed the child—one to do it and one to keep the one who does it company. Now it takes two parents to take the child to the doctor—one to do it and one to keep the one who does it from becoming resentful about having to do it. Now it takes two parents to fight over who gets to be the first person to introduce solids or the last person to notice the diaper has to be changed or the one who cares most about limiting sugar snacks or the one who cares least about conventional discipline.

No one ever tells you these things—not that we would have listened had anyone tried. We were so smart. We were so old. We were so happy. We had it knocked.

"Can you feel this?" the doctor said.

"No."

He was cutting now. Far, far away. A minute passed. Then two. Let the baby be okay, please let him be okay. I opened my eyes and saw a nurse crossing the room to the pediatrician. In her arms I could see the baby's wet head and spiky black hair. I could see an arm, such a skinny arm. Long skinny legs. *Move. Please move.* A flutter kick. A noise like a tiny cough. A tiny cry.

Nathaniel.

I closed my eyes.

He was fine, I could hear them saying that.

He's fine. He's going to be fine.

So. Nathaniel was early. I could hardly blame him. Something was dying inside me, and he had to get out.

Twelve

It was a complicated Caesarean, and there were complications. Nathaniel was on the eighth floor of the hospital, with tubes and monitors stuck all over his little froggy body, and I was on the fifth, with tubes and monitors all over mine. I lay in bed in a Percodan haze; I spent hours turning my marriage over in my mind. What had happened? What had gone wrong? *He was crazy.* I kept coming back to that. It was a simple enough answer, but accepting that answer meant accepting that I would never really know what had happened, accepting the mystery. I hate mystery, and I'm not the only one who does. Nature abhors a mystery too.

Vera flew to Washington. She spent a day with me in the hospital. She rubbed my head and listened while I floated trial balloons at her. I told her I thought I had spent too much time cooking and not enough time paying attention. I told her I thought that having a baby had changed our lives together. I told her I had been impatient and mean and snappish and irritable, and that it was no wonder Mark was drawn to someone who hadn't heard all his stories before and didn't shoot him a reproving look every time he uttered an opinion he had stolen from his best friend.

"All this may be true," Vera said, "but it isn't the point. The point is to figure out what you want."

"Maybe we just ran out of things to renovate," I said. "Maybe that was the problem. Maybe if we'd just gone on buying houses and fighting with contractors and arguing over whether to bleach the floor or stain it dark, we would have lived happily ever after."

"Did you hear me?" Vera said.

"I actually believed it was possible to have a good marriage," I said.

"It is possible," said Vera.

"No it's not," I said. "And don't tell me about your marriage, I don't want to hear about it. You got the last good one. For the rest of us, it's hopeless. I know that, but I never really get it. I go right on. I think to myself: I was wrong about the last one, but I'll try harder to be right about the next one."

"That's not the worst lesson to take through life," said Vera.

"But it doesn't work," I said. "It's kreplach. Remember?"

Vera looked at me, and her eyes filled with tears. She does this sometimes, especially when I'm being hateful and difficult; she responds by having all the feelings I'm refusing to have. Now she reached over and took my hand, and we both began to cry.

Mark came to the hospital every day. Every day except for Thelma's birthday. On Thelma's birthday, he called to say he had to go to New York for an interview. I know it was Thelma's birthday because Betty called the next day to tell me all about it. It seems that Jonathan Rice had planned a surprise birthday lunch for Thelma, and everyone gathered in the restaurant, ready to pop out from under the table when she arrived, but she never turned up.

"Can you imagine?" said Betty.

"I'm afraid I can," I said.

"I wish I could figure out who she's sleeping with," Betty said.

"It's probably Mark," I said.

Betty laughed. "Rachel, wait till I tell that to Mark," she said. "It'll kill him."

"I'll tell him myself," I said. "He just turned up."

"What was that about?" Mark said.

Stifle yourself, Rachel.

"Nothing," I said. "Just the Ladies' Central."

I got out of bed and into a wheelchair. Mark wheeled me and my intravenous equipment to the elevator and we went up to see the baby. We were lucky. I kept telling myself that. Nathaniel was on a floor with newborns who had real problems—there were blue babies, babies missing kidneys, babies with holes in their hearts—and there was nothing wrong with him except that he was small. He wasn't even the smallest. Still, he was ours, and he looked like a sack of bones. They'd shaved his head for the monitors, and there were tiny Band-Aids all over his body, taping the tubes here and there. We couldn't hold him. All we could do was reach in through the holes with our hexachlorophene-scrubbed hands and feed him, awkwardly propping up his floppy body by the neck. He had weighed four pounds when he was born. He was feeding well, catching up, but he was such a tiny thing. I waved a little red clown we'd put into the Isolette in front of his face. Maybe he saw it. Mark sang him a song. *Hush-a-bye, don't you cry, go to sleep-y, little baby.* I wondered where they had gone to celebrate her birthday. *When you wake you shall have all the pretty little horses.* I wondered what he had given her for her birthday. *Blacks and bays, dapples and grays, all the pretty little horses.* I wish I'd known it was Thelma's birthday; I would have sent her a present myself. *Hush-a-bye, don't you cry, go to sleep-y, little baby.* A garrote.

Arthur and Julie came to see me. One day while I was in the hospital, they discovered that their decorator had taken the four thousand dollars they had given him for furniture and spent it all on cocaine. The next day, their daughter was suspended from school for flushing six gerbils down the lavatory toilet. The next day, a bat moved into their kitchen. They brought me all of it, every day, and Julie rustled up a hairdresser to come wash my hair, and Arthur made rice pudding the day they took the tube out of my nose and I could eat bland food. Rice pudding is the only thing Arthur cooks, but he cooks it perfectly, with exactly the right proportion of rice to raisins. There's an awful lot of nursery food in this book already, so I won't give you the recipe. My feeling about rice pudding is that if you like it, you already have a good recipe; and if you don't, there's no way anyone will ever get you to eat it, unless you fall in love with someone who likes rice pudding, which I once did, and then you learn to love it, too.

My last day in the hospital, Marvin, my obstetrician, took out the stitches. Then he swiped an apple from a big basket of fruit Betty's boyfriend had sent me, and he sat down in a leatherette chair. I suspected he was going to ask if I was having a postpartum depression, but the last thing I wanted was for my obstetrician to know that in my case a postpartum depression would be superfluous. I am very fond of Marvin, even though he once asked me to endorse his book on premenstrual tension, but I wasn't up for a heart-to-heart talk with him.

"Do you believe in love?" said my obstetrician.

This is what I get for calling him by his first name, I thought. This is the price I pay for insisting that if he's going to call me by my first name I get to call him by his. Do I ask him if he gets turned on sticking his hands into ladies' pussies? Do I ask him if he gets off feeling their breasts for lumps?

"What?" I said.

"Do you believe in love?" he said.

Sometimes I believe that love dies but hope springs eternal. Sometimes I believe that hope dies but love springs eternal. Sometimes I believe that sex plus guilt equals love, and sometimes I believe that sex plus guilt equals good sex. Sometimes I believe that love is as natural as the tides, and sometimes I believe that love is an act of will. Sometimes I believe that some people are better at love than others, and sometimes I believe that everyone is faking it. Sometimes I believe that love is essential, and sometimes I believe that the only reason love is essential is that otherwise you spend all your time looking for it.

"Yes," I said. "I do."

I went home.

Nathaniel stayed in the hospital.

Both of us got stronger.

I behaved myself.

I said very little.

I attempted to follow the budget debate.

I went to a dinner party and held up my end.

They took Nathaniel out of the Isolette and I could hold him and feed him.

I read Sam a lot of stories about baby brothers.

I did not say, how are you, how are we, do you still love her, do you love me at all, are you still thinking of buying a house with her, what did you get her for her birthday, is it over with her, is it ever going to be over.

Two weeks passed.

Betty called. She asked if we wanted to come to dinner. "We have lobsters," she said. "You bring dessert. Bring one of your Key lime pies."

Thirteen

If I had it to do over again, I would have made a different kind of pie. The pie I threw at Mark made a terrific mess, but a blueberry pie would have been even better, since it would have permanently ruined his new blazer, the one he bought with Thelma. But Betty said bring a Key lime pie, so I did. The Key lime pie is very simple to make. First you line a 9-inch pie plate with a graham cracker crust. Then beat 6 egg yolks. Add 1 cup lime juice (even bottled lime juice will do), two 14-ounce cans sweetened condensed milk, and 1 tablespoon grated lime rind. Pour into the pie shell and freeze. Remove from freezer and spread with whipped cream. Let sit five minutes before serving.

I realize now that I should have thrown the pie (or at least done the thinking that led to the throwing of the pie) several weeks earlier than I did, but it's very hard to throw a pie at someone when you're pregnant, because you feel so vulnerable. Also, let's face it, I wasn't ready to throw the pie. I should add that the pie was hardly the first thing I'd thought of throwing at Mark, but every other time I'd wanted to throw something at him, I couldn't bring myself to do it. Once, for example, right after I found out about him and Thelma, I'd been seized by a violent impulse, but the only thing I could see to throw at the time was a signed Thonet chair, and I am far too bourgeois to throw a signed Thonet anything at anyone. Some time later, especially while I was in the hospital, I gave considerable thought to smashing Mark's head in with a very good frying pan I had bought at the Bridge kitchenware company, but I always knew I would never do anything of the sort, and in any case, smashing your husband's head in with a frying pan seems slightly too fraught with feminist content, if you know what I mean.

(Even now, I wonder if I would have thrown the pie had we been eating in Betty's dining room. Probably not. On the floor in Betty's dining room is a beautiful Oriental rug, and I would have been far too concerned about staining it. Fortunately, though, we were eating in the kitchen, and the kitchen has a linoleum floor. That's how bourgeois I am: at the split second I picked up the pie to throw it at Mark, at the split second I was about to do the bravest—albeit the most derivative—thing I had ever done in my life, I thought to myself: Thank God the floor is linoleum and can be wiped up.)

On Saturday afternoon, after Betty called, I went out for a walk to buy the pie ingredients. I took Sam with me. We had a long talk about how Nathaniel would be coming home from the hospital on Monday, and how much Sam was going to love him, and how he was going to feed him some delicious spiders. We bought the food at Neam's. It was a beautiful day, so we decided to walk down to the toy store on M Street. On the way we passed the jewelry store where Mark had bought me the diamond ring, and I remembered that I hadn't yet taken it in to have it fixed. It was in a little envelope in my purse.

I could see Leo Rothman, the owner, sitting on a stool behind the counter—Leo, the dear, white-haired man who had marched with the Abraham Lincoln Brigade in the thirties and been thrown out of the Labor Department in the forties and was now a millionaire jeweler who buzzed only white people through his electronically operated door. He buzzed me in and gave me a big kiss. When Mark was courting me, when he was pursuing me with flowers and balloons and jewels, Leo was the man Mark bought the jewels from, and as a result Leo felt almost proprietary about our marriage: he had outfitted the courtship, the wedding, the birth of the first child, the first child's silver spoon; and he didn't seem to mind that except for the diamond ring, none of Mark's purchases had amounted to more than a few hundred dollars.

I told Leo about the robbery, and he said it would take just a minute to reset the stone. Sam and I waited while he got out his instruments and went to work. We were making conversation. Chitchat. Nothing much. He said did I know the diamond in the ring was a perfect stone. I said Mark had told me that. He said it wasn't the kind of diamond I'd ever have trouble selling if I ever wanted to—he had told Mark he'd be glad to buy it back for what Mark had paid for it. I said I was glad to hear that. He asked me how I liked the necklace. The necklace, I said. Leo looked up, and the loup dropped from his eye. "I must be thinking of another customer," he said.

"No you're not," I said. "I knew Mark had bought something while I was in the hospital." So he had bought her a necklace for her birthday. I was lying in the hospital with a tube up my nose and he had bought her a necklace. "That rascal," I said.

"I shouldn't have said anything," Leo said.

"I'm glad you did," I said. "Now I know what to be prepared for. There's nothing worse than opening a box with a necklace in it when you're not in the mood for a necklace." I kept talking, I couldn't stop. "Once," I said, "I was in the mood for a nightgown, and Mark kept dropping hints about what he'd gotten me for my birthday, and finally

I said, 'I don't care what it is as long as it's not a suitcase,' and it was a suitcase. Was my face red." Leo was focused on the ring again; I'd bored him so thoroughly he barely grunted a response. He finished resetting the stone and handed the ring back to me. It was such a beautiful ring. The diamond caught the afternoon sun and made a rainbow on the wall of the store. Sam ran to the reflection, and I waved the ring this way and that, moving the rainbow while he giggled and leapt and tried to catch it in his hands.

"How much?" I said.

"No charge," Leo said.

"How much for the ring?" I said. "How much would you give me for the ring?"

Leo looked at me.

"You don't really want to sell it," he said.

"I really want to sell it," I said. "Do you really want to buy it?"

"Of course," he said.

"I love the ring, Leo," I said, "but it really doesn't go with my life. It would never have been stolen in the first place if I hadn't been wearing it on the subway, and if you've got a ring you can't wear on the subway, what's the point of having it? It's sort of like a mink coat. If I had a mink coat, I'd have to take cabs every time I was in New York, and the next thing you know we'd be even broker than we are now. Mark's so romantic, he probably spent every penny of his savings on the necklace."

Leo nodded. "For the down payment," he said.

"For the down payment," I said.

"It's a beautiful necklace," said Leo.

"Now I'll have a necklace I won't be able to wear on the subway either," I said. "How much for the ring?"

"Fifteen thousand," Leo said.

"Fifteen thousand," I said.

"That's what Mark paid for it," Leo said.

Right after my mother left my father and ran off to New Mexico with Mel, my father gave me some money. It was quite unexpected. I had gone over to visit him—I was married to Charlie at the time—and in the middle of a long and rather sentimental conversation about how termites had once eaten the entire garage door of our house in Beverly Hills one Sunday when we weren't looking, my father whipped out his checkbook and wrote me a check for three thousand dollars. "But why?" I said, hoping he wouldn't notice I had snatched it from his hands and stuffed it into my back pocket. "Because you're a good girl," said my father. I put my hand over the pocket, as if the check were going to fly right out and back into the checkbook and erase itself. I could feel the paper through the cloth; I kept running my finger over the outside of the pocket and feeling the check crinkle inside. My heart started to pound: I realized I had just been given the means to walk out of my marriage.

"Fifteen thousand it is," I said to Leo. Ten years had passed; the cost of walking out of a marriage had gone up.

I went home with Leo's check and made the pie. I was in a trance. Well, perhaps it wasn't a trance, but it was as close to a trance as I'll ever get: I was speechless. I said nothing—nothing at all—for several hours. At eight, Mark and I took the pie to Betty's. It was just us—me, Mark, Betty, and Dmitri, whom Betty lives with. Dmitri used to be the Yugoslavian ambassador to the United States. When his tour ended, he went back to Belgrade and opened a chain of laundromats. Then he moved back to Washington and went into high-priced sherbet. Mark always used to throw Dmitri in my face as an example of someone who managed to be interested in food and politics simultaneously, but the truth is that what Dmitri was really interested in was money; to the extent that he was at all political, it lay in his understanding that in a socialist country you can get rich by providing necessities, while in a capitalist country you can get rich by providing luxuries. Dmitri is the most good-natured man I have ever known, which infuriates Betty, which makes Dmitri laugh, which makes Betty laugh. They seem very happy together. Not that you can tell. Look at all the people who thought Mark and I were happy. Me included.

When we got to Betty's, Mark and Dmitri went into the kitchen to boil the lobsters, and Betty and I sat in the living room while Betty talked about the dance she and Thelma and I were apparently giving. Apparently we were giving it at the Sulgrave Club. Apparently the crepe man had already been booked. Apparently all that was lacking was my guest list: Thelma and Betty had already drawn up theirs. Apparently the Kissingers were on Thelma's list, just as I'd predicted. I sat and listened and drank an entire bottle of white wine as Betty went on and on, and by the time I got to dinner, I was tipsy. We ate the lobsters. I don't remember the conversation. I do remember realizing that no one seemed to be noticing that I hadn't said anything the entire evening, and that no one seemed to mind. I must try this again, I thought; I must try again someday to sit still and not say a word. Maybe when I'm dead.

After the lobsters, I took the Key lime pie out of the freezer and put the whipped cream on it and sat it in front of me. I was going to give it five minutes to thaw slightly (see recipe). And that's when Betty turned to me and said, "Rachel, you didn't tell me about Richard and Helen!"

"What about Richard and Helen?" said Mark.

"They're getting a divorce," said Betty. "I bumped into him this week in New York."

"I always hated that woman," said Mark.

"I sort of liked her," said Dmitri.

"When did you meet her?" said Betty.

"Here," said Dmitri. "Rachel and Mark brought them over one night. No one else would talk to her, so I did. She wasn't so bad."

"You're the only person on this earth who's ever found anything even halfway nice to say about her," said Betty.

"I did think she was a dyke," said Dmitri.

"That makes me so furious!" Betty screamed. "Why didn't you tell me?"

"I did tell you," said Dmitri, "and you said, 'Don't be ridiculous.'"

"Goddammit," said Betty.

"Why are you angry at Dmitri?" said Mark.

"Because she *is* a dyke," said Betty.

"No shit," said Mark.

"And if Dmitri wasn't so good-natured about everything, he would have put it more forcefully, and I might have believed him, and then none of this would have come as a surprise to me." She glared at Dmitri. "I hate surprises," she said.

Dmitri stood up to go make the coffee and on his way he kissed Betty on the neck. "Don't try to make up to me," said Betty. She was smiling.

"Helen's a dyke?" said Mark.

"She left Richard for her secretary," said Betty.

"Did you know this, Rachel?" said Mark.

I nodded.

"I couldn't get over it," said Betty. "I kept thinking about it on the shuttle on the way home. How could you know someone for that long . . . how long have they been together?"

"As long as Rachel and I have," said Mark.

"Exactly," said Betty. "How could you be with someone that long, be *married* to them, and not know?"

"He has to have known," said Dmitri. "*I* knew."

"He says he didn't know," said Betty. "But how could he not? How could you be married to someone and not know something like that?"

"Maybe it wasn't true when he first met her," said Dmitri.

"Of course it was true," said Betty. "You don't just become a dyke, bang, like that."

"Sure you do," said Dmitri. "It's like being allergic to strawberries. You eat strawberries all your life and then one day, bang, you get hives."

"Don't be ridiculous," said Betty.

"The last time you said 'Don't be ridiculous' to me, I was trying to tell you that Richard's wife was a dyke," said Dmitri.

"And now you're trying to tell me she was merely an incipient dyke," said Betty. "Which is it?"

"I have no idea," said Dmitri. "I'm just trying to drive you crazy." He kissed her again.

"I don't believe people change that much," said Betty. "And don't tell me they do, Rachel. Don't give me that New York psychological bullshit about how people are capable of it. They aren't. Which brings me back to my question: How is it possible to be married to someone and not know something so fundamental?"

I was starting to get dizzy.

Perhaps I ought to say something, I thought. Either that or I'm going to fall into the pie. Perhaps I ought to say that it *is* possible. I could hear Mark changing the subject. He was saying something about Zbigniew Brzezinski. Perhaps I ought to say that you can love someone—or want to love someone—so much that you don't see anything at all. You decide to love him, you decide to trust him, you're in the marriage, in the day-to-dayness of the marriage, and you kind of notice that things aren't what they were, but it's a distant bell, it's through a filter. And then when something does turn out to be wrong, it isn't that you knew all along, it's that you were somewhere else.

"He must have been living in a dream," said Betty. She stood up to get the coffee cups. Mark and Dmitri were discussing détente.

In a dream. I suppose so. And then the dream breaks into a million tiny pieces. The dream dies. Which leaves you with a choice: you can settle for reality, or you can go off, like a fool, and dream another dream.

I looked across the table at Mark. I still love you, I thought. I still look at that dopey face of yours, with that silly striped beard, and think you are the handsomest man I've ever known. I still find you interesting, even if right now you are being more boring than the Martin Agronsky show. But someday I won't anymore. And in the meantime, I'm getting out. I am no beauty, and I'm getting on in years, and I have just about enough money to last me sixty days, and I am terrified of being alone, and I can't bear the idea of divorce, but I would rather die than sit here and pretend it's okay, I would rather die than sit here figuring out how to get you to love me again, I would rather die than spend five more minutes going through your drawers and wondering where you are and anticipating the next betrayal and worrying about whether my poor, beat-up, middle-aged body with its Caesarean scars will ever turn you on again. I can't stand feeling sorry for myself. I can't stand feeling like a victim. I can't stand hoping against hope. I can't stand sitting here with all this rage turning to hurt and then to tears. I CAN'T STAND NOT TALKING!

I looked at the pie sitting right there in front of me and suddenly it began to throb. They were talking about the State Department now. If I throw this pie at him, I thought to myself, he will never love me. And then it hit me: he *doesn't* love me. It hit me with a shimmering clarity: that was all there was to it. It didn't matter if he was crazy. It didn't matter if I was innocent or guilty. Nothing mattered except that he didn't love me. *If I throw this pie at him, he will never love me. But he doesn't love me anyway. So I can throw the pie if I want to.* I picked up the pie, thanked God for the linoleum floor, and threw it. It landed mostly on the right side of Mark's face, but that was good enough. The cream and the lime filling clung to his beard and his nose and his eyelashes, and pieces of crust dropped onto his blazer. I started to laugh. Mark started to laugh, too; I must say he handled it very well. He laughed as if all this were part of a running joke we'd forgotten to let Betty and Dmitri in on. He wiped himself off. He said, "I think it's time for us to go home." He stood up. So did I. I turned to Betty, who was staring wide-eyed at the two of us. "By the way," I said, "I'm not coming to the dance." And we went home.

Of course I'm writing this later, much much later, and it worries me that I've done what I usually do—hidden the anger, covered the pain, pretended it wasn't there for the sake of the story. "Why do you feel you have to turn everything into a story?" Vera once asked me. I remember when she asked me, in fact. It was right after my marriage to Charlie broke up, and I was living in an apartment where everything made into something else—the couch made into a bed, the coffee table made into a dining table, the end table made into a stool. "How are you?" people would ask me, in that intimate way people asked the question in those days. How *are* you. I couldn't bear it. So I told them about my apartment where everything made into something else. Then a friend called and said, "I have one piece of advice for you. I give it to all my friends whose marriages break up: Don't buy anything at Azuma." I added that to my repertoire.

Vera said: "Why do you feel you have to turn everything into a story?"

So I told her why:

Because if I tell the story, I control the version.

Because if I tell the story, I can make you laugh, and I would rather have you laugh at me than feel sorry for me.

Because if I tell the story, it doesn't hurt as much.

Because if I tell the story, I can get on with it.

My last day in Washington I read the Sunday papers. I made French toast for Sam. I went to the hospital to see Nathaniel. I asked the pediatrician if Nathaniel could go to New York when he got out of the hospital the next day. The pediatrician said he could if he took the train. I called Nathaniel's baby nurse and told her we would be going to New York on the train the next day. I called Richard in New York and told him we would be moving in for a few weeks, until I found an apartment. I came home and started dinner. I made a bouillabaisse, and crème brulée, and in between there was a salad. I taught Mark to make the vinaigrette. Mix 2 tablespoons Grey Poupon mustard with 2 tablespoons good red wine vinegar. Then, whisking constantly with a fork, slowly add 6 tablespoons olive oil, until the vinaigrette is thick and creamy; this makes a very strong vinaigrette that's perfect for salad greens like arugola and watercress and endive.

We got into bed and Mark put his arms around me. "That was a lovely evening," he said. He fell asleep. I lay there. Two years earlier, when I had been pregnant with Sam, Mark would sing me a song every night and every morning. We called it the Petunia song. It was a dumb song, really dumb. Mark would make up a different tune and lyrics each time, but it never rhymed, and it was never remotely melodious. *I sing to you, Petunia, I sing a song of love, I sing to you even though you are bigger than the last time I sang the Petunia song to you.* Something like that. Or: *Oh, Petunia, I sing to thee, even though it's much too early and I have a hangover.* You get the idea. Really dumb, but every time Mark sang it, I felt secure and loved in a way I had never dreamed possible. I had always meant to write down some of the words, because they were so silly and funny and made me feel so happy; but I never did. And now I couldn't remember them. I could remember the feeling, but I couldn't really remember the words.

Which was not the worst way to begin to forget.

RECIPE INDEX

—May 1983

✳ *The Playwright*

Lucky Guy

A Play in Two Acts

CHARACTERS

MIKE McALARY, a columnist
JOHN COTTER, an editor
MICHAEL DALY, a columnist
JIM DWYER, a columnist
HAP HAIRSTON, an editor
EDDIE HAYES, a lawyer
ALICE McALARY, a housewife
LOUISE IMERMAN, a reporter
DEBBY KRENEK, an editor
BOB DRURY, a reporter
JERRY NACHMAN, an editor
STANLEY JOYCE, an editor
JOHN MILLER, deputy commissioner for public information, NYPD
ABNER LOUIMA, a security guard

The ensemble also plays other parts: JIMMY BRESLIN, DINO
TORTORICI, BRIAN O'REGAN, miscellaneous REPORTERS, a DOCTOR.

ON STAGE RIGHT, THE MAKINGS OF
    A bar—sometimes the bar is Elaine's, sometimes it's Ryan's,
    sometimes it's McGuire's, or the Lion's Head, sometimes it's
    just a bar. A neon sign indicates which bar it is. A couple of
    chairs, a table or two, the bar itself, possibly a couple of bar
    stools. A small TV over the bar.

ON STAGE LEFT, THE MAKINGS OF
    A newsroom—sometimes the newsroom is Newsday, *sometimes*
    the New York Daily News, *sometimes the* New York Post.

*A projection of the logo on the back wall tells us which
newsroom. A few chairs, desks, tables, computer terminals,
just enough to indicate where we are. A small TV on the
editor's desk. A big* NO SMOKING *sign.*

LATER IN THE PLAY WE'LL NEED:
  *A bedroom—sometimes in Brooklyn, sometimes in Bellport.
    The beds become more well-appointed as the play progresses.
  A kitchen—first in Brooklyn with an old table and chairs and an
    old refrigerator, then in Bellport with a new table, chairs, and
    a sub-zero refrigerator.
  A diner.
  A white porch in Bellport.
  A podium.
  Various offices—a doctor's, a police department official's.
  A hospital room.
  The sets are minimal. A lot of black and white.
  In some abstract way, the play should feel like an homage to
    an old newspaper movie like* Deadline–U.S.A. *Stagehands
    move the set dressing in and out during the action, which is
    continuous. The play should be lit like a noir movie, with
    sharp contrast, overhead spots, etc.*

ACT I

A Bar

*An ensemble of about eight men at the bar. They will play
the male parts. Among them are the journalists* MIKE
McALARY, JIM DWYER, HAP HAIRSTON, MICHAEL DALY, JERRY
NACHMAN, BOB DRURY, *and* JOHN COTTER. HAIRSTON *is
black. They sing an Irish song:*
THE ENSEMBLE: *(Sings.)*
  I've been a wild rover for many's the year,
  I've spent all me money on whiskey and beer,
  But now I'm returning with gold in great store,
  And I never will play the wild rover no more.
  And it's no, nay, never,

No nay never no more,
Will I play the wild rover,
No never no more.
I went to an alehouse I used to frequent
And I told the landlady me money was spent.
I asked her for credit she answered me 'Nay'
Such custom as you I can have any day
And it's no, nay, never,
No nay never no more,
Will I play the wild rover,
No never no more.

JIM DWYER: So the question is, where to begin?

BOB DRURY: Always hard to know where the story begins.

MICHAEL DALY: Although we know how it ends.

JIM DWYER: This is a true story—

HAP HAIRSTON: To the extent that any story is true—

JERRY NACHMAN: Yeah, yeah, yeah.

HAP HAIRSTON: It begins before. Before he became—

JIM DWYER: —famous—

BOB DRURY: —a columnist—

JERRY NACHMAN: —reckless—

HAP HAIRSTON: —bad—

MICHAEL DALY: —before he became Mike McAlary—

JERRY NACHMAN: —with his picture on the side of the truck.

JIM DWYER: But even before, we all talked about him when he wasn't there, way more than we ever talked about anybody else—

MICHAEL DALY: Because we all knew it was going to be a fucking mess someday.

HAP HAIRSTON: Messy, messy story, nothing neat about this story. So it starts in 1985. New York City is totally polarized. Rich, poor. Black, white. The crack epidemic is just beginning. The murder rate is rising. The city is a shithole. It was a grand and glorious time to be in the tabloid business. *(Holds up a copy of the* New York Times.) This is the *New York Times*. This is a serious newspaper. Fuck it. (HAIRSTON *holds up a copy of the* Daily News, *by way of illustration.)* This is a tabloid. Small paper. Big headline. High energy. Blood, guts, dirt, fires, floods. Champion of da people. *(Beat.)* New York City is a tabloid town—lots of newsstands, a working class that rides the subway—and in 1985 it had two scrappy tabloids, the *Post* and the *News*. But in 1985,

Newsday, out on Long Island, decided to move into the city and start a third tabloid. They lost a hundred million bucks in the process but that took five years. *(Beat.)*
    Stagehands and actors carry in desks, computers, a very small television set, transforming the space into the—

Newsday *Newsroom*

HAP HAIRSTON: *(To audience.)* Meanwhile we were hiring people left and right. *(Identifying himself.)* Hap Hairston, city editor.

JIM DWYER: Jim Dwyer. I was writing a column.

JOHN COTTER: John Cotter. Managing editor—

HAP HAIRSTON: Cotter is drunk.

JOHN COTTER: We're rocking.

JIM DWYER: He was drunk twenty-four hours a day.

JOHN COTTER: Where's my nun-rape? Who's got the subway slasher? I need the red meat. More red meat.

JERRY NACHMAN: If you held the guy up to the light, you could see the olive.

JOHN COTTER: *(Singling out a reporter's story.)* Ahhh, Red Meat!

HAP HAIRSTON: *(To the rest of the ensemble.)* The rest of you can stay at the bar. We got good cops, bad cops, reporters, columnists, criminals—

    We see MIKE McALARY *now. A tall, handsome guy with a mustache.*

McALARY: What about me?

HAP HAIRSTON: We're working up to you.

McALARY: McAlary. It's my story. McAlary. Mike McAlary. Zealous, hard-working, true-blue. Police reporter.

HAP HAIRSTON: I'm setting it up, okay?

McALARY: All I ever wanted to be was a reporter in New York City. You get to be at the center of everything that's happening that day. A plane crash on Bergen Street in Brooklyn. You see it. The Stones arrive, you're there. Whatever's happening, you go out, you get it, and write it, and millions of people read it. And then you get to go sit in the bar and tell everyone the stuff that the lawyers didn't let you put in the paper. And, most important of all, the next day you get to go out and do it all over again, except everything is new.

HAP HAIRSTON: McAlary—

McALARY: —you are God's fucking messenger—

HAP HAIRSTON: Relax.

MCALARY: It's New York City, who can relax? Are you relaxed?—

HAP HAIRSTON: Just let me set the fucking thing up. Louise.

MCALARY: Why do you need Louise?

HAP HAIRSTON: In my story, Louise is a character.

> LOUISE IMERMAN *enters, but just barely.*

LOUISE IMERMAN: McAlary's right. You don't really need me. *(To audience.)* This is a story about guys, guys with cops, cops with guys. It's a very guy thing. *(To* HAP *and the ensemble.)* The reason they were all hung up on McAlary is he made them think they could go back to the days when there were no women around, none, just Irish guys at the bar all night long. You don't need me at all.

HAP HAIRSTON: *(Prompting her.)* So—

LOUISE IMERMAN: *(With feeling.)* —Kiss my ass.

HAP HAIRSTON: And—

LOUISE IMERMAN: *(With feeling.)* —Fuck you.

HAP HAIRSTON: That's it. *(To audience.)* That's Louise.

> *She sits down at a desk.*

Smoke.

> *Everyone lights cigarettes and picks up the phones.*

More smoke.

> *A stagehand brings in a smoke machine and turns it on.*
>
> *A cacophony of phones ringing, editors and reporters shouting back and forth as* MCALARY *leaves the bar and works his way into the newsroom.*
>
> *Reporters and editors overlapping:*

JOHN COTTER: Who's at City Hall?

JIM DWYER: Koch is meeting with the Lubavitchers in Williamsburg.

HAP HAIRSTON: Dwyer, Vinnie's on three. He's got a jumper at Twenty-ninth and Park.

REPORTER #1: Donald Trump is opening his hotel.

HALF THE REPORTERS: Fuck him.

THE OTHER HALF: Who cares!

JOHN COTTER: Got two dead in a bodega robbery—

HAP HAIRSTON: I'm sending Tommy.

JOHN COTTER: —and a riot at Rikers.

> MIKE MCALARY *reaches* HAP *at the City Desk, stands there.* HAP *is on the phone.*

MCALARY: Did you see my piece?

HAP HAIRSTON: *(To* MCALARY.*)* I don't have time for you. *(Shouting over to* LOUISE.*)* Louise, what are you doing?

LOUISE IMERMAN: *(Shouting back.)* Who the fuck wants to know?

McALARY: About the hospital in Flushing. Did you read it?

HAP HAIRSTON: *(To McALARY.)* You're lurking. Stop lurking.

McALARY: *(To HAIRSTON.)* Could you even find it on page forty-eight, next to the Word Jumble? I deserve better.

JIM DWYER: *(To audience.)* Mac was good. He was hungry. He'd been a sportswriter at the *New York Post*, spent a couple of years covering the Yankees, driving George Steinbrenner crazy.

McALARY: I drove him nuts. I may have shortened his life.

JIM DWYER: *(To audience.)* They thought maybe he would make a police reporter. And they brought in Bob Drury—

McALARY: We'd both covered sports at the *Post*.

BOB DRURY, *a tall, good-looking reporter, at his computer.*

BOB DRURY: *(To audience.)* We both took pay cuts to come here.

McALARY: Anything to get out of sports.

BOB DRURY: Anything to keep from spending our lives wearing plaid jackets interviewing a bunch of fucking morons.

JIM DWYER: *(To audience.)* McAlary was a rookie, so they sent him out to Queens—

BOB DRURY: To the middle of nowhere, to be a neighborhood reporter.

JIM DWYER: *(To audience.)* He was miserable out there—

McALARY: *(To audience.)* —covering the borough president's office and school board demonstrations and tertiary sewage treatment facilities. *(To HAP.)* I do not belong in the outer boroughs. I belong here!

JIM DWYER: At five o'clock on Fridays, he'd come in from Rego Park and do this thing we called "Desk Hawking."

McALARY *pops up into* HAP HAIRSTON's *eye line, index fingers pointing toward himself.*

McALARY: Hey, Hap.

HAP HAIRSTON: *(Not looking at him.)* I see you, McAlary. *(To a reporter in the newsroom.)* When am I getting that gas explosion?

BOB DRURY: In ten—

HAP HAIRSTON: *(to DRURY)* Is this a weekly?

McALARY: I am here. Just want to say that—

HAP HAIRSTON: I need it. I need it now—

BOB DRURY: All right—

McALARY: —Just in case something comes up I am right here, doing nothing. Ready to go to work—

HAP HAIRSTON: McAlary, go sit down or I'll send you to cover the Board of Estimates.

MCALARY: I don't have a desk.

HAP HAIRSTON: You have a desk. You have a desk in Queens.

MCALARY: *(Hamming.)* Please, Mr. Hairston, don't send me back to Queens.

HAP HAIRSTON: Sit down somewhere. Find a chair as far away from me as possible and sit in it.

> MCALARY *sits down at someone else's desk. His leg jiggles. He tries to catch* HAIRSTON's *eye.* HAIRSTON *won't look at him.* MCALARY *stands up.*

Sit down, you dickhead.

> MCALARY *sits down. Starts jiggling.*

(To audience.) Late one Friday night, people all over the country started dropping dead from cyanide in poisoned Tylenol. Including some nineteen-year-old girl in Yonkers, which made it local.

MCALARY: Which made it local.

HAP HAIRSTON: I wanted to send someone to see the family. I asked three or four of the solid prima donna types, but they were all giving birth to kids, or their mothers had just died, every excuse you could think of not to end up on something that might kill the weekend.

LOUISE IMERMAN: Fuck you, kiss my fucking ass, I have plans. It's Friday. Did you ever fucking hear of Friday?

> HAP *looks around.*
> MCALARY *is standing, pointing to himself with both index fingers.*

HAP HAIRSTON: Okay, go. *(To audience.)* He raced up there and managed to get an interview with the boyfriend of the victim, which nobody else got because they all went home. McAlary sat in front of the guy's house until two in the morning and got him to talk.

The Stoop

> MCALARY *talking to a young man,* DINO TORTORICI. MCALARY *has his notebook out, as he does during all interviews.*

MCALARY: Dino, Mike McAlary, *Newsday.* I don't want to bother you. I just want to check what I've got against what really happened so it's accurate. *(To the audience, by way of explanation.)* I didn't really have anything, but you always pretend you do, that you're going to write it whether they talk to you or not— *(Back to the interview.)* You probably spent the day answering questions with the cops— *(To audience.)* What you're saying is, you're not a cop, you're a friend, you feel for them . . . which you do, most of the time. *(Back to the interview.)* You're exhausted and upset, I get that. But you're going to want all of this to be right. Otherwise the wrong stuff gets printed and it's there forever. *(To audience.)* See, the guy has no control whatsoever over whatever fucking nightmare just happened, but you're saying if you work with me, you can have some control— *(Back to the interview.)* Okay?

TORTORICI *nods.*

(To audience.) Finally you ask a question, a harmless, easy question— *(Back to the interview.)* She was your girlfriend?

DINO TORTORICI: Since seventh grade.

McALARY: *(To audience.)* They talk to you. You learn that early. Bad things happen, and you think, nobody's going to want to talk about it, but they do.

TORTORICI: I gave her the pills. I opened the bottle. She had a headache, and I said, I'll get you some Tylenol, and I went downstairs and got it out of my mother's bathroom. It was brand-new. I had to open it with my teeth.

HAP HAIRSTON: It was a great story.

> *Headline on* Newsday: INSIDE THE TYLENOL CASE *by Mike McAlary.*

Mac talked to everyone up in Yonkers and we kicked ass for four or five days.

Newsday *Newsroom*

> McALARY *walks into the newsroom. High fives. "Great story."*
> *Walks over to* HAIRSTON.

HAP HAIRSTON: There's your desk. You're not going back to Queens.

McALARY: But they said I had to be in Queens for six months—

HAP HAIRSTON: Fuck that.

> McALARY, *elated, lifts his hands in the air.*

(To audience.) So that's the beginning of the story, as I tell it.

JIM DWYER: *(To audience.)* He was a very generous guy—

BOB DRURY: You could not help liking him. He checked in every morning—

JIM DWYER: Twice a day—

BOB DRURY: Five times a day—

McALARY: Hey, Drury, last night I ran into a detective I know on that Sheepshead Bay drug case. He said to give him a a call. Who wants soup? Louise, you are looking stunning.

LOUISE IMERMAN: Fuck you.

McALARY: Hey, Dwyer, is today your birthday? Everybody, it's Dwyer's birthday—

> McALARY *whips out a cake with a candle on it, puts it in front of* DWYER, *lights the candle with his Bic lighter.* DWYER *blows it out. Everyone claps.*

JIM DWYER: He knew your mother's name—

BOB DRURY: —if you were mustard or mayo—

JIM DWYER: —Yankees or Mets—

HAP HAIRSTON: —beer or Bourbon—

McALARY: *(To the other reporters.)* Put your money away. I'm buying. I am buying.

McFadden's Bar

> *In the bar,* MICHAEL DALY *stands.*

MICHAEL DALY: *(To audience.)* Michael Daly. I was a columnist at the *Daily News.* I'd known McAlary from when he was covering sports and when he went to *Newsday* we started hanging around together—

> *A group of reporters sit at a table.* McALARY *joins his pretty wife,* ALICE, *and* MICHAEL DALY *at the bar.*

McALARY: *(Lifts his glass.)* Gentlemen, the former Alice Argento of North Massapequa—

ALICE: —which is not to be confused with Massapequa.

MICHAEL DALY: *(To audience.)* I was crazy about McAlary's wife.

ALICE: Michael and I first met in college.

McALARY: At Syracuse.

ALICE: At this mixer.

McALARY: She caused me to spill my drink.

ALICE: Accidentally.

McALARY: So I said—

ALICE: He had the nerve to tell me I had to buy him another drink. Which I did! And for the rest of the night we talked and laughed—

McALARY: We had a great time—

ALICE: And agreed to meet a week later.

MCALARY: On an official date.

ALICE: I showed up looking really good—

MCALARY: Here's the thing, there was this sophomore named Lisa—

ALICE: Here's the thing, I found him dancing with another girl! I'm not a doormat. So I grabbed my coat, very dramatic, and walked out.

MCALARY: Nice view. I followed.

ALICE: We've been together ever since.

MCALARY: My wife can recite all the stops on the Long Island Railroad in a conductor's voice—

MICHAEL DALY: She could. She absolutely could—

MCALARY: Do it, babe—

ALICE: I'm not doing it.

MCALARY: I love it when you say Ronkonkoma. C'mon, do it.

> *Okay, she'll do it.*

ALICE: *(Long Island accent.)* The 7:01 to Babylon, now departing on Track 16. Woodside, Jamaica, Saint Albans, Lynbrook, Rockville Center, Baldwin, Freeport, Merrick, Bellmore, Wantagh, Seaford, Massapequa, Massapequa Park, Amityville, Copiague, Lindenhurst, and Babylon.

> MCALARY *and* DALY *are entranced. But:*

MCALARY: What about Ronkonkoma?

ALICE: It's not on the Babylon Line.

> MCALARY *looks at her imploringly.*

It's not.

MCALARY: Sweetheart, honeybunch, love of my life—

ALICE: Ronkonkoma.

MCALARY: Beau-ti-ful.

MICHAEL DALY: *(To audience.)* We all said that. Bee-you-tee-ful. Because Breslin said it. Jimmy Breslin was the greatest newspaper columnist who ever lived.

BOB DRURY: Remember his columns on Marvin the Torch and Fat Thomas, and the one on the guy who dug Kennedy's grave?

MICHAEL DALY: If we had some cop on the line, he had the chief. While we were grilling some flunky, Jimmy had the governor on hold.

JIM DWYER: He had the story while the rest of us were still chasing the facts.

MICHAEL DALY: He was Irish, we were Irish. We were all trying to be him, every minute of the day—

BOB DRURY: —especially Mac.

MICHAEL DALY: So there we were, at the bar one night—

McALARY: Hey, is that Jimmy over there?

MICHAEL DALY: *(To audience.)* It was. It was Breslin himself. *(To McALARY.)* Want to meet him?

McALARY: Nah.

ALICE: You don't want to meet Jimmy Breslin?

McALARY: I already met Breslin.

MICHAEL DALY: When?

McALARY: Last week. We were covering that mafia murder in Coney Island.

MICHAEL DALY: And?

> McALARY *doesn't even want to tell the story.*

MICHAEL DALY AND ALICE: What? Come on. Tell us, etc.

McALARY: I go up to him, say my name, tell him how when I would come stay with my uncle Tim in Brooklyn, he would never even say good morning when you came down for breakfast, he would just say, "Read Breslin." I'm prepared to quote Breslin to Breslin, and you know what he says to me?

MICHAEL DALY: What?

McALARY: Nothing. He just grunts.

MICHAEL DALY: That's what Breslin does. He grunts. It's his way of hello.

McALARY: It wasn't a hello kind of a grunt. It was more of a fuck-you kind of a grunt. I worship the guy, I always have, and he turns out to be a total prick, so fuck him, and then the next day I read his piece, and it's about a hundred times better than my piece, it's a hundred times better than anything I ever wrote, or ever will, and it's not even one of his best columns—

ALICE: Well, he's Jimmy Breslin.

McALARY: And I'm not, fuck.

> *They look over at the bar where a group of reporters is standing.*

MICHAEL DALY: Hey, be Breslin for a minute.

> *The ensemble opens and we see one of them, as Breslin.*

Light up.

> *Breslin lights a cigar.*

Lean back.

> *Breslin exhales.*
>
> *A big guy in a haze of smoke.*

Hands behind your head.
    He puts his hands behind his head, leans against the wall.
    McALARY *watches, entranced.*
(To audience.) And McAlary said—
McALARY: One day.

Ryan's Bar

    McALARY *surrounded by a group of detectives, dressed similarly in trench coats. They are all smoking.*
MICHAEL DALY: *(To audience.)* In 1986 I decided to take a leave of absence to write a novel. McAlary had helped me on a couple of stories so I took him around and introduced him to all of the detectives I knew. I told him, if you have five detectives, one in every borough, you can cover the entire city.
McALARY: Detectives are heroes. My father was from East Flatbush out by Holy Cross Cemetery. He moved us up to New Hampshire when I was a kid, otherwise I would have been a cop—
MICHAEL DALY: He looked like a cop, walked like a cop—
McALARY: I even eat like a cop, fast. Growing up, everybody I knew was either a cop or married to one. Half-Stitch Delaney, this reporter with the *Journal American*, was married to a lady cop, Pussy Bumper Delaney. She made lots of arrests. She got the nickname because, on the subway, she would bump up against guys and arrest them as perverts. She never stopped. Story is, even on their anniversary, they wound up in Night Court instead of a restaurant, because Pussy Bumper Delaney nailed some guy on the subway. Pussy Bumper Delaney!
    They all toast to Pussy Bumper Delaney.
MICHAEL DALY: They loved him and he loved them.
McALARY: The best training for writing about cops is writing about sports—
MICHAEL DALY: *(To audience.)* —which is one of the things that got him into trouble eventually. Because sports is all black hats and white hats and New York City is way more complicated than that. But in 1986, nothing got in his way. He just ripped through the whole crack era.

Bronx Montage

>As McALARY *works at his desk, a series of projections of front-page headlines. Projection:* SIX KILLED IN QUEENS CRACK DEN *by Mike McAlary.*

McALARY: "On the east side of Phelan Place you have a row of crack houses. On the west side, a drug rehabilitation center. Only in the Bronx where good and bad are on opposite sides of the same street can there be such a thin line between the saved and the doomed."

MICHAEL DALY: —He'd go places cops wouldn't go. Bed-Stuy, the Bronx; climbing stairs, banging on doors.

>*Projection:* CITY ON CRACK *by Mike McAlary.*

McALARY: "Today with nearly 900 murders in the first three months, this promises to be the city's most murderous year. Seven years ago there were 1,826 murders in New York City total. But that was B.C.—before crack."

>*More headlines, and then, projection of a newscast:*

SUE SIMMONS: *(A recording.)* They began turning in their badges and guns tonight. All are accused of shaking down drug dealers.

MIKE TAIBBI: *(A recording.)* It reportedly began about a year ago when a couple of drug dealers in this neighborhood started talking and making noises about cops shaking them down. The internal affairs division of the police department listened to those noises and then began questioning some of the cops. Two specifically, we are told, who agreed to cooperate with an investigation that continues to this day. But tonight cops from this Brooklyn precinct, cops in civilian clothes, consoled and perhaps protected each other. We were told the shorter man, the one in the blue shirt, was among those suspended.

Newsday *Newsroom*

>HAP HAIRSTON *at his desk. Also in the room:* BOB DRURY, LOUISE IMERMAN, McALARY.

HAP HAIRSTON: *(To audience.)* When you have a breaking story like the Seven-Seven, which was the biggest police scandal in years, you've got to get the cops to talk to you. So the first day we sent everyone out. Bob Drury went to find this cop who was one of the two key guys in the case. His name was Henry Winter, he was a total lowlife, and he'd worn a wire and gotten half the precinct indicted—

BOB DRURY: *(To audience.)* I went out to Henry Winter's on Long Island, and there's a big boat sitting in the driveway, and three sets of his daughters' pink sneakers drying in the sun. So I write a story about how could this guy afford a boat like this on a cop's salary. And I put in the little pink sneakers.

> DRURY *exits.*

HAP HAIRSTON: *(To audience.)* The next day the phone rings, and the guy on the other end says he's calling "as a friend of Henry Winter's," and on behalf of his "friend" Henry Winter he wants to say why the fuck did we have to drag in the little pink sneakers, and it's clear the guy's not a *friend* of Henry Winter's, he's Henry Winter. Which he finally admits. So I tell him I'll send one of our finest reporters—

> HAP HAIRSTON *looks around the city room, waves* LOUISE *over to the desk.*

(To audience.) —and I call Louise over to give it to her. Because she had seniority. The night before, she'd taken the Deputy Police Commissioner to dinner and managed to get the list of cops who were being indicted and faxed it from the restaurant.

> LOUISE IMERMAN *comes over to the desk and looks at* HAP.

LOUISE IMERMAN: Yeah, what is it?

HAP HAIRSTON: *(To* LOUISE.*)* I've got one of the cops. He's in the D.A.'s office in Brooklyn. *(To audience.)* So by now you know what Louise is going to say.

LOUISE IMERMAN: *(To* HAP.*)* Fuck you, kiss my ass, I'm not doing another fucking thing on this story. I was up all night getting that list, I'm not going home late again because I had to spend the day holding some cop's dick. *(To audience.)* And by the way, that is the end of me in this story.

> *She starts to exit, stops.*

Although—

HAP HAIRSTON: What?

LOUISE IMERMAN: He spoke to my journalism class at CUNY. McAlary. Years later.

HAP HAIRSTON: *You* taught a journalism class? You're shitting me.

LOUISE IMERMAN: Kiss my ass, fuck you.

> LOUISE *exits.*

HAP HAIRSTON *looks around. There's* McALARY. *Pointing to himself with his index fingers.*

HAP HAIRSTON: So the point is—

McALARY: I got the story.

McALARY *exits.*

HAP HAIRSTON: *(To audience.)* An hour later—

DRURY *walks in.*

Your cop called. He's mad. He wants to talk.

BOB DRURY: Great. Where is he?

HAP HAIRSTON: At the D.A.'s office. You weren't in yet, so I sent McAlary.

BOB DRURY: You gave it to McAlary?

HAP HAIRSTON: You weren't in. He was.

BOB DRURY: I don't believe this shit.

HAP HAIRSTON: You weren't. He was.

BOB DRURY: You couldn't wait an hour?

HAP HAIRSTON: How did I know you were going to be here in an hour?

BOB DRURY: Shit! Fuck!

HAP HAIRSTON: *(To audience.)* And he kicked over his wastebasket.

DRURY *walks away, kicks over his wastebasket.*

Bang.

Then he turns back to HAP.

BOB DRURY: Oh, wait a minute, that's not really what happened. I wasn't that mad, Hap. *(To audience.)* I wasn't. Swear to God.

HAP HAIRSTON: Sure you were. Admit it. If you'd been there an hour earlier, you would have had McAlary's career—

BOB DRURY: *(Overlapping.)* Bullshit, bullshit—

HAP HAIRSTON: Did that ever cross your mind? Come on, tell the truth.

BOB DRURY: *(Overlapping.)* No, it never crossed my mind. And I did not kick over the wastebasket. Fuck you.

HAP HAIRSTON: Fuck you. *(To audience.)* The point is, McAlary went up to see Henry Winter and say whatever you want about McAlary, the guy could get you to talk. Winter told him everything.

The other REPORTERS *read from* McALARY's *article—*

MICHAEL DALY: "Henry Winter let it be known to everybody: We're bad in the Seven-Seven. Whatever you got to sell, we'll buy."

JIM DWYER: *(Reading.)* "You got drugs, we'll buy drugs. You want to get guns, we'll buy guns."

BOB DRURY: *(Reading.)* "You got stolen property, we'll buy stolen property. If there's a break-in at night at a video store, we'll buy tapes. That's how it worked."

HAP HAIRSTON: *(To audience.)* McAlary wrote one story after another about this group of cops in the Seven-Seven who called themselves the Buddy Boys and who turned out to be the biggest drug dealers in the city.

Lion's Head

> *The newsstand guy tosses the tabloids on the bar, everyone dives into them.*

McALARY: You pussies at the *News* and the *Post* are going to shoot yourselves when you see what we've got.

JIM DWYER: *(To audience.)* McAlary started to live for the wood.

McALARY: *(Flashing the headline.)* "Rogue Cop Talks" by Mike McAlary.

JIM DWYER: The wood is slang for the front-page headline. The type was so big they had to make the letters out of wood.

McALARY: "Buddy Boys of the 7-7" by Mike McAlary.

JIM DWYER: It was cops and scandal, cops and scandal, nothing else mattered. The Mets won the World Series that year, I don't even think he cared.

McALARY: "It's Worse: Probe Goes Beyond Drugs to Guns, Hot Cars, Stolen VCRs; At Least 49 Officers Involved; Federal Agencies Join Inquiry" by—

ALL BUT DRURY: Mike McAlary.

> *High fives from everybody.* McALARY *and his friends all sing an Irish song:*

McALARY/FRIENDS: *(Sing.)*
Look at the coffin, with golden handles.
Isn't it grand, boys, to be bloody-well dead.
Let's not have a sniffle,
Let's have a bloody good cry,
And always remember, the longer you live,
The sooner you'll bloody well die.

HAP HAIRSTON: The wood became his drug of choice. Making headlines during the day—

JOHN COTTER: McAlary!

HAP HAIRSTON: And then staying up all night with Cotter.

> McALARY *sits at a table in the bar with* COTTER.

JOHN COTTER: Mac! McAlary, my boy. What reporters think, okay, is that there's this thing called the truth, and their job is to go out and get it.

McALARY: Right.

JOHN COTTER: Wrong. Any story you're on has only one real truth. Go to the morgue and count the bodies. Count the bodies.

McALARY: That's great. That's great. *(A beat.)* What does it mean?

JOHN COTTER: You're born, you die. Everything in between is subject to interpretation.

McALARY: Everything?

JOHN COTTER: *(Overlapping.)* Everything in between is how you tell the story and who's telling the story and what they think is important and which order to put it in and where they're coming from.

McALARY: What about facts? We believe in facts. Don't we believe in facts? We're journalists. Who, what, where, when. We write, like, the first draft of history. The voice of da people. If it wasn't for us, we'd be living in a dictatorship.

JOHN COTTER: You're making me sick. I may throw up. McAlary, I want you to try to wrap your thick skull around this philosophical point I'm trying to make—

McALARY: Oh, philosophical. Fuck you.

JOHN COTTER: Except for a few hard-core things, which for want of a better word we will call facts, like what time it was when the shot was fired, and is the guy alive or dead, everything's a story. For example, what's your story? The story of McAlary.

McALARY: I'm a newspaper reporter. I love my job. I'm doing God's work, serving the public, telling people what happened yesterday, telling them the facts, rewarding the good guys and putting the bad guys away, and fuck you, Cotter, there is such a thing as the facts. That's my story.

JOHN COTTER: Your story is you're a kid with a bad case of Breslinitis and you're probably never going to get over it.

McALARY: That's how *you* tell the story.

JOHN COTTER: Exactly. You've also got a gut for red meat, you get people to talk who don't want to talk, and someday you're going to have your own column.

McALARY: You think so? 'Cause I swear, that is all I ever wanted. Writing a column in New York. Everything else is second place— You really think it might happen?

JOHN COTTER: I do.

McALARY: And when it does, that will be a fact. *(Beat.)* I got a wife and kid. You left that out of the story.

JOHN COTTER: So did you.

Queens Diner

MICHAEL DALY: *(To audience.)* One night I got a call from McAlary. He was going to see one of the Buddy Boys, a cop who'd been indicted named Brian O'Regan. By now I'd finished my novel and I was working at *New York* magazine. So we go out to Queens and we meet O'Regan, and we do our thing.

    DALY *and* McALARY *sit at a table with* BRIAN O'REGAN.
       McALARY *and* DALY *stand, circle, double-team him, blow smoke.*

McALARY: We'll take care of you.

MICHAEL DALY: We'll tell your story.

McALARY: You'll have a Michael Daly piece in *New York* magazine.

MICHAEL DALY: A Mike McAlary story in *Newsday.*

McALARY: You could not be in better hands.

MICHAEL DALY: You think you're the only guy in the department who had your hand out?

McALARY: Everybody makes mistakes.

MICHAEL DALY: We all fuck up.

McALARY: Pressures of the job—

MICHAEL DALY: Pressures of the culture—

McALARY: More coffee?—

MICHAEL DALY: Have another cup of coffee—

McALARY: We know what you're going through. An article like this could help you in your sentencing.

MICHAEL DALY: The story's going to come out anyway, it should be on your terms.

McALARY: Word for word—

MICHAEL DALY: As you tell it—

McALARY: You are safe with us.

MICHAEL DALY: *(To audience.)* So O'Regan tells us the whole thing about how he got involved at the Seven-Seven. How they'd rob drug dealers and then deal the drugs.

BRIAN O'REGAN: Sometimes I used to get a feeling—a deep, deep feeling of guilt. But then I'd get back on patrol, and it would go away. I got so I just didn't care.

MICHAEL DALY: *(To audience.)* We spent two or three hours with him. After it's over, we walk out to the parking lot and he opens the trunk of his car. His uniform is in it. He asks if either of us wants it. He's supposed to turn himself in tomorrow.

> *Front-page headline:* CONFESSION OF A SCARED COP *by Mike McAlary, a* Newsday *exclusive.*

(To audience.) The next day O'Regan reads McAlary's story, drives out to Southampton and checks into a motel, locks the door, and pours himself a Seven & Seven, Seagram's Seven Crown and 7Up. How corny is that?

> *A gunshot.*

Newsday *Newsroom*

> JOHN COTTER *and* McALARY.

McALARY: *(Stunned.)* Cotter! Jesus Christ, Cotter, what the hell did I do?

JOHN COTTER: Don't flatter yourself. This shit can happen. You gotta divorce yourself from it like cops do.

McALARY: I don't know how to do that.

JOHN COTTER: Go write the story, or I'll assign it to somebody else and they'll get the byline.

JIM DWYER: *(To audience.)* He did a draft. And then he and Hap went through it for adjectives.

> HAP *and* McALARY *go through the piece together.*
> *A projection of the computer copy of* McALARY's *story as* HAIRSTON *edits it.*

HAP HAIRSTON: How tall was he?

McALARY: About my height.

> *Projection of* McALARY's *story on the computer as* HAP HAIRSTON *inserts the word "tall" into the text.*

HAP HAIRSTON: How many cups of coffee?

McALARY: Six or eight.

> HAIRSTON *inserts the words "eight cups of" into the text.*

HAP HAIRSTON: How hard was it raining?

McALARY: I don't know. Hard.

> *The words "pouring down" are inserted.*
> *The word "nervously" is inserted.*

The word "all-night" is inserted in front of "diner."

HAP HAIRSTON: What else did he say? Come on, come on, come on, focus—

McALARY: "You tell me why I did this."

HAP HAIRSTON: He said that? He said, "You tell me why I did this"?

McALARY: Yeah.

HAP HAIRSTON: Did he really say it? Is that in your notebook?

McALARY: He said it, he definitely said it.

"You tell me why I did this" is inserted.

A beat.

HAP HAIRSTON: The uniform he offered you. Was it, like, on a hanger, in a box, what?

McALARY: On a hanger, in, like, a dry-cleaning bag . . . Jesus, Hap.

"In a plastic dry-cleaning bag" is inserted.

JIM DWYER: *(To the audience.)* Mac was devastated—

HAP HAIRSTON: *(To audience.)* He was. He was devastated. And in the tradition of all truly devastated reporters whose sources kill themselves, he somehow managed to do a bunch of television appearances on the subject that day.

A television crew interviews McALARY.

McALARY: It was pouring rain, and he got into his car and drove away.

Another television crew interviews McALARY.

JIM DWYER: *(To* HAP.*)* That's not fair. He was really upset—

HAP HAIRSTON: —because he thought people were blaming *him*—

McALARY: I probably should have known, because he opened the trunk of his car and showed us his uniform, in a plastic bag—

JIM DWYER: That's really not fair. He carried O'Regan's mass card in his wallet for years.

HAP HAIRSTON: He loved being asked about it over and over again. *(To audience.)* He even suggested they tape one of the interviews in Battery Park, because he liked the vista.

Another television crew, in Battery Park.

McALARY: *(On TV.)* I keep asking myself what I could have done.

JIM DWYER: *(To* HAP.*)* But he was devastated.

HAP HAIRSTON: I'm just saying.

JIM DWYER: What are you just saying, Hap?

HAP HAIRSTON: You know what I'm saying. It was a great story. He got the wood.

Projection of a front-page headline: A SCARED COP'S LAST ACT OF DESPERATION *by Mike McAlary.*

The Sound of Bagpipes

> *A group of pallbearers in police uniform carry Brian O'Regan's coffin out of the church.*
> McALARY *and* DALY, *under umbrellas, watch.*
> *The bagpipes continue as the coffin passes.*

Brooklyn Bedroom

> *As the bagpipes end.*
> ALICE McALARY *asleep in a chair next to the bed. She's wrapped in a shawl.*
> *There's a double stroller on the way to the bedroom.*
> McALARY *walks in, knocks over the stroller.*
> ALICE *wakes up.*

ALICE: Hey.

McALARY: Hey.

ALICE: It's three in the morning.

McALARY: I was at the funeral.

> *He sits down near her, on the edge of the bed.*

Down at the paper, everyone keeps coming over to me and saying, "How do you feel? You must feel terrible. It's not your fault." Then they go over to the water cooler and they say, "McAlary killed the guy." Then they come over and go, "Oh man, it must be terrible."

ALICE: Do people think it was your fault?

McALARY: We went and interviewed an unstable guy in a diner and we got what we wanted and then we were done. We had to know what he was going to do.

ALICE: How could you know? You couldn't know.

McALARY: We had to know. We had to. You should have heard us. "You're safe with us. You could not be in better hands."

ALICE: What were you supposed to do? Move in with him? Give him the name of a good shrink, which you yourself do not know the name of?

> *A beat.*

McALARY: He left a note. By the bed. It said, "McAlary wrote too much."

ALICE: When did you find that out?

McALARY: At the funeral home today. After the funeral.

ALICE: Michael. This is ridiculous. Did you misquote the guy?

McALARY: No.

ALICE: Was he drunk when he talked to you?

McALARY: No.

ALICE: Did you call him or did he call you?

McALARY: He called me.

ALICE: The man was a crook. He was selling drugs to kids—

McALARY: Not really—

ALICE: He stole drugs from drug dealers and where do you think those drugs ended up? With kids. He was going to jail. His life was over. If you wrote too much, it's because he told you too much.

    A beat.

    He gives her a little kiss.

McALARY: I love you.

    The thing is, I got the story right. And that's all that matters.

ALICE: You got the story right.

McALARY: Hey, how are you?

ALICE: I have a double stroller in the bedroom, I have two babies in what used to be the dining room, and I walk up and down four flights of stairs at least three times a day with the babies and stroller. Other than that, I'm happy you're home.

    They kiss again.

Newsday *Newsroom/Bellport*

HAP HAIRSTON: *(To audience.)* Which brings us to the house.

BOB DRURY: I hated that fucking house. Let's cut to the part where Mac—

HAP HAIRSTON: Can't tell the story of McAlary if you leave out the house, 'cause this is where everything starts to turn.

    McALARY *enters, carrying a copy of the* Times *Real Estate section, and walks over to* COTTER.

McALARY: Hey, Cotter, you know about this guy Eddie Hayes?

JOHN COTTER: Sure. He's a lawyer. Everybody knows him. He's a character.

McALARY: He's selling a house I want to buy for Alice. Is he a good guy or a bad guy?

JOHN COTTER: Good guy/bad guy does not apply when it comes to Eddie Hayes. He's got a motto. His motto is "I can get you out of anything."

HAP HAIRSTON: *(To ensemble.)* Who wants to play Eddie Hayes?
> *He looks over at the ensemble.* COTTER *raises his hand while a few ensemble enter, volunteering.*
> EDDIE HAYES *enters. A very dapper man, Turnbull & Asser shirt, tailored suit, a hat.*

EDDIE HAYES: Me. I play me. None of these guys can play me. Look at all you. Look at this.
> McALARY *walks over to the Bellport house, where* EDDIE HAYES *is waiting. The house should be suggested by a front porch.*

McAlary. *(Mispronounces as Mick-allery, rhyming with gallery.)* You ever been to Bellport before?

McALARY: Nope. McAlary. *(Pronounced Mac-a-lair-ee.)*

EDDIE HAYES: The editor of the *New York Times*, Abe Rosenthal, lives three blocks away. Anna Wintour, the editor of *Vogue*, over there. *(Waves his hand.)* Beautiful front porch, six thousand square feet, someday there will be a lawn and the Dumpster will be gone. I live right down the block. Anything goes wrong, I'll get you a plumber. You have kids?

McALARY: Two.

EDDIE HAYES: This is good for you, it's good for you. You could have six kids in this house. Eight, if they aren't too big.

McALARY: How much is it?

EDDIE HAYES: Five hundred fifty thousand. But for you, five hundred fifty thousand.

McALARY: Okay, explain to me about a mortgage.

EDDIE HAYES: How much are you planning to put down?
> *The stagehands push a huge sub-zero onstage.*

(Indicating the refrigerator.) Sub-zero.
> EDDIE HAYES *opens the refrigerator.*
> McALARY *looks into its vast, empty interior.*

McALARY: Jesus, Mary, mother of God, you could live in this—
(Beat.) What do you mean, "put down?"

EDDIE HAYES: Cash cash. Like, say, two hundred thousand, just to pluck a figure out of the air. Then you get a mortgage for the rest. On which you pay interest. Do you have two hundred thousand?

McALARY: No, I do not.

EDDIE HAYES: What's your salary?

McALARY: Fifty-eight thousand a year.

EDDIE HAYES: How much do you have in the bank?

McALARY: I got about three thousand in the bank.

EDDIE HAYES: This is a five-hundred-fifty-thousand-dollar house. You can't afford it. *(Indicating the mudroom.)* Mudroom.

McALARY: What the fuck is a mudroom?

HAYES *looks at* McALARY.

And don't go on like you grew up knowing what a mudroom was, you were once a dumb Mick just like me—

HAYES *laughs.*

EDDIE HAYES: A mudroom, you dumb Mick, is the room where you take off your muddy boots if it happens to be muddy outside.

McALARY: Just what we need.

EDDIE HAYES: Trust me, once you have one you'll never know how you lived without it.

McALARY: I got an idea. I retain you. Isn't that what people do with lawyers, retain them? I hereby retain you as my lawyer, and now it's your job to figure out a way for me to pay for this house.

EDDIE HAYES: Get out of here—

McALARY: This is my house, I'm not going anywhere—

EDDIE HAYES: Get the fuck out of my house—

McALARY: You get the fuck out of *my* house—

EDDIE HAYES: Who are you?

McALARY: You know that scandal at the Seventy-seventh Precinct? I'm the guy that uncovered it—

EDDIE HAYES: You uncovered it?

McALARY: I am that guy.

EDDIE HAYES *is impressed.*

I'm not going to be a reporter forever. At some point I'm going to have a column.

EDDIE HAYES: The next Jimmy Breslin.

McALARY: Bigger than Breslin. And when it happens, you can do my contract. I want a big expense account, and start thinking now about other things I might want.

EDDIE HAYES: Like a car.

McALARY: Like a car. Only I've got a car.

EDDIE HAYES: We'll get you a better car. What else? A car for your wife. Does your wife have a car?

McALARY: You're going to get the paper to pay for a car for my wife?

EDDIE HAYES: It's feasible, it's feasible. A pied-à-terre.

McALARY: Yeah! What is that?

EDDIE HAYES: An apartment in town.

McALARY: Sure. *(Laughs.)* Let's do this.

McALARY *walks off.*

EDDIE HAYES: *(To audience.)* So long story short, I lent him the two hundred thousand down payment and deferred the interest and second-mortgage payments. I said at the end of three years he'll have enough to pay me back. So when I called him, I said, I found a way for you to buy the house. For two reasons: you're a great writer, and you're fucking crazy.

    BOB DRURY, *dressed for a day at the beach, enters—*

BOB DRURY: *(To audience.)* So we all went out there.

    Followed by the other journalists, also in shorts, T-shirts,
      baseball hats, etc. They move in a clump.

HAP HAIRSTON: *(To audience.)* We all went out to see the spec house Eddie Hayes conned Mac into buying.

MICHAEL DALY: It was way the hell out.

ALICE: All right, who's hungry? I got burgers and franks, lasagna— my mother's recipe.

    A chaise longue is wheeled out. EDDIE, *still perfectly dressed,*
      lies on it.

JIM DWYER: *(To audience.)* Eddie Hayes was holding court out back, taking credit for selling Mac the house.

EDDIE HAYES: It's good for him, it's good for him, it's going to force him to make more money, because otherwise he'd spend his life in a Brooklyn apartment looking out at a fire escape—

HAP HAIRSTON: *(To audience.)* Like all of us. So that went over big.

ALICE: Lemonade? Soda? Beer?

    The guys all respond to beer.

JIM DWYER: *(To audience.)* Eddie kept talking about his clothes—

EDDIE HAYES: I like to dress well, I like to spend money on clothes. I think I deserve it.

MICHAEL DALY: And how great it was for Mac—

EDDIE HAYES: It's good for him, it's good for him—

MCALARY: It's good for me, it's good for me.

HAP HAIRSTON: *(To audience.)* Although, by implication, the rest of us were going to be on the breadline—

BOB DRURY: *(To audience.)* —the rest of us were schmucks—

MICHAEL DALY: *(To audience.)* —schmucks who had no idea you could get rich in the newspaper business.

HAP HAIRSTON: Which we didn't.

BOB DRURY: *(To audience.)* Nobody made much money, but we all made enough money—

JIM DWYER: *(To audience.)* We all thought we'd succeeded, and suddenly, we all felt like failures.

MCALARY: And hey, if you guys ever need anything, Eddie will do it
for you, right?

EDDIE HAYES: I'll get you out of anything. Although not gratis.
The sub-zero refrigerator magically appears. MCALARY *closes
the refrigerator door and then opens it again.*

BOB DRURY: *(To audience.)* He kept showing us the refrigerator.

MCALARY: Check this out! It's bigger than my first apartment. Alice
should have a place she really loves. I just need a career to pay for
this.

HAP HAIRSTON: *(To audience.)* All I could think was, not only has
this guy mortgaged his whole fucking future, but himself as well.

JIM DWYER: *(To audience.)* But then Mac, being Mac, luckiest guy
on the planet—what happens next?—
*Projections: A series of headlines about Breslin winning the
Pulitzer Prize and leaving the* Daily News.

Bar

JIM DWYER: Jimmy Breslin quits. He'd just won the Pulitzer Prize, his
long-awaited Pulitzer Prize and decided to leave the *Daily News*
and take his column to *Newsday*. So Cotter called up the editor of
the *News*, a guy named Jim Willse, and said, "Hey, I've got this
kid over here, I think he could write a column for you guys."

MCALARY: Can you fucking believe this?
MCALARY *to all the guys—*DALY, DRURY, HAIRSTON, EDDIE, *a
few others.*
I got a column. I got a column in New York City. Page three.
Breslin's slot. Fuck. Now I have to write it.
Everybody laughs.

BOB DRURY: Do you know how to write a column, because there's a
big difference between a column and all of that good cop/bad cop
bullshit.

MCALARY: Don't rain on my parade, Drury. Whatever I don't know,
Hap will teach me.

HAP HAIRSTON: I'm going there, too.

BOB DRURY: Seriously, you're going to teach McAlary to write a
column?

HAP HAIRSTON: I'm going to be city editor—

MCALARY: Willse and I have had extensive conversations and the idea
is to combine being a police reporter with being a columnist.

BOB DRURY: Seriously?

McALARY: Seriously, let's have lobsters tonight. Go someplace really expensive and have two lobsters each!

EDDIE HAYES: I did the contract. One hundred twenty-five thousand a year, plus an expense account, plus a car, and he started dressing better. It was good, it was good.

JIM DWYER: He started out a little shaky at the *News*, but then he found a rhythm, started getting a lot of big stories and a big—

BOB DRURY: *(From McGuire's.)* —head. He was getting a big head.

DRURY *is in McGuire's bar, with a group of journalists.*

JIM DWYER: I was going to say a big reputation.

BOB DRURY: I'm going to go and say head.

Daily News *Newsroom*

McALARY *passes* WILLSE's *desk, looks at his computer.*

McALARY: Hey, Willse, this front page needs something.

WILLSE *presses a button.* McALARY's *picture appears on the projection, at the top of the front page.*

Just the thing.

BOB DRURY: Head.

Subway Station

A poster in the subway with McALARY's *face:* MIKE McALARY IN THE DAILY NEWS.

JIM DWYER: One night I was writing about a hot dog stand, the only twenty-four-hour operation left in the subway system that was being shut down and of course because it was a twenty-four-hour operation, you had to cover it at two in the morning. So I'm standing by the newsstand and there's a guy reading the *News*, and on page one, there's this huge McAlary story about Mike Tyson trying to commit suicide. I remember looking at it and wondering what in God's name was I doing with my life. At which moment this woman comes along and buys a hot dog for her kid. So I decide I'll interview her about the tragic end of the all-night hot dog stand, and she turns out to be Mike Tyson's third cousin. McAlary's on page one with Mike Tyson, and I'm underground in the middle of the fucking night with Mike Tyson's homeless third cousin, Latifa. I wanted to kill myself. Yeah, I was jealous. Yeah. That's what I'm saying. Nobody wants to cop to that, but yeah.

McGuire's Bar

Journalists laughing as McALARY *enters.*

McALARY: Hey, Drury, did you see the column? Did you see what I got? Did you see what I got? Did you see what I got?

BOB DRURY: *(To the other reporters.)* I told you. I told you he'd be proud of it. *(To* McALARY.*)* You got an exclusive interview with Donald Trump. On the occasion of his divorce. Way to go. You probably had to stake out the Trump Tower for hours.

McALARY: I had to drink a lot of espresso, waiting for the Donald to send that elevator down.

BOB DRURY: Is that what you do now? You write about Trump?

McALARY: Who's everybody talking about? Donald Trump. You think I'm not going to write about Donald Trump? Of course I am.

BOB DRURY: You write for the *Daily News.* The voice of da people. You don't flack for rich assholes who give you "exclusive interviews." *(*DRURY *reaches for a* Daily News *on the bar.)* Note that it is open to the page. Because we were reading it out loud. We took a vote, and our favorite sentence was, "Trump continued talking in a soft voice, his manner surprisingly delicate."

The reporters in the bar all laugh.

Here's the deal. In the future—just give me your stuff, give me your stuff, I'll write it. If you write it, it's shit.

McALARY: —And yet I am the one with the column. How did that happen?—

BOB DRURY: That is one of the enduring mysteries, especially after reading crap like this.

McALARY: If I want to write about Donald Trump I can write about Donald Trump—

BOB DRURY: Because "I'm Mike McAlary and you're not"?

McALARY: I am Mike McAlary and you're not. How many columns a week do you write? Just out of curiosity, how many?

McALARY *holds up his hand in a zero sign.*

BOB DRURY: What the fuck happened to you? Where did you go? What happened to McAlary? Listen to this shit. "This is not as the song goes. '. . . the same old story, a fight for love and glory.' Mostly it's the story about not being thirty years old anymore." No, mostly it's the story of a two-bit hack who got Breslin's slot, but not his talent.

McALARY: Fuck you.

BOB DRURY: Fuck you.

McALARY: Fuck you.

> McALARY *hits* DRURY. DRURY *hits him back. They end up on the floor and roll out of the bar.*

Bellport Bedroom

> ALICE *in bed asleep as* McALARY *comes up into the bedroom.*
> ALICE *wakes up.*
> *He has the beginning of a black eye and a cut on his face.*

McALARY: I was at McGuire's. I didn't want to wake you so I didn't call. I got in a fight with Drury.

> *He goes into the bathroom.*

(*Offstage.*) Some guy from the *Post* was there, and it's going to be on Page Six. I called Eddie to see if he could kill it, and he said, why would I kill it, it's good for us, it's good for us, Page Six is good for us.

ALICE: You're on Page Six of the *New York Post* and I'm off exit sixty-six on the Long Island Expressway.

> *He comes out of the bathroom in his T-shirt and boxers.*

McALARY: What are you saying?

ALICE: I refuse to let you do this to me—

McALARY: What are we talking about?

ALICE: . . . Turn me into one of those women who sit around wondering when their man is gonna come home. Is that why we bought this house, Michael, so that you could stick me out here?

McALARY: Don't you like it here? We were going crazy in that little apartment, remember? You wanted space.

ALICE: We have kids, Michael. You can't put kids in a drawer—

McALARY: You wanted a house, you wanted a porch.

ALICE: I love my house, I love my porch, I love my children. I love my husband. What I don't love is you being gone four, five days at a time.

McALARY: I'm at Hap's. I'm on the couch at Hap's. It's a long drive. I'd fall asleep on the way back.

ALICE: We lead separate lives. We're married but lead separate lives.

McALARY: When I'm here, I am here. Last Sunday, I was on the front lawn with Ryan, kicking the ball for three and a half hours.

ALICE: But when you're not here, you're not here. That may be okay for Cotter's wife or, or, Daly's wife, but it is not fine by me.

McALARY: I'm a columnist, I go to the bars, I meet cops, I stay up late—

ALICE: Bullshit, Michael. Bullshit.

McALARY:	ALICE:
I pick stuff up, I'm always looking, I'm writing three, four times a week. It's what I care about, the column. It's my life.	This is not about that. It's about being a father and a—

McALARY: (Overlapping.) I have to be in the city. I can't get my ideas here . . .

ALICE: Then I suggest you go back out there where no one's gonna tell you how full of shit you are.

Down the hall, Carla, the baby, starts to cry.

I'm going to go feed the baby.

She leaves the bedroom. In a moment, the baby stops crying.

Daily News *Newsroom*

> HAP HAIRSTON *and* JIM WILLSE *at their desks. We hear the picketers outside cheering and shouting:* "Don't buy the Daily News, *don't buy the* Daily News," *while videos of the protests are projected.*

HAP HAIRSTON: (To audience.) The *Daily News* strike began in 1990 and lasted four months, and there are people who still don't speak to each other because of it. The drivers struck and the Newspaper Guild refused to cross the picket lines. Before the strike, they made me go to Scab School in Fort Lauderdale. I made the mistake of telling McAlary about it.

> *A projection of* McALARY's *rally:*

McALARY: (Live on video.) They sent Hairston to Scab School!

> *The crowd "boos."*

(Live on video.) They gave him lessons in strike-breaking. They taught him how to cross a picket line.

> *The crowd cries "Scab!"*

(Live on video.) Hap Hairston. Can you believe that?

> McALARY *enters and sees* HAP *watching the rally on TV. We continue to hear:*

McALARY: *(Recorded.)* The right to organize is as basic as freedom of the press— We will hang tough and hang together. Don't give up—Boycott the *Daily News*!

> *On the TV, we hear the crowd's cheer:* "Boycott the Daily News."
>
> HAP *turns off the TV.*

HAP HAIRSTON: You owe me an apology—

McALARY: Because I didn't keep your secret?

HAP HAIRSTON: I told you because I was upset about it. I hated it—

McALARY: So why did you go?

HAP HAIRSTON: They told me to go. I'm management. What was I supposed to do?

McALARY: You can work anywhere—

HAP HAIRSTON: I like it here. I like the *Daily News*. I even like being your editor, you prick—

McALARY: You like telling people you invented me. You like telling people if it wasn't for you, there would be no Mike McAlary—

HAP HAIRSTON: Yeah, well there are days when you turn in your column and I have no fucking idea what it's about—

McALARY: You tell people you write my column—

HAP HAIRSTON: Some days I do—

McALARY: Bullshit. *I* write my column. Some days you fix my column. And I am so grateful to you, Mr. Hairston. But that is your job. News flash—if it wasn't for you, I would still be—

HAP HAIRSTON:	McALARY:
—Mike McAlary—	—writing a column.

McALARY: Fuckin' A. And some other guy would be editing it and it would be just as big—

HAP HAIRSTON: Tell me something, just out of curiosity, are you speaking to Willse?

McALARY: Why would I not speak to Willse? He didn't go to Scab School—

HAP HAIRSTON: They don't make the editor in chief go to Scab School—

McALARY: They didn't make *you* go. You didn't have to go. They can't fire *you*, Hap. Don't make me spell it out.

HAP HAIRSTON: You're saying I didn't have to go to Scab School because I'm black?

McALARY: Am I saying that? Yes, I am saying that.

HAP HAIRSTON: Fuck you. I never got a break because of that. You have no idea how hard I had to work. How many white guys had to forget I was black for me to get where I am—

McALARY: My heart is bleeding—

HAP HAIRSTON: You're an asshole, McAlary, you're an asshole—

McALARY: I absolutely am. You know why? Because I confused you with me. That was my mistake. I never confused Willse. I confused you, because we close the bars. Because we once almost drove off the Brooklyn Bridge. Because last summer—

HAP HAIRSTON: So because we're friends, you get to sell me out. Is that what you're saying? I get to hang out with a bunch of fucking borderline psychotic racist Irish drunk pussies, and you get to sell me out when it's convenient.

McALARY: I'm just speaking the truth—

HAP HAIRSTON: The truth is you don't give a shit about anybody or anything but yourself. You're just climbing the greasy pole, you fuck. Ready for your close-up. Soon you'll be wearing makeup on the picket line.

> McALARY *puts an imaginary knife to his chest.*

You said you wouldn't tell anyone I went to Florida—

McALARY: I did. I promised.

HAP HAIRSTON: You promised.

McALARY: And then you know what? I changed my mind.

> *He walks away.*
> HAIRSTON *stands there.*
> *The crowd: "Don't buy the* Daily News.*" "Solidarity forever."*
>   *"Scab." Louder and louder.*
> McALARY *walks into:*

A Restaurant

> *He sits down with* EDDIE HAYES. *Starts stripping out of his coat, scarf, gloves, etc.*

EDDIE HAYES: I have the solution. The *New York Post* wants to hire you. They're hiring Cotter as city editor.

McALARY: I would kill to write for Cotter again.

EDDIE HAYES: So are we going to the *Post*?

McALARY: Absolutely not. We can't do that.

EDDIE HAYES: Because . . . ?

McALARY: Because we're on strike.

> *He signals for a drink.*

EDDIE HAYES: Do you want to hear what they're offering you?

McALARY: There is no point. I mean, tell them thank you, but no.
Thank you, but— *(Shakes his head no.)*

EDDIE HAYES: No.

McALARY: *(It's obvious.)* No.

EDDIE HAYES: No, as in N-O.

McALARY: I can't leave. Everybody's out there on the picket line
freezing their butts off, they're looking to me. Solidarity—

EDDIE HAYES: —forever.

> *A beer arrives.* McALARY *takes a swig.*

But the timing is good. For a move.

McALARY: Eddie Eddie Eddie.

EDDIE HAYES: Mac Mac Mac. What?

McALARY: I can't leave the *News*. They gave me a column. I owe
them. *(On the other hand.)* I love Cotter. I love the guy.

EDDIE HAYES: It was Cotter who suggested they hire you in the
first place. As a columnist. In case it slipped your mind. So you
owe him, too. Although as far as I'm concerned, you don't owe
anybody anything. I mean, follow the logic: If you really owed the
News, would you be on the picket line? Or am I crazy?

McALARY: *(Emphatic.)* You don't cross a picket line.

EDDIE HAYES: Okay, okay.

> *A beat.*

You'd have fun.

McALARY: I know, I know.

EDDIE HAYES: You wouldn't have Hap sitting on every fucking
comma.

McALARY: I wouldn't have Hap. Who is not speaking to me. Or else
I'm not speaking to him.

EDDIE HAYES: Well, this would solve that problem. Which is not a
reason to leave. There are a million reasons to leave.

> McALARY *looks at* EDDIE.

Okay, I exaggerated. Eight hundred thousand reasons, give or
take. Over three years.

McALARY: Can I get that thing?

EDDIE HAYES: What thing?

McALARY: A little place in town. I forget the word.

EDDIE HAYES: A pied-à-terre. It's French.

> *Projection: A* New York Post *truck with a big sign:* STARTING
> THIS WEEK: MIKE McALARY IN THE NEW YORK POST.
> *As he walks into:*

New York Post *Newsroom*

> *The scruffiest newsroom of all.* COTTER *walks through, leans over a reporter at his computer, pats another on the back, salutes the editor,* JERRY NACHMAN.

JERRY NACHMAN: *(Introducing himself to audience.)* Jerry Nachman.

ALL: Jerry!

JERRY NACHMAN: When I became editor of the *New York Post*, everybody said you've gotta meet this guy named John Cotter. You know about Cotter, right?

ENSEMBLE:	JOHN COTTER:
They know.	We're rocking.

JERRY NACHMAN: I hired him as city editor and the first thing he does is hire McAlary and then they create an unsuccessful putsch to throw me out of my job. Anyway—

ALL: Anyway—

> COTTER *smiles, salutes, walks off.*

Elaine's

JERRY NACHMAN: Every night McAlary, Cotter, the whole pack, would travel up to Elaine's, that's where they were hanging out, Elaine's, and they'd continue in their hopeless attempt to oust me and replace me with Cotter. I don't think McAlary thought I was bad at my job—he just wanted Cotter to have it. It was crazy drunken Irish stuff. I'd see them sitting there plotting against me. I'd wave, they'd wave back—

> NACHMAN *waves.* McALARY *and his group wave back.*

McALARY:	ALL:
Jerry, baby—	Hey!

JERRY NACHMAN: Tell the truth, you're plotting against me, right?
> *Everyone denies it. No way, Jerry. Are you crazy? What are you talking about?*

McALARY:	JOHN COTTER:
Your name has not come up.	Paranoid Nachman?

JERRY NACHMAN: Yeah, yeah, yeah. Bullshit.
> *They go back to plotting.*

(To audience.) The *Post* was always more fun to work at than anyplace else. See, Cotter was a great editor and McAlary was on a roll. Every time he scratched his nuts he was on page one. He knew who the gangsters were. Knew which cops would talk. He got the first interview with Joey Buttafuoco. And then he attacked Breslin.

JOHN COTTER: Breslin goes around telling everybody you stole beauti-ful from him?

JERRY NACHMAN: Cotter egged him into it one night at Elaine's—

McALARY: He says that?

JOHN COTTER: He's always talking about you. McAlary copies my style—c'mon, he says it to everyone.

McALARY: He says that?

JOHN COTTER: Says it to everyone, Mac.

McALARY: Where's my pen, gimme a pen. Take this down. *(Scribbling like mad.)* "It's good to hear people finally talking about Breslin again. Unfortunately it's Breslin himself who's doing most of the talking."

Laughter.

JOHN COTTER: Good one. Pretty good.

McALARY, *spurred on by* COTTER, *alternates between writing lines and shouting them out to the crowd.*

McALARY: I hear Breslin runs around town saying I copy his style. We are both white and Irish but that's about it. I do not write one life and live another. I do not cross a picket line to write about the workingman.

Laughter/cheering.

(On a roll/ragging.) Breslin has become the most despised creature in journalism; a bully-boy, out-of-control hypocrite!

Headline: THE TABLOID WAR HAS BEGUN: BULLY-BOY BRESLIN AN OUT-OF-CONTROL HYPOCRITE *by Mike McAlary. Part One.*

JERRY NACHMAN: It was fucking Oedipal. Attacking the guy he spent his entire life trying to become. Everybody came down on him. But then, being McAlary, he bounced right back—

McALARY: —with a huge story on the NYPD and turned the department upside down.

Projection: Post *front-page headline:* THE NEW SERPICO; COP UNCOVERED MASSIVE CORRUPTION—BUT NYPD WOULDN'T LISTEN—A MIKE McALARY EXCLUSIVE.

JERRY NACHMAN: *(To audience.)* They had to appoint a commission because of Mike McAlary—

McALARY: —and I even figured out who should run it.

> *Projection:* Post *front-page headline:* I CREATED THE MOLLEN COMMISSION *by Mike McAlary.*

McALARY AND NACHMAN: It was a great time to be in the tabloid business.

JERRY NACHMAN: When they write the history of journalism, they won't include it, because the guys who write about the history of journalism don't understand places like the *New York Post* in those days. And then, one day, to everybody's shock—

> McALARY *and* COTTER *at a table.*

McALARY: I don't fucking believe this. I left the *News* to come to the *Post* because of you and now you're leaving the *Post* to go to the *News*?

JOHN COTTER: I've got kids. They're offering me a one-hundred-thousand-dollar signing bonus.

McALARY: You're an editor. Who gives editors signing bonuses?

JOHN COTTER: I know.

> *They both laugh.*

McALARY: I hope you're going to use some of it to get your teeth fixed. Fuck. It's the politburo over there, you're going to hate it. *(Beat while it sinks in.)* Hey, it's great. But fuck you.

JOHN COTTER: You'll come back there, I'll bring everyone we care about back there with me—

McALARY: I like the *Post*. I can't go back to the *News*. Plus I have a contract . . . I can't get out of my contract.

JOHN COTTER: Eddie can get you out of anything.

> *A beat.*

McALARY: You know what I love about you?

JOHN COTTER: Yeah. I do. I'm a sick twisted fuck. I'm a heartless prick. I'll do anything for a good story. I've seen too many movies about journalism and I believed them all— *(Waving for another drink.)* Deadline–U.S.A. Humphrey Bogart. As me. Although considerably nobler. *(Quoting Bogart.)* "So you want to be a reporter. Well, don't ever change your mind."

McALARY: That's the worst Bogart I ever heard. *(Beat.)* I'm better when I write for you. I don't know if I'm any good without you.

JOHN COTTER: You're my finest creation.

McALARY: You know what I mean.

JOHN COTTER: Nah, Eddie will get you out, we'll all make out like bandits.

MCALARY: Hey. It's great. Congratulations. Hey.

> *They clink glasses.*

MICHAEL DALY: *(To audience.)* Cotter never wore socks, did anyone tell you that?

BOB DRURY: *(To audience.)* They told him he had to give up gin, so he switched to vodka.

MICHAEL DALY: *(To audience.)* They told him he had to give up vodka, so he switched to gin.

JERRY NACHMAN: He used to call you up, and if you weren't home he'd say to your kid, "You know what your daddy told me he's getting you for Christmas? A pony."

JOHN COTTER: We're dinosaurs, you know that? We're blacksmiths.

MCALARY: I love you, man.

JOHN COTTER: Don't get sloppy.

> MCALARY *stands.* COTTER *stands. They hug.* MCALARY *exits.* COTTER *sits back down, smiles happily, sips his drink, in a spotlight all his own.*

JIM DWYER: *(To audience.)* He'd already had one heart attack, and he was wearing the nitrogen patch you're supposed to wear, and they told him he had to stop drinking, so every five drinks he'd just slap on another patch.

JERRY NACHMAN: *(To audience.)* Cotter used to say, any story has only one real truth. Go to the morgue and count the bodies.

JOHN COTTER: *(To audience.)* Count the bodies.

> *The spotlight on* COTTER *goes out.*
> *As the guys once again sing an Irish song,* MCALARY *stands motionless, silent.*

ENSEMBLE: *(Sings.)*
"Let's not have a sniffle,
Let's have a bloody good cry,
And always remember, the longer you live,
The sooner you'll bloody well die."

JERRY NACHMAN: The day after Cotter quit the *Post*, we took his name off of the masthead. The next day, he died. The day after, we put it back on so his family could qualify for the death payment.

JIM DWYER: What happened next—

BOB DRURY: Everyone knew it would happen.

MICHAEL DALY: We all saw it coming.

JERRY NACHMAN: Inevitable.

JIM DWYER: It was only a matter of time.

New York Post *Newsroom*

> *Lights up on* McALARY *at his desk, working and drinking and working and drinking.*
> *Phones ring throughout.*

McALARY: Do-it-do-it-do-it-do-it.

JIM DWYER: *(To audience.)* One day, the owner of the *Post* ran out of money and sold the paper, to a snake oil salesman who was running a Ponzi scheme.

McALARY: *(Into phone.)* Get me the fuck out of here, Eddie, the ship is sinking—

JIM DWYER: It looked like the *Post* was going under, so Mac decided to go back to the *News*—

McALARY: *(In a bar.)* Where's Dinkins? I'll tell you where: He's out practicing his backhand. Giuliani's going to beat him and it will be Mussolini time. *(Into phone.)* Eddie, what gives?

EDDIE HAYES: *(To audience.)* —I'm going to get you three hundred thousand a year—

McALARY: *(To* EDDIE.*)* Plus a signing bonus, I want a signing bonus, don't forget it—

EDDIE HAYES: —plus a fifty-thousand-dollar signing bonus.

McALARY: —Enough for Alice and the kids to move back to a house in Brooklyn *and* keep the place in Bellport.

EDITORS: McAlary!

JIM DWYER: *(To audience.)* But Mac wasn't happy at the *News*.

EDITORS: McAlary!

JIM DWYER: Jim Willse was gone—

McALARY: *(On the phone.)* It's not the same place, Eddie. I'm dying, Eddie, I can't breathe—

JERRY NACHMAN: —So he decided he wanted to go back to the *Post*, which Rupert Murdoch had just bought.

> *In the bar,* McALARY *plots with* DWYER.

McALARY: Here's the plan, Dwyer. I go to the *Post*, you come to the *News*, you'll get my slot, we'll make Giuliani's first term a misery. It'll be perfect. One-two, one-two.

> *He signals for another round.*

JIM DWYER: *(To audience.)* That summer he had a spectacular run of stories.

McALARY: Five days in a row.

BOB DRURY: —about a police scandal in Brooklyn.

McALARY: "KNUCKLEHEADS VS ROGUE COPS by Mike McAlary. PBA BOSS A HYPOCRITE by Mike McAlary. GET KELLY COMMISH OUTTA THERE by Mike McAlary."

JIM DWYER: He got the wood every single day.

EDITOR #1: McAlary!

JERRY NACHMAN: It was like watching Michael Jordan.

McALARY: *(Into phone.)* Alice, Alice, I love you—

EDITOR #2: McAlary!

McALARY: I'm almost done. *(Into phone.)* But I am chained to my desk.

EDDIE HAYES: He was driving his price up. It was absolutely methodical.

McALARY: All I want—all I want is to be the highest-paid columnist in New York City.

EDDIE HAYES: It's feasible. It's feasible.

JIM DWYER: *(To audience.)* The *Post* offered him a million dollars over three years.

EDDIE HAYES: Plus I got you a relocation fee—

BOB DRURY: For what?

McALARY: Moving three cardboard boxes from the *News* to the *Post*. *(To everyone. Hands in the air.)* Put your money away. I'm buying! I am buying!

JIM DWYER: So Mac quit.

JERRY NACHMAN: The *News* sued McAlary.

BOB DRURY: The *Post* sued the *News*.

MICHAEL DALY: There was an injunction.

EDDIE HAYES: Everybody was writing about it. "What was McAlary going to do?"

> *The phones all stop ringing.*

McGuire's

> McALARY *is drunk at the bar. He sings.*

McALARY: *(Sings.)* Look at the widow, *(Quietly singing during below.)* Bloody great woman.
Isn't it grand, boys, to be bloody well dead?
Let's not have a sniffle,

Let's have a bloody good cry,
And always remember the longer you live
The sooner you'll bloody well die.

MICHAEL DALY: September 18, 1993. He went to a Yankee game.

HAP HAIRSTON: Fact.

BOB DRURY: He drank beer at the game.

HAP HAIRSTON: Fact.

JIM DWYER: He went to McGuire's after the game.

BOB DRURY: And drank more beer.

HAP HAIRSTON: More facts.

JERRY NACHMAN: He was out-of-his-mind drunk.

HAP HAIRSTON: Story.

JIM DWYER: He'd been drinking, but he was taking painkillers for a
    pinched nerve in his neck.

HAP HAIRSTON: Conflicting story.

BOB DRURY: He'd just gotten a million-dollar offer and he was out of
    control.

HAP HAIRSTON: One way of looking at it.

BOB DRURY: Icarus.

HAP HAIRSTON: Full-of-shit way of looking at it.

JERRY NACHMAN: Inevitable.

McALARY: *(Sings.)* Look at the tombstone,

McALARY: *(Cont'd.)*	BOB DRURY:
Bloody great boulder	Everyone knew it would happen.

MICHAEL DALY: We all saw it coming.

JERRY NACHMAN: Yeah, yeah, yeah.

McALARY:	JIM DWYER:
Isn't it grand, boys . . .	He should never have been driving.

HAP HAIRSTON: We'll all agree to that.
    McALARY *leaves the bar. The sound of hard rain falling.*

McALARY:
    To be bloody well dead?
    Let's not have a sniffle,
    Let's have a bloody good cry

MICHAEL DALY: It was raining.

JIM DWYER: It was two in the morning.

BOB DRURY: He was traveling south on the FDR.

MICHAEL DALY: Going at least seventy.

BOB DRURY: At least.

JIM DWYER: We don't really know that.

HAP HAIRSTON: Sure we do.

McALARY: And always remember, the longer you live—
The sound of a car skidding out of control.
A HUGE CRASH.
The sound of the rain.
A phone starts to ring.

McAlary Bedroom in Brooklyn

The light goes on.
ALICE McALARY *wakes up alone in bed. She reaches over to*
McALARY'*s side of the bed, answers the phone.*

ALICE: Hello?

BLACKOUT

ACT II

Bar/Hospital

A barrage of PROJECTION HEADLINES *from multiple*
newspapers: COLUMNIST CRITICALLY INJURED IN CAR
CRASH.
HAP HAIRSTON, JIM DWYER, MICHAEL DALY, JERRY NACHMAN,
and EDDIE HAYES *are in the bar.*

JERRY NACHMAN: So. Not dead.

MICHAEL DALY: But he died—

JERRY NACHMAN: He did not die—

JIM DWYER: They thought he was dead.

MICHAEL DALY: He stopped breathing—

EDDIE HAYES: They gave him last rites—

MICHAEL DALY: —twice—

JERRY NACHMAN: He stopped breathing for a couple of minutes—

EDDIE HAYES: —Seven minutes—

JIM DWYER: At least a minute—

EDDIE HAYES: Nobody knew if he was going to make it—

MICHAEL DALY: Or if he had health insurance. Because he was between jobs. He'd quit the *Post* for the *News*—

JERRY NACHMAN: —the *News* for the *Post*—

MICHAEL DALY: —who could keep track of any of it?

EDDIE HAYES: And the *News* was suing him for quitting.

JIM DWYER: They gave him an emergency tracheotomy—

JERRY NACHMAN: There was massive internal bleeding—

MICHAEL DALY: What I remember is being in an elevator in the hospital and somebody said, "Good news, there's no swelling on the brain."

JIM DWYER: And I said, "Are they sure it's really McAlary?"

> McALARY *appears stage right. He's in a hospital gown and he has a walker. He's with* ALICE, *starting to walk.*
> *She takes the walker away.*

McALARY: *(His speech is slightly slurred.)* I don't know how to walk.

ALICE: Sure you do.

McALARY: I don't . . . I—

ALICE: Michael . . . Michael—

McALARY: —don't know what I'm supposed to do with my legs.

ALICE: *(Looking him directly in the eye.)* You just put one foot in front of the other. C'mon.

> *He stands stock-still.*

Walk—walk, you bastard.

> *He starts to walk across the stage. Now that* McALARY *is no longer looking at her, she starts to cry.*

That's it. Keep going.

JIM DWYER: So, not dead.

EDDIE HAYES: But different.

JIM DWYER: And his speech—

MICHAEL DALY: He wasn't as fast.

EDDIE HAYES: He had trouble with some words. He was a little—

JIM DWYER: Stroke-y.

> *They all nod.*

MICHAEL DALY: But you had to have known him before—

JIM DWYER: It was like a millisecond slower, a hitch—

EDDIE HAYES: If you didn't know him before, you wouldn't know.

MICHAEL DALY: But if you knew him before, you knew.

> *Waiting for him is* HAP.
> McALARY *stands there.*

McALARY: Back when I was smart, before I was dead, I could figure this out.

HAP HAIRSTON: You were never smart.

> HAP *holds out his arm and he and* McALARY *walk slowly together back across the stage.*

I ever tell you about my dog?

McALARY: You got a dog? Poor dog.

> As McALARY *struggles to walk—*

HAP HAIRSTON: Stella. Just went blind. Dealing a hell of a lot better than you or I would. To her, loss of sight is just the next thing in her life she has to confront. That's where you are, dealing with the next thing you've gotta confront. Nothing more.

McALARY: Nah. Feels like I'm being punished, for being an asshole.

HAP HAIRSTON: I can see that.

McALARY: Thanks for coming.

HAP HAIRSTON: By the way, this doesn't mean I'm not still pissed off at you.

ALICE: He went to Rusk for rehab. After a few months, he was still struggling. I tried to convince him not to, but—

JIM DWYER: He went back to work at the *Daily News*, where he'd just quit, right before the accident.

Daily News *Newsroom*

> *There are big TV sets all over the newsroom.*
> *There's a* NO SMOKING *sign. No one is smoking.*

JIM DWYER: It's 1994. Giuliani has just been elected. *New York Newsday* folded, and a lot of us ended up at the *News*. Willse was gone and the paper was essentially being run by a charming gentleman named Stanley Joyce. *(To audience.)* The weekend before McAlary came back to work, he wrote a column from home— *(Quoting the column.)* "One day you wake up and you are not dead. It's funny, but the first thing you forget when you are struggling to reclaim your mind are all those mindless feuds that made you so miserably happy."—

McALARY: —All my enemies went away. Or seemed to. You just wake up one day and the hate slate is clean.

> McALARY *walks in, sits down at the desk next to* JIM DWYER.

JIM DWYER: Good column.

McALARY: Thanks.

McALARY *has just the slightest difficulty talking. Very slight.*

JIM DWYER: Had to see you now that you were done hating. You made a lot of promises when you were talking to God, but I couldn't help saying to myself, when he's feeling better he's going to say to himself, fuck this.

McALARY *smiles. He stands to hug* DWYER.

McALARY: Gimme a hug.

JIM DWYER: Don't give me one of those nelly hugs of yours, McAlary.

McALARY: I love you man.

McALARY *laughs, sits back down.*

STANLEY JOYCE *appears in the newsroom.*

JIM DWYER: You heard Stanley is running the joint.

McALARY: The guy hates me.

JIM DWYER: But luckily you don't hate him anymore. Because you are done hating. *(To audience.)* McAlary once wrote a column calling him "the most overrated talent in the history of journalism," so that was kind of a problem.

McALARY: Where's Hap?

JIM DWYER: In Business. They made him Business editor.

McALARY: What does Hap know about business?

JIM DWYER: The interest rate on overdue credit card payments. What are you writing for tomorrow?

McALARY: I don't know. Something. There's always something. Patrick Ewing. He's a bum.

He starts to type.

JIM DWYER: You can't do Patrick Ewing.

McALARY: I have a feud with Patrick Ewing. It's famous.

McALARY *goes on typing.*

JIM DWYER: You can't do Patrick Ewing again. Tell me you're not doing Patrick Ewing.

McALARY *goes on typing.*

HAP *walks into the newsroom.*

HAP HAIRSTON: *(To audience.)* So. Two people who figure into this part of the story—Debby Krenek. She's an editor. Eventually, she's going to end up running the place.

HAP *points to* DEBBY KRENEK, *who turns to* STANLEY JOYCE, *waves her hand meekly to get his attention.*

STANLEY JOYCE: What is it, Debby?

HAP HAIRSTON: Stanley Joyce. The managing editor. Who did hate McAlary.

DEBBY KRENEK: McAlary's column—

STANLEY JOYCE: What about it?

DEBBY KRENEK: It's about Patrick Ewing? The basketball player?

STANLEY JOYCE: I know who Patrick Ewing is.

DEBBY KRENEK: McAlary's written this column before—"Patrick Ewing is a bum."

STANLEY JOYCE: And?

DEBBY KRENEK: It's not well-written, and I'm just concerned—

STANLEY JOYCE: This is coming as a big surprise to you? He's overrated, he's overpaid, I wish he wasn't here. What did I leave out?
   A beat.

DEBBY KRENEK: O-kay. *(To audience.)* The editors were all treating him very gingerly. And the reporters . . . Well, there was a sense he was all for himself, that he didn't stand for the paper. He stood for whatever was best for him. And all of this came into play with the Jane Doe case.

Bar

HAP HAIRSTON: The Jane Doe case. How the fuck do we tell this part of it?

JIM DWYER: Shit.

EDDIE HAYES: Why don't we just skip over it?

HAP HAIRSTON: We can't skip over it.

EDDIE HAYES: Sure we can. No one even remembers—

HAP HAIRSTON: But it happened.

EDDIE HAYES: Fuck. You're going to need Miller.

MICHAEL DALY: It wasn't only Miller's fault.

HAP HAIRSTON: So you tell the story.

MICHAEL DALY: I don't want to tell the story. I had nothing to do with it. I just want to get my theory in, early.

HAP HAIRSTON: Which is?

MICHAEL DALY: What McAlary never understood is, cops; good cops, bad cops, doesn't matter. They all piss in your pocket and say it's raining. He never understood, cops fuck everything up.

HAP HAIRSTON: Noted.

Police Headquarters

The clamor of a press conference at NYPD.

JOHN MILLER *appears at the podium. There's an NYPD shield hanging on the front of the podium.*

REPORTER #1: What's the story on the Jane Doe in Prospect Park?

HAP HAIRSTON: *(To audience.)* This is where the whole mess starts, at a press briefing at NYPD.

JOHN MILLER: We don't know. Things don't quite add up, apparently. So if I were you, I would go easy on it—

REPORTER #1: Meaning what?

JOHN MILLER: Meaning there are problems with the case. But I never said it.

HAP HAIRSTON: *(To audience.)* John Miller. Deputy commissioner for public information.

REPORTER #2: Can you give us any details?

JOHN MILLER: For your guidance. Not for publication, okay? The Jane Doe says she was walking home from the grocery store when she was dragged up a hill and raped, but the police couldn't find the bags or the groceries, there were no grass stains on her clothes, no injuries consistent with the struggle she described. Look, all I'm saying is, don't go to the wood.

A phone starts to ring.

MILLER *leaves the podium and walks to his office at NYPD Headquarters, answers the phone.*

Miller.

McALARY *on the phone at his desk at the* News.

McALARY: McAlary. I hear the police don't think too much of this rape in Brooklyn—

JOHN MILLER: They think it's bullshit. But you didn't hear it from me.

McALARY: I'm on it. I'll call you later.

McALARY *hangs up.*

JOHN MILLER: *(To audience.)* When McAlary called me back later he had a lot of stuff about the Jane Doe—

McALARY: *(On phone.)* She's gay, she's black, she's scheduled to speak at a lesbian rally about rape this weekend—

JOHN MILLER: *(To audience.)* Apparently she'd told the police her rapist was a black guy—

McALARY: *(On phone.)* —and when the cops stopped a black guy for questioning she got pissed and said they only picked the guy up because he was black.

JOHN MILLER: Clearly he was getting his information from someone in the department who knew way more than I did. It was classic McAlary.

Daily News *Newsroom*

McALARY: Stanley?

STANLEY JOYCE: What?

McALARY: That rape in Prospect Park is bullshit. She's speaking at a rally on rape this weekend and she told the cops, I'm going to use this in my speech. She invented it to promote a rally on rape. I have it cold.

STANLEY JOYCE: What about the semen test?

McALARY: No results yet. Maybe tomorrow.

STANLEY JOYCE: So wait a day.

McALARY: I'm writing for tomorrow. She made it up, Stanley. She could be arrested.

STANLEY JOYCE: Who's your source?

McALARY: Who's my source?

STANLEY JOYCE: Yeah.

McALARY: The chief of detectives. Plus, the chief of department. Plus Miller. You want me to get another source? Who else do you want? How about the Cardinal?

STANLEY JOYCE: So another Tawana?

JIM DWYER: *(To audience.)* The Tawana Brawley thing had happened a couple of years earlier.

EDDIE HAYES: Tawana Brawley was also a black woman who said she'd been raped, but she was lying.

McALARY: Yes, another Tawana.

MICHAEL DALY: It was a huge story and kind of a precedent for a maybe-she's-lying scenario.

McALARY: It's that big.

STANLEY JOYCE: Okay.

> *Projection: page one of the* Daily News: RAPE HOAX THE REAL CRIME *by Mike McAlary.*
> *Everyone onstage looks up at the projection and then back at the audience.*

HAP HAIRSTON: *(To audience.)* I looked at that column and said, this is going to be a nightmare.

JIM DWYER: That doesn't make you a genius. We all knew it.

HAP HAIRSTON: If I'd been his editor, it never would have happened.

JIM DWYER: The next day, the police released the results of the semen test—

JOHN MILLER: *(At podium.)* She tested positive for semen—
  McALARY *with the editors.*

McALARY: Don't believe it. She tested *negative.*

STANLEY JOYCE: Negative? But Miller said positive. Which is it?

McALARY: Negative.
  The editors look completely confused.

STANLEY JOYCE: So the Department spokesman is saying positive—

McALARY: And the chief of detectives is saying negative—

STANLEY JOYCE: The chief of detectives said this to you? The chief of detectives said, the sperm test is negative?

McALARY: The chief of detectives said this to my guy—

STANLEY JOYCE: To your guy. Who is your guy today?

McALARY: The chief of department. Who got it from the chief of detectives.

STANLEY JOYCE: So why is Miller saying it's positive? Is he lying? Is he out of the loop? Is he a nut? Which is it?

McALARY: He's saying what he has to say. *(Beat.)* Look, the chief of detectives' office handles the material, *they* check the evidence, not the PR guy. My sources are the real sources. Which is why—

STANLEY JOYCE: *(Finishing the sentence.)* —they pay you the fucking big bucks.
  The phone rings.

McALARY: —which is why this story is true. And fuck you, Stanley.
  McALARY *walks back to his desk.*
  STANLEY JOYCE *answers the phone.*

STANLEY JOYCE: Mike McAlary has a long record of solid authoritative reporting and we stand by his column.

MICHAEL DALY: The thing is, she was raped.

EDDIE HAYES: She wasn't raped.

MICHAEL DALY: She was raped.

EDDIE HAYES: She might have been raped, she might not have been raped.

JIM DWYER: Shut the fuck up, Eddie.

HAP HAIRSTON: *(To audience.)* The lawyers were involved. Everybody was in on it. Everyone except—

JIM DWYER: You.

HAP HAIRSTON: If I'd been his editor, I would have said, did you try to contact this woman? Did you talk to anyone in the precinct?

Did you go to Prospect Park? Did you call the grocery store
she says she went to? I would have said to the editors, do you
understand this is sexist, and racist? Hello? Nobody's antennae
went up because they all are white boys. I would have said
something—

MICHAEL DALY: Look, he didn't do the legwork.

JIM DWYER: He couldn't do the legwork. He came back to work too
soon.

MICHAEL DALY: Long story short: the cops fucked up and he
fucked up.

EDDIE HAYES: You know what they say about the Irish? The Irish are
their own worst—

HAP HAIRSTON: This hasn't got one damn thing to do with the
Irish and everything to do with McAlary looking for a big story,
trying to prove he still had it. And all the people in the past who
protected Mac from Mac weren't around.

MICHAEL DALY: Including you.

HAP HAIRSTON: I'm just saying.

> *A beat.*

DEBBY KRENEK: *(To audience.)* The next day we ran a news story
that said the police were saying the rape had happened—

> *Projection of page five of the* Daily News *and the headline:*
> EVIDENCE BACKS RAPE.

And on the opposite page, we had McAlary's column saying it
hadn't happened.

> *Projection of headline reads:* NO EASY TASK EXPOSING LIE *by*
> *Mike McAlary.*

> *On the television set, a projection of the police commissioner,*
> *Bill Bratton.*

HAP HAIRSTON: And then everything went nuts. Bill Bratton, the
police commissioner, apologized—he apologized in this weird,
elliptical, convoluted way—

> *Bill Bratton: "It's unfortunate that apparently a member of*
> *this department shared some thoughts with others that were*
> *reported in the media. I can comfortably offer an apology*
> *in terms of, if there was any police role in this, it should not*
> *have been."*

> *A phone rings.*

STANLEY JOYCE: *(On the phone.)* Mike McAlary has a long record of
solid authoritative reporting and we stand by his column.

DEBBY KRENEK: But here was the thing—McAlary's sources in the police department stuck with the story—

McALARY *and* STANLEY JOYCE *at* McALARY's *desk.*

STANLEY JOYCE: I don't get this.

McALARY: There was no semen.

STANLEY JOYCE: Explain it to me.

McALARY: I'm telling you what the lab report really says.

STANLEY JOYCE: Doesn't the police commissioner read the lab report?

McALARY: He's fucking me. He's fucking me because he has to say that.

STANLEY JOYCE: Why? Why?

McALARY: He's running for mayor? He doesn't want to lose the black vote? How do I know? All I can tell you is, the lab report says—

McALARY:	STANLEY JOYCE:
No semen.	No semen.

STANLEY JOYCE: I hate that word.

McALARY: I know.

STANLEY JOYCE: Did you talk to the lawyers?

McALARY: I'm sleeping with the lawyers. I've got the lawyers checking every word I write—

DEBBY KRENEK: *(To audience.)* And then, the petition. A bunch of reporters at the paper signed a petition condemning McAlary. Two of the reporters who wrote the petition showed it to me. They were proud of themselves. I couldn't believe it. I said, "Do you really want to do this?" I mean, this never happens, reporters turning on a fellow reporter.

"McAlary's column—

DEBBY, REPORTER/PETITIONER: —and the *Daily News*'s hypocritical performance—

DEBBY, REPORTERS/PETITIONERS: —are a disgrace.—

REPORTERS/PETITIONERS: —No reporter, whether writing an opinion column—

—or a news story,—

REPORTER/PETITIONER: —should be allowed to—

DEBBY, REPORTERS/PETITIONERS: —rush to judgment—

REPORTER/PETITIONER: —without at least trying to hear the opposing views.—

REPORTERS/PETITIONERS: —Without speaking to the victim,—

—McAlary was allowed to—

DEBBY, REPORTERS/PETITIONERS: —judge and convict her."
DEBBY KRENEK: The *Times* wrote about it. Everybody wrote about it.
DEBBY, REPORTERS/PETITIONERS: "We demand an apology."

McAlary Living Room

> MCALARY *and* ALICE *in the kitchen.* MCALARY *has the petition.*

MCALARY: *(Exploding.)* "We demand an apology!" Just look at all the names. Catherine Ellis. I got her moved from Sports to the Metro Desk. I got her her first freelance magazine assignment. Even had Eddie negotiate her deal.
ALICE: "Without speaking to the victim, McAlary was allowed to judge and . . ."
MCALARY: Carl Marino. I wrote about his book seven times at least, and it's fucking unreadable. Joe Martinez. How many times did I help you, Joe?
ALICE: What does it matter? As long as you got the story right, right?
MCALARY: Tim Bradley—he used to work at the *Voice*, what the fuck does he know? Fuck!

Daily News *Newsroom*

HAP HAIRSTON: And then he wrote a third column, which had nothing to do with the tenets of journalism and everything to do with McAlary feeling under attack.

> *Projection:* I'M RIGHT BUT THAT'S NO REASON TO CHEER *by Mike McAlary.*

And nobody can tell me if I was his editor that third column would have run. Is anyone going to tell me that?

> *No one is going to contradict him.*
> *A projection of Police Commissioner Bratton.*
> *Everyone turns to look at the television set.*
> *A projection of the police commissioner Bill Bratton, who also appears on all the TV screens in the office:* "A rape took place. There is physical evidence that a rape occurred. Unfortunately there was some confusion in the police department about the lab report and its significance"—

STANLEY JOYCE: Confusion?
DEBBY KRENEK: —the confusion being that the chief of detectives couldn't read a lab report. And he'd gotten confused about semen

versus sperm. Turns out sperm is not always present in semen, so the semen test turned out to be positive but the sperm test was negative. It was a disaster.

HAP HAIRSTON: Although we all ended up knowing way more about semen than we knew before, so it wasn't a total loss.

McALARY: I'm getting smoked.

MICHAEL DALY: What can you do?

JIM DWYER: See if Miller will bail you out. He was a source, get him to say so.

McALARY: He's not going to do that.

MICHAEL DALY: Did you ask him?

McALARY: Yeah, I asked him.

MICHAEL DALY: It's not libel if you had a credible source.

McALARY: I can't give up my sources. They'll never trust me again. No one will.

JIM DWYER: Ask him again.

McALARY: You think there's going to be a libel suit?

MICHAEL DALY: Do I think there's going to be a libel suit?

   Silence. A beat as it sinks in.

HAP HAIRSTON: *(To audience.)* So she sued for libel. For twelve million dollars. And here's what happens when you get sued for libel, here's what happens even if everyone involved knows you got the story wrong—

   STANLEY JOYCE *on the phone.*

STANLEY JOYCE: Mike McAlary has a long record of solid authoritative reporting and we stand by his column.

   STANLEY JOYCE *hangs up. Stands there for a moment.*
Fuck.

HAP HAIRSTON: *(To audience.)* The *Post* was calling him Mike Malarkey.

JIM DWYER: The *Times* was trashing him.

MICHAEL DALY: The cops had backed away from the story they'd given him. They put him out on a limb and left him there.

EDDIE HAYES: People were writing stories saying, "This woman is being re-raped in the *Daily News*."

ALICE: *(To audience.)* One morning, I was walking the kids to school and there were big lemon-yellow posters up and down the block with Michael's picture on them. Wanted posters. WANTED FOR CRIMES AGAINST WOMEN. I said to the older kids, "Not everybody is going to agree with what Daddy writes; sometimes Daddy is going to write things and people are going to react." So we all decided to just ignore it, but the baby kept pointing, saying, "There's Daddy, there's my daddy."

HAP HAIRSTON: *(To audience.)* They made me his editor again. So now I was the Business editor, and I was the McAlary editor. The lawyers were reading everything the guy wrote. They were making grammatical suggestions. They were editing the column, and then when they got done, Stanley Joyce would bury it in the back of the paper.

Diner

> McALARY *on a cell phone. He's having breakfast with* EDDIE HAYES.

McALARY: Hap, this is Mike McAlary. Where'd they play me?

HAP HAIRSTON: I'll tell you, but don't hang up on me.

McALARY: Okay.

HAP HAIRSTON: Promise?

McALARY: Promise.

HAP HAIRSTON: Page seventeen.

> McALARY *hangs up.*

McALARY: I'm having a major demise.

EDDIE HAYES: They're just waiting for the lawsuit to sort itself out. We'll be fine.

> *Before* McALARY *can object—*

We'll be fine. Now that I got Miller to agree to testify, they can't say it's libel if you printed what he told you. At some point they'll fire Stanley Joyce.

McALARY: He's never going to get fired. He's like an inkblot, he never goes away—

> McALARY *lights a cigarette.*

EDDIE HAYES: You not eating your bacon?

McALARY: Have it. Here. You want the toast too?

EDDIE HAYES: I'm on a diet. All the bacon you can eat but no toast.

McALARY: How is it possible you can eat all the bacon you want?

EDDIE HAYES: Don't ask me. There's a book, I'll get it for you.

McALARY: Am I ever going to get lucky again? Have I used it all up? Is there just so much and—

EDDIE HAYES: We went to Tough Guy School, we'll ride it out. What's the worst that could happen?

McALARY: I could end up a rewrite man on the lobster shift typing press releases and obits all night long. No byline. No money.

Nothing. I'd be one of those zombies I see staggering out of the office every morning looking for a breakfast special of cheap rye and beer chasers. *(Beat.)* I feel like shit. I'm not sleeping, I've got chills. I've got the runs.

EDDIE HAYES: Did you have a flu shot?

McALARY: I forgot.

EDDIE HAYES: Go see a doctor. You've probably got the flu. You need a doctor, I've got a doctor.

McALARY: I don't need a doctor to tell me what's wrong with me. Stanley Joyce is what's wrong with me. It's a low-grade fever, that's all. And the fucking lawsuit.

He takes out a bottle of Advil and pops a couple, drinks some water.

McAlary Living Room

ALICE *in a wing-back chair.*

ALICE: *(To audience.)* One night we went to a dinner party and I looked across the table at Michael and suddenly realized something was very wrong. He was gray. I just hadn't seen it because I'd been living with it. The next day we called my doctor and he went to see her. She called me from Brookhaven Hospital and said they were giving him some blood because he was anemic. I thought, anemic, that explains everything. And then she said she was going to stop by. I didn't think much about it—she was a friend. She came over and she said, "I've got to talk to you." I didn't know what was happening. She sat down in the living room and she said, "Michael has an adenocarcinoma of the sigmoid colon with metastasis to the liver and the bladder." I said, okay, what are you saying, say it in English, and she said, "Michael has cancer." The next thing I remember, I was running from the house. I got into the car and I just began driving wildly. I had no idea where I was going. There was a church, and I stopped and walked into the chapel. I couldn't take one more thing. We'd gone through so much, and after you go through so much, life is supposed to be grand. And then my phone rang, and it was one of my kids saying, "Mommy, where are you? What happened?" I snapped out of it and I went home.

Doctor's Office/Hospital

McALARY *and* EDDIE HAYES *with a* DOCTOR.

DOCTOR: We're going to operate and then we're going to give you chemotherapy and radiation. It'll be very powerful, you'll be nauseous, you'll probably become sterile—

McALARY: I can live with sterile. I got three kids.

EDDIE HAYES: You've got a shot.

McALARY: But the odds—

DOCTOR: Don't think about the odds. You've got a shot. There's no cure now, but there's stuff in the pipeline.

EDDIE HAYES: If we can just keep you alive for a few years, some Asian guy will find a cure.

An orderly wheels a hospital bed onstage and when the bed is in place we see that the patient in the bed is HAP HAIRSTON.

HAP HAIRSTON: *(To audience.)* In December 1996 he had his first big operation. I'd had open heart surgery and my sternum wouldn't knit and they couldn't get it to knit. I went into St. Vincent's on a Thursday morning and I woke up on a Sunday. Freaked out. I wasn't just in Intensive Care, I was in the Intensive Care where the nurse only has two patients. My first call was from McAlary. *(Picking up a phone.)* Hairston.

McALARY *is on the phone in another hospital bed.*

McALARY: This sucks huh?

HAP HAIRSTON: Yeah. It's really pissing me off.

McALARY: But on the bright side, Hap, they found your heart, which is a surprise to some of us.

HAP HAIRSTON: I'm going to make it through. So are you. Even if it kills us. Both of us can not go down.

McALARY: And meanwhile, we've got morphine.

They've both got morphine pumps.

Does yours have a regulator?

HAP HAIRSTON: Sure. I guess so.

McALARY: What's it set to?

HAP HAIRSTON: Six.

McALARY: Press the Exit button. See the main menu? Press the up arrow till it says thirteen.

HAP HAIRSTON: Okay.

HAP *presses the button.*

McALARY: Let's do it.

HAP HAIRSTON: One, two, three.

MCALARY: Beam me up, Scotty.

>*They both hit their morphine pumps.*
>
>*Another beat.*

You know what, Hap?

HAP HAIRSTON: What?

MCALARY: Journalism has lost its charm.

HAP HAIRSTON: It's like my first wife.

MCALARY: How is it like your first wife?

HAP HAIRSTON: I know I used to love her, but I can't remember why.

MCALARY: Even so—I always knew I was going to live in the city. Knew I was going to write for a newspaper. Didn't know which one, but I knew. Knew I'd have a column. I even knew I was going to be edited by a balding black man who drank almost as much as me. What I didn't know, was all the other stuff that would come along as well.

>*Silence.*

HAP HAIRSTON: So what's the story?

MCALARY: It's looking not good. They got most of it. There's something on the liver—but there's this new chemo—there's stuff in the pipeline.

McAlary Living Room

ALICE: The prognosis wasn't good, but Michael's outlook was positive. I thought, okay, we've got a grip on this. I did some reading, and then I stopped. I thought, this is Michael, this is not a statistic. The chemo was brutal but the tumors were shrinking. And the doctors weren't right about everything—I was pregnant. After a few months, Michael went back to work at the *Daily News*—

Daily News *Newsroom*

DEBBY KRENEK: —Where I'd taken over as executive editor.

>MCALARY *at his desk, typing. He looks up. There's* DEBBY KRENEK.

Good news. The lawsuit was dismissed.

MCALARY: We won?

DEBBY KRENEK: We won in that it's over and it was dismissed. It says you reported what the police department told you so it's not libel. But the cops were wrong to tell you what they told you. It's over, that's the main thing.

> *A beat.*

McALARY: What a relief. It's all I thought about until I got sick. Good things have to happen every so often. I gotta call Alice. What a fucking anticlimax.

DEBBY KRENEK: Also, and this is unrelated I promise you, we have a problem. They're making cutbacks. The owner.

> *A beat.*

McALARY: He wants to fire me?

DEBBY KRENEK: But we have an idea—

McALARY: I have a contract.

DEBBY KRENEK: What if you wrote only once a week? They'd pay you less, but you'd hold on to your health insurance. And you could do magazine articles, you could write a book—

McALARY: *(Re: the owner.)* The prick.

DEBBY KRENEK: Owners. What can you do?

> *A beat.*

McALARY: I do have an idea for a novel.

DEBBY KRENEK: So we'll work it out with Eddie?

> McALARY *nods.*

This way you stay here. We need you here.

> DEBBY *walks off.*

Bellport Kitchen

> ALICE *in the kitchen. She's making toast.* McALARY *walks into the kitchen.*

ALICE: What's your day?

> McALARY *picks up the phone and dials his office to play his messages.*

McALARY: *(Listening to the phone message.)* Chemo at eight. Then I gotta do some radio show and an interview with the *Bellport Bulletin.*

ALICE: Big-time. I'm making you toast.

> McALARY *doesn't respond. He's still listening to his message.*

Not hearing an answer, I am moving forward in the toast area.

> McALARY *hangs up.*
> *Stands by the phone, thinking.*

Michael? *(Turns and sees he's distracted.)* Are you feeling okay?

McALARY: *(To* ALICE.*)* Listen to this.

He hits the speaker-phone button on the phone.

PHONE MESSAGE: McAlary. Mike McAlary. You don't know me but I am calling you because in the Seven-O Precinct in Brooklyn, on August the ninth at 0400 hours, they, the cops there, sodomized a prisoner. The patient is currently at Coney Island Hospital. His name, his last name, is L-O-U-I-M-A. Now they are trying to cover this up, because it was two white officers. And they did this to a black guy who they locked up for disorderly conduct. And now they are charging him with assault in the second. All this information can be verified if you call Coney Island Hospital or the Seven-O Precinct. I will not call you again.

He hangs up the phone and looks at ALICE. *After a beat—*

McALARY: It probably didn't happen.

ALICE: It sounds like it happened. Like something happened.

McALARY: We had something like it a couple of years ago, some livery drivers in Rockaway cooked up a story about a cop they said had sodomized them, it didn't check out.

ALICE: If it did happen and you ignore it, you'll never be able to look at yourself again.

McALARY: I'll phone it in to Corky and pass it on to the desk.

ALICE: You're gonna let someone else write it? What is going on here?

McALARY: I'm done with cop stuff.

ALICE: What the hell does that mean? You're "done with cop stuff"?

McALARY: I'm only doing one column a week. I am done with cops.

ALICE: No, no, no. This is bigger than "I am only doing one column a week and I'm done with cops." Who are these people going to call if they can't call you? You're the guy they call. Your whole career is about being the guy they call.

ALICE *hands him his pad.*

I'm changing your appointment.

McALARY: And I got that radio interview.

ALICE: Yeah, that radio thing.

McALARY: And the—

ALICE: *Bellport Bulletin.* Got it.

McALARY: On my way to chemo I start working the phone. Call a guy at the DMV, and I get him to run the name Louima. L-O-U-I-M-A. Ten Louimas. I call six or seven till I get to Fanie Louima, who turns out to be the guy's aunt and she gives me his first name,

Abner, and the name of his lawyer. So now I'm in chemo, and I reach the lawyer, and he tells me the name of the arresting officer and the room number at the hospital. Which I need because they don't tell you the room number at the front desk if it's a guy who just got arrested. They don't even let you on the elevator, but I get around that.

Hospital Room

> LOUIMA *is a delicate Haitian. He's wearing a white hospital smock. His right wrist is handcuffed to the side of the bed.* McALARY *is next to him, close by.*

ABNER LOUIMA: They threw me in the car. They kicked me, they beat me with their radios. One said, "You scum, I am going to teach you to respect a cop." "Why do you niggers come to this country if you can't speak English?"

McALARY: Who were the cops?

ABNER LOUIMA: I don't know.

McALARY: Did you see their name tags?

ABNER LOUIMA: No name tags. They took off my clothes at the station. My pants were down at my ankles in front of them. They walked me over to the bathroom and closed the door. There were two cops. One said, "You niggers have to learn to respect police officers." The other one said, "If you yell or make any noise, I will kill you."

> *He stops for a moment.*

McALARY: Take your time. *(Sits.)* I'm not going anywhere.

ABNER LOUIMA: Then one held me and the other one stuck the stick up my behind. He said, "Take this, nigger." I was screaming. Then the cop pulled it out. There was blood and shit on it. He shoved it in my mouth, broke my teeth and said, "That's your shit, nigger."

McALARY: What kind of a nightstick are we talking about?

ABNER LOUIMA: Not a nightstick. It was the plunger from the policemen's bathroom.

McALARY: How do you know?

ABNER LOUIMA: I seen the rubber thing on the bottom.

McALARY: Where's the Brooklyn D.A.?

ABNER LOUIMA: My lawyer is calling him.

McALARY: Be sure to tell him a reporter was here. Tell him it was me, okay? Mike McAlary.

Daily News *Newsroom*

HAP HAIRSTON, DEBBY KRENEK, STANLEY JOYCE *at the table.*
STANLEY JOYCE: No. Absolutely not. It shouldn't be the wood.
HAP HAIRSTON: It shouldn't be the wood? What else have you got for the wood?
STANLEY JOYCE: We've got the Duchess of Windsor. They're auctioning off her jewels.
HAP HAIRSTON: Great.
STANLEY JOYCE: How do we know it's true?
HAP HAIRSTON: We've got Louima, we're the only ones who talked to the guy. The police confirmed he was arrested. Which part of it do we not know is true?
STANLEY JOYCE: How do we know he was really raped?
HAP HAIRSTON: His asshole is bleeding. Look, the story's solid. We're already thinking about follow-up. I don't see the problem.
STANLEY JOYCE: The problem is obvious, isn't it? The problem is McAlary.
A long pause.
HAP HAIRSTON: It's not your call, Stanley.
They turn to look at DEBBY KRENEK.
DEBBY KRENEK: *(To audience.)* It was my call. The editor in chief, Pete Hamill, was on vacation, and I was the acting editor. I couldn't believe it. We've got this great story and we have to figure out how to play it and unfortunately all I'm thinking is, why me? *(To the other editors.)* I think we should read it first. *(A beat.)* And the lawyers obviously have to read it.
STANLEY JOYCE: Obviously.
DEBBY KRENEK: I'll see if I can find Pete.
HAP HAIRSTON: *(To audience.)* We turned the story in at six. Everyone was still nervous. The lawyers had a million petty and obscure suggestions. Stanley was still talking about the Duchess of Windsor. But Debby found Pete, and he said, go with McAlary. By then, the cops knew Mac had the story, so they put out a statement.
The volume comes up on all the television sets in the newsroom. Everyone in the newsroom turns to watch.
NEW YORK 1 REPORTER: The NYPD announced late today it was suspending two policemen in Brooklyn pending an investigation into an incident following an arrest in a Flatbush nightclub.

The volume drops but everyone continues to watch the New York 1 Reporter.

HAP HAIRSTON: *(To audience.)* Big sigh of relief. They're thrilled. It must be true—it's on television. It's the moment you know, if you didn't already know, that it's over. The newspaper business. The glory days.

McALARY: But here's the thing about being a reporter. "It's not the oldest job in the world, but it's the best job in the world." Because—

JIM DWYER: —because what you do matters—

HAP HAIRSTON: —because every day is different—

JERRY NACHMAN: —because everybody is smart, even the dumb ones—

MICHAEL DALY: —because of the action—

BOB DRURY: —because of the deadlines—

JERRY NACHMAN: —because of the guys—

MICHAEL DALY: —because of the stories—

HAP HAIRSTON: —because you never have to go home—

McALARY: —because beneath that cynicism there's the same sweet fantasy we all have about this business—that we're knights, that we right wrongs, and then afterwards we go out and have a drink because that's what we do.

Headline on Daily News *front page:* SECURITY GUARD TELLS McALARY HE WAS TORTURED BY COPS.

McALARY *at his computer, typing.*

DEBBY KRENEK: *(To audience.)* It was a huge story.

Headline on Daily News *front page:* ACCUSED COP TALKS TO McALARY ABOUT TORTURE SCANDAL.

McALARY *at his computer, typing.*

HAP HAIRSTON: *(To audience.)* Nobody had what Mac had.

Headline on Daily News *front page:* RUDY AND BRASS REAP HARVEST OF HATE *by Mike McAlary.*

MICHAEL DALY: Every connection he'd ever made paid off.

DEBBY KRENEK: And he had the wood for the next four days.

JIM DWYER: *(To audience.)* That summer, the McAlarys came up to the Poconos for a visit. Mac's novel had just been published, he was looking healthy and happy. The kids called him Zipper Man because of all his scars. He played tennis. So we were all out at the pool and their son Ryan wanted to do a flip, and he was nervous, and Mac said, "When you do these things you can't be nervous—

if you think about what can go wrong, if you think about the belly flop, or you think you'll land on your back, that's what'll happen. You just have to do it. I'll show you." So he went out to the end of the diving board. Poor Alice, she covered her eyes. She couldn't even look at this, she couldn't even watch. Mac took two steps, bounces up into the sun, and he's not just doing a flip, he's doing a one-and-a-half gainer. He comes out of the water laughing. And he said to Ryan—I can see him, putting his fingers in the air—he always put his fingers in the air—he said, "Ryan, the important thing is, don't be afraid. Just do the dive."

> DWYER *puts his fingers up in the air, like* McALARY.
>
> As ALICE *helps a weakened* McALARY *get dressed*—

HAP HAIRSTON: I first heard from Debby—

BOB DRURY: Daly told me—

MICHAEL DALY: After Alice had called me.

DEBBY KRENEK: It was a Friday.

HAP HAIRSTON: *(Elated.)* The first words out of my mouth were son-of-a-bitch! That lucky bastard has gone and won himself the Pulitzer Prize!

Daily News *Newsroom*

DEBBY KRENEK: *(To audience.)* We planned a celebration in the newsroom and everybody showed up. He walked in and—

> McALARY *walks in. He's very obviously sick, his shirt is way too big for his neck, and he's walking with difficulty.*
>
> *The ensemble is in the newsroom. Everyone starts to applaud.*

JIM DWYER: *(To audience.)* He was so thin.

HAP HAIRSTON: *(To audience.)* He was emaciated.

MICHAEL DALY: *(To audience.)* His shirt collar was way too big for his neck.

DEBBY KRENEK: *(To audience.)* Everyone was shocked.

HAP HAIRSTON: *(To audience.)* People were shocked, especially the ones who hadn't seen him.

JIM DWYER: *(To audience.)* Alice was wearing red.

> ALICE *is wearing red.*

DEBBY KRENEK: *(To audience.)* I spoke first. Then the publisher said something. And then Mac said, "A mistake has been made"—

> McALARY *stands in front of the newsroom. He's nervous and shaking.*

McALARY: A mistake has been made. That's what I keep telling myself. I was on the phone with the office every ten minutes yesterday asking, "Is it still true?" And then we would scream. I told my parents they must have the wrong Mike. They must mean Daly, who along with Cotter taught me to write a column. It could and should have been any of you. Catherine, Carl, Joe, Tim—

HAP HAIRSTON: *(To the audience.)* He mentioned a whole bunch of people. A lot of them had signed the petition against him, but he mentioned them anyway.

EDDIE HAYES: *(To the audience.)* He even mentioned me.

McALARY: On the other hand, as my lawyer and friend Eddie Hayes said, "I don't know if I'm ready to live in a world where McAlary is admired and respected."

    Everyone laughs, including EDDIE.

So they made a mistake. But I won't ask for a correction. *(Beat.)* I got sick a couple of years ago. They removed a tumor from my colon. Finding out you have cancer is a little like waking up on death row. I had chemotherapy the day I heard about Abner Louima. Drove directly from my doctor's office to his hospital room. It wasn't my day to write. But Hap Hairston, my genius editor—

HAP HAIRSTON: *(To audience.)* —He called me the best editor in the United States, bar none—

McALARY: —the best editor in the United States, bar none—cleared the decks and Debby rode the column into the paper.

    HAP HAIRSTON *is crying.*

I might not have done it if Alice hadn't pushed me the morning we heard the taped message. This is her win too.

    ALICE *is crying.*

So yes, maybe it was a mistake. But I am a couple of people's mistakes. Jim Willse listened to my late friend John Cotter and gave me the chance to follow Breslin. We believed that you could do a column differently. Mostly we believed this because we weren't smart enough to do it any other way. You could write a column and break news. And a lot of days we did that. Reporting was the key. The story's the thing. And you have to go get it. Basic reporting. Go find out. There are no stories in the newsroom. Get your butt into the street. Knock on doors, ask questions at two in the morning. Red meat.

    McALARY *is crying now.*

I have lived the life I dreamed about, but there's so much more I want to do. I want to dance at my daughter's wedding. I want to see my son Ryan graduate from college. I want to walk old and gray on the beach with my wife. *(Beat.)* I know I am unworthy. But please forgive me if I don't protest this Pulitzer Prize. This is a mistake I can live with.

> *He smiles.*
> *Everyone starts to applaud.*
> *Applause stops as* McALARY *puts his fingers in the air.*

(To audience.) I was in Room 918 in the Milstein Hospital at Columbia-Presbyterian, the floor where they put the rich people. There's an atrium with a big grand piano. They serve tea every day at four and some guy who can't play the piano plays the piano. It's Christmas Eve and there's a little tree in the room. My legs are swollen. Everything hurts. They want to put a tube down my throat but I won't let them.

> *A beat.*

Count the bodies.

> JOHN COTTER *raises his hand. Projection:* JOHN COTTER 1943–
> 1991.
> HAP HAIRSTON *raises his hand. Projection:* HAP HAIRSTON
> 1949–2002.
> McALARY *raises his hand. Projection:* MIKE McALARY 1957–
> 1998.
> *And then the sound of bagpipes and everyone sings "Wild*
> *Rover":*

JOHN COTTER: *(Sings.)*
I'll go home to my parents,
Confess what I've done,
And ask them to pardon
Their prodigal son,
ENSEMBLE: *(Sings.)*
And when they've caressed me
As oft times before,
I never will play
The wild rover no more.
And it's no, nay, never,
No nay never no more,
Will I play the wild rover,
No never no more.

And it's no, nay, never,
No nay never no more,
Will I play the wild rover,
No never no more.

CURTAIN

✳ *The Screenwriter*

When Harry Met Sally . . .

FADE IN:

DOCUMENTARY FOOTAGE
of an OLDER COUPLE, *a* MAN *and a* WOMAN. *They're sitting
together on a love seat looking straight at the* CAMERA.

MAN: I was sitting with my friend Arthur Kornblum, in a restaurant,
it was a Horn and Hardart cafeteria, and this beautiful girl walked
in— *(He points to the woman beside him.)* —and I turned to
Arthur and I said, "Arthur, you see that girl? I'm going to marry
her." And two weeks later we were married. And it's over fifty
years later and we're still married.

FADE OUT.

FADE IN:

EXTERIOR. UNIVERSITY OF CHICAGO CAMPUS—DAY
CARD: UNIVERSITY OF CHICAGO—1977
A couple in a clinch.
The young man involved is named HARRY BURNS. *He's twenty-
six years old, just graduated from law school. Wearing jeans
and a sweatshirt.*
He's kissing a young woman named AMANDA. *She has long,
straight hair that she irons. She's about twenty. The embrace
is fairly melodramatic. They pull back to look at one
another.*

AMANDA: I love you.

HARRY: I love you.

They begin to kiss again.
A car pulls up right beside them. Stops. Sits there.
Driving the car is SALLY ALBRIGHT. *She's twenty-one years old.
She's very pretty although not necessarily in an obvious way.
She sits there waiting for the kiss to end. It doesn't end. She
clears her throat.*

AMANDA *sees* SALLY, *and she and* HARRY *move over to the car.*

AMANDA: Oh. Hi, Sally. Sally, this is Harry Burns. Harry, this is Sally Albright.

HARRY: Nice to meet you.

They shake hands.

SALLY: *(To* HARRY.*)* You want to drive the first shift?

HARRY: No, no, you're there already, you can start.

SALLY: Back's open.

HARRY *looks meaningfully at* AMANDA.

Then he starts to put his stuff—a duffel bag, a box of records— into the backseat of the car, where SALLY'*s stuff is, too— suitcases, stereo speakers, a guitar, boxes of books, a small TV.*

AMANDA: Call me.

HARRY: I'll call as soon as I get there.

AMANDA: Call me from the road.

HARRY: I'll call before that.

HARRY *and* AMANDA *exchange longing looks outside the car.*

AMANDA: I love you.

HARRY: I love you.

They kiss again.

SALLY *sits waiting, waiting. She shifts position and accidentally-on-purpose hits the car HORN, which beeps and startles* AMANDA *and* HARRY *into breaking off their clinch.*

SALLY: Sorry.

HARRY: I miss you already.

AMANDA: I miss you.

HARRY: Bye.

HARRY *gets into the car, and* AMANDA *watches it pull away.*

CUT TO:

INTERIOR. CAR—DAY

HARRY *takes out a bunch of grapes, starts to eat them.*

SALLY: I have it all figured out. It's an eighteen-hour trip, which breaks down to six shifts of three hours each. Or, alternatively, we could break it down by mileage. There's a map on the visor that I've marked to show the locations where we change shifts.

HARRY: *(Offering her one.)* Grape?

SALLY: No. I don't like to eat between meals.

HARRY *spits a grape seed out the window, which doesn't happen to be down.*

HARRY: I'll roll down the window.

> *After a lengthy silence.*

Why don't you tell me the story of your life.

SALLY: The story of my life.

HARRY: We've got eighteen hours to kill before we hit New York.

SALLY: The story of my life isn't even going to get us out of Chicago. I mean, nothing's happened to me yet. That's why I'm going to New York.

HARRY: So something can happen to you?

SALLY: Yes.

HARRY: Like what?

SALLY: Like I'm going to go to journalism school to become a reporter.

HARRY: So you can write about things that happen to other people.

SALLY: *(After a beat.)* That's one way to look at it.

HARRY: Suppose nothing happens to you. Suppose you live there your whole life and nothing happens. You never meet anyone, you never become anything, and finally you die one of those New York deaths where nobody notices for two weeks until the smell drifts out into the hallway.

> SALLY *looks over at* HARRY. *Who am I stuck in this car with? She looks back at the road.*

EXTERIOR. CAR—TRAVELING SHOT—DAY

> *As the car turns onto the highway.*

SALLY: *(Voice-over.)* Amanda mentioned you had a dark side.

HARRY: That's what drew her to me.

SALLY: Your dark side?

HARRY: Sure. Why? Don't you have a dark side? I know, you're probably one of those cheerful people who dot their "i's" with little hearts.

SALLY: *(Defensively.)* I have just as much of a dark side as the next person—

HARRY: *(Pleased with himself.)* Oh, really? When I buy a new book, I read the last page first. That way, in case I die before I finish, I know how it ends. That, my friend, is a dark side.

SALLY: *(Irritated now.)* That doesn't mean you're deep or anything. I mean, yes, basically I'm a happy person . . .

HARRY: *(Cheerfully.)* So am I.

SALLY: . . . and I don't see that there's anything wrong with that.

HARRY: Of course not. You're too busy being happy. Do you ever think about death?

SALLY: Yes.

HARRY: Sure you do. A fleeting thought that drifts in and out of the transom of your mind. I spend hours, I spend days—

SALLY: (Interrupting.) —and you think this makes you a better person?

HARRY: Look, when the shit comes down, I'm going to be prepared and you're not, that's all I'm saying.

SALLY: And in the meantime, you're going to ruin your whole life waiting for it.

DISSOLVE TO:

EXTERIOR. CAR—DAY

The car tooling along a beautiful stretch of highway.

SALLY: (Voice-over.) You're wrong.

HARRY: (Voice-over.) I'm not wrong.

SALLY: (Voice-over.) You're wrong.

HARRY: (Voice-over.) He wants her to leave. That's why he puts her on the plane.

SALLY: (Voice-over.) I don't think *she* wants to stay.

HARRY: (Voice-over.) Of course she wants to stay. Wouldn't you rather be with Humphrey Bogart than that other guy?

EXTERIOR.—CAR EXITING (INDUSTRIAL)—MAGIC HOUR

EXTERIOR.—DINER—NIGHT

SALLY's car rounds the corner near some refinery tanks, heads into a diner parking lot.

SALLY: (Voice-over.) I don't want to spend the rest of my life in Casablanca married to a man who runs a bar. That probably sounds very snobbish to you, but I don't.

The car pulls up in front of a diner straight out of the fifties, HARRY driving.

HARRY: (Voice-over.) You'd rather have a passionless marriage—

SALLY: (Voice-over.) —and be First Lady of Czechoslovakia—

HARRY: (Voice-over.) —than live with the man . . .

INTERIOR. CAR—NIGHT

HARRY: . . . you've had the greatest sex of your life with, just because he owns a bar and that's all he does.

SALLY: Yes, and so would any woman in her right mind. Women are very practical.

> SALLY *takes out a can of hairspray, sprays her hair.*

Even Ingrid Bergman, which is why she gets on that plane at the end of the movie.

EXTERIOR. DINER PARKING LOT—NIGHT

HARRY: *(Getting out of car.)* Oh, I understand.

SALLY: *(Getting out of car.)* What? What?

HARRY: Nothing.

> HARRY *crosses toward the diner.* SALLY *follows after him.*

SALLY: What?

HARRY: Forget about it.

SALLY: What? What? Forget about what?

> *He doesn't answer and heads up the stairs to the diner,* SALLY
> *following.*

Now just tell me.

HARRY: Obviously you haven't had great sex.

> *He goes inside the diner. She follows.*

INTERIOR. DINER—NIGHT

HARRY: *(To the hostess.)* Table for two.

SALLY: Yes, I have.

HARRY: No, you haven't.

> *He crosses away from her toward the table.*

SALLY: It just so happens I have had plenty of good sex.

> *This doesn't go unheard by the hostess and other diners.* SALLY
> *walks to the table, sits down.*

HARRY: With whom?

SALLY: What?

HARRY: With whom have you had this great sex?

SALLY: *(Embarrassed.)* I'm not going to tell you that.

HARRY: Fine. Don't tell me.

> *A long silence.* HARRY *looks at the menu.* SALLY *opens hers but*
> *doesn't read it.*

SALLY: Shel Gordon.

HARRY: Shel. Sheldon? No. You did not have great sex with Sheldon.

SALLY: I did too.

HARRY: No, you didn't. A Sheldon can do your taxes. If you need a root canal, Sheldon is your man, but humping and pumping is not Sheldon's strong suit. It's the name. "Do it to me, Sheldon." "You're an animal, Sheldon." "Ride me, big Sheldon." It doesn't work.

A WAITRESS *approaches the table.*

WAITRESS: What can I get you?

HARRY: I'll have the Number Three.

The WAITRESS *turns to* SALLY.

SALLY: I'd like the chef salad, please, with the oil and vinegar on the side. And the apple pie à la mode.

WAITRESS: *(Writing.)* Chef and apple à la mode.

SALLY: But I'd like the pie heated, and I don't want the ice cream on top, I want it on the side. And I'd like strawberry instead of vanilla if you have it. If not, then no ice cream, just whipped cream, but only if it's real. If it's out of a can, then nothing.

WAITRESS: Not even the pie?

SALLY: No, just the pie. But then not heated.

As the WAITRESS *leaves,* HARRY *stares in disbelief at* SALLY. What?

HARRY: Nothing. Nothing. So how come you broke up with Sheldon?

SALLY: How do you know we broke up?

HARRY: Because if you didn't break up, you wouldn't be with me, you'd be off with Sheldon the Wonder Schlong.

SALLY: First of all, I'm not *with* you. And second of all, it's none of your business why we broke up.

HARRY: You're right, you're right. I don't want to know.

After a beat:

SALLY: Well, if you must know, it was because he was very jealous and I had these Days of the Week underpants.

HARRY: *(Makes a buzzer sound.)* I'm sorry, I need a judge's ruling on this. Days of the Week underpants?

SALLY: Yes. They had the days of the week on them, I thought they were sort of funny—and one day Sheldon says to me, "You never wear Sunday." He's all suspicious. Where was Sunday? Where had I left Sunday? And I told him, and he didn't believe me.

HARRY: What?

SALLY: They don't make Sunday.

HARRY: Why not?

SALLY: Because of God.

DISSOLVE TO:

EXTERIOR. DINER—NIGHT—REESTABLISH
INTERIOR. DINER—NIGHT

> *They are finishing their meal.* SALLY *figures out her portion of the bill.*

SALLY: Fifteen percent of my share is . . . *(Writes.)* Six-ninety . . . leave seven. . . .

> *She notices* HARRY *just staring at her.*
> *(Thinking she might have some food on her face, she nervously wipes.)*

What? Do I have something on my face?

HARRY: You're a very attractive person.

SALLY: Thank you.

HARRY: Amanda never said how attractive you were.

SALLY: Well, maybe she doesn't think I'm attractive.

HARRY: I don't think it's a matter of opinion. Empirically, you are attractive.

> *They get up to leave.*

SALLY: Amanda is my friend.

> HARRY *throws down a crumpled bill, and they head for the door.*

HARRY: So?

SALLY: So you're going with her.

HARRY: So?

SALLY: So you're coming on to me.

EXTERIOR. DINER—NIGHT

HARRY: *(Coming out of door.)* No, I wasn't.

> SALLY *looks at him.*

What? Can't a man say a woman is attractive without it being a come-on?

> HARRY *walks to the driver's side as* SALLY *is unlocking the passenger door.*

All right, all right.

> *Both walk into the foreground, meeting.* SALLY *moves away from him, upset.*

Let's just say, just for the sake of argument, that it was a come-on. Okay. What do you want me to do about it? I take it back, okay? I take it back.

SALLY: You can't take it back.

HARRY: Why not?

SALLY: Because it's already out there.

An awkward pause.

HARRY: Oh, jeez. What are we supposed to do? Call the cops? It's already out there!

SALLY: Just let it lie, okay?

HARRY: Great! Let it lie. That's my policy. That's what I always say.
They both get in the car.

INTERIOR. CAR—NIGHT

HARRY: Let it lie. *(Beat.)* Want to spend the night in a motel?
SALLY *glares at him.*

See what I did? I didn't let it lie.

SALLY: Harry—

HARRY: I said I would and then I didn't—

SALLY: Harry—

HARRY: I went the other way—

SALLY: Harry—

HARRY: What?

SALLY: We are just going to be friends, okay?

HARRY: Great. Friends. The best thing.
As the car starts up and pulls out, we—

CUT TO:

EXTERIOR. HIGHWAY—NIGHT
As the car tools along, we hear:

HARRY: *(Voice-over.)* You realize, of course, that we could never be friends.

SALLY: *(Voice-over.)* Why not?

INTERIOR. CAR—NIGHT
SALLY *is driving.*

HARRY: What I'm saying—and this is not a come-on in any way, shape, or form—is that men and women can't be friends, because the sex part always gets in the way.

SALLY: That's not true. I have a number of men friends and there's no sex involved.

HARRY: No, you don't.

SALLY: Yes, I do.

HARRY: No, you don't.

SALLY: Yes, I do.

HARRY: You only think you do.

SALLY: You're saying I'm having sex with these men without my knowledge?

HARRY: No, I'm saying they all *want* to have sex with you.

SALLY: They do not.

HARRY: Do too.

SALLY: They do not.

HARRY: Do too.

SALLY: How do you know?

HARRY: Because no man can be friends with a woman he finds attractive. He always wants to have sex with her.

SALLY: So you're saying a man *can* be friends with a woman he finds unattractive.

HARRY: No. You pretty much want to nail them, too.

SALLY: What if *they* don't want to have sex with *you*?

HARRY: Doesn't matter, because the sex thing is already out there, so the friendship is ultimately doomed, and that is the end of the story.

SALLY: Well, I guess we're not going to be friends, then.

HARRY: Guess not.

SALLY: That's too bad. *(Beat.)* You were the only person I knew in New York.

DISSOLVE TO:

EXTERIOR. NEW YORK SKYLINE—DAWN
   As the car comes over the George Washington Bridge. A
   gorgeous day.

DISSOLVE TO:

EXTERIOR. NEW YORK STREET CORNER—DAY
   Downtown near Washington Square. The car pulls up and
   HARRY *hops out, grabbing his stuff.* SALLY *also walks to the*
   back of the car.

HARRY: Thanks for the ride.

SALLY: Yeah. It was interesting.

HARRY: It was nice knowing you.

SALLY: Yeah.
   SALLY *nods. Harry nods. An awkward moment.*
   SALLY *holds out her hand. They shake.*
Well, have a nice life.

HARRY: You too.

HARRY *starts to walk off.*
As she drives off.

FADE OUT.

FADE IN:

DOCUMENTARY FOOTAGE
Another OLDER COUPLE *sitting together on the same love seat
we saw earlier.*
SECOND WOMAN: We fell in love in high school—
SECOND MAN: Yeah, we were high school sweethearts.
SECOND WOMAN: But then after our junior year, his parents moved
away.
SECOND MAN: I never forgot her.
SECOND WOMAN: He never forgot me.
SECOND MAN: Her face was burned on my brain. And it was thirty-
four years later that I was walking down Broadway and I see her
coming out of Toffenetti's.
SECOND WOMAN: And we both looked at each other, and it was just
as though not a single day had gone by.
SECOND MAN: She was just as beautiful as she was at sixteen.
SECOND WOMAN: He was just the same. He looked exactly the same.

FADE OUT.

FADE IN:

INTERIOR. LA GUARDIA AIRPORT—DAY
IT'S FIVE YEARS LATER.
A couple in a clinch.
The woman is SALLY *at twenty-six. She looks great, she's a
stylish young woman.*
*She's kissing a very attractive man, although it's not that easy
to see him at the moment. His name is* JOE.
HARRY *is coming down the hallway of the airline terminal.
He's wearing a suit and tie and trench coat; he has a kind
of attractive-but-rumpled demeanor. He notices the couple
kissing. Goes past them. Then stops. Backs up. He recognizes
them.*
They're still kissing.
HARRY *comes closer, peers at the two of them from slightly too
close. It's not easy to see either of their faces.*
Finally, SALLY *and* JOE *become aware that someone is standing
nearby, and they stop kissing to look at* HARRY.

HARRY: Joe—I thought it was you. I thought it was you! *(Shaking hands.)* Harry Burns.

JOE: Harry, Harry, how ya doing?

HARRY: Good. How you doing?

JOE: I'm just fine. I'm doing fine.

HARRY: I was just walking by, and I thought it was you, and here it is, it's you.

JOE: Yeah, yeah, it was.

HARRY: You still with the D.A.'s Office?

JOE: No, I switched to the other side.

HARRY: Oh.

JOE: What about you?

HARRY: I'm working with this small company, doing political consulting.

JOE: Oh yeah?

HARRY: Yeah, it's been great. Yeah.

> JOE *nods.* HARRY *nods. An awkward pause.* SALLY *just standing there, wondering if* HARRY *remembers her.*

JOE: Oh, Harry, this is Sally Albright. Harry Burns.

> HARRY *nods and smiles.*

Harry and I used to live in the same building.

> SALLY *nods.* HARRY *knows he's seen her someplace but he can't remember where.*

HARRY: Well, listen, I got a plane to catch. It was really good to see you, Joe.

JOE: You too, Harry.

HARRY: *(To* SALLY.*)* Bye.

> HARRY *starts down the long corridor for his plane.* JOE *and* SALLY *look at each other.*

SALLY: Thank God he couldn't place me. I drove from college to New York with him five years ago and it was the longest night of my life.

JOE: What happened?

SALLY: He made a pass at me, and when I said no—he was going with a girlfriend of mine—oh God, I can't remember her name. Don't get involved with me, Joe, I'm twenty-six years old and I can't even remember the name of the girl I was such good friends with that I wouldn't get involved with her boyfriend.

JOE: So what happened?

SALLY: When?

JOE: When he made a pass at you and you said no.

SALLY: Uh . . . I said we could just be friends, and—this part I remember—he said men and women could never really be friends.

    JOE *smiles, shakes his head.*

  Do you think that's true?

JOE: No.

SALLY: Do you have any women friends? Just friends?

JOE: No, but I'll get one if it's important to you.

    SALLY *smiles, then she and* JOE *move close to kiss. Suddenly* SALLY *pulls back.*

SALLY: Amanda Reese. Thank God.

JOE: I'm going to miss you. *(Beat.)* I love you.

SALLY: *(It's the first time he's said it.)* You do?

JOE: Yes.

SALLY: I love you.

    They kiss.

CUT TO:

  INTERIOR. AIRPLANE—DAY

    The plane is in flight, en route from New York to Washington.

    SALLY *is in a middle seat in a crowded all-coach plane. She has the* New York Times *on her lap, but she's staring into the middle distance, a little smile on her face.*

    There's a MAN ON THE AISLE *next to her.*

    In the row in back of her, in the aisle seat, is HARRY. *His head pops up.*

    SALLY *starts to read the newspaper. The* MAN ON THE AISLE *looks up at* HARRY, *who's still looming over him, trying to place* SALLY. HARRY *pops down.*

    The STEWARDESS *comes down the aisle with the drink cart.*

STEWARDESS: And what would you like to drink?

SALLY: Do you have any Bloody Mary mix?

STEWARDESS: Yes.

    She starts to pour.

SALLY: No, wait. Here's what I want. Regular tomato juice, filled about three quarters, and add a splash of Bloody Mary mix, just a splash, and . . .

    HARRY's *head starts to rise again.*

  . . . a little piece of lime, but on the side.

HARRY: The University of Chicago, right?

    SALLY *turns, sees* HARRY, *then turns back around.*

SALLY: Yes.

HARRY: Did you look this good at the University of Chicago?

SALLY: No.

HARRY: *(He's being mischievous here.)* Did we ever—?

SALLY: *(Laughing; she can't believe him.)* No. No! *(To* MAN ON THE AISLE.*)* We drove from Chicago to New York together after graduation.

> *The* MAN ON THE AISLE *has been listening and watching all this.*

MAN ON THE AISLE: *(To* HARRY.*)* Would you two like to sit together?

SALLY: No.

HARRY: Great! Thank you.

> HARRY *and the* MAN ON THE AISLE *change seats and* HARRY *sits down next to* SALLY.

You were a friend of . . . um . . .

> *He can't remember her name.*

SALLY: Amanda's. I can't believe you can't remember her name.

HARRY: What do you mean? I can remember. Amanda. Right? Amanda Rice.

SALLY: Reese.

HARRY: Reese, right. That's what I said. Whatever happened to her?

SALLY: I have no idea.

HARRY: You have no idea? You were really good friends with her. We didn't make it because you were such good friends.

SALLY: You went with her.

HARRY: And was it worth it? This sacrifice for a friend you haven't even kept in touch with?

SALLY: Harry, you might not believe this, but I never considered not sleeping with you a sacrifice.

HARRY: Fair enough, fair enough.

> *After a beat:*

You were going to be a gymnast.

SALLY: A journalist.

HARRY: Right, that's what I said. And?

SALLY: I'm a journalist. I work at the *News.*

HARRY: Great. And you're with Joe.

> SALLY *nods.*

Well, that's great. Great. You're together—what—three weeks?

SALLY: A month. How did you know that?

HARRY: You take someone to the airport, it's clearly the beginning of a relationship. That's why I've never taken anyone to the airport at the beginning of a relationship.

SALLY: Why?

HARRY: Because eventually things move on and you don't take someone to the airport, and I never wanted anyone to say to me, "How come you never take me to the airport anymore?"

SALLY: It's amazing. You look like a normal person, but actually you're the Angel of Death.

HARRY: Are you going to marry him?

SALLY: We've only known each other a month, and besides, neither one of us is looking to get married right now.

HARRY: I'm getting married.

SALLY: You are?

HARRY: (Matter-of-factly.) Um-hmm.

SALLY: *You* are?

HARRY: Yeah.

SALLY: Who is she?

HARRY: Helen Hillson. She's a lawyer. She's keeping her name.

SALLY: (Shakes her head.) You're getting married.
        She laughs.

HARRY: Yeah. What's so funny about it?

SALLY: It's just so optimistic of you, Harry.

HARRY: Well, you'd be amazed what falling madly in love can do for you.

SALLY: Well, it's wonderful. It's nice to see you embracing life in this manner.

HARRY: Yeah, plus, you know, you just get to a certain point where you get tired of the whole thing.

SALLY: What whole thing?

HARRY: The whole life-of-a-single-guy thing. You meet someone, you have the safe lunch, you decide you like each other enough to move on to dinner, you go dancing, you do the white man's overbite, you go back to her place, you have sex, and the minute you're finished, you know what goes through your mind? (SALLY *shakes her head no.*) How long do I have to lie here and hold her before I can get up and go home? Is thirty seconds enough?

SALLY: That's what you're thinking? Is that true?

HARRY: Sure. All men think that. How long do you like to be held afterwards? All night, right? See, that's the problem. Somewhere between thirty seconds and all night is your problem.

SALLY: I don't have a problem.

HARRY: Yeah you do.

                                                            CUT TO:

EXTERIOR. NATIONAL AIRPORT—DAY
As the plane lands.

INTERIOR. NATIONAL AIRPORT—DAY
HARRY *and* SALLY *are on a moving sidewalk,* HARRY *several steps behind* SALLY. *He makes his way past the other passengers to stand by her.*

HARRY: Staying over?

SALLY: Yes.

HARRY: Would you like to have dinner?
SALLY *looks at him suspiciously.*
Just friends.

SALLY: I thought you didn't believe men and women could be friends.

HARRY: When did I say that?

SALLY: On the ride to New York.

HARRY: No, no, no, no. I never said that. *(Reconsiders.)* Yes, that's right. They can't be friends . . . *(Figuring this out.)* . . . unless both of them are involved with other people. Then they can. This is an amendment to the earlier rule. If the two people are in relationships, the pressure of possible involvement is lifted. *(Thinking this over.)* That doesn't work either. Because what happens then, the person you're involved with doesn't understand why you need to be friends with the person you're just friends with, like it means something is missing from the relationship and you have to go outside to get it. Then when you say, "No, no, no, it's not true, nothing is missing from the relationship," the person you're involved with then accuses you of being secretly attracted to the person you're just friends with, which you probably are—I mean, come on, who the hell are we kidding, let's face it—which brings us back to the earlier rule before the amendment, that men and women can't be friends. So where does that leave us?

SALLY: Harry—

HARRY: What?

SALLY: Goodbye.

HARRY: Okay.
They look at each other. Though they have said goodbye, they are now in that awkward place of still going in the same direction next to each other on the moving sidewalk. After a beat:
I'll just stop walking, I'll let you go ahead.

FADE OUT.

FADE IN:

DOCUMENTARY FOOTAGE
Another OLDER COUPLE *sitting on a love seat, looking at the* CAMERA.

THIRD MAN: We were married forty years ago. We were married three years. We got a divorce. Then I married Marjorie.

THIRD WOMAN: But first you lived with Barbara.

THIRD MAN: Right. Barbara. But I didn't marry Barbara. I married Marjorie.

THIRD WOMAN: Then you got a divorce.

THIRD MAN: Right. Then I married Katie.

THIRD WOMAN: Another divorce.

THIRD MAN: Then, a couple of years later at Eddie Callichio's funeral, I ran into her. I was with some girl I don't even remember.

THIRD WOMAN: Roberta.

THIRD MAN: Right. Roberta. But I couldn't take my eyes off you. *(Beat.)* I remember, I snuck over to her and I said—what did I say?

THIRD WOMAN: You said, "What are you doing after?"

THIRD MAN: Right. So I ditched Roberta, we go for coffee, a month later we're married.

THIRD WOMAN: Thirty-five years to the day after our first marriage.

FADE OUT.

EXTERIOR. NEW YORK RESTAURANT WITH VIEW—DAY
IT'S FIVE YEARS LATER.
SALLY *is sitting at a table with two other women,* MARIE *and* ALICE. MARIE *is a dark-haired, dark-eyed beauty.* ALICE *is cute and plump, a married lady.*

MARIE: So, I go through his pockets, okay?

ALICE: Marie, why do you go through his pockets?

MARIE: You know what I found?

ALICE: No, what?

MARIE: They just bought a dining-room table. He and his wife just went out and spent $1,600 on a dining-room table.

ALICE: Where?

MARIE: The point isn't where, Alice. The point is, he's never going to leave her.

ALICE: So what else is new? You've known this for two years.

MARIE: *(Glumly.)* You're right, you're right. I know you're right.

ALICE: Why can't you find someone single? When I was single, I knew lots of nice, single men. There must be someone. Sally found someone.

MARIE: Sally got the last good one.

SALLY: *(Matter-of-factly.)* Joe and I broke up.

ALICE: What?

MARIE: When?

SALLY: Monday.

ALICE: You waited three days to tell us?

MARIE: You mean Joe's available?

ALICE: For God's sake, Marie—don't you have any feelings about this? She's obviously upset.

SALLY: I'm not that upset. We've been growing apart for quite a while.

MARIE: *(Horrified.)* But you guys were a couple. You had someone to go places with. You had a date on national holidays.

SALLY: I said to myself, you deserve more than this, you're thirty-one years old—

MARIE: —and the clock is ticking.

SALLY: No, the clock doesn't really start to tick until you're thirty-six.

ALICE: God. You're in such great shape.

SALLY: Well, I've had a few days to get used to it, and I feel okay.

MARIE: Good. Then you're ready.

> MARIE *takes her Rolodex out of her satchel and starts to look through it.*

ALICE: *(Aghast.)* Really, Marie.

MARIE: Well, how else do you think you do it?

> *She flips through the Rolodex and pulls out a card.*

I've got the perfect guy. I don't happen to find him attractive, but you might. *(To* ALICE, *indicating* SALLY.*)* She doesn't have a problem with chins.

SALLY: Marie, I'm not ready yet.

MARIE: But you just said you were over him.

SALLY: I am over him. But I am in a mourning period. *(Beat.)* Who is it?

MARIE: Alex Anderson.

SALLY: You fixed me up with him six years ago.

MARIE: Sorry . . .

SALLY: God.

MARIE: *(Pulls another card.)* All right, wait. Here—here we go. Ken Darman.

SALLY: He's been married for over a year.

MARIE: Really? Married.

> MARIE *takes Ken Darman's Rolodex card and dog-ears a corner of it and places it in a section at the back of the box. Then she pulls out another card.*

Oh wait, wait, wait, I got one.

SALLY: Look, there is no point in my going out with someone I might really like if I met him at the right time but who right now has no chance of being anything to me but a transitional man.

MARIE: Okay. But don't wait too long. Remember what happened to David Warsaw? His wife left him, and everyone said, give him some time, don't move in too fast. *Six months later he was dead.*

SALLY: What are you saying? I should get married to someone right away in case he's about to die?

ALICE: At least you can say you were married.

MARIE: I'm saying that the right man for you might be out there right now and if you don't grab him, someone else will, and you'll have to spend the rest of your life knowing that someone else is married to your husband.

CUT TO:

EXTERIOR. GIANTS STADIUM—DAY

> *A wave is in progress. It sweeps around the stadium and passes by* HARRY *and his friend* JESS, *sitting in the second deck surrounded by Giants fans. It's fall, they're both wearing jeans and windbreakers.*
>
> HARRY *is very despondent.*

JESS: When did this happen?

HARRY: Friday, Helen comes home from work, and she says, "I don't know if I want to be married anymore." Like it's the institution, you know, like it's nothing personal, just something she's been thinking about in a casual way. I'm calm. I say, "Why don't we take some time to think about it?" You know, don't rush into anything.

JESS: Yeah, right.

HARRY: Next day she says she's thought about it, and she wants a trial separation. She just wants to *try* it, she says. But we can still date, she says, like this is supposed to cushion the blow. I mean,

I got married so I could stop dating, so I don't see where "we can still date" is a big incentive, since the last thing you want to do is date your wife, who's supposed to love you, which is what I'm saying to her when it occurs to me that maybe she doesn't, so I say to her, "Don't you love me anymore?" and you know what she says? "I don't know if I've ever loved you."

> *A wave comes through the crowd, and* HARRY *and* JESS *stand and wave their hands.*

JESS: Ooh, that's harsh.

> *They sit down.*

You don't bounce back from that right away.

HARRY: Thanks, Jess.

JESS: No, I'm a writer, I know dialogue, and that's particularly harsh.

HARRY: Then she tells me that someone in her office is going to South America, and she can sublet his apartment. I can't believe this. And the doorbell rings. "I can sublet his apartment." The words are still hanging in the air, you know, like in a balloon connected to her mouth.

JESS: Like in a cartoon.

HARRY: Right. So I'm going to the door, and there are moving men there. Now I start to get suspicious. I say, "Helen, when did you call these movers?" And she doesn't say anything, so I ask the movers, "When did this woman book you for this gig?" and they're just standing there, three huge guys, one of them wearing a T-shirt that says "Don't fuck with Mister Zero." So I said, "Helen, when did you make this arrangement?" She says, "A week ago." I said, "You've known for a week, and you didn't tell me?" And she says, "I didn't want to ruin your birthday."

> *A second wave comes through and* HARRY *and* JESS *stand and wave their hands.*

JESS: You're saying Mister Zero knew you were getting a divorce a week before you did?

HARRY: Mister Zero knew.

JESS: I can't believe this.

HARRY: I haven't told you the bad part yet.

JESS: What could be worse than Mister Zero knowing?

HARRY: It's all a lie. She's in love with somebody else, some tax attorney. She moved in with him.

JESS: How did you find out?

HARRY: I followed her. I stood outside the building.

JESS: So humiliating.

HARRY: Tell me about it. *(Beat.)* And you know, I knew. I knew the whole time that even though we were happy, it was just an illusion and one day she would kick the shit out of me.

JESS: Marriages don't break up on account of infidelity—it's just a symptom that something else is wrong.

HARRY: Really? Well, that symptom is fucking my wife.

Another wave comes through, and they stand up. They sit down.

CUT TO:

INTERIOR. SHAKESPEARE & CO. BOOKSTORE—DAY

SALLY and MARIE standing in the bookstore in a section called Personal Relationships. A table full of books. MARIE is looking at something like Smart Women, Foolish Choices. *SALLY is looking at something like* Safe Sex in Dangerous Times.

MARIE: So I just happened to see his American Express bill.

SALLY: What do you mean, you just happened to see it?

MARIE: Well, he was shaving, and there it was in his briefcase.

SALLY: What if he came out and saw you looking through his briefcase?

MARIE: You're missing the point. I'm telling you what I found. *(Beat.)* He just spent $120 on a new nightgown for his wife. *(Beat.)* I don't think he's ever going to leave her.

SALLY: No one thinks he's ever going to leave her.

MARIE: You're right, you're right. I know you're right.

MARIE looks up for a moment for a new book, sees something. Someone is staring at you in Personal Growth.

SALLY glances over to the Personal Growth section. There's HARRY.

SALLY: I know him. You'd like him. He's married.

MARIE: Who is he?

SALLY: Harry Burns. He's a political consultant.

MARIE: He's cute.

SALLY: You think he's cute?

MARIE: How do you know he's married?

SALLY: Because the last time I saw him, he was getting married.

MARIE: When was that?

SALLY: Six years ago.

MARIE: So he might not be married anymore.

SALLY: Also he's obnoxious.

MARIE: This is just like in the movies, remember, like *The Lady Vanishes*, where she says to him, "You are the most obnoxious man I have ever met"—

SALLY: *(Correcting her.)* —"the most contemptible"—

MARIE: And then they fall madly in love.

SALLY: Also, he never remembers me.

HARRY: Sally Albright—

SALLY: Hi, Harry—

HARRY: I thought it was you.

SALLY: It is. This is Marie . . .

> MARIE *is exiting down the stairs. She waves goodbye.*

. . . *was* MARIE.

> SALLY *turns back to* HARRY.

HARRY: How are you?

SALLY: Fine.

HARRY: How's Joe?

SALLY: Fine. I hear he's fine.

HARRY: You're not with Joe anymore?

SALLY: We just broke up.

HARRY: Oh, I'm sorry. That's too bad.

SALLY: Yeah, well, you know. Yeah. *(Beat.)* So, what about you?

HARRY: I'm fine.

SALLY: How's married life?

HARRY: Not so good. I'm getting a divorce.

SALLY: Oh, I'm sorry. I'm really sorry.

HARRY: Yeah. Well. What are you going to do? What happened with you guys?

CUT TO:

INTERIOR. RESTAURANT—DAY
> SALLY *and* HARRY *having a glass of wine.*

SALLY: When Joe and I started seeing each other, we wanted exactly the same thing. We wanted to live together, but we didn't want to get married because every time anyone we knew got married, it ruined their relationship. They practically never had sex again. It's true, it's one of the secrets no one ever tells you. I would sit around with my girlfriends who have kids—well, actually, my one girlfriend who has kids, Alice—and she would complain about how she and Gary never did it anymore. She didn't even complain about it, now that I think about it. She just said it matter-of-factly.

She said they were up all night, they were both exhausted all the time, the kids just took every sexual impulse they had out of them. And Joe and I used to talk about it, and we'd say we were so lucky to have this wonderful relationship, we can have sex on the kitchen floor and not worry about the kids walking in, we can fly off to Rome on a moment's notice. And then one day I was taking Alice's little girl for the afternoon because I'd promised to take her to the circus, and we were in a cab playing "I Spy"—I spy a mailbox, I spy a lamppost—and she looked out the window and she saw this man and this woman with these two little kids, the man had one of the kids on his shoulders, and Alice's little girl said, "I spy a family," and I started to cry. You know, I just started crying. And I went home, and I said, "The thing is, Joe, we never do fly off to Rome on a moment's notice."

HARRY: And the kitchen floor?

SALLY: Not once. It's this very cold, hard Mexican ceramic tile. Anyway, we talked about it for a long time, and I said, this is what I want, and he said, well, I don't, and I said, well, I guess it's over, and he left. And the thing is, I feel really fine. I am over him. I mean, I really am over him. That was it for him, that was the most he could give, and every time I think about it, I'm more and more convinced I did the right thing.

HARRY: Boy, you sound really healthy.

SALLY: *(Not totally.)* Yeah.

                                                              CUT TO:

EXTERIOR. 77TH STREET WALK—DUSK

  HARRY *and* SALLY *walking together. The sun is setting.*

SALLY: At least I got the apartment.

HARRY: That's what everybody says to me, too. But really, what's so hard about finding an apartment? What you do is, you read the obituary column. Yeah. You find out who died, go to the building, and then you tip the doorman. What they can do to make it easier is to combine the obituaries with the real estate section, see, and then you have, "Mr. Klein died today, leaving a wife, two children, and a spacious three-bedroom apartment with a wood-burning fireplace."

  SALLY *laughing. A nice moment.*

HARRY: You know, the first time we met, I really didn't like you that much—

SALLY: *I* didn't like *you.*

HARRY: Yeah, you did. You were just so uptight then. You're much softer now.

SALLY: You know, I hate that kind of remark. It sounds like a compliment, but really it's an insult.

HARRY: Okay, you're still as hard as nails.

SALLY: I just didn't want to sleep with you, so you had to write it off as a character flaw instead of dealing with the possibility that it might have something to do with you.

HARRY: What's the statute of limitations on apologies?

SALLY: Ten years.

HARRY: Ooh. I can just get in under the wire.

> SALLY *smiles, then after a beat, she makes the smallest of moves.*

SALLY: Would you like to have dinner with me sometime?

HARRY: *(Not knowing quite how to take this.)* Are we becoming friends now?

SALLY: Well, *(This is not what she meant.)* yeah.

HARRY: Great. A woman friend. You know, you may be the first attractive woman I've not wanted to sleep with in my entire life.

SALLY: *(Slightly rejected.)* That's wonderful, Harry.

> *As they continue to walk along, we—*

FADE OUT.

FADE IN:

DOCUMENTARY FOOTAGE

> *An* OLDER COUPLE *on a love seat.*

FOURTH MAN: We were both born in the same hospital.

FOURTH WOMAN: *(Overlaps.)* In 1921.

FOURTH MAN: Seven days apart.

FOURTH WOMAN: In the same hospital.

FOURTH MAN: We both grew up one block away from each other.

FOURTH WOMAN: *(Overlaps.)* We both lived in tenements.

FOURTH MAN: On the Lower East Side.

FOURTH WOMAN: On Delancey Street.

FOURTH MAN: My family moved to the Bronx when I was ten.

FOURTH WOMAN: *(Overlaps.)* He lived on Fordham Road.

FOURTH MAN: Hers moved when she was eleven.

FOURTH WOMAN: *(Overlaps.)* I lived on 183rd Street.

FOURTH MAN: For six years she worked on the fifteenth floor—

FOURTH MAN:—as a nurse where I had a practice on the fourteenth floor of the very same building.

FOURTH MAN: We never met.

FOURTH WOMAN: I worked for a very prominent neurologist, Dr. Bemmelman.

FOURTH WOMAN: We never met. Can you imagine that?

FOURTH MAN: You know where we met? In an elevator—

FOURTH WOMAN: I was visiting family.

FOURTH MAN: —in the Ambassador Hotel in Chicago, Illinois.

FOURTH WOMAN: (Overlaps.) He was on the third floor, I was on the twelfth.

FOURTH MAN: I rode up nine extra floors just to keep talking to her.

FOURTH WOMAN: Nine extra floors.

FADE OUT.

FADE IN:

> A TIGHT SHOT of one of those toy felt birds that somehow is able to miraculously keep dunking its beak into a glass of water.

WIDER TO REVEAL:

> INTERIOR. HARRY'S OFFICE—DAY
>> HARRY is sitting in his office staring blankly at this ornithological phenomenon. As HARRY stares, we hear the sound of a phone RINGING. It is picked up by SALLY.

SALLY: (Voice-over.) Hello.

HARRY: (Voice-over.) You sleeping?

SALLY: (Voice-over.) No, I was watching Casablanca.

HARRY: (Voice-over.) Channel, please.

SALLY: (Voice-over.) Eleven.

HARRY: (Voice-over.) Thank you. Got it.

> As HARRY continues to stare at the bird, we hear a few lines of dialogue from CASABLANCA: "Of all the gin joints . . . ," etc. As the CASABLANCA dialogue continues, we—

CUT TO:

> INTERIOR. SALLY'S OFFICE—DAY
>> SALLY is at her desk, doing business on the telephone. A woman walks in, hands her something.

HARRY: (Voice-over.) Now, you're telling me you would be happier with Victor Laszlo than with Humphrey Bogart?

> The woman walks offscreen as SALLY looks at the magazine on her desk, hangs up phone.

SALLY: *(Voice-over.)* When did I say that?

HARRY: *(Voice-over.)* When we drove to New York.

> SALLY *turns to her computer terminal.*

CUT TO:

INTERIOR. KOREAN GREENGROCERY—DAY

> SALLY *moves along the salad bar, very selectively assembling a salad.*

SALLY: *(Voice-over.)* I never said that. I would never have said that.

HARRY: *(Voice-over.)* All right, fine. Have it your way.

CUT TO:

INTERIOR. HARRY'S APARTMENT—DAY

> HARRY *sits on the floor with a deck of cards, pitching them into a bowl.*

HARRY: *(Voice-over.)* Have you been sleeping?

SALLY: *(Voice-over.)* Why?

HARRY: *(Voice-over.)* 'Cause I haven't been sleeping.

> HARRY *continues pitching the cards. We see the room is bare except for a couple of chairs.*

I really miss Helen. Maybe I'm coming down with something. Last night I was up at four in the morning watching *Leave It to Beaver* in Spanish.

CUT TO:

INTERIOR. HARRY'S APARTMENT—DAY

> HARRY *is sitting in a chair, trying to read a book. He has a thermometer in his mouth. He can't concentrate. He keeps reading the same paragraph over and over.*

HARRY: *(Voice-over.)* "Buenos días, Señora Cleaver. Dónde están Wallace y Theodore?"

> *Finally,* HARRY *flips to the last page and reads it.*

I'm not well.

CUT TO:

INTERIOR. FITNESS CLUB—DAY

> SALLY *in a tap-dancing class.*

SALLY: *(Voice-over.)* Well, I went to bed at seven-thirty last night. I haven't done that since the third grade.

HARRY: *(Voice-over.)* That's the good thing about depression. You get your rest.

SALLY: *(Voice-over.)* I'm not depressed.

HARRY: *(Voice-over.)* Okay, fine.

CUT TO:

EXTERIOR. CHINESE RESTAURANT—NIGHT

> *Through the window, we see* SALLY *is going through a very detailed ordering session. The waiter's trying to keep up.* HARRY *just stares.*

HARRY: *(Voice-over.)* Do you still sleep on the same side of the bed?

SALLY: *(Voice-over.)* I did for a while, but now I'm pretty much using the whole bed.

HARRY: *(Voice-over.)* God, that's great. I feel weird when just my leg wanders over.

CUT TO:

EXTERIOR. STREET—DAY

> SALLY *is putting mail into a mailbox, one letter at a time, checking to see that each letter has safely entered the box.* HARRY *stands impatiently waiting.*

HARRY: *(Voice-over.)* I miss her.

SALLY: *(Voice-over.)* I don't miss him. I really don't.

HARRY: *(Voice-over.)* Not even a little?

> HARRY *is getting impatient.*

SALLY: *(Voice-over.)* You know what I miss? I miss the idea of him.

> HARRY *moves around beside* SALLY *and rests his elbow on top of the mailbox, watching incredulously as she continues the ritual.*

HARRY: *(Voice-over.)* Maybe I only miss the idea of her. No, I miss the whole Helen.

> HARRY'S *impatience with* SALLY'S *letter mailing gets the best of him. He impulsively grabs the remaining letters in her hand, opens the box, shoves them in, then hustles her off.*

SALLY: *(Voice-over.)* Last scene.

AND NOW SPLIT SCREEN:

INTERIOR. SALLY'S BEDROOM—NIGHT

> SALLY *in bed on the phone watching* Casablanca *on TV and talking to:*

INTERIOR. HARRY'S BEDROOM—NIGHT
>HARRY *in bed on the phone watching* Casablanca.

HARRY: Ingrid Bergman. Now *she's* low maintenance.

SALLY: Low maintenance?

HARRY: Yeah. There are two kinds of women: high maintenance and low maintenance.

SALLY: And Ingrid Bergman is low maintenance?

HARRY: An L.M. Definitely.

SALLY: Which am I?

HARRY: You're the worst kind. You're high maintenance, but you think you're low maintenance.

SALLY: I don't see that.

HARRY: You don't see that? *(Mimicking her.)* "Waiter, I'll begin with the house salad, but I don't want the regular dressing. I'll have the balsamic vinegar and oil, but on the side, and then the salmon with mustard sauce, but I want the mustard sauce on the side." "On the side" is a very big thing for you.

SALLY: Well, I just want it the way I want it.

HARRY: I know. High maintenance.
>SALLY *smiling.*
>*Bogart says, "Louie, this could be the beginning of a beautiful friendship."*
Ooh. Best last line of a movie, ever.
>*As the movie ends.*
I'm definitely coming down with something. Probably a twenty-four-hour tumor. They're going around.

SALLY: You don't have a tumor.

HARRY: How do you know?

SALLY: If you're so worried, go see a doctor.

HARRY: No, he'll just tell me it's nothing.

SALLY: Will you be able to sleep?

HARRY: If not, I'll be okay.

SALLY: What'll you do?

HARRY: I'll stay up and moan. Maybe I should practice now.
>*He starts moaning.*

SALLY: Good night, Harry.

HARRY: Good night.
>*They hang up.* HARRY *remains in his place among the pillows on his bed. He moans again.*
>SALLY *turns off the light by her bed, and as she does, her side of the screen goes BLACK.*

Another moan from HARRY.

FADE OUT.

FADE IN:

EXTERIOR. STREET—DAY

HARRY *and* SALLY *walking in front of pillars and a building.*

HARRY: I had my dream again. Where I'm making love, and the Olympic judges are watching. I've nailed the compulsories, so this is it. The finals. I get a 9.8 from the Canadian. I get a perfect 10 from the American. And my mother, disguised as an East German judge, gives me a 5.6. Must have been the dismount.

CUT TO:

EXTERIOR. CENTRAL PARK ARBOR—DAY

HARRY *and* SALLY *in the park on a gorgeous fall day.*

SALLY: Basically it's the same one I've been having since I was twelve.

HARRY: What happens?

SALLY: No, it's too embarrassing.

HARRY: Don't tell me.

SALLY: Okay. There's this guy.

HARRY: What's he look like?

SALLY: I don't know. He's just kind of faceless.

HARRY: A faceless guy. Okay. Then what happens?

SALLY: He rips off my clothes.

HARRY: Then what happens?

SALLY: That's it.

HARRY: That's it? A faceless guy rips off your clothes. And that's the sex fantasy you've been having since you were twelve? Exactly the same?

SALLY: Well, sometimes I vary it a little.

HARRY: Which part?

SALLY: What I'm wearing.

HARRY *reacts.*

What?

HARRY: Nothing.

CUT TO:

INTERIOR. METROPOLITAN MUSEUM OF ART—DUSK

HARRY *and* SALLY *are walking through the Egyptian Temple exhibit.*

HARRY: *(In a funny voice.)* I've decided that for the rest of the day we are going to talk like this.

SALLY: *(Trying to imitate him.)* Like this.

HARRY: *(Funny voice.)* No, please. To repeat after me. Pepper.

SALLY: *(Trying to imitate.)* Pepper.

HARRY: *(Funny voice.)* Pepper.

SALLY: *(Laughing, still trying.)* Pepper.

HARRY: *(Funny voice.)* Pepper.

SALLY: *(Imitating.)* Pepper.

HARRY: *(Funny voice.)* Pepper.

SALLY: *(Imitating.)* Pepper.

HARRY: *(Funny voice.)* Waiter, there is too much pepper on my paprikash.

SALLY: *(Imitating.)* Waiter, there is too much pepper . . .

HARRY: *(Funny voice.)* . . . there is too much pepper . . . on my paprikash.

SALLY: *(Imitating.)* . . . on my paprikash.

HARRY: *(Funny voice.)* But I would be proud to partake of your pecan pie.

> HARRY *smiles, waits for her to repeat.* SALLY *shakes her head.* *(Funny voice.)* But I would be proud . . .

SALLY: *(Imitating.)* But I would be proud . . .

HARRY: *(Funny voice.)* . . . to partake . . .

SALLY: *(Imitating.)* . . . to partake . . .

HARRY: *(Funny voice.)* . . . of your pecan pie.

SALLY: *(Imitating.)* . . . of your pecan pie.

HARRY: *(Funny voice.)* Pecan pie.

SALLY: *(Imitating.)* Pecan pie.

HARRY: *(Funny voice.)* Pecan pie.

SALLY: *(Imitating.)* Pecan pie.

HARRY: *(Funny voice.)* Would you like to go to the movies with me tonight?

SALLY: *(Imitating.)* Would . . . you . . . like . . . to go . . .

HARRY: *(Funny voice.)* Not to repeat, please, to answer. Would you like to go to the movies . . . with me tonight?

SALLY: *(In her regular voice.)* Oh, oh, oh, I'd love to, Harry, but I can't.

HARRY: *(Still in funny voice.)* What do you have, a hot date?

SALLY: Well, yeah. Yeah.

HARRY: *(In his regular voice.)* Really?

SALLY: Yeah, I was going to tell you, but . . . I don't know. I felt
   strange about it.

HARRY: Why?

SALLY: Well, because we've been spending so much time together . . .

HARRY: Well, I think it's great you have a date.

SALLY: You do?

HARRY: Yeah. *(Leaning in conspiratorially.)* Is that what you're going
   to wear?

SALLY: Yeah. Well, I don't know. Why?

HARRY: I think you should wear skirts more. You look really good in
   skirts.

SALLY: I do?

HARRY: Yeah. You know, I have a theory that hieroglyphics are really
   an ancient comic strip about a character named Sphinxy.

SALLY: You know, Harry, you should get out there, too.

HARRY: *(In the funny voice again.)* Oh, I'm not ready.

SALLY: You should.

HARRY: *(Funny voice.)* I would not be good for anybody right now.

SALLY: It's time.

                                                          CUT TO:

INTERIOR. HARRY'S APARTMENT—DAY
   HARRY *and* SALLY *are unrolling a new rug.*

HARRY: It was the most uncomfortable night of my life.

SALLY: Well, the first date back is always the toughest, Harry.

HARRY: You only had one date. How do you know it's not going to
   get worse?

SALLY: How much worse can it get than finishing dinner, having him
   reach over, pull a hair out of my head, and start flossing with it at
   the table?

HARRY: You're talking dream date compared to my horror. It started
   out fine, she's a very nice person, and we're sitting and we're
   talking in this Ethiopian restaurant she wanted to go to. I was
   making jokes, like, "Hey, I didn't know they had food in Ethiopia.
   This'll be a quick meal. I'll order two empty plates and we can
   leave." Nothing from her, not even a smile. So I downshift into
   small talk, and I ask her where she went to school and she says
   Michigan State and this reminds me of Helen. All of a sudden I'm
   in the middle of this massive anxiety attack, my heart's beating
   like a wild man, and I'm sweating like a pig.

SALLY: Helen went to Michigan State?

HARRY: No. She went to Northwestern. But they're both Big Ten schools. *(Beat.)* I was so upset, I had to leave the restaurant.

SALLY: Harry, I think it takes a long time. It might be months before we're actually able to enjoy going out with someone new.

HARRY: Yeah.

SALLY: And maybe even longer before we'll be actually able to go to bed with someone new.

HARRY: Oh, I went to bed with her.

SALLY: You went to bed with her?

HARRY: Sure.

SALLY: Oh.

CUT TO:

INTERIOR. BATTING CAGE IN QUEENS—DAY
   HARRY *and* JESS *with bats in hand as the machine pitches.*

JESS: I don't understand this relationship.

HARRY: What do you mean?

JESS: You enjoy being with her?

HARRY: Yeah.

JESS: You find her attractive?

HARRY: Yeah.

JESS: And you're not sleeping with her?

HARRY: No.

JESS: You're afraid to let yourself be happy.

HARRY: Why can't you give me credit for this? This is a big thing for me, I've never had a relationship with a woman that didn't involve sex. I feel like I'm growing.

   One NINE-YEAR-OLD *is waiting to use the batting cage and is watching* HARRY *and* JESS *just stand there.*

NINE-YEAR-OLD: Are you finished?

HARRY: I got a whole stack of quarters and I was here first.

NINE-YEAR-OLD: Were not.

HARRY: Was too.

NINE-YEAR-OLD: Were not.

HARRY: Was too.

NINE-YEAR-OLD: You jerk.

HARRY: Creep. *(Back to* JESS.) Where was I?

JESS: You were growing.

HARRY: Yeah. It's very freeing. I can say anything to her.

JESS: Are you saying you can say things to her you can't say to me?

HARRY: No, it's just different. It's a whole different perspective. I get the woman's point of view on things. She tells me about the men she goes out with and I can talk to her about the women I see.

JESS: You tell her about other women?

HARRY: Yeah. Like the other night I made love to this woman and it was so incredible, I took her to a place that wasn't human. She actually meowed.

JESS: You made a woman meow?

HARRY: Yes. That's the point. I can say these things to her. And the great thing is, I don't have to lie because I'm not always thinking about how to get her into bed. I can just be myself.

JESS: You made a woman meow?

CUT TO:

INTERIOR. CARNEGIE DELICATESSEN—DAY
   HARRY *and* SALLY *are seated at a table, waiting for their sandwiches.*

SALLY: What do you do with these women? Do you just get up out of bed and leave?

HARRY: Sure.

SALLY: Well, explain to me how you do it. What do you say?
   A waiter brings their order.

HARRY: I say, I have an early meeting, an early haircut, an early squash game.

SALLY: You don't play squash.

HARRY: They don't know that. They just met me.

SALLY: *(Rearranging the meat on her sandwich.)* That's disgusting.

HARRY: I know. I feel terrible. *(Takes a bite of sandwich.)*

SALLY: You know, I am so glad I never got involved with you. I just would have ended up being some woman you had to get up out of bed and leave at three o'clock in the morning and go clean your andirons. And you don't even have a fireplace. *(Quite irritated now, slapping the meat over more quickly.)* Not that I would know this.

HARRY: Why are you getting so upset? This is not about you.

SALLY: Yes, it is. You're a human affront to all women. And I'm a woman. *(Bites into sandwich.)*

HARRY: Hey, I don't feel great about this, but I don't hear anyone complaining.

SALLY: Of course not. You're out the door too fast.

HARRY: I think they have an okay time.

SALLY: How do you know?

HARRY: What do you mean, how do I know? I know.

SALLY: Because they . . . ? *(She makes a gesture with her hands.)*

HARRY: Yes, because they . . . *(He makes the same gesture back.)*

SALLY: How do you know they're really . . . *(She makes the same gesture.)*

HARRY: What are you saying, they fake orgasm?

SALLY: It's possible.

HARRY: Get outta here.

SALLY: Why? Most women, at one time or another, have faked it.

HARRY: Well, they haven't faked it with me.

SALLY: How do you know?

HARRY: Because I know.

SALLY: Oh right. *(Sets her sandwich down.)* That's right. I forgot. You're a man.

HARRY: What's that supposed to mean?

SALLY: Nothing. It's just that all men are sure it never happens to them, and most women at one time or another have done it, so you do the math.

HARRY: You don't think I can tell the difference?

SALLY: No.

HARRY: Get outta here.

> HARRY *bites into his sandwich.* SALLY *just stares at him. A seductive look comes onto her face.*

SALLY: Oooh!

> HARRY, *sandwich in hand, chewing his food, looks up at* SALLY.

Oh! Oooh!

HARRY: Are you okay?

> SALLY, *her eyes closed, ruffles her hair seductively.*

SALLY: Oh, God!

> HARRY *is beginning to figure out what* SALLY *is doing.*

Oooh! Oh, God!

> SALLY *tilts her head back.*

Oh!

> *Her eyes closed, she runs her hand over her face, down her neck.*

Oh, my God! Oh, yeah, right there.

> HARRY *looks around, noticing that others in the deli are noticing* SALLY. *She's really making a show now.*

(Gasps.) Oh!
> *A man in the background turns to look at her.*

Oh! Oh! *(Gasps.)* Oh God! Oh! Yes!
> HARRY, *embarrassed, stares at her in disbelief.*

(Pounding the table.) Yes! Yes!
> *The man in the background is now watching intently.*

(Pounding the table with both hands.) Yes! Yes! Yes!
> HARRY *looks around, very embarrassed, smiles at customers. An* OLDER WOMAN *seated nearby stares.*

Yes! Yes!
> *By now, the place is totally silent and everyone is watching.*

Yes! Oh! *(Still thumping table.)* Yes, yes, yes!
> SALLY *leans her head back, as though experiencing the final ecstatic convulsions of an orgasm.*

Yes! Yes! Yes!
> *She finally tosses her head forward.*

Oh. Oh. Oh.
> SALLY *sinks down into her chair, tousling her hair, rubbing her hand down her neck to her chest.*

Oh, God.
> *Then, suddenly, the act is over.* SALLY *calmly picks up her fork, digs into her coleslaw, and smiles innocently at* HARRY.
> *A waiter approaches the* OLDER WOMAN *to take her food order. The woman looks at him.*

OLDER WOMAN: I'll have what she's having.

> FADE OUT.

FADE IN:

EXTERIOR. CENTRAL PARK—DAY
> *Various scenes of the snow-blanketed park: A horse pulls a carriage, people bundled up in winter clothing walk along the snow-covered paths, and a lone cross-country skier crosses a large expanse.*

> CUT TO:

EXTERIOR. ROCKEFELLER PLAZA—NIGHT
> *The huge Christmas tree in the square; a woman skating expertly in the center of the ice rink.*

> CUT TO:

EXTERIOR. STREET—NIGHT
A store window with a Christmas display; families admiring it.

CUT TO:

EXTERIOR. PARK—DAY
Children riding sleds and toboggans down a hill.

CUT TO:

EXTERIOR. STREET—NIGHT
*Pedestrians, huddled against the cold, walking by lighted
Christmas trees.*

CUT TO:

EXTERIOR. PARK—DAY
*The Wollman Rink, full of skaters. A man walks his dog
outside the fence.*

CUT TO:

EXTERIOR. CHRISTMAS TREE LOT—DAY
SALLY *is paying for a tree. Then she and* HARRY *pick it up, he
holding the top and she the bottom, and carry it to* SALLY'*s.
Together.*

CUT TO:

INTERIOR. NEW YEAR'S EVE PARTY—NIGHT
Champagne is popped.
*We know it's New Year's Eve because people are wearing funny
hats and there's one of those mirrored things hanging from
the ceiling and casting twinkle lights on a fairly large crowd of
revelers in a penthouse apartment somewhere in Manhattan.*
A band is PLAYING. HARRY *and* SALLY *are dancing.*
He dips her.
SALLY: I really want to thank you for taking me out tonight.
HARRY: Oh, don't be silly. And next year, if neither of us is with
somebody, you've got a date.
SALLY: Deal. See, now we can dance cheek to cheek.
They dance a moment and then the MUSIC ENDS. *They go
on dancing a bit longer and for a split second we see the
beginnings of something . . . an inkling . . . a little tender
moment. Then—*

VOICE: *(Offscreen.)* Hey, everybody, ten seconds to the New Year!
> *The* CROWD *begins to count down:*

CROWD: Ten, nine . . .

HARRY: Want to get some air?

SALLY: Yeah.

CROWD: . . . eight, seven, six . . .

EXTERIOR. NEW YEAR'S EVE PARTY—NIGHT
. . . five, four . . .
> HARRY *and* SALLY *go out onto the balcony.*

. . . three, two, Happy New Year!
> *All around* HARRY *and* SALLY, *couples are hugging, kissing, celebrating. It is slightly uncomfortable.*

HARRY: Happy New Year.

SALLY: Happy New Year.
> *They kiss quickly and awkwardly.*

FADE OUT.

FADE IN:

DOCUMENTARY FOOTAGE
> *A* COUPLE *on a love seat.*

FIFTH WOMAN: He was the head counselor at the boys' camp, and I was the head counselor at the girls' camp. They had a social one night. *(Beat.)* And he walked across the room. I thought he was coming to talk to my friend Maxine, because people were always walking across rooms to talk to Maxine, but he was coming to talk to me. And he said—

FIFTH MAN: I'm Ben Small of the Coney Island Smalls.

FIFTH WOMAN: And at that moment, I knew, I knew the way you know about a good melon.

FADE OUT.

FADE IN:

EXTERIOR. WEST BROADWAY, NEAR RESTAURANT—EARLY EVENING
> SALLY *and her friend* MARIE *walking down the street on their way to a restaurant.*

SALLY: You sent flowers to yourself?

MARIE: Sixty dollars I spend on this big stupid arrangement of flowers, and I wrote a card that I planned to leave out on the front table where Arthur would just happen to see it—

SALLY: What did the card say?

MARIE: "Please say yes. Love, Jonathan."

SALLY: Did it work?

MARIE: He never even came over. He forgot this charity thing that his wife was chairman of. *(Beat.)* He's never going to leave her.

SALLY: Of course he isn't.

MARIE: You're right, you're right. I know you're right. *(Beat.)* Where is this place?

SALLY: Somewhere in the next block.

MARIE: Oh, I can't believe I'm doing this.

SALLY: Look, Harry is one of my best friends, and you are one of my best friends, and if by some chance you two hit it off, we could all still be friends instead of drifting apart the way you do when you get involved with someone who doesn't know your friends.

MARIE: You and I haven't drifted apart since I started seeing Arthur.

SALLY: If Arthur ever left his wife and I actually met him, I'm sure you and I would drift apart.

MARIE: He's never going to leave her.

SALLY: Of course he isn't.

MARIE: You're right, you're right, I know you're right.

CUT TO:

EXTERIOR. WEST BROADWAY, NEAR RESTAURANT—NIGHT
  HARRY *and his friend* JESS *coming down the street.*

JESS: I don't know about this.

HARRY: It's just a dinner.

JESS: You know, I've finally gotten to a place in my life where I'm comfortable with the fact that it's just me and my work. *(They walk on.)* If she's so great, why aren't *you* taking her out?

HARRY: How many times do I have to tell you, we're just friends.

JESS: So you're saying she's not that attractive?

HARRY: No, I told you she is attractive.

JESS: But you also said she had a good personality.

HARRY: She has a good personality.

  JESS *makes a "precisely my point" gesture.*
  What?

JESS: When someone's not attractive, they're always described as having a good personality.

HARRY: Look. If you had asked me what does she look like and I said, she has a good personality, *that* means she's not attractive. But just because I happen to mention she has a good personality,

she could be either. She could be attractive with a good
personality, or not attractive with a good personality.

JESS: So which one is she?

HARRY: Attractive.

JESS: But not beautiful, right?

    HARRY *glares at him.*

CUT TO:

INTERIOR. RESTAURANT—NIGHT

    HARRY, JESS, SALLY, *and* MARIE *at a table. A waiter has just
brought them drinks. It is clear from the arrangement at
the table that* HARRY *is meant to be with* MARIE *and* JESS
is meant to be with SALLY. JESS *and* SALLY *are talking to
each other, while* HARRY *and* MARIE *carry on their own
conversation.*

JESS: *(To* SALLY.) It's like whenever I read Jimmy Breslin, it's as if he's
leaving some kind of wake-up call for the city of New York.

SALLY: What do you mean by a wake-up call?

    They continue talking as we now focus on HARRY *and* MARIE'S
conversation:

HARRY: Would I have seen any of your windows?

MARIE: Well, just a couple of weeks ago, I did a thing with hostages.

HARRY: Oh, the thing with people in blindfolds.

    Back to JESS *and* SALLY, *who obviously is not enjoying or
agreeing with what he is saying.*

SALLY: *(To* JESS.) Uh, let's just say I'm . . . I'm really not a big fan of
Jimmy Breslin.

JESS: Well, he's the reason I became a writer, but that's not
important.

    A little pause.

SALLY: Harry, you and Marie are both from New Jersey.

MARIE: Really?

HARRY: Where are you from?

MARIE: South Orange.

HARRY: Haddonfield.

MARIE: Oh.

    They all look at each other.

    Then they look at their menus.

HARRY: So what are we going to order?

SALLY: I'm going to start with the grilled radicchio.

HARRY: Jess, Sally is a great orderer. Not only does she always pick the best thing on the menu, but she orders it in a way that even the chef didn't know how good it would be.

SALLY *shoots* HARRY *a look.*

JESS: I think restaurants have become too important.

MARIE: Oh, I agree. "Restaurants are to people in the eighties what theater was to people in the sixties." I read that in a magazine.

JESS: I wrote that.

MARIE: Get outta here.

JESS: No, I did. I wrote that.

MARIE: I never quoted anything from a magazine in my life. That's amazing. Don't you think that's amazing? And you wrote it?

JESS: I also wrote, "Pesto is the quiche of the eighties."

MARIE: Get over yourself.

JESS: I did.

MARIE: Where did I read that?

JESS: *New York* magazine.

HARRY: Sally writes for *New York* magazine.

MARIE: Do you know, that piece had a real impact on me. I don't know that much about writing, but . . .

JESS: Look, it spoke to you, and that pleases me.

MARIE: It had a wonderful, unique—is the word "style"?

JESS: If you say that's the word, that's the word.

MARIE: I . . . I mean . . . I really have to admire people who can be as . . . as . . . articulate . . .

JESS: Nobody's ever quoted me back to me before.

CUT TO:

EXTERIOR. WEST BROADWAY—NIGHT

HARRY, JESS, MARIE, *and* SALLY *are walking up the avenue, all four of them in a row, ad-libbing about the meal and what a nice night it is. They walk past a shoe store, and* MARIE *suddenly yanks* SALLY *over.*

MARIE: Oooo, I've been looking for a red suede pump. *(Beat.)* What do you think of Jess?

The two men keep walking.

SALLY: Well, uh . . .

MARIE: *(Interrupting.)* Do you think you could go out with him?

SALLY: I don't know . . .

MARIE: —because I feel really comfortable with him.

SALLY: You want to go out with Jess?

MARIE: If it's all right with you.

SALLY: Sure. Sure. I'm just worried about Harry. He's very sensitive, he's going through a rough period, and I just don't want you to reject him right now.

MARIE: I wouldn't. I totally understand.

SALLY: Okay.

EXTERIOR. WEST BROADWAY—NIGHT

> HARRY *and* JESS *apparently in the midst of an identical conversation. They're stopped in front of a running-equipment store.*

JESS: If you don't think you're going to call Marie, do you mind if I call her?

HARRY: No.

JESS: Good, good.

HARRY: But for tonight you shouldn't . . . I mean, Sally's very vulnerable right now. I mean, you can call Marie, it's fine, but just, like, wait a week or so, you know? Don't make any moves tonight.

JESS: Fine. No problem. I wasn't even thinking about tonight.

> *The women join them.*

Well. *(Beat.)* I don't feel like walking anymore, I think I'll get a cab.

MARIE: I'll go with you.

JESS: Great. *(He leaps into the street as he spots a cab.)* Taxi!

> *The cab SCREECHES to a halt, and* JESS *and* MARIE *get into it and it pulls away, leaving* SALLY *and* HARRY *on the curb.*

FADE OUT.

FADE IN:

DOCUMENTARY FOOTAGE

> *Another* OLDER COUPLE, *both Asian, sitting together on the love seat.*

ASIAN MAN: A man came to me and said, "I found nice girl for you. She lives in the next village, and she is ready for marriage." We were not supposed to meet until the wedding. But I wanted to make sure, so I sneaked into her village and hid behind a tree and watched her wash the clothes. I think, if I don't like the way she looks, I don't marry her. But she looked really nice to me. So I said okay to the man, we get married. We are married for fifty-five years.

FADE OUT.

FADE IN:

EXTERIOR. THE SHARPER IMAGE—DAY—ESTABLISHING
INTERIOR. THE SHARPER IMAGE—DAY

> *One of those places with gifts for people who have everything.*
> HARRY *and* SALLY *are browsing through. He shoots a*
> *basketball into a mini-sized hoop.*

HARRY: I have to get this, I have to.

SALLY: Harry, we're here for Jess and Marie.

HARRY: I know we'll find them something, there's great stuff here.

SALLY: We should've gone to the plant store.

> *He picks up a pith helmet with a battery-operated fan in it and*
> *puts it on* SALLY'*s head.*

HARRY: Here. Perfect for them.

SALLY: What's that?

HARRY: Battery-operated pith helmet, with fan.

SALLY: Why is this necessary in life?

HARRY: I don't know. Look, look at this. *(Indicating fan.)* It also
makes great fries.

> *He spots something across the aisle.*

Oh, oh, oh.

> *He heads toward it.*

Good. Call off the dogs. The hunt is over.

> *He goes to one of those machines that allow you to sing the*
> *lead to the backup vocal and instrumental on a song.*

Sally, this is the greatest. *(Into the microphone.)* Sally, please
report to me. Look at this. This is incredible. They're gonna love
this. This is a singing machine.

> HARRY *puts in one of the cassettes. The INSTRUMENTAL for*
> *"The Surrey with the Fringe on Top" comes on.*

Look. You sing the lead, and this has the backup and everything.
This is from *Oklahoma!* Here's the lyrics right here.

SALLY: *(Reading.)* "Surrey with the Fringe on Top."

HARRY: Yeah, this is perfect.

> *He starts singing giddily.*

"Chicks and ducks and geese better scurry,
When I take you out in the surrey,
When I take you out in the surrey
With the fringe on top." *(Pointing to* SALLY.*)* Now you.

> *She starts to sing.*

SALLY: *(Singing.)* "Watch that fringe and . . ."
> HARRY *resumes singing, too, as the absurd and dizzy*
> *instrumental continues. They both get more and more idiotic.*

HARRY AND SALLY: *(Singing.)* ". . . see how it flutters,
When I drive them high steppin' strutters,
Nosey pokes'll peek through their shutters and their eyes will
  pop!"
> *Suddenly* HARRY *turns pale and stops singing.*

SALLY: *(Continuing to sing.)* "The wheels are yeller, the upholstery's
brown,
The dashboard's gen-u-ine leather
With isinglass curtains y'can roll . . ."
> SALLY *notices something's wrong.*
> *The* BACKUP *MUSIC CONTINUES as she stops, too.*

What? It's my voice, isn't it? You hate my voice. I know it's
terrible. Joe hated it. . . .

HARRY: It's Helen.

SALLY: Helen?

HARRY: She's coming right toward me.
> *The BACKUP VOCAL CONTINUES as we see coming*
> *toward* HARRY *a dark-haired, very chic woman,* HELEN,
> *accompanied by a tall, attractive man,* IRA.

HELEN: How are you, Harry?

HARRY: *(He swallows.)* Fine. I'm fine.

HELEN: This is Ira Stone. Harry Burns.

IRA: Harry.
> *They shake hands. It's very awkward.* HARRY *suddenly*
> *remembers* SALLY.

HARRY: I'm sorry. This is Sally Albright. Helen Hillson and Ira.

IRA: Sally.

HELEN: Nice to meet you.

SALLY: Hi.
> *A terrible moment.*

HELEN: Well, see you.

HARRY: Yeah. Nice to meet you, Ira.
> *A smile, and they move on. HOLD on* HARRY, *about to faint.*

SALLY: You okay?

HARRY: Yeah, I'm perfect.
> HARRY *looks like one of those cartoon characters who's been*
> *struck on the head with a mallet.*

She looked weird, didn't she? She looked really weird. She looked very weird.

SALLY: I've never seen her before.

HARRY: Trust me, she looked weird. Her legs looked heavy. Really, she must be retaining water.

SALLY: Harry.

HARRY: Believe me, the woman saved everything.

CUT TO:

EXTERIOR. PLANT SHOP—DAY
    SALLY *is paying for a plant.* HARRY *is just staring blankly into a ficus.* SALLY *approaches.*

SALLY: You sure you're okay?

HARRY: Oh, I'm fine. Look, it had to happen at some point. In a city of eight million people you're bound to run into your ex-wife. So, boom, it happened. And now I'm fine.

CUT TO:

INTERIOR. JESS AND MARIE'S APARTMENT—DAY
    A nice West Side floor-through with a beautiful fireplace and a great deal of furniture—about twice as much furniture as is necessary, as a matter of fact.
    MARIE *and* JESS *in sneakers, jeans, baggy shirts, are clearly in the middle of some sort of dispute.* HARRY *is still distracted. There are a few unpacked boxes—some books, a couple of ashtrays, a glass, etc.*

JESS: It works. I like it. It says home to me.

MARIE: *(To* JESS.*)* Okay, okay, we'll let Harry and Sally be the judge. *(To* SALLY *and* HARRY.*)* What do *you* think?
    MARIE *points to a large wagon wheel that's been made into a coffee table with a round plate of glass over it.*
    HARRY *looks at* JESS, *who's glaring at him.*

HARRY: It's nice.

JESS: Case closed.
    JESS *smiles, victorious.*

MARIE: Of course he likes it. He's a guy. Sally?
    SALLY *crinkles up her nose.*

JESS: What's so awful about it?

MARIE: It's so awful there's no way even to begin to explain what is so awful about it.

JESS: Honey, I don't object to any of *your* things.

MARIE: If we had an extra room, we could put all your things in it, including your bar stools, and . . .

JESS: Wait, wait, honey, honey, wait, wait. You don't like my bar stools?

> MARIE *looks at him. Of course she doesn't like his bar stools.*
> JESS *turns to* HARRY *for help.*
> HARRY, *we now see, has wandered away and stands by the window and he's staring out like a forlorn figure in a Magritte painting.*

JESS: Harry, come on. *(Beat.)* Someone has to be on my side.

> *No response from* HARRY.

MARIE: I'm on your side. I'm just trying to help you have good taste.

JESS: I have good taste.

MARIE: Everybody thinks they have good taste and a sense of humor, but they couldn't possibly all.

> HARRY *stands up, looks around the room.*

HARRY: You know, it's funny—we started out like this, Helen and I. We had blank walls. We hung things. We picked out tiles together. Then you know what happens? Six years later you find yourself singing "Surrey with the Fringe on Top" in front of Ira.

SALLY: Do we have to talk about this right now?

HARRY: Yes, I think that right now is actually the perfect time to talk about this, because I want our friends to benefit from the wisdom of my experience. *(He's becoming more and more upset.)* Right now everything is great. Everyone is happy. Everyone is in love. And that's wonderful. But you gotta know that sooner or later you're gonna be screaming at each other about who's gonna get this dish. *(He picks up a cracked ashtray.)* This eight-dollar dish will cost you a thousand dollars in phone calls to the legal firm of "That's mine, this is yours."

SALLY: Harry—

HARRY: *(To* SALLY.*)* Please. *(To* JESS *and* MARIE.*)* Jess, Marie, do me a favor. For your own good. *Put your name in your books.* Right now. Before they get mixed up and you don't know whose is whose. Because someday, believe it or not, you'll go fifteen rounds over who's going to get this coffee table, this stupid wagon-wheel, Roy Rogers, garage-sale coffee table.

JESS: I thought you liked it.

HARRY: *(Still shouting.)* I was being nice.

HARRY *slams out the door.*

SALLY *looks at* JESS *and* MARIE.

SALLY: He just bumped into Helen.

SALLY *goes out the door, leaving* JESS *and* MARIE.

MARIE: I want you to know that I will never want that wagon-wheel coffee table.

CUT TO:

EXTERIOR. JESS AND MARIE'S APARTMENT—DAY

HARRY *is sitting on the stoop.* SALLY *comes down the steps.*

HARRY: I know, I know. I shouldn't have done that.

SALLY: Harry, you're going to have to try and find a way of not expressing every feeling that you have every moment that you have them.

HARRY: Oh, really.

SALLY: Yes. There are times and places for things.

HARRY: Well, the next time you're giving a lecture series in social graces, would you let me know, 'cause I'll sign up.

SALLY: You don't have to take your anger out on me.

HARRY: Oh, I think I'm entitled to throw a little anger your way. Especially when I'm being told how to live my life by Miss Hospital Corners.

SALLY: What is that supposed to mean?

HARRY: I mean, nothing bothers you. You never get upset about anything.

SALLY: Don't be ridiculous.

HARRY: What? You never get upset about Joe. I never see that back up on you. How is that possible? Don't you experience any feelings of loss?

SALLY: I don't have to take this crap from you.

SALLY *storms back to the building.* HARRY *follows.*

HARRY: If you're so over Joe, why aren't you seeing anyone?

SALLY: I see people.

HARRY: See people? Have you slept with *one* person since you broke up with Joe?

SALLY: What the hell does that have to do with anything? That will prove that I'm over Joe? Because I fuck somebody? Harry, you're going to have to move back to New Jersey because you've slept with everybody in New York, and I don't see that turning Helen into a faint memory for you. Besides, I will make love to someone when it's making love, not the way you do it, like you're out for revenge or something.

HARRY: Are you finished now?

SALLY: Yes.

HARRY: Can I say something?

SALLY: Yes.

HARRY: I'm sorry.

> *He walks over and gives her a hug.*
>
> *They walk back up the steps toward the house.* JESS *passes them, coming down the stairs carrying out the wagon-wheel coffee table.*

JESS: Don't say a word.

CUT TO:

INTERIOR. JESS AND MARIE'S APARTMENT—NIGHT

> *It's all furnished now, very comfortable, not lavish. A corduroy couch, lots of books and records, a couple of quilts hanging over the backs of chairs. No wagon-wheel coffee table. A game of Win, Lose or Draw is in progress.* SALLY's *team consists of* HARRY, ALICE, *and* JESS. EMILY, HARRY's *date, is snuggled up against him.* ALICE's *husband,* GARY, MARIE, *and* JULIAN, SALLY's *date, are part of the other team.*
>
> SALLY *is feverishly drawing what is supposed to be a baby.*

JESS: It's a monkey. It's a monkey. Monkey see, monkey do.

> SALLY *shakes her head no and keeps drawing.*

It's an ape. Going ape.

ALICE: It's a baby.

> SALLY *nods yes.*

JESS: *Planet of the Apes.*

> SALLY *writes the word "BABY" on the paper. She continues to draw what looks like a big mouth.*

HARRY: *Planet of the Apes.* She just said it's a baby. How about planet of the dopes?

JESS: It doesn't look like a baby.

> SALLY *now has drawn what look like arrows on lines coming out of the mouth.*

HARRY: It's a big-mouth baby. Mick Jagger as a baby.

JESS: Baby ape! Baby ape!

ALICE: Baby's breath.

HARRY: *(Overlap.)* Rosemary's Baby's mouth.

JESS: "Won't you come home, Bill Baby?"

ALICE: *(Overlap.)* Kiss the baby!

HARRY: Melancholy Baby's mouth!

JESS: Baby fish mouth!

JULIAN: Fifteen seconds.

ALICE: Baby boom!

>SALLY *is getting frustrated, can do nothing but draw more arrows out of the mouth.*

JESS: Draw something resembling anything!

ALICE: . . . Kiss the baby . . .

HARRY: *(Overlap.)* Baby spitting up. Exorcist baby!

ALICE: "Yes, sir, that's my baby."

HARRY: "No, sir, don't mean maybe."

JULIAN: That's it. Time's up.

SALLY: Baby talk.

JESS: Baby talk? What's that? That's not a saying.

HARRY: Oh, but "baby fish mouth" is sweeping the nation.

GARY: Final score: our team, 110, you guys, 60.

SALLY: *(To JULIAN.)* I can't draw.

JULIAN: No. That's a baby, and that's a baby talking. You're wonderful.

>*He puts his arms around her.*

MARIE: All right, who wants coffee?

>SALLY *and* JULIAN *kiss.* HARRY *looks on.*

JESS: I do, and I love you.

ALICE: Do you have any tea?

MARIE: One tea.

>HARRY *holds up his hand.*

HARRY: Industrial strength.

EMILY: I'll have tea also.

SALLY: I'll help you. *(To JULIAN.)* Decaf?

JULIAN: Yeah.

ALICE: Cream.

EMILY: *(To MARIE.)* Where's the bathroom?

MARIE: Through that door, down the hall.

>EMILY *and* HARRY *kiss as she heads away.* SALLY *notices this.*
>
>JESS *and* JULIAN *are at the drawing board, examining* SALLY's *"baby" drawing.*

JESS: Never looked like a baby to me.

JULIAN: Which part?

JESS: All of it.

HARRY: Hey, Jess, you were going to show me the cover art for your book.

JESS: Oh, yeah, yeah. It's in the den. *(To* JULIAN.*)* Look, uh, Julian, help yourself—have some more wine, whatever you like, okay? *(To* HARRY.*)* I like saying it's in the den. It's got a nice ring to it.

INTERIOR. KITCHEN—NIGHT

    SALLY *and* MARIE *go about getting the coffee ready.*

SALLY: Emily's a little young for Harry, don't you think?

MARIE: Well, she's young, but look what she's done.

SALLY: What has she done? She makes desserts.

INTERIOR. DEN—NIGHT

HARRY: Does Julian seem a little stuffy to you?

JESS: He's a good guy. You should talk to him, get to know him.

HARRY: He's too tall to talk to.

INTERIOR. KITCHEN—NIGHT

MARIE: She makes 3,500 chocolate mousse pies a week.

SALLY: Emily is *Aunt* Emily?

INTERIOR. DEN—NIGHT

JESS: He took us all to a Mets game last week. It was great.

HARRY: You all went to a Mets game together?

JESS: It was a last-minute thing.

HARRY: But Sally hates baseball.

INTERIOR. KITCHEN—NIGHT

SALLY: Harry doesn't even like sweets.

MARIE: Julian is great.

SALLY: I know. He's a grown-up.

INTERIOR. DEN—NIGHT

JESS: Emily is terrific.

HARRY: Yeah. Of course, when I asked her where she was when Kennedy was shot, she said, "Ted Kennedy was shot?"

JESS: No.

                                        CUT TO:

INTERIOR. HARRY'S BEDROOM—NIGHT

HARRY *in bed reading, trying not to look at the last page, but finally he can't help himself. As he flips to the last page, the phone RINGS. He reaches for the phone and answers it.*

HARRY: Hello.

SALLY: *(Through filter.)* Are you alone?

HARRY: Yeah. I was just finishing a book.

SALLY: *(Through filter.)* Could you come over?

HARRY: What's the matter?

INTERIOR. SALLY'S BEDROOM—NIGHT

SALLY: He's getting married.

HARRY: *(Through filter.)* Who?

SALLY: Joe.

INTERIOR. HARRY'S BEDROOM—NIGHT

HARRY: I'll be right there.

CUT TO:

INTERIOR. HALLWAY OUTSIDE SALLY'S APARTMENT—NIGHT

SALLY *opens the door. She wears a bathrobe. She is crying and looks terrible.*

SALLY: Hi.

HARRY: Are you all right?

SALLY: Come on in.

HARRY *follows her inside and closes the door.*

INTERIOR. SALLY'S APARTMENT—NIGHT

SALLY: *(Through tears.)* I'm sorry to call you so late.

HARRY: It's all right.

She goes on sobbing, then pulls back and gives a huge wheeze.

SALLY: I need a Kleenex.

HARRY: Okay.

SALLY: Okay.

SALLY *starts into the bedroom.*

INTERIOR. SALLY'S BEDROOM—NIGHT

SALLY *enters the room, looks for the Kleenex.* HARRY *sits on the bed.*

SALLY: He just called me up. Just wanted to see how you were. Fine, how are you? Fine. . . . His secretary's on vacation, everything's all backed up, he's got a big case in Newark, blah blah blah, and I'm thinking, I'm over him, I really am over him, I can't believe I was ever remotely interested in any of this, and then he said, "I have some news."

> SALLY *starts to cry again.*

She works in his office. She's a paralegal. Her name is Kimberly. *He just met her.* She's supposed to be his transitional person, she's not supposed to be the one. *(Beat.)* All this time I've been saying he didn't want to get married. *(Beat.)* But the truth is he didn't want to marry *me.* He didn't love *me.*

HARRY: If you could take him back right now, would you?

SALLY: No. But why didn't he want to marry me? What's the matter with me?

HARRY: Nothing.

SALLY: I'm difficult.

HARRY: You're challenging.

SALLY: I'm too structured. I'm completely closed off.

HARRY: But in a good way.

SALLY: No, no, no. I drove him away.

> *Crying even harder now.*

And I'm going to be forty.

HARRY: When?

SALLY: Someday.

HARRY: In eight years.

SALLY: But it's there, it's just sitting there like this big dead end. It's not the same for men. Charlie Chaplin had babies when he was seventy-three.

HARRY: Yeah, but he was too old to pick them up.

> *She smiles a little, then starts crying again.*

Oh, c'mere, c'mere. *(He gives her a hug.)* It's going to be okay. You're gonna be fine, you'll see.

> SALLY *sniffles into* HARRY'*s shirt.*

Go ahead, it's not one of my favorites anyway. It's gonna be okay.

> HARRY *holds her. He gives her a kiss, starts to break the hug.*

I'll make you some tea.

SALLY: Harry, could you just hold me a little longer?

HARRY: Oh, sure. There.

> HARRY *holds her. After a beat,* SALLY *looks up at him, almost searching for something. She kisses him. A hungry, needy*

kiss. HARRY *is caught slightly off guard, but returns the kiss.*
As they begin to make love—

CUT TO:

INTERIOR. SALLY'S BEDROOM—LATER

They've made love. Both of them lying in bed, SALLY *is in*
HARRY's *arms.* SALLY *has a smile on her face.* HARRY *stares*
straight ahead.

SALLY: Are you comfortable?

HARRY *nods.*

HARRY: Sure.

After a pause.

SALLY: Do you want something to drink or something?

HARRY: No, I'm okay.

SALLY: *(Getting up.)* Well, I'm going to get up for some water, so it's
really no trouble.

HARRY: Okay. Water.

INTERIOR. KITCHEN—NIGHT

SALLY *enters and gets a bottle of water from the refrigerator.*
She goes to the cabinet and takes out two glasses and pours.

INTERIOR. BEDROOM—NIGHT

HARRY *lying in* SALLY's *bed, still staring straight ahead. Finally,*
he looks around and reaches for a file box he sees. He opens
it and looks inside.

INTERIOR. KITCHEN—NIGHT

As SALLY *stands thinking, a little smile on her face.*

INTERIOR. BEDROOM—NIGHT

HARRY *is sitting up in bed with the light on, looking through*
the box of index cards.

SALLY *comes in with the glasses of water.*

HARRY: *(Looking up from the box.)* You have all your videotapes
alphabetized and on index cards.

SALLY *hands him the water.*

Thank you.

A silence while HARRY *desultorily goes through the box.*
Unbelievably awkward.

Every SOUND is louder than it actually is. The riffle of the index cards. SALLY *taking a gulp of water.* HARRY *rearranging his pillow.*

SALLY: Do you want to watch something?

HARRY: No, not unless you do.

SALLY: No, that's okay.

A pause. He puts the file box back. SALLY *slides back into bed, nestles into his shoulder.*

Do you want to go to sleep?

HARRY: Okay.

She turns off the lamp and settles in beside HARRY.

CUT TO:

INTERIOR. BEDROOM—DAY

SALLY *wakes up. Sees the other half of the bed empty. Where's* HARRY? *She turns over and sees him getting dressed.*

SALLY: Where are you going?

HARRY: I gotta go.

SALLY *stares at him.*

I gotta go home, I gotta change my clothes, and then I have to go to work and so do you, but after work I'd like to take you out to dinner if you're free. Are you free?

SALLY: Yes.

HARRY: Fine. I'll call you later.

SALLY: Fine.

HARRY: Fine.

HARRY *gives her a little kiss, walks out.*

HOLD *on her in bed as the door SLAMS.*

Next to her is the phone.

INTERIOR. JESS AND MARIE'S BEDROOM—MORNING

A bed with a phone on each side. JESS *and* MARIE *asleep in bed. The phone on* MARIE's *side of the bed starts to RING.* MARIE *and* JESS *both wake up, look at the clock. They can't believe how early it is.*

It RINGS again.

JESS: *(Accusingly.)* Yours.

MARIE *picks up the phone, pulls the phone onto the bed.*

MARIE: Hello.

WIPE IN FROM RIGHT:

   SALLY *sitting up in bed, talking on phone.*
SALLY: I'm sorry to call so early—
MARIE: Are you all right?
JESS: No one I know would call at this hour.
   The phone RINGS on JESS*'s side of the bed.*
SALLY: I did something terrible.
   JESS *picks up the phone.*
MARIE: What did you do?

WIPE IN FROM LEFT:

   HARRY *standing at public phone. Now we see all four of them*
      on-screen, MARIE *and* JESS *in their bed on their phones,*
      talking to SALLY, *in her apartment at the far right, and*
      HARRY, *on a pay phone in the street at the far left.*
JESS: *(Into phone.)* No one I know would call at this hour.
SALLY: It's so awful.
HARRY: I need to talk.
MARIE: What happened?
JESS: What's the matter?
SALLY: Harry came over last night . . .
HARRY: I went over to Sally's last night . . .
SALLY: . . . because I was upset that Joe was getting married . . .
HARRY: . . . and one thing led to another . . .
SALLY: . . . and before I knew it, we were kissing . . . and
   then . . . *(She shakes her head in horror, remembering.)*
HARRY: . . . to make a long story short . . .

SALLY:	HARRY:
We did it.	We did it.
JESS: *(Whispering to* MARIE.*)*	MARIE: *(Whispering to* JESS.*)*
They did it.	They did it.

MARIE: *(Back to* SALLY.*)* That's great, Sally.
JESS: *(Back to* HARRY.*)* We've been praying for it.
MARIE: You should have done it in the first place.
JESS: For months we've been saying, you should do it.
MARIE: You guys belong together.
JESS: It's like killing two birds with one stone.
MARIE: It's like two wrongs make a right.

JESS:	MARIE:
How was it?	How was it?

HARRY: The during part was good . . .
SALLY: I thought it was good . . .
HARRY: . . . but then I felt suffocated.
SALLY: . . . but then I guess it wasn't.
JESS: Jesus, I'm sorry.
MARIE: The worst.
HARRY: I just wanted to get out of there.
SALLY: He just disappeared.
HARRY: I feel so bad.
SALLY: I'm so embarrassed.
JESS: I don't blame you.
MARIE: That's horrible.
HARRY: I think I'm coming down with something.
SALLY: I think I'm catching a cold.
JESS: Look, it would have been great if it had worked out, but it didn't.
MARIE: You should never go to bed with anyone when you've found out your last boyfriend is getting married.
HARRY: Who's that talking?
JESS: Who?
SALLY: Is that Jess on the phone?
JESS: It's Jane Fonda on the VCR.
MARIE: It's Bryant Gumbel.

JESS:	MARIE:
Do you want to come over for breakfast?	Do you want to come over for breakfast?

MARIE *and* JESS *look at each other, horrified.*
HARRY: No, I'm not up to it.
SALLY: No, I feel too awful.

JESS:	MARIE:
Good.	Good.

MARIE: I mean, it's so early.
JESS: Call me later if you want.
MARIE: I'll call you later, okay?
HARRY: Okay, bye.

SALLY: Bye.
JESS: Bye.
MARIE: Bye.
> *Everyone hangs up.* HARRY *and* SALLY *frames WIPE*
> *OFFSCREEN LEFT AND RIGHT, leaving* JESS *and* MARIE
> *on-screen.*
> *HOLD on* MARIE *and* JESS.
> MARIE *looks at* JESS.

MARIE: God.
JESS: I know.
MARIE: Tell me I'll never have to be out there again.
> JESS *puts his arms around her and holds her.*

JESS: You'll never have to be out there again.
> *They kiss.*

CUT TO:

INTERIOR. SALLY'S BATHROOM—DAY
> SALLY *looking at herself in the mirror as she puts on makeup.*

SALLY: *(Voice-over.)* I'll just say we made a mistake—

CUT TO:

INTERIOR. HARRY'S BATHROOM—DAY
> HARRY *is showering.*

HARRY: *(Voice-over.)* Sally, it was a mistake—

CUT TO:

INTERIOR. SALLY'S BATHROOM—DAY
> *As before.*

SALLY: *(Voice-over.)* I just hope I get to say it first.

CUT TO:

INTERIOR. HARRY'S BATHROOM—DAY
> HARRY *still showering.*

HARRY: *(Voice-over.)* I hope she says it before I do.

CUT TO:

INTERIOR. RESTAURANT—NIGHT
> SALLY *and* HARRY *sit, silently, with their drinks. Long pause.*

SALLY: It was a mistake.
HARRY: I'm so relieved that you think so, too.

Both of them take swigs of their water.
I'm not saying last night wasn't great.

SALLY: It was.

HARRY: Yes, it was.

SALLY: We just never should've done it.

HARRY: I couldn't agree more.

> SALLY *nods.*
> *A pause.*

SALLY: I'm so relieved.

HARRY: Great.

SALLY: Yeah.

> HARRY *nodding.*
> SALLY *nodding.*
> *Well, that's that.*
> *A* WAITER *brings their salads.*

WAITER: Two mixed green salads.

> *They start to eat.*
> *They eat.*
> *Silence.*
> *We hear the* FORKS *against the plates.*
> *More silence.*

HARRY: It is so nice when you can sit with someone and not have to talk.

> *HOLD on the scene as they go on eating in silence.*
> *HOLD.*
> *HOLD.*

CUT TO:

EXTERIOR. CENTRAL PARK—BETHESDA FOUNTAIN—DAY

> HARRY *and* JESS *fast-walking along.*

HARRY: It's just like, most of the time you go to bed with someone and then she tells you all her stories, you tell her your stories, but with Sally and me we'd already heard each other's stories, so once we went to bed, we didn't know what we were supposed to do, you know?

JESS: Sure, Harry.

EXTERIOR. STREET—RAINING

> HARRY *and* JESS *crossing the street.*

HARRY: I don't know, you get to a certain point in a relationship where it's just too late to have sex, you know?

CUT TO:

INTERIOR. DEPARTMENT STORE FITTING ROOM—DAY
We can see MARIE *standing at a mirror,* SALLY *in a chair.*
SALLY: Is Harry bringing anyone to the wedding?
MARIE: I don't think so.
SALLY: Is he seeing anyone?
MARIE: He was seeing this anthropologist, but . . .
SALLY: What did she look like?
MARIE: Thin. Pretty. Big tits. Your basic nightmare. So what do you think?
　　MARIE *is trying on a very traditional white wedding dress with a train and veil.*
SALLY: Oh, Marie.
MARIE: Tell me the truth.
　　SALLY's *eyes start to well with tears.*
SALLY: It's just beautiful.

CUT TO:

INTERIOR. WEDDING—AFTERNOON
The wedding. A winter wedding with pine boughs and holly.
MARIE *in her wedding dress with a gorgeous bouquet of flowers comes down the aisle with her father and* SALLY, *who's the maid of honor.*
A chamber MUSIC quartet is playing something by Mozart as they come down the aisle to a JUDGE *who's standing at the head of the aisle next to* JESS *and* HARRY, *his best man.*
The ceremony begins. HARRY *looks at* SALLY. *She looks at him for a moment, then looks away.*
JUDGE: We are gathered here today to celebrate the marriage of Marie and Jess and to consecrate their vows of matrimony. The vows they will take will join their lives, the wine they will share binds all their hopes together, and by the rings they will wear, they will be known to all as husband and wife.

CUT TO:

INTERIOR. PUCK BUILDING—WEDDING RECEPTION—
AFTERNOON
A band is PLAYING.
HARRY *approaches* SALLY.
HARRY: Hi.

SALLY: Hello.

HARRY: Nice ceremony.

SALLY: Beautiful.

> SALLY *is clearly uncomfortable. She's going to behave like someone who simply is not going to get involved or even pretend interest in the conversation.*

HARRY: Boy, the holidays are rough. Every year I just try to get from the day before Thanksgiving to the day after New Year's.

> SALLY *nods.*

SALLY: A lot of suicides.

> HARRY *nods.* SALLY *nods.*
>
> *A* WAITER *comes up with a tray of hors d'oeuvres.*

WAITER: Would you like a pea pod with shrimp?

SALLY: *(With all the warmth she hasn't been showing* HARRY.*)* Thank you.

> *She takes one.* WAITER *turns the tray to* HARRY.

HARRY: No thanks.

> *The* WAITER *leaves.*

HARRY: How've you been?

SALLY: Fine.

> *A pause.*

HARRY: Are you seeing anybody?

> SALLY *looks at him.*

SALLY: Harry—

HARRY: What?

SALLY: *(Cutting him off.)* I don't want to talk about this.

HARRY: Why not?

SALLY: I don't want to talk about it.

> SALLY *turns and walks away.* HARRY *follows.*

HARRY: Why can't we get past this? I mean, are we gonna carry this thing around forever?

> SALLY *stops, whirls around to face him.*

SALLY: Forever? It just happened.

HARRY: It happened three weeks ago.

> SALLY *looks at him disbelievingly.*

You know how a year to a person is like seven years to a dog?

SALLY: Yes.

> HARRY *throws up his hands as if it's self-explanatory.*

Is one of us supposed to be a dog in this scenario?

HARRY: Yes.

SALLY: Who is the dog?

HARRY: You are.

SALLY: I am? I'm the dog?

HARRY: Um-hmm.

SALLY: I am the dog?

> *People are starting to notice the intensity of the conversation.*
> SALLY *is really furious now. She starts toward the large doors*
> *in the background, thinking they can get some privacy there.*
> *Once in front of the doors, she stands angrily with her hands*
> *on her hips, away from the guests.*

I don't see that, Harry. If anybody is the dog, you are the dog. You want to act like what happened didn't mean anything.

HARRY: I'm not saying it didn't mean anything. I'm saying why does it have to mean *everything*?

SALLY: Because it does, and you should know that better than anyone because the minute that it happened, you walked right out the door.

HARRY: I didn't walk out—

SALLY: No, sprinted is more like it.

HARRY: We both agreed it was a mistake—

SALLY: The worst mistake I ever made.

INTERIOR. KITCHEN—DAY

> *They go through the doors* SALLY *was heading for and now*
> *they're in the kitchen. Waiters are banging by with trays,*
> *dumping glasses into the sink, opening champagne, etc.*
> HARRY *and* SALLY *shouting now over the* DIN.

HARRY: What do you want from me?

SALLY: I don't want anything from you.

HARRY: Fine, fine, but let's just get one thing straight. I didn't go over there that night to make love to you. That's not why I went there. But you looked at me with those big, weepy eyes. "Don't go home tonight, Harry. Hold me a little longer, Harry." What was I supposed to do?

SALLY: What are you saying? You took pity on me?

HARRY: No, I . . .

SALLY: Fuck you!

> SALLY *slaps* HARRY *across the face. Then bursts out of the*
> *kitchen with a stunned* HARRY *right behind her.*

INTERIOR. PUCK BUILDING—WEDDING RECEPTION—DAY
  The entire wedding party is assembled around the bandstand.
  The band is PLAYING *some kind of musical riff that signals*
  that attention must be paid. SALLY *stomps through the room,*
  HARRY *just behind. There's a crowd of guests assembled in*
  a knot with JESS *and* MARIE, *their arms around each other,*
  standing there with their champagne glasses. JESS *is in front*
  of the microphone.

JESS: Everybody, could I have your attention, please? I want to
  propose a toast to Harry and Sally.

  SALLY, *surprised, comes to a halt, as does* HARRY. *The entire*
  crowd turns toward the two of them.

If Marie or I had found either of them remotely attractive, we
  would not be here today.

  Everyone laughs and raises their glasses to HARRY *and* SALLY.

FADE OUT.

MUSIC HERE.
FADE IN:

EXTERIOR. 96TH STREET—CHRISTMAS TREE STAND—DAY
  SALLY, *in jeans and a plain jacket, has just bought her Christmas*
  tree, and the salesman has finished putting plastic netting
  around it. SALLY *starts to carry the tree. It's very heavy; the*
  top of it is dragging slightly behind her, and she's leaving a
  little trail of pine needles behind her as she starts home, but
  she's going to carry this damn tree home alone if it kills her.

CUT TO:

INTERIOR. HARRY'S APARTMENT—DAY
  HARRY *paces in the kitchen, the phone to his ear, as he makes a*
  cup of tea.

HARRY: *(Into phone.)* Hi, it's me. It's the holiday season, and I
  thought I might remind you that this is the season of charity and
  forgiveness . . .

INTERIOR. SALLY'S APARTMENT—DAY
  SALLY *brings in the tree.*

HARRY'S VOICE: *(On answering machine.)* . . . and although it's
  not widely known, it's also the season of groveling. So if you felt
  like calling me back, I'd be all too happy to do the traditional
  Christmas grovel. Give me a call.

INTERIOR. HARRY'S APARTMENT—DAY
>HARRY *at the counter, hangs up, carries his cup to the table, sits, and looks through his mail.*

>>>>>>>>>>>>CUT TO:

INTERIOR. SALLY'S APARTMENT—DAY
>SALLY *works at her computer. The phone RINGS. She stops working and listens to the answering machine.*

SALLY'S VOICE: *(On answering machine.)* Hi, I'm not home right now. Call you right back.
>*Machine BEEPS.*

HARRY'S VOICE: *(On answering machine.)* If you're there, please pick up the phone. I really want to talk to you.

INTERIOR. HARRY'S APARTMENT—DAY
>HARRY *is lying on his bed, talking on the phone.*

HARRY: The fact that you're not answering leads me to believe you're either (a) not at home, (b) home but don't want to talk to me, or (c) . . .

INTERIOR. SALLY'S APARTMENT—DAY
>SALLY, *not picking up.*

HARRY'S VOICE: *(On answering machine.)* . . . home, desperately want to talk to me but trapped under something heavy. If it's (a) or (c), call me back.
>*The phone CLICKS off. HOLD on* SALLY.

>>>>>>>>>>>>CUT TO:

EXTERIOR. STREET—HOT DOG STAND—DAY
>HARRY *and* JESS *are stopped at a hot dog stand.*

HARRY: Obviously she doesn't want to talk to me. What do I have to do? Get hit over the head? If she wants to call me, she'll call me. I'm through making a schmuck out of myself.

>>>>>>>>>>>>CUT TO:

INTERIOR. HARRY'S APARTMENT—DAY
>HARRY *singing on the phone. The backup MUSIC machine is going.*

HARRY: *(Singing.)* "If you're feeling sad and lonely, there's a service I can render . . .

INTERIOR. SALLY'S APARTMENT—DAY
> SALLY *is getting ready to leave. She glances at her machine as she hears:*

HARRY'S VOICE: *(Singing, on answering machine.)* "Tell the one who digs you only, I can be so warm and tender—Call me, maybe it's late but just call me . . ."

INTERIOR. HARRY'S APARTMENT—DAY
HARRY: *(Singing into the phone.)* "Don't be afraid to just phone *moi . . .*"

INTERIOR. SALLY'S APARTMENT—DAY
HARRY'S VOICE: *(Singing, on answering machine.)* "Call me and I'll be around."
> SALLY *just stares.*

INTERIOR. HARRY'S APARTMENT—DAY
HARRY: *(Into phone, speaking.)* Give me a call.
> *He switches off the song machine.*

SALLY: *(Through filter.)* Hi, Harry.
HARRY: Hello! Hi, hi! I didn't think that you would . . . that you were there.

INTERIOR. SALLY'S APARTMENT—DAY
HARRY: *(Through filter.)* What are you doing?
SALLY: I was just on my way out.
HARRY: *(Through filter.)* Where are you going?
SALLY: What do you want, Harry?

INTERIOR. HARRY'S APARTMENT—DAY
HARRY: Nothing. Nothing, I just called to say I'm sorry.

INTERIOR. SALLY'S APARTMENT—DAY
SALLY: Okay.
> *She waits for him to seize the moment. Which he doesn't.*

INTERIOR. HARRY'S APARTMENT—DAY
> *He doesn't know what else to say.*

INTERIOR. SALLY'S APARTMENT—DAY
SALLY: I gotta go.

INTERIOR. HARRY'S APARTMENT—DAY
HARRY: Wait a second . . . wait a second. What are you doing for
New Year's? Are you going to the Tylers' party? 'Cause I don't
have a date, and if you don't have a date, we always said that if
neither one of us had a date . . .

INTERIOR. SALLY'S APARTMENT—DAY
HARRY: *(Through filter.)* . . . we could be together for New Year's,
and . . .
SALLY: Harry, I can't do this anymore. I am not your consolation
prize. Goodbye.
She hangs up.

INTERIOR. HARRY'S APARTMENT—DAY
HARRY *stands there, listening to the DIAL TONE.*

FADE OUT.

FADE IN:

INTERIOR. HARRY'S APARTMENT—NIGHT
A tight shot, on television, of DICK CLARK.
DICK CLARK: *(On television.)* And here we are, once again, the
sixteenth annual New Year's Rockin' Eve, coming to you live from
the heart . . .
We PULL BACK TO REVEAL
HARRY *lying in bed eating Mallomars and watching Dick Clark
on television.*
HARRY: *(Voice-over.)* What's so bad about this? You have Dick
Clark, that's tradition, you have Mallomars, the greatest cookie
of all time, and you're about to give the Knicks their first
championship since 1973.
HARRY *aims a toy basketball at a plastic basket mounted on the
wall.*
He misses.
He looks back at the television set.

CUT TO:

INTERIOR. NEW YEAR'S EVE PARTY—NIGHT
*A great big New Year's Eve party, just like the one we were at a
year earlier. The mirrored ball is twirling. Twinkly lights on
everyone's face.*
SALLY *dancing with a tall man. He dips her. She's appalled.*

Upright again, she catches MARIE's *eye as the tall man swoops her about the floor.* MARIE *is dancing with* JESS.

SALLY: I don't know why I let you drag me to this.
And she's yanked out of frame.

CUT TO:

EXTERIOR. STREET—STOREFRONTS—NIGHT
HARRY *walks along an empty street.*

EXTERIOR. DOWNTOWN STREET—NIGHT
HARRY *walking down the street past shop windows.*

HARRY: *(Voice-over.)* This is much better. Fresh air. I have the streets all to myself. Who needs to be at a big, crowded party pretending to have a good time? Plus this is the perfect time to catch up on my window shopping. This is good.
He sees a couple across the street standing with their arms around each other in front of a store window. The woman laughs.

CUT TO:

INTERIOR. NEW YEAR'S EVE PARTY—NIGHT
SALLY *is leaning against a pillar facing a* MAN AT THE PARTY, *who is telling her a joke.*

MAN AT THE PARTY: So the guy says, "Read the card."
SALLY *leans around the pillar toward* MARIE, *who's on the other side.*

SALLY: I'm going home.
MARIE: You'll never get a taxi.

CUT TO:

EXTERIOR. WASHINGTON SQUARE—NIGHT
HARRY *is walking along the same place he was dropped off by* SALLY *eleven years ago. He has an ice-cream cone. He dumps the ice cream in a trash can. He stops and looks up at the Washington Square Arch.*

HARRY: *(Voice-over flashback.)* You realize, of course, that we could never be friends.

FLASHBACK—DAY
At the Square under the Arch, SALLY *and* HARRY *are at the back of her car, facing each other.* SALLY *extends her hand to* HARRY.

SALLY: *(Voice-over flashback.)* Why not?
    HARRY *shakes* SALLY's *hand.*
HARRY: *(Voice-over flashback.)* What I'm saying . . . is that men and women . . .

FLASHBACK—DAY
    SALLY *and* HARRY *in the airplane.*
HARRY: *(Voice-over flashback.)* . . . can't be friends, because the sex part always gets in the way.

FLASHBACK—DAY
    HARRY *and* SALLY *walking down the street.*
SALLY: *(Voice-over flashback.)* That's not true.
HARRY: *(Voice-over flashback.)* No man can be friends with . . .

FLASHBACK—DAY
    HARRY *and* SALLY *walking in the park.*
HARRY: *(Voice-over flashback.)* . . . a woman he finds attractive. He always wants to have sex with her.

FLASHBACK—DAY
    HARRY *and* SALLY *in the museum—she is laughing.*
SALLY: *(Voice-over flashback.)* What if *they* don't want to have sex with *you?*
HARRY: *(Voice-over flashback.)* Doesn't matter . . .

FLASHBACK—DAY
    HARRY *and* SALLY *in deli, when* SALLY *is faking an orgasm as other customers look on.*
HARRY: *(Voice-over flashback.)* . . . because the sex thing is already out there, so the friendship is ultimately doomed . . .

FLASHBACK—NIGHT
    HARRY *and* SALLY *kissing in her bedroom.*
HARRY: *(Voice-over flashback.)* . . . and that is the end of the story.
SALLY: *(Voice-over flashback.)* Well, I guess we're not going to be friends, then.
HARRY: *(Voice-over flashback.)* Guess not.
SALLY: *(Voice-over flashback.)* That's too bad. You were the only person I knew in New York.

EXTERIOR. WASHINGTON SQUARE—NIGHT
> HARRY *back in reality. Thinking about what just happened in his mind. He feels the cold and turns his collar up, then starts walking slowly away from the Arch. We stay with* HARRY *as his pace starts to quicken and finally ends with him running down the street.*

> CUT TO:

INTERIOR. NEW YEAR'S EVE PARTY—NIGHT
> *It's almost midnight. Balloons, confetti, the mirrored ball spinning slowly around.*
> *The excitement in the room builds as we approach midnight.*
> *We see* SALLY *standing alone in the crowd.*
> *She decides to leave. She makes her way to* JESS *and* MARIE.

> CUT TO:

EXTERIOR. STREET—NIGHT
> HARRY *running.*

> CUT TO:

INTERIOR. NEW YEAR'S EVE PARTY—NIGHT
SALLY: *(Going for her coat.)* I'm going.
MARIE: It's almost midnight.
SALLY: The thought of not kissing somebody is just . . .
JESS: I'll kiss you.

> CUT TO:

EXTERIOR. STREET—NIGHT
> HARRY *is looking for a cab. He can't find one. He keeps running.*

> CUT TO:

INTERIOR. NEW YEAR'S EVE PARTY—NIGHT
JESS: C'mon, stay. Please.
SALLY: Thanks, Jess. I just . . . I have to go.
MARIE: Oh, wait two minutes.
SALLY: I'll call you tomorrow.
> *They kiss each other on the cheek, and* SALLY *heads off.*

> CUT TO:

EXTERIOR. STREET—NIGHT

> HARRY *runs along the street, rounds the corner, and runs into the hotel and through the lobby.*

CUT TO:

INTERIOR. NEW YEAR'S EVE PARTY—NIGHT

> SALLY *is making her way through the crowd when she stops dead in her tracks. It's* HARRY. *Slowly he comes toward her and stops in front of her.*

HARRY: I've been doing a lot of thinking. And the thing is, I love you.

SALLY: What?

HARRY: I love you.

SALLY: How do you expect me to respond to this?

HARRY: How about you love me, too?

SALLY: How about, I'm leaving.

> SALLY *turns and walks off, parting the crowd.* HARRY *follows her like a terrier.*

HARRY: Doesn't what I said mean anything to you?

> SALLY *stops and turns to face him. During the following, we hear the* COUNTDOWN *to the New Year, after which everyone breaks into "HAPPY NEW YEAR," confetti flies, everyone is kissing and breaking into "AULD LANG SYNE."*

SALLY: I'm sorry, Harry. I know it's New Year's Eve, and I know you're feeling lonely, but you just can't show up here, tell me you love me, and expect to make everything all right. It doesn't work that way.

HARRY: Well, how does it work?

SALLY: I don't know, but not this way.

> SALLY *turns to go, but* HARRY *grabs her, stopping her.*

HARRY: How about this way? I love how you get cold when it's seventy-one degrees out. I love that it takes you an hour and a half to order a sandwich. I love that you get a little crinkle right there when you're looking at me like I'm nuts. I love that after I spend the day with you, I can still smell your perfume on my clothes. And I love that you're the last person I want to talk to before I go to sleep at night. And it's not because I'm lonely. And it's not because it's New Year's Eve. I came here tonight because when you realize you want to spend the rest of your life with somebody, you want the rest of your life to start as soon as possible.

SALLY: *(Furious.)* That is just like you, Harry. You say things like that, and you make it impossible for me to hate you, and I hate you, Harry. I really hate you. I hate you.
>   HARRY *puts his arms around her.*
>   *They kiss.*
>   *A long kiss.*
>   *The twinkle ball goes around, twinkling.*
>   *They go on kissing.*
>   *"AULD LANG SYNE" continues in the background.*

HARRY: What does this song mean? My whole life, I have never known what this song means. I mean, "Should old acquaintance be forgot"? Does that mean we should forget old acquaintances, or does it mean if we happened to forget them, we should remember them, which is not possible because we already forgot them?

SALLY: Well, maybe it just means that we should remember that we forgot them or something. Anyway, it's about old friends.
>   *They start to kiss again.*
>   *And as the camera PULLS UP away from them:*

HARRY: *(Voice-over.)* The first time we met we hated each other.

SALLY: *(Voice-over.)* You didn't hate me, I hated you. *(Beat.)* And the second time we met, you didn't even remember me.

HARRY: *(Voice-over.)* I did too, I remembered you. *(A long beat.)* The third time we met, we became friends.

SALLY: *(Voice-over.)* We were friends for a long time.

HARRY: *(Voice-over.)* And then we weren't.

SALLY: *(Voice-over.)* And then we fell in love.

>   CUT TO:

>   A COUPLE *on a love seat*
>   HARRY *and* SALLY *together.*

SALLY: Three months later we got married.

HARRY: It only took three months.

SALLY: Twelve years and three months.

HARRY: We had this . . . really wonderful wedding.

SALLY: It really was.

HARRY: It was great. We had this enormous coconut cake.

SALLY: Huge coconut cake with the tiers, and there was this very rich chocolate sauce on the side.

HARRY: Right. Because not everybody likes it on the cake, because it makes it very soggy.

SALLY: Particularly coconut. It soaks up a lot of that stuff. It's
    important to keep it on the side.
HARRY: Right . . .
    And as they continue on, we—

FADE OUT.

THE END

Afterword

This screenplay has my name on it, but it was very much a collabo-
ration, and before I write a word about the movie itself, I want
to write about how it got started. It began in October 1984, when I
got a call from my agent that Rob Reiner and his producing partner
Andrew Scheinman wanted to have lunch to discuss a project. So we
had a lunch, and they told me about an idea they had for a movie about
a lawyer. I've forgotten the details. The point is, it didn't interest me at
all, and I couldn't imagine why they'd thought of me in connection with
it. I remember being slightly perplexed about whether to say straight
off that the idea didn't interest me or whether to play along for an hour
so as not to have that horrible awkwardness that can happen when the
meeting is over but the lunch must go on. I decided on the former; and
we then spent the rest of the lunch talking about ourselves. Well, that
isn't entirely true: we spent the rest of the lunch talking about Rob and
Andy. Rob was divorced, and Andy was a bachelor—and they were
both extremely funny and candid about their lives as single men in Los
Angeles. When the lunch ended, we still didn't have an idea for a movie;
but we decided to meet again the next time they were in New York.

And so, a month later, we got together. And threw around some
more ideas, none of which I remember. But finally, Rob said he had
an idea—he wanted to make a movie about a man and a woman who
become friends, as opposed to lovers; they make a deliberate decision
not to have sex because sex ruins everything; and then they have sex
and it ruins everything. And I said, let's do it.

So we made a deal, and in February, Andy and Rob came back to

New York and we sat around for several days and they told me some things. Appalling things. They told me, for instance, that when they finished having sex, they wanted to get up out of bed and go home. (Which became: HARRY: "How long do I have to lie here and hold her before I can get up and go home? Is thirty seconds enough? . . . How long do you like to be held afterwards? All night, right? . . . Somewhere between thirty seconds and all night is your problem." SALLY: "I don't have a problem.") They told me about the endless series of excuses they had concocted in order to make a middle-of-the-night getaway. (SALLY: "You know, I am so glad I never got involved with you. I just would have ended up being some woman you had to get up out of bed and leave at three o'clock in the morning and go clean your andirons. And you don't even have a fireplace. Not that I would know this.") They also told me that the reason they thought men and women couldn't be friends was that a man always wanted to sleep with a woman. Any woman. (HARRY: "No man can be friends with a woman he finds attractive. He always wants to have sex with her." SALLY: "So you're saying a man *can* be friends with a woman he finds unattractive." HARRY: "No. You pretty much want to nail them, too.") I say that these things were appalling, but the truth is that they weren't really a surprise; they were sort of my wildest nightmares of what men thought.

Rob and Andy and I noodled for hours over the questions raised by friendship, and sex, and life in general; and as we did, I realized—long before I had any idea of what was actually going to happen in the movie itself—that I had found a wonderful character in Rob Reiner. Rob is a very strange person. He is extremely funny, but he is also extremely depressed—or at least he was at the time; he talked constantly about how depressed he was. "You know how women have a base of makeup," he said to me. "I have a base of depression. Sometimes I sink below it. Sometimes I rise above it." This line went right into the first draft of the movie, but somewhere along the line Rob cut it. A mistake, I think, but never mind. Here's another from Rob on his depression: "I think I'm not ready for a relationship. When you're as depressed as I am . . . If the depression was lifted, I would be able to be with someone on my level. But it's like playing tennis on a windy day with someone who's worse than you are. They can do all right against you, they can win a couple of games, but there's too much wind. You know what I mean?" I have no idea what Rob was talking about, but as I wrote those words in my notebook I knew that I would use the lines somehow. And I did, and they were cut, and it was a mistake, and never mind.

The point is that Rob was depressed; but he wasn't at all depressed about being depressed; in fact, he loved his depression. And so does Harry. Harry honestly believes that he is a better person than Sally because he has what Sally generously calls a dark side. "Suppose nothing happens to you," he says in the first sequence of the movie. "Suppose you live there [New York] your whole life and nothing happens. You never meet anyone, you never become anything, and finally you die one of those New York deaths where nobody notices for two weeks until the smell drifts out into the hallway." Harry is genuinely proud to have thought of that possibility and to lay it at the feet of this shallow young woman he is stuck in a car with for eighteen hours. He is thrilled to be the prince of darkness, the master of the worst-case scenario, the man who is happy to tell you, as you find yourself in the beginning of a love affair, that what follows lust, inevitably, is post-lust: "You take someone to the airport, it's clearly the beginning of a relationship. That's why I've never taken anyone to the airport at the beginning of a relationship. . . . Because eventually things move on and you don't take someone to the airport, and I never wanted anyone to say to me, 'How come you never take me to the airport anymore?'"

So I began with a Harry, based on Rob. And because Harry was bleak and depressed, it followed absolutely that Sally would be cheerful and chirpy and relentlessly, pointlessly, unrealistically, idiotically optimistic. Which is, it turns out, very much like me. I'm not precisely chirpy, but I am the sort of person who is fine, I'm just fine, everything's fine. "I am over him," Sally says, when she isn't over him at all; I have uttered that line far too many times in my life, and far too many times I've made the mistake of believing it was true. Sally loves control—and I'm sorry to say that I do too. And inevitably, Sally's need to control her environment is connected to food. I say inevitably because food has always been something I write about—in part because it's the only thing I'm an expert on. But it wasn't my idea to use the way I order food as a character trait for Sally; well along in the process—third or fourth draft or so—Rob and Andy and I were ordering lunch for the fifth day in a row, and for the fifth day in a row my lunch order—for an avocado and bacon sandwich—consisted of an endless series of parenthetical remarks. I wanted the mayonnaise on the side. I wanted the bread toasted and slightly burnt. I wanted the bacon crisp. "I just like it the way I like it," I said, defensively, when the pattern was pointed out to me—and the line went into the script.

But all that came much later. In the beginning, I was more or less alone—with a male character based somewhat on Rob, and a female character based somewhat on me. And a subject. Which was not, by the way, whether men and women could be friends. The movie instead was a way for me to write about being single—about the difficult, frustrating, awful, funny search for happiness in an American city where the primary emotion is unrequited love. This is from my notes, February 5, 1985, Rob speaking: "This is a talk piece. There are no chase scenes. No food fights. This is walks, apartments, phones, restaurants, movies." Also from my notes, Rob again: "We're talking about a movie about two people who get each other from the breakup of the first big relationship in their lives to the beginning of the second. Transitional on some level. Who are friends, who don't have sex, who nurse each other and comfort each other and talk to each other and then finally do it and it's a mistake and recover from it and move into second relationships." Here's a scene from the first draft; it bit the dust early, too self-conscious, but I toss it in partly because I can't stand to waste anything, and partly because it perfectly sums up the movie I was trying to write:

SALLY: I think we should write a movie about our relationship.

HARRY: What's the plot?

SALLY: There are only two plots. The first is, an appealing character strives against great odds to achieve a worthwhile goal, and the second is, the bluebird of happiness is right in your own backyard. We're the first.

HARRY: An appealing character—

SALLY: *Two* appealing characters strive against great odds to achieve a worthwhile goal. Two people become friends at the end of the first major relationship of their lives and get each other to the next major relationship of their lives.

HARRY: I don't know anything about writing movies.

SALLY: Neither do I.

HARRY: But on the face of it—I don't want to be negative about it—

SALLY: Sure you do. You love being negative, it's who you are, embrace it—

HARRY: —but it seems to me that movies are supposed to be visual. We don't do anything visual. We just sit in restaurants and talk, or we sit on the phone and talk, or we sit in your apartment or my apartment and talk.

SALLY: In French movies they just talk.

HARRY: Do you speak French?

SALLY: Not really.

HARRY: What happens to the friends when each of them gets to the next major relationship of their lives?

SALLY: They're still going to be friends. They're going to be friends forever.

HARRY: I don't know, Sally. You know what happens. You meet somebody new and you take them to meet your friend, and you want them to like each other as much as you do, but they never do, they always see the friend as a threat to your relationship, and you try to stay just as good friends with your friend but eventually you don't really need each other as much because you've got a new friend, you've got someone you can talk to *and* fuck—

SALLY: Forget I mentioned it, okay?

   They smile at each other.

HARRY: I love you. You know that.

SALLY: I love you too.

HARRY: When I say, "I love you," you know what I mean—

SALLY: I know what you mean. I know.

When Harry Met Sally started shooting in August 1988, almost four years after my first meeting with Rob and Andy. In the meantime I wrote a first draft about two people who get each other from the breakup of the first big relationship in their lives to the beginning of the second. Rob went off and made *Stand By Me*. We met again and decided that Harry and Sally belonged together. I wrote a second draft. Rob went off and made *The Princess Bride*. And then we all went to work together on the next (at least) five drafts of the movie. What had been called *Just Friends* and then *Play Melancholy Baby* went on to be called *Boy Meets Girl*; *Words of Love*; *It Had to Be You*; and *Harry, This Is Sally*. To name just a few of the titles. Mostly we called it "Untitled Rob Reiner Project." Rob suggested that we try inserting some older couples talking about how they met. *How They Met* was another title we considered for at least a day. And gradually, the script began to change, from something that was mostly mine, to something else.

Here is what I always say about screenwriting. When you write a script, it's like delivering a great big beautiful plain pizza, the one with only cheese and tomatoes. And then you give it to the director, and the director says, "I love this pizza. I am willing to commit to this pizza. But I really think this pizza should have mushrooms on it." And you say, "Mushrooms! Of course! I meant to put mushrooms on the pizza! Why didn't I think of that? Let's put some on immediately." And then someone else comes along and says, "I love this pizza too, but it really needs green peppers." "Great," you say. "Green peppers. Just the thing." And then someone else says, "Anchovies." There's always a fight over the anchovies. And when you get done, what you have is a pizza with everything. Sometimes it's wonderful. And sometimes you look at it and you think, I knew we shouldn't have put the green peppers onto it. Why didn't I say so at the time? Why didn't I lie down in traffic to prevent anyone's putting green peppers onto the pizza?

All this is a long way of saying that movies generally start out belonging to the writer and end up belonging to the director. If you're very lucky as a writer, you look at the director's movie and feel that it's your movie, too. As Rob and Andy and I worked on the movie, it changed: it became less quirky and much funnier; it became less mine and more theirs. But what made it possible for me to live through this process— which is actually called "The Process," a polite expression for the period when the writer, generally, gets screwed—was that Rob and I each had a character we owned. On most movies, what normally happens in the course of The Process is that the writer says one thing and the director says another thing, and in the end the most the writer can hope for is a compromise; what made this movie different was that Rob had a character who could say whatever he believed, and if I disagreed, I had Sally to say so for me.

And much as I would like to take full credit for what Sally says in the movie, the fact is that many of her best moments went into the script after the three of us began work on it together. "We told you about men," Rob and Andy said to me one day. "Now tell us about women." So I said, "Well, we could do something about sex fantasies." And I wrote the scene about Sally's sex fantasy. "What else?" they said. "Well," I said, "women send flowers to themselves in order to fool their boyfriends into thinking they have other suitors." And I wrote the scene about Marie sending flowers to herself. "What else?" Rob and Andy said. "Well," I said, "women fake orgasms." "Really?" they said. "Yes," I said. There was a long pause. I think I am correct in remembering the long pause. "All women?" they said. "Most women," I said. "At one time or another."

A few days later, Rob called. He and Andy had written a sequence about faking orgasms and they wanted to insert it at the end of the scene that was known (up to that time) as the andirons scene. He read it over the phone. I loved it. It went into the script. A few weeks later, we had our first actors' reading, and Meg Ryan, who by then was our Sally, suggested that Sally actually fake an orgasm in the delicatessen at the end of the scene. We loved it. It went into the script. And then Billy Crystal, our Harry, provided the funniest of the dozens of funny lines he brought with him to the movie; he suggested that a woman customer turn to a waiter, when Sally's orgasm was over, and say: "I'll have what she's having." The line, by the way, was delivered in the movie by Estelle Reiner, Rob's mother. So there you have it—a perfect example of how The Process works on the occasions when it works.

I don't want to sound Pollyannaish about any of this. Rob and I disagreed. We disagreed all the time. Rob believes that men and women can't be friends (HARRY: "Men and women can't be friends, because the sex part always gets in the way"). I disagree (SALLY: "That's not true. I have plenty of men friends and there's no sex involved"). And both of us are right. Which brings me to what *When Harry Met Sally* is really about—not, as I said, whether men and women can be friends, but about how different men and women are. The truth is that men don't want to be friends with women. Men know they don't understand women, and they don't much care. They want women as lovers, as wives, as mothers, but they're not really interested in them as friends. They have friends. Men are their friends. And they talk to their male friends about sports, and I have no idea what else.

Women, on the other hand, are dying to be friends with men. Women know they don't understand men, and it bothers them: they think that if only they could be friends with them, they would understand them and, what's more (and this is their gravest mistake), it would help. Women think if they could just understand men, they could *do something*. Women are always trying to *do something*. There are entire industries based on this premise, the most obvious one being the women's magazines—there are hundreds of them, there are probably five of them in darkest Zaire alone—that are based completely on the notion that women can *do something* where men are concerned: cook a perfect steak, or wear a perfect skirt, or dab a little perfume behind the knee. "Rub your thighs together when you walk," someone once wrote in *Cosmopolitan* magazine. "The squish-squish sound of nylon has a frenzying effect."

When a movie like *When Harry Met Sally* opens, people come to ask you questions about it. And for a few brief weeks, you become an expert. You seem quite wise. You give the impression that you knew what you were doing all along. You become an expert on friends, on the possibilities of love, on the differences between men and women. But the truth is that when you work on a movie, you don't sit around thinking, We're making a movie about the difference between men and women. Or whatever. You just do it. You say, this scene works for me, but this one doesn't. You say, this is good, but this could be funnier. You say, it's a little slow here, what could we do to speed it up? You say, this scene is long, and this scene isn't story, and we need a better button on this one.

And then they go off and shoot the movie and cut the movie and sometimes you get a movie that you're happy with. It's my experience that this happens very rarely. Once in a blue moon. *Blue Moon* was another title we considered for a minute or two. I mention it now so you will understand that even when you have a movie you're happy with, there's always something—in this case, the title—that you wish you could fix. But never mind.

—February 1990

The Foodie

Serial Monogamy: A Memoir

My mother gave me my first cookbook. It was 1962, and I began my New York life with her gift of *The Gourmet Cookbook* (volume 1) and several sets of sheets and pillowcases (white, with scallops). *The Gourmet Cookbook* was enormous, a tome, with a gloomy reddish brown binding. It was assembled by the editors of *Gourmet* magazine and punctuated by the splendid, reverent, slightly lugubrious pictures of food the magazine was famous for. Simply owning it had changed my mother's life. Until the book appeared, in the fifties, she had been content to keep as far from the kitchen as possible. We had a wonderful Southern cook named Evelyn Hall, who cooked American classics like roast beef and fried chicken and a world-class apple pie. But thanks to *The Gourmet Cookbook*, Evelyn began to cook chicken Marengo and crème caramel; before long, my mother herself was in the kitchen, whipping up Chinese egg rolls from scratch. A recipe for them appears in the book, but it doesn't begin to convey how stressful and time-consuming an endeavor it is to make egg rolls, nor does it begin to suggest how much tension a person can create in a household by serving egg rolls that take hours to make and are not nearly as good as Chinese takeout.

Owning *The Gourmet Cookbook* made me feel tremendously sophisticated. For years I gave it to friends as a wedding present. It was an emblem of adulthood, a way of being smart and chic and college-educated where food was concerned, but I never really used it in the way you're supposed to use a cookbook—by propping it open on the kitchen counter, cooking from it, staining its pages with spattered butter and chocolate splotches, conducting a unilateral dialogue with the book itself—in short, by having a relationship with it.

The cookbook I used most my first year in New York was a small volume called *The Flavour of France*. It was given to me by a powerful older woman I'll call Jane, whom I met my first summer in the city. She was twenty-five, and she took me in hand and introduced me not just to the cookbook but also to Brie and *vitello tonnato* and the famous omelet place in the East Sixties. In fact, the first time I went to the omelet place, which was called Madame Romaine de Lyon, I was a mail girl at *Newsweek,* making $55 a week, and I almost fainted when I saw that an omelet cost $3.45. Jane also introduced me to the concept of One Away. You were One Away from someone if you had both slept with the same man. Jane had slept with a number of up-and-coming journalists, editors, and novelists, the most famous of whom, at the end of their one night together, gave her a copy of one of his books, a box of which was conveniently located right next to his front door. According to Jane, his exact words, as she made her way to the exit, were "Take one on your way out."

The night President Kennedy was shot, Jane was having a dinner party, which went forward in spite of the tragedy, as these things tend to do. Jane served as an appetizer *céleri rémoulade*, a dish that I had never before encountered and that remains a mystery to me. A few months later, I had a thing with someone Jane had had a thing with. Jane and I were now One Away from each other, and interestingly, that was the end of our friendship, though not the end of my connection to *The Flavour of France*.

The Flavour of France was the size of a date book, only six by eight inches. It contained small blocks of recipe text by Narcissa Chamberlain and her daughter Narcisse, and large black-and-white travel photographs of France taken by Narcissa's husband (and Narcisse's father), Samuel Chamberlain. I didn't focus much on the mysterious Chamberlain family as I cooked my way through their cookbook, and when I did, I usually hit a wall. For openers, I couldn't imagine why anyone named Narcissa would name her daughter Narcisse. Also, I couldn't figure out how they collaborated. Did the three of them drive around France together, fighting over whose turn it was to sit in the backseat? Did Narcisse like working with her parents? And if so, was she crazy? But the Chamberlains' recipes were simple and foolproof. I learned to make a perfect chocolate mousse that took about five minutes, and a wonderful dessert of caramelized baked pears with cream. I made those pears for years, although chocolate mousse eventually faded from my repertory when the crème brûlée years began.

Just before I'd moved to New York, two historic events had occurred: The birth control pill had been invented, and the first Julia Child cookbook was published. As a result, everyone was having sex, and when the sex was over, you cooked something. One of my girlfriends moved in with a man she was in love with. Her mother was distraught and warned that he would never marry her because she had already slept with him. "Whatever you do," my friend's mother said, "don't cook for him." But it was too late. She cooked for him. He married her anyway. This was right around the time endive was discovered, which was followed by arugula, which was followed by radicchio, which was followed by frisée, which was followed by the three *M*'s—mesclun, mâche, and microgreens—and that, in a nutshell, is the history of the last forty years from the point of view of lettuce. But I'm getting ahead of the story.

By the mid-sixties, Julia Child's *Mastering the Art of French Cooking,* Craig Claiborne's *New York Times Cookbook*, and *Michael Field's Cooking School* had become the holy trinity of cookbooks. At this point I was working as a newspaper reporter at the *New York Post* and living in the Village. If I was home alone at night, I cooked myself an entire meal from one of these cookbooks. Then I sat down in front of the television set and ate it. I felt very brave and plucky as I ate my perfect dinner. Okay, I didn't have a date, but at least I wasn't one of those lonely women who sat home with a pathetic container of yogurt. Eating an entire meal for four that I had cooked for myself was probably equally pathetic, but that never crossed my mind.

I cooked every single recipe in Michael Field's book and at least half the recipes in the first Julia, and as I cooked, I had imaginary conversations with them both. Julia was nicer and more forgiving—she was by then on television and famous for dropping food, picking it up, and throwing it right back into the pan. Michael Field was sterner and more meticulous; in fact, he was almost fascistic. He was full of prejudice about things like the garlic press (he believed that using one made the garlic bitter), and I threw mine away for fear he would suddenly materialize in my kitchen and disapprove. His recipes were precise, and I followed them to the letter; I was young, and I believed that if you changed even a hair on a recipe's head, it wouldn't turn out right. When I had people to dinner, I loved to serve Michael's complicated recipe for chicken curry, accompanied by condiments and pappadums—although I sometimes served instead a marginally simpler Craig Claiborne recipe for lamb curry that had appeared in Craig's Sunday column in the *New York Times Magazine*. There were bananas in it, and heavy cream. I made it recently and it was horrible.

Craig Claiborne worked at the *New York Times* not just as the chief food writer but also as the restaurant critic; he was enormously powerful and influential, and I developed something of an obsession with him. Craig—everyone called him Craig even if they'd never met the man—was famous for championing ethnic cuisine, and as his devoted acolyte, I learned to cook things like moussaka and tabbouleh. Everyone lived for his Sunday recipes; it was the first page I turned to in the Sunday *Times*. Everyone knew he had a Techbuilt house on the bay in East Hampton, that he'd added a new kitchen to it, that he usually cooked with the French chef Pierre Franey, and that he despised iceberg lettuce. You can't really discuss the history of lettuce in the last forty years without mentioning Craig; he played a seminal role. I have always had a weakness for iceberg lettuce with Roquefort dressing, and that's one of the things I used to have imaginary arguments with Craig about.

For a long time, I hoped that Craig and I would meet and become friends. I gave a lot of thought to this eventuality, most of it concerning what I would cook if he came to my house for dinner. I was confused about whether to serve him something from one of his cookbooks or something from someone else's cookbook. Perhaps there was a protocol for such things; if so, I didn't know what it was. It occurred to me that I ought to serve him something that was "my" recipe, but I didn't have any recipes that were truly mine—with the possible exception of my mother's barbecue sauce, which mostly consisted of Heinz ketchup. But I desperately wanted him to come over. I'd read somewhere that people were afraid to invite him to dinner. I wasn't; I just didn't know the man. I must confess that my fantasy included the hope that after he came to dinner, he would write an article about me and of course include my recipes; but as I said, I didn't have any.

Meanwhile, we all began to cook in a wildly neurotic and competitive way. We were looking for applause, we were constantly performing, we were desperate to be all things to all people. Was this the grand climax of the post–World War II domestic counterrevolution or the beginning of a pathological strain of feminist overreaching? No one knew. We were too busy slicing and dicing.

I got married and entered into a series of absolutely insane culinary episodes. I made the Brazilian national dish. I wrapped things in phyllo. I stuffed grape leaves. There were soufflés. I took a course in how to use a Cuisinart food processor. I even cooked an entire Chinese banquet that included Lee Lum's lemon chicken. Lee Lum was the chef at Pearl's, the famous Chinese restaurant where no one could get a table. If you did get a table, you remembered the meal forever because there was so much MSG in the food that you were awake for years afterward. Lee Lum's recipe for lemon chicken involved dipping strips of chicken breast in water-chestnut flour, frying it, plunging it into a sauce that included crushed pineapple, and dousing the entire concoction with a one-ounce bottle of lemon extract. Once again, the recipe was from the Sunday *Times* column written by Craig Claiborne. Craig of course had no difficulty getting a table at Pearl's, and I looked forward to going there with him someday, after we had actually met and become close personal friends. I'd gone to Pearl's once and was stunned to discover that it was not only impossible to get a table if you weren't famous but that being famous was not enough—there were degrees of famous. There was famous enough to get a table, and then there was famous enough to get Pearl to come to the table to tell you the nightly specials, and then there was true fame, top-of-the-line fame, which was famous enough to get Pearl to allow you to order the sweet-and-pungent crispy fish. This was what it came down to in New York: You had to have pull to order a fish.

I became a freelance magazine writer. One of my first pieces, for *New York* magazine, was about Craig Claiborne and Michael Field, who turned out to be at war with each other. As a result, I met Craig Claiborne, and after the article appeared, he invited me to his house. What he served for dinner was not memorable, and in any case, I don't remember it. Then Claiborne came to our house for dinner, and I served a recipe from one of his cookbooks, a Chilean seafood-and-bread casserole that was a recipe of Leonard Bernstein's wife, Felicia Montealegre. I can't believe I remember her name, much less how to spell it, especially given the fact that her recipe was a gluey, milky, disappointing concoction that practically bankrupted me.

I don't think it was Felicia Montealegre's fault that Craig and I never became friends, but there was no question in my mind after our two meals that we had no future together. Craig was a nice guy, don't get me wrong, but he was so low-key that once I'd gotten to know him, I was almost completely unable to have even imaginary conversations with him while cooking his recipes.

Around this time I met a man named Lee Bailey, and I guess I would have to say that if there were any embers burning in the Craig Claiborne department, they were completely extinguished the moment I met Lee. Lee Bailey was a friend of my friend Liz Smith, who believed that everyone she knew should be friends with everyone else she knew. So one night, she invited us to Lee's house for dinner. Lee lived in the East Forties, in a floor-through below the ground, and what I distinctly remember about it was that it had some sort of straw matting on the walls that probably came from Azuma, and it was just about the most fabulous place I'd ever seen. It was simple, and easy on the eyes, and comfortable, but nothing was expensive, and there was no art to speak of, and no color at all. Everything was beige. As Lee once said, "Be very careful about color."

And then dinner was served. Pork chops, grits, collard greens, and a dish of tiny baked crab apples. It was delicious. It was so straightforward and plain and honest and at the same time so playful. Those crab apples! They were adorable! The entire evening was mortifying, a revelation, a rebuke in its way to every single thing I had ever bought and every dinner I had ever served. My couch was purple. I owned a collection of brightly painted wooden Mexican animals. I had red plates and a shag rug. My menus were overwrought and overthought. Would Lee Bailey ever in a million years consider cooking the Brazilian national dish? Or Lee Lum's lemon chicken? Certainly not. It was horribly clear that my entire life up to that point had been a mistake.

I immediately got a divorce, gave my ex-husband all the furniture, and began to make a study of Lee Bailey. I bought the chairs he told me to buy, and the round dining room table that seemed to be part of the secret of why Lee's dinner parties were more fun than anyone else's. When Lee opened a store at Henri Bendel, I bought the white plates, seersucker napkins, and wood-handled stainless flatware that were just like his. I bought new furniture, and all of it was beige. I became Lee's love slave, culinarily speaking. Long before he began to write the series of cookbooks that made him well known, he had replaced all my previous imaginary friends in the kitchen, and whenever I cooked dinner and anything threatened to go wrong, I could hear him telling me to calm down, it didn't matter, pour another drink, no one will care. I stopped serving hors d'oeuvres, just like Lee, and as a result, my guests were chewing the wood off the walls before dinner, just like Lee's. I began to osmose from a neurotic cook with a confusing repertory of ethnic dishes to a very relaxed one specializing in faintly Southern food.

The most important thing I learned from Lee was something I call the Rule of Four. Most people serve three things for dinner—some sort of meat, some sort of starch, and some sort of vegetable—but Lee always served four. And the fourth thing was always unexpected, like those crab apples. A casserole of lima beans and pears cooked for hours with brown sugar and molasses. Peaches with cayenne pepper. Sliced tomatoes with honey. Biscuits. Savory bread pudding. Spoon bread. Whatever it was, that fourth thing seemed to have an almost magical effect on the eating process. You never got tired of the food because there was always another taste on the plate that seemed simultaneously to match it and contradict it. You could go from taste to taste; you could mix a little of this with a little of that. And when you finished eating, you always wanted more, so that you could go from taste to taste all over again. At Lee Bailey's you could eat forever. This was important. This was crucial. There's nothing worse than having people to a dinner that they all just polish off and before you know it, they're done eating and dinner is over and it's only ten o'clock and everyone leaves and it's just you and the dishes. (And that was another thing about dinner at Lee's: On top of everything else, he had fewer dishes to wash, because he never ever served a first course or a cheese course; and if he served salad, it just went onto the plate along with everything else.)

And by the way, Lee never served fish, so I never served fish, and I'll tell you why: It's too easy to eat fish. Bim bam boom you're done with a piece of fish, and you're right out the door. When people come to dinner, it should be fun, and part of the fun should be the food. Fish—and I'm sorry to say this but it's true—is no fun. People like to play with their food, and it's virtually impossible to play with fish. If you must have fish, order it at a restaurant.

You might think that having Lee as a real friend might have made it superfluous to have him as an imaginary friend, but you would be wrong. As I conducted my inner conversations with Lee—about what to serve, or what would be the perfect fourth thing to accompany what I was serving—it never occurred to me to pick up the phone and ask him. Lee was much too easygoing; he would just have laughed and said, anything you feel like, honey. He was, in his way, as close to a Zen master as I've ever had, and all of us who fell under his influence began with his style and eventually ended up with our own.

I always secretly wished that Lee would include a recipe of mine in one of his cookbooks—he frequently came to dinner and was always fantastically kind about the food—but he never asked for any of my recipes. He did take a photograph of my backyard for one of his cookbooks, and he used my napkins and plates in the photograph; but of course, I'd bought them at his store in Bendel's, so it didn't really count.

Meanwhile, I got married again, and divorced again. I wrote a thinly disguised novel about the end of my marriage, and it contained recipes. By then, I'd come to realize that no one was ever going to put my recipes into a book, so I'd have to do it myself. I included Lee's recipe for lima beans and pears (unfortunately I left out the brown sugar, and for years people told me they'd tried cooking the recipe and it didn't work), along with my family cook Evelyn's recipe for cheesecake, which I'm fairly sure she got from the back of the Philadelphia cream cheese package. A food writer who wrote about the book carped that the recipes were not particularly original, but it seemed to me she missed the point. The point wasn't about the recipes. The point (I was starting to realize) was about putting it together. The point was about making people feel at home, about finding your own style, whatever it was, and committing to it. The point was about giving up neurosis where food was concerned. The point was about finding a way that food fit into your life.

And after a while, I didn't have to have long internal dialogues with Lee—I'd incorporated what I learned from him and moved on. Four things were not enough; I went to five, and sometimes to six. I liked salad and cheese, so I served salad and cheese. So there were more dishes to wash—so what? On the design front, I left behind beige, and as a result I made all the decorating mistakes that are possible once you do.

And I got married again, by the way. In the course of my third marriage, I have had a series of culinary liaisons. I went through a stretch with Marcella Hazan, a brilliant cookbook author whom I had a somewhat unsatisfactory connection to; with Martha Stewart, whom I worshipped and had long, long imaginary talks with, mostly having to do with my slavish adulation of her; and only last year with Nigella Lawson, whose style of cooking is very similar to mine. I gave up on Nigella when one of her cupcake recipes failed in a big way, but I admire her willingness to use store-bought items in recipes, her lackadaisical qualities when it comes to how things look, and her fondness for home cooking. I especially like making her roast beef dinner, which is very much like my mother's, except for the Yorkshire pudding. My mother didn't serve Yorkshire pudding, although there is a recipe for it on page 61 of *The Gourmet Cookbook*. My mother served potato pancakes instead. I serve Yorkshire pudding *and* potato pancakes. Why not? You only live once.

—February 2006

Baking Off

Roxanne Frisbie brought her own pan to the twenty-fourth annual Pillsbury Bake-Off. "I feel like a nut," she said. "It's just a plain old dumb pan, but everything I do is in that crazy pan." As it happens, Mrs. Frisbie had no cause whatsoever to feel like a nut: it seemed that at least half the one hundred finalists in the Bake-It-Easy Bake-Off had brought something with them—their own sausages, their own pie pans, their own apples. Edna Buckley, who was fresh from representing New

York State at the National Chicken Cooking Contest, where her recipe for fried chicken in a batter of beer, cheese, and crushed pretzels had gone down to defeat, brought with her a lucky handkerchief, a lucky horseshoe, a lucky dime for her shoe, a potholder with the Pillsbury Poppin' Fresh Doughboy on it, an Our Blessed Lady pin, and all of her jewelry, including a silver charm also in the shape of the doughboy. Mrs. Frisbie and Mrs. Buckley and the other finalists came to the Bake-Off to bake off for $65,000 in cash prizes; in Mrs. Frisbie's case, this meant making something she created herself and named Butterscotch Crescent Rolls—and which Pillsbury promptly, and to Mrs. Frisbie's dismay, renamed Sweet 'n Creamy Crescent Crisps. Almost all the recipes in the finals were renamed by Pillsbury using a lot of crispy snicky snacky words. An exception to this was Sharon Schubert's Wiki Wiki Coffee Cake, a name which ought to have been snicky snacky enough; but Pillsbury, in a moment of restraint, renamed it One-Step Tropical Fruit Cake. As it turned out, Mrs. Schubert ended up winning $5,000 for her cake, which made everybody pretty mad, even the contestants who had been saying for days that they did not care who won, that winning meant nothing and was quite beside the point; the fact was that Sharon Schubert was a previous Bake-Off winner, having won $10,000 three years before for her Crescent Apple Snacks, and in addition had walked off with a trip to Puerto Vallarta in the course of this year's festivities. Most of the contestants felt she had won a little more than was really fair. But I'm getting ahead of the story.

The Pillsbury Company has been holding Bake-Offs since 1948, when Eleanor Roosevelt, for reasons that are not clear, came to give the first one her blessing. This year's took place from Saturday, February 24, through Tuesday, February 27, at the Beverly Hilton Hotel in Beverly Hills. One hundred contestants—ninety-seven of them women, two twelve-year-old boys, and one male graduate student—were winnowed down from a field of almost a hundred thousand entrants to compete for prizes in five categories: flour, frosting mix, crescent main dish, crescent dessert, and hot-roll mix. They were all brought, or flown, to Los Angeles for the Bake-Off itself, which took place on Monday, and a round of activities that included a tour of Universal Studios, a mini-version of television's *Let's Make a Deal* with Monty Hall himself, and a trip to Disneyland. The event is also attended by some one hundred food editors, who turn it from a mere contest into the incredible publicity stunt Pillsbury intends it to be, and spend much of their time talking to each other about sixty-five new ways to use tuna fish and listening to various speakers lecture on the consumer movement and food and the appliance business. General Electric is co-sponsor of the event and donates a stove to each finalist, as well as the stoves for the Bake-Off; this year, it promoted a little Bake-Off of its own for the microwave oven, an appliance we were repeatedly told was the biggest improvement in cooking since the invention of the Willoughby System. Every one of the food editors seemed to know what the Willoughby System was, just as everyone seemed to know what Bundt pans were. "You will all be happy to hear," we were told at one point, "that only one of the finalists this year used a Bundt pan." The food editors burst into laughter at that point; I am not sure why. One Miss Alex Allard of San Antonio, Texas, had already won the microwave contest and $5,000, and she spent most of the Bake-Off turning out one Honey Drizzle Cake after another in the microwave ovens that ringed the Grand Ballroom of the Beverly Hilton Hotel. I never did taste the Honey Drizzle Cake, largely because I suspected—and this was weeks before the *Consumers Union* article on the subject—that microwave ovens were dangerous and probably caused peculiar diseases. If God had wanted us to make bacon in four minutes, He would have made bacon that cooked in four minutes.

"The Bake-Off is America," a General Electric executive announced just minutes before it began. "It's family. It's real people doing real things." Yes. The Pillsbury Bake-Off is an America that exists less and less, but exists nonetheless. It is women who still live on farms, who have six and seven children, who enter county fairs and sponsor 4-H Clubs. It is Grace Ferguson of Palm Springs, Florida, who entered the Bake-Off seventeen years in a row before reaching the finals this year, and who cooks at night and prays at the same time. It is Carol Hamilton, who once won a trip on a Greyhound bus to Hollywood for being the most popular girl in Youngstown, Ohio. There was a lot of talk at the Bake-Off about how the Bake-It-Easy theme had attracted a new breed of contestants this year, younger contestants—housewives, yes, but housewives who used whole-wheat flour and Granola and sour cream and similar supposedly hip ingredients in their recipes and were therefore somewhat more sophisticated, or urban, or something-of-the-sort, than your usual Bake-Off contestant. There were a few of these—two, to be exact: Barbara Goldstein of New York City and Bonnie Brooks of Salisbury, Maryland, who actually visited the Los Angeles County Art Museum during a free afternoon. But there was also Suzie Sisson of Palatine, Illinois, twenty-five years old and the only Bundt-pan person in the finals, and her sentiments about life were the same as those that Bake-Off finalists presumably have had for years. "These are the beautiful people," she said, looking around the ballroom as she waited for her Bundt cake to come out of the oven. "They're not the little tiny rich people. They're nice and happy and religious types and family-oriented. Everyone talks about women's lib, which is ridiculous. If you're nice to your husband, he'll be nice to you. Your family is your job. They come first."

I was seven years old when the Pillsbury Bake-Off began, and as I grew up reading the advertisements for it in the women's magazines that were lying around the house, it always seemed to me that going to a Bake-Off would be the closest thing to a childhood fantasy of mine, which was to be locked overnight in a bakery. In reality, going to a Bake-Off *is* like being locked overnight in a bakery—a very bad bakery. I almost became sick right there on Range 95 after my sixth carbohydrate-packed sample—which happened, by coincidence, to be a taste of the aforementioned Mrs. Frisbie's aforementioned Sweet 'n Creamy Crescent Crisps.

But what is interesting about the Bake-Off—what is even significant about the event—is that it is, for the American housewife, what the Miss America contest used to represent to teenagers. The pinnacle of a certain kind of achievement. The best in field. To win the Pillsbury Bake-Off, even to be merely a finalist in it, is to be a great housewife. And a creative housewife. "Cooking is very creative." I must have heard that line thirty times as I interviewed the finalists. I don't happen to think that cooking is very creative—what interests me about it is, on the contrary, its utter mindlessness and mathematical certainty. "Cooking is very relaxing"—that's my bromide. On the other hand, I have to admit that some of the recipes that were concocted for the Bake-Off, amazing combinations of frosting mix and marshmallows and peanut butter and brown sugar and chocolate, were practically awe-inspiring. And cooking, it is quite clear, is only a small part of the apparently frenzied creativity that flourishes in these women's homes. I spent quite a bit of time at the Bake-Off chatting with Laura Aspis of Shaker Heights, Ohio, a seven-time Bake-Off finalist and duplicate-bridge player, and after we had discussed her high-protein macaroons made with coconut-almond frosting mix and Granola, I noticed that Mrs. Aspis was wearing green nail polish. On the theory that no one who wears green nail polish wants it to go unremarked upon, I remarked upon it.

"That's not green nail polish," Mrs. Aspis said. "It's platinum nail polish that I mix with green food coloring."

"Oh," I said.

"And the thing of it is," she went on, "when it chips, it doesn't matter."

"Why is that?" I asked.

"Because it stains your nails permanently," Mrs. Aspis said.

"You mean your nails are permanently green?"

"Well, not exactly," said Mrs. Aspis. "You see, last week they were blue, and the week before I made purple, so now my nails are a combination of all three. It looks like I'm in the last throes of something."

On Sunday afternoon, most of the finalists chose to spend their free time sitting around the hotel and socializing. Two of them—Marjorie Johnson of Robbinsdale, Minnesota, and Mary Finnegan of Minneota, Minnesota—were seated at a little round table just off the Hilton ballroom talking about a number of things, including Tupperware. Both of them love Tupperware.

"When I built my new house," Mrs. Johnson said, "I had so much Tupperware I had to build a cupboard just for it." Mrs. Johnson is a very tiny, fortyish mother of three, and she and her dentist husband have just moved into a fifteen-room house she cannot seem to stop talking about. "We have this first-floor kitchen, harvest gold and blue, and it's almost finished. Now I have a second kitchen on my walk-out level and that's going to be harvest gold and blue, too. Do you know about the new wax Congoleum? I think that's what I put in—either that or Shinyl Vinyl. I haven't had to wash my floors in three months. The house isn't done yet because of the Bake-Off. My husband says if I'd spent as much time on it as I did on the Bake-Off, we'd be finished. I sent in sixteen recipes—it took me nearly a year to do it."

"That's nothing," said Mrs. Finnegan. "It took me twenty years before I cracked it. I'm a contest nut. I'm a thirty-times winner in the *Better Homes & Gardens* contest. I won a thousand dollars from Fleischmann's Yeast. I won Jell-O this year, I'm getting a hundred and twenty-five dollars' worth of Revere cookware for that. The Knox Gelatine contest. I've won seven blenders and a quintisserie. It does four things—fries, bakes, roasts, there's a griddle. I sold the darn thing before I even used it."

"Don't tell me," said Mrs. Johnson. "Did you enter the Crystal Sugar Name the Lake Home contest?"

"Did I enter?" said Mrs. Finnegan. "Wait till you see this." She took a pen and wrote her submission on a napkin and held it up for Mrs. Johnson. The napkin read "Our Entry Hall." "I should have won that one," said Mrs. Finnegan. "I did win the Crystal Sugar Name the Dessert contest. I called it 'Signtation Squares.' I think I got a blender on that one."

"Okay," said Mrs. Johnson. "They've got a contest now, Crystal Sugar Name a Sauce. It has pineapple in it."

"I don't think I won that," said Mrs. Finnegan, "but I'll show you what I sent in." She held up the napkin and this time what she had written made sense. "Hawaiian More Chant," it said.

"Oh, you're clever," said Mrs. Johnson.

"They have three more contests so I haven't given up," said Mrs. Finnegan.

On Monday morning at exactly 9:00 a.m., the one hundred finalists marched four abreast into the Hilton ballroom, led by Philip Pillsbury, former chairman of the board of the company. The band played "Nothin' Says Lovin' Like Somethin' from the Oven," and when it finished, Pillsbury announced: "Now you one hundred winners can go to your ranges."

Chaos. Shrieking. Frenzy. Furious activity. Cracking eggs. Chopping onions. Melting butter. Mixing, beating, blending. The band perking along with such carefully selected tunes as "If I Knew You Were Coming I'd Have Baked a Cake." Contestants running to the refrigerators for more supplies. Floor assistants rushing dirty dishes off to unseen dishwashers. All two hundred members of the working press, plus television's Bob Barker, interviewing any finalist they could get to drop a spoon. At 9:34 a.m., Mrs. Lorraine Walmann submitted her Cheesy Crescent Twist-Ups to the judges and became the first finalist to finish. At 10:00 a.m., all the stoves were on, the television lights were blasting, the temperature in the ballroom was up to the mid-nineties, and Mrs. Marjorie Johnson, in the course of giving an interview about her house to the *Minneapolis Star*, had forgotten whether she had put one cup of sugar or two into her Crispy Apple Bake. "You know, we're building this new house," she was saying. "When I go back, I have to buy living-room furniture." By 11:00 a.m., Mae Wilkinson had burned her skillet corn bread and was at work on a second. Laura Aspis had lost her potholder. Barbara Bellhorn was distraught because she was not used to California apples. Alex Allard was turning out yet another Honey Drizzle Cake. Dough and flour were all over the floor. Mary Finnegan was fussing because the crumbs on her Lemon Cream Bars were too coarse. Marjorie Johnson was in the midst of yet another interview on her house. "Well, let me tell you," she was saying, "the shelves in the kitchen are built low. . . . " One by one, the contestants, who were each given seven hours and four tries to produce two perfect samples of their recipes, began to finish up and deliver one tray to the judges and one tray to the photographer. There were samples everywhere, try this, try that, but after six tries, climaxed by Mrs. Frisbie's creation, I stopped sampling. The overkill was unbearable: none of the recipes seemed to contain one cup of sugar when two would do, or a delicate cheese when Kraft American would do, or an actual minced onion when instant minced onions would do. It was snack time. It was convenience-food time. It was less-work-for-Mother time. All I could think about was a steak.

By 3:00 p.m., there were only two contestants left—Mrs. Johnson, whose dessert took only five minutes to make but whose interviews took considerably longer, and Bonnie Brooks, whose third sour-cream-and-banana cake was still in the oven. Mrs. Brooks brought her cake in last, at 3:27 p.m., and as she did, the packing began. The skillets went into brown cartons, the measuring spoons into barrels, the stoves were dismantled. The Bake-Off itself was over—and all that remained was the trip to Disneyland, and the breakfast at the Brown Derby . . . and the prizes.

And so it is Tuesday morning, and the judges have reached a decision, and any second now, Bob Barker is going to announce the five winners over national television. All the contestants are wearing their best dresses and smiling, trying to smile anyway, good sports all, and now Bob Barker is announcing the winners. Bonnie Brooks and her cake and Albina Flieller and her Quick Pecan Pie win $25,000 each. Sharon Schubert and two others win $5,000. And suddenly the show is over and it is time to go home, and the ninety-five people who did not win the twenty-fourth annual Pillsbury Bake-Off are plucking the orchids from the centerpieces, signing each other's programs, and grumbling. They are grumbling about Sharon Schubert. And for a moment, as I hear the grumbling everywhere—"It really isn't fair. . . ." "After all, she won the trip to Mexico"—I think that perhaps I am wrong about these women: perhaps they are capable of anger after all, or jealousy, or competitiveness, or something I think of as a human trait I can relate to. But the grumbling stops after a few minutes, and I find myself listening to Marjorie Johnson. "I'm so glad I didn't win the grand prize," she is saying, "because if you win that, you don't get to come back to the next Bake-Off. I'm gonna start now on my recipes for next year. I'm gonna think of something really good." She stopped for a moment. "You know," she said, "it's going to be very difficult to get back to normal living."

—July 1973

I Just Want to Say: The Egg-White Omelette

There's a new book out about diet, and it apparently says what I've known all my life—protein is good for you, carbohydrates are bad, and fat is highly overrated as a dangerous substance. Well, it's about time. As my mother used to say, you can never have too much butter.

For example, here's how we cook steak in our house: First you coat the steak in kosher salt. Then you cook the steak in a very hot frying pan. When it's done, you throw a huge pat of butter on top of it. That's it. And by the way, I'm not talking about sweet butter, I'm talking about salted butter.

Here's another thing it says in this book: dietary cholesterol has nothing whatsoever to do with your cholesterol count. This is another thing I've known all my life, which is why you will not find me lying on my deathbed regretting not having eaten enough chopped liver. Let me explain this: You can eat all sorts of things that are high in dietary cholesterol (like lobster and avocado and eggs) and they have NO EFFECT WHATSOEVER on your cholesterol count. NONE. WHATSOEVER. DID YOU HEAR ME? I'm sorry to have to resort to capital letters, but what is wrong with you people?

Which brings me to the point of this: the egg-white omelette. I have friends who eat egg-white omelettes. Every time I'm forced to watch them eat egg-white omelettes, I feel bad for them. In the first place, egg-white omelettes are tasteless. In the second place, the people who eat them think they are doing something virtuous when they are instead merely misinformed. Sometimes I try to explain that what they're doing makes no sense, but they pay no attention to me because they have all been told to avoid dietary cholesterol by their doctors. According to the *New York Times*, the doctors are not deliberately misinforming their patients; instead, they're the victims of something known as the informational cascade, which turns out to be something that's repeated so many times that it becomes true even though it isn't. (Why isn't it called the misinformational cascade, I wonder.) In any case, the true victims of this misinformation are not the doctors but the people I know who've been brainwashed into thinking that egg-white omelettes are good for you.

So this is my moment to say what's been in my heart for years: it's time to put a halt to the egg-white omelette. I don't want to confuse this with something actually important, like the war in Afghanistan, which it's also time to put a halt to, but I don't seem be able to do anything about the war, whereas I have a shot at cutting down consumption of egg-white omelettes, especially with the wind of this new book in my sails.

You don't make an omelette by taking out the yolks. You make one by putting additional yolks in. A really great omelette has two whole eggs and one extra yolk, and by the way, the same thing goes for scrambled eggs. As for egg salad, here's our recipe: boil eighteen eggs, peel them, and send six of the egg whites to friends in California who persist in thinking that egg whites matter in any way. Chop the remaining twelve eggs and six yolks coarsely with a knife, and add Hellmann's mayonnaise and salt and pepper to taste.

—November 2010

Gourmet *Magazine*

I'm not sure you can make a generalization on this basis, which is the basis of twice, but here goes: whenever I get married, I start buying *Gourmet* magazine. I think of it as my own personal bride's disease. The first time I started buying it was in 1967, when everyone my age in New York City spent hours talking about things like where to buy the best pistachio nuts. Someone recently told me that his marriage broke up during that period on account of veal Orloff, and I knew exactly what he meant. Hostesses were always making dinners that made you feel guilty, meals that took days to prepare and contained endless numbers of courses requiring endless numbers of plates resulting in an endless series of guests rising to help clear. Every time the conversation veered away from the food, the hostess looked hurt.

I got very involved in this stuff. Once I served a six-course Chinese dinner to twelve people, none of whom I still speak to, although not because of the dinner. I also specialized in little Greek appetizers that involved a great deal of playing with rice, and I once produced something known as the Brazilian national dish. Then, one night at a dinner party, a man I know looked up from his chocolate mousse and said, "Is this Julia's?" and I knew it was time to get off.

I can date that moment almost precisely—it was in December 1972—because that's when I stopped buying *Gourmet* the first time around. And I can date that last *Gourmet* precisely because I have never thrown out a copy of the magazine. At the end of each month, I place it on the top of the kitchen bookshelf, and there it lies, undisturbed, forever. I have never once looked at a copy of *Gourmet* after its month was up. But I keep them because you never know when you might need to. One of the tricky things about the recipes in *Gourmet* is that they often refer back to recipes in previous copies of the magazine: for example, once a year, usually in January, *Gourmet* prints the recipe for pâte brisée, and if you throw out your January issue, you're sunk for the year. All the tart recipes thereafter call for "one recipe pâte brisée (January 1976)" and that's that. The same thing holds for chicken stock. I realize that I have begun to sound as if I actually use the recipes in *Gourmet*, so I must stop here and correct that impression. I don't. I also realize that I have begun to sound as if I actually read *Gourmet*, and I'd better correct that impression too. I don't actually read it. I sort of look at it in a fairly ritualistic manner.

The first thing I turn to in *Gourmet* is the centerfold. The centerfold of the magazine contains the *Gourmet* menu of the month, followed by four color pages of pictures, followed by the recipes. In December the menu is usually for Christmas dinner, in November for Thanksgiving, in July for the Fourth, and in April—when I bought my first *Gourmet* in four years owing to my marriage that month to a man with a Cuisinart Food Processor—for Easter. The rest of the year there are fall luncheons and spring breakfasts, and so forth. But the point is not the menus but the pictures. The first picture each month is of the table of the month, and it is laid with the china and crystal and silver of the month. That most of the manufacturers of this china and crystal and silver advertise in *Gourmet* should not concern us now; that comes later in the ritual. The table and all the things on it look remarkably similar every issue: very formal, slightly stuffy, and extremely elegant in a cut-glass, old-moneyed way. The three pages of pictures that follow are of the food, which looks just as stuffy and formal and elegant as the table itself. It would never occur to anyone at *Gourmet* to take the kind of sleek, witty food photographs I associate with the *Life* "Great Dinners" series, or the crammed, decadent pictures the women's magazines specialize in. *Gourmet* gives you a full-page color picture of an incredibly serious rack of lamb *persillé* sitting on a somber Blue Canton platter by Mottahedeh Historic Charleston Reproductions sitting on a stiff eighteenth-century English mahogany table from Charles Deacon & Son—and it's no wonder I never cook anything from this magazine: the pictures are so reverent I almost feel I ought to pray to them.

After the centerfold I always turn to a section called "Sugar and Spice." This is the letters-to-the-editor department, and by all rights it should be called just plain "Sugar." I have never seen a letter in *Gourmet* that was remotely spicy, much less moderately critical. "I have culled so many fine recipes from your magazine that I feel it's time to do the sharing. . . ." "My husband and I have had many pleasant meals from recipes in *Gourmet* and we hope your readers will enjoy the following. . . ." Mrs. S. C. Rooney of Vancouver, B.C., writes to say that she and her husband leaf through *Gourmet* before every trip and would never have seen the Amalfi Drive but for the February 1972 issue. "It is truly remarkable how you maintain such a high standard for every issue," she says. Almost every letter then goes on to present the writer's recipe—brownies Weinstein, piquant mushrooms Potthoff, golden marinade Wyeth, Parmesan puff Jupenlaz. "Sirs," writes Margy Newman of Beverly Hills, "recently I found myself with two ripe bananas, an upcoming weekend out of town, and an hour until dinnertime. With one eye on my food processor and the other on some prunes, I proceeded to invent Prune Banana Whip Newman." The recipe for one prune banana whip Newman (April 1976) followed.

"You Asked For It" comes next. This is the section where readers write in for recipes from restaurants they have frequented and *Gourmet* provides them. I look at this section for two reasons: first, on the chance that someone has written in for the recipe for the tarte Tatin at Maxwell's Plum in New York, which I would like to know how to make, and second, for the puns. "Here is the scoop du jour," goes the introduction to peach ice cream Jordan Pond House. "We'd be berry happy," *Gourmet* writes in the course of delivering a recipe for blueberry blintzes. "Rather than waffling about, here is a recipe for chocolate waffles." "To satisfy your yen for tempura, here is Hibachi's shrimp tempura." I could go on, but I won't; I do want to mention, though, that the person who writes these also seems to write the headlines on the "Sugar and Spice" column—at least I think I detect the same fine hand in such headlines as "Curry Favor," "The Berry Best," and "Something Fishy."

I skip the travel pieces, many of which are written by ladies with three names. "If Provence did not exist, the poets would be forced to invent it, for it is a lyrical landscape and to know it is to be its loving captive for life." Like that. Then I skip the restaurant reviews. *Gourmet* never prints unfavorable restaurant reviews; in fact, one of its critics is so determined not to find fault anywhere that he recently blamed himself for a bad dish he was served at the Soho Charcuterie: "The potatoes that came with it (savoyarde?—hard to tell) were disappointingly nondescript and cold, but I seemed to be having bad luck with potatoes *wherever* I went." Then I skip the special features on eggplant and dill and the like, because I have to get on to the ads.

Gourmet carries advertisements for a wide array of upper-class consumer goods (Rolls-Royce, De Beers diamonds, Galliano, etc.); the thing is to compare these ads to the editorial content of the magazine. I start by checking out the *Gourmet* holiday of the month—in May 1976, for example, it was Helsinki—and then I count the number of ads in the magazine for things Finnish. Then I like to check the restaurants reviewed in the front against the restaurant ads in the back. Then, of course, I compare the china, silver, and crystal in the menu of the month against the china, silver, and crystal ads. All this is quite satisfying and turns out about the way you might suspect.

After that, I am pretty much through looking at *Gourmet* magazine. And where has it gotten me, you may ask. I've been trying to figure that out myself. Last April, when I began my second round, I think I expected that this time I would get around to cooking something from it. Then May passed and I failed to make the rhubarb tart pictured in the centerfold and I gave up in the recipe department. At that point, it occurred to me that perhaps I bought *Gourmet* because I figured it was the closest I would ever get to being a gentile. But that's not it either. The real reason, I'm afraid, has simply to do with food and life, particularly married life. "Does everyone who gets married talk about furniture?" my friend Bud Trillin once asked. No. Only for a while. After that you talk about pistachio nuts.

—December 1976

A Sandwich

The hot pastrami sandwich served at Langer's Delicatessen in down-town Los Angeles is the finest hot pastrami sandwich in the world. This is not just my opinion, although most people who know about Langer's will simply say it's the finest hot pastrami sandwich in Los Angeles because they don't dare to claim that something like a hot pastrami sandwich could possibly be the best version of itself in a city where until recently you couldn't get anything resembling a New York bagel, and the only reason you can get one now is that New York bagels have deteriorated.

Langer's is a medium-sized place—it seats a hundred and thirty-five people—and it is decorated, although "decorated" is probably not the word that applies, in tufted brown vinyl. The view out the windows is of the intersection of Seventh and Alvarado and the bright-red-and-yellow signage of a Hispanic neighborhood—bodegas, check-cashing store-fronts, and pawnshops. Just down the block is a spot notorious for being the place to go in L.A. if you need a fake I.D. The Rampart division's main police station, the headquarters of the city's second-most-recent police scandal, is a mile away. Even in 1947, when Langer's opened, the neighborhood was not an obvious place for an old-style Jewish delica-tessen, but in the early nineties things got worse. Gangs moved in. The crime rate rose. The Langers—the founder, Al, now eighty-nine, and his son Norm, fifty-seven—were forced to cut the number of employees, close the restaurant nights and Sundays, and put coin-operated locks on the restroom doors. The opening of the Los Angeles subway system—one of its stops is half a block from the restaurant—has helped business slightly, as has the option of having your sandwich brought out to your car. But Langer's always seems to be just barely hanging on. If it were in New York, it would be a shrine, with lines around the block and tour buses standing double-parked outside. Pilgrims would come—as they do, for example, to Arthur Bryant's in Kansas City and Sonny Bryan's in Dallas—and they would report on their conversion. But in Los Ange-les a surprising number of people don't even know about Langer's, and many of those who do wouldn't be caught dead at the corner of Seventh and Alvarado, even though it's not a particularly dangerous intersection during daytime hours.

Pastrami, I should point out for the uninitiated, is made from a cut of beef that is brined like corned beef, coated with pepper and an assortment of spices, and then smoked. It is characterized by two things. The first is that it is not something anyone's mother whips up and serves at home; it's strictly restaurant fare, and it's served exclusively as a sandwich, usually on Russian rye bread with mustard. The second crucial thing about pastrami is that it is almost never good. In fact, it usually tastes like a bunch of smoked rubber bands.

The Langers buy their pastrami from a supplier in Burbank. "When we get it, it's edible," Norm Langer says, "but it's like eating a racquetball. It's hard as a rock. What do we do with it? What makes us such wizards? The average delicatessen will take this piece of meat and put it into a steamer for thirty to forty-five minutes and warm it. But you've still got a hard piece of rubber. You haven't broken down the tissues. You haven't made it tender. We take that same piece of pastrami, put it into our steamer, and steam it for almost three hours. It will shrink 25 to 30 percent, but it's now tender—so tender it can't be sliced thin in a machine because it will fall apart. It has to be hand-sliced."

So: tender and hand-sliced. That's half the secret of the Langer's sandwich. The other secret is the bread. The bread is hot. Years ago, in the nineteen-thirties, Al Langer owned a delicatessen in Palm Springs, and, because there were no Jewish bakers in the vicinity, he was forced to bus in the rye bread. "I was serving day-old bread," Al Langer says, "so I put it into the oven to make it fresher. Hot crispy bread. Juicy soft pastrami. How can you lose?"

Today, Langer's buys its rye bread from a bakery called Fred's, on South Robertson, which bakes it on bricks until it's ten minutes from being done. Langer's bakes the loaf the rest of the way, before slicing it hot for sandwiches. The rye bread, faintly sour, perfumed with caraway seeds, lightly dusted with cornmeal, is as good as any rye bread on the planet, and Langer's puts about seven ounces of pastrami on it, the proper proportion of meat to bread. The resulting sandwich, slathered with Gulden's mustard, is an exquisite combination of textures and tastes. It's soft but crispy, tender but chewy, peppery but sour, smoky but tangy. It's a symphony orchestra, different instruments brought together to play one perfect chord. It costs eight-fifty and is, in short, a work of art.

—August 2002

I Just Want to Say: Teflon

I feel bad about Teflon.

It was great while it lasted.

Now it turns out to be bad for you.

Or, to put it more exactly, now it turns out that a chemical that's released when you heat up Teflon gets into your bloodstream and probably causes cancer and birth defects.

I loved Teflon. I loved the no-carb ricotta pancake I invented last year, which can be cooked only on Teflon. I loved my Silverstone Teflon-coated frying pan, which makes a beautiful steak. I loved Teflon as an adjective; it gave us a Teflon president (Ronald Reagan) and it even gave us a Teflon Don (John Gotti), whose Teflonness eventually wore out, making him an almost exact metaphorical duplicate of my Teflon pans. I loved the fact that Teflon was invented by someone named Roy J. Plunkett, whose name alone should have ensured Teflon against ever becoming a dangerous product.

But recently DuPont, the manufacturer of polytetrafluoroethylene (PTFE) resin, which is what Teflon was called when it first popped up as a laboratory accident back in 1938, reached a $16.5 million settlement with the Environmental Protection Agency; it seems the company knew all along that Teflon was bad for you. It's an American cliché by now: a publicly traded company holds the patent on a scientific breakthrough, it turns out to cause medical problems, and the company knew all along. You can go to the bank on it.

But it's sad about Teflon.

When it first came onto the market, Teflon wasn't good. The pans were light and skimpy and didn't compare to copper or cast iron. They were great for omelettes, and, of course, nothing stuck to them, but they were nowhere near as good for cooking things that were meant to be browned, like steaks. But then manufacturers like Silverstone produced Teflon pans that were heavy-duty, and you could produce a steak that was as dark and delicious as one made on the barbecue. Unfortunately, this involved heating your Teflon pan up to a very high temperature before adding the steak, which happens to be the very way perfluoroctanoic acid (PFOA) is released into the environment. PFOA is the bad guy here, and DuPont has promised to eliminate it from all Teflon products by 2015. I'm sure that will be a comfort to those of you under the age of forty, but to me it simply means that my last years on this planet will be spent, at least in part, scraping debris off my non-Teflon frying pans.

Rumors about Teflon have been circulating for a long time, but I couldn't help hoping they were going to turn out like the rumors about aluminum, which people thought (for a while, back in the nineties) caused Alzheimer's. That was a bad moment, since never mind giving up aluminum pots and pans, it would also have meant giving up aluminum foil, disposable aluminum baking pans, and, most crucial of all, antiperspirants. I rode out that rumor, and I'm pleased to report that it went away.

But this rumor is clearly for real, so I suppose I am going to have to throw away my Teflon pans.

Meanwhile, I am going to make one last ricotta pancake breakfast:

Beat one egg, add one-third cup fresh whole-milk ricotta, and whisk together. Heat up a Teflon pan until carcinogenic gas is released into the air. Spoon tablespoons of batter into the frying pan and cook about two minutes on one side, until brown. Carefully flip. Cook for another minute to brown the other side. Eat with jam, if you don't care about carbs, or just eat unadorned. Serves one.

—June 2006

The Food Establishment:
Life in the Land of the Rising Soufflé
(Or Is It the Rising Meringue?)

One day, I awoke having had my first in a long series of food anxiety dreams (the way it goes is this: there are eight people coming to dinner in twenty minutes, and I am in an utter panic because I have forgotten to buy the food, plan the menu, set the table, and clean the house, and the supermarket is closed). I knew that I had become a victim of the dreaded food obsession syndrome and would have to do something about it. This article is what I did.

Incidentally, I anticipated that my interviews on this

would be sublime gourmet experiences, with each of my
subjects forcing little goodies down my throat. But no. All
I got from over twenty interviews were two raw potatoes
that were guaranteed by their owner (who kept them in a
special burlap bag on her terrace) to be the only potatoes
worth eating in all the world. Perhaps they were. I don't
know, though; they tasted exactly like the other potatoes
I've had in my life.

You might have thought they'd have been polite enough not to mention it at all. Or that they'd wait at least until they got through
the reception line before starting to discuss it. Or that they'd hold off
at least until after they had tasted the food—four tables of it, spread
about the four corners of the Four Seasons—and gotten drinks in hand.
But people in the Food Establishment are not noted for their manners
or their patience, particularly when there is fresh gossip. And none of
them had come to the party because of the food.

They had come, most of them, because they were associated with
the Time-Life Cookbooks, a massive, high-budget venture that has
managed to involve nearly everyone who is anyone in the food world.
Julia Child was a consultant on the first book. And James Beard had
signed on to another. And Paula Peck, who bakes. And Nika Hazelton,
who reviews cookbooks for the *New York Times Book Review*. And
M.F.K. Fisher, usually of *The New Yorker*. And Waverley Root of Paris,
France. And Pierre Franey, the former chef of Le Pavillon who is now
head chef at Howard Johnson's. And in charge of it all, Michael Field,
the birdlike, bespectacled, frenzied gourmet cook and cookbook writer,
who stood in the reception line where everyone was beginning to discuss
it. Michael was a wreck. A wreck, a wreck, a wreck, as he himself might
have put it. Just that morning, the very morning of the party, Craig
Claiborne of the *New York Times*, who had told the Time-Life people
he would not be a consultant for their cookbooks even if they paid him
a hundred thousand dollars, had ripped the first Time-Life cookbook
to shreds and tatters. *Merde alors*, as Craig himself might have put it,
how that man did rip that book to shreds and tatters. He said that the
recipes, which were supposed to represent the best of French provincial
cooking, were not even provincial. He said that everyone connected
with the venture ought to be ashamed of himself. He was rumored to
be going about town telling everyone that the picture of the soufflé on

the front of the cookbook was not even a soufflé—it was a meringue! *Merde alors!* He attacked Julia Child, the hitherto unknockable. He referred to Field, who runs a cooking school and is author of two cookbooks, merely as a "former piano player." Not that Field wasn't a former piano player. But actually identifying him as one—*well!* "As far as Craig and I are concerned," Field was saying as the reception line went on, "the gauntlet is down." And worst of all—or at least it seemed worst of all that day—Craig had chosen the day of the party for his review. Poor Michael. How simply frightful! How humiliating! How delightful! "Why did he have to do it today?" moaned Field to Claiborne's close friend, chef Pierre Franey. "Why? Why? Why?"

Why indeed?

The theories ranged from Gothic to Byzantine. Those given to the historical perspective said that Craig had never had much respect for Michael, and they traced the beginnings of the rift back to 1965, when Claiborne had gone to a restaurant Field was running in East Hampton and given it *one* measly star. Perhaps, said some. But why include Julia in the blast? Craig had done that, came the reply, because he had never liked Michael and wanted to tell Julia to get out of Field's den of thieves. Perhaps, said still others. But mightn't he also have done it because his friend Franey had signed on as a consultant to the *Time-Life Cookbook of Haute Cuisine* just a few weeks before, and Craig wanted to tell *him* to get out of that den of thieves? Perhaps, said others. But it might be even more complicated. Perhaps Craig had done it because he was furious at Michael Field's terrible review in the *New York Review of Books* of Gloria Bley Miller's *The Thousand Recipe Chinese Cookbook*, which Craig had praised in the *Times*.

Now, while all this was becoming more and more arcane, there were a few who secretly believed that Craig had done the deed because the Time-Life cookbook was as awful as he thought it was. But most of those people were not in the Food Establishment. Things in the Food Establishment are rarely explained that simply. They are never what they seem. People who seem to be friends are not. People who admire each other call each other Old Lemonface and Cranky Craig behind backs. People who tell you they love Julia Child will add in the next breath that of course her husband *is* a Republican and her orange Bavarian cream recipe just doesn't work. People who tell you Craig Claiborne is a genius will insist he had little or nothing to do with *The New York Times Cook Book*, which bears his name. People will tell you that Michael Field is delightful but that some people do not take success quite as well as they might. People who claim that Dione Lucas is the most brilliant food technician of all time further claim that when she puts everything together it comes out tasting bland. People who love Paula Peck will go on to tell you—but let one of *them* tell you. "I love Paula," one of them is saying, "but *no* one, absolutely *no* one understands what it is between Paula and monosodium glutamate."

Bitchy? Gossipy? Devious?

"It's a world of self-generating hysteria," says Nika Hazelton. And those who say the food world is no more ingrown than the theater world and the music world are wrong. The food world is smaller. Much more self-involved. And people in the theater and in music are part of a culture that has been popularly accepted for centuries; people in the food world are riding the crest of a trend that began less than twenty years ago.

In the beginning, just about the time the Food Establishment began to earn money and fight with each other and review each other's books and say nasty things about each other's recipes and feel rotten about each other's good fortune, just about that time, there came curry. Some think it was beef Stroganoff, but in fact, beef Stroganoff had nothing to do with it. It began with curry. Curry with fifteen little condiments and Major Grey's mango chutney. The year of the curry is an elusive one to pinpoint, but this much is clear: it was before the year of quiche Lorraine, the year of paella, the year of *vitello tonnato,* the year of *boeuf* Bourguignon, the year of blanquette *de veau,* and the year of beef Wellington. It was before Michael stopped playing the piano, before Julia opened L'École des Trois Gourmandes, and before Craig had left his job as a bartender in Nyack, New York. It was the beginning, and in the beginning there was James Beard and there was curry and that was about all.

Historical explanations of the rise of the Food Establishment do not usually begin with curry. They begin with the standard background on the gourmet explosion—background that includes the traveling fighting men of World War II, the postwar travel boom, and the shortage of domestic help, all of which are said to have combined to drive the housewives of America into the kitchen.

This background is well and good, but it leaves out the curry development. In the 1950s, suddenly, no one knew quite why or how, everyone began to serve curry. Dinner parties in fashionable homes featured curried lobster. Dinner parties in middle-income homes featured curried chicken. Dinner parties in frozen-food compartments featured curried rice. And with the arrival of curry, the first fashionable international food, food acquired a chic, a gloss of snobbery it had hitherto possessed only in certain upper-income groups. Hostesses were expected to know that iceberg lettuce was *déclassé* and tunafish casseroles *de trop*. Lancers sparkling rosé and Manischewitz were replaced on the table by Bordeaux. Overnight, *rumaki* had a fling and became a cliché.

The American hostess, content serving frozen spinach for her family, learned to make a spinach soufflé for her guests. Publication of cookbooks tripled, quadrupled, quintupled; the first cookbook-of-the-month club, the Cookbook Guild, flourished. At the same time, American industry realized that certain members of the food world—like James Beard, whose name began to have a certain celebrity—could help make foods popular. The French's mustard people turned to Beard. The can-opener people turned to Poppy Cannon. Pan American Airways turned to Myra Waldo. The Potato Council turned to Helen McCully. The Northwest Pear Association and the Poultry and Egg Board and the Bourbon Institute besieged food editors for more recipes containing their products. Cookbook authors were retained, at sizable fees, to think of new ways to cook with bananas. Or scallions. Or peanut butter. "You know," one of them would say, looking up from a dinner made during the peanut-butter period, "it would never have occurred to me to put peanut butter on lamb, but actually, it's rather nice."

Before long, American men and women were cooking along with Julia Child, subscribing to the Shallot-of-the-Month Club, and learning to mince garlic instead of pushing it through a press. Cheeses, herbs, and spices that had formerly been available only in Bloomingdale's delicacy department cropped up around New York, and then around the country. Food became, for dinner-party conversations in the sixties, what abstract expressionism had been in the fifties. And liberated men and women who used to brag that sex was their greatest pleasure began to suspect that food might be pulling ahead in the ultimate taste test.

Generally speaking, the Food Establishment—which is not to be confused with the Restaurant Establishment, the Chef Establishment, the Food-Industry Establishment, the Gourmet Establishment, or the Wine Establishment—consists of those people who write about food or restaurants on a regular basis, either in books, magazines, or certain newspapers, and thus have the power to start trends and, in some cases, begin and end careers. Most of them earn additional money through lecture tours, cooking schools, and consultancies for restaurants and industry. A few appear on radio and television.

The typical member of the Food Establishment lives in Greenwich Village, buys his vegetables at Balducci's, his bread at the Zito bakery, and his cheese at Bloomingdale's. He dines at the Coach House. He is given to telling you, apropos of nothing, how many soufflés he has been known to make in a short period of time. He is driven mad by a refrain he hears several times a week: "I'd love to have you for dinner," it goes, "but I'd be afraid to cook for you." He insists that there is no such thing as an original recipe; the important thing, he says, is point of view. He lists as one of his favorite cookbooks the original *Joy of Cooking* by Irma Rombauer, and adds that he wouldn't be caught dead using the revised edition currently on the market. His cookbook library runs to several hundred volumes. He gossips a good deal about his colleagues, about what they are cooking, writing, and eating, and whom they are talking to; about everything, in fact, except the one thing everyone else in the universe gossips about—who is sleeping with whom. In any case, he claims that he really does not spend much time with other members of the Food Establishment, though he does bump into them occasionally at Sunday lunch at Jim Beard's or at one of the publishing parties he is obligated to attend. His publisher, if he is lucky, is Alfred A. Knopf.

He takes himself and food very very seriously. He has been known to debate for hours such subjects as whether nectarines are peaches or plums, and whether the vegetables that Michael Field, Julia Child, and James Beard had one night at La Caravelle and said were canned were in fact canned. He roundly condemns anyone who writes more than one cookbook a year. He squarely condemns anyone who writes a cookbook containing untested recipes. Colleagues who break the rules and succeed are hailed almost as if they had happened on a new galaxy. "Paula Peck," he will say, in hushed tones of awe, "broke the rules in puff paste." If the Food Establishmentarian makes a breakthrough in cooking methods—no matter how minor and superfluous it may seem—he will celebrate. "I have just made a completely and utterly revolutionary discovery," said Poppy Cannon triumphantly one day. "I have just developed a new way of cooking asparagus."

There are two wings to the Food Establishment, in mortal combat with the other. On the one side are the revolutionaries—as they like to think of themselves: the home economists and writers and magazine editors who are industry-minded and primarily concerned with the needs of the average housewife. Their virtues are performance, availability of product, and less work for mother; their concern is with improving American food. "There is an awe about Frenchiness in food which is terribly precious and has kept American food from being as good as it could be," says Poppy Cannon, the leader of the revolutionaries. "People think French cooking is gooking it up. All this kowtowing to so-called French food has really been a hindrance rather than a help." The revolutionaries pride themselves on discovering shortcuts and developing convenience foods; they justify the compromises they make and the loss of taste that results by insisting that their recipes, while unquestionably not as good as the originals, are probably a good deal better than what the American housewife would prepare if left to her own devices. When revolutionaries get together, they talk about the technical aspects of food: how to ripen a tomato, for example; and whether the extra volume provided by beating eggs with a wire whisk justifies not using the more convenient electric beater.

On the other side are the purists or traditionalists, who see themselves as the last holdouts for haute cuisine. Their virtue is taste; their concern primarily French food. They are almost missionary-like, championing the cause of great food against the rising tide of the TV dinner, clamoring for better palates as they watch the children of America raised on a steady diet of SpaghettiOs. Their contempt for the revolutionaries is eloquent: "These people, these home economists," said Michael Field distastefully, "—they skim the iridescent froth off the gourmet department, and it comes out tasting like hell." When purists meet, they discuss each other; very occasionally, they talk about food: whether one ought to put orange peel into *boeuf* Bourguignon, for example, and why lamb tastes better rare.

Although the purists do not reach the massive market available to the revolutionaries, they are virtually celebrities. Their names conjure up a sense of style and taste; their appearance at a benefit can mean thousands of dollars for hospitals, charities, and politicians. The Big Four of the Food Establishment are all purists—James Beard, Julia Child, Michael Field, and Craig Claiborne.

Claiborne, a Mississippi-born man who speaks softly, wears half-glasses, and has a cherubic reddish face that resembles a Georgia peach, is probably the most powerful man in the Food Establishment. From his position as food editor of the *New York Times*, he has been able to bring down at least one restaurant (Claude Philippe's Pavillon), crowd customers into others, and play a critical part in developing new food tastes. He has singlehandedly revived sorrel and cilantro, and, if he could have his way, he would singlehandedly stamp out iceberg lettuce and garlic powder. To his dismay, he played a large part in bringing about the year of beef Wellington. "I hate the stuff," he says.

In his thirties, after too many unhappy years in public relations and the armed forces, Claiborne entered the Lausanne Hotel School to study cooking. On his return—and after a brief fling bartending—he began to write for *Gourmet* magazine and work for Ann Seranne's public-relations firm, handling such products as the Waring Blender and Fluffo the Golden Shortening. In 1957 he was hired by the *Times*, and he unabashedly admits that his job has been a dream come true. He loves it, almost as much as he loves eating, though not nearly as much as he loves cooking.

Claiborne is happiest in his Techbuilt house in Springs, East Hampton, which overlooks an herb garden, an oversized swimming pool, and Gardiner's Bay. There, he, his next-door neighbor Pierre Franey—whom he calls "my arm and my dear friend"—and a number of other chefs go fishing, swap recipes, and whip up meals for fifty guests at a time. The menus are logged into a small leatherbound notebook in which Claiborne records every meal he eats throughout the year. During the winter, Claiborne lives in Greenwich Village. His breakfasts often consist of Sara Lee frozen croissants. His other daily meals are taken in restaurants, and he discusses them as if he were serving penance. "That," he says firmly, "is the thing I like least about my job."

Six years ago Claiborne began visiting New York restaurants incognito and reviewing them on a star system in the Friday *Times*; since that time, he has become the most envied, admired, and cursed man in the food world. Restaurant owners decry his Francophilia and can barely control their tempers while discussing his prejudice against large-management corporations and in favor of tiny, ethnic restaurants. His nit-picking constantly irritates. Among some of the more famous nits: his censure of a Pavillon waiter who allowed his pencil to peek out; his disapproval of the salt and pepper shakers at L'Étoile; and this remark about Lutèce: "One could wish that the owner, Monsieur Surmain, would dress in a more reserved and elegant style to better match his surroundings."

Surmain, a debonair man who wears stylish striped shirts, sputters when Claiborne's name is mentioned. "He said in a restaurant of this sort I should wear a tuxedo," said Surmain. "What a bitchy thing. He wants me to act like a headwaiter."

The slings and arrows of outrage fly at Claiborne—and not only from restaurateurs. Carping about Craig is practically a parlor game in the food world. Everything he writes is pored over for its true significance. It is suggested, for example, that the reason Craig criticized proprietor Stuart Levin's clothes in his recent review of Le Pavillon had to do with the fact that Levin fawned over him during his two visits to the restaurant. It is suggested that the reason Craig praised the clothes of Charles Masson of Grenouille in the same review had to do with the fact that Masson ignores Craig entirely too much. It is suggested that Craig is not a nice person; and a story is offered to support the thesis, all about the time he reviewed a new restaurant owned by a friend after the friend begged him to wait a few weeks. His criticisms, it is said, drove the friend to drink.

But the fact of the matter is that Craig Claiborne does what he does better than anyone else. He is a delight to read. And the very things that make him superb as a food critic—his integrity and his utter incorruptibility—are what make his colleagues loathe him.

"Everyone thinks about Craig too much," says cookbook author and consultant Mimi Sheraton. "The truth is that he is his own man and there is no way to be a friend of his. He is the only writer who is really honest. Whether or not he's reliable, whether or not you like him, he is honest. I know *Cue* isn't—I used to write for them. *Gourmet* isn't. And Michael Field is just writing for Craig Claiborne."

Whenever members of the Food Establishment tire of discussing Craig they move on to discuss Craig's feuds—though in all fairness, it must be said that Claiborne is usually the less active party to the feuds. The feud currently absorbing the Food Establishment is between Claiborne and Michael Field. Field, who burst into stardom in the Food Establishment after a career as half of the piano team of Appleton & Field, is an energetic, amusing, frenetic man whose recent rise and subsequent candor have won him few friends in the food world. Those who are not his admirers have taken to passing around the shocking tidbit—untrue—that Field had not been to Europe until 1967, when he visited Julia Child in Provence.

"Essentially," says Field, "the whole Food Establishment is a mindless one, inarticulate and not very cultivated. These idiots who attack me are furious because they think I just fell into it. Well, let me tell you, I used to make forty soufflés in one day and throw them out, just to find the right recipe."

Shortly after his first cookbook was published, Field began reviewing cookbooks for the *New York Review of Books*, a plum assignment. One of his first articles, an attack on *The Fannie Farmer Cookbook* which centered on its fondue recipe, set off a fracas that produced a furious series of argumentative letters, in themselves a hilarious inadvertent parody of letters to highbrow magazines. Recently, he reviewed

The Thousand Recipe Chinese Cookbook—a volume that was voted winner of the R. T. French (mustard) Tastemaker Award (chosen by one hundred newspaper food editors and roughly analogous in meaning to landing on the Best Dressed List). In his attack on Gloria Bley Miller's book, he wrote: "It would be interesting to know why, for example, Mrs. Miller's recipe for hot mustard requires the cook to bring one cup of water to a boil and then allow it to cool before adding one half cup of dry mustard? Surely Mrs. Miller must be aware that drinking and cooking water in China was boiled because it was often contaminated. . . ."

Mrs. Miller wrote in reply: "I can only suggest to Mr. Field . . . that he immerse his typewriter immediately in boiling water. There are many types of virulence in the world, and 'boiling the water first' is one of the best ways to disinfect anything."

The feud between Field and Claiborne had been simmering for several years, but Claiborne's review of the Time-Life cookbook turned it up to full boil. "He has a perfect right to dislike the book," said Field. "But his attack went far beyond that, into personalities." A few months after the review was published, Field counterpunched, with an article in *McCall's* entitled "New York's Ten Most Overrated Restaurants." It is in almost total opposition to Claiborne's *Guide to New York Restaurants*; in fact, reading Field's piece without having Claiborne's book alongside is a little like reading *Finnegans Wake* without the key.

For his part, Claiborne would just as soon not discuss Field—"Don't get me started," he said. And his attitude toward the Time-Life series has mellowed somewhat: he has finally consented to write the text of the *Time-Life Cookbook of Haute Cuisine* along with Franey. But some time ago, when asked, he was only too glad to defend his review. "Helen McCully (food editor of *House Beautiful*) said to me, 'How could you be so mean to Michael?'" he recalled. "I don't give a good God damn about Michael." His face turned deep red, his fists clenched, he stood to pace the room. "The misinformation! The inaccuracies in that book! I made a stack of notes thicker than the book itself on the errors in it. It's shameful."

Claiborne was so furious about the book, in fact, that he managed to intensify what was, until then, a one-sided feud between James Beard and himself. Beard, a genial, large, round man who receives guests in his Tenth Street house while seated, Buddha-like, on a large pouf, had been carrying on a mild tiff with Claiborne for some time. Just before the first Time-Life cookbook was published, the two men appeared together on the *David Susskind Show*, and in the course of the program, Beard held up the book and plugged it on the air. Afterward, Claiborne wrote a letter to Susskind, with carbon copy to Beard, saying that if he had known he was going to appear on the same show with the Time-Life cookbook, he never would have consented to go on.

(That Julia Child has managed thus far to remain above the internecine struggles of the food world probably has more to do with the fact that she lives in Cambridge, Massachusetts, well away from it all, than with her charming personality.)

The success of the Time-Life cookbook series is guaranteed, Claiborne's review notwithstanding. Offered by mail order to subscribers who care not one whit whether the soufflé on the cover is actually a meringue, the series rapidly signed up five hundred thousand takers—for all eighteen books! (*The New York Times Cook Book*, itself a blockbuster, has sold only two hundred thousand copies.) "The books, whatever their limits, are of enormous quality," says Field. "Every recipe works and is honestly conceived." Yet a number of those intimately connected with the books have complained about the limits Field parenthetically refers to, and most particularly about the technique of group journalism that has produced the books: apparently, the text, recipes, and photographs of some of the cookbooks have been done independently of each other.

"It's a joke," said Nika Hazelton, who is writing the text for the *Time-Life German Cookbook*. "First there is the writer—me, in this case, but I have nothing to do with the recipes or illustrations. Then there is the photographic staff, which takes recipes from old cookbooks, changes them a little, and photographs them. Then there is the kitchen, under Michael Field's supervision. I think Michael knows about French and Italian food, but he doesn't know quite as much about other cookery. The cook is John Clancy, a former cook in a short-order house who once worked for Jim Beard. I'm the only person connected with the project who knows languages besides French. There is a consultant who hasn't been in Germany for thirty years. My researcher's background is spending three years with the Morgan Bank. It's hilarious. I'm doing it only for the money."

The money that is available to members of the Food Establishment is not quite as much as they would have you think, but it is definitely enough to keep every last one of them in truffles. James Beard—who commands the highest fees and, though a purist, has the most ties with industry—recently turned down a hundred-thousand-dollar offer to endorse Aunt Jemima mixes because he didn't believe in their products. Retainers offered lesser stars are considerably smaller, but there are many jobs, and they suffice. Nevertheless, the impression persists that there are not enough jobs to go around. And because everyone in the food world is freelancing and concerned with putting as many eggs into his basket as possible, it happens that every time someone gets a job, the rest feel that they have lost one.

Which brings us to the case of Myra Waldo. An attractive, chic woman who lives on upper Fifth Avenue, Miss Waldo published her first cookbook in 1954, and since then she has been responsible for forty-two others. Forty-three cookbooks! In addition, she does four radio spots a day for WCBS, is roving editor of *Family Circle* magazine, is retained by Pan American Airways, and recently landed the late Clementine Paddleford's job as food editor of *This Week* magazine. Myra Waldo has never been a favorite in the Food Establishment: she is far too successful. Furthermore, although *she* once made forty-eight soufflés over a July Fourth weekend, she is not a truly serious cook. (To a visitor who wanted a recipe for a dinner party, she suggested duck in a sauce made of frozen orange juice, Melba sauce, red wine, cognac, lemon juice, and a can of Franco-American beef gravy.) For years it has been rumored that Miss Waldo produces as many cookbooks as she does because she clips recipes and pastes them right onto her manuscript pages, or because she has a gigantic staff—charges she denies. But when she landed the *This Week* job, one that nearly everyone else in the Food Establishment had applied for, the gang decided that too much was too much. Shortly afterward, she went to the Cookbook Guild party, and no one except James Beard even said hello to her.

Said Beard: "You could barely move around at that party for fear someone would bite you in the back."

How much longer life in the Food Establishment—with its back-biting, lip-smacking, and pocket-jingling—will go on is hard to tell. There are some who believe the gourmet explosion that began it all is here to stay and that fine cooking is on the increase. "Of course it will last," said Poppy Cannon, "just in the way sculpture will last. We need it. It is a basic art. We ought to have a National Academy of the Arts to represent the art of cooking."

Others are less sure. They claim that the food of the future will be quite different: precooked, reconstituted, and frozen dishes with portion control. "The old cuisine is gone for good and dying out," says Mrs. Hazelton. "Ultimately, cooking will be like an indoor sport, just like making lace and handiwork."

Whatever happens, the Food Establishment at this moment has the power to change the way America eats. And in fact, about all it is doing is showing how to make a better piecrust and fill a bigger breadbox.

"What fascinates me," says Mimi Sheraton, "is that the more interest there is in gourmet food, the more terrible food is for sale in the markets. You can't buy an unwaxed cucumber in this country, the bread thing everyone knows about, we buy overtenderized meat and frozen chicken. You can't buy a really fresh egg because they've all been washed in hot water so the shells will be clean. And the influence of color photography on food! Oil is brushed on to make it glow. When we make a stew, the meat won't sit on top, so we have to prop it up with oatmeal. Some poor clod makes it at home and it's like buying a dress a model has posed in with the back pinned closed. As a result, food is marketed and grown for the purpose of appearances. We are really the last generation who even has a vague memory of what food is supposed to taste like.

"There have been three revolutionary changes in the food world in past years," Miss Sheraton continued. "The pressure groups have succeeded in changing the labeling of foods, they've succeeded in cutting down the amounts of pesticides used on foods, and they've changed the oversized packages used by the cereal and cracker people. To me, it's interesting that not one of these stories began with a food writer. Where are they, these food writers? They're off wondering about the *boeuf en daube* and whether the quiche was authentic."

Yes, that's exactly where they are. "Isn't it all a little too precious?" asks Restaurant Associates president Joseph Baum. "It's so elegant and recherché, it's like overbreeding a collie." But, after all, someone has to worry about the *boeuf en daube* and whether the quiche was authentic—right? And there is so much more to do. So many soufflés to test and throw out. So many ways of cooking asparagus to discover. So many patés to concoct. And so many things to talk about. Myra's new book. The record Poppy is making. Why Craig finally signed on to Time-Life Cookbooks. Michael's latest article. So much more to do. So many things to talk about. . . .

—September 1968

About Having People to Dinner

When I started out cooking, my biggest fear was that nothing would come out at the same time as anything else.

This proved to be a ridiculous fear, but it took me years to realize that you can keep food warm for quite a long time without really harming it in any way. There is an awful lot of mumbo-jumbo in cookbooks that completely terrifies you—cookbook writers always insisting that you must serve something right away and that you can't possibly reheat things—but with the possible exception of mashed potatoes, most everything you cook can be kept warm for a while without any serious consequences. And even mashed potatoes can sit covered with foil in a 300-degree oven for a while without losing a whole lot. Just make sure you have the oven turned on in advance.

Of course, a thing you can do if this is at all worrisome to you is to plan a dinner where everything isn't hot. This is one of the things that's so great about the ham dinner theory—the ham doesn't have to be hot, and just about everything served with it doesn't have to be hot.

On the other hand, I almost never serve anything like roast beef or leg of lamb for a large number of people, because there's no way that the meat won't be cold by the time you serve everyone. And roast beef is just not as good when it's cold.

So what am I saying here? I think what I'm saying is that you should try to relax about having people over. I have friends who are nervous hostesses, and it just contaminates the entire mood of the evening. They are always rushing from the room to check things and have a wild look in their eyes when they return from the kitchen.

Another thing I'm saying is, try to make things easy for yourself. Don't overreach. Don't ever cook a meal that has more than one complicated item on the menu. Try to plan menus where most things can be done in advance and where all you have to do is reheat the main dish and cook the pasta (or potatoes or rice) just before dinner. I am also a big believer in buying delicious things that you are either truthful about (because if people love what they're eating, they have a huge amount of respect for you for simply finding good food) or, of course, passing them off as something you made. Fried chicken, for example, is something I cannot make as well as several take-out places in New York and Los Angeles, including a supermarket on Santa Monica Boulevard. So I just buy it and serve it, along with things I make to go with it, like monkey bread.

I believe in the Rule of Four. Most dinners consist of three things—a meat or fish, a starch, and a vegetable. I think you must always have a fourth—applesauce, or cornsticks, or chutney, or biscuits, or tiny little baked apples, or monkey bread. Not that you should pay attention to these rules of mine; you have to find your own way to entertain. But even if you're just serving spaghetti and a salad, I'd try to do something with bread—with garlic or rosemary or oregano—to give the meal just a little extra taste.

I try to be very loose about lots of things, but what I mostly believe is that when you have people to dinner, it should be fun, and part of the fun should be in what you eat. It's sad when you go to someone's house and they serve something—like a piece of fish, for example—that's so straightforward that you finish eating dinner in about three minutes. This, actually, is one of my main objections to fish: it's just too easy to eat, and therefore you should never serve it. People like to play with their food (which is why I go on serving curry and lots of condiments to people years after curry ceased to be chic). They like lots of different tastes. Your hope always is that your guests will go back for seconds and won't have any trouble staying late and making you believe it was worth it to go to the trouble to have them to your home.

I have learned over the years that:

> It is never fun if people in monkey suits serve dinner by going around the table and passing the food. This is why I always just put the food out on a table and let everyone help themselves.
>
> It is absolutely essential to have a round table. If you have people to dinner and make good food and then put your guests at a long rectangular table where people can't hear what's going on at the other end of the table and are pretty much trapped talking to the person on either side of themselves . . . well, what is the point? The perfect round table is a sixty-inch round, which serves ten people comfortably, but a fifty-two-inch round, which serves eight people, is also nice, and a forty-eight- or forty-two-inch round, which will serve six, is also nice. Any round table is nicer than any table with corners.

People like to have a seating plan. They get very nervous when there isn't one. This doesn't mean you have to have place cards (although place cards are nice, especially if you use odd things to make them out of, like postcards or something), but it does mean you should have a plan. And it also means you should keep an eye on what's happening before dinner, and if two of your guests that you'd planned to seat together spend the entire cocktail hour talking to one another, change the seating plan and separate them. Or tell them before dinner that you've seated them together at dinner so they can mix with other people beforehand.

A thing I like to do when I have a big round table of twelve people, or two round tables, is change the seats just before dessert. This is a wonderful thing to do because everyone has new people to talk to.

It is very easy to seat a small dinner at a round table. It's just a question of math most of the time. The rules are: don't seat anyone next to the person they came with or live with or go with or don't speak to. It's nice to seat boy/girl, but I have a friend who seats boy/girl/girl/boy/boy/girl, etc., so that everyone is seated next to one boy and one girl. In California, of course, they never break up couples at dinner for fear of what might happen if someone's husband were seated next to someone else's very young girlfriend; but dinners with couples seated next to one another are always deadly dull, which is why there are almost no good dinner parties in the entire state of California.

✳ *The Blogger*

The First Annual "Tell Us What You're Cooking This Year for Thanksgiving Dinner That You Didn't Cook Last Year"

Here's the deal about Thanksgiving dinner at our house: it's the same every year, except for one thing. Every year one thing changes.

Sometimes we try something new and it stays forever, like the apricot Jell-O mold that's been a guilty pleasure of our Thanksgiving dinner for at least fourteen years.

Sometimes it's something that makes the cut for several years—like sweet potatoes with pecan praline—and then, for no real reason, falls off the menu never to be spoken of again.

And sometimes it's a mistake, like the pearl onions in balsamic vinegar, which turned out to be a dish that was far too full of itself.

Anyway, here's what we're doing on *Huffington Post*: the first annual "Tell Us What You're Cooking This Year for Thanksgiving Dinner That You Didn't Cook Last Year."

Send in your recipe. Send in the thing you've never cooked before on Thanksgiving Day, the thing that proves conclusively that you're up for change, that you're not your mother, that you're open to new ideas, that you're flexible and full of surprises and with-it food-wise, even though the truth about Thanksgiving is the exact opposite—it's about ritual and tradition and the same-old same-old.

This year, in our house, we're cooking our version of Suzanne Goin's succotash. Of course Suzanne Goin doesn't call it succotash; in her book *Sunday Suppers at Lucques*, she calls it sweet corn, green cabbage, and bacon. We call it succotash because we throw in some lima beans and way more butter:

Cut 6 thick slices of bacon into small pieces and cook in a casserole until crispy. Remove and drain. Melt 1 stick of butter in the remaining bacon grease, and add 1 sliced onion and some salt and pepper. Sauté for a few minutes, then add half a small green cabbage, sliced, and cook until wilted. Add 2 packages of cooked frozen lima beans and 2 packages of frozen corn. Cook about 5 minutes, stirring, till the corn is done. You can do this in advance. Reheat gently and add the bacon.

—November 18, 2007

Hello. By the Way. Whatever.

I don't really have anything much to say today, but I thought I'd write anyway because last Sunday I opened up the *New York Times Magazine* and discovered that *Daily Kos* had taken a pop at me in an interview with Deborah Solomon:

> Q: Do you read your fellow liberal bloggers, like those who write for *Huffington Post*?
>
> A: To me, *Huffington Post* gives voice to the voice. They're celebrities who don't need a platform.
>
> Q: That's not fair. You can't discredit bloggers like Jane Smiley or Nora Ephron just because they have a reputation outside politics.
>
> A: These people don't have trouble being heard if they want to be heard.

Well, excuse me but my feelings were a little hurt. I like *Daily Kos*, even though he is under a major delusion about the political future of Mark Warner. And I thought the whole point of the blogosphere was that it was a big wide-open place like the world itself where everyone was welcome. Only a few days ago, someone in the Internet world told me there were 62,000 new blogs a day. Isn't that amazing? (I'm pretty sure that's what he said. I wrote the number down on a piece of paper and promptly lost it.) It's clear that at this rate, everyone in the world will have a blog. It's what we'll give babies when they're born, instead of rattles.

It has not been a good week for bloggers, so I don't want to make it seem as if it was any worse for me just because I was attacked by a blogger. Judy Miller was back in an article in *Vanity Fair*, blaming the bloggers, and Donald Rumsfeld was on CBS, blaming the bloggers, and Joe Lieberman is quoted (in *Daily Kos*, by Kos himself) blaming the bloggers. And of course, there was what is now called Clooneygate, about which may I say if there was ever a celebrity who didn't need a platform to be heard it's George Clooney, and I was still happy to see him blogging, and sad to discover that he didn't actually mean to be doing it.

Bloggers—aka the pajama people—are now the class everyone loves to beat up on, the bottom of the barrel, the writers even journalists can look down on, and now bloggers are even bashing other bloggers just for blogging.

But it seems to me that Kos is missing the point of blogs. Not that there's only one point about blogs, there are thousands. But there are two I'd like to make. One is that, yes, it's true that some people who blog can probably get their blogs printed elsewhere. But where? First you have to send the blog elsewhere. Then you have to get someone elsewhere to read it. That person is what's known as an editor, who might or might not like what you have sent in. If he likes it, he probably has to show it to another person. Then they have to get back to you. (They might even have "suggestions" or "changes," God forbid.) Days and weeks can pass in this manner. If you have sent your writing to a place that publishes only occasionally, weeks or months might pass before your words are printed anywhere, by which time you stand a good chance of being even less relevant and truthful than you were in the first place. I mean, time is of the essence, and not just when it comes to things of this sort.

But the other point I want to make is that getting heard outside the world of blogs occasionally requires that you have something to say. And one of the most delicious things about the profoundly parasitical world of blogs is that you don't have to have anything much to say. Or you just have to have a little tiny thing to say. You just might want to say hello. I'm here. And by the way. On the other hand. Nevertheless. Did you see this? Whatever. A blog is sort of like an exhale. What you hope is that whatever you're saying is true for about as long as you're saying it. Even if it's not much.

—March 23, 2006

Deep Throat and Me: Now It Can Be Told, and Not for the First Time Either

For many years, I have lived with the secret of Deep Throat's identity. It has been hell, and I have dealt with the situation by telling pretty much anyone who asked me, including total strangers, who Deep Throat was. Not for nothing is indiscretion my middle name.

I knew that Deep Throat was Mark Felt because I figured it out. Carl Bernstein, to whom I was married for a brief time, certainly would never have told me; he was far too intelligent to tell me a secret like that. He refused to tell his children, too, who are also my children, so I told them, and they told others, and even so, years passed and no one really listened to any of us. Years passed while unbelievably idiotic ideas of who Deep Throat was were floated by otherwise intelligent people. There were theories about John Dean, and David Gergen, and Alexander Haig, and L. Patrick Gray and Diane Sawyer and Ron Ziegler (Ron Ziegler!), and I'm pretty sure even Henry Kissinger's name came up. I mean, really. Why these people with these ludicrous theories didn't call me I cannot imagine. I am listed.

Only the other day, a well-known and credible journalist who shall be nameless suggested to me that Deep Throat did not exist, that he was a composite character invented by Bob Woodward. I tried to explain to him that Bob Woodward would never have invented anything, much less a composite character, but as I say, no one listened.

The clues to Deep Throat's identity were clear:

- Bob and Carl wrote in *All the President's Men* that Woodward's code name for their source—before he was christened Deep Throat by *Washington Post* managing editor Howard Simons—was My Friend. Hello.
- Long before Bob and Carl had become Woodward and Bernstein, they told writer Timothy Crouse that their anonymous source for their early stories worked in the Justice Department, and Crouse printed it in *The Boys on the Bus*, his book about the press and the 1972 presidential campaign.
- If you read *All the President's Men* carefully, you can see that whoever Deep Throat was had access to FBI files within days of the Watergate break-in, and that the most obvious suspect was probably a high-level official at the FBI.
- Mark Felt was a navy veteran, and so was Woodward.

I can see just from reading the early coverage about Mark Felt's revelation that he has had a hard time living with this secret, too. For years, he has had to hear the constant refrain from Woodward that Deep Throat's identity would not be revealed until Deep Throat died; I don't know about you, but if I were Deep Throat, that would start to get on my nerves. So Felt began to tell the people in his family the truth. "I'm the guy they used to call Deep Throat," he allegedly said to them. My guess is that they reacted with incredulity; after all, that's how people have reacted to me over the years. And then, inevitably, they probably began to wonder about who was going to own the rights to the television movie.

So Mark Felt and his family let *Vanity Fair* have the story, and now everyone has admitted it's true, and all I can say is that this is a huge load off my mind. Mark Felt is Deep Throat. Don't say I didn't try to tell you.

—May 31, 2005

The Curious Incident of the Veep in the Summertime

For some time I've been wondering whether anyone is going to explain the true mystery of what happened after Hurricane Katrina struck. I read thousands of words on the subject in this morning's *New York Times*, and I still don't get it. Where was the president? And more to the point, where was the vice president? And don't tell me Crawford, Texas, and on a ranch in Wyoming. For days there was an absolute vacuum at the top. Why? What was going on?

You'll be happy to hear that I have a theory. Is it possible that the president and the vice president have fallen out? I mean, I'm just asking. But if you remember September 11, 2001—and I'm sure you do—the president had no idea what to do, but the vice president did. The vice president took over. He didn't even consult with the president. He put the president on Air Force One and the president spent the day flying from one airport to another, which was something that even the president eventually understood made him look as if he wasn't in charge.

The relationship between Cheney and Bush has always reminded me of a moment I witnessed in the movie business many years ago. I had written a script for an actress, and she had decided she wanted to direct it. This was a terrible idea, because she was famous for dithering, but there was no question that the studio would make the movie if she directed it. "Don't worry about it," the producer of the movie said to me when I asked if she was remotely capable of directing a movie. "We can walk her through it."

It's always been clear to me that five years ago, when all those Republican guys got together and realized that George Bush could be elected president—and that he wasn't remotely capable—they came to an understanding: they would walk him through it. I'm sure it seemed like a swell idea, especially because it meant that they'd be in a perfect position to convince him to do all sorts of exciting things they had always wanted to do.

Cheney was the point man. Cheney was the guy they put on *Meet the Press*. Cheney was the person who seemed always to be the first responder. Cheney was the official they put into the bunker last May when a plane flew too close to the White House; Bush, who was bicycling in Maryland, wasn't even told about the episode until forty minutes after it was over. Even Laura Bush, who was in the bunker with Cheney, publicly questioned the decision to keep the president in the dark.

But if you look at the chart in Sunday's *New York Times*, which tells you who was where when Katrina struck, Cheney doesn't even get a listing. It's Bush, Chertoff, Brown. Bush I and Bill Clinton were summoned to help. But Cheney didn't even turn up back in Washington until last week, when he was sent off for a day of spouting platitudes while touring the flood zone.

Like the curious incident of the dog that didn't bark in the famous Sherlock Holmes story, Cheney's the missing person in this event, and one has to wonder why. If he were a woman, I would guess he'd been busy recovering from a face-lift, but he's not. So I can only suppose that something has gone wrong. Could the president be irritated that Cheney helped con him into Iraq? Oh, all right, probably not. Could Cheney—and not just his aides—possibly be involved in the Valerie Plame episode? Is Cheney not speaking to Karl Rove? Does the airplane/bicycle incident figure into this in any way? And how is it possible that the president is off on vacation and the vice president is, too? Not that it matters that much if the president is on vacation; on some level, the president is always on vacation. But where was Cheney?

Just asking.

—September 11, 2005

Hooked on Anonymity

*"The frustration throughout the week was getting good,
reliable information," said the aide, who demanded
anonymity so as not to be identified in disclosing inner
workings of the White House. "Getting truth on the
ground in New Orleans was very difficult."*

From a *New York Times* piece September 10, 2005,
by Elisabeth Bumiller, on the White House decision to remove
Michael Brown of FEMA from ongoing supervision of hurricane relief.

I've become hooked on the excuses the *New York Times* is providing
for using anonymous sources. Of course, the *Times* doesn't think of
them as excuses—they think of them as motivations. "Whenever anonymity is granted, it should be the subject of energetic negotiation to
arrive at phrasing that will tell the reader as much as possible about the
placement and motivation of the source"—this is from the new set of
Times standards instituted after the Jayson Blair fiasco two years ago.

Allan M. Siegal, the standards editor at the *Times*, whose position
was created After Blair, gave an interview a couple of weeks ago to the
public editor at the *Times*. In it, Siegal elaborated further on the question of anonymity, and said that he spends part of each day randomly
vetting the next day's stories for anonymous sources and occasionally
calling editors to ask about them. Last Saturday, when a motive for anonymity failed to appear in Elisabeth Bumiller's story about the White
House decision to remove Michael Brown—and then turned up inserted
in the article in subsequent editions (as quoted above)—I amused myself
imagining the last-minute phone call and "energetic negotiation" that
were probably involved. It reminded me of my days as a reporter writing profiles at the *New York Post*. The then-owner of the *Post*, Dorothy
Schiff, was obsessed with mixed marriages, and every time a profile
of a Jewish man who'd married a gentile woman was about to appear,
she would phone the editor and demand we call the interview subject
to find out what religion his children were being raised as, and whether
actual bar mitzvahs were going to be involved. We were constantly having to scramble at the last minute to reach the person we were profiling,
and to explain—mortified—why we were calling.

My own feeling about the *Times*'s policy is that it's misguided and naive and will someday make a fine chapter in a book about this era of transparency we're currently enduring. Where the notion of transparency originated is a mystery to me, but I first recall seeing the word in a mea culpa the *Times* issued at the time of the Blair episode. I was puzzled that anyone could possibly believe that a corporation, much less a newspaper, could possibly benefit in any way from making its process visible. My own experience at newspapers—and I will grant that the *New York Post* in the 1960s was a peculiar place—was that much of what the editors did consisted of sending reporters to journalistic Siberia, which at the *Post* involved writing about dead people or the Board of Education.

Enough nostalgia. Here's the point: anonymous sources are never going to admit the truth about why they prefer to be anonymous. They are never going to say, the reason I'm willing to be your anonymous source is that I'm in a power struggle with the person I'm giving you information about. They are never going to say, I'm willing to talk to you about Fred (but don't use my name) because he slept with my ex-wife. They're never going to say, the reason I'm talking to you off the record is that I'm a malicious gossip and have nothing better to do. They're never going to say, I'm talking to you on background in the hopes of convincing you that my version of events is true, although it probably isn't. Or, I'm talking to you on background because I'm essentially shilling for the president, but if I make the quote anonymous it will sound as if I've told you something top secret. They're certainly never going to say (as Ahmed Chalabi ought to have when he spent so many years being the most effective anonymous source since Deep Throat), I'm talking to you on condition of anonymity because I hope to plant false information about weapons of mass destruction in your very powerful newspaper in order to con the United States government into going to war against Saddam Hussein so I can return to Iraq and become part of the new government and steal a whole bunch more money than I already have.

And by the way, sources aren't the only people who opt for anonymity. Reporters, especially beat reporters, often have only a few reliable sources, whom they use day after day. One traditional way of cultivating them is to keep their names out of the newspapers. No one with a job likes to be known as a reliable source. And no reporter likes it known that he has only a few sources. What's more, anonymity protects the reporter from losing his reliable source to other bird-dogging reporters.

Of course, it's possible that the pendulum will swing back, and the

Times—and some of the other national publications that have followed suit—will give all this up and go back to being the delightfully opaque places they used to be. But in the meantime, the odd thing about this policy is that it almost seems to have the opposite effect of what's intended. Since sources are never really going to admit their true motives for wanting to remain anonymous, they will lie. They will lie because the *New York Times* is going to persuade them to lie, urge them to lie, enable them to lie, demand they lie, and furthermore even negotiate the lie. And then the *New York Times* is going to print the lie and call it a motivation. But it's not a motivation. At best, it's an excuse—a bland, misleading excuse. But it's nowhere near the whole truth.

—September 14, 2005

One Small Blog

The World Is One Big Blog, that's what the panel was called that I went to today. Here was the idea of the panel, articulated by moderator Ken Auletta: "Some say blogs are a way to democratize the media. . . . Others say they may rob democracy of a common sense of . . . " something or other. I don't know what that something or other was, because I can't read my notes and all I can hear on my tape recorder are some indistinct voices and the sound of someone coughing. Actually, it's me coughing. I could call Ken Auletta and ask him what it was he said exactly, but that would involve reporting, and I learned this morning at the panel on blogs that when you are a blogger, you are so busy blogging that you don't have time to report.

Anyway, you get the idea of the panel, and as with all panels the moderator framed the question beautifully, and then the panel went on to other things. We never really did find out about the effect of blogs on democracy. (I don't think we did, anyway.)

On the panel were Ana Marie Cox, *Wonkette* herself, and Jason Calacanis, cofounder of Weblogs, dressed perfectly in a pair of ripped jeans (I am not one of you) and a blazer (on the other hand, I am one of you). Arianna Huffington was supposed to be on the panel, too, but had to cancel and was replaced by her *Huffington Post* business partner Ken Lerer. They spoke at Condé Nast to a room full of (mostly) men, (mostly) in blazers, all this sponsored by *The New Yorker* magazine and the Newhouse School.

We establish from the beginning that the best thing about being a blogger, besides not having to do reporting, is that you never actually have to get dressed—you can work in your pajamas (Wonkette) or your bathrobe (Calacanis). "Blogging is ridiculously easy to do," Wonkette says. "My cat could do it." We also learn almost immediately that Calacanis is flirting with a number of companies that apparently are going to buy him out for (I guess) millions of dollars. He gives us a list of the companies that are in the bidding for Weblogs, this, too, lost in the ether of my tape recorder; my memory is that Rupert Murdoch's News Corporation is at the top of the list.

Calacanis is very impressive and confident, reeling off endless thrilling acronyms and technical terms that are Greek to me. He says that what blogs are really good at is getting to the truth. He says that if Jayson Blair's fraudulent articles had appeared on the Internet instead of in the *New York Times*, he would have been nailed immediately. I guess this is the case, although I can't help but think Calacanis is missing the delicious point about truth and blogs. It's not that the blogosphere doesn't care about the truth, but that truth is a very limited, overrated concept, and nowhere is this more clear than on the Internet. It's true, for example, that there was a panel discussion about blogs this morning at Condé Nast moderated by Ken Auletta, and it's also true that certain things were said at it, many of them not picked up by my tape recorder. But what actually happened this morning? Nothing? Anything? Something? Everything? That depends on how you look at it. Which, by the way, is, to me, the point of blogs, and it's what makes their relationship to the truth so interesting.

My favorite thing Calacanis said is that he thought the *New York Times* was idiotic to charge people to read op-ed material, that the paper was putting up a wall around part of their product, and as a result, the *Times*'s columnists wouldn't even be Google-able. Apparently the worst thing that can happen to you in the history of the world if you are a blogger is to not be easily accessible on Google. By the way, Calacanis told everyone to buy Google stock.

Wonkette spent some time drawing a distinction between bloggers and journalists. I think she said you could be a journalist but not write journalism, or else she said you could be in journalism but not be a journalist. She definitely said a blogger could perform an act of journalism without being a journalist exactly. It was sort of existential and reminded me of the question "Is a play a play if it isn't being performed?" She also spoke eloquently about drinking, being drunk, being hungover, and never being anywhere without a miniature bottle of Jim Beam. She was fantastically fast and funny, and if I were a straight man or a gay woman I would have gotten a huge, pathetic crush on her. She has written a novel and showed me the manuscript, which was in her tote bag. Her tote bag was pretty messy, and so was mine, so that made things even more exciting. I don't have a clue how she has had time to write a novel, what with the blogging and the drinking, but I guess you save a lot of time not having to do any reporting.

As for Ken Lerer, he said that the Internet and the explosion of blogs isn't really new, it's just the next new thing to evolve, sort of like what happened two hundred years ago when people first started writing broadsides and pamphlets. I completely disagree with this, although I didn't raise my hand during the question period to say so for fear that I would start coughing again. But I happen to think the Internet is a cosmic, seismic, amazing change, unlike anything that's gone before. Way more than television, it's changing the culture, it's changing the way people think, it's changing the way their brains work, it's changing pretty much everything. Although it doesn't seem to have changed panel discussions.

—September 28, 2005

On Bill Clinton

I broke up with Bill a long time ago. It's always hard to remember love—years pass and you say to yourself, was I really in love or was I just kidding myself? Was I really in love or was I just pretending he was the man of my dreams? Was I really in love or was I just desperate? But when it came to Bill, I'm pretty sure it was the real deal. I loved the guy.

As for Bill, I have to be honest: he did not love me. In fact, I never even crossed his mind. Not once. But in the beginning that didn't stop me. I loved him, I believed in him, and I didn't even think he was a liar. Of course, I knew he'd lied about his thing with Gennifer, but at the time I believed that lies of that sort didn't count. How stupid was that?

Anyway, I fell out of love with Bill early in the game—over gays in the military. That was in 1993, after he was inaugurated, and at that moment my heart turned to stone. People use that expression and mean it metaphorically, but if your heart can turn to stone and not have it be metaphorical, that's how stony my heart was where Bill was concerned. I'd had faith in him. I'd been positive he'd never back down. How could he? But then he did, he backed down just like that. He turned out to be just like the others. So that was it. Goodbye, big guy. I'm out of here. Don't even think about calling. And by the way, if your phone rings and your wife answers and the caller hangs up, don't think it's me because it's not.

By the time Bill got involved with Monica, you'd have thought I was past being hurt by him. You'd have thought I'd have shrugged and said, I told you so, you can't trust the guy as far as you can spit. But much to my surprise, Bill broke my heart all over again. I couldn't believe how betrayed I felt. He'd had it all, he'd had everything, and he'd thrown it away, and here's the thing: it wasn't his to throw away. It was ours. We'd given it to him, and he'd squandered it.

Years passed. I'd sit around with friends at dinner talking about How We Got Here and Whose Fault Was It? Was it Nader's fault? Or Gore's? Or Scalia's? Even Monica got onto the list, because after all, she delivered the pizza, and that pizza was truly the beginning of the end. Most of my friends had a hard time narrowing it down to a choice, but not me: only one person was at fault, and it was Bill. I drew a straight line from that pizza to the war. The way I saw it, if Bill had behaved, Al would have been elected, and thousands and thousands of people would be alive today who are instead dead.

I bring all this up because I bumped into Bill the other day. I was watching the Sunday news programs, and there he was. I have to say, he looked good. And he was succinct, none of that wordy blah-blah thing that used to drive me nuts. He'd invited a whole bunch of people to a conference in New York and they'd spent the week talking about global warming, and poverty, and all sorts of obscure places he knows a huge amount about.

When Bill described the conference, it was riveting. I could see how much he cared; and of course, I could see how smart he was. It was so refreshing. It was practically moving. To my amazement, I could even see why I'd loved the guy in the first place. It made me sadder than I can say. It's much easier to get over someone if you can delude yourself into thinking you never really cared that much.

Then, later in the week, I was reading about Bill's conference, and I came upon something that made me think, for just a moment, that Bill might even want me back. "I've reached an age now where it doesn't matter whatever happens to me," he said. "I just don't want anyone to die before their time anymore." It almost really got to me. But then I came to my senses. And instead I just wanted to pick up the phone and call him and say, if you genuinely believe that, you hypocrite, why don't you stand up and take a position against this war?

But I'm not calling. I haven't called in years and I'm not starting now.

—September 29, 2005

A Million Little Embellishments

There are a lot of bad things going on in the world this week, but Angelina and Brad are not among them. For one thing, I actually know who Angelina and Brad are. She has huge lips, and those lips stay pretty much the same no matter what. Even when Angelina dyes her hair blond, I know it's her. Also, there's the baby, stapled to her midsection, which is a fashion accessory that I'm sure will last long after her youngest child is old enough to run in a marathon; this, too, helps me identify her, and I am grateful.

Today's paper says Angelina is pregnant. I'm a little shocked but I'm dealing with it. Last week I read in *Us* magazine that Brad and Angelina were fighting over whether to become pregnant, and that Angelina's position on the question was that she was not willing to become pregnant if there was even one orphan left in the world. I loved that! I really got into that! It was so Angelina! Of course, it turns out not to be "true" in the literal sense of the word, which is to say that it seems unlikely Angelina actually "said" those words last week, or meant them if she did say them, but so what? Why carp over details? Who cares? It's the kind of thing Angelina might have said at some point. And at least I know what the woman looks like.

Which is more than I can say for Britney. Who is Britney? What has she done to have so many blowsy pictures of herself in magazines? I usually know it's Britney because her name is right next to her picture, but I feel as if I walked in late in the plot of her life, and no one bothered to explain to me what she's doing here, much less why she spells her name that way. Is she the one involved with Kevin Federline or someone else? I'll tell you who I really miss: that country singer who married Renée Zellweger. I liked that guy because he looked exactly like Renée in a hat, so you could pretty much tell who he was, but he lasted only a second and then he was gone. Oh well.

Meanwhile, I was planning to read the piece about Lindsay Lohan and her anorexia in this month's *Vanity Fair*. I sort of know who Lindsay Lohan is; she's the one with the horrible father. Or else she's the one with the horrible stepfather. Father, stepfather, it's a detail. But yesterday, just as I was about to read the article, Lindsay issued a statement through her publicist claiming that she did not say many of the quotes that are attributed to her in it. What is this woman's problem? Why bother denying quotes? No one cares whether what she said is true or not: Get with it, girl! And if she's truly into denying things, why not claim she had nothing whatsoever to do with the photographs either? Since the photographs don't look like Lindsay Lohan, why not claim they're actually of someone else, like an Olsen twin? Why stop there? Why not claim the pictures are of that person who poses for pictures of JT LeRoy? Of course Lindsay Lohan has probably never heard of JT LeRoy. But neither had I until very recently.

Which brings me to James Frey and his best-selling book *A Million Little Pieces*. I meant to read that book. I have a sneaker for books on the best-seller list, and I'm a fairly pathetic follower of Oprah, who turned Frey's book into a best seller. Last summer, along with thousands of other slavish Oprah acolytes, I read *Anna Karenina*, and let me tell you that is one swell book. By the way, *Anna Karenina* is a novel. That means it's fiction. But why get hung up on such distinctions? No one else does. Frey himself was on *Larry King* last night, with his mother no less, and he said, "In the memoir genre the writer generally takes liberties." What a great quote! And he came right out and admitted he changed a few "details." In his book, for example, Frey says he spent three months in jail, but it turns out he spent only one night in jail. In his book he says he was arrested for smoking crack, but it turns out he was arrested for being drunk. I'm with Oprah, who called the *Larry King* show to support Frey, and said that the whole concern over whether he was telling the truth or not was just "much ado about nothing." I feel the same way about what the president says about how we're doing in the war. I mean, big deal. We have got to get past these details and focus on what is important.

And by the way, how great that Frey let his mother—who undoubtedly at some point encouraged him in his gift for a million little embellishing details—appear on the *Larry King* show with him. Now if I could just get Frey's face straight in my head I'd be completely happy.

—January 12, 2006

Scooter, Rosa Lopez, and the Grassy Knoll

I have a small dog, a Chihuahua, and I know exactly when we got her. It was during O. J., and the reason I know this is that for a while, we thought about naming the dog Rosa Lopez. Rosa Lopez, in case you've forgotten, was the housekeeper who lived across the street from O. J. Simpson, on Rockingham; she testified in a famously incoherent way at the first trial. I remember her name because of the dog we didn't name her after, but I've managed to forget nearly everything else I ever knew about the Simpson murder case, and let me tell you, I knew a lot; I knew just about all there was to know, and every bit of it was lodged in my head, in a part of my brain that I now think of as the grassy knoll.

The O. J. Simpson case was not the beginning of my life on the grassy knoll; Watergate was. I never really got it about the actual, original, mother-of-all-grassy-knolls—the grassy knoll itself, in Dallas, Texas. I was a reporter at the *New York Post* the day JFK was shot, and for years afterward I believed that Lee Harvey Oswald did it, acting alone. At the time, in 1963, I was a journalist, and I had an instinctive contempt for conspiracy theory. Most things that were thought of as conspiracies were—in my opinion—a series of incompetent acts coming together in a perfect storm. (It was especially easy to believe in the power of incompetent acts if you worked at the *New York Post* in that period.) So I never became a student of trajectories and how many bullet fragments and the role of Carlos Marcello and any of the rest of it, even after certain aspects of a conspiracy theory became somewhat compelling.

Then along came Watergate. Watergate was a revelation. It was an honest-to-God conspiracy, and the detail that clinched it was the break-in at Daniel Ellsberg's psychiatrist's office. When the people behind the Watergate burglary turned out to be behind the break-in at Ellsberg's psychiatrist's months earlier, I realized that my natural antipathy to conspiracy was something I would probably have to give up: life was coming up with way too much evidence on the other side. My brain instantly expanded and made room for vast quantities of sheer speculation, narrative scenarios that led nowhere, and useless bits of information. I knew the name of Chuck Colson's wife, I knew the details of Ken Clawson's circumcision, and I knew so much about Howard Hunt that I eventually came to believe it was a shame I had never really become an expert on the Kennedy assassination because, no question, he was involved in it but it was too late for me to figure out how. Howard Hunt was truly Zelig, it seemed to me, and if you turned over almost any rock in American life from November 22, 1963, to the Watergate break-in on June 17, 1972, you'd find him lurking underneath.

(Eventually, I came to believe the same thing about Lucianne Goldberg, who first crossed my consciousness in the early days of the women's movement, when she was one member of a two-member organization that opposed feminism and whose motto was "A lamb chop, not a karate chop." Later she popped up in Watergate, as part of a dirty-tricks team, and then of course she was a key figure in Monicagate, which it's no exaggeration to say would never have happened but for her.)

Anyway, this week, as I welcomed Plamegate back to the news cycle—and back to my brain—I realized that I'd somehow managed to forget exactly what Scooter Libby was under indictment for. Yes, I know: lying. But about what? I couldn't remember. I couldn't believe it. Back in October I knew everything about Plamegate, I even knew the name of Judy Miller's new dog, and now I'd forgotten exactly what it was Libby was under indictment for.

My grassy knoll is full. It is crammed to bursting. Jared Paul Stern just turned up, and he's trying to sell Anita Busch a T-shirt, but she's busy because she just found a dead fish on her car windshield. There's a Woodstock typewriter, and a pumpkin patch, both left there by my parents, and somewhere David Greenglass is lurking. Leslie Abramson just wandered off; where did she go? What happened to her? Jean Harris will be here soon, under the influence of drugs given to her by Dr. Herman Tarnower. Kato Kaelin is doing a commercial for No Excuses jeans. Monica is on the way, wearing a purple thong. Ron Perelman isn't going to hire her; he's giving the job to Richard Johnson's fiancée instead. Hillary is upstairs in the residential quarters; she's just discovered a big box of papers she thought she'd lost. In some way, Tim Russert is involved, but no one knows how; meanwhile, let's blame him for asking the wrong questions on Sunday. Will Anthony Pellicano rat out

Bert Fields? Is Bert Fields upset because Howard Weitzman walked out of his law firm? Will Michael Ovitz go to jail? Is Katie Holmes pregnant or is it a beach ball? Did George Bush have a clue what Scooter Libby was going to say to Judy Miller? Is Dick Cheney behind everything? Does Richard Perle ever lose a night's sleep? Does Jack Bauer ever go to the bathroom? I'm dizzy. I'm overloaded. Too much is happening.

—April 11, 2006

Reflections on Reading the Results of President Bush's Annual Physical Examination

Try to imagine what it would be like.
They said it would be easy but it turned out to be hard.
They said everyone would love you but it turns out they don't.
They said Dick Cheney would take care of everything, but he
    screwed everything up.
They said, just stand next to Tony Blair and let him do the talk-
    ing, but whenever he did, you looked like a moron.
They said it would be a piece of cake, but it turned out to be a
    quagmire.
They said it would cost $50 billion, but it's costing $400 billion.
They said it would be good for Israel, they said slam dunk, they
    said dancing in the streets, they said minimal casualties.
Try to imagine what it would be like.
And then you tell me how it's possible for anyone under these
    conditions to have a resting heart rate of forty-six beats per
    minute.
And yet he *does*. How is it possible?

—August 1, 2006

My Weekend in Vegas

A couple of weekends ago, we went to Las Vegas. It was a small group of us who can never get enough Vegas. We stayed at the Wynn, where we always stay. We like the Wynn and we like Steve and Elaine Wynn, who own the Wynn, and we like the breakfast buffet at the Wynn, which is the greatest breakfast buffet in Las Vegas and therefore in the world. It's even better than the breakfast buffet at the Bellagio Hotel, which Steve Wynn used to own. The day you die and go to heaven, there will not be a breakfast buffet as good as the one at the Wynn.

We got there Friday night and went straight to dinner at the SW Steakhouse, which is of course named after Steve Wynn. I'd never been there. It has a strip steak that I honestly thought was the finest steak of my life, and let me tell you, I eat a lot of steak. (This reminds me, someone at our table ordered a steak made of grass-fed beef; it was the second time I'd had grass-fed beef in less than a week, it's become a big trend, and may I say that someone should stamp out grass-fed beef because it has no taste whatsoever.) Anyway, while we were eating, Steve and Elaine Wynn stopped by the table. Wynn was in a very good mood because, he told us, he had just sold a Picasso for $139 million. I was surprised he'd sold it, because the Picasso in question was not just any old Picasso but the famous painting *Le Rêve,* which used to hang in the museum at the Bellagio when Wynn owned it, and no question it was Wynn's favorite painting. He'd practically named his new hotel after it, but at some point in the course of construction he'd changed his mind and decided to name the hotel after himself, which, when you think of it, was a good idea, what with the homonym and all. Meanwhile, he named the Cirque de Soleil show at the Wynn after *Le Rêve.*

The buyer of the painting, Wynn told us, was a man named Steven Cohen. Everyone seemed to know who Steven Cohen was, a hedge fund billionaire who lived in Connecticut in a house with a fabulous art collection he had just recently amassed. "This is the most money ever paid for a painting," Steve Wynn said. The price was $4 million more than Ronald Lauder had recently paid for a Klimt. Oh, that Klimt. It had set a bar, no question of that, and Wynn was thrilled to have beaten it. He invited us to come see the painting before it moved to Connecticut, never to be seen again by anyone but people who know Steven Cohen.

The next day, after an excellent lunch at Chinois in the Forum mall, which is the eighth wonder of the world, we all trooped back to our hotel to see the painting. We went into Wynn's office, which is just off the casino, past a waiting area with a group of fantastic Warhols, past a secretary's desk with a Matisse over it (a Matisse over a secretary's desk!) (and by the way a Renoir over another secretary's desk!), and into Wynn's office. There, on the wall, were two large Picassos, one of them *Le Rêve*. Steve Wynn launched into a long story about the painting—he told us that it was a painting of Picasso's mistress, Marie-Thérèse Walter, that it was extremely erotic, and that if you looked at it carefully (which I did, for the first time, although I'd seen it before at the Bellagio) you could see that the head of Marie-Thérèse was divided in two sections and that one of them was a penis. This was not a good moment for me vis-à-vis the painting. In fact, I would have to say that it made me pretty much think I wouldn't pay five dollars for it. Wynn went on to tell us about the provenance of the painting—who'd first bought it and who'd then bought it. This brought us to the famous Victor and Sally Ganz, a New York couple who are a sort of ongoing caution to the sorts of people who currently populate the art world, because the Ganzes managed to accumulate a spectacular art collection in a small New York apartment with no money at all. The Ganz collection went up for auction in 1997, Wynn was saying—he was standing in front of the painting at this point, facing us. He raised his hand to show us something about the painting—and at that moment, his elbow crashed backward right through the canvas.

There was a terrible noise.

Wynn stepped away from the painting, and there, smack in the middle of Marie-Thérèse Walter's plump and allegedly erotic forearm, was a black hole the size of a silver dollar—or, to be more exact, the size of the tip of Steve Wynn's elbow—with two three-inch-long rips coming off it in either direction. Steve Wynn has retinitis pigmentosa, an eye disease that damages peripheral vision, but he could see quite clearly what had happened.

"Oh shit," he said. "Look what I've done."

The rest of us were speechless.

"Thank God it was me," he said.

For sure.

The word "money" was mentioned by someone, or perhaps it was the word "deal."

Wynn said: "This has nothing to do with money. The money

means nothing to me. It's that I had this painting in my care and I've damaged it."

I felt that I was in a room where something very private had happened that I had no right to be at. I felt absolutely terrible.

At the same time I was holding my digital camera in my hand—I'd just taken several pictures of the Picasso—and I wanted to take a picture of the Picasso with the hole in it so badly that my camera was literally quivering. But I didn't see how I could take a picture—it seemed to me I'd witnessed a tragedy, and what's more, that my flash would go off if I did and give me away.

Steve Wynn picked up the phone and left a message for his art dealer. Then he called his wife, Elaine. "You'll never believe what I just did," he said to her. From where we stood, on the other end of the phone call, Elaine seemed to take the news calmly and did not yell at her husband. This was particularly impressive to my own husband. There was a conversation about whether the painting could be restored—Wynn seemed to think it could be—and about the two people in America who were capable of restoring it. We all promised we would keep the story quiet—not, you understand, to cover it up, but to make sure that Wynn was able to deal with the episode as he wished to until it came out. We all knew it would come out eventually. It would have to. There were too many of us in the room, plus all the people in the art world who were eventually going to hear about it.

Meanwhile, we were not going to tell anyone.

We promised.

I promised.

That night we went to dinner, once again at SW because that's how great it is; it's worth going to two nights in a row. They were serving creamed corn with truffles, which was amazing. Once again the Wynns joined us. They were in a terrifically jolly mood, all things considered, and Wynn told us that he planned to tell Steve Cohen the next day that of course Cohen was released from the deal because the painting had been damaged.

After dinner I threw eight or nine passes at the craps table, one of which included a hard ten.

The next day one of my sons came to meet us in Las Vegas, and we went to Joe's Stone Crab, which is excellent, and where the Key lime pie may be even better than the Key lime pie at Joe's Stone Crab in Miami Beach, if such a thing is possible. I told my son the story of what had happened to the painting, but it didn't really count because my son is completely trustworthy.

Nine days passed and I told no one else. It was the most painful experience of my life. But I felt good, too, because, as I say, I knew the story would come out eventually and when it did, I didn't want it to be my fault. And the story did come out. Ten days after Wynn put his elbow through the painting, there was an item about it on Page Six of the *New York Post*. It was very clear who had given Page Six the item, and it wasn't me. I was thrilled that I had managed to keep the story (more or less) to myself and celebrated by calling several friends and telling them my version of what had happened.

Two days later, I got a call from a reporter at *The New Yorker* who said he was going to write a piece about the episode. I still didn't feel comfortable discussing the event, but I called Elaine Wynn and told her *The New Yorker* was going to write a story and that Steve should call the reporter back and tell him about it, since no question the story was out there.

Elaine told me that she was glad I'd called because she had awakened that morning with the realization that Steve's putting his elbow through the painting had been a sign that they were meant to keep the painting. So they were going to.

Now, in today's *New Yorker*, there's a very charming piece about the incident, and as far as I'm concerned I am entirely released from my vow of silence on the matter.

So there it is.

My weekend in Vegas.

—October 16, 2006

O. J. Again

By now I've forgotten many of the mysteries of the O. J. Simpson case, but a few of them linger in a sort of quiescent way. For example, I have never really understood those three thumps on Kato Kaelin's wall, but I don't lose sleep over them. I certainly used to, though. Back in 1995, the Simpson case threw the country (and me) into a national dither, and it took the place of life, conversation, and community. While it lasted, it became a form of bliss. To this day, when I drive the south-north route on Bundy Drive that O. J. took on his way home from having murdered Nicole, I'm in Nancy Drew mode—I look carefully on both sides of the street along the way just in case I spot O. J.'s bloody clothes that have been missing for twelve years now. You never know. I might find them. And then I, too, could become part of the story.

All sorts of people have become part of the O. J. story; in fact, many of them have careers almost entirely because Nicole Brown Simpson and Ronald Goldman were murdered. I like to amuse myself by wondering—if those people could be given the magical power to bring Nicole and Ron back to life, would they do it, given that their careers would never have happened? Oh well. Why even ask the question?

In any case, the Simpson case Cast of Characters now has a new member, and I would like to take this moment to welcome her to the mix. She is, as you no doubt know, the publisher Judith Regan, who announced this week that she would be publishing a book (and interviewing O. J. in connection with it) called *If I Did It*. Apparently it's a confession of sorts.

I should declare a bias—I've met Judith Regan on several occasions, and we have something in common: we both survived bad divorces without having to move to Connecticut. She has spent her life working hard and (as a sideline, or is it the other way around?) popping up in many dramas, the most compelling of which is her own personal life, which has contained a number of exciting episodes, including her bad divorce, a major run-in with the New York police over a parking space that led (as I recall) to a night in jail, and a very messy affair with the former (now discredited) New York City police commissioner Bernard Kerik (whom she also published), which, in its happy beginnings, included his dispatching the police department to retrieve her lost cell phone, and which, at its end, involved stalking (on his part), once again with the help of the police. (Along the way, there were a series of trysts in a downtown apartment that was donated to the city in order to give Kerik a place to lay his weary head during his investigative work in the aftermath of 9/11.)

In any case, I like Judith Regan; I can't help it. And I was sad this week when she felt she had to defend her decision to publish and interview O. J. by issuing a 2,200-word statement on the subject, most of which appeared in Friday's *New York Post*. (Ms. Regan's publishing house is owned by Rupert Murdoch.) In it, Regan claims that she published O. J. because, having been beaten up by a former boyfriend, she's on a personal crusade against domestic abuse:

> I did the book and sat face to face with the killer because I wanted him and the men who broke my heart and your hearts

to tell the truth . . . to confess to their sins, to do penance and to amend their lives. Amen. Fifty-three years prepared me for this conversation. The men who lied and cheated and beat me. They were all there in the room. And the people who denied it, they were there, too. And though it might sound a little strange, Nicole and Ron were in my heart.

I wish Judith Regan had checked with me before issuing this statement. I'm a big believer in not explaining any more than you have to. I'm also a believer in not using the word "Amen," although I'm guilty of it from time to time. And I don't think you have to go all the way to *Mein Kampf* (which Regan used as an example of a book that is still in print after all these years, having also been written by a less-than-likeable author) to defend publishing whatever this thing is that O. J. and his ghostwriter have come up with. I don't really think you have to defend publishing this book at all. It's news. Just get it out there.

And while you're at it, please find out what those three thumps were on Kato Kaelin's window.

I'd really like to know.

—April 18, 2006

Say It Ain't So, Rupe

He pulled it? Rupert Murdoch pulled the O. J. book and the O. J. special? And Rupert Murdoch personally issued a statement of apology for causing pain to the families of the victims? Is this possible? When you live in New York City, when you read Murdoch's *New York Post* every day, it's hard to imagine that there's anything that could possibly make Rupert Murdoch lose his tabloid nerve or apologize for causing pain to anyone. I mean, what is a tabloid? It's a paper that causes pain to at least half the people it writes about every single day.

What a shame. I wasn't planning to watch O. J. on television or buy the book, but I was certainly planning to read about it. I didn't expect the book to be good, and I certainly didn't expect it to sell enough copies to justify whatever Judith Regan was paying to publish it, but I was looking forward to another bath of O. J. stuff. These American mysteries have a way of washing back every so often—the death of Marilyn Monroe has a half-life more powerful than plutonium—and in some weird way, they're like old acquaintances. Now that Murdoch has lost his nerve, isn't anyone going to publish this garbage? Where's Lyle Stuart now that we need him? Oh well.

—November 20, 2006

Melancholy Babies

So according to Robert Novak, Donald Rumsfeld received a standing ovation at the *American Spectator* dinner last week—not because of his performance as defense secretary but because the audience wanted to make Rummy feel better because they knew that President Bush had hurt his feelings.

"The day after the election," Novak writes of Rumsfeld, "he had seemed devastated—the familiar confident grin gone and his voice breaking. According to administration officials, only three or four people knew he would be fired—and Rumsfeld was not one of them. His fellow presidential appointees, including some who did not applaud Rumsfeld's performance in office, were taken aback by his treatment."

Good gracious me. Donald Rumsfeld, who to the best of my knowledge has not lost a wink of sleep since he helped lead us into this sorry war, spent a whole day on the verge of tears because of the way he was fired? Because no one had the courtesy to tell him in advance? Because he believed it when Bush told the press that Rumsfeld would serve until the end of his presidency?

I love this.

People actually think that there's a good way to be fired.

They get fired, and no matter what they were doing before being fired—losing an unwinnable war, running things into the ground, failing to meet the metrics, or merely holding on to a job that was destined for downsizing—they complain afterward about the way they were fired instead of about what really bothers them, which is that they were fired at all. After years of wielding power, personally firing people right and left, and, in Rumsfeld's case, actually authorizing the illegal torture of prisoners, they try to worm their way to a scenario meant to entitle them to a wave of sympathy that will obliterate whatever reasons they were fired for in the first place.

My favorite of these Firing Victim scenarios is the one called "They fired me on my birthday." You can't imagine how many people walk around complaining that they were fired on their birthdays. "They fired me while I was in the hospital." "They fired me a week after my mother's funeral." "They fired me right before Christmas." Almost any firing can be made into a Firing Victim scenario, especially if you throw in national holidays. I recently bumped into a Very Powerful Woman who complained bitterly that she had just been fired while her partner was in labor. I mean, I'm sorry the woman was fired, but how was anyone to know that her partner was in labor? Was this common knowledge? Had the labor been going on for days? And how long would the person who fired this woman have had to wait? Until the epidural wore off? Until the baby was home from the hospital?

Here's my point: there's no good way to be fired and there's no good day to be fired.

But here are all these Republicans at the *American Spectator* dinner, making the mistake of believing that at the very least ("at the very least" being a key phrase in such episodes) Rumsfeld was entitled to be treated better because of his loyalty to the president.

By the way, Novak writes that Rumsfeld isn't the only member of the Bush Administration who has Lost His Happy: Vice President Cheney is "profoundly disturbed" at the way Rumsfeld was treated and recently "appeared melancholy." We will leave aside the question of how anyone can evaluate the levels of Dick Cheney's melancholy and instead wonder whether Cheney is feeling bad because he sees the handwriting on wall. Who knows? Maybe the rumor is true, and he's next.

—November 26, 2006

Take My Secretary of State, Please

I met Condoleezza Rice last weekend. She was much prettier than I thought she was going to be. This was at the State Department dinner the night before the Kennedy Center Honors. She was wearing a beautiful green evening dress, and she looked great. That gap between her front teeth is not as bad in person as it is on television. I've always wanted to talk to Condi about that gap because it's very easy to fix and I know a good celebrity dentist who can do the job in less than twenty-four hours. He's expensive but Condi makes a decent salary, and let's face it, she hasn't picked up a check for the last six years, so she can afford it.

Anyway, Condi was the hostess of the dinner, and she stood up to speak about each of the honorees. She was completely competent. She was, however, not at all funny. She tried to be, but she wasn't. She was what I call not just "not funny" but "NF," which is far worse—it's truly, deeply, tragically not funny. I mention this because it may help explain why Christopher Hitchens has written a piece called "Why Women Aren't Funny" in this month's *Vanity Fair*. I can only assume that it's because he's spent too much time living in the same city with Condoleezza Rice.

Hitchens's thesis (let's be honest about it) has a germ of truth. There are plenty of funny women, way more than there used to be, but as a rule women are not as funny as men. The reasons are simple, and fairly boring. Hitchens quotes at length from a Stanford University study that proves conclusively that women don't respond to punch lines as enthusiastically as men do; I can't imagine why he even brings up the study unless he has a word count he's trying to meet. Why not just get right down to it? Men love jokes, women don't. Men tell jokes, women can't. Men have cocks, women don't. End of story.

By the way, I should confess I love Christopher Hitchens, but the man once wrote that Bob Hope was not funny. That is not true. Bob Hope is empirically funny.

But my subject is Condi, not Bob Hope. Condoleezza Rice was once a provost, and if there's ever been a job description that doesn't require humor, it's provost. She was an expert on the Soviet Union. I mean, what would that be like? You spend your academic life becoming an expert on something that one day just ceases to exist. Everything you once knew turns out to be outdated, irrelevant, and wrong. That alone could cause you to lose your gift for humor, if you ever had one.

But what Condi is really good at is making nice, which is the opposite of being funny. I've always believed that women of my generation (and hers) were literally trained to make nice. It wasn't really important for us to have opinions of our own; instead, we were supposed to preside over dinner parties, and when two men at the table disagreed violently with each other, we were supposed to step in and point out the remarkable similarities between their opposing positions.

Condoleezza Rice's compulsion to make nice is discussed in the same January *Vanity Fair* in which the Hitchens piece appears, in an amazing article by David Rose about the neocons and their remorse about the Iraq War. Why this piece hasn't been on the front page of every newspaper is mystifying. It's full of jaw-dropping interviews with people like Richard Perle, Kenneth Adelman, and David Frum, all of them blaming everyone in sight (including themselves) for this mess we've made. According to neocon Michael Ledeen, Condi saw her job as "conflict resolution, so that when Powell and Rumsfeld disagreed, which did happen from time to time, she would say to Hadley or whomever, 'Okay, try to find some middle ground where they can both agree.' So then it would descend at least one level in the bureaucracy, and people would be asked to draft new memos. . . . Thousands of hours were wasted by searching for middle ground, which most of the time will not exist." Ledeen claims that the best way to understand the Bush Administration is to look at who the most powerful people in the White House are: "They are women who are in love with the President: Laura, Condi, Harriet Miers and Karen Hughes."

I don't actually believe that we went to war in Iraq because of the women in the White House—if there was ever an episode caused by misplaced testosterone, this was it. And I don't think you can blame Condoleezza Rice for trying to find a middle ground—after all, that's part of what politics is. But it's increasingly clear that the search for a middle ground when it comes to Iraq is fruitless and, what's more, that all the middle-ground solutions (like waiting to leave until the Iraqi military functions on its own) will simply lead to months and years of quagmire.

Meanwhile, the woman is still with us, more powerful and more disconnected from reality than ever. She apparently still believes there's no point in talking to Syria and Iran. She still believes that democracy is a feasible goal in Iraq. At the State Department dinner, I watched her speak about the arts. "Arts flourish most when they happen in a democracy," she said. "The arts give expression to human spirit and give expression to human freedom."

This remark—coming as it does from a key figure in an administration that's done more to cut back on funding for the arts than any in recent history—would be funny if it weren't so serious. As it is, it's not just "not funny," it's "NF."

—December 9, 2006

On Being Named Person of the Year

It never crossed my mind that when I was finally named Person of the Year by *Time* magazine, which I seem to have been, I would find it out by reading the morning newspaper on the actual day *Time* magazine appeared. It never occurred to me that they would be able to assemble an entire article about me without even calling. I was busy this week, it's true, I had a lot of Christmas shopping, but I could have squeezed them in. But I realize now that this was just part of how brilliant it all is on the part of *Time*, how fantastically cutting-edge and New Media! Do an article about someone and don't even call them! It's so now! It's so bloggy! Ontology recapitulates phylogeny! If you know what I mean!

Still, I can't quite believe it. I'm easy to reach. I so have things to say about being Person of the Year. *Time* might want to know how I manage to Do It All, which I do. They might want my favorite new recipe, for leek bread pudding (although they could copy it out of the December *Martha Stewart*, where I got it). They might want to know about my favorite new ice cream flavor (Häagen-Dazs caramel cone), although I already mentioned it in a recent blog; God forbid there should be any fact about me that isn't known to just about everyone. I mean, that's how it is here in the new digital democracy: we tell everyone everything.

But as I said, they did it without me. The Person of the Year is me. Of course the person of the year is also you. Actually the person of the year is "You," as in YouTube and MySpace, as in the World Wide Web—"for seizing the reins of the global media, for founding and framing the new digital democracy, for working for nothing and beating the pros at their own game." Don't you love it? I especially love the part about "working for nothing"; I especially love the condescension in that phrase, the dead giveaway about how *Time* magazine really feels about the giant collective unwashed, unpaid You out Here that is nonetheless making life a misery for Them in There—for the Old Media scrambling to figure out What It Means for things like the future of print, the paper business, network television, privacy, and their jobs, for which (it goes without saying) they are paid.

I feel happy of course to be the Person of the Year, and at some point I will celebrate by doing what I always do on Sunday morning. I will make breakfast (What to cook? Biscuits? Waffles? Eggs?) and watch the morning talk shows. The morning talk shows will remind me (not that I need to be reminded) that the world is currently in the midst of a total meltdown, that we have the worst president in current history, that the elation of the recent election has passed to a numbing foreboding that nothing is going to change and that innocent people will continue to die in this hateful, violent episode we've unleashed. Less than two weeks ago, the long-awaited Baker Commission report was issued, and it died faster than *Snakes on a Plane*.

But I am not going to focus on any of these things, because I am the Person of the Year. It's me, me, me—or, as *Time* magazine insists on putting it, you, you, you. Last year, *Time*'s Person of the Year was actually three people—Bill and Melinda Gates, and Bono. I thought they were a brilliant choice, and the selection had a way of focusing the year and making me view the world in a different way, as smart, brave editorial selections sometimes do. "You," *Time* tells us, beat out Iran's president Ahmadinejad, China's president Hu Jintao, North Korea's Kim Jong Il, and my own candidates—the Fab Four: President Bush, Donald Rumsfeld, Dick Cheney, and Condoleezza Rice.

I'm proud of me. I'm proud of "You." I'm proud of us. But like all people who stand before you holding a trophy, I feel compelled to say that I can't help thinking a mistake has been made, and unlike most of the people who utter those bromidic words, I actually believe them.

—December 17, 2006

Condi's Diary

What a week! First of all, Harriet's gone! Yay! A big victory *pour moi*. They forced her out. Goodbye, Harriet, good riddance to you and your royal blue suit! Now if only I could just get rid of that Karen. She left once, in 2002, and do you know what she said when she resigned? She said she needed to spend more time with her family. Was that a dig at me, Dear Diary? Of course it was. I didn't realize it at the time, but now I do. (Two years later, when Karen insisted on coming back, I was worried she would retake her place in the P.'s heart, so I suggested she go on a never-ending mission to make people in the Middle East love America. Ha ha ha ha ha.)

But what a week! We had lots and lots o' meetings. What should we do? Should we do less? Should we do more? Less? More? Less? More? No one knew. So this is a quagmire! You hear about quagmires but until you're in one you just have no idea! And here's the best thing about those meetings: no Laura. Ever since I accidentally called her husband "my husband," things have been a little bit sticky between me and Laura. A couple of months ago she was asked if she thought I should be president, and do you know what she said? She said: "Dr. Rice, who I think would be a really good candidate, is not interested. Probably because she is single, her parents are no longer living, she's an only child. You need a very supportive family and supportive friends to have this job." Was that a dig at me, Dear Diary? Of course it was. I didn't realize it at the time, but now I do.

But back to what I was saying: *quelle semaine!* The P. spoke in the library. It was so cute, him standing against the background of the books and stuff. Then, the very next day, I got to defend him. And it was hard, it was sooooo hard, but I did it! I saw myself on television later, and I was all hunched over like I expected everyone to hit me. And they did hit me. But I didn't care because I was defending the P. and his new policy, which I forgot to mention we finally decided on—the More option, not the Less option. When my testimony was over, all I could think was, I hope the P. was watching me. I hope he knows I'd do anything for him, absolutely anything, and that includes you know what. (I know he's never going to leave her, but a girl can't help hoping!)

Then I got back to the office afterward, and there were all these messages from the White House. I was sure they were calling to tell me how much the P. loved my testimony. But it turned out he hadn't seen any of it—he'd spent the entire day on the treadmill watching the World Series of Poker on the TiVo.

But Tony Snow and Karl Rove had seen me, and they were calling to ask about what Barbara Boxer said to me at the hearing. I felt so dumb, Dear Diary. It turned out she had really insulted me, but I was so busy wrinkling my forehead I hadn't really clocked it. She'd been asking me about the war, and she'd said to me: "The issue is who pays the price? I'm not going to pay a personal price. My kids are too old and my grandchild is too young. You're not going to pay a particular price, as I understand it, with an immediate family. So who pays the price? The American military and their families."

Karl and Tony said: "How does that make you feel? Doesn't it make you feel terrible?"

"Not as terrible as Chuck Hagel made me feel," I said. "Chuck Hagel actually insulted our policy! He insulted the P.!"

"Never mind that," Karl Rove said. "Barbara Boxer insulted you."

"Not really," I said. "All she was saying was that the war was being conducted by people with nothing to lose."

But Karl and Tony disagreed. "What's more," said Tony Snow, "it's a setback for feminism."

"Feminism?" I said. "Do we care about feminism?"

"We do," said Tony Snow. "Now we do."

"No one told me," I said.

I got so irritated I almost lost my temper. I mean, guys, just tell me what you want me to say and I'll say it! But I can't say it if you don't tell me!!!!!

The next day I told the *New York Times* that I'd been insulted by Barbara Boxer. I said it was a setback for feminism. "I thought it was okay to be single," I said. "I thought it was okay to not have children and I thought you could still make good decisions on behalf of the country if you were single and didn't have children."

I hope the P. sees what I said. I doubt if he will, though, because he doesn't read the papers. But still, I'm glad I struck back at that Senator Boxer. Was that a dig at me, Dear Diary? Of course it was. I didn't realize it at the time, but now I do.

—January 14, 2007

Some People

"Some people" are saying that Katie Couric went too far on *60 Minutes*. I don't actually know who those people are, because I haven't done any reporting on it. Why bother? "Some people" must be saying it. "Some people" will say anything. And there's no real need to mention their names, because I can just say that "some people" are saying it and get away with it.

Last night on *60 Minutes*, Katie Couric kept referring to "some people." She said that "some" were saying the Edwardses were courageous, and "others" were saying they were callous and ambitious. She said that some people were wondering how someone could be president if he was "distracted" by his wife's health. (This question, in a year when there are two presidential candidates who are themselves cancer survivors, seemed particularly disingenuous.) (And never mind that it was being asked by someone who managed to keep working while dealing with her own husband's terminal illness.)

I kept waiting for John or Elizabeth Edwards to ask her who "some people" were exactly, but they didn't. They cheerfully answered her questions. Elizabeth Edwards said, "We're all going to die." And: "I pretty much know what I'm going to die of now." She said that on hearing that her cancer had recurred, she realized she had a choice—to go on living her life, or begin dying. She said she had chosen to go on living her life. Katie Couric looked at her as if someone had set off a stink-bomb in the room and then asked another "some people" question, this one about whether the Edwardses were "in denial."

I don't know what some people think, but I myself think it's weird to question the Edwardses as if there's some right way to deal with cancer. There's no real way to know how one is going to deal with such things until they happen, and even then, there's no way to apply the way one person chooses to deal with mortal illness to another. And I disagree with Elizabeth Edwards when she says that there are only two choices—to go on living, or begin dying. What I believe instead is that at a certain point in life, whether or not you've been diagnosed with illness, you enter into a conscious, ongoing, unending, eternal, puzzling, confusing negotiation between the two. Some days one of them wins, and some days the other. This negotiation often includes decisions as trivial as whether to eat a second piece of pie, and as important as whether to have medical treatment that may or may not prolong your life.

I also believe that nothing anyone says in such circumstances means anything except at that very moment—and even then, perhaps not. These decisions are private in the most serious sense of the word, which is not to say that they are nobody's business—if you run for president everything you do is somebody's business—but that they reside in an area where things change, where people are not bound to whatever course of action they committed to the day before yesterday. It's a zone of privacy that's like no other and is therefore (or should be) virtually immune to judgment.

Last night on *60 Minutes*, Katie Couric quoted John Edwards's remark earlier in the week—that he was in the race "for the duration"— and asked him, "How can you say that, Senator Edwards, with such certainty? If, God forbid, Elizabeth doesn't respond to whatever treatment is recommended, if her health deteriorates, would you really say that?" Thank you, Katie. Thank you for asking that question. The world could not have survived had you not asked it. Of course, "some people" were undoubtedly thinking it. And it would have been a tragedy not to have given voice to that thought, wouldn't it? Or would it?

—March 26, 2007

What Did You Do in the War?

One of the things I've always wondered about was what it was like to live in the United States during World War II. It was one of the things I'd have most wanted to ask my parents about if they were still alive—my own particular "What did you do in the war, Daddy?" question.

I don't literally want to know what my parents did during the war. I know. My father had flat feet, so he was 4F. But what I truly wondered was what they knew and when they knew it—about the Holocaust, for example, and the Japanese internment camps. It was a complete mystery to me. I read a half-dozen books on the subject of the United States and the Holocaust and I could never imagine how so many people could have known what they knew and done nothing. Did my parents know? Probably they did. Did they do anything? Probably they didn't. And why not?

In any case, I don't much wonder about this anymore, because I know the answer. I know because Guantánamo prison is now more than five years old, five years of our holding and torturing prisoners without bail and without the rights of habeus corpus. Of the 385 men detained at Guantánamo, only ten have been charged. How is this possible? In the United States of America? You can blame Bush/Cheney if you want; you can blame our justice system, which moves sluggishly through the Guantánamo cases, deferring to the legislative branch, which then does nothing. But what about us? What are we doing about Guantánamo? Nothing, just as my parents did nothing about the injustices they knew about. And why not? It's simple. We're too busy.

The news in this morning's paper that thirteen Guantánamo prisoners have started a hunger strike and are being force-fed is heartbreaking, because these prisoners are assuming that somewhere out there is a way of reaching the American people, triggering a sense of injustice, and eventually causing a wave of international opprobrium to smack into the White House and somehow affect the war criminals who are running the country. This, of course, will never come to pass: the only good thing that's happened to George Bush since the glory days of 9/11 is that the terrorists haven't attacked us again here in America, and the reason they haven't (in the Bush/Cheney scenario) is that we've managed to lock them all up on an island no one can get to. This was a brilliant move, by the way, and you have to hand it to the guys who thought it up: the prisoners can't be seen (by us or by the press) and most of them are faceless and stateless.

On Friday night we went downtown to see the writer Lawrence Wright, the author of *The Looming Tower*, perform his one-man show called *My Trip to Al-Qaeda*. It's a completely riveting evening, and it begins with Wright's story about *The Siege*, a Denzel Washington movie about terrorism that Wright wrote and which some blamed for inciting a terrorist act that resulted in the death of one person and the crippling of another. It was a stupid, mindless act on the part of the terrorists, obviously, but Wright understands that if he hadn't written the movie, it might never have happened. It led him to write his brilliant book, and then, to write and perform his play about terrorism and torture and his own response to what he's learned. The evening is full of chilling observations about the enemy. "Perhaps Al-Qaeda can best be understood as an engine that runs on the despair of the Muslim world, especially its young men, whose lives are so futile and unexpressed," Wright says. "Al-Qaeda offers them a chance to make history. All they have to do is die." But it's equally chilling about us—the evening ends with an image of Abu Ghraib projected on a screen onstage, of American soldiers threatening a naked, blindfolded prisoner with a wild dog.

We will never be able to tell our children that we didn't know it was happening. And what will we say when they ask what we did about it? Will we tell them the truth—that we were too busy?

—April 9, 2007

How to Foil a Terrorist Plot
in Seven Simple Steps

1. In order to foil a terrorist plot, you must first find a terrorist plot. This is not easy.

2. Not just anyone can find and then foil a terrorist plot. You must have an incentive. The best incentive is to be an accused felon, looking at a long prison term. Under such circumstances, your lawyer will explain to you, you may be able to reduce your sentence by acting as an informant in a criminal case, preferably one involving terrorists.

3. The fact that you do not know any actual terrorists should not in any way deter you. Necessity is the mother of invention: if you can find the right raw material—a sad, sick, lonely, drunk, deranged, disgruntled, or just plain anti-American Muslim somewhere in the United States—you can make your very own terrorist.

4. Now the good part begins. Money! The FBI will give you lots of money to take your very own terrorist out to lots of dinners where you, wearing a wire, can record yourself making recommendations to him about possible targets and weapons that might be used in the impending terrorist attack that your very own terrorist is going to mastermind, with your help. It will even buy you a computer so you can go to Google Earth in order to show your very own terrorist a "top secret" aerial image of the target you have suggested.

5. More money!! The FBI will give you even more money to travel to foreign countries with your very own terrorist, and it will make suggestions about terrorist groups you can meet while in said foreign countries.

6. Months and even years will pass in this fashion, while you essentially get the FBI to pay for everything you do. (Incidentally, be sure your lawyer negotiates your expense account well in advance, or you may be forced—as the informant was in the Buffalo terrorist case—to protest your inadequate remuneration by setting yourself on fire in front of the White House.)

7. At a certain point, something will go wrong. You may have

trouble recruiting other people to collaborate with your very own terrorist, who is, as you yourself know, just an ordinary guy in a really bad mood. Or, alternatively, the terrorist cell you have carefully cobbled together may malfunction and fail to move forward—probably as a result of sheer incompetence or of simply not having been genuinely serious about the acts of terrorism you were urging it to commit. At this point, you may worry that the FBI is going to realize that there isn't much of a terrorist plot going on here at all, just a case of entrapment. Do not despair: the FBI is way ahead of you. The FBI knows perfectly well what's going on. The FBI has as much at stake as you do. So before it can be obvious to the world that there's no case, the FBI will arrest your very own terrorist, hold a press conference, and announce that a huge terrorist plot has been foiled. It will of course be forced to admit that this plot did not proceed beyond the preplanning stage, that no actual weapons or money were involved, and that the plot itself was "not technically feasible," but that will not stop the story from becoming a front-page episode all over America and, within hours, boilerplate for all the Republican politicians who believe that you need to arrest a "homegrown" terrorist now and then to justify the continuing war in Iraq. Everyone will be happy, except for the schmuck you shmekeled into becoming a terrorist, and no one really cares about him anyway. So congratulations. You have foiled a terrorist plot. Way to go.

—June 4, 2007

My Top Ten New Year's Resolutions

I just read my New Year's resolutions from last year, and I'm sorry to say that I managed to carry out almost none of them. I vowed to lose two pounds; I didn't. I was going to cook a timballo; I didn't. I promised myself I would leave America Online, and I almost succeeded, but after deciding where to go, I discovered that I couldn't even get my own name as a handle, so that was pretty much that. Last year I even resolved to become a better human being, but then I promptly forgot all about it.

It's discouraging that I couldn't manage to carry out any of these resolutions, which are minimal and personal and easily achievable, to put it mildly, and it crossed my mind that perhaps my problem is that I'm aiming too low—I'm doing the traditional thing, which is to resolve to do something I have control over, as opposed to something that's completely out of reach.

So here's a list of my resolutions for 2008, which it seems to me I have as good a chance of carrying out as last year's:

1. End the war in Iraq. I've wanted to do this for a long time, and I'm not talking about a slow withdrawal, I'm talking about just getting the hell out. This resolution involves my becoming Speaker of the House and majority leader of the Senate and whipping the entire Democratic membership of Congress into a brilliant frenzy of opposition that includes (but is not limited to) refusing to fund a penny more for the war.

2. Make sure a Democrat is elected president. Any Democrat. I wish it were going to be Chris Dodd, who would make a great president, but he doesn't have a shot. But I'll take anyone who's running. And I promise to try not to find fault with the candidate, whoever he or she is, even though it will be hard and will probably require a personality transplant on my part.

3. In the meantime, while George Bush is still president, I will persuade him to get behind the threat of global warming. I plan to do this by slipping into the White House in the dead of night, tying the president naked to a bedpost, and forcing him to watch footage of the melting polar ice cap until he concedes.

4. Close the prison at Guantánamo Bay and then, in my capacity as special prosecutor, indict and convict all the American officials who condoned torture, from Rumsfeld on down.

5. Get William Kristol fired from the *New York Times*. I don't think any actual work is going to be required in this area; this will come to pass as soon as he starts writing for the paper and whoever hired him actually reads his copy. But how did this happen? I have been watching this supercilious man smirk on Fox News for years, but it never crossed my mind that I would someday have to waste a perfectly good New Year's resolution on him.

6. Kill Osama bin Laden. Everyone has almost forgotten about him, but I haven't. I would send a SWAT team headed by Kiefer

Sutherland and Matt Damon into Afghanistan or Pakistan or wherever, and although the two of them would continually disagree about methods, they would eventually get their man.

7. Decide whether I would rather impeach Dick Cheney or Clarence Thomas. I always have a hard time figuring out which of these two I would rather do without, but this year I am definitely going to make a decision on the question, and there's no telling what might happen once I do. At the moment I'm leaning toward Clarence Thomas, but that's because I just read *The Nine* by Jeffrey Toobin (which I highly recommend) and the Supreme Court is on my mind. (By the way, if I choose to impeach Clarence Thomas, my scenario includes another brave moment from the Democrats in Congress, who under my leadership refuse to approve Bush's nominee to the Court and hold up the appointment until the next president is elected.)

8. Start a universal health care program and put Oprah Winfrey in charge of it. She can figure the whole thing out, and I, therefore, won't have to.

9. Get the United States government to fund an endowment to lend money, interest-free, to anyone who wants to go to college, and to refinance (also interest-free) the college loans of all the adults who are walking around saddled with interest payments on their tuition debt. This might require my becoming education czar, which in turn would require my becoming involved in improving school lunches, which would be good for everyone involved, trust me.

10. Cook a timballo.

—January 1, 2008

Hooked on Hillary

I would like to put myself among the growing chorus of people demanding that Hillary Clinton withdraw from the election. I don't really think it's fair to ask her to withdraw, and I certainly don't believe she's going to; she'll hang in there 'til the last dog dies, or 'til she runs out of money, whichever comes first. I'm not asking her to withdraw because I prefer Obama, and I don't think she should withdraw "for the sake of party unity," or whatever current bromide is being flung at her to get her to pull out. I think she should withdraw because I'm losing my mind.

Don't get me wrong, this primary election has been swell. Like Michelle Obama, I feel proud of my country for the first time in a long time. I loved Dennis Kucinich, and I had a big sneaker for Chris Dodd. But now that we're down to two contenders, it's turned into an unending last episode of *Survivor*. They're eating rats and they're frying bugs, and they're frying rats and they're eating bugs; no one is ever going to get off the island and I can't take it anymore.

I am particularly sensitive to this because I'm a woman of a certain age, and this means that part of the pie that passes for my brain contains a large slice called Hillary. I've been thinking about her in a fairly pathological way ever since 1992 and dreaming about her as well. She is me, and then again she's not. I used to love her and I no longer do, but unlike what usually happens when love dies, I still think about her far too much. When she tells a big lie, like her recent Bosnia episode, I can lose hours trying to figure out why. I mean, why? Was it one of those things that she'd said so often that she'd come to believe it? Was it a story that had worked in the past so she thought she'd gotten away with it? Did she honestly think that no one would rat her out? Does she not understand that if you're famous, there's almost nothing you do that someone doesn't have a picture of? I have no idea what the answer is to any of this because I'm not a liar and she is. (By the way, I don't think she was always a liar, the way some kids are born liars and never get over it. I think she was once a truthful person and her lying skills were forged in the early years of her marriage, forged in the crucible of Bill's infidelities and in her role as point person in dealing with them. This is what happens when you marry a narcissist: he spills the milk, you clean it up, and your love grows. And then you end up a liar, just like him.)

But the point is that it doesn't matter why Hillary lied; what matters is that I'm hooked on Hillary and on the Rorschach process that defines my relationship with her: she does something, I spend far too much time thinking about it, I superimpose my life and my choices onto hers, I decide how I feel about what she's done, I bore friends witless with my theories, and then, instead of moving on, I'm confronted with yet another episode of her behavior and am forced to devote more hours to developing new theories about her behavior. I don't have time for this.

I understand that asking Hillary to withdraw from the race has more to do with me than it does with her, but that's my point.

—March 30, 2008

White Men

Here's another thing I don't like about this primary: now that there are only two Democratic candidates, it's suddenly horribly absolutely crystal-clear that this is an election about gender and race. This may have always been true, but weeks ago it wasn't so obvious—once upon a time there were eight candidates, and although six of them withered away, their presence in the campaign managed to obscure things. Even around the time of Ohio, when there were primarily three candidates, the outlines were murky, because Edwards was still in there, picking up votes from all sectors.

But now there are two and we're facing Pennsylvania and whom are we kidding? This is an election about whether the people of Pennsylvania hate blacks more than they hate women. And when I say people, I don't mean people, I mean white men. How ironic is this? After all this time, after all these stupid articles about how powerless white men are and how they can't even get into college because of overachieving women and affirmative action and mean lady teachers who expected them to sit still in the third grade even though they were all suffering from terminal attention deficit disorder—after all this, they turn out (surprise!) to have all the power. (As they always did, by the way; I hope you didn't believe any of those articles.)

To put it bluntly, the next president will be elected by them: the outcome of Tuesday's primary will depend on whether they go for Hillary or Obama, and the outcome of the general election will depend on whether enough of them vote for McCain. A lot of them will: white men cannot be relied on, as all of us know who have spent a lifetime dating them. And McCain is a compelling candidate, particularly because of the Torture Thing. As for the Democratic hope that McCain's temper will be a problem, don't bet on it. A lot of white men have terrible tempers, and what's more, they think it's normal.

If Hillary pulls it out in Pennsylvania, and she could, and if she follows it up in Indiana, she can make a credible case that she deserves to be the candidate; these last primaries will show which of the two Democratic candidates is better at overcoming the bias of a vast chunk of the population that has never in its history had to vote for anyone but a candidate who could have been their father or their brother or their son, and that has never had to think of the president of the United States as anyone other than someone they might have been had circumstances been just slightly different.

Hillary's case is not an attractive one, because what she'll essentially be saying (and has been saying, although very carefully) is that she can attract more racist white male voters than Obama can. Nonetheless, and as I said, she has a case.

I spent the weekend listening to one commentator after another saying that Obama has it locked up, it's a done deal. I dunno. Hillary is the true whack-a-mole and if she survives on Tuesday, it will be a whole new ball game. And it will be all because of white men. *Plus ça change*.

—April 20, 2008

It Ought to Be a Word

It's true what he said: we misunderestimated him.

George Bush came into his presidency with a huge wave of goodwill. Not from me, but from the others. An amazing number of people who should have known better thought of him as a charming guy whose intellectual limitations would somehow be as benign as Ronald Reagan's, whose promise of a fairly passive presidency would be as survivable as Dwight Eisenhower's. So he couldn't seem to get a sentence out straight, so what? And as for his religious rigidity, that was simply his way of dealing with an alcohol problem without the sloppy conventions of AA.

He was misunderestimated in every way. It was hard to imagine that this feckless leader could do so much damage. But even as the worst emerged, he was given the benefit of the doubt because of the ongoing mysteries of his administration—mysteries that have remained unsolved in spite of the skills of hundreds of gifted journalists who have attempted to uncover them:

- Who exactly was running the country these last eight years?
- What did the president know, if anything, and when did he know it, if ever?
- Was he capable in any way of even one sleepless night, much less the ongoing insomnia that any sentient person would suffer after so many wrong decisions and pointless deaths?
- Did he mispronounce the word "nuclear" (1) on purpose, in order to make himself seem folksy, (2) because he actually thought he was pronouncing it correctly, or (3) just to piss us off?

The exit appearances that Bush has made in recent weeks will be something future presidents will refer to as often as Lincoln's Second Inaugural, although for different reasons. Here's what he said:

- We did the best we could under the circumstances.
- It's not easy being president.
- It wasn't completely my fault.
- Everyone makes mistakes.
- I kept America safe, except for this one time.
- After that one time I worked really, really hard almost every day and had to read a lot of stuff about foreign countries.

This is Bush's legacy—a stunning series of alibis. This is what he will crawl off to Texas with, hoping that it will fool a publisher into giving him a substantial book advance and contributors into giving him money for a library full of pilfered papers.

On Monday, we will have to get used to a different thing entirely, a president who's in the loop, who reads history, who speaks decent English. He will rob of us of something—of the burning anger that has sustained us the last eight years—and that will take some adjusting to. But we're up for it; after all these years in the dark, we're ready for a little overestimation. Which is, unlike "misunderestimation," an actual word. But come to think of it, "misunderestimation" ought to be a word. I certainly know what it means.

—January 16, 2009

✳ *Personal*

The Story of My Life in 3,500 Words or Less

If I can just get back to New York, I'll be fine

I'm five years old. We've just moved from New York to Los Angeles, and I'm outside, at a playground, at my new school on Doheny Drive in Beverly Hills. The sunlight dapples through the trees, and happy laughing blond children surround me. All I can think is, What am I doing here?

What my mother said

My mother says these words at least five hundred times in the course of my growing up: "Everything is copy."

She also says, "Never ever buy a red coat."

What my teacher said

My high school journalism teacher, whose name is Charles O. Simms, is teaching us to write a lead—the first sentence or paragraph of a newspaper story. He writes the words "Who What Where When Why and How" on the blackboard. Then he dictates a set of facts to us that goes something like this: "Kenneth L. Peters, the principal of Beverly Hills High School, announced today that the faculty of the high school will travel to Sacramento on Thursday for a colloquium in new teaching methods. Speaking there will be anthropologist Margaret Mead and Robert Maynard Hutchins, the president of the University of Chicago." We all sit at our typewriters and write a lead, most of us inverting the set of facts so that they read something like this, "Anthropologist Margaret Mead and University of Chicago president Robert Maynard Hutchins will address the faculty Thursday in Sacramento at a colloquium on new teaching methods, the principal of the high school Kenneth L. Peters announced today." We turn in our leads. We're very proud. Mr. Simms looks at what we've done and then tosses everything into the garbage. He says: "The lead to the story is 'There will be no school Thursday.'" An electric lightbulb turns itself on in the balloon over my head. I decide at this moment that I am going to be a journalist. A few months later I enter a citywide contest to write an essay in fifty words or less on why I want to be a journalist. I win first prize, two tickets to the world premiere of a Doris Day movie.

I swear to God Janice Glabman will never laugh at me again

I go off to college. I weigh 106 pounds. I come back from college three months later. I weigh 126 pounds. I was once thin and shapeless. Now I am fat and, ironically, equally shapeless. Nothing fits, except for my wool plaid Pendleton pleated skirt, which makes me look even fatter. It's tragic. My father takes one look at me as I get off the plane and says to my mother, "Well, maybe someone will marry her for her personality."

I go back to college. I stay fat. There's a machine in the dormitory cafeteria called The Cow, and when you press a nozzle, out comes the coldest, most delicious milk you've ever tasted. Also there are sticky buns and popovers and scones. I have never been exposed to such wonders. I love them. I have seconds. I have thirds. There's butter everywhere you look, and of course, that cold, delicious milk. We're not talking low-fat milk, my friends. This was so long ago no one even knew about low-fat milk.

Anyway, months pass. I come home for the summer. I'm as fat as ever. None of my clothes fit. I already said that, and it's still true. And because it's summer, I can't even wear my wool plaid Pendleton pleated skirt. So I go over to my friend Janice Glabman's to borrow some clothes from her. Janice has always been overweight. I try on a pair of her pants. They're too small. They're way too small. I can't even zip them up. Janice laughs at me. These are Janice's exact words: "Ha ha ha ha ha." The next day I go on a diet. In six months my weight drops back to 106. I have been on a diet ever since.

I have not seen Janice in more than forty years, but if I do see her, I'm ready. I'm thin. Although I now weigh 126 pounds, the exact amount I weighed when I came home from college having become a butterball. I can't explain this.

I am not going to marry Stanley J. Fleck

I'm working as a summer intern in the Kennedy White House, and I'm engaged to be married to a young lawyer named Stanley J. Fleck. Everyone I know is engaged to be married. My fiancé is visiting me in Washington, and I give him a tour of the White House, which I have a pass to roam freely. I show him the Red Room. I show him the Blue

Room. I show him the beautiful portrait of Grace Coolidge. I show him the Rose Garden. At the end of the tour, he says, "No wife of mine is ever going to work at a place like this."

Sunday in the park

I'm in a rowboat on the lake in Central Park. Fortunately I'm not rowing the boat. I'm still in college, but soon I won't be, soon I'll be living here, in New York City. I look up at all the buildings surrounding the park, and it crosses my mind that except for the man rowing the boat, I don't know anyone in New York City. And I barely know the man in the boat. I wonder if I'm going to end up being one of those people you read about in newspapers, who lives in New York and never meets anyone and eventually dies and no one even notices until days later, when the smell drifts out into the hallway. I vow that someday I will know someone in New York City.

I'm going to be a newspaper reporter forever

It's 1963. I've written a piece for a parody of the *New York Post* during a long newspaper strike. The editors of the *Post* are upset about the parody, but the publisher of the *Post* is amused. "If they can parody the *Post*, they can write for it," she says. "Hire them." When the strike ends, I'm given a one-week tryout at the *Post*. The city room is dusty, dingy, and dark. The desks are dilapidated and falling apart. It smells terrible. There aren't enough phones. The city editor sends me to the Coney Island aquarium to cover the story of two hooded seals who've been brought together to mate but have refused to have anything to do with each other. I write a story. I think it's funny. I turn it in. I hear laughter from the city desk. They think it's funny too. I am hired permanently. I have never been happier. I have achieved my life's ambition, and I am twenty-two years old.

I may not be a newspaper reporter forever

One night I go to a bar near the *Post* with one of my fellow reporters and the managing editor. It's been raining. After quite a few drinks, the managing editor invites us to his home in Brooklyn Heights. When we get there, he tells me to stand on the stoop in front of the house. There's an awning over one of the windows. As I step into position, he lowers the awning, and about ten gallons of water drench me from head to toe. He thinks this is hilarious.

My life changes

I write a magazine article about having small breasts. I am now a writer.

What my mother said (2)

I now believe that what my mother meant when she said "Everything is copy" is this: When you slip on a banana peel, people laugh at you; but when you tell people you slipped on a banana peel, it's your laugh. So you become the hero rather than the victim of the joke.

I think that's what she meant.

On the other hand, she may merely have meant, "Everything is copy."

When she was in the hospital, dying, she said to me, "You're a reporter, Nora. Take notes." It seems to me this is not quite the same as "Everything is copy."

My mother died of cirrhosis, but the immediate cause of her death was an overdose of sleeping pills administered by my father. At the time this didn't seem to me to fall under the rubric of "Everything is copy." Although it did to my sister Amy, and she put it into a novel. Who can blame her?

How she died: my version

My mother is in the hospital. Every day, my father calls and says, this is it, they're pulling the plug. But there is no plug. My mother comes home. Several days pass. One day my father says, I'm going to give the nurse the night off. Late that night, he calls to tell me my mother has died. The funeral home has already come and taken away her body. I go to their apartment. It's four in the morning. I sit with my father for a while, and then we both decide to take a nap before the next day begins. My father reaches into the pocket of his bathrobe and pulls out a bottle of sleeping pills. "The doctor gave me these in case I was having trouble sleeping," he says. "Flush them down the toilet." I go into the bathroom and flush them down the toilet. The next morning, when my sisters arrive, I tell them about the pills. My sister Amy says to me, "Did you count the pills?"

"No," I say.

"Duh," she says.

I was married to him for six years

My first husband is a perfectly nice person, although he's pathologically attached to his cats. It's 1972, the height of the women's movement, and everyone is getting a divorce, even people whose husbands don't have pathological attachments to their cats. My husband is planning for us to take a photo safari through Africa, and I say to him, "I can't go on this trip."

"Why not?" he says.

"Because it's very expensive and we're probably going to split up and I'll feel horribly guilty that you spent all this money taking me to Africa."

"Don't be crazy," my husband says. "I love you and you love me and we're not getting a divorce and even if we do, you're the only person I want to go to Africa with. We're going."

So we go to Africa. It's a wonderful trip. When we come back, I tell my husband that I want a divorce. "But I took you to Africa!" he says.

You can't make this stuff up

I'm working on a magazine story about a woman who was fired from her job as president of Bennington College. I have read a story about her in the *New York Times* that says she's been fired—along with her husband, the vice president of Bennington—because of her brave stand against tenure. I suspect her firing has nothing to do with her brave stand against tenure, although I don't have a clue what the real reason is. I go to Bennington and discover that she has in fact been fired because she's been having an affair with a professor at Bennington, that they taught a class on Hawthorne together, and that they both wore matching T-shirts in class with scarlet *A*'s on them. What's more, I learn that the faculty hated her from the very beginning because she had a party for them and served lukewarm lasagna and unthawed Sara Lee banana cake. I can't get over this aspect of journalism. I can't believe how real life never lets you down. I can't understand why anyone would write fiction when what actually happens is so amazing.

Everything is copy

I'm seven months pregnant with my second child, and I've just discovered that my second husband is in love with someone else. She too is married. Her husband telephones me. He's the British ambassador to the

United States. I'm not kidding. He happens to be the kind of person who tends to see almost everything in global terms. He suggests lunch. We meet outside a Chinese restaurant on Connecticut Avenue and fall into each other's arms, weeping. "Oh, Peter," I say to him, "isn't it awful?"

"It's awful," he says. "What's happening to this country?"

I'm crying hysterically, but I'm thinking, someday this will be a funny story.

I was married to him for two years and eight months

I fly to New York to see my shrink. I walk into her office and burst into tears. I tell her what my husband has done to me. I tell her my heart is broken. I tell her I'm a total mess and I will never be the same. I can't stop crying. She looks at me and says, "You have to understand something: You were going to leave him eventually."

On the other hand, perhaps you can make this stuff up

So I write a novel. I change my first husband's cats into hamsters, and I change the British ambassador into an undersecretary of state, and I give my second husband a beard.

One of the saddest things about divorce

My sister Delia says this, and it's true. When we were growing up, we used to love to hear the story of how our parents met and fell in love and eloped one summer when they were both camp counselors. It was so much a part of our lives, a song sung again and again, and no matter what happened, no matter how awful things became between the two of them, we always knew that our parents had once been madly in love.

But in a divorce, you never tell your children that you were once madly in love with their father because it would be too confusing.

And then, after a while, you can't even remember whether you were.

A man and a woman live in a house on a deserted peninsula

Alice Arlen and I have written a script for the movie *Silkwood*. It's based on the true story of Karen Silkwood, who worked at a plutonium plant in Oklahoma; she died in a mysterious automobile accident while on her way to meet a *New York Times* reporter to talk about conditions in the plant. Mike Nichols is going to direct it; he was supposed to direct a Broadway musical instead, but it all fell through because he was betrayed by a close friend who was involved with the show. We will call the close friend Jane Doe for the purposes of this story.

So we all start to work together on the next draft of the script, and Mike keeps suggesting scenes for the movie that involve Karen Silkwood's being betrayed by a close woman friend. He has a million ideas along these lines, none of which really bear any resemblance to what happened to Karen Silkwood but all of which bear a resemblance to what happened between Mike and his friend Jane. I finally say, "Mike, Jane Doe did not kill Karen Silkwood."

"Yes," Mike says, "I see what you're saying. It's the peninsula story."

And he tells us the peninsula story:

A man and a woman live in a house on a deserted peninsula. The man's mother comes to stay with them, and the man goes off on a business trip. The woman takes the ferry to the mainland and goes to see her lover. They make love. When they finish, she realizes it's late, and she gets up, dresses, and rushes to catch the last ferry home. But she misses the boat. She pleads with the ferryboat captain. He tells her he will take her back to the peninsula if she gives him six times the normal fare. But she doesn't have the money. So she's forced to walk home, and on the way, she's raped and killed by a stranger.

And the question is: Who is responsible for her death, and in what order—the woman, the man, the mother, the ferryboat captain, the lover, or the rapist?

The question is a Rorschach, Mike says, and if you ask your friends to answer it, they will all answer differently.

Another lightbulb moment.

This one marks the end of my love affair with journalism and the beginning of my understanding that just about everything is a story.

Or, as E. L. Doctorow once wrote, far more succinctly

"I am led to the proposition that there is no fiction or nonfiction as we commonly understand the distinction; there is only narrative."

From my script for When Harry Met Sally

HARRY: Why don't you tell me the story of your life?
SALLY: The story of my life?
HARRY: We've got eighteen hours to kill before we hit New York.

SALLY: The story of my life isn't even going to get us out of Chicago. I mean, nothing's happened to me yet. That's why I'm going to New York.

HARRY: So something can happen to you?

SALLY: Yes.

HARRY: Like what?

SALLY: Like I'm going to go to journalism school to become a reporter.

HARRY: So you can write about things that happen to other people.

SALLY: *(After a beat.)* That's one way to look at it.

HARRY: Suppose nothing happens to you. Suppose you live there your whole life and nothing happens. You never meet anyone, you never become anything, and finally you die one of those New York deaths where nobody notices for two weeks until the smell drifts out into the hallway.

A guy walks into a restaurant

I'm having dinner at a restaurant with friends. A man I know comes over to the table. He's a famously nice guy. His marriage broke up at about the same time mine did. He says, "How can I find you?"

We can't do everything

I'm sitting in a small screening room waiting for a movie to begin. The room fills up. There aren't enough seats. People are bunching up in the aisles and looking around helplessly. I'm next to my friend Bob Gottlieb, watching all this. The director of the movie decides to solve the problem by asking all the children at the screening to share seats. I watch in mounting frustration. Finally, I say to Bob, "It's really very simple. Someone should go get some folding chairs and set them up in the aisles."

Bob looks at me. "Nora," he says, "we can't do everything."

My brain clears in an amazing way.

Nora. We can't do everything.

I have been given the secret of life.

Although it's probably a little late.

And by the way

The other day I bought a red coat, on sale. But I haven't worn it yet.

—August 2006

The Legend

I grew up in Beverly Hills, in a Spanish house in the flats. My parents had a large group of friends, almost all of them transplanted New Yorkers who were in the business. That's what it was known as—the business. (People who were not in the business were known as civilians.) The men were screenwriters or television writers. Their wives did nothing. They were known at the time as housewives, but none of them did housework—they all had cooks and maids and laundresses. Our mother had household help too, but she was different: she worked. "You'll just have to tell them your mother can't be there because she has to work." My mother uttered that sentence several times a year; it was meant to get her off the hook for PTA meetings and such, but it was also meant to make us understand that she was a cut above the other mothers. She was even a cut above the other career women—there were a few in the business, including the costume designer Edith Head, whom my mother once took me to lunch with, but none of them had careers *and* children. My mother did. Also, she served delicious food, which was another way she liked to rub it in. And she could keep help. What's more, she dressed beautifully.

This was long before the concept of having it all, but my mother had it all. And then she ruined the narrative by becoming a crazy drunk. But that came later.

Every day my parents came home from work, and we all gathered in the den. My parents had drinks and there were crudités for us—although they were not called crudités at the time, they were called carrots and celery. Then we had dinner in the dining room. The plates were heated, and there were butter balls made with wooden paddles. There was an appetizer, a main course, and dessert. We thought everyone lived like this.

At our dinner table, we discussed politics and what we were reading. We told cheerful stories of what had happened in school that day. We played charades. My mother, once a camp counselor, would lead us in song. "Under the spreading chestnut tree," we would sing, and we would spread our arms and bang our chests. Or we would sing, "The bells they all go tingalingaling," and we'd clink our spoons against our glasses. We learned to believe in Lucy Stone, the New Deal, Norman Thomas, and Edward R. Murrow. We were taught that organized religion was the root of all evil and that Adlai Stevenson was God. We were indoctrinated in my mother's rules: Never buy a red coat. Red meat keeps your hair from turning gray. You *can* leave the table but you *may not* leave the table. Girdles ruin your stomach muscles. The means and the end are the same.

And there were stories, the stories we grew up on. How my parents met and fell in love. How they ran away from the camp where they were counselors and got married so they could sleep in the same tent. How my mother's aunt Minnie became the first woman dentist in the history of the world. And finally—and this is where this is all leading—how my mother threw Lillian Ross out of our house.

This was not just a story, it was a legend.

It seemed that Lillian Ross had come to one of my parents' parties. About once a year they had a big sit-down dinner for about forty people, with tables and chairs from Abbey Rents. They served their delicious food cooked by their longtime housekeeper, and my mother wore a Galanos dress bought for the occasion. All their friends were invited— Julius J. Epstein (*Casablanca*), Richard Maibaum (*The Big Clock* and, eventually, the Bond movies), Richard Breen (*Dragnet*), Charles Brackett (*Ninotchka, Sunset Boulevard*), and Albert Hackett and his wife, Frances Goodrich, who had the greatest credits of all (*The Thin Man, Seven Brides for Seven Brothers, It's a Wonderful Life, The Diary of Anne Frank*). I would stand on the second floor and look over the banister down at the parties, and listen to Herbie Baker (*The Girl Can't Help It*) play the piano after dinner. Once I caught a glimpse of Shelley Winters, who was dating Liam O'Brien (*Young at Heart*), and once Marge and Gower Champion turned up. That was as starry as it ever got.

One night, St. Clair McKelway was invited to one of my parents' parties. McKelway was a well-known *New Yorker* magazine writer who'd written a couple of movies. He called beforehand to ask if he could bring a friend, Lillian Ross. Did my mother know who she was? he asked. My mother certainly knew who she was. *The New Yorker* arrived by mail every week. Along with the Sunday *New York Times* and the *Saturday Review of Literature,* it was required reading for the diaspora of smart people living in Hollywood; reading it made them feel they hadn't lost a step, that they could move back East at a moment's notice.

Lillian Ross was young at the time, but she was already famous for her reporting in *The New Yorker,* and for her ability to make her subjects sound like fools. She had just published her devastating profile of Ernest Hemingway and was in Los Angeles reporting her piece on John Huston and the making of *The Red Badge of Courage.* My mother told St. Clair McKelway that he was welcome to bring Lillian Ross to dinner but that Ross had to agree that the party would be off the record.

So Lillian Ross came to the party. Before dinner, she asked my mother for a tour of the house. My mother showed her around, and at a certain point, Ross came upon a picture of my three sisters and me.

"Are these your children?" she asked my mother.

"Yes," my mother said.

"Do you ever see them?" Lillian Ross asked.

That did it.

My mother walked Lillian Ross downstairs and back to McKelway. "Out," she said.

And Lillian Ross and St. Clair McKelway left.

That was the legend of my mother and Lillian Ross. My mother loved to tell it. It was practically a cowboy movie. We'd been raised to believe that a woman could do everything and Lillian Ross had dared to question it. In our house. So my mother threw her out.

I loved this story. I loved all stories that proved that my mother was right and everyone else was wrong, especially since there was a piece of me that couldn't help wishing she was exactly like everyone else's mother.

It was at least ten years before I began to wonder about it. Had it ever actually happened? There are all sorts of stories you grow up with, and then you get older, and there's just something about them that doesn't pass the nose test. They're somehow too perfect. And the most nagging part is the coup de grâce, the perfectly chosen last line. My father wrote a memoir once, and in it are several completely unbelievable episodes in which he tells people like Darryl Zanuck to go fuck themselves. This legend of my mother and Lillian Ross was in some way a version of those stories. It was too good to be true.

My mother became an alcoholic when I was fifteen. It was odd. One day she wasn't an alcoholic, and the next day she was a complete lush.

She drank a bottle of scotch every night. Around midnight she would come flying out of her bedroom, banging and screaming and terrorizing us all. My father drank too, but he was a sloppy, sentimental drunk, and somehow his alcoholism was more benign.

By the time I went off to Wellesley, their movie work had dried up, but somehow they were sober enough in the daytime to collaborate; they wrote a successful play called *Take Her, She's Mine*, about a Southern California family whose daughter goes off to an eastern women's college. It quoted the letters I'd written from college, and it opened on Broadway during my senior year, starring Art Carney as the father and Elizabeth Ashley as the daughter. Everyone at Wellesley knew about it and about my remarkable mother, the writer who could do everything.

I didn't expect either of my parents to turn up at my graduation, but a few days before it, my mother called to say she'd decided to come. She arrived in all her stylish glory. She wore her suit, and her three-inch heels, and her clip-on earrings that matched her brooch. She slept in the dormitory, in the room next to mine, for two nights. I lay in my bed and listened through the paper-thin wall to her drunken mutterings. I was terrified that she'd burst from her room into the halls of Tower Court and mortify me in front of my classmates, that she'd stagger down the hall banging and screaming, and my friends would learn the truth.

But what was the truth?

I was invested in the original narrative; I was a true believer. My mother was a goddess.

But my mother was an alcoholic.

Alcoholic parents are so confusing. They're your parents, so you love them; but they're drunks, so you hate them. But you love them. But you hate them. They have moments when they're still the people you grew up idolizing; they have moments when you can't imagine they were ever anything but monsters. And then, after a while, they're monsters full-time. The people they used to be have enormous power over you—it will be forty years before you buy a red coat (and even then, you will wear it only once)—but the people they've turned into have no power over you at all.

For a long time before she died, I wished my mother were dead. And then she died, and it wasn't one of those things where I thought, Why did I think that? What was wrong with me? What kind of person would wish her mother dead? No, it wasn't one of those things at all. My mother had become a complete nightmare. She drank herself to death at the age of fifty-seven.

I was thirty when she died. After five years as a newspaper reporter, I'd become a freelance magazine writer. I wrote for *Esquire* in the last days of editor Harold Hayes and for *New York* magazine in the first days of Clay Felker. It was a heady time. Magazines like *Esquire* and *New York* were the zeitgeist, and the (mostly) men who wrote for them were cocky and full of beans. They thought they had invented nonfiction, which they hadn't, and they even thought they had invented hanging out together in restaurants and staying up late. It was an era when people really cared about magazines, when the arrival of a new *Esquire* on the newsstands was a bombshell, and it was seriously fun to be part of it. I became an *Esquire* writer. I wrote a column there, about women. In the world of print, the small world where I lived, I became a little bit famous.

I had never met Lillian Ross, but I wondered about her from time to time. I'd read all her early work and admired it greatly, but she'd stopped doing bylined profiles and wrote mostly unsigned "Talk of the Town" pieces in *The New Yorker.* She was rumored to be having an affair with the editor of the magazine, William Shawn, and she seemed (from a distance) to have fallen under the evil spell of blandness that he'd cast over the magazine.

At the time, there was a cold war in the magazine world, between those of us at *Esquire* and *New York,* and those of them at *The New Yorker.* They lived enviable lives—they had contracts and health insurance, and they could take months writing pieces; we, on the other hand, were always overextended and scrambling for dough. They were feigning modesty and disdaining success; we were self-aggrandizing and climbing the greasy pole. They were the anointed; we were pagans. They worshipped the famously reclusive "Mr. Shawn," and they dropped his name in hushed tones as if he were the Ba'al Shem Tov; we, on the other hand, jumped from Harold to Clay and back again. They thought we were egomaniacs; we thought they were weird.

I was the sort of person Lillian Ross would hate, if she even knew who I was, or so it seemed to me one night in 1978 when I was pulled across a room to meet her. I was at a party at the home of Lorne Michaels, the producer of *Saturday Night Live.* Lillian Ross had been reporting a profile of Lorne for eight years. "You two must meet," Lorne was saying, as he brought us together. I could see in an instant that Lillian Ross did not share this imperative. "You have so much in common," he said, as he sat us down on the sofa.

"It's so nice to meet you," I said.

"And you," she said.

She was a tiny woman with short curly hair and bright blue eyes, and she smiled and waited for me to begin.

I had one goal: to find out if my mother's story was true and to find it out without giving anything away. I didn't want Lillian Ross to know that she was a character in our family saga, and I didn't want to betray my mother by giving away the fact that Ross had lingered on, in our home, for so many years after her cameo appearance there. I wanted my mother to win the duel, whether or not it had actually happened.

But how to ask the question? "Is it true my mother threw you out of the house?" seemed a little bold. "I think you once met my mother" seemed coy, especially if Ross remembered the incident.

I couldn't figure out what to do.

So I began by saying that I was a huge fan. She said thank you and waited for me to say something else. I took this to mean she'd never read anything I'd written, or that she hated my work, or perhaps—I was reaching for straws here—she had no idea that I was a writer.

I asked her about her son and I told her about mine. It's my experience that no one but your very close friends is truly interested in your children, but we went on pretending for a while.

Then I asked her if she was still writing the profile of Lorne, as I'd heard. Yes, she said, she was. Another pause. It was clear that Lillian Ross was not even going to meet me halfway. I was starting to become irritated. Was it true that she was now in her eighth year of writing about Lorne, I asked. Yes, she was, she said. When do you think you'll be done with it, I asked. I asked this in what I hoped was an innocent manner, but I didn't fool her. She had no idea, she replied. We don't have to rush things at *The New Yorker*.

That cleared up one thing: she knew who I was.

I plowed on: I asked her why she'd stopped writing signed profiles. I asked the question cleverly, I thought. Honey dripped from my lips. I said I had loved her long pieces so much and missed reading them and wondered why she had stopped writing them. She replied that she'd stopped writing bylined articles because she believed that too much magazine journalism these days was egotistical and self-promoting.

I had to hand it to her: that was good.

And then Lillian Ross answered the question I hadn't asked.

"I went to your house once," she said. "I met your mother."

"Really?" I said, feigning absolute ignorance.

"Didn't see much of you, though," she said.

So there it was.

No question.

It had happened.

I have met Lillian Ross many times since that night. She still writes for *The New Yorker,* although *The New Yorker* no longer publishes unsigned pieces. She eventually wrote a first-person confessional about her relationship with Mr. Shawn, so on some level she threw off the veil. I consider her to be as egotistical and self-promoting as the rest of us, and that's a compliment.

But this is not about Lillian Ross, really. It's about my mother. Long before she died, I'd given up on her. But that night with Lillian Ross, I got her back; I got back the mother I'd idolized before it had all gone to hell. I got back the simple version. She'd thrown Lillian Ross out of our house for all the right reasons. The legend was true.

—October 2010

Me and JFK: Now It Can Be Told

JFK intern admits all

John F. Kennedy's intern admitted to the Daily News *yesterday: "I am the Mimi."*

Marion (Mimi) Fahnestock, now 60, called it a huge weight off her shoulders to finally reveal her affair with the dashing young president four decades ago. "The gift for me is that this allowed me to tell my two married daughters a secret that I've been holding for 41 years," she said. "It's a huge relief. And now I will have no further comment on this subject. I request that the media respect my privacy and that of my family."

I was an intern in the JFK White House. I was. This is not one of those humor pieces where the writer pretends to some experience currently in the news in order to make an "amusing" point. It was 1961, and I was hired by Pierre Salinger to work in the White House press office, the very same place where Mimi Fahnestock was to work the following year. And now that Mimi Fahnestock has been forced to come forward and admit that she had an affair with JFK, I might as well tell my story too.

I notice that all the articles about poor Mimi quote another woman in the press office, Barbara Gamarekian, who fingered Fahnestock in the oral history archives at the Kennedy Library. Gamarekian cattily pointed out, according to the newspapers, that Mimi "couldn't type." Well, all I can say to that is: Ha. In fact: Double ha. There were, when I worked there, six women in Pierre Salinger's office. One of them was called Faddle (her best friend, Fiddle, worked for Kennedy), and her entire job, as far as I could tell, was autographing Pierre Salinger's photographs. Fiddle's job was autographing Kennedy's. Typing was not a skill that anyone seemed to need, and it certainly wasn't necessary for interns like me (and Mimi, dare I say), because THERE WAS NO DESK FOR AN INTERN TO SIT AT AND THEREFORE NO TYPEWRITER TO TYPE ON.

Yes, I am still bitter about it! Because there I was, not just the only young woman in the White House who was unable to afford an endless succession of A-line sleeveless linen dresses just like Jackie's, but also the only person in the press office with nowhere to sit. And then, as now, I could type one hundred words a minute. Every eight-hour day there were theoretically forty-eight thousand words that weren't being typed because I DIDN'T HAVE A DESK.

Also, I had a really bad permanent wave. This is an important fact for later in the story, when things heat up.

I met the president within minutes of going to "work" in the White House. My first morning there, he flew to Annapolis to give the commencement address, and Salinger invited me to come along with the press pool in the press helicopter. When I got back to the White House, Pierre took me in to meet Kennedy. He was the handsomest man I had ever seen. I don't remember the details of our conversation, but perhaps they are included in Salinger's reminiscences in the Kennedy Library. Someday I will look them up. What I do remember is that the meeting was short, perhaps ten or fifteen seconds. After it, I went back to the press office and discovered what you, reader, already know: that there was no place for me to sit.

So I spent my summer internship lurking in the hall near the file cabinet. I read most of the things that were in the file cabinet, including some interesting memos that were marked "Top Secret" and "Eyes

Only." Right next to the file cabinet was the men's room, and one day the speaker of the House, Sam Rayburn, inadvertently locked himself into it. Had I not been nearby, he might be there still.

From time to time I went into the Oval Office and watched the president be photographed with various foreign leaders. Sometimes, I am pretty sure, he noticed me watching him.

Which brings me to my crucial encounter with JFK, the one that no one at the Kennedy Library has come to ask me about. It was a Friday afternoon, and because I had nowhere to sit (see above) and nothing to do (ditto), I decided to go out and watch the president leave by helicopter for a weekend in Hyannis Port. It was a beautiful day, and I stood out under the portico overlooking the Rose Garden, just outside the Oval Office. The helicopter landed. The noise was deafening. The wind from the chopper blades was blowing hard (although my permanent wave kept my hair glued tightly to my head). And then suddenly, instead of coming out of the living quarters, the president emerged from his office and walked right past me to get to the helicopter. He turned. He saw me. He recognized me. The noise was deafening but he spoke to me. I couldn't hear a thing, but I could read his lips, and I'm pretty sure what he said was "How are you coming along?" But I wasn't positive. So I replied as best I could. "What?" I said.

And that was it. He turned and went off to the helicopter, and I went back to standing around the White House until the summer was over. I never saw him again.

Now that I have read the articles about Mimi Fahnestock, it has become horribly clear to me that I am probably the only young woman who ever worked in the Kennedy White House that the president did not make a pass at. Perhaps it was my permanent wave, which was a truly unfortunate mistake. Perhaps it was my wardrobe, which mostly consisted of multicolored Dynel dresses that looked like distilled Velveeta cheese. Perhaps it's because I'm Jewish. Don't laugh; think about it— think about that long, long list of women JFK slept with. Were any of them Jewish? I don't think so.

On the other hand, perhaps nothing happened between us simply because JFK somehow sensed that discretion was not my middle name. I mean, I assure you that if anything had gone on between the two of us, you would not have had to wait this long to find it out.

Anyway, that's my story. I might as well go public with it, although I have told it to pretty much everyone I have ever met in the last forty-two years. And now, like Mimi Fahnestock, I will have no further comment on this subject. I request that the media respect my privacy and that of my family.

—May 2003

A Few Words About Breasts

I have to begin with a few words about androgyny. In grammar school, in the fifth and sixth grades, we were all tyrannized by a rigid set of rules that supposedly determined whether we were boys or girls. The episode in *Huckleberry Finn* where Huck is disguised as a girl and gives himself away by the way he threads a needle and catches a ball—that kind of thing. We learned that the way you sat, crossed your legs, held a cigarette, and looked at your nails—the way you did these things instinctively was absolute proof of your sex. Now obviously most children did not take this literally, but I did. I thought that just one slip, just one incorrect cross of my legs or flick of an imaginary cigarette ash would turn me from whatever I was into the other thing; that would be all it took, really. Even though I was outwardly a girl and had many of the trappings generally associated with girldom—a girl's name, for example, and dresses, my own telephone, an autograph book—I spent the early years of my adolescence absolutely certain that I might at any point gum it up. I did not feel at all like a girl. I was boyish. I was athletic, ambitious, outspoken, competitive, noisy, rambunctious. I had scabs on my knees and my socks slid into my loafers and I could throw a football. I wanted desperately not to be that way, not to be a mixture of both things, but instead just one, a girl, a definite indisputable girl. As soft and as pink as a nursery. And nothing would do that for me, I felt, but breasts.

I was about six months younger than everyone else in my class, and so for about six months after it began, for six months after my friends had begun to develop (that was the word we used, develop), I was not partic-ularly worried. I would sit in the bathtub and look down at my breasts and know that any day now, any second now, they would start growing like everyone else's. They didn't. "I want to buy a bra," I said to my mother one night. "What for?" she said. My mother was really hateful about bras, and by the time my third sister had gotten to the point where she was ready to want one, my mother had worked the whole business into a comedy routine. "Why not use a Band-Aid instead?" she would say. It was a source of great pride to my mother that she had never even had to wear a brassiere until she had her fourth child, and then only because her gynecologist made her. It was incomprehensible to me that anyone could ever be proud of something like that. It was the 1950s, for God's sake. Jane Russell. Cashmere sweaters. Couldn't my mother see that? "*I am too old to wear an undershirt.*" Screaming. Weeping. Shouting. "Then don't wear an undershirt," said my mother. "But I want to buy a bra." "What for?"

I suppose that for most girls, breasts, brassieres, that entire thing, has more trauma, more to do with the coming of adolescence, with becoming a woman, than anything else. Certainly more than getting your period, although that, too, was traumatic, symbolic. But you could see breasts; they were there; they were visible. Whereas a girl could claim to have her period for months before she actually got it and nobody would ever know the difference. Which is exactly what I did. All you had to do was make a great fuss over having enough nickels for the Kotex machine and walk around clutching your stomach and moaning for three to five days a month about The Curse and you could convince anybody. There is a school of thought somewhere in the women's lib/women's mag/gynecology establishment that claims that menstrual cramps are purely psychological, and I lean toward it. Not that I didn't have them finally. Agonizing cramps, heating-pad cramps, go-down-to-the-school-nurse-and-lie-on-the-cot cramps. But, unlike any pain I had ever suffered, I adored the pain of cramps, welcomed it, wallowed in it, bragged about it. "I can't go. I have cramps." "I can't do that. I have cramps." And most of all, gigglingly, blushingly: "I can't swim. I have cramps." Nobody ever used the hard-core word. Menstruation. God, what an awful word. Never that. "I have cramps."

The morning I first got my period, I went into my mother's bedroom to tell her. And my mother, my utterly-hateful-about-bras mother, burst into tears. It was really a lovely moment, and I remember it so clearly not just because it was one of the two times I ever saw my mother cry on my account (the other was when I was caught being a six-year-old kleptomaniac), but also because the incident did not mean to me what it meant to her. Her little girl, her firstborn, had finally become a woman. That was what she was crying about. My reaction to the event, however, was that I might well be a woman in some scientific, textbook sense (and could at least stop faking every month and stop wasting all those nickels). But in another sense—in a visible sense—I was as androgynous and as liable to tip over into boyhood as ever.

I started with a 28 AA bra. I don't think they made them any smaller in those days, although I gather that now you can buy bras for five-year-olds that don't have any cups whatsoever in them; trainer bras they are called. My first brassiere came from Robinson's Department Store in Beverly Hills. I went there alone, shaking, positive they would look me over and smile and tell me to come back next year. An actual fitter took me into the dressing room and stood over me while I took off my blouse and tried the first one on. The little puffs stood out on my chest. "Lean over," said the fitter. (To this day, I am not sure what fitters in bra departments do except to tell you to lean over.) I leaned over, with the fleeting hope that my breasts would miraculously fall out of my body and into the puffs. Nothing.

"Don't worry about it," said my friend Libby some months later, when things had not improved. "You'll get them after you're married."

"What are you talking about?" I said.

"When you get married," Libby explained, "your husband will touch your breasts and rub them and kiss them and they'll grow."

That was the killer. Necking I could deal with. Intercourse I could deal with. But it had never crossed my mind that a man was going to touch my breasts, that breasts had something to do with all that, petting, my God, they never mentioned petting in my little sex manual about the fertilization of the ovum. I became dizzy. For I knew instantly—as naive as I had been only a moment before—that only part of what she was saying was true: the touching, rubbing, kissing part, not the growing part. And I knew that no one would ever want to marry me. I had no breasts. I would never have breasts.

My best friend in school was Diana Raskob. She lived a block from me in a house full of wonders. English muffins, for instance. The Raskobs were the first people in Beverly Hills to have English muffins for breakfast. They also had an apricot tree in the back, and a badminton court, and a subscription to *Seventeen* magazine, and hundreds of games, like Sorry and Parcheesi and Treasure Hunt and Anagrams. Diana and I spent three or four afternoons a week in their den reading and playing and eating. Diana's mother's kitchen was full of the most colossal assortment of junk food I have ever been exposed to. My house was full of apples and peaches and milk and homemade chocolate-chip cookies—which were nice, and good for you, but-not-right-before-dinner-or-you'll-spoil-your-appetite. Diana's house had nothing in it that was good for you, and what's more, you could stuff it in right up until dinner and nobody cared. Bar-B-Q potato chips (they were the first in them, too), giant bottles of ginger ale, fresh popcorn with melted butter, hot fudge sauce on Baskin-Robbins Jamoca ice cream, powdered-sugar doughnuts from Van de Kamp's. Diana and I had been best friends since we were seven; we were about equally popular in school (which is to say, not particularly), we had about the same success with boys (extremely intermittent), and we looked much the same. Dark. Tall. Gangly.

It is September, just before school begins. I am eleven years old, about to enter the seventh grade, and Diana and I have not seen each other all summer. I have been to camp and she has been somewhere like Banff with her parents. We are meeting, as we often do, on the street midway between our two houses, and we will walk back to Diana's and eat junk and talk about what has happened to each of us that summer. I am walking down Walden Drive in my jeans and my father's shirt hanging out and my old red loafers with the socks falling into them and coming toward me is . . . I take a deep breath . . . a young woman. Diana. Her hair is curled and she has a waist and hips and a bust and she is wearing a straight skirt, an article of clothing I have been repeatedly told I will be unable to wear until I have the hips to hold it up. My jaw drops, and suddenly I am crying, crying hysterically, can't catch my breath sobbing. My best friend has betrayed me. She has gone ahead without me and done it. She has shaped up.

Here are some things I did to help:
Bought a Mark Eden Bust Developer.
Slept on my back for four years.
Splashed cold water on them every night because some French actress said in *Life* magazine that that was what *she* did for her perfect bustline.
Ultimately, I resigned myself to a bad toss and began to wear padded bras. I think about them now, think about all those years in high school I went around in them, my three padded bras, every single one of them

with different-sized breasts. Each time I changed bras I changed sizes: one week nice perky but not too obtrusive breasts, the next medium-sized slightly pointy ones, the next week knockers, true knockers; all the time, whatever size I was, carrying around this rubberized append-age on my chest that occasionally crashed into a wall and was poked inward and had to be poked outward—I think about all that and won-der how anyone kept a straight face through it. My parents, who nor-mally had no restraints about needling me—why did they say nothing as they watched my chest go up and down? My friends, who would periodically inspect my breasts for signs of growth and reassure me—why didn't they at least counsel consistency?

And the bathing suits. I die when I think about the bathing suits. That was the era when you could lay an uninhabited bathing suit on the beach and someone would make a pass at it. I would put one on, an absurd swimsuit with its enormous bust built into it, the bones from the suit stabbing me in the rib cage and leaving little red welts on my body, and there I would be, my chest plunging straight downward absolutely vertically from my collarbone to the top of my suit and then suddenly, wham, out came all that padding and material and wiring absolutely horizontally.

Buster Klepper was the first boy who ever touched them. He was my boyfriend my senior year of high school. There is a picture of him in my high-school yearbook that makes him look quite attractive in a Jewish, horn-rimmed-glasses sort of way, but the picture does not show the pimples, which were air-brushed out, or the dumbness. Well, that isn't really fair. He wasn't dumb. He just wasn't terribly bright. His mother refused to accept it, refused to accept the relentlessly average report cards, refused to deal with her son's inevitable destiny in some junior college or other. "He was tested," she would say to me, apropos of noth-ing, "and it came out a hundred and forty-five. That's near-genius." Had the word "underachiever" been coined, she probably would have lobbed that one at me, too. Anyway, Buster was really very sweet—which is, I know, damning with faint praise, but there it is. I was the editor of the front page of the high-school newspaper and he was editor of the back page; we had to work together, side by side, in the print shop, and that was how it started. On our first date, we went to see *April Love*, starring Pat Boone. Then we started going together. Buster had a green coupe, a 1950 Ford with an engine he had hand-chromed

490 THE MOST OF NORA EPHRON

until it shone, dazzled, reflected the image of anyone who looked into it, anyone usually being Buster polishing it or the gas-station attendants he constantly asked to check the oil in order for them to be overwhelmed by the sparkle on the valves. The car also had a boot stretched over the backseat for reasons I never understood; hanging from the rear-view mirror, as was the custom, was a pair of angora dice. A previous girlfriend named Solange, who was famous throughout Beverly Hills High School for having no pigment in her right eyebrow, had knitted them for him. Buster and I would ride around town, the two of us seated to the left of the steering wheel. I would shift gears. It was nice.

There was necking. Terrific necking. First in the car, overlooking Los Angeles from what is now the Trousdale Estates. Then on the bed of his parents' cabana at Ocean House. Incredibly wonderful, frustrating necking, I loved it, really, but no further than necking, please don't, please, because there I was, absolutely terrified of the general implications of going-a-step-further with a near-dummy and also terrified of his finding out there was next to nothing there (which he knew, of course; he wasn't that dumb).

I broke up with him at one point. I think we were apart for about two weeks. At the end of that time, I drove down to see a friend at a boarding school in Palos Verdes Estates and a disc jockey played "April Love" on the radio four times during the trip. I took it as a sign. I drove straight back to Griffith Park to a golf tournament Buster was playing in (he was the sixth-seeded teen age golf player in Southern California) and presented myself back to him on the green of the eighteenth hole. It was all very dramatic. That night we went to a drive-in and I let him get his hand under my protuberances and onto my breasts. He really didn't seem to mind at all.

"Do you want to marry my son?" the woman asked me.

"Yes," I said.

I was nineteen years old, a virgin, going with this woman's son, this big strange woman who was married to a Lutheran minister in New Hampshire and pretended she was gentile and had this son, by her first husband, this total fool of a son who ran the hero-sandwich concession at Harvard Business School and whom for one moment one December in New Hampshire I said—as much out of politeness as anything else—that I wanted to marry.

"Fine," she said. "Now, here's what you do. Always make sure you're on top of him so you won't seem so small. My bust is very large, you see, so I always lie on my back to make it look smaller, but you'll have to be on top most of the time."

I nodded. "Thank you," I said.

"I have a book for you to read," she went on. "Take it with you when you leave. Keep it." She went to the bookshelf, found it, and gave it to me. It was a book on frigidity.

"Thank you," I said.

That is a true story. Everything in this article is a true story, but I feel I have to point out that that story in particular is true. It happened on December 30, 1960. I think about it often. When it first happened, I naturally assumed that the woman's son, my boyfriend, was responsible. I invented a scenario where he had had a little heart-to-heart with his mother and had confessed that his only objection to me was that my breasts were small; his mother then took it upon herself to help out. Now I think I was wrong about the incident. The mother was acting on her own, I think: that was her way of being cruel and competitive under the guise of being helpful and maternal. You have small breasts, she was saying; therefore you will never make him as happy as I have. Or you have small breasts; therefore you will doubtless have sexual problems. Or you have small breasts; therefore you are less woman than I am. She was, as it happens, only the first of what seems to me to be a never-ending string of women who have made competitive remarks to me about breast size. "I would love to wear a dress like that," my friend Emily says to me, "but my bust is too big." Like that. Why do women say these things to me? Do I attract these remarks the way other women attract married men or alcoholics or homosexuals? This summer, for example. I am at a party in East Hampton and I am introduced to a woman from Washington. She is a minor celebrity, very pretty and Southern and blond and outspoken, and I am flattered because she has read something I have written. We are talking animatedly, we have been talking no more than five minutes, when a man comes up to join us. "Look at the two of us," the woman says to the man, indicating me and her. "The two of us together couldn't fill an A cup." Why does she say that? It isn't even true, dammit, so why? Is she even more addled than I am on this subject? Does she honestly believe there is something wrong with her size breasts, which, it seems to me, now that I look hard at them, are just right? Do I unconsciously bring out competitiveness in women? In that form? What did I do to deserve it?

As for men.

There were men who minded and let me know that they minded. There were men who did not mind. In any case, *I* always minded.

And even now, now that I have been countlessly reassured that my figure is a good one, now that I am grown-up enough to understand that most of my feelings have very little to do with the reality of my shape, I am nonetheless obsessed by breasts. I cannot help it. I grew up in the terrible fifties—with rigid stereotypical sex roles, the insistence that men be men and dress like men and women be women and dress like women, the intolerance of androgyny—and I cannot shake it, cannot shake my feelings of inadequacy. Well, that time is gone, right? All those exaggerated examples of breast worship are gone, right? Those women were freaks, right? I know all that. And yet here I am, stuck with the psychological remains of it all, stuck with my own peculiar version of breast worship. You probably think I am crazy to go on like this: here I have set out to write a confession that is meant to hit you with the shock of recognition, and instead you are sitting there thinking I am thoroughly warped. Well, what can I tell you? If I had had them, I would have been a completely different person. I honestly believe that.

After I went into therapy, a process that made it possible for me to tell total strangers at cocktail parties that breasts were the hang-up of my life, I was often told that I was insane to have been bothered by my condition. I was also frequently told, by close friends, that I was extremely boring on the subject. And my girlfriends, the ones with nice big breasts, would go on endlessly about how their lives had been far more miserable than mine. Their bra straps were snapped in class. They couldn't sleep on their stomachs. They were stared at whenever the word "mountain" cropped up in geography. And *Evangeline*, good God what they went through every time someone had to stand up and recite the Prologue to Longfellow's *Evangeline*: " . . . stand like druids of eld . . . / With beards that rest on their bosoms." It was much worse for them, they tell me. They had a terrible time of it, they assure me. I don't know how lucky I was, they say.

I have thought about their remarks, tried to put myself in their place, considered their point of view. I think they are full of shit.

—May 1972

The Mink Coat

I think it was about 1954 when my mother got her mink. A Beverly Hills furrier had run into some difficulty with the Internal Revenue Service and he was selling off his coats. My mother would never have bought anything wholesale—she disapproved of it on grounds that I never understood but later came to suspect had something to do with being the daughter of a garment salesman—but there was a distinction between buying wholesale and getting a good price. She got a good price. It was an enormous mink. A tent. It came to her ankles, and at least two people could have fitted under it. The skins were worked vertically. I did not know this at the time. I did not know much of anything at the time, much less anything about the way mink skins were worked. A few years later, when I knew, all the furriers in America decided to work the skins horizontally; when I heard about it, I instantly understood that it would not make her happy to be wearing an Old Mink. But she always pretended that things like that meant nothing to her. She was a career woman who was defiant about not being like the other mothers, the other mothers who played canasta all day and went to P.T.A. meetings and wore perfume and talked of hemlines; she hated to shop, hated buying clothes. Once a year, after my father had nagged her into it, she would go off to a fashionable ladies' clothing store on Wilshire Boulevard and submit to having a year's supply of clothing brought to her in a dressing room larger than my current apartment. She grumbled throughout. I thought she was mad. Now I understand.

My guess is that my father paid for the mink, wrote the check for it—but he did not *buy* it for her. My parents worked together, wrote together, and there was no separation between his money and hers. That was important. Beverly Hills was a place where the other mothers wore minks their husbands had bought them. They would come to dinner. The maid would bring the coats upstairs and lay them on my mother's bed. Dozens of them, silver, brown, black, all of them lined with what seemed like satin and monogrammed by hand with initials. I would creep into the bedroom and lie on the bed and roll over them and smell the odd and indescribable smell of the fur. Other children grow up loving the smell of fresh-cut grass and raked leaves; I grew up in Beverly Hills loving the smell of mink, the smell of the pavement after it rained, and the smell of dollar bills. A few years ago, I went back to

Beverly Hills and all I could smell was jasmine, and I realized that that smell had always been there and I had never known it.

My mother wore the mink for years. She wore it through the horizontal period and into another vertical period, but it never became fashionable again; by the time vertical skins were back, furriers were cutting minks close and fitted. Eventually, she stopped wearing it and went back to cloth coats. She and my father had moved back to New York and she had less patience than ever for shopping. And then she was sick and went to bed. One Thanksgiving she was too sick to come to the table. My mother loved Thanksgiving almost as much as she loved making a show of normal family life. I knew she was dying.

The months went by, and she hung on. In the hospital, then out, then back in. She was drugged, and wretchedly thin, and her throat was so dry, or so clogged with mucus, that I could not understand anything she tried to say to me. If I nodded at her as if I understood, she would become furious because she knew I hadn't; if I said, "What?" or, "I don't understand," she would become furious at the effort it would take to say it again. And I was furious, too, because I was there for some kind of answer—what kind of answer? what was the question? I don't know, but I wanted one, a big one, and there was no chance of getting it. The Thorazine kept her quiet and groggy and hallucinating. When the nurse would bring in lunch, soft food, no salt allowed, she would look around almost brightly and say, "I think I'll take it in the living room." I would become so angry at her at moments like that, so impatient. I wanted to say, damn you, there is no living room, you're in a hospital, you're dying, you're going off without having explained any of it. And she would look up and open her mouth just slightly, and I would put another spoonful into it.

Then it was September. Fall. The room had a nice view of Gracie Mansion and the leaves were turning. It was a corner room on the sixth floor, which is, for those who care, a little like being seated at the right table. She did care. She managed, almost until the end, to keep up appearances. If the nurse was new, she would raise herself a bit, lift her arm in a dear and pathetic waft, and introduce us formally. "Miss Browning," she would say, "my daughter, Mrs. Greenburg." (My mother and the fish market were the only people who ever thought of me as Mrs. Greenburg.) Then she would collapse back into the pillow and manage a bare flicker of a smile. I found it unbearable to be there and unbearable not to be there. I was conscious that I was going through an experience that writers write about, that I should be acutely aware of what was happening, but I hated that consciousness. And I could not look at her. She would moan with pain, and the nurse would reach under her, move her slightly, and the sheet would fall away and I would catch a glimpse of her legs, her beautiful legs now drained of muscle tone, gone to bones. The hallucinations went on. Then, one day, suddenly, she came into focus, knew exactly who I was, and like a witch, what I was thinking. "You're a reporter," she said to me. "Take notes."

Two days after she died, my sisters and I spent an afternoon—how to put this?—disposing of her possessions. It was an extremely odd day. People kept dropping in, somber people, to pay their respects to my father; in the bedroom were the four of us, not at all somber, relieved, really, that it was finally over, and finding a small and genuine pleasure in the trivial problem of what to do with her things.

Most of my mother's clothes were sent to charity. And the evening dresses, the beautiful chiffon Galanos dresses my father had bought her, were too big for any of us. But there was the mink. And there I was. The eldest. The most grown-up. It occurred to me I could cut it down to size or line another coat with it. Something. I took it.

A few weeks later, one of my sisters called. Did I take the mink? she asked. Yes. It's not fair, she said. She didn't even have a winter coat and I had hundreds and a big apartment and a rich husband and now I had the mink, too. You can have half of it, I said. She didn't want half of it. She didn't have the money for a winter coat much less the money to turn half a mink into something. What do you want? I said. She didn't know. There were three more phone calls, each uglier and more vituperative, thirty years of sibling rivalry come to a head over an eighteen-year-old mink. I have to make it clear that I was as awful as she was. I wanted the mink.

Finally, one day, we met in front of the Ritz Thrift Shop on Fifty-seventh Street. I was carrying the mink. She was barely speaking to me. We went inside, and a lady came over. We said we wanted to sell the mink. The lady took the fur in her hands and turned it over, peeling away the coat lining to look at the underside of the skins. She spent a good half second with it. "I won't give you a nickel for it," she said. The skins were worthless. Shot. Something like that. We walked out onto Fifty-seventh Street carrying the mink. It was suddenly a burden, a useless assemblage of old worn-out pelts. I didn't want it. She didn't want it. A year later, my maid asked for it and I gave it to her. Shortly thereafter, my maid's apartment was robbed and the burglar got the mink.

I will never have one. I know that now. And like a lot of things I will never have, I have mixed feelings about it. I mean, I could have one if I wanted one. I could squirrel away every extra nickel and buy myself, maybe not a perfect mink, but something made of mink noses or mink eyes or whatever spare parts make up that category of coats they call fun furs. But I don't really want one: a mink coat is serious, and I would have to change my life to go with it.

But I love her for having bought one. She had the only kind of mink worth having, the kind you pay for yourself. That is not the answer I was looking for, but it will have to do.

—December 1975

Parenting in Three Stages

Stage One: *The Child Is Born*

I want to begin by saying that when I gave birth to my children, which was not that long ago, there was almost no such thing as parenting as we know it today. There were parents, of course, and there were mothers and fathers (and mothering and fathering), but the concept of parenting was in its very early stages, if it existed at all.

Here's what a parent is: A parent is a person who has children. Here's what's involved in being a parent: You love your children, you hang out with them from time to time, you throw balls, you read stories, you make sure they know which utensil is the salad fork, you teach them to say please and thank you, you see that they have an occasional haircut, and you ask if they did their homework. Every so often, sentences you never expected to say (because your parents said them to you) fall from your lips, sentences like:

DO YOU HAVE ANY IDEA WHAT THAT COST?

BECAUSE I SAY SO. THAT'S WHY.

I SAID NOW.

STOP THAT THIS MINUTE.

GO TO YOUR ROOM.

I DON'T CARE WHAT JESSICA'S MOTHER LETS HER DO.

A TIARA? YOU WANT A TIARA?

Back in the day when there were merely parents, as opposed to people who were engaged in parenting, being a parent was fairly straightforward. You didn't need a book, and if you owned one, it was by Dr. Spock, a pediatrician, and you rarely looked at it unless your child had a temperature of 103, or the croup, or both. You understood that your child had a personality. His very own personality. He was born with it. For a certain period, this child would live with you and your personality, and you would do your best to survive each other.

"They never really change," people often said (back in those days) about babies. This was a somewhat mystifying concept when you first had a baby. Exactly what was it about the baby that would never change? After all, it's incredibly difficult to tell what a baby's exact personality is when it's merely a baby. (I'm using the word *personality* in the broadest sense, the one that means "the whole ball of wax.") But eventually the baby in question began to manifest its personality, and sure enough, remarkably enough, that personality never changed. For example, when the police arrived to inform you that your eight-year-old had just dropped a dozen eggs from your fifth-floor window onto West End Avenue, you couldn't help but be reminded of the fourteen-month-old baby he used to be, who knocked all the string beans from the high chair to the floor and thought it was a total riot.

Back in those days—and once again, let me stress that I am not talking about the nineteenth century here, it was just a few years ago—no one believed that you could turn your child into a different human being from the one he started out being. T. Berry Brazelton, the pediatrician who supplanted Spock in the 1980s, was a disciple of Piaget, and his books divided babies into three types—active, average, and quiet. He never suggested that your quiet baby would ever become an active one, or vice versa. Your baby was your baby, and if he ran you ragged, he ran you ragged; and if he lay in his crib staring happily at his mobile, that was about what you could expect.

All this changed around the time I had children. You can blame the women's movement for it—one of the bedrock tenets of the women's movement was that because so many women were entering the workforce, men and women should share in the raising of children; thus

498 · THE MOST OF NORA EPHRON

the gender-neutral word *parenting,* and the necessity of elevating child rearing to something more than the endless hours of quantity time it actually consists of. Conversely, you can blame the backlash against the women's movement—lots of women didn't feel like entering into the workforce (or even sharing the raising of children with their husbands), but they felt guilty about this, so they were compelled to elevate full-time parenthood to a sacrament.

In any event, suddenly, one day, there was this thing called parenting. Parenting was serious. Parenting was fierce. Parenting was solemn. *Parenting* was a participle, like *going* and *doing* and *crusading* and *worrying*; it was active, it was energetic, it was unrelenting. Parenting meant playing Mozart CDs while you were pregnant, doing without the epidural, and breast-feeding your child until it was old enough to unbutton your blouse. Parenting began with the assumption that your baby was a lump of clay that could be molded (through hard work, input, and positive reinforcement) into a perfect person who would someday be admitted to the college of your choice. Parenting was not simply about raising a child, it was about transforming a child, force-feeding it like a foie gras goose, altering, modifying, modulating, manipulating, smoothing out, improving. (Interestingly, the culture came to believe in the perfectibility of the child just as it also came to believe in the conflicting theory that virtually everything in human nature was genetic—thus proving that whoever said that a sign of intelligence was the ability to hold two contradictory thoughts simultaneously did not know what he was talking about.)

And by the way, all sorts of additional personnel were required to achieve the transformational effect that was the goal of parenting—baby whisperers, sleep counselors, shrinks, learning therapists, family therapists, speech therapists, tutors—and, if necessary, behavior-altering medication, which, coincidentally or uncoincidentally, was invented at almost the exact moment that parenting came into being.

Parenting carried with it the implicit assumption that any time is quality time if the parent is in attendance. As a result, you were required to be in attendance at the most mundane activities—to watch, cheerlead, and, if necessary, coach, even if this meant throwing your weekend away by driving three hours and twenty minutes in each direction so that you could sit in a dark, hot locker room next door to a gym where your beloved child was going down to resounding defeat in a chess tournament you were not allowed to observe because your mere presence in the room would put unfair pressure on him or her. (The willingness on the part of both parents to be present at any place at any time had the interesting side effect of causing schools to rely on parents to oversee all sorts of events that used to be supervised by trained professionals.)

Parenting meant that whether or not your children understood you, your obligation was to understand them; understanding was the key to everything. If your children believed you understood them, or at least tried to understand them, they wouldn't hate you when they became adolescents; what's more, they would grow up to be happy, well-adjusted adults who would never have to squander their money (or, far more likely, yours) on psychoanalysis or whatever fashion in self-improvement had come along to take its place.

Parenting used entirely different language from just plain parent-hood, language you would never write in big capital letters in order to make clear that it had been uttered impulsively or in anger. So it went more or less like this:

I'm sure you didn't mean to break Mommy's antique vase, sweetheart.

We should talk about this.

I know how frustrated and angry you must feel right now.

Why don't you go to your room and take a time-out and come back when you're feeling better.

If you want, I'll call Jessica's mother to see what her reasoning is.

If you finish your homework, we can talk about the tiara.

Stage Two: *The Child Is an Adolescent*

Adolescence comes as a gigantic shock to the modern parent, in large part because it seems so much like the adolescence you yourself went through. Your adolescent is sullen. Your adolescent is angry. Your adolescent is mean. In fact, your adolescent is mean to you.

Your adolescent says words you were not allowed to say while grow-ing up, not that you had even heard of them until you read *The Catcher in the Rye.* Your adolescent is probably smoking marijuana, which you may have smoked too, but not until you were at least eighteen. Your

adolescent is undoubtedly having completely inappropriate and mean-
ingless sex, which you didn't have until you were in your twenties,
if then. Your adolescent is embarrassed by you and walks ten steps
ahead of you so that no one thinks you are remotely acquainted with
each other. Your adolescent is ungrateful. You have a vague memory
of having been accused by your parents of being ungrateful, but what
did you have to be grateful for? Almost nothing. Your parents weren't
into parenting. They were merely parents. At least one of them drank
like a fish. Whereas you are exemplary. You've devoted years to making your children feel that you care about every single emotion they've
ever felt. You've filled every waking second of their lives with cultural
activities. The words "I'm bored" have never crossed their lips, because
they haven't had time to be bored. Your children have had everything you could give—everything and more, if you count the sneakers.
You love them wildly, way more than your parents loved you. And
yet they seem to have turned out exactly the way adolescents have
always turned out. Only worse. How did this happen? What did you do
wrong?

Furthermore, thanks to modern nutritional advances, your adolescent is large, probably larger than you. Your adolescent's weekly allow-
ance is the size of the gross national product of Burkina Faso, a small,
poverty-stricken African country neither you nor your adolescent had
ever heard of until recently, when you both spent several days working
on a social studies report about it.

Your adolescent has changed, but not in any of the ways you'd hoped
for when you set about to mold your child. And you have changed too.
You have changed from a moderately neurotic, fairly cheerful human
being to an irritable, crabby, abused wreck.

But not to worry. There's somewhere you can go for help. You can
go to all the therapists and counselors you consulted in the years before
your children became adolescents, the therapists and counselors who've
put their own children through college and probably law school thanks
to your ongoing reliance on them.

Here's what they will say:

- Adolescence is for adolescents, not for parents.
- It was invented to help attached—or overattached—children
  to separate, in preparation for the inevitable moment when
  they leave the nest.
- There are things you can do to make life easier for yourself.

This advice will cost you hundreds—or thousands—of dollars, depending on whether you live in a major metropolitan area or a minor one. And it's completely untrue:

- Adolescence is for parents, not adolescents.
- It was invented to help attached—or overattached—*parents* to separate, in preparation for the inevitable moment when their children leave the nest.
- There is almost nothing you can do to make life easier for yourself except wait until it's over.

Incidentally, there's an old joke that was probably invented by someone with adolescent children. Not that I'm good at telling jokes. And if I were, you still wouldn't know how good this joke is, because it takes quite a long time to tell it and requires one of those Yiddish accents people use when telling jokes about old rabbis. But anyway, this married couple goes to see a rabbi. What can I do for you, the rabbi says. We're having a terrible problem, Rabbi, the couple says. We have five children and we all live in a one-room house and we're driving each other crazy. The rabbi says, Move in a sheep. So they move a sheep into the house. A week later they go see the rabbi and tell him that things are worse than ever, plus there's a sheep. Move in a cow, the rabbi says. The next week they go to complain once again, because things are so much worse now that there's a cow. Move in a horse, the rabbi says. The next week the couple goes to see the rabbi to tell him that things are the worst they've ever been. "You're ready for the solution," the rabbi says. "Move the animals out."

Stage Three: *The Child Is Gone*

Oh, the drama of the empty nest. The anxiety. The apprehension. What will life be like? Will the two of you have anything to talk about once your children are gone? Will you have sex now that the presence of your children is no longer an excuse for not having sex?

The day finally comes. Your child goes off to college. You wait for the melancholy. But before it strikes—before it even has time to strike—a shocking thing happens: Your child comes right back. The academic year in American colleges seems to consist of a series of short episodes of classroom attendance interrupted by long vacations. These vacations aren't called "vacations," they're called "breaks" and "reading periods." There are colleges that even have October breaks. Who ever heard of an October break? On a strictly per diem basis, your child could be staying at a nice Paris hotel for about what you're paying in boarding expenses.

In any event, four years quickly pass in this manner. Your children go. Your children come back. Their tuition is raised.

But eventually college ends, and they're gone for good.

The nest is actually empty.

You're still a parent, but your parenting days are over.

Now what?

There must be something you can do.

But there isn't.

There is nothing you can do.

Trust me.

If you find yourself nostalgic for the ongoing, day-to-day activities required of the modern parent, there's a solution: Get a dog. I don't recommend it, because dogs require tremendous commitment, but they definitely give you something to do. Plus they're very loveable and, more important, uncritical. And they can be trained.

But that's about all you can do.

Meanwhile, you have an extra room. Your child's room. Do not under any circumstances leave your child's room as is. Your child's room is not a shrine. It's not going to the Smithsonian. Turn it into a den, a gym, a guest room, or (if you already have all three) a room for wrapping Christmas presents. Do this as soon as possible. Leaving your child's room as is may encourage your child to return. You do not want this.

Meanwhile, every so often, your children come to visit. They are, amazingly, completely charming people. You can't believe you're lucky enough to know them. They make you laugh. They make you proud. You love them madly. They survived you. You survived them. It crosses your mind that on some level, you spent hours and days and months and years without laying a glove on them, but don't dwell. There's no point. It's over.

Except for the worrying.

The worrying is forever.

—August 2006

The D Word

The most important thing about me, for quite a long chunk of my life, was that I was divorced. Even after I was no longer divorced but remarried, this was true. I have now been married to my third husband for more than twenty years. But when you've had children with someone you're divorced from, divorce defines everything; it's the lurking fact, a slice of anger in the pie of your brain.

Of course, there are good divorces, where everything is civil, even friendly. Child support payments arrive. Visitations take place on schedule. Your ex-husband rings the doorbell and stays on the other side of the threshold; he never walks in without knocking and helps himself to the coffee. In my next life I must get one of those divorces.

One good thing I'd like to say about divorce is that it sometimes makes it possible for you to be a much better wife to your next husband because you have a place for your anger; it's not directed at the person you're currently with.

Another good thing about divorce is that it makes clear something that marriage obscures, which is that you're on your own. There's no power struggle over which of you is going to get up in the middle of the night; you are.

But I can't think of anything good about divorce as far as the children are concerned. You can't kid yourself about that, although many people do. They say things like, It's better for children not to grow up with their parents in an unhappy marriage. But unless the parents are beating each other up, or abusing the children, kids are better off if their parents are together. Children are much too young to shuttle between houses. They're too young to handle the idea that the two people they love most in the world don't love each other anymore, if they ever did. They're too young to understand that all the wishful thinking in the world won't bring their parents back together. And the newfangled rigmarole of joint custody doesn't do anything to ease the cold reality: in order to see one parent, the divorced child must walk out on the other.

The best divorce is the kind where there are no children. That was my first divorce. You walk out the door and you never look back. There were cats, cats I was wildly attached to; my husband and I spoke in cat voices. Once the marriage was over, I never thought of the cats again (until I wrote about them in a novel and disguised them as hamsters).

A few months before my first husband and I broke up, I had a magazine assignment to write about the actors Rod Steiger and Claire Bloom and their fabulous marriage. I went to see them at their Fifth Avenue apartment, and they insisted on being interviewed separately. This should have been some sort of clue. But I was clueless. In fact, looking back, it seems to me that I was clueless until I was about fifty years old. Anyway, I interviewed the two of them in separate rooms. They seemed very happy. I wrote the piece, I turned it in, the magazine accepted it, they sent me a check, I cashed the check, and a day later, Rod Steiger and Claire Bloom announced they were getting a divorce. I couldn't believe it. Why hadn't they told me? Why had they gone forward with a magazine piece about their marriage when they were getting a divorce?

But then my own marriage ended, and about a week later a photographer turned up at my former apartment to take a picture of my husband and me for an article about our kitchen. I wasn't there, of course. I'd moved out. What's more, I'd forgotten the appointment. The reporter involved with the article was livid that I hadn't remembered, hadn't called, hadn't told her, and was no doubt angry that I'd agreed to do the interview about my marital kitchen when I had to have known I was getting a divorce. But the truth is you don't always know you're getting a divorce. For years, you're married. Then, one day, the concept of divorce enters your head. It sits there for a while. You lean toward it and then you lean away. You make lists. You calculate how much it will cost. You tote up grievances, and pluses and minuses. You have an affair. You start seeing a shrink. The two of you start seeing a shrink. And then you end the marriage, not because anything in particular happened that was worse than what had happened the day before, but simply because you suddenly have a place to stay while you look for an apartment, or $3,000 your father has unexpectedly given you.

I don't mean to leave out the context. My first marriage ended in the early 1970s, at the height of the women's movement. Jules Feiffer used to draw cartoons of young women dancing wildly around looking for themselves, and that's what we were all like. We took things way too seriously. We drew up contracts that were meant to divide the household tasks in a more equitable fashion. We joined consciousness-raising groups and sat in a circle and pretended we weren't jealous of one another. We read tracts that said the personal is political. And by the way, the personal *is* political, although not as much as we wanted to believe it was.

But the main problem with our marriages was not that our husbands wouldn't share the housework but that we were unbelievably irritable young women and our husbands irritated us unbelievably.

A thing I remember from my consciousness-raising group is that one of the women in it burst into tears one day because her husband had given her a frying pan for her birthday.

She, somehow, never got a divorce.

But the rest of us did.

We'd grown up in an era when no one was divorced, and suddenly everyone was divorced.

My second divorce was the worst kind of divorce. There were two children; one had just been born. My husband was in love with someone else. I found out about him and his affair when I was still pregnant. I had gone to New York for the day and had had a meeting with a writer-producer named Jay Presson Allen. I was about to go to LaGuardia to take the Eastern shuttle back to Washington when she handed me a script she happened to have lying around, by an English writer named Frederic Raphael. "Read this," she said. "You'll like it."

I opened it on the plane. It began with a married couple at a dinner party. I can't remember their names, but for the sake of the story, let's call them Clive and Lavinia. It was a very sophisticated dinner party and everyone at it was smart and brittle and chattering brilliantly. Clive and Lavinia were particularly clever, and they bantered with each other in a charming, flirtatious way. Everyone in the room admired them, and their marriage. The guests sat down to dinner and the patter continued. In the middle of the dinner, a man seated next to Lavinia put his hand on her leg. She put her cigarette out on his hand. The glittering conversation continued. When the dinner ended, Clive and Lavinia got into their car to drive home. The talk ceased, and they drove in absolute silence. They had nothing to say to each other. And then Lavinia said: "All right. Who is she?"

That was on page 8 of the screenplay.

I closed the script. I couldn't breathe. I knew at that moment that my husband was having an affair. I sat there, stunned, for the rest of the flight. The plane landed, and I went home and straight to his office in our apartment. There was a locked drawer. Of course. I knew there would be. I found the key. I opened the drawer and there was the evidence—a book of children's stories she'd given him, with an incredibly stupid inscription about their enduring love. I wrote about all this in a novel called *Heartburn*, and it's a very funny book, but it wasn't funny at the time. I was insane with grief. My heart was broken. I was terrified about what was going to happen to my children and me. I felt gaslighted, and idiotic, and completely mortified. I wondered if I was going to become one of those divorced women who's forced to move with her children to Connecticut and is never heard from again.

I walked out dramatically, and I came back after promises were made. My husband entered into the usual cycle for this sort of thing—lies, lies, and more lies. I myself entered into surveillance, steaming open American Express bills, swearing friends to secrecy, finding out that the friends I'd sworn to secrecy couldn't keep a secret, and so forth. There was a mysterious receipt from James Robinson Antiques. I called James Robinson and pretended to be my husband's assistant and claimed I needed to know exactly what the receipt was for so that I could insure it. The receipt turned out to be for an antique porcelain box that said "I Love You Truly" on it. It was presumably not unlike the antique porcelain box my husband had bought for me a couple of years earlier that said "Forever and Ever." I mention all this so you will understand that this is part of the process: once you find out he's cheated on you, you have to keep finding it out, over and over and over again, until you've degraded yourself so completely that there's nothing left to do but walk out.

When my second marriage ended, I was angry and hurt and shocked.

Now I think, Of course.

I think, Who can possibly be faithful when they're young?

I think, Stuff happens.

I think, People are careless and there are almost never any consequences (except for the children, which I already said).

And I survived. My religion is Get Over It. I turned it into a rollicking story. I wrote a novel. I bought a house with the money from the novel.

People always say that once it goes away, you forget the pain. It's a cliché of childbirth: you forget the pain. I don't happen to agree. I remember the pain. What you really forget is love.

Divorce seems as if it will last forever, and then suddenly, one day, your children grow up, move out, and make lives for themselves, and except for an occasional flare, you have no contact at all with your ex-husband. The divorce has lasted way longer than the marriage, but finally it's over.

Enough about that.

The point is that for a long time, the fact that I was divorced was the most important thing about me.

And now it's not.

Now the most important thing about me is that I'm old.

—November 2010

Fantasies

One of the trump cards that men who are threatened by women's liberation are always dredging up is the question of whether there is sex after liberation. I have heard at least five or six experts or writers or spokesmen or some such stand up at various meetings and wonder aloud what happens to sex between men and women when the revolution comes. These men are always hooted down by the women present; in fact, I am usually one of the women present hooting them down, sniggering snide remarks to whoever is next to me like well-we-certainly-know-how-sure-of-himself-*he*-is. This fall, at the *Playboy* Writers' Convocation, an author named Morton Hunt uttered the magic words at a panel on The Future of Sex, and even in that room, full of male chauvinism and *Playboy* philosophers, the animosity against him was audible.

I spend a great deal of my energy these days trying to fit feminism into marriage, or vice versa—I'm never sure which way the priorities lie; it depends on my mood—but as truly committed as I am to the movement and as violent as I have become toward people who knock it, I think it is unfair to dismiss these men. They deserve some kind of answer. Okay. The answer is, nobody knows what happens to sex after liberation. It's a big mystery. And now that I have gotten that out of the way, I can go on to what really interests and puzzles me about sex and liberation—which is that it is difficult for me to see how sexual behavior and relations between the sexes can change at all unless our sexual fantasies change. So many of the conscious and unconscious ways men and women treat each other have to do with romantic and sexual fantasies that are deeply ingrained, not just in society but in literature. The movement may manage to clean up the mess in society, but I don't know whether it can ever clean up the mess in our minds.

I am somewhat liberated by current standards, but I have in my head this dreadful unliberated sex fantasy. One of the women in my consciousness-raising group is always referring to her "rich fantasy life," by which I suppose she means that in her fantasies she makes it in costume, or in exotic places, or with luminaries like Mao Tse-tung in a large bowl of warm Wheatena. My fantasy life is unfortunately nowhere near that interesting.

Several years ago, I went to interview photographer Philippe Halsman, whose notable achievements include a charming book containing photographs of celebrities jumping. The jumps are quite revealing in a predictable sort of way—Richard Nixon with his rigid, constricted jump, the Duke and Duchess of Windsor in a deeply dependent jump. And so forth. In the course of the interview, Halsman asked me if I wanted to jump for him; seeing it as a way to avoid possibly years of psychoanalysis, I agreed. I did what I thought was my quintessential jump. "Do it again," said Halsman. I did, attempting to duplicate exactly what I had done before. "Again," he said, and I did. "Well," said Halsman, "I can see from your jump that you are a very determined, ambitious, directed person, but you will never write a novel." "Why is that?" I asked. "Because you have only one jump in you," he said.

At the time, I thought that was really unfair—I had, after all, thought he wanted to see the *same* jump, not a different one every time; but I see now that he was exactly right. I have only one jump in me. I see this more and more every day. I am no longer interested in thirty-one flavors; I stick with English toffee. More to the point, I have had the same sex fantasy, with truly minor variations, since I was about eleven years old. It is really a little weird to be stuck with something so crucially important for so long; I have managed to rid myself of all the other accouterments of being eleven—I have pimples more or less under control, I can walk fairly capably in high heels—but I find myself with this appalling fantasy that has burrowed in and has absolutely nothing to do with my life.

I have never told anyone the exact details of my particular sex fantasy: it is my only secret and I am not going to divulge it here. I once told *almost* all of it to my former therapist; he died last year, and when I saw his obituary I felt a great sense of relief: the only person in the world who almost knew how crazy I am was gone and I was safe. Anyway, without giving away any of the juicy parts, I can tell you that in its broad outlines it has largely to do with being dominated by faceless males who rip my clothes off. That's just about all they have to do. Stare at me in this faceless way, go mad with desire, and rip my clothes off. It's terrific. In my sex fantasy, nobody ever loves me for my mind.

The fantasy of rape—of which mine is in a kind of prepubescent subcategory—is common enough among women and (in mirror image) among men. And what I don't understand is that with so many of us stuck with these clichéd feminine/masculine, submissive/dominant, masochistic/sadistic fantasies, how are we ever going to adjust fully to the less thrilling but more desirable reality of equality? A few months ago, someone named B. Lyman Stewart, a urologist at Cedars of Lebanon Hospital in Los Angeles, attributed the rising frequency of impotence among his male patients to the women's movement, which he called an effort to dominate men. The movement is nothing of the kind; but it and a variety of other events in society have certainly brought about a change in the way women behave in bed. A young man who grows up expecting to dominate sexually is bound to be somewhat startled by a young woman who wants sex as much as he does, and multi-orgasmic sex at that. By the same token, I suspect that a great deal of the difficulty women report in achieving orgasm is traceable—sadly—to the possibility that a man who is a tender fellow with implicit capabilities for impotence hardly fits into classic fantasies of big brutes with implicit capabilities for violence. A close friend who has the worst marriage I know—her husband beats her up regularly—reports that her sex life is wonderful. I am hardly suggesting that women ask their men to beat them—nor am I advocating the course apparently preferred by one of the most prominent members of the women's movement, who makes it mainly with blue-collar workers and semiliterates. But I wonder how we will ever break free from all the nonsense we grew up with; I wonder if our fantasies can ever catch up to what we all want for our lives.

It is possible, through sheer willpower, to stop having unhealthy sex fantasies. I have several friends who did just that. "What do you have instead?" I asked. "Nothing," they replied. Well, I don't know. I'm not at all sure I wouldn't rather have an unhealthy sex fantasy than no sex fantasy at all. But my real question is whether it is possible, having discarded the fantasy, to discard the thinking and expectations it represents. In my case, I'm afraid it wouldn't be. I have no desire to be dominated. Honestly I don't. And yet I find myself becoming angry when I'm not. My husband has trouble hailing a cab or flagging a waiter, and suddenly I feel a kind of rage; ball-breaking anger rises to my T-zone. I wish he were better at hailing taxis than I am; on the other hand, I realize that expectation is culturally conditioned, utterly foolish, has nothing to do with anything, is exactly the kind of thinking that ought to be got rid of in our society; on still another hand, having that insight into my reaction does not seem to calm my irritation.

My husband is fond of reminding me of the story of Moses, who kept the Israelites in the desert for forty years because he knew a slave generation could not found a new free society. The comparison with the women's movement is extremely apt, I think; I doubt that it will ever be possible for the women of my generation to escape from our own particular slave mentality. For the next generation, life may indeed be freer. After all, if society changes, the fantasies will change; where women are truly equal, where their status has nothing to do with whom they marry, when the issues of masculine/feminine cease to exist, some of this absurd reliance on role playing will be eliminated. But not all of it. Because even after the revolution, we will be left with all the literature. "What will happen to the literature?" Helen Dudar of the *New York Post* once asked Ti-Grace Atkinson. "What does it matter what happens?" Ms. Atkinson replied. But it does. You are what you eat. After liberation, we will still have to reckon with the Sleeping Beauty and Cinderella. Granted there will also be a new batch of fairy tales about princesses who refuse to have ladies-in-waiting because it is exploitative of the lower classes—but that sounds awfully tedious, doesn't it? Short of a mass book burning, which no one wants, things may well go on as they are now: women pulled between the intellectual attraction of liberation and the emotional, psychological, and cultural mishmash it's hard to escape growing up with; men trying to cope with these two extremes, and with their own ambivalence besides. It's not much fun this way, but at least it's not boring.

—July 1972

On Maintenance

I have been trying for weeks to write about maintenance, but it hasn't been easy, and for a simple reason: Maintenance takes up so much of my life that I barely have time to sit down at the computer.

You know what maintenance is, I'm sure. Maintenance is what they mean when they say, "After a certain point, it's just patch patch patch." Maintenance is what you have to do just so you can walk out the door knowing that if you go to the market and bump into a guy who once rejected you, you won't have to hide behind a stack of canned food. I don't mean to be too literal about this. There are a couple of old boyfriends whom I always worry about bumping into, but there's no chance—if I ever did—that I would recognize either of them. On top of which they live in other cities. But the point is that I still think about them every time I'm tempted to leave the house without eyeliner.

There are two types of maintenance, of course. There's Status Quo Maintenance—the things you have to do daily, or weekly, or monthly, just to stay more or less even. And then there's the maintenance you have to do monthly, or yearly, or every couple of years or so—maintenance I think of as Pathetic Attempts to Turn Back the Clock. Into this category fall such things as face-lifts, liposuction, Botox, major dental work, and Removal of Unsightly Things—of varicose veins, for instance, and skin tags, and those irritating little red spots that crop up on your torso after a certain age for no real reason. I'm not going to discuss such issues here. For now, I'm concentrating only on the routine, everyday things required just to keep you from looking like someone who no longer cares.

Hair

We begin, I'm sorry to say, with hair. I'm sorry to say it because the amount of maintenance involving hair is genuinely overwhelming. Sometimes I think that not having to worry about your hair anymore is the secret upside of death.

Tell the truth. Aren't you sick of your hair? Aren't you tired of washing and drying it? I know people who wash their hair every day, and I don't get it. Your hair doesn't need to be washed every day, any more than your black pants have to be dry-cleaned every time you wear them. But no one listens to me. It takes some of my friends an hour a day, seven days a week, just to wash and blow-dry their hair. How they manage to have any sort of life at all is a mystery. I mean, we're talking about 365 hours a year! Nine workweeks! Maybe this made sense when we were young, when the amount of time we spent making ourselves look good bore some correlation to the number of hours we spent having sex (which was, after all, one of the reasons for our spending so much time on grooming). But now that we're older, whom are we kidding?

On top of which, have you tried buying shampoo lately? I mean, good luck to you. Good luck finding anything that says on the label, simply, shampoo. There are shampoos for dry but oily hair and shampoos for coarse but fine hair, and then there are the conditioners and the straighteners and the volumizers. How damaged does your hair have to be to qualify as "damaged"? Why are some shampoos for blondes? Do the blondes get better shampoos than the rest of us? It's totally dizzying, shelf after shelf of products, not one of them capable of doing the job alone.

I deal with all this confusion by taking draconian measures to reduce the amount of time I spend on my hair. I never do my own hair if I can help it, and I try my best to avoid situations that would require me to. Every so often a rich friend asks me if I'd like to go on a trip involving a boat, and all I can think about is the misery of five days in a small cabin struggling with a blow-dryer. And I am never going back to Africa; the last time I was there, in 1972, there were no hairdressers out in the bush, and as far as I was concerned, that was the end of that place.

I'm in awe of the women I know who have magical haircuts that require next to no maintenance. I envy all Asian women—I mean, have you ever seen an Asian woman whose hair looks bad? (No, you haven't. Why is this?) I once read an interview with a well-known actress who said that the thing she was proudest of was that she could blow-dry her own hair, and I was depressed for days afterward. I'm completely inept at blow-drying my own hair. I have the equipment and the products, I assure you. I own blow-dryers with special attachments, and hot rollers and Velcro rollers, and gel and mousse and spray, but my hair looks absolutely awful if I do it myself.

So, twice a week, I go to a beauty salon and have my hair blown dry. It's cheaper by far than psychoanalysis, and much more uplifting. What's more, it takes much less time than washing and drying your own hair every single day, especially if, like me, you live in a large city where a good and reasonably priced hairdresser is just around the corner. Still, at the end of the year, I've spent at least eighty hours just keeping my hair clean and pressed. That's two workweeks. There's no telling what I could be doing with all that time. I could be on eBay, for instance, buying something that will turn out to be worth much less than I bid for it. I could be reading good books. Of course, I could be reading good books while having my hair done—but I don't. I always mean to. I always take one with me when I go to the salon. But instead I end up reading the fashion magazines that are lying around, and I mostly concentrate on articles about cosmetic and surgical procedures. Once I picked up a copy of *Vogue* while having my hair done, and it cost me twenty thousand dollars. But you should see my teeth.

Hair Dye

Many years ago, when Gloria Steinem turned forty, someone complimented her on how remarkably young she looked, and she replied, "This is what forty looks like." It was a great line, and I wish I'd said it. "This is what forty looks like" led, inevitably, to its most significant corollary, "Forty is the new thirty," which led to many other corollaries: "Fifty is the new forty," "Sixty is the new fifty," and even "Restaurants are the new theater," "Focaccia is the new quiche," et cetera.

Anyway, here's the point: There's a reason why forty, fifty, and sixty don't look the way they used to, and it's not because of feminism, or better living through exercise. It's because of hair dye. In the 1950s only 7 percent of American women dyed their hair; today there are parts of Manhattan and Los Angeles where there are no gray-haired women at all. (Once, some years ago, I went to Le Cirque, a well-known New York restaurant, to a lunch in honor of a woman named Jean Harris, who had just that week been released from twelve years in prison for murdering her diet-doctor boyfriend, and she was the only woman in the restaurant with gray hair.)

Hair dye has changed everything, but it almost never gets the credit. It's the most powerful weapon older women have against the youth culture, and because it actually succeeds at stopping the clock (at least where your hair color is concerned), it makes women open to far more drastic procedures (like face-lifts). I can make a case that it's at least partly responsible for the number of women entering (and managing to stay in) the job market in middle and late middle age, as well as for all sorts of fashion trends. For example, it's one of the reasons women don't wear hats anymore, and it's entirely the reason that everyone I know has a closet full of black clothes. Think about it. Fifty years ago, women of a certain age almost never wore black. Black was for widows, specifically for Italian war widows, and even Gloria Steinem might concede that the average Italian war widow made you believe that sixty was the new seventy-five. If you have gray hair, black makes you look not just older but sadder. But black looks great on older women with dark hair—so great, in fact, that even younger women with dark hair now wear black. Even blondes wear black. Even women in L.A. wear black. Most everyone wears black—except for anchorwomen, United States senators, and residents of Texas, and I feel really bad for them. I mean, black makes your life so much simpler. Everything matches black, especially black.

But back to hair dye. I began having my hair dyed about fifteen years ago, and for many years, I was categorized by my colorist as a single-process customer—whatever was being done to me (which I honestly have no idea how to describe) did not involve peroxide and therefore took "only" ninety minutes every six weeks or so. Whenever I complained about how long it took, I was told that I was lucky I wasn't blond. Where hair dye is concerned, being blond is practically a career.

Oh, the poor blondes! They were sitting there at the colorist's when I arrived, and they were still sitting there when I left. Their scalps were sectioned off and dotted with little aluminum-foil packets; they had to sit under hair-dryers; they complained bitterly about their dry and damaged hair and their chronic split ends. I felt superior to them in every way. For the first time in my life, it seemed, there was an advantage to being a brunette.

But then, about a year ago, my colorist gave me several highlights as a present. Highlights, you probably know, are little episodes of blondness that are scattered about your head. They involve peroxide. They extend the length of time involved in hair dying from unbearable to unendurable. As I sat in the chair, waiting for my highlights to sink in, I was bored witless. Hours passed. I couldn't imagine why I had been conned into agreeing to this free trial. I vowed that I would never ever even be tempted to have highlights again, much less to pay money for them. (They are, in addition to being time-consuming, wildly expensive. Naturally.)

But—you will probably not be surprised to hear this—those highlights were a little like that first sip of brandy Alexander that Lee Remick drank in *Days of Wine and Roses*. I emerged onto Madison Avenue with four tiny, virtually invisible blondish streaks in my hair, and was so thrilled and overwhelmed by the change in my appearance that I honestly thought that when I came home, my husband wouldn't recognize me. As it happened, he didn't even notice I'd done anything to myself. But it didn't matter; from that moment on, I was hooked. As a result, my hair-dying habit now takes at least three hours every six weeks or so, and because my hair colorist is (in her world) only slightly less famous than Hillary Clinton, it costs more per year than my first automobile.

Nails

I want to ask a question: When and how did it happen that you absolutely had to have a manicure? I don't begin to know the answer, but I want to leave the question out there, floating around in the atmosphere, as a reminder that just when you think you know exactly how many things you have to do to yourself where maintenance is concerned, another can just pop up out of nowhere and take a huge bite out of your life.

I spent the first forty-five years of my life never thinking about my nails. Occasionally I filed them with the one lone wretched emery board I owned. (A side note on this subject: One of the compelling mysteries of the world, right up there with the missing socks, is what happens to all the other emery boards in the box of emery boards you bought so that you would have more than just one lone wretched emery board.) Anyway, occasionally I filed my nails, put a little polish on them, and went out into the world. This process took about three minutes, twice a year. (Just kidding. But not by much.) I knew there were women who had manicures on a regular basis, but in my opinion they were indolent women who had nothing better to do. Or they were under the mistaken impression that painted nails were glamorous. They were certainly not women who made their living at a typewriter, the machine that was the sworn enemy of long nails.

And then one day, like mushrooms, a trillion nail places appeared in Manhattan. Suddenly there were more nail places than there were liquor stores, or Kinko's, or opticians, or dry cleaners, or locksmiths, and there are way more of all of those in Manhattan than you can ever understand. Sometimes it seemed there were more nail places in Manhattan than there were nails. Most of these nail places were staffed by young Korean women, all of whom could do a manicure quickly and efficiently and not eat up the clock in any way by feigning the remotest interest in their customers. And they were incredibly cheap—eight or ten dollars at most for a regular manicure.

Soon everyone was getting manicures. If your nails weren't manicured (as opposed to merely clean), you felt ungroomed. You felt ashamed. You felt like sitting on your hands. And so it became necessary to have manicures once a week. Which brings me, alas, to pedicures.

The best thing about a pedicure is that most of the year, from September to May to be exact, no one except your loved one knows if you have had one. The second best thing about a pedicure is that while you're having your feet done, you have the use of your hands and can easily read or even talk on a cell phone. The third best thing about a pedicure is that when it's over, your feet really do look adorable.

The worst thing about pedicures is that they take way too much time and then, just when you think you're done, you have to wait for your toenails to dry. It takes almost as long for your toenails to dry as it does to have a pedicure. So there you sit, for what seems like eternity, and finally you can't stand waiting one more minute so you gently slip on your sandals and leave and on the way home you absolutely ruin the polish on your big toe and since your big toe is really the only thing anyone notices as far as your feet are concerned, you might as well not have had a pedicure in the first place.

Unwanted Hair

I'm sorry to report that I have a mustache. The truth is, I probably always had a mustache, but for years it was sort of dormant, or incipient, or threatening, in the way a cloudy sky threatens to rain. On a few occasions in my younger years it turned dark and stormy, and when it did, I dealt with it by going to the drugstore and buying a much-too-large jar of something called Jolen creme bleach. (I always tried to buy a *small* jar of Jolen creme bleach, but no one stocks it, for the obvious reason that it costs less than the big jar.) This trip to the store was usually followed, almost immediately, by the discovery of several other barely used, perfectly good much-too-large jars of Jolen creme bleach, which turned out to have been right there all along, under the bathroom sink, where I had just looked for them—I swear I had—and yet didn't see them. Jolen creme bleach turns the mustache on your upper lip to the exact color of Richard Gephardt's hair, which is better than its looking like Frida Kahlo's mustache, but it's still slightly hairier than you mean it to be.

But then, along came menopause. And with it, my mustache changed: It was no longer dormant, incipient, and threatening; it was now just plain there. Fortunately, at the time, I was going to a lovely Russian-born hairdresser named Nina on the Upper West Side of Manhattan who, as it turned out, specialized in something called threading, a fantastic and thrilling method of hair removal she had learned in Russia and which, as far as I can tell, is the only thing the Russians managed to outdo us at in fifty years of the Cold War. Threading involves thread—

garden-variety sewing thread—a long strand of which is twisted and maneuvered in a sort of cat's cradle configuration so as to remove hair in a way that is quick and painful (although not, I should point out, as painful as, say, labor). The results last about a month.

For a long time, threading seemed like a wonderful and not particularly burdensome addition to my maintenance regime. Nina did my hair twice a week, so it took only five additional minutes for her to thread my mustache—plus, of course, ten additional minutes to thread my eyebrows, not that I needed my eyebrows threaded because my bangs are so long you can't even tell whether I have eyebrows, much less whether they need weeding. But as long as Nina was doing the mustache it seemed to her (and let's face it, to me) that she might as well do the eyebrows too. Having your eyebrows threaded is much more expensive and much more painful (although not, I should point out, as painful as labor), and causes you to sneeze uncontrollably. But that's a small price to pay. In fact, the cost of threading is a small price to pay for the smooth and lovely result.

Unfortunately, though, a couple of years ago, I moved away from the Upper West Side to the Upper East Side of Manhattan, taking my mustache with me but leaving behind Nina and her compelling geographical convenience. So now I must add the travel time (and cab fare) to the cost of threading.

On the other hand, where unwanted hair is concerned, I'm duty-bound to report that I spend considerably less time having myself waxed than I used to because (and you don't see a whole lot of this in those cheerful, idiotic books on menopause), at a certain point, you have less hair in all sorts of places you used to have quite a lot. When I was growing up, I had a friend who was a pioneer in waxing—she first had her legs waxed when she was fifteen, and this was in 1956, when waxing was really practically unknown. She assured me that if I didn't start getting my legs waxed—if I persisted in simply shaving like all the other commoners in the world—the hair would grow in faster and faster and faster and faster and eventually I would look like a bear. This turns out not to be true. You can shave your legs for many years, and they don't really get a whole lot hairier than when they started. And then, at a certain age, they get less hairy. My guess is that by the time I'm eighty, I will be able to handle any offending hair on my legs with two plucks of an eyebrow tweezer.

As for waxing what I like to call my bikini, it has become but a brief episode in what the fashion magazines refer to as my beauty regimen, and owing to my ability to avoid wearing a bathing suit except on rare occasions, I rarely need to do it anymore. (In the old days, however, a bikini wax was not just painful—it was truly as painful as labor. I dealt with the pain by using the breathing exercises I learned in Lamaze classes. I recommend them highly, although not for childbirth, for which they are virtually useless.) I understand that some young women have their pubic hair removed entirely, or shaped, like topiary, into triangles and hearts and the like. I am too old for this, thank God.

Speaking of the pain of labor, which I seem to be, I would like to interject a short, irrelevant note: Why do people always say you forget the pain of labor? I haven't forgotten the pain of labor. Labor hurt. It hurt a lot. The fact that I am not currently in pain and cannot simulate the pain of labor doesn't mean I don't remember it. I am currently not eating a wonderful piece of grilled chicken I once had in Asolo, Italy, in 1982, but I remember it well. It was delicious. I can tell you exactly what it tasted like, and except for the time when I returned to the restaurant six years later and ordered it again (and it turned out, amazingly, to be exactly as wonderful as I remembered), I have never tasted chicken that was crisper, tastier, or juicier. The song has ended, but the melody lingers on, and that goes for the pain of labor—but not in a good way.

Exercise

I would like to be in shape. I have a friend who gets up every morning at 5 a.m. and essentially does a triathlon. I'm not exaggerating. She is Ironwoman. She lifts weights. She runs marathons. She bicycles for hours. Last summer she took swimming lessons, and within a week she was talking about swimming around the island of Manhattan. A few summers ago I decided to do some swimming, and within a week I had swimmer's ear. Have you ever had it? It's torture. Water rattles around in your ear and itches so much that it wakes you up at night, and there's absolutely no way you can scratch it short of plunging your finger into your brain stem. My own theory about Van Gogh is that he cut off his ear because he'd made the mistake of taking up swimming.

In any case, I would like to be in shape. I would. But every time I try to get into shape, something goes wrong and makes it impossible. Let me make this clear: Every time I get into shape, something breaks.

Exercise, as you no doubt know, is a late arrival in the history of civilization. Until around 1910, people exercised all the time, but they didn't think of it as exercise—they thought of it as life itself. They had to get from one place to the other, usually on foot, and harvest the crop, and wage war, and so on. But then the automobile was invented (not to mention the Sherman tank), and that pretty much led to what we have today—a country full of underexercised (and often overweight) people—and a parallel universe of overexercised (but not necessarily underweight) people. I myself swing between the two universes. I spend time getting into shape; then something breaks, and then I spend time recovering and not being in shape; then I recover and I get into shape; then something new breaks. So far, in the breakage department, I have managed the following: I pulled my lower back doing sit-ups; I threw out my right hip on the treadmill; I got shin splints from jogging; and I entirely destroyed my neck just from rolling over in bed. A few years ago, during a wild and committed period of exercise, I happened to be sent a tape of the movie *Chicago*, and I made the mistake of confusing it with an exercise video. It was, without question, the greatest exercise video I have ever worked out to. I could lift weights forever while watching it. For the first time in my exercising life, I was never bored. I could be Catherine Zeta-Jones, and then I could be Renée Zellweger. I pranced around the apartment waving my five-pound weights here and there and singing "All That Jazz." I have never been happier exercising. But after three weeks, I woke up one morning in horrible pain and discovered I couldn't move my arms. Millions of dollars in doctor's fees later, it turned out that I had not one but two frozen shoulders, the result (naturally) of lifting too many weights for far too long. It took two years for these frozen shoulders to mostly thaw, and in the meantime, I had pretty much resigned myself to the prospect of never being able to scratch my own back (or zip up a dress). (Not that I wear dresses, but if I did.) But I am now exercising again. I have a trainer. I have my treadmill. I have my TV set over the treadmill. I exercise almost four hours a week, and I would rather be in Philadelphia (although not in labor).

Skin

In my bathroom there are many bottles. There are also many jars. Most of these bottles and jars contain products for the skin, although none of them contain something that is called, merely, "skin cream." Instead they contain face cream, or hand lotion, or body lotion, or foot cream. Remember when we were young? There was only Nivea. Life was so simple. I know in my heart that all these labels on these bottles and jars are whimsical and arbitrary and designed to make vulnerable, pitiable women like me shell out astronomical sums of money for useless products; on the other hand, you will probably never see me using foot cream on my face, just in case.

Here, for example, right next to the sink, is a bottle of something called StriVectin-SD. For exactly five minutes in 2004 StriVectin-SD was thought to be the Fountain of Youth. It instead turned out to be simply skin lotion, a bottle of which cost an arm and a leg. But meanwhile, for one brief shining moment, I believed it was the answer to everything. The woman who sold it to me at the cosmetics counter behaved as if she were slipping me a bottle of aged whiskey during Prohibition. It had just come in, she whispered. It was down in the basement. They couldn't put it out on display, or it would be gone in a twinkling. Only certain customers were being allowed to have it.

Now it sits on the bathroom counter, taking up space, alongside similar testaments to my gullibility—relics of the Retin-A years and the glycolic-acid era and the La Prairie period. One of my good friends once gave me a tiny jar of La Mer cream, which I think cost about a hundred dollars a teaspoon. I still have it, since it is way too valuable to use.

The point is, I have cream for my face. I have lotions for my arms and legs. I have oil for my bath. I have Vaseline for my feet. I cannot begin to tell you how much time I spend rubbing these moisturizers into myself. But I still get pimples on my face and rough patches on my arms and legs. What's more, the skin on my back is so dry that when I take off a black sweater it looks as if it's been in a snowstorm, and the skin on my heels has the consistency of a loofah.

I have no doubt omitted something where maintenance is concerned. The world of maintenance is changing every second, and I may not know about all sorts of things that women my age are up to. (The other day, for instance, I had lunch with a friend who assured me that I hadn't lived until I had tried having some sort of facial that seems to include a mild form of electroshock.)

What I know is that I spend a huge amount of time with my finger in the dike, and that doesn't begin to include all the things I promised not to go into—the pathetic things. I have done any number of things that fall just short of plastic surgery. I even had all the fillings in my mouth replaced with white material, and I swear to God it took six months off my age. From time to time my dermatologist shoots a hypodermic needle full of something called Restylane into my chin, and it sort of fills in the saggy parts. I have had Botox twice, in a wrinkle in my forehead.

Once I even had my lips plumped up with a fat injection, but I looked like a Ubangi, so I never did it again.

But the other day, on the street, I passed a homeless woman. I have never understood the feminists who insisted they were terrified of becoming bag ladies, but as I watched this woman shuffle down the street, I finally understood at least my version of it. I don't want to be melodramatic; I am never going to become a bag lady. But I am only about eight hours a week away from looking exactly like that woman on the street—with frizzled flyaway gray hair I would probably have if I stopped dyeing mine; with a potbelly I would definitely develop if I ate just half of what I think about eating every day; with the dirty nails and chapped lips and mustache and bushy eyebrows that would be my destiny if I ever spent two weeks on a desert island.

Eight hours a week and counting. By the time I reach my seventies, I'm sure it will take at least twice as long. The only consolation I have in any of this is that when I'm very old and virtually unemployable, I will at least have something to do. Assuming, of course, that I haven't spent all my money doing it.

—October 2005

The Six Stages of E-mail

Stage One: Infatuation

I just got e-mail! I can't believe it! It's so great! Here's my handle. Write me. Who said letter-writing was dead? Were they ever wrong. I'm writing letters like crazy for the first time in years. I come home and ignore all my loved ones and go straight to the computer to make contact with total strangers. And how great is AOL? It's so easy. It's so friendly. It's a community. Wheeeee! I've got mail!

Stage Two: Clarification

Okay, I'm starting to understand—e-mail isn't letter-writing at all, it's something else entirely. It was just invented, it was just born, and overnight it turns out to have a form and a set of rules and a language all its own. Not since the printing press. Not since television. It's revolutionary. It's life-altering. It's shorthand. Cut to the chase. Get to the point. It saves so much time. It takes five seconds to accomplish in an e-mail something that takes five minutes on the telephone. The phone requires you to converse, to say things like hello and goodbye, to pretend to some semblance of interest in the person on the other end of the line. Worst of all, the phone occasionally forces you to make actual plans with the people you talk to—to suggest lunch or dinner—even if you have no desire whatsoever to see them. No danger of that with e-mail. E-mail is a whole new way of being friends with people: intimate but not, chatty but not, communicative but not; in short, friends but not. What a breakthrough. How did we ever live without it? I have more to say on this subject, but I have to answer an instant message from someone I almost know.

Stage Three: Confusion

I have done nothing to deserve any of this: Viagra!!!!! Best Web source for Vioxx. Spend a week in Cancún. Have a rich beautiful lawn. Astrid would like to be added as one of your friends. XXXXXXXVideos. Add three inches to the length of your penis. The Democratic National Committee needs you. Virus Alert. FW: This will make you laugh. FW: This is funny. FW: This is hilarious. FW: Grapes and raisins toxic for dogs. FW: Gabriel García Márquez's Final Farewell. FW: Kurt Vonnegut's Commencement Address. FW: The Neiman Marcus Chocolate Chip Cookie recipe. AOL Member: We value your opinion. A message from Barack Obama. Find low mortgage payments, Nora. Nora, it's your time to shine. Need to fight off bills, Nora? Yvette would like to be added as one of your friends. You have failed to establish a full connection to AOL.

Stage Four: Disenchantment

Help! I'm drowning. I have 112 unanswered e-mails. I'm a writer—imagine how many unanswered e-mails I would have if I had a real job. Imagine how much writing I could do if I didn't have to answer all this e-mail. My eyes are dim. My wrist hurts. I can't focus. Every time I start to write something, the e-mail icon starts bobbing up and down and I'm compelled to check whether anything good or interesting has arrived.

It hasn't. Still, it might, any second now. And yes, it's true—I can do in a few seconds with e-mail what would take much longer on the phone, but most of my e-mails are from people who don't have my phone number and would never call me in the first place. In the brief time it took me to write this paragraph, three more e-mails arrived. Now I have 115 unanswered e-mails. Strike that: 116. Glub glub glub glub glub.

Stage Five: Accommodation

Yes. No. Can't. No way. Maybe. Doubtful. Sorry. So sorry. Thanks. No thanks. Out of town. OOT. Try me in a month. Try me in the fall. Try me in a year. NoraE@aol.com can now be reached at NoraE81082@gmail.com.

Stage Six: Death

Call me.

—July 2007

Considering the Alternative

When I turned sixty, I had a big birthday party in Las Vegas, which happens to be one of my top five places. We spent the weekend eating and drinking and gambling and having fun. One of my friends threw twelve passes at the craps table and we all made some money and screamed and yelled and I went to bed deliriously happy. The spell lasted for several days, and as a result, I managed to avoid thinking about what it all meant. Denial has been a way of life for me for many years. I actually believe in denial. It seemed to me that the only way to deal with a birthday of this sort was to do everything possible to push it from my mind. Nothing else about me is better than it was at fifty, or forty, or thirty, but I definitely have the best haircut I've ever had, I like my new apartment, and, as the expression goes, consider the alternative.

I have been sixty for four years now, and by the time you read this I will probably have been sixty for five. I survived turning sixty, I was not thrilled to turn sixty-one, I was less thrilled to turn sixty-two, I didn't much like being sixty-three, I loathed being sixty-four, and I will hate being sixty-five. I don't let on about such things in person; in person, I am cheerful and Pollyannaish. But the honest truth is that it's sad to be over sixty. The long shadows are everywhere—friends dying and battling illness. A miasma of melancholy hangs there, forcing you to deal with the fact that your life, however happy and successful, has been full of disappointments and mistakes, little ones and big ones. There are dreams that are never quite going to come true, ambitions that will never quite be realized. There are, in short, regrets. Edith Piaf was famous for singing a song called "Non, je ne regrette rien." It's a good song. I know what she meant. I can get into it; I can make a case that I regret nothing. After all, most of my mistakes turned out to be things I survived, or turned into funny stories, or, on occasion, even made money from. But the truth is that *je regrette beaucoup*.

There are all sorts of books written for older women. They are, as far as I can tell, uniformly upbeat and full of bromides and homilies about how pleasant life can be once one is free from all the nagging obligations of children, monthly periods, and, in some cases, full-time jobs. I find these books utterly useless, just as I found all the books I once read about menopause utterly useless. Why do people write books that say it's better to be older than to be younger? It's not better. Even if you have all your marbles, you're constantly reaching for the name of the person you met the day before yesterday. Even if you're in great shape, you can't chop an onion the way you used to and you can't ride a bicycle several miles without becoming a candidate for traction. If you work, you're surrounded by young people who are plugged into the marketplace, the demographic, the zeitgeist; they want your job and someday soon they're going to get it. If you're fortunate enough to be in a sexual relationship, you're not going to have the sex you once had. Plus, you can't wear a bikini. Oh, how I regret not having worn a bikini for the entire year I was twenty-six. If anyone young is reading this, go, right this minute, put on a bikini, and don't take it off until you're thirty-four.

A magazine editor called me the other day, an editor who, like me, is over sixty. Her magazine was going to do an issue on Age, and she wanted me to write something for it. We began to talk about the subject, and she said, "You know what drives me nuts? Why do women our age say, 'In my day . . .'? *This* is our day."

But it isn't our day. It's *their* day. We're just hanging on. We can't wear tank tops, we have no idea who 50 Cent is, and we don't know how to use almost any of the functions on our cell phones. If we hit the wrong button on the remote control and the television screen turns to snow, we have no idea how to get the television set back to where it was in the first place. (This is the true nightmare of the empty nest: Your children are gone, and they were the only people in the house who knew how to use the remote control.) Technology is a bitch. I can no longer even figure out how to get the buttons on the car radio to play my favorite stations. The gears on my bicycle mystify me. On my bicycle! And thank God no one has given me a digital wristwatch. In fact, if any of my friends are reading this, please don't ever give me a digital anything.

Just the other day I went shopping at a store in Los Angeles that happens to stock jeans that actually come all the way up to my waist, and I was stunned to discover that the customer just before me was Nancy Reagan. That's how old I am: Nancy Reagan and I shop in the same store.

Anyway, I said to this editor, you're wrong, you are so wrong, this is not *our* day, this is *their* day. But she was undaunted. She said to me, well then, I have another idea: Why don't you write about Age Shame? I said to her, get someone who is only fifty to write about Age Shame. I am way past Age Shame, if I ever had it. I'm just happy to be here at all.

Anyway, the point is, I don't know why so much nonsense about age is written—although I can certainly understand that no one really wants to read anything that says aging sucks. We are a generation that has learned to believe we can do something about almost everything. We are active—hell, we are proactive. We are positive thinkers. We have the power. We will take any suggestion seriously. If a pill will help, we will take it. If being in the Zone will help, we will enter the Zone. When we hear about the latest ludicrously expensive face cream that is alleged to turn back the clock, we will go out and buy it even though we know that the last five face creams we fell for were completely ineffectual. We will do crossword puzzles to ward off Alzheimer's and eat six almonds a day to ward off cancer; we will scan ourselves to find whatever can be nipped in the bud. We are in control. Behind the wheel. On the cutting edge. We make lists. We seek out the options. We surf the net.

But there are some things that are absolutely, definitively, entirely uncontrollable.

I am dancing around the D word, but I don't mean to be coy. When you cross into your sixties, your odds of dying—or of merely getting horribly sick on the way to dying—spike. Death is a sniper. It strikes people you love, people you like, people you know, it's everywhere. You could be next. But then you turn out not to be. But then again you could be.

Meanwhile, your friends die, and you're left not just bereft, not just grieving, not just guilty, but utterly helpless. There is nothing you can do. Everybody dies.

"What is the answer?" Gertrude Stein asked Alice B. Toklas as Stein was dying.

There was no reply.

"In that case, what is the question?" Stein asked.

Well, exactly.

Well, not quite exactly. Here are some questions I am constantly noodling over: Do you splurge or do you hoard? Do you live every day as if it's your last, or do you save your money on the chance you'll live twenty more years? Is life too short, or is it going to be too long? Do you work as hard as you can, or do you slow down to smell the roses? And where do carbohydrates fit into all this? Are we really going to have to spend our last years avoiding bread, especially now that bread in America is so unbelievably delicious? And what about chocolate? There's a question for you, Gertrude Stein—what about chocolate?

My friend Judy died last year. She was the person I told everything to. She was my best friend, my extra sister, my true mother, sometimes even my daughter, she was all these things, and one day she called up to say, the weirdest thing has happened, there's a lump on my tongue. Less than a year later, she was dead. She was sixty-six years old. She had no interest in dying, right to the end. She died horribly. And now she's gone. I think of her every day, sometimes six or seven times a day. This is the weekend she and I usually went to the spring garden and antiques show in Bridgehampton together. The fire screen in the next room is something she spotted in a corner of that antiques show, and above the fireplace is a poster of a seagull that she gave me only two summers ago. It's June now; this is the month one or the other of us would make cornbread pudding, a ridiculous recipe we both loved that's made with cornbread mix and canned cream corn. She made hers with sour cream, and I made mine without. "Hi, hon," she would say when she called. "Hi, doll." "Hello, my darling." I don't think she ever called me, or anyone else she knew, by their actual name. I have her white cashmere shawl. I wore it for days after her death; I wrapped myself up in it; I even slept in it. But now I can't bear to wear it because it feels as if that's all there is left of my Judy. I want to talk to her. I want to have lunch with her. I want her to give me a book she just read and loved. She is my phantom limb, and I can't believe I'm here without her.

A few months before they found the lump on her tongue, Judy and I went out to lunch to celebrate a friend's birthday. It had been a difficult year: barely a week had passed without some terrible news about someone's health. I said at lunch, What are we going to do about this? Shouldn't we talk about this? This is what our lives have become. Death is everywhere. How do we deal with it? Our birthday friend said, Oh, please, let's not be morbid.

Yes. Let's not be morbid.

Let's not.

On the other hand, I meant to have a conversation with Judy about death. Before either of us was sick or dying. I meant to have one of those straightforward conversations where you discuss What You Want in the eventuality—well, I say "the eventuality," but that's one of the oddest things about this whole subject. Death doesn't really feel eventual or inevitable. It still feels . . . avoidable somehow. But it's not. We know in one part of our brains that we are all going to die, but on some level we don't quite believe it.

But I meant to have that conversation with Judy, so that when the inevitable happened we would know what our intentions were, so that we could help each other die in whatever way we wanted to die. But of course, once they found the lump, there was no having the conversation. Living wills are much easier to draft when you are living instead of possibly dying; they're the ultimate hypotheticals. And what difference would it have made if we'd had that conversation? Before you get sick, you have absolutely no idea of how you're going to feel once you do. You can imagine you'll be brave, but it's just as possible you'll be terrified. You can hope that you'll find a way to accept death, but you could just as easily end up raging against it. You have no idea what your particular prognosis is going to be, or how you'll react to it, or what options you'll have. You have no clue whether you will ever even know the truth about your prognosis, because the real question is, What is the truth, and who is going to tell it to us, and are we even going to want to hear it?

My friend Henry died a few months ago. He was what we refer to as one of the lucky ones. He died at eighty-two, having lived a full, rich, and successful life. He had coped brilliantly with macular degeneration—for almost two years, most of his friends had no idea he couldn't see—and then he wrote a book about going blind that will probably outlast all the rest of his accomplishments, which were considerable. He died of heart failure, peacefully, in his sleep, with his adoring family around him. The day before his death, he asked to be brought a large brown accordion folder he kept in his office. In it were love letters he had received when he was younger. He sent them back to the women who'd written them, wrote them all lovely notes, and destroyed the rest. What's more, he left complete, detailed instructions for his funeral, including the music he wanted—all of this laid out explicitly in a file on his computer he called "Exit."

I so admire Henry and the way he handled his death. It's inspirational. And yet I can't quite figure out how any of it applies. For one thing, I have managed to lose all my love letters. Not that there were that many. And if I ever found them and sent them back to the men who wrote them to me, I promise you they would be completely mystified. I haven't heard from any of these men in years, and on the evidence, they all seem to have done an extremely good job of getting over me. As for instructions for my funeral, I suppose I could come up with a few. For example, if there's a reception afterward, I know what sort of food I would like served: those little finger sandwiches from this place on Lexington Avenue called William Poll. And champagne would be nice. I love champagne. It's so festive. But otherwise I don't have a clue. I haven't even figured out whether I want to be buried or cremated—largely because I've always worried that cremation in some way lowers your chances of being reincarnated. (If there is such a thing.) (Which I know there isn't.) (And yet.)

"I don't want to die," Judy said.

"I believe in miracles," she said.

"I love you," she said.

"Can you believe this?" she said.

No, I can't believe it. I still can't believe it.

But let's not be morbid.

Let's put little smiley faces on our faces.

LOL.

Eat, drink, and be merry.

Seize the day.

Life goes on.

It could be worse.

And the ever popular "Consider the alternative."

And meanwhile, here we are.

What is to be done?

I don't know. I hope that's clear. In a few minutes I will be through with writing this piece, and I will go back to life itself. Squirrels have made a hole in the roof, and we don't quite know what to do about it. Soon it will rain; we should probably take the cushions inside. I need more bath oil. And that reminds me to say something about bath oil. I use this bath oil I happen to love. It's called Dr. Hauschka's lemon bath. It costs about twenty dollars a bottle, which is enough for about two weeks of baths if you follow the instructions. The instructions say one capful per bath. But a capful gets you nowhere. A capful is not enough. I have known this for a long time. But if the events of the last few years have taught me anything, it's that I'm going to feel like an idiot if I die tomorrow and I skimped on bath oil today. So I use quite a lot of bath oil. More than you could ever imagine. After I take a bath, my bathtub is as dangerous as an oil slick. But thanks to the bath oil, I'm as smooth as silk. I am going out to buy more, right now. Goodbye.

—June 2006

On Rapture

I've just surfaced from spending several days in a state of rapture— with a book. I loved this book. I loved every second of it. I was transported into its world. I was reminded of all sorts of things in my own life. I was in anguish over the fate of its characters. I felt alive, and engaged, and positively brilliant, bursting with ideas, brimming with memories of other books I've loved. I composed a dozen imaginary letters to the author, letters I'll never write, much less send. I wrote letters of praise. I wrote letters relating entirely inappropriate personal information about my own experiences with the author's subject matter. I even wrote a letter of recrimination when one of the characters died and I was grief-stricken. But mostly I wrote letters of gratitude: the state of rapture I experience when I read a wonderful book is one of the main reasons I read, but it doesn't happen every time or even every other time, and when it does happen, I'm truly beside myself.

When I was a child, nearly every book I read sent me into rapture. Can I be romanticizing my early reading experiences? I don't think so. I can tick off so many books that I read and re-read when I was growing up—foremost among them the Oz books, which obsessed me—but so many others that were favorites in the most compelling way. I wanted so badly to *be* Jane Banks, growing up in London with Mary Poppins for a nanny, or Homer Price, growing up in Centerburg with an uncle who owned a donut machine that wouldn't stop making donuts. Little Sara Crewe in Frances Hodgson Burnett's classic *A Little Princess* was my alter ego—not in any real way, you understand; she was a much better-behaved child than I ever was—but I was so entranced by the story of the little rich girl who was sent up to the garret to be the scullery maid at the fancy boarding school where she'd been a pampered student before her father died. Oh, how I wanted to be an orphan! I read *The Nun's Story*, and oh, how I wanted to be a nun! I wanted to be shipwrecked on a desert island and stranded in Krakatoa! I wanted to be Ozma, and Jo March, and Anne Frank, and Nancy Drew, and Eloise, and Anne of Green Gables—and in my imagination, at least, I could be.

I did most of my reading as a child on my bed or on a rattan sofa in the sunroom of the house I grew up in. Here's a strange thing: Whenever I read a book I love, I start to remember all the other books that have sent me into rapture, and I can remember where I was living and the couch I was sitting on when I read them. After college, living in Greenwich Village, I sat on my brand-new wide-wale corduroy couch and read *The Golden Notebook* by Doris Lessing, the extraordinary novel that changed my life and the lives of so many other young women in the 1960s. I have the paperback copy I read at the time, and it's dog-eared, epiphany after epiphany marked so that I could easily refer back to them. Does anyone read *The Golden Notebook* nowadays? I don't know, but at the time, just before the second stage of the women's movement burst into being, I was electrified by Lessing's heroine, Anna, and her struggle to become a free woman. Work, friendship, love, sex, politics, psychoanalysis, writing—all the things that preoccupied me were Lessing's subjects, and I can remember how many times I put the book down, reeling from its brilliance and insights.

Cut to a few years later. The couch is covered with purple slipcovers, and I'm reading for pure pleasure—it's *The Godfather* by Mario Puzo, a divine book that sweeps me off into a wave of romantic delirium. I want to be a mafioso! No, that's not quite right. Okay then, I want to be a mafioso's wife!

A few years later, I'm divorced. No surprise there. The couch and I have moved to a dark apartment in the West Fifties. It's a summer weekend, I have nothing whatsoever to do, and I should be lonely but I'm not—I'm reading the collected works of Raymond Chandler.

Six years later, another divorce. For weeks I've been unable to focus, to settle down, to read anything at all. A friend I'm staying with gives me the bound galleys of *Smiley's People*. I sink into bed in the guest bedroom and happily surrender to John le Carré. I love John le Carré, but I'm even more in love with his hero, George Smiley, the spy with the broken heart. I want George Smiley to get over his broken heart. I want him to get over his horrible ex-wife who betrayed him. I want George Smiley to fall in love. I want George Smiley to fall in love with me. George Smiley, come to think of it, is exactly the sort of person I ought to marry and never do. I make a mental note to write John le Carré a letter giving him the benefit of my wisdom on this score.

But meanwhile, my purple couch is lost in the divorce and I buy a new couch, a wonderful squishy thing covered with a warm, cozy fabric, with arms you can lie back on and cushions you can sink into, depending on whether you want to read sitting up or lying down. On it I read most of Anthony Trollope and all of Edith Wharton, both of whom are dead and can't be written to. Too bad; I'd like to tell them their books are as contemporary as they were when they were written. I read all of Jane Austen, six novels back to back, and spend days blissfully worrying over whether the lovers in each book will ever overcome the misunderstandings, objections, misapprehensions, character flaws, class distinctions, and all the other obstacles to love. I read these novels in a state of suspense so intense that you would never guess I have read them all at least ten times before.

And finally, one day, I read the novel that is probably the most rapture-inducing book of my adult life. On a chaise longue at the beach on a beautiful summer day, I open Wilkie Collins's masterpiece, *The Woman in White*, probably the first great work of mystery fiction ever written (although that description hardly does it justice), and I am instantly lost to the world. Days pass as I savor every word. Each minute I spend away from the book pretending to be interested in everyday life is a misery. How could I have waited so long to read this book? When can I get back to it? Halfway through, I return to New York to work, to finish a movie, and I sit in the mix studio unable to focus on anything but whether my favorite character in the book will survive. I will not be able to bear it if anything bad happens to my beloved Marian Halcombe. Every so often I look up from the book and see a roomful of people waiting for me to make a decision about whether the music is too soft or the thunder is too loud, and I can't believe they don't understand that what I'm doing is Much More Important. I'm reading the most wonderful book.

There's something called the rapture of the deep, and it refers to what happens when a deep-sea diver spends too much time at the bottom of the ocean and can't tell which way is up. When he surfaces, he's liable to have a condition called the bends, where the body can't adapt to the oxygen levels in the atmosphere. All this happens to me when I surface from a great book. The book I've currently surfaced from—the one I mentioned at the beginning of this piece—is called *The Amazing Adventures of Kavalier and Clay* by Michael Chabon. It's about two men who create comic-book characters, but it's also about how artists create fantastic and magical things from the events of everyday life. At one point in the book there's a roomful of moths, and then a few pages later there's a huge luna moth sitting in a maple tree in Union Square Park— and all of this is reinvented a few pages later as a female comic-book heroine named Luna Moth. The moment where the image turns from ordinary to fantastic was so magical that I had to put down the book. I was dazed by the playfulness of the author and his ability to do something so difficult with such apparent ease. Chabon's novel takes place in New York City in the 1940s, and though I finished reading it more than a week ago, I'm still there. I'm smoking Camels, and Salvador Dalí is at a party in the next room. Eventually, I'll have to start breathing the air in today's New York again, but on the other hand, perhaps I won't have to. I'll find another book I love and disappear into it. Wish me luck.

—June 2002

Revision and Life:
Take It from the Top—Again

I have been asked to write something for a textbook that is meant to teach college students something about writing and revision. I am happy to do this because I believe in revision. I have also been asked to save the early drafts of whatever I write, presumably to show these students the actual process of revision. This too I am happy to do. On the other hand, I suspect that there is just so much you can teach college students about revision; a gift for revision may be a developmental stage—like a two-year-old's sudden ability to place one block on top of another—that comes along somewhat later, in one's mid-twenties, say; most people may not be particularly good at it, or even interested in it, until then.

When I was in college, I revised nothing. I wrote out my papers in longhand, typed them up, and turned them in. It would never have crossed my mind that what I had produced was only a first draft and that I had more work to do; the idea was to get to the end, and once you had got to the end you were finished. The same thinking, I might add, applied in life:

I went pell-mell through my four years in college without a thought about whether I ought to do anything differently; the idea was to get to the end—to get out of school and become a journalist.

Which I became, in fairly short order. I learned as a journalist to revise on deadline. I learned to write an article a paragraph at a time—and to turn it in a paragraph at a time—and I arrived at the kind of writing and revising I do, which is basically a kind of typing and retyping. I am a great believer in this technique for the simple reason that I type faster than the wind. What I generally do is start an article and get as far as I can—sometimes no farther in than a sentence or two—before running out of steam, ripping the piece of paper from the typewriter, and starting all over again. I type over and over until I have got the beginning of the piece to the point where I am happy with it. I then am ready to plunge into the body of the article itself. This plunge usually requires something known as a transition. I approach a transition by completely retyping the opening of the article leading up to it in the hope that the ferocious speed of my typing will somehow catapult me into the next section of the piece. This does not work—what in fact catapults me into the next section is a concrete thought about what the next section ought to be about—but until I have the thought the typing keeps me busy, and keeps me from feeling something known as blocked. Typing and retyping as if you know where you're going is a version of what therapists tell you to do when they suggest that you try changing from the outside in—that if you can't master the total commitment to whatever change you want to make, you can at least do all the extraneous things connected with it, which make it that much easier to get there. I was twenty-five years old the first time a therapist suggested that I try changing from the outside in. In those days, I used to spend quite a lot of time lying awake at night wondering what I should have said earlier in the evening and revising my lines. I mention this not just because it's a way of illustrating that a gift for revision is practically instinctive, but also (once again) because it's possible that a genuine ability at it doesn't really come into play until one is older—or at least older than twenty-five, when it seemed to me that all that was required in my life and my work was the chance to change a few lines.

In my thirties, I began to write essays, one a month for *Esquire* magazine, and I am not exaggerating when I say that in the course of writing a short essay—fifteen hundred words; that's only six double-spaced typewritten pages—I often used three hundred or four hundred pieces of typing paper, so often did I type and retype and catapult and re-catapult myself, sometimes on each retyping moving not even a sentence farther from the spot I had reached the last time through. At the same time, though, I was polishing what I had already written: as I struggled with the middle of the article, I kept putting the beginning through the typewriter; as I approached the ending, the middle got its turn. (This is a kind of polishing that the word processor all but eliminates, which is why I don't use one. Word processors make it possible for a writer to change the sentences that clearly need changing without having to retype the rest, but I believe that you can't always tell whether a sentence needs work until it rises up in revolt against your fingers as you retype it.) By the time I had produced what you might call a first draft—an entire article with a beginning, middle, and end—the beginning was in more like forty-fifth draft, the middle in twentieth, and the end was almost newborn. For this reason, the beginnings of my essays are considerably better written than the ends, although I like to think no one ever notices this but me.

As I learned the essay form, writing became harder for me. I was finding a personal style, a voice if you will, a way of writing that looked chatty and informal. That wasn't the hard part—the hard part was that having found a voice, I had to work hard month to month not to seem as if I were repeating myself. At this point in this essay it will not surprise you to learn that the same sort of thing was operating in my life. I don't mean that my life had become harder—but that it was becoming clear that I had many more choices than had occurred to me when I was marching through my twenties. I no longer lost sleep over what I should have said. Not that I didn't care—it was just that I had moved to a new plane of late-night anxiety: I now wondered what I should have done. Whole areas of possible revision opened before me. What should I have done instead? What could I have done? What if I hadn't done it the way I did? What if I had a chance to do it over? What if I had a chance to do it over as a different person? These were the sorts of questions that kept me awake and led me into fiction, which at the very least (the level at which I practice it) is a chance to rework the events of your life so that you give the illusion of being the intelligence at the center of it, simultaneously managing to slip in all the lines that occurred to you later. Fiction, I suppose, is the ultimate shot at revision.

Now I am in my forties and I write screenplays. Screenplays—if they are made into movies—are essentially collaborations, and movies are not a writer's medium; we all know this, and I don't want to dwell on the craft of screenwriting except insofar as it relates to revision. Because the moment you stop work on a script seems to be determined not by whether you think the draft is good but simply by whether shooting is about to begin: if it is, you get to call your script a final draft; and if it's not, you can always write another revision. This might seem to be a hateful way to live, but the odd thing is that it's somehow comforting; as long as you're revising, the project isn't dead. And by the same token, neither are you. It was, as it happens, while thinking about all this one recent sleepless night that I figured out how to write this particular essay. I say "recent" in order to give a sense of immediacy and energy to the preceding sentence, but the truth is that I am finishing this article four months after the sleepless night in question, and the letter asking me to write it, from George Miller of the University of Delaware, arrived almost two years ago, so for all I know Mr. Miller has managed to assemble his textbook on revision without me.

Oh, well. That's how it goes when you start thinking about revision. That's the danger of it, in fact. You can spend so much time thinking about how to switch things around that the main event has passed you by. But it doesn't matter. Because by the time you reach middle age, you want more than anything for things not to come to an end; and as long as you're still revising, they don't.

I'm sorry to end so morbidly—dancing as I am around the subject of death—but there are advantages to it. For one thing, I have managed to move fairly effortlessly and logically from the beginning of this piece through the middle and to the end. And for another, I am able to close with an exhortation, something I rarely manage, which is this: Revise now, before it's too late.

—November 1986

I Feel Bad About My Neck

I feel bad about my neck. Truly I do. If you saw my neck, you might feel bad about it too, but you'd probably be too polite to let on. If I said something to you on the subject—something like "I absolutely cannot stand my neck"—you'd undoubtedly respond by saying something nice, like "I don't know what you're talking about." You'd be lying, of course, but I forgive you. I tell lies like that all the time—mostly to friends who tell me they're upset because they have little pouches under their eyes, or jowls, or wrinkles, or flab around the middle, and do I think they should have an eye job, or a face-lift, or Botox, or liposuction. My experience is that "I don't know what you're talking about" is code for "I see what you mean, but if you think you're going to trap me into engaging on this subject, you're crazy." It's dangerous to engage on such subjects, and we all know it. Because if I said, "Yes, I see exactly what you mean," my friend might go out and have her eyes done, for instance, and it might not work, and she might end up being one of those people you read about in tabloids who ends up in court suing their plastic surgeons because they can never close their eyes again. Furthermore, and this is the point: It would be All My Fault. I am particularly sensitive to the All My Fault aspect of things, since I have never forgiven one of my friends for telling me not to buy a perfectly good apartment on East Seventy-fifth Street in 1976.

Sometimes I go out to lunch with my girlfriends—I got that far into the sentence and caught myself. I suppose I mean my women friends. We are no longer girls and have not been girls for forty years. Anyway, sometimes we go out to lunch and I look around the table and realize we're all wearing turtleneck sweaters. Sometimes, instead, we're all wearing scarves, like Katharine Hepburn in *On Golden Pond*. Sometimes we're all wearing mandarin collars and look like a white ladies' version of the Joy Luck Club. It's sort of funny and it's sort of sad, because we're not neurotic about age—none of us lies about how old she is, for instance, and none of us dresses in a way that's inappropriate for our years. We all look good for our age. Except for our necks.

Oh, the necks. There are chicken necks. There are turkey gobbler necks. There are elephant necks. There are necks with wattles and necks with creases that are on the verge of becoming wattles. There are scrawny necks and fat necks, loose necks, crepey necks, banded necks, wrinkled necks, stringy necks, saggy necks, flabby necks, mottled necks. There are necks that are an amazing combination of all of the above. According to my dermatologist, the neck starts to go at forty-three, and that's that. You can put makeup on your face and concealer under your eyes and dye on your hair, you can shoot collagen and Botox and Restylane into your wrinkles and creases, but short of surgery, there's not a damn thing you can do about a neck. The neck is a dead giveaway. Our faces are lies and our necks are the truth. You have to cut open a redwood tree to see how old it is, but you wouldn't have to if it had a neck.

My own experience with my neck began shortly before I turned forty-three. I had an operation that left me with a terrible scar just above the collarbone. It was shocking, because I learned the hard way that just because a doctor was a famous surgeon didn't mean he had any gift for sewing people up. If you learn nothing else from reading this essay, dear reader, learn this: Never have an operation on any part of your body without asking a plastic surgeon to come stand by in the operating room and keep an eye out. Because even if you are being operated on for something serious or potentially serious, even if you honestly believe that your health is more important than vanity, even if you wake up in the hospital room thrilled beyond imagining that it wasn't cancer, even if you feel elated, grateful to be alive, full of blinding insight about what's important and what's not, even if you vow to be eternally joyful about being on the planet Earth and promise never to complain about anything ever again, I promise you that one day soon, sooner than you can imagine, you will look in the mirror and think, I hate this scar.

Assuming, of course, that you look in the mirror. That's another thing about being a certain age that I've noticed: I try as much as possible not to look in the mirror. If I pass a mirror, I avert my eyes. If I must look into it, I begin by squinting, so that if anything really bad is looking back at me, I am already halfway to closing my eyes to ward off the sight. And if the light is good (which I hope it's not), I often do what so many women my age do when stuck in front of a mirror: I gently pull the skin of my neck back and stare wistfully at a younger version of myself. (Here's something else I've noticed, by the way: If you want to get really, really depressed about your neck, sit in the backseat of a car, right behind the driver, and look at yourself in the rearview mirror. What is it about rearview mirrors? I have no idea why, but there are no worse mirrors where necks are concerned. It's one of the genuinely compelling mysteries of modern life, right up there with why the cold water in the bathroom is colder than the cold water in the kitchen.)

But my neck. This is about my neck. And I know what you're thinking: Why not go to a plastic surgeon? I'll tell you why not. If you go to a plastic surgeon and say, I'd like you just to fix my neck, he will tell you flat out that he can't do it without giving you a face-lift too. And he's not lying. He's not trying to con you into spending more money. The fact is, it's all one big ball of wax. If you tighten up the neck, you've also got to tighten up the face. But I don't want a face-lift. If I were a muffin and had a nice round puffy face, I would bite the bullet—muffins are perfect candidates for this sort of thing. But I am, alas, a bird, and if I had a face-lift, my neck would be improved, no question, but my face would end up pulled and tight. I would rather squint at this sorry face and neck of mine in the mirror than confront a stranger who looks suspiciously like a drum pad.

Every so often I read a book about age, and whoever's writing it says it's great to be old. It's great to be wise and sage and mellow; it's great to be at the point where you understand just what matters in life. I can't stand people who say things like this. What can they be thinking? Don't they have necks? Aren't they tired of compensatory dressing? Don't they mind that 90 percent of the clothes they might otherwise buy have to be eliminated simply because of the necklines? Don't they feel sad about having to buy chokers? One of my biggest regrets—bigger even than not buying the apartment on East Seventy-fifth Street, bigger even than my worst romantic catastrophe—is that I didn't spend my youth staring lovingly at my neck. It never crossed my mind to be grateful for it. It never crossed my mind that I would be nostalgic about a part of my body that I took completely for granted.

Of course it's true that now that I'm older, I'm wise and sage and mellow. And it's also true that I honestly do understand just what matters in life. But guess what? It's my neck.

—August 2003

What I Wish I'd Known

People have only one way to be.

Buy, don't rent.

Never marry a man you wouldn't want to be divorced from.

Don't cover a couch with anything that isn't more or less beige.

Don't buy anything that is 100 percent wool even if it seems to be very soft and not particularly itchy when you try it on in the store.

You can't be friends with people who call after 11 p.m.

Block everyone on your instant mail.

The world's greatest babysitter burns out after two and a half years.

You never know.

The last four years of psychoanalysis are a waste of money.

The plane is not going to crash.

Anything you think is wrong with your body at the age of thirty-five you will be nostalgic for at the age of forty-five.

At the age of fifty-five you will get a saggy roll just above your waist even if you are painfully thin.

This saggy roll just above your waist will be especially visible from the back and will force you to reevaluate half the clothes in your closet, especially the white shirts.

Write everything down.

Keep a journal.

Take more pictures.

The empty nest is underrated.

You can order more than one dessert.

You can't own too many black turtleneck sweaters.

If the shoe doesn't fit in the shoe store, it's never going to fit.

When your children are teenagers, it's important to have a dog so that someone in the house is happy to see you.

Back up your files.

Overinsure everything.

Whenever someone says the words "Our friendship is more important than this," watch out, because it almost never is.

There's no point in making piecrust from scratch.

The reason you're waking up in the middle of the night is the second glass of wine.

The minute you decide to get divorced, go see a lawyer and file the papers.

Overtip.

Never let them know.

If only one third of your clothes are mistakes, you're ahead of the game.

If friends ask you to be their child's guardian in case they die in a plane crash, you can say no.

There are no secrets.

—August 2006

I Hate My Purse

I hate my purse. I absolutely hate it. If you're one of those women who think there's something great about purses, don't even bother reading this because there will be nothing here for you. This is for women who hate their purses, who are bad at purses, who understand that their purses are reflections of negligent housekeeping, hopeless disorganization, a chronic inability to throw anything away, and an ongoing failure to handle the obligations of a demanding and difficult accessory (the obligation, for example, that it should in some way match what you're wearing). This is for women whose purses are a morass of loose Tic Tacs, solitary Advils, lipsticks without tops, ChapSticks of unknown vintage, little bits of tobacco even though there has been no smoking going on for at least ten years, tampons that have come loose from their wrappings, English coins from a trip to London last October, boarding passes from long-forgotten airplane trips, hotel keys from God-knows-what hotel, leaky ballpoint pens, Kleenexes that either have or have not been used but there's no way to be sure one way or another, scratched eyeglasses, an old tea bag, several crumpled personal checks that have come loose from the checkbook and are covered with smudge marks, and an unprotected toothbrush that looks as if it has been used to polish silver.

This is for women who in mid-July realize they still haven't bought a summer purse or who in midwinter are still carrying around a straw bag.

This is for women who find it appalling that a purse might cost five or six hundred dollars—never mind that top-of-the-line thing called a Birkin bag that costs ten thousand dollars, not that it's relevant because you can't even get on the waiting list for one. On the waiting list! For a purse! For a ten-thousand-dollar purse that will end up full of old Tic Tacs!

This is for those of you who understand, in short, that your purse is, in some absolutely horrible way, you. Or, as Louis XIV might have put it but didn't because he was much too smart to have a purse, *Le sac, c'est moi.*

I realized many years ago that I was no good at purses, and for quite a while I managed to do without one. I was a freelance writer, and I spent most of my time at home. I didn't need a purse to walk into my own kitchen. When I went out, usually at night, I frequently managed with only a lipstick, a twenty-dollar bill, and a credit card tucked into my pocket. That's about all you can squeeze into an evening bag anyway, and it saved me a huge amount of money because I didn't have to buy an evening bag. Evening bags, for reasons that are obscure unless you're a Marxist, cost even more than regular bags.

But unfortunately, there were times when I needed to leave the house with more than the basics. I solved this problem by purchasing an overcoat with large pockets. This, I realize, turned my coat into a purse, but it was still better than carrying a purse. Anything is better than carrying a purse.

Because here's what happens with a purse. You start small. You start pledging yourself to neatness. You start vowing that This Time It Will Be Different. You start with the things you absolutely need—your wallet and a few cosmetics that you have actually put into a brand-new shiny cosmetics bag, the kind used by your friends who are competent enough to manage more than one purse at a time. But within seconds, your purse has accumulated the debris of a lifetime. The cosmetics have somehow fallen out of the shiny cosmetics bag (okay, you forgot to zip it up), the coins have fallen from the wallet (okay, you forgot to fasten the coin compartment), the credit cards are somewhere in the abyss (okay, you forgot to put your Visa card back into your wallet after you bought the sunblock that is now oozing into the lining because you forgot to put the top back onto it after you applied it to your hands while driving seventy miles an hour down the highway). What's more, a huge amount of space in your purse is being taken up by a technological marvel that holds your address book and calendar—or would, but the batteries in it have died. And there's half a bottle of water, along with several snacks you saved from an airplane trip just in case you ever found yourself starving and unaccountably craving a piece of cheese that tastes like plastic. Perhaps you can fit your sneakers into your purse. Yes, by God, you can! Before you know it, your purse weighs twenty pounds and you are in grave danger of getting bursitis and needing an operation just from carrying it around. Everything you own is in your purse. You could flee the Cossacks with your purse. But when you open it up, you can't find a thing in it—your purse is just a big dark hole full of stuff that you spend hours fishing around for. A flashlight would help, but if you were to put one into your purse, you'd never find it.

What's the solution? I'm no longer a freelance writer who sits home all day; I need stuff. I need stuff for work. I need cosmetics to tide me over. I need a book to keep me company. I need, sad to say, a purse. For a while, I searched for an answer. Like those Hollywood women who are willing to fling themselves into the Kabbalah, or Scientology, or yoga, I read just about any article about purses that promised me some sort of salvation from this misery. At one point I thought, Perhaps the solution is not one purse but two. So I tried having two purses, one for personal things and one for work things. (Yes, I know: The second purse is usually called a briefcase.) This system works for most people but not for me, and for a fairly obvious reason, which I've already disclosed: I'm not an organized human being. Another solution I tried involved spending quite a lot of money on a purse, on the theory that having an expensive purse would inspire me to change my personality, but that didn't work either. I also tried one of those Prada-style semi-backpack purses, but I bought it just when it was going out of fashion, and in any case I put so much into it that I looked like a sherpa.

And then, one day, I found myself in Paris with a friend who announced that her goal for the week was to buy a Kelly bag. Perhaps you know what a Kelly bag is. I didn't. I had never heard of one. What is a Kelly bag? I asked. My friend looked at me as if I had spent the century asleep in a cave. And she explained: A Kelly bag is an Hermès bag first made in the 1950s that Grace Kelly had made famous; hence the name. It is a classic. It is the purse equivalent of the world's most perfect string of pearls. It's still being manufactured, but my friend didn't want a new one, she wanted a vintage Kelly bag. She'd heard that there was a dealer in the flea market who had several for sale. The flea market is open on weekends only, so we spent several days eating, drinking, sightseeing, all of it (as far as my friend was concerned) mere prelude to the main event. How much is this purse going to cost? I asked. I practically expired when she told me: about three thousand dollars. Three thousand dollars for an old purse, plus (if you're counting, which I was) plane fare?

Well, finally we went to the flea market and there was the Kelly bag. I didn't know what to say. It looked like the sort of bag my mother used to carry. It barely held anything, and it hung stiffly on my friend's arm. I may not be good at purses, but I know that any purse that hangs stiffly on your arm (instead of on your shoulder) adds ten years to your age, and furthermore immobilizes half your body. In a modern world, your arms have to be free. I don't want to get too serious here, but a purse (like a pair of high heels) actually impinges on your mobility. That's one of many reasons why you don't see the guys-with-purses trend catching on. If one of your hands is stuck carrying your purse, it means it's not free for all sorts of exciting things you could be using it for, like shoving your way through crowds, throwing your arms around loved ones, climbing the greasy pole to success, and waving madly for taxis.

Anyway, my friend bought her Kelly bag. She paid twenty-six hundred dollars for it. The color wasn't exactly what she wanted, but it was in wonderful shape. Of course it would have to be waterproofed immediately because it would lose half its value if it got caught in the rain. Waterproofed? Caught in the rain? It had never crossed my mind to worry about a purse being caught in the rain, much less being water-proofed. For a moment I thought once again about how my mother had failed to teach me anything about purses, and I almost felt sorry for myself. But it was time for lunch.

The two of us went to a bistro, and the Kelly bag was placed in the center of the table, where it sat like a small shrine to a shopping victory. And then, outside, it began to rain. My friend's eyes began to well with tears. Her lips closed tightly. In fact, to be completely truthful, her lips actually *pursed*. It was pouring rain and she hadn't had the Kelly bag waterproofed. She would have to sit there all afternoon and wait for the rain to end rather than expose the bag to a droplet of moisture. It crossed my mind that she and her Kelly bag might have to sit there forever. Years would pass and the rain would continue to fall. She would get old (although her Kelly bag would not) and eventually she and the bag would, like some modern version of Lot's wife, metamorphose into a monument to what happens to people who care too much about purses. Country songs would be written about her, and parables. At that point I stopped worrying about purses and gave up.

I came back to New York and bought myself a purse. Well, it's not a purse exactly; it's a bag. It's definitely the best bag I have ever owned. On it is the image of a New York City MetroCard—it's yellow (taxicab yellow, to be exact) and blue (the most horrible blue of all, royal blue)—so it matches nothing at all and therefore, on a deep level, matches everything. It's made of plastic and is therefore completely waterproof. It's equally unattractive in all seasons of the year. It cost next to nothing (twenty-six dollars), and I will never have to replace it because it seems to be completely indestructible. What's more, never having been in style, it can never go out of style.

It doesn't work for everything, I admit; on rare occasions, I'm forced to use a purse, one that I hate. But mostly I go everywhere with my MetroCard bag. And wherever I go, people say to me, I love that bag. Where did you get that bag? And I tell them I bought it at the Transit Museum in Grand Central station, and that all proceeds from it go toward making the New York City subway system even better than it is already. For all I know, they've all gone off and bought one. Or else they haven't. It doesn't matter. I'm very happy.

—September 2002

Christmas Dinner

We have a traditional Christmas dinner. We've been doing it for twenty-two years. There are fourteen people involved—eight parents and six children—and we all get together at Jim and Phoebe's* during Christmas week. For one night a year, we're a family, a cheerful, makeshift family, a family of friends. We exchange modest presents, we make predictions about events in the coming year, and we eat.

Each of us brings part of the dinner. Maggie brings the hors d'oeuvres. Like all people assigned to bring hors d'oeuvres, Maggie is not really into cooking, but she happens to be an exceptional purchaser of hors d'oeuvres. Jim and Phoebe do the main course because the dinner is at their house. This year they're cooking a turkey. Ruthie and I were always in charge of desserts. Ruthie's specialty was a wonderful bread pudding. I can never settle on just one dessert, so I often make three—something chocolate (like a chocolate cream pie), a fruit pie (like a tarte tatin), and a plum pudding that no one ever eats but me. I love making desserts for Christmas dinner, and I have always believed that I make excellent desserts. But now that everything has gone to hell and I've been forced to replay the last twenty-two years of Christmas dinners, I realize that the only dessert anyone ate with real enthusiasm was Ruthie's bread pudding; no one ever said anything complimentary about any of mine. How I could have sat through Christmas dinner all this time and not realized this simple truth is one of the most puzzling aspects of this story.

A little over a year ago, Ruthie died. Ruthie was my best friend. She was also Maggie's best friend and Phoebe's best friend. We were all devastated. A month after her death, we had our traditional Christmas dinner, but it wasn't the same without Ruthie—life wasn't the same, Christmas dinner wasn't the same, and Ruthie's bread pudding (which I reproduced, from her recipe) wasn't the same either. This year, when we opened negotiations about when our Christmas dinner would take place, I told Phoebe that I'd decided I didn't want to make Ruthie's bread pudding again because it made me feel even worse about her death than I already did.

Anyway, we settled on a night for the dinner. But then Ruthie's hus-

---

* Nora changed certain names in this piece out of tactful affection.

band, Stanley, announced that he didn't want to be there. He said he was too sad. So Phoebe decided to invite another family instead. She asked Walter and Priscilla and their kids to join us. Walter and Priscilla are good friends of ours, but four years ago Priscilla announced that she didn't like living in New York anymore and was moving, with the children, to England. Priscilla is English and therefore entitled to prefer England to New York; still, it was hard not to take it personally. But she and the kids were coming to Manhattan to join Walter for Christmas, and they accepted the invitation to our Christmas dinner. A few days later Phoebe called to tell me that she'd asked Priscilla to do one of the desserts. I was thunderstruck. I do the desserts. I love doing the desserts. I make excellent desserts. Priscilla hates doing desserts. The only dessert Priscilla ever makes is trifle, and when she serves it she always announces that she hates trifle and never eats it.

"But she will make her trifle," I said.

"She won't make her trifle," Phoebe said.

"How do you know?" I said.

"I will tell her not to make her trifle," Phoebe said. "Meanwhile, are you good at mashed potatoes?"

"Sure," I said.

"Bring mashed potatoes," Phoebe said, "because Jim and I don't have any luck with them."

"Fine," I said.

Several days passed while I thought about what desserts I would bring to Christmas dinner. I read the new Martha Stewart baking book and found a recipe for cherry pie. I went on the Internet and ordered pie cherries from Wisconsin. I bought the ingredients for the plum pudding that no one eats but me. I was thinking about making a peppermint pie. And then a shocking thing happened: Phoebe e-mailed to say that since I was doing the mashed potatoes, she'd asked Priscilla to make all the desserts. I couldn't believe it. Stripped of the desserts and down-graded to mashed potatoes? I was a legendary cook—how was this possible? It crossed my mind that Phoebe was using Ruthie's death to get me to stop making desserts. She'd probably been trying to do this for years; it was only a matter of time before I would be reassigned to hors d'oeuvres, displacing Maggie, who would doubtless be relegated to mixed nuts.

I took a bath in order to contemplate this blow to my self-image.

I got out of the bathtub and wrote an e-mail in reply to Phoebe. It said, simply, "WHAT?" I thought it was understated and brilliant and would get her attention.

Minutes later the phone rang. It was Phoebe. She wasn't calling about my e-mail at all.

"I can't believe this," she said. "I just got an e-mail from Priscilla in England saying that she's not making dessert. Instead, Walter has gone to London and bought mince pies. He's bringing them to New York. I hate mince pies. I absolutely hate them. Didn't you once make a mince pie that no one ate?"

"It was a raisin pie," I said. "And I liked it."

"Mince pies!" Phoebe said. "Who's going to eat mince pies?"

"What are you going to do?" I said.

"I've already done it," Phoebe said. "I e-mailed her back and told her the mince pies were out of the question and that she should order a Yule log and a coconut cake from Eli's and just have them delivered to me. Mince pies. Really."

"I can't believe this," I said. "I think we must be talking about the cruelest woman on the planet."

"Who?" Phoebe said.

"You," I said. "Why am I not doing the desserts? I liked doing desserts. Last year my peppermint pie was a huge hit."

"I remember that pie," Phoebe said.

"This year I ordered cherries from Wisconsin," I said. "The shipping alone cost fifty-two dollars."

"If you want to bring dessert, bring dessert," said Phoebe.

"But we don't need dessert because there are mince pies and a Yule log—"

"And a coconut cake," said Phoebe. "We've got to have a coconut cake. But you can bring anything else you want."

I hung up the phone. I was reeling. To make matters worse, I'd already gone out and bought four pints of peppermint stick ice cream for the peppermint pie I was now not going to make unless I wanted to prove that I was the all-time world champion in the can't-take-a-hint department of life. I stood there, missing Ruthie desperately. If she were alive, none of this would ever have happened. She was the glue, she was the thing that gave us the illusion that we were a family, she was the mother who loved us all so much that we loved one another, she was the spirit of Christmas. Now we were a group of raging siblings; her death had released us all to be the worst possible versions of ourselves.

I went to my computer and pulled up the pictures from the last Christmas we'd all been together. There we were, so happy, crowded together, overlapping. There was Ruthie. She had the most beautiful smile.

The next day, Walter called. He'd just arrived in New York with

fourteen mince pies, and he was bringing them to Christmas dinner come hell or high water. "I love mince pie," he said. "It wouldn't be Christmas without mince pie."

I know how he feels.

RUTHIE'S BREAD AND BUTTER PUDDING

5 large eggs
4 egg yolks
1 cup granulated sugar
¼ teaspoon salt
1 quart whole milk
1 cup heavy cream, plus 1 cup for
   serving

1 teaspoon vanilla extract
Twelve ½-inch-thick slices brioche,
   crusts removed, buttered
   generously on one side
½ cup confectioners' sugar

Preheat the oven to 375 degrees. Butter a shallow two-quart baking dish.

Gently beat the eggs, egg yolks, granulated sugar, and salt until thoroughly blended.

Scald the milk and cream in a saucepan over high heat. Don't boil. When you tip the pan and the mixture spits or makes a sizzling noise, remove from the heat and stir in the vanilla extract. STIR GENTLY, don't beat, into the egg mixture until blended.

Overlap the bread, butter side up, in the prepared baking dish and pour the egg mixture over the bread. Set in a larger pan with enough hot water to come halfway up the side of the dish. Bake for about 45 minutes, or until the bread is golden-brown and a sharp knife inserted in the middle comes out clean. The bread should be golden and the pudding puffed up. This can be done early in the day. Do not chill.

Before serving, sprinkle with confectioners' sugar and place under the broiler. Don't walk away; this takes only a minute or so. Or you can use one of those crème brûlée gadgets to brown the sugar.

Serve with a pitcher of heavy cream.

—December 2006

I Remember Nothing

I have been forgetting things for years—at least since I was in my thirties. I know this because I wrote something about it at the time. I have proof. Of course, I can't remember exactly where I wrote about it, or when, but I could probably hunt it up if I had to.

In my early days of forgetting things, words would slip away, and names. I did what you normally do when this happens: I scrolled through a mental dictionary, trying to figure out what letter the word began with, and how many syllables were involved. Eventually the lost thing would float back into my head, recaptured. I never took such lapses as harbingers of doom, or old age, or actual senescence. I always knew that whatever I'd forgotten was going to come back to me sooner or later. Once I went to a store to buy a book about Alzheimer's disease and forgot the name of it. I thought it was funny. And it was, at the time.

Here's a thing I've never been able to remember: the title of that movie with Jeremy Irons. The one about Claus von Bülow. You know the one. All I ever succeeded in remembering was that it was three words long, and the middle word was "of." For many years, this did not bother me at all, because no one I knew could ever think of the title either. One night, eight of us were at the theater together, and not one of us could retrieve it. Finally, at intermission, someone went out to the street and Googled it; we were all informed of the title and we all vowed to remember it forever. For all I know, the other seven did. I, on the other hand, am back to remembering that it's three words long with an "of" in the middle.

By the way, when we finally learned the title that night, we all agreed it was a bad title. No wonder we didn't remember it.

I am going to Google for the name of that movie. Be right back. . . .

It's *Reversal of Fortune*.

How is one to remember that title? It has nothing to do with anything.

But here's the point: I have been forgetting things for years, but now I forget in a new way. I used to believe I could eventually retrieve whatever was lost and then commit it to memory. Now I know I can't possibly. Whatever's gone is hopelessly gone. And what's new doesn't stick.

The other night I met a man who informed me that he had a neurological disorder and couldn't remember the faces of people he'd met. He said that sometimes he looked at himself in a mirror and had no idea whom he was looking at. I don't mean to minimize this man's ailment, which I'm sure is a bona fide syndrome with a long name that's capitalized, but all I could think was, Welcome to my world. A couple of years ago, the actor Ryan O'Neal confessed that he'd recently failed to recognize his own daughter, Tatum, at a funeral and had accidentally made a pass at her. Everyone was judgmental about this, but not me. A month earlier, I'd found myself in a mall in Las Vegas when I saw a very pleasant-looking woman coming toward me, smiling, her arms outstretched, and I thought, Who is this woman? Where do I know her from? Then she spoke and I realized it was my sister Amy.

You might think, Well, how was she to know her sister would be in Las Vegas? I'm sorry to report that not only did I know, but she was the person I was meeting in the mall.

All this makes me feel sad, and wistful, but mostly it makes me feel old. I have many symptoms of old age, aside from the physical. I occasionally repeat myself. I use the expression "When I was young." Often I don't get the joke, although I pretend that I do. If I go see a play or a movie for a second time, it's as if I didn't see it at all the first time, even if the first time was just recently. I have no idea who anyone in *People* magazine is.

I used to think my problem was that my disk was full; now I'm forced to conclude that the opposite is true: it's becoming empty.

I have not yet reached the nadir of old age, the Land of Anecdote, but I'm approaching it.

I know, I know, I should have kept a journal. I should have saved the love letters. I should have taken a storage room somewhere in Long Island City for all the papers I thought I'd never need to look at again.

But I didn't.

And sometimes I'm forced to conclude that I remember nothing.

For example: I met Eleanor Roosevelt. It was June 1961, and I was on my way to a political internship at the Kennedy White House. All the Wellesley/Vassar interns drove to Hyde Park to meet the former first lady. I was dying to meet her. I'd grown up with a photograph in our den of her standing with my parents backstage at a play they'd written. My mother was wearing a corsage and Eleanor wore pearls. It was a photograph I always thought of as iconic, if I'm using the word correctly, which, if I am, it will be for the first time. We were among the thousands of Americans (mostly Jews) who had dens, and, in their dens, photos of Eleanor Roosevelt. I idolized the woman. I couldn't believe I was going to be in the same room with her. So what was she like that day in Hyde Park, you may wonder. I HAVE NO IDEA. I can't remember what she said or what she wore; I can barely summon up a mental picture of the room where we met her, although I have a very vague memory of drapes. But here's what I do remember: I got lost on the way. And ever since, every time I've been on the Taconic State Parkway, I'm reminded that I got lost there on the way to meet Eleanor Roosevelt. But I don't remember a thing about Eleanor Roosevelt herself.

In 1964 the Beatles came to New York for the first time. I was a newspaper reporter and I was sent to the airport to cover their arrival. It was a Friday. I spent the weekend following them around. Sunday night they appeared on *The Ed Sullivan Show*. You could make an argument that the sixties began that night, on *The Ed Sullivan Show*. It was a historic night. I was there. I stood in the back of the Ed Sullivan Theater and watched. I remember how amazingly obnoxious the fans were—the teenage girls who screamed and yelled and behaved like idiots. But how were the Beatles, you may ask. Well, you are asking the wrong person. I could barely hear them.

I marched on Washington to protest the war in Vietnam. This was in 1967, and it was the most significant event of the antiwar movement. Thousands and thousands of people were there. I went with a lawyer I was dating. We spent most of the day in a hotel room having sex. I am not proud of this, but I mention it because it explains why I honestly cannot remember anything about the protest, including whether I ever even got to the Pentagon. I don't think I did. I don't think I've ever been to the Pentagon. But I wouldn't bet a nickel on it one way or the other.

Norman Mailer wrote an entire book about this march, called *The Armies of the Night*. It was 288 pages long. It won the Pulitzer Prize. And I can barely write two paragraphs about it. If you knew Norman Mailer and me and were asked to guess which of us cared more about sex, you would, of course, pick Norman Mailer. How wrong you would be.

Here are some people I met that I remember nothing about:

Justice Hugo Black
Ethel Merman
Jimmy Stewart
Alger Hiss
Senator Hubert Humphrey
Cary Grant
Benny Goodman
Peter Ustinov
Harry Kurnitz

George Abbott
Dorothy Parker

I went to the Bobby Riggs–Billie Jean King tennis match and couldn't really see anything from where I was sitting.

I went to stand in front of the White House the night Nixon resigned and here's what I have to tell you about it: my wallet was stolen.

I went to many legendary rock concerts and spent them wondering when they would end and where we would eat afterward and whether the restaurant would still be open and what I would order.

I went to at least one hundred Knicks games and I remember only the night that Reggie Miller scored eight points in the last nine seconds.

I went to cover the war in Israel in 1973 but my therapist absolutely forbid me to go to the front.

I was not at Woodstock, but I might as well have been because I wouldn't remember it anyway.

On some level, my life has been wasted on me. After all, if I can't remember it, who can?

The past is slipping away and the present is a constant affront. I can't possibly keep up. When I was younger, I managed to overcome my resistance to new things. After a short period of negativity, I flung myself at the Cuisinart food processor. I was curious about technology. I became a champion of e-mail and blogs—I found them romantic; I even made movies about them. But now I believe that almost anything new has been put on the earth in order to make me feel bad about my dwindling memory, and I've erected a wall to protect myself from most of it.

On the other side of that wall are many things, pinging. For the most part I pay no attention. For a long time, I didn't know the difference between the Sunnis and the Shias, but there were so many pings I was finally forced to learn. But I can't help wondering, Why did I bother? Wasn't it enough to know they didn't like each other? And in any case, I have now forgotten.

At this moment, some of the things I'm refusing to know anything about include:

The former Soviet republics
The Kardashians
Twitter
All Housewives, Survivors, American Idols, and Bachelors
Karzai's brother
Soccer

Monkfish

Jay-Z

Every drink invented since the Cosmopolitan

Especially the drink made with crushed mint leaves. You know
the one.

I am going to Google the name of that drink. Be right back. . . .

The Mojito.

I am living in the Google years, no question of that. And there are
advantages to it. When you forget something, you can whip out your
iPhone and go to Google. The Senior Moment has become the Google
moment, and it has a much nicer, hipper, younger, more contemporary
sound, doesn't it? By handling the obligations of the search mechanism,
you almost prove you can keep up. You can delude yourself that no
one at the table thinks of you as a geezer. And finding the missing bit is
so quick. There's none of the nightmare of the true Senior Moment—
the long search for the answer, the guessing, the self-recrimination, the
head-slapping mystification, the frustrated finger-snapping. You just go
to Google and retrieve it.

You can't retrieve your life (unless you're on Wikipedia, in which
case you can retrieve an inaccurate version of it).

But you can retrieve the name of that actor who was in that movie,
the one about World War II. And the name of that writer who wrote
that book, the one about her affair with that painter. Or the name of
that song that was sung by that singer, the one about love.

You know the one.

—November 2010

The O Word

I'm old.
I am sixty-nine years old.
I'm not really old, of course.
Really old is eighty.
But if you are young, you would definitely think that I'm old.

No one actually likes to admit that they're old.

The most they will cop to is that they're older. Or oldish.

In these days of physical fitness, hair dye, and plastic surgery, you can live much of your life without feeling or even looking old.

But then one day, your knee goes, or your shoulder, or your back, or your hip. Your hot flashes come to an end; things droop. Spots appear. Your cleavage looks like a peach pit. If your elbows faced forward, you would kill yourself. You're two inches shorter than you used to be. You're ten pounds fatter and you cannot lose a pound of it to save your soul. Your hands don't work as well as they once did and you can't open bottles, jars, wrappers, and especially those gadgets that are encased tightly in what seems to be molded Mylar. If you were stranded on a desert island and your food were sealed in plastic packaging, you would starve to death. You take so many pills in the morning you don't have room for breakfast.

Meanwhile, there is a new conversation, about CAT scans and MRIs. Everywhere you look there's cancer. Once a week there's some sort of bad news. Once a month there's a funeral. You lose close friends and discover one of the worst truths of old age: they're irreplaceable. People who run four miles a day and eat only nuts and berries drop dead. People who drink a quart of whiskey and smoke two packs of cigarettes a day drop dead. You are suddenly in a lottery, the ultimate game of chance, and someday your luck will run out. Everybody dies. There's nothing you can do about it. Whether or not you eat six almonds a day. Whether or not you believe in God.

(Although there's no question a belief in God would come in handy. It would be great to think there's a plan, and that everything happens for a reason. I don't happen to believe that. And every time one of my friends says to me, "Everything happens for a reason," I would like to smack her.)

At some point I will be not just old, older, or oldish—I will be really old. I will be actively impaired by age: something will make it impossible for me to read, or speak, or hear what's being said, or eat what I want, or walk around the block. My memory, which I can still make jokes about, will be so dim that I will have to pretend I know what's going on.

The realization that I may have only a few good years remaining has hit me with real force, and I have done a lot of thinking as a result. I would like to have come up with something profound, but I haven't. I try to figure out what I really want to do every day, I try to say to myself,

If this is one of the last days of my life, am I doing exactly what I want to be doing? I aim low. My idea of a perfect day is a frozen custard at Shake Shack and a walk in the park. (Followed by a Lactaid.) My idea of a perfect night is a good play and dinner at Orso. (But no garlic, or I won't be able to sleep.) The other day I found a bakery that bakes my favorite childhood cake, and it was everything I remembered; it made my week. The other night we were coming up the FDR Drive and Manhattan was doing its fabulous, magical, twinkling thing, and all I could think was how lucky I've been to spend my adult life in New York City.

We used to go to our house on Long Island every summer. We would drive out with the kids the day they got out of school and we wouldn't come back until Labor Day. We were always there for the end of June, my favorite time of the year, when the sun doesn't set until nine-thirty at night and you feel as if you will live forever. On July Fourth, there were fireworks at the beach, and we would pack a picnic, dig a hole in the sand, build a fire, sing songs—in short, experience a night when we felt like a conventional American family (instead of the divorced, patched-together, psychoanalyzed, oh-so-modern family we were).

In mid-July, the geese would turn up. They would fly overhead in formation, their wings beating the air in a series of heart-stopping whooshes. I was elated by the sound. The geese were not yet flying south, mostly they were just moving from one pond to another, but that moment of realizing (from the mere sound of beating wings) that birds were overhead was one of the things that made the summers out there so magical.

In time, of course, the kids grew up and it was just me and Nick in the house on Long Island. The sound of geese became a different thing—the first sign that summer was not going to last forever, and soon another year would be over. Then, I'm sorry to say, they became a sign not just that summer would come to an end, but that so would everything else. As a result, I stopped liking the geese. In fact, I began to hate them. I especially began to hate their sound, which was not beating wings—how could I have ever thought it was?—but a lot of uneuphonious honks.

Now we don't go to Long Island in the summer and I don't hear the geese. Sometimes, instead, we go to Los Angeles, where there are hummingbirds, and I love to watch them because they're so busy getting the most out of life.

—November 2010

What I Won't Miss

Dry skin
Bad dinners like the one we went to last night
E-mail
Technology in general
My closet
Washing my hair
Bras
Funerals
Illness everywhere
Polls that show that 32 percent of the American people
    believe in creationism
Polls
Fox
The collapse of the dollar
Joe Lieberman
Clarence Thomas
Bar mitzvahs
Mammograms
Dead flowers
The sound of the vacuum cleaner
Bills
E-mail. I know I already said it, but I want to emphasize it.
Small print
Panels on Women in Film
Taking off makeup every night

—November 2010

What I Will Miss

My kids
Nick
Spring
Fall
Waffles
The concept of waffles
Bacon
A walk in the park
The idea of a walk in the park
The park
Shakespeare in the Park
The bed
Reading in bed
Fireworks
Laughs
The view out the window
Twinkle lights
Butter
Dinner at home just the two of us
Dinner with friends
Dinner with friends in cities where none of us lives
Paris
Next year in Istanbul
Pride and Prejudice
The Christmas tree
Thanksgiving dinner
One for the table
The dogwood
Taking a bath
Coming over the bridge to Manhattan
Pie

—November 2010

These pieces originally appeared in:

Esquire: "How to Write a Newsmagazine Cover Story," "The Assassination Reporters," "The *Palm Beach Social Pictorial*," "The Boston Photographs," "Russell Baker," "The *Detroit News*," "The *Ontario Bulletin*," "Gentlemen's Agreement," "The Making of Theodore H. White," "Vaginal Politics," "Miami," "Reunion," "Helen Gurley Brown: 'If You're a Little Mouseburger, Come with Me . . . ',," "Dorothy Schiff and the *New York Post*," "Dorothy Parker," "Baking Off," "*Gourmet* Magazine," "A Few Words About Breasts," "The Mink Coat," "Fantasies"

Harper's Bazaar: "I Hate My Purse"

The Huffington Post: "I Just Want to Say: The World Is Not Flat," "I Just Want to Say: The Egg-White Omelette," "I Just Want to Say: Teflon," "The First Annual 'Tell Us What You're Cooking This Year for Thanksgiving Dinner That You Didn't Cook Last Year,' " "Hello. By the Way. Whatever.," "Deep Throat and Me: Now It Can Be Told, and Not for the First Time Either," "The Curious Incident of the Veep in the Summertime," "Hooked on Anonymity," "One Small Blog," "On Bill Clinton," "A Million Little Embellishments," "Scooter, Rosa Lopez, and the Grassy Knoll," "Reflections on Reading the Results of President Bush's Annual Physical Examination," "My Weekend in Vegas," "O.J. Again," "Say It Ain't So, Rupe," "Melancholy Babies," "Take My Secretary of State, Please," "On Being Named Person of the Year," "Condi's Diary," "Some People," "What Did You Do in the War?" "How to Foil a Terrorist Plot in Seven Simple Steps," "My Top Ten New Year's Resolutions," "Hooked on Hillary," "White Men," "It Ought to Be a Word," "The D Word," "Christmas Dinner"

I Feel Bad About My Neck: "The Story of My Life in 3,500 Words or Less," "Parenting in Three Stages," "What I Wish I'd Known"

I Remember Nothing: "Journalism: A Love Story," "Lillian Helman: *Pentimento*," "I Remember Nothing," "The O Word," "What I Won't Miss," "What I Will Miss"

New York Magazine: "Pat Loud: No, But I Read the Book," "Julie Nixon Eisenhower: The Littlest Nixon," "The Food Establishment: Life in the Land of the Rising Soufflé (Or Is It the Rising Meringue?)"

The New Yorker: "Lisbeth Salander: The Girl Who Fixed the Umlaut," "Serial Monogamy: A Memoir," "A Sandwich"

The New York Times: "Me and JFK: Now It Can Be Told," "The Six Stages of E-mail," "Revision and Life: Take It from the Top—Again"

O, The Oprah Magazine: "On Maintenance," "On Rapture"

Rolling Stone: "Jan Morris: *Conundrum*"

Vogue: "The Legend," "Considering the Alternative," "I Feel Bad About My Neck"

Wallflower at the Orgy: "Introduction"

Previously unpublished:
"About Having People to Dinner"
"Commencement Address to Wellesley Class of 1996"
Lucky Guy

A NOTE ON THE TYPE

The text of this book was set in Sabon, a typeface designed by Jan
Tschichold (1902–1974). Based on the original designs by Claude
Garamond (c. 1480–1561), Sabon was named for the Lyons
punch cutter Jacques Sabon, who brought some of Garamond's
matrices to Frankfurt.

Composed by North Market Street Graphics, Lancaster, Pennsylvania

Printed and bound by Berryville Graphics, Berryville, Virginia

Designed by Maggie Hinders